The Foundations of American Civilization

A HISTORY OF COLONIAL AMERICA

Max Savelle

STANFORD UNIVERSITY

GREENWOOD PRESS, PUBLISHERS
WESTPORT, CONNECTICUT

To

PITÍN

CITIZEN OF THE NEW WORLD

La historia es la narrativa del pasado;
La juventud es la esperanza del futuro.

Preface

M Y REASONS for writing a new survey of American colonial history are four. First, it has been my experience in teaching this field that it is very difficult to arrive at a satisfactory understanding of this phase of the history of the western hemisphere without considering the British Empire as a whole. The relations of the continental colonies with the British West Indies were so close, and these relations so profoundly influenced the history of the settlements on the continent, that I am convinced that any treatment which omits the British West Indies inevitably results in distortion of the story. For this reason it seems to me advisable to include in a history of the British colonies in America a treatment of the West Indies and their relationships to the continental colonies.

A second reason for assuming responsibility for a new treatment of American colonial history is the fact that none of the texts thus far published presents any considerable treatment of the diplomatic aspects of early American history. It seems to me that it is just as important to consider the diplomatic history of the American colonies as it is to include diplomatic history in any account of the evolution of the United States after independence. Not only were the colonies important to the diplomatic history of Europe, but it should also be emphasized that in their relationships with each other, with the mother country, and with the colonies of other nations, such as France, Holland, and Spain, the British colonies formulated certain embryonic diplomatic ideas and practices which eventually developed into the diplomatic policies of the United States. It is for these reasons that I have included in this book certain chapters devoted to this aspect of the evolving American civilization.

Recent developments in the study of human history have led to an increased emphasis upon the economic and social factors that contribute to the progress of events in any time and place. A great deal has yet to be done in connection with the history of colonial America before we may thoroughly understand all the social forces at work to determine the characteristics of the later American culture. But the main outlines and tendencies of economic and social development in the colonial epoch in the history of Anglo-American civilization are fairly clear, and every citizen of that culture will find a knowledge of them to contribute to his understanding of the nationality of which he is a member. It has seemed to me advisable to include in this book a broader and more thoroughgoing treatment of economic and social phenomena than has been customary in the past.

Finally, it has seemed to me desirable to attempt a somewhat interpretative treatment of forces and conditions that contributed to the origins of our American civilization. Our economic institutions and practices, our political institutions, our social forms and ideals, our literary and cultural outlook, and our diplomatic policies, all have their origins deep in the experiences of the Anglo-Saxons who first came to America. The civilization of the United States cannot be adequately understood without a consideration of the relationship of our present scene to these remote origins. It has been my desire to suggest in this book some of these origins and our own relationships to them.

In the preparation of this survey I have leaned heavily upon the monumental works of Charles McLean Andrews, Herbert E. Osgood, Lawrence H. Gipson and Edward Channing, and upon volumes I and VI of *The Cambridge History of the British Empire*. But I have also endeavored to use and follow, wherever possible, the best monographic materials available. In teaching this field of history I have used texts by Marcus Jernegan, Evarts B. Greene, Curtis Nettels, Oliver Chitwood, Herbert E. Bolton, and Jennings B. Sanders, and it goes without saying that my thinking has been affected in important ways by all of them. The chapters dealing with the diplomatic history of America lean heavily upon the work of Frances G. Davenport for the period prior to the Peace of Utrecht, and chiefly upon my own researches for the period from that time to the Revolution.

I have included a carefully selected list of references at the end of each chapter for the use of students who may wish to pursue farther the subject treated there. But I have avoided the use of footnotes as having a tendency to confuse the narrative for the undergraduate, besides being of no practical use to him. Where quotations are given—and they have been used sparingly—every effort has been made to make sure of their accuracy.

Besides my indebtedness to the authors named above, it is a pleasure to acknowledge my gratitude to the Carnegie Institution of Washington and to the American Geographical Society for permission to reproduce certain materials in C. O. Paullin, ed., *Atlas of the Historical Geography of the United States,* and to Mr. Herman R. Friis for permission to reproduce certain materials in his *Series of Population Maps of the Colonies and the United States, 1625-1790.* To Herbert E. Bolton is due my sincere thanks for permission to reproduce some of the maps in his syllabus of the *History of the Americas;* similarly, I am indebted to Frank W. Pitman for permission to reproduce certain materials in his book, *The Development of the British West Indies, 1700-1763,* to Little, Brown and Company for permission to reproduce one of the maps in James T. Adams, *The Founding of New England,* and to the Arthur H. Clark Company for permission to adapt certain materials taken from the maps in C. V. Alvord's *The Mississippi Valley in British Politics.*

Professors Charles McLean Andrews, Evarts B. Greene, Thomas A. Bailey, Charles A. Barker, and Beverley McAnear read the manuscript in its entirety or in part, and made many helpful suggestions. Such errors as may appear, however, are my own responsibility. My gratitude to these scholars is profound; the great and generous assistance they have been able to give me is a testimonial of the sincere and cooperative desire to find and present the truth that characterizes the members of the brotherhood of history scholars everywhere.

I owe a special debt of gratitude to George Harmon Knoles, Professor of History at Colorado State Teachers College at Greeley, Colorado. Mr. Knoles not only read the manuscript at every stage of its preparation; he also wrote Chapter 47 in its entirety, and made countless valuable criticisms and suggestions with regard to the book as a whole. Without his assistance this book could not have appeared in its present form.

I am also indebted to Miss Winifred Webster, who rendered valuable editorial and bibliographical assistance in the preparation of the manuscript and to Miss Martha Jane Thornton, who so patiently and loyally helped in the making of the index.

M. S.

May 20, 1942
Stanford University

Contents

CONTENTS

1

Introduction

IN THE last two hundred years many men have tried to solve the riddle of the human past. Peering back into the very beginnings of human civilization, they have sought to see what plan, if any, is to be found in the unfolding history of human culture. Nearly all historians have agreed that the study of the past sheds a greater light of understanding upon the problems of the present. As Thucydides put it in the fifth century, B.C., "the accurate knowledge of what has happened will be useful, because, according to human probability, similar things will happen again."

That—as far as it goes—is what might be called the "pragmatic" justification of the study of history. But there are other justifications of that pleasant study, and, besides, the pragmatic justification of the study of history does not go far enough in the direction of explaining just how a knowledge of the past is to be useful—in other words, what are the lessons from the past that may help us in solving the riddles of the present.

It is just here that the historical philosophers disagree. Some have thought that we can observe the plan of God for the salvation of man in the unfolding pages of human history; others see in history the story of the development of the "world spirit." Others, again, under the influence of rationalism, have seen history as the record of human progress, under the direction of natural law, toward a higher, more perfect condition of life. Still others, under the influence of nineteenth-century naturalistic science, have seen history as the story of the evolution of the animal man in the process of adapting himself to his environment, and nothing more. Karl Marx, impressed by the effects of the industrial revolution, found history to be the record of a long sociological struggle between classes of exploiters and exploited workers for the control of the means of production and distribution of the products of industry.

The twentieth-century historians—some of whom, to be sure, do cling to the older theories of the meaning of human history—seem for the most part to be largely under the domination of the last two groups of ideas. Discarding, or at least accepting with great caution, the idea of progress, twentieth-century historians incline to disregard metaphysical influences because of lack of evidence and to treat

1

man merely as an animal whose history has been determined in large measure by the struggle for survival in a variety of environments. This is not to say, of course, that certain "spiritual" (in the sense of mental) or "social" or "ethical" or other psychological factors have not strongly influenced human actions and institutions. Nor is it to say, either, that the natural environment is the only environment to which the animal man has had to adapt himself. For by the use of tools, which distinguishes man from the other animals, he has been able to irrigate arid valleys and bridge impassable rivers; and in the social aspects of his living, man has set up institutions that have had tremendous directional force in the shaping of the course of history—even long after the institutions themselves have passed the zenith of their own usefulness. Thus the word environment, as here used, means not only the natural physical environment, but also the modifications in that environment created by man himself, as well as the social environment that consists of language, the family, religion, government, education, and similar institutions, all created, more or less consciously, by man himself.

In other words, a very considerable number of modern historians have come to consider man as an entirely natural phenomenon, and his history, however complicated, as the record of this animal's efforts to survive in a physical universe that neither is conscious of man's existence, nor cares. In his struggle for survival, man has been directed by several major impulses: (1) the economic, or the impulse that springs from the necessity of securing his food supply and shelter from his environment; (2) the social impulse to form, for his own protection and greater happiness, social groups—of which the family is perhaps the most primitive and fundamental; (3) the political urge or tendency to form, more or less by consent of the social groups concerned, governments of some sort for the regulation of relations between individuals within the groups; (4) the religio-scientific impulse, which seeks to understand and explain the nature of the universe and man's relation to it. Finally, a fifth impulse might be added, as that urge in man—the esthetic—to portray in tangible, visible form the aspects of the universe that he has found beautiful—in literature, in art, or in music.

Almost nowhere else in the entirety of human history is there such a complete and well-documented record of human adaptation as in the American hemisphere in the first three centuries of its recorded history. The story is perfectly clear from the beginning; and the record is fairly complete. The history of European colonization in America is the history of adaptation writ large. For not only are the five impulses listed above to be seen working themselves out in adaptation—sometimes rapid, sometimes amazingly swift—to a new environment. Quite clearly, also, are to be seen the elements that went into the making of a new culture: the men themselves, and the ideas and the institutions they brought with them, ready made; the variety of environments in the new world to which they had to re-adapt themselves and their ideas; and the effects of the new institutions—such, for example, as the plantation system in the South—in shaping the course of history after they were once fixed and stabilized in the new home. Finally, here is a clear record of the sort of accomplishment of which—after centuries of effort, to be sure—men are capable. Here may be observed the result of two centuries of a more or less conscious struggle at adaptation, not only for mere survival, but also for the conscious betterment and enrichment of the conditions of life—social, intellectual, and economic—in this new world.

From the "pragmatic" point of view, a study of the origins of American civilization must inevitably contribute to an understanding of American life in the present. But that is not its only justification: the study of early American history is interesting in itself; it is to be hoped that that alone should justify it to many. Such a study, also, should not only imbue the student with the spirit of adaptation—that same willingness to consider new ideals and new means for the enrichment of human life which lay at the very heart of the motivation of our ancestors. The realistic study of the lives of the "giants" in our history, while revealing that they were merely ordinary men, no better and no worse than our contemporaries, might also be expected to be a matter of inspiration to the men of the twentieth century, if only by showing what ordinary men may do.

American civilization is an offshoot of European civilization. Or, to put it another way, the cultures of the various national societies in the western hemisphere are component units in the broader complex we call "western civilization" as distinguished from "oriental civilization." For the differences between the national cultures that compose the civilization of the western (European and American) world are far less marked than those which distinguish the civilization of the west from that of the east. The culture of the United States, the origins of which are the major subject of this book, is but one of the national cultures that make up the whole of western civilization. It originated, along with those of Canada and the

British West Indies, with which it is almost identical, as an offshoot from the civilization of England. But under the stress of adaptation to the new environment of North America and the admixture of other European streams, the original English culture became diversified; it split up into a variety of forms that were at once different from their mother-culture and from one another. It was only by growth, and by expansion until they touched each other, and by the uniting effect of common enemies and common problems of law, commerce, government and defense, that they came at last, at the end of two centuries, to coalesce into a culture which, though internally still diversified, could now in a very real sense be called an American civilization.

Thus, in the course of our treatment of the appearance of an American civilization, we shall be under the necessity of considering certain questions. First, who were the people who laid the foundations of an American culture, and why did they cross three thousand miles of a dangerous ocean to set up a civilization in a wilderness? Some came because of a desire to make a living in a country where there was an abundance of free land to be had for the taking. Others came because they had failed or were in some way uncomfortable in the mother country and desired to set up a new home in a new land. Many others came because they wished to escape from the economic or political or religious disturbances that marked the history of the seventeenth century in Europe or to avoid the constant and universal threat of war. In such a study, also, it will be necessary to ask the question, not only why the individuals who came to America did so, but why there were to be found so many men willing to supply the necessary capital for colonial enterprises. Thus the first problem involved in a history of English colonial America is to understand the motives of the men who came to found the new civilization, as well as the motives of the men who gave them the necessary financial and political support.

The second problem in our history must be the question, what did these men do when they arrived in America? In what sorts of economic activities did they engage, and why? What sorts of social institutions did they formulate in this new land and why did they take the peculiar forms that they did? Why was it, for example, that political institutions in the colonies in the eighteenth century were probably more liberal than any others in the world—even in England? Religion, also, has been one of the most dominant and constant factors in American history, and yet the history of religion in this country has been paralleled by an increasing breadth of religious toleration, and one of the most typical aspects of our civilization has been this broad tolerance. Our treatment of the growing colonial society, therefore, must include a considerable emphasis upon the religion of the people who settled in America and the growth of religious tolerance. Again, a thoroughgoing discussion of this new civilization must include a study of the emergence and development of an intellectual life that is genuinely American. The intellectual background of the first colonies was English; but the qualities of their intellectual life declined after the first generation, and the second and third generations present an intellectual and cultural life somewhat below the level of that of their fathers and grandfathers. By the end of the seventeenth century, however, the Americans had begun to develop an indigenous, if primitive, culture of their own; and from that point forward it may be said that an American, as distinguished from an English or a European civilization has continued to exist and to grow on this continent.

In their adaptation of themselves and their institutions to the new world, through the course of two centuries, the people who settled the British empire in America perfected certain economic, social, political, and intellectual institutions and ideals which were different from the corresponding aspects of European institutions. They were different, indeed, from each other; and by the middle of the eighteenth century there had appeared in New England, in New York and Pennsylvania, in Virginia and the Carolinas, and in the West Indies, at least four new cultures which were different both from the European culture from which they sprang and from one another.

By that time, however, there had appeared among the thirteen older colonies on the continent a tendency toward unification and certain aspects of these societies overlapped sectional differences. This tendency toward union, stimulated by conflict with the Indians and the French on the one side, and conflict and an increasingly bitter contest with the mother country on the other, eventually produced a civilization upon the continent of North America that may be called national as distinguished from any of its compound cultural sectors, and this American national culture has been moving from that time to this in the direction of greater and greater uniformity. It was this continental nucleus that resisted the attempts of Great Britain to tighten up its mercantilistic imperial administration following the Seven Years War. On the other hand, the British West Indies had become increasingly dependent upon the mother country for economic regulation and military protection, and they therefore felt little incentive to secede from the empire along with the continental colonies. The new French and Spanish areas of the empire, added in the Peace of Paris of 1763, also refused, for reasons of their own, to join in the American revolution. The revolution thus became a struggle of one segment of the British empire against the mother country for recognition of a young nationhood which that segment alone, among the parts of the empire, had achieved.

Once they had won a recognition of their independence, the thirteen former colonies found themselves faced with the necessity for a final adaptation. That was the formulation of some institution with power to regulate and govern their common interests for the benefit of all of them and with the dignity and the sovereignty that were necessary in order to command the respect of the other members of the family of nations. The result was the establishment in 1789 of the constitution of the United States of America.

It was a long and diverse drama that started with a few scattered settlements along the coast of America from Guiana to Newfoundland and passed through the various phases of growth and conflict to culminate at last in the splitting of the British empire and the emergence of a relatively small part of it as a united independent state. It was a drama, indeed, that might well be called the birth of an American nation out of an empire that was British.

PART I

America in the Expansion of Europe

THE CIVILIZATION of America is an offshoot of the civilization of Europe. The history of America, therefore, begins with the stirrings of the western European peoples that brought them first to a phenomenal expansion of Europe's internal economic life, with a resultant growth of cities, national states, and new social classes, and then carried them far and wide over the seven seas to discover the rest of the world, to them, hitherto, unknown. It is this swarming of Europeans overseas, first on voyages of discovery, plunder and commerce, and then with the object of forming new homes for themselves in the "new world," that raises the curtain upon the drama that is the story of America.

2

The European Background of American History

IN THE year 986 A.D. a Norseman named Bjarni Heriulfsson sailed from Iceland for the Norse colonies in Greenland. Having been blown off his course, Bjarni saw a hitherto unknown land to the westward. But he was in a hurry, and did not stop to explore. Some fourteen years later, or about the year 1000 A.D., Leif Ericsson sailed to the new land that Bjarni had seen from the sea. There he landed, and having discovered that it was a very pleasant country, abounding in wild grapes, he called it Vineland. After Leif there came other Norsemen, and some even settled in Vineland, which was probably the northeastern part of North America. But the Norsemen got into difficulties with the Indians, and their interest in Vineland gradually diminished. Thus, while their voyages seem to have continued at intervals down to about the year 1362, the Norse adventure had little or no permanent significance in American history. If the news of Leif's discovery ever reached the countries of southern Europe, it excited little interest; for Europeans were not disposed, as yet, to engage in westward expansion. On the contrary, only ninety-six years after Leif's expedition, there took place the first of a long series of semi-predatory, semi-religious expeditions eastward, called the Crusades. The Crusades may, indeed, be taken as one of the early signs of European interest in expansion. This expansion, however, was directed toward the countries around the eastern Mediterranean.

Four hundred and seventy-two years after Leif, a Dane named John Scolp sailed westward and landed in what seems to have been the same territory that Leif had visited in the year 1000. Scolp, however, had sailed from Denmark for very different reasons from those of Leif, and he was disappointed when he landed in Vineland, since he had set out to find the way to Asia by sailing westward. Twenty years after Scolp, Christopher Columbus, a Genoese in the employ of the king and queen of Spain, sailed westward across the Atlantic for the same purpose and suffered the same disappointment. For Columbus, too, was seeking a highway to the east by sailing westward across the Atlantic. Columbus made a series of voyages in his attempt to find a way past the land barrier on the westward route to the Indies, but he died without realizing that the land he had discovered was only less than half way to the riches of Cathay. News of the exploits of Columbus, however, excited a great wave of interest in the countries of western Europe, and there followed a long line of explorers who eventually brought to the knowledge of Europeans the geographic nature of North and South America, as well as a realization of the existence and enormous extent of the Pacific Ocean.

What had happened between the time of Leif Ericsson, when Europeans failed to show any interest in westward expansion, and the time of Columbus, when news of discoveries to the west excited the cupidity of the adventurers in every court of western Europe? Four developments of major historical significance had taken place to bring about this fundamental change in attitude toward western discovery.

THE REVIVAL OF COMMERCE AND THE CAPITALISTIC SPIRIT

The beginning of European expansion goes back at least to the Crusades, and has gone on almost continuously and with increasing momentum from that time until the present. The modes and the methods have changed, to be sure, but the eventual result has ever been the same—that is, the establishment of some sort of hegemony of European civilization over non-European areas of the globe, for the purposes, primarily, of economic exploitation. The Crusades had their beginning in the great expedition that set out from Europe to recover the holy places for Christianity in 1096. While the first Crusade succeeded in its primary objective, its greatest significance for the history of civilization lies not in that, but rather in the stimulus it gave to knowledge and to culture, and the impetus it gave to the revival of commerce between the west and the east.

The Italian cities—Naples, Venice, Pisa, Florence, and Genoa, together with Marseilles in France and Barcelona in Spain—had begun, indeed, to enjoy a revival of commercial prosperity with the re-establishment of relative order in the Mediterranean and western Europe as early as the ninth century, after the Moorish invasions. These cities (except Florence, which owed its prosperity more to industry than to seaborne commerce) were the logical points of departure for the great crusading military expeditions that set out for the eastern Mediterranean throughout the twelfth century, and the first effect of the Crusades upon these cities was to make them rapidly wealthy by the profits derived from furnishing the armies with supplies, arms, and ships.

The Crusades had done two things to stimulate an expansion of European commerce: they had provided much of the necessary capital in the hands of the Mediterranean merchants—who needed no urging to expand—and they had greatly quickened and enlarged the demand for eastern goods in western Europe. Thus the Mediterranean cities became the great emporiums, or middlemen, between Europe and the near east in a flourishing intercontinental trade. This trade was itself a remarkable expansion of European life and commerce. But the Italian cities were the promoters, and for nearly three hundred years they enjoyed a monopoly of the intercourse between east and west. It is no wonder that they accumulated vast wealth, or that, as a result, life took on an increasingly secular interest. Nor is it surprising that here, in these wealthy urban centers, learning and art should have found the fertile soil from which sprang the flower of the Italian Renaissance.

Year after year the goods of the south and east passed northward and westward to the fairs and the towns of Spain, France, the Low Countries, the Germanies, and the British Isles. Pack-trains of horses bearing such products as rugs, perfumes, spices, and jewels from the east, and glassware, fine textiles of silk or wool, wares of gold and silver and wine from the Mediterranean countries made their toilsome journeys over the Alps and down the Rhine, or up the Rhone Valley and down the Seine or the branches of the Rhine, to the market-towns and the fairs of France and Germany. Little villages, that had long been the marketplaces for the exchange of country products for crude handmade local manufactures, gradually reaching farther and farther afield, both to buy and to sell, came to be able to offer to their townsmen the products, first of the Mediterranean, then of the near and the distant east. And to the itinerant merchants who brought those goods they gave in return their rough woolen cloth, linen, tin, leather or fur from the more distant north, and gold and silver coin to make up the adverse balance.

The towns that had been market villages flourished in modern cities; such were the towns of Augsburg, Paris, Lyons, Bruges, Brussels, Ypres, Rheims, and many others. But the towns that stood on good harbors facing the ocean westward and northward where the land and river routes met the sea were the most fortunate, for they became not only trading centers for their own localities, but also transfer stations for goods coming from or going to points farther on. Such were the ports of Bordeaux, Rouen, Amsterdam, Antwerp, Hamburg, Lübeck, Danzig, and, in England, London, Southampton and Bristol. Cadiz, in southern Castile, and Lisbon, in Portugal, became the transfer points for trade in and out of the Mediterranean and to and from the North Sea and the Baltic—especially after 1317, when Venice began to send its annual "Flanders fleets" to Southampton and the Low Countries all the way by sea to avoid the⁄expenses and the dangers of land transport. Just as the Mediterranean cities had become the great exchange points for commerce through the Mediterranean toward the east, so the cities along the western coast of Europe became the great exchange points for commerce over the Atlantic toward the north.

As these cities flourished and became wealthy, they achieved great power. Many were able to win their practical independence by the power of money or by the strength of their hired armies, and their power was still more greatly increased by their custom of joining together in leagues. The most famous of all these confederations of commercial cities was the Hanseatic League, which at one time included upward of eighty cities, supported a powerful army and navy, and made successful war against pirates and interlopers, and even challenged the power of over-restrictive kings. The League made rules governing the commerce of its city-members; it regulated weights and coins, and collected and published to its members data and maps to aid in navigation along the coasts. Its ships were to be found in every important port from Cape St. Vincent to North Cape; over many of these places, indeed, it held the power of life or death through its monopoly of their trade.

It was in these cities of the Atlantic that wealth and culture accumulated, and that surplus capital was amassed that made possible the "venturing" of considerable sums in search of new routes and new markets for trade; it was from them that men were sent to set up the first European colonies overseas. It was around the commercial towns as nuclei, moreover, that were formed the gradually emerging and expanding unified political states, with their centralized governments and their all-powerful kings, that were slowly but surely replacing the old feudal system of government and sapping the power and the importance of the old feudal aristocracy, whose power had been built upon the ownership of land.

For in the cities the changing nature of economic life had created a new social class, the "bourgeoisie," or bourg(city)-dwellers. These were the merchants, the tradesmen, the artisans, and, later, the lawyers and officials who were dependent upon the affairs of commerce for their existence, both individually and as a class. As trade continued to expand, the bourgeoisie became wealthy; they became the money-lenders, even for kings, and the entrepreneurs of new enterprise. In a word, they became the capitalists of the new era.

Capitalism had long since been dead. It had flourished in ancient Rome, of course, and it was still flourishing in Byzantium. But it had become practically defunct with the collapse of commercial life during the long "depression" that followed the disintegration of Roman authority in the west. But with the revival of commerce in western Europe capitalism came to life again, and with it were revived old Roman commercial methods and Roman commercial law. Some new methods were invented. At first, the great merchants were also bankers. But banking finally became specialized and, naturally enough, the first true bankers appeared in Italy. The houses of Buonsignori of Siena, and the Peruzzi, the Bardi, and the Alfani of Florence were banking houses with branches all over Europe. They transferred money from one country to another by means of bills of exchange or letters of credit, thus avoiding the dangers and the inconveniences attendant upon the transfer of cumbersome sacks of gold or silver coin from place to place. They collected and remitted moneys for the popes, and they made great loans to the ever-indigent kings. They took the bonds of kings, merchants, or cities for the repayment of loans, charging interest and penalties for failure to repay on time—penalties ranging sometimes as high as twenty-five percent of the principal, or even more. Often enough the kings repudiated their bonds, with consequent ruin for the bankers. As time went on, and the emerging unified states became more and more stable, national bankers arose beside the great international houses, and much of the wealth was kept at home. Thus Jacques Coeur, greatest of French medieval merchant-princes, became the national financier of France in the Hundred Years War; and France, with all of Joan of Arc's heroism, could probably not have driven out the English had it not been for him. Later, the Fuggers of Augsburg became the best-known and most successful international bankers of the north.

Along with banking went other developments in the conduct of business. Insurance, for example, was extended to ships and enterprises. "Bourses" or "exchanges" were established in some of the more important trading centers such as Lyons, Bruges and Antwerp, first for trading in bills of exchange, and later for the exchange of stocks of commodities, in which there took place a considerable amount of speculation. Of most direct importance, however, for the history of colonial expansion, was the appearance of great companies of investors for carrying on enterprises too great or too risky to be undertaken by a single merchant.

All this expansion of commercial, industrial and financial life would not have been possible without an expanding and flexible supply of negotiable money. This necessary medium of exchange was supplied, at first, in Italy, by the profits of a favorable balance of trade. Later the supply of gold and silver coin was expanded by the discovery of mines in Bohemia and Germany. After the conquest of America by the Spaniards and the Portuguese, the flood of treasure from the new world caused a considerable rise in prices. The number of the new coins was legion, and their variety was infinite; but the most famous and the most widely used in international commerce was the florin, created by the city of Florence about the middle of the thirteenth century. The florin was a gold coin containing about fifty-four grains of gold (a little over three times the content of the American dollar since 1934). The English pound was one pound of silver, coined into 240 silver pennies!

THE EMERGENCE OF THE INTEGRATED POLITICAL STATE

Hand in hand with the emerging capitalists went the "national" kings. For, beginning about the thirteenth century, certain of the local kings of western Europe began to emerge as more powerful or more important than their feudal equals and underlings, and, step by step, they succeeded in extending their possessions and their power at the expense of their feudal retainers. In this process they generally had the active aid and support of the bourgeoisie of the cities. For the cities and the merchants in them were deeply concerned with the winning of self-government for themselves, independence from the power of their feudal lords, and the maintenance of law and order all over the areas where they did their trading. It thus came about that the towns more or less willingly furnished money to the king for the prosecution of his wars, both domestic and foreign, and received in return certain privileges and immunities, including a large measure of self-government and a release from feudal responsibility to their former lords; failing that, they became direct fiefs of the king himself, under his direct protection. Often the cities would form leagues for mutual assistance in the maintenance of order and the protection of commerce and for the support of the interests of the king. This was notably true particularly in Castile and Aragon, where the leagues were called *hermandades*. In France, Germany, and England, middle-class cooperation with the national kings followed much the same pattern.

The result of this support upon the fortunes of the king was that he was enabled thereby to hire professional armies for his wars, and thus became independent of the old feudal levies. His increasing power made it possible for him to suppress the resistance and the decentralizing tendencies of the nobles. Finally, he was able to bring larger and larger areas under his sway, so that there gradually emerged from the chaos of feudal decentralization the centralized and integrated European states as we know them today.

It was by such a process that Portugal, which during the Middle Ages had been a fief of the king of Leon, broke off and became an independent state. The kings of Portugal were able to take Lisbon from the Moors in 1147 and to drive them entirely from the country about 1262. Thereafter, with the aid of the commercial interests of Lisbon and Oporto, they consolidated their power despite the opposition of the nobles and the church. In this the great national kings had the support of the merchants, and the process of national unification and progress was further promoted by a series of measures for the encouragement of commerce. King Diniz, for example, encouraged agriculture and commerce, signed a commercial treaty with England in 1294, and established a Portuguese navy under the command of a Genoese admiral in 1317, the year of the first Venetian "Flanders fleet." John I, the father of Prince Henry the Navigator, offered bounties, timber, and exemptions from military service to shipbuilders, built a navy for the protection of commerce, and bound his country closely to England by marrying an English princess, the daughter of John of Gaunt, and by making a treaty of commerce with that country in 1386. The rise of an integrated Portugal was thus bound up with the interests of the merchants, and it was a combination of forces between the merchants and the state that brought the Portuguese search for new trade routes and new lands to its final complete success.

Similarly, the unification of Spain into four or five small kingdoms, then two, and then one, is the story of the gradual rise of the kings above the power of the nobles. The process was consummated, after the marriage of Ferdinand of Aragon and Isabella of Castile in 1469, when they ascended the throne of a united Spain in 1474. They began a program of consolidation of their power which completely reduced the power of the nobles and finally drove the Moors from the peninsula in 1492. Ferdinand and Isabella made effective use of the *hermandades* in bringing about these results, and gave the cities and the merchants certain city rights and mercantile encouragements that made for the growth of both internal and external trade. Barcelona, indeed, had long been one of the proudest and most cultured of the Mediterranean cities—the first city to have a bank of deposit and the home of the first code of maritime law— the *Consolato del Mare*. With the unification of the Spanish state and the Reconquest, the cities of the west and south, and particularly Seville and Cadiz, became centers of foreign trade. By the middle of the fifteenth century Cadiz was sending its merchant ships down the coast of Africa and up the coast of Europe; and this overseas expansion, long before the time of Columbus, was the result of the capitalistic and political cooperation of the merchants and the kings.

The unification of France was carried forward in the thirteenth century by several kings, of whom Philip Augustus is perhaps the most notable. Beginning with the Île de France and the city of Paris, the French kings gradually extended their sway and their language over the center, the east, and the south of France. They fought the Hundred Years War to eject the English claimants to the French throne, which they finally succeeded in doing in 1453. Thereafter, the process of integration was completed by the annexation of Anjou and other areas in the second half of the same century by crafty Louis XI. Here, again, the kings began the subjugation of the nobles with the aid of the cities, but here as elsewhere, also, the cities eventually found that they had to submit to the power of the state they had helped to create just as the nobles had done. But it was relatively easy for the towns to allow themselves to become amalgamated in the national France. For the now national kings encouraged their commerce; and, when the time came, they encouraged and even subsidized voyages of exploration and created monopolies for the exploitation and the colonization of the "new world" overseas.

The national integration of England was probably promoted by England's defeat in the Hundred Years War. For English effort, economic and political, was henceforth to be concentrated upon England itself, rather than upon the old dynastic claims of English kings in France. The country was torn by the civil Wars of the Roses until 1485, when Henry Tudor, as King Henry VII, ascended the throne and turned his attention to the economic stabilization of the country. He had the cooperation of the merchants—he was interested in business himself—and promoted their prosperity both at home and in his diplomacy. In the latter case, the *Intercursus Magnus* (1496), a treaty made with the Dukes of Burgundy, then rulers of the Low Countries, had as its objective the expansion of the continental market for English woolen cloth. And it was this same merchant-king, Henry VII, who sent John Cabot out in 1497 to search for a northerly route westward to Cathay.

Thus the political state lent its power, protection and support to the movements of commercial expansion. By the adoption of national economic policies, every encouragement was given to the national merchants. Export and import could be carried on only by royal license; foreign merchants were limited in their activities, and sometimes their establishments were closed in favor of the home merchants—as, for example, in England, when the Steelyard, agency of the once all-powerful Hanseatic League, finally came to its end. The export of money was limited or prohibited. Native industry was encouraged, and native products were given advantages over foreign products. For this was the period in which the notion of economic nationalism was germinating. The national interest was seen to lie in the promotion of economic life, and this conviction led eventually to the set of ideas and practices known as mercantilism. Not only that, the thoughtful portions of the population were coming to be conscious of a difference between their own and "foreign" peoples—differences of language, it may be, or of social customs, or of traditions, or of government. And some men began to feel that somehow the glory and the honor of their nation was their own, and that exploits and missions and conquests in foreign seas could only redound to the "national" glory. It would of course be too much to say that the mass of the people felt much of this distinctly modern emotion; that had to await the invention of modern means for the communication of ideas and feelings. But the kings and the enlightened bourgeoisie, and even the nobles, began to share in the consciousness of national identity, and to take a nationalistic interest in overseas expansion.

THE AWAKENING OF POPULAR INTEREST
IN OVERSEAS ADVENTURE

Another prerequisite to vigorous European expansion overseas was the development of a widespread popular interest. The Crusades had taken many Europeans into the lands bordering the Mediterranean to the eastward, and contact with a higher culture had stimulated the tastes and the intellectual interests of the crusaders in many things besides religion. And the tales of wealth, splendor, and adventure told by the returning crusaders doubtless fired the imagination and the wanderlust of many others.

In the first half of the thirteenth century events in Asia became propitious for closer contacts between the east and the west. For the Tartars, under the leadership of Genghis Khan, swept out of central Asia eastward and westward, with the result that, by 1241, all the territory from the Vistula to the China Sea had come momentarily under the sway of one man, and a traveler might go from one end of this vast empire to the other without fear of serious molestation. The Pope, Innocent IV, in 1245 sent to the court of the Great Khan at Kara Korum an embassy, headed by John of Plano Carpini; and Louis IX, king of France, sent another, under William de Rubruquis, in 1253. Thereafter, missions were established in several places in China; by 1306 there were three Christian Churches in Peking and two in Amoy, with others elsewhere in China, as well as scattered Christian "houses" in Turkestan and India. These missions did not last; but the missionaries left narratives of their travels that were of absorbing interest to the Europeans who were able to read them.

But contacts between east and west were not all of a missionary or religious nature. There had been commerce across the plains of central Asia from antiquity, and far-eastern goods had found their way through the markets of the trading towns of the Caspian and Black Sea regions and thence westward. Thus it was that the Polo brothers of Venice were engaged in trade with Black Sea ports by way of Constantinople. In 1260 Maffeo and Nicolo Polo made a trading expedition to Serai, Tartar capital on the Volga. While there they were temporarily cut off from return by the outbreak of war to the south, and decided to accept the invitation of the Great Khan to go to Peking. The Great Khan received them well, and sent them back, armed with a letter of safe-conduct, to request the Christian Pope to send to his court 100 missionaries and some oil from the Holy Sepulchre at Jerusalem. The brothers were not successful in getting the missionaries, but on their return to China in 1271 they took with them Marco Polo, son of Nicolo, then a boy of sixteen. Marco found special favor in the eyes of the Great Khan, and became a trusted official. He remained in China about twenty years, and came to know it well. After his return to Europe by way of India in 1292, he wrote an account of his travels that became the most famous travel-book of all time, and had a profound influence upon the work of later explorers, very probably upon the Portuguese Prince Henry and certainly upon Christopher Columbus.

For Marco Polo described the wonders of Cathay and of Asia in terms that could not fail to excite the curiosity, the religious interest, or the cupidity of his European readers. He described the Tartars and their kingdoms, the fabled Christian kingdom of Prester John, and the splendor and magnificence of Kamboluc (Peking) and the court of the Great Khan. Of China he described the principal cities, and his descriptions are based on personal observation: Nanking, whose people used paper money and manufactured tissues of silver and gold; Quinsay (Hangchow), "the celestial city," which surpassed all other cities of the world by its grandeur and magnificence, with its great market squares where fifty to sixty thousand people assembled at one time, its courtesans who made the city a sort of paradise, and the wealth of its merchants; Zayton (Amoy), one of the largest and busiest ports of the world, where vast quantities of pepper and other commodities were imported from India and Java, and drugs, sandalwood, silks, porcelain, jewels, and other fine manufactures were exported. Marco described, also, India and Persia, which he visited on his way home, and the isles of the ocean, including even distant Madagascar and Zanzibar, of which he heard reports and with which the Arab traders of the Red Sea and the Persian Gulf had developed a steady trade. Many of the passages in Polo's book were marked by Christopher Columbus in the copy he took with him to America. In his journal Columbus noted, on November 1, 1492, after having seen several of the islands of the West Indies, "I am in front of Zayton and Quinsay." Marco Polo heard of Japan, but never went there; he described it as being rich, and as being some 1,500 miles to the eastward of China. Both Columbus and John Cabot, who probably also had read Polo's book, thought they were in the neighborhood of Japan when they arrived in America.

Marco Polo's book, even though printing had not yet been invented, was copied many times over, and after the invention of printing about 1450 it was one of the first books to be printed, in practically every European tongue. But this was only the greatest and most influential of a considerable number of books descriptive of the east. There were numerous compilations of "travels," and guidebooks for travelers. The most significant of the latter was the *Practica della Mercatura*, a sort of guidebook for merchants by Francesco Balducci Pegolotti of Florence, written about 1335, giving descriptions of the routes to the far east, and widely used by traveling merchants during the fourteenth century. Perhaps the most notorious of the travel books was the one called *The Travels of Sir John Mandeville,* written about 1360 by a French plagiarizer who 'had never been in the regions he described, but whose fantastic descriptions of the lands of the east were read, and probably believed, by a very great number of people.

These books, and many others, were being widely read by those who could read in western Europe during the fourteenth and fifteenth centuries. It must be remembered, to be sure, that the percentage of literacy was very small; but those who could read the books evidently passed on the contents to those who could not. For by the beginning of the fifteenth century there was a very considerable popular interest in travel and adventure in lands outside Europe; indeed, many voyages of exploration had already been made.

THE DEVELOPMENT OF NAVAL AND GEOGRAPHIC SCIENCE

The popular interest in travel and adventure abroad, that sent men upon exploring expeditions into regions where Europeans had never gone before, was one aspect of the intellectual era that has come to be called the Renaissance. Another aspect of the Renaissance, and one of supreme importance to exploration and cultural expansion, was the revival of applied science, or invention. For it was the development of instruments of astronomy and navigation in the thirteenth, fourteenth, and fifteenth centuries that for the first time made long voyages over the uncharted ocean practicable.

Long before the Mediterranean merchants knew of it, the Arab navigators of the Indian Ocean had learned, perhaps from the Chinese, that a needle rubbed with lodestone seemed always to point directly at the pole-star. This was the beginning of the compass. Already, by the time of Marco Polo, the magnetized needle was in use by the Sicilians, who improved it by mounting the needle, or metal "fish" formerly allowed to float free in a basin of water, upon a fixed post in a box. By the beginning of the fourteenth century the compass was in general use by ships sailing the Mediterranean, although some of the sailors looked upon it with horror as a device of the devil, and in some cases even refused to sail in ships that carried it. The English mariners seem to have adopted the use of the compass during the fourteenth century, and by the fifteenth it was in general use all along the Atlantic coast of Europe.

Another instrument of inestimable value to the navigators of the ocean was the astrolabe, direct ancestor of the modern sextant. This instrument, making possible a fairly accurate calculation of the altitude of the sun, and, therefore, of latitude, was probably known to the ancients. The Arabs, who passed it on to the Europeans, seem to have gotten it from the Greeks in the first place, but it had not been used, and it became current only with the revival of the sciences of geography and cartography and astronomy—the "ptolemaic renaissance." This instrument came into general use in the thirteenth and fourteenth centuries, and its use was assisted by the tables of solar declination or ephemerides published by Regiomontanus (Jean de Koenigsberg) in 1473. The quadrant was a simplification of the astrolabe; the "Jacob's staff" was an instrument that calculated the sun's altitude by a sliding disk on a graduated bar of wood. Longitude was much more difficult to calculate than latitude, and it was not until the eighteenth century, with the perfection of the chronometer, that it could be done with a satisfactory degree of accuracy.

All these instruments contributed to the assurance which, for the first time, men began to feel in venturing far out over the western ocean. But contemporaneously with the invention of instruments of navigation there also took place a revival of the study of geography and of astronomy. The revival of interest in the study of the ancient geographers was an integral part of the revival of ancient learning, and a widespread discussion of the nature, shape and extent of the earth was the result, particularly among the Italians and Catalans who were in daily contact with commerce and far-sailing ships. Similarly, the revival of the study of astronomy resulted in new knowledge with regard to the stars, culminating in the work of Regiomontanus, Copernicus, and Galileo. From the mariner's point of view, the greatest practical result was the publication of tables of the altitude of the sun and the positions of the stars, and, most especially, the improvement in map-making.

The improvement in maps was the result of efforts by both the practical navigators and the theoretical geographers. The ancestor of the accurate modern map is, indeed, the *portolano*, or small handbook, containing descriptions of harbors, shorelines, and channels, together with very accurate outline maps of the shoreline, carried by the Italian navigators. (Eventually, the name *portolano* came to be given to the maps, as well as the books.) But with the advance of geographic knowledge, the map-makers were able to include more and more of the area of the earth with a certain amount of dependability. The most famous geographers of antiquity, Eratosthenes of Alexandria (276-196 B.C.) and Ptolemy (C. 151-127 B.C.), had both showed that the earth was round, and Eratosthenes had calculated its circumference almost exactly. With the revival of ancient knowledge and the appearance of a Latin translation of Ptolemy in 1409, his work was brought again to the attention of Europeans. His map of the world prolonged Asia much too far to the eastward, and this accident is probably one of the causes of the voyages of Columbus. Ptolemy's map was successively modified in other directions, however, long before Columbus, by the cartographers who incorporated in their maps the results of the rapid expansion of geographic knowledge. The revived science of cartography seems to have had its chief centers, during the fourteenth and fifteenth centuries, at Genoa and Majorca. One of the most interesting of the maps of this period is the "Catalan Map" of 1375, which already showed the islands in the Atlantic off the coast of Africa. It is probable that this map may have had a very considerable influence upon the work of Prince Henry the Navigator.

One other technical improvement contributed to what might be called the revolution of navigation. That was the change that took place in the construction and in the sailing of ships. For the boats that sailed or were rowed over the relatively smooth waters of the Mediterranean were not capable of constant service in the rough and stormy waters of the Atlantic. In the ports along the Atlantic, and particularly in Portugal, ships became larger and rounder. Because of the relatively steady winds, an increasing dependence upon sail made for the disappearance of oars, and this tendency was hastened by the difficulty of rowing great ships in the ocean where huge waves made the use of oars practically impossible. Finally, invention of the fore-and-aft rig and the perfection of tacking—by Fletcher of Rye, in 1539—a technique that made it possible to sail much closer to the wind than the older ships could do, made the handling of sailing ships so easy that the doom of the Mediterranean galley was sealed, even though it hung on for a century or more longer. There is a direct connection between the so-called "commercial revolution," marked by the movement of the commercial center of gravity out of the Mediterranean into the Atlantic, and the revolution in ship construction.

In any case, the revival of ancient knowledge, the study of astronomy and geography and cartography, the invention of the compass, the astrolabe and the chronometer, and the evolution of shipbuilding, all contributed to the solution of the practical problems of navigation that had to be solved before men could venture with comparative safety out upon the unknown and uncharted ocean waters. Indeed, it is difficult to see how the practical work of the explorers could have been done without this intellectual and technical preparation.

RECOMMENDED BOOKS FOR FURTHER READING

CONTEMPORARY NARRATIVES

Julius E. Olson and Edward G. Bourne, eds., *The Northmen, Columbus and Cabot,* pp. 3-74.

Marco Polo, *The Book of Ser Marco Polo, the Venetian,* edited by Henry Yule.

MODERN ACCOUNTS

Wilbur C. Abbott, *The Expansion of Europe,* I, Chapters 1-2, 4.

Charles R. Beazley, "Marco Polo and the European Expansion of the Middle Ages," in *Atlantic Monthly,* CIV, 493-501.

Edward P. Cheyney, *The Dawn of a New Era, 1250-1453.*

Edward P. Cheyney, *European Background of American History, 1300-1600.*

Clive Day, *A History of Commerce,* Parts II and III.

John Fiske, *The Discovery of America.*

Geoffrey M. Gathorne-Hardy, *The Norse Discoverers of America, the Wineland Sagas.*

Carleton J. H. Hayes, *A Political and Cultural History of Modern Europe,* I, Chapters 1-3.

Herbert Heaton, *Economic History of Europe,* Chapters 5-11.

Hjalmer R. Holand, *Westward from Vineland.*

Edward M. Hulme, *The Renaissance, the Protestant Revolution and the Catholic Reformation in Continental Europe,* Chapters 1-9, 11.

Arthur P. Newton, ed., *Travel and Travellers of the Middle Ages.*

Laurence B. Packard, *The Commercial Revolution, 1440-1776.*

Albert F. Pollard, *Factors in Modern History.*

Henri Pirenne, *Economic and Social History of Medieval Europe.*

Henri Pirenne, *Medieval Cities.*

Preserved Smith, *The Age of the Reformation,* Chapter 11.

John K. Wright, *The Geographical Lore of the Time of the Crusades.*

3

The Age of Exploration

O NE OF the most profoundly significant events in the entire history of western civilization was its expansion outside the bounds of Europe, first around the shores of the Atlantic basin, and eventually entirely around the world. In the course of about three centuries the civilization of Europe sent out branches from which, reaching around the world, sprang new cultures, fundamentally European in nature, but which eventually became independent, with distinguishing characteristics peculiarly their own. This process is still going on, despite the fact that the outward-flowing waves of European influence have at certain points beat upon a resistance of incompatible native cultures that is driving the European influences back upon themselves. But the most dramatic and romantic phase of the European overseas adventure was its beginnings, the ages of discovery and of overseas colonization, long since ended, when Europeans seemed to take to the water like a flock of young ducks, and when the world overseas, in their eyes, was new.

THE ITALIAN PHASE OF THE AGE OF EXPLORATION

During the thirteenth and fourteenth centuries, as a result of the circumstances described in the preceding chapter, the commerce of Europe with the Near East enjoyed a rapid growth. But this was not enough to absorb the expanding supply of new capital. Europeans began to look for new markets and for new sources of goods that would sell at a profit in Europe. And it was only natural that the Italians should have been the first to go out in search of new lands, new markets, and new routes of trade; nor is it strange that the Italian navigators, with their long training and experience, should have been the teachers of the exploring merchants and mariners of the cities and states on the Atlantic seaboard.

The Arabs, indeed, had already done much to expand the bounds of geographic knowledge and to improve the science of navigation. For, besides bringing the primitive compass and the astrolabe to European sailors, they had explored the shores of the Indian Ocean eastward to India and southward, along the eastern shore of Africa, as far as Zanzibar and Madagascar, before the time of Marco Polo. Edresi, greatest of Arab geographers (born 1099), lived at the court of Palermo, in Italy, and doubtless exercised a considerable influence upon the growth of geographic knowledge there. But the Arab geographers were followers of Ptolemy—whom they liked, it was said, because Ptolemy did so well and accurately all that he knew and did all that he did not know so much better! The new geographic knowledge was to be based upon accurate observation rather than imagination; and the Italians superseded the Arabs precisely by the accuracy of their maps, the improvements they made in the instruments of navigation, and by their slow and steady accumulation of geographic knowledge and seamanship that made them for two centuries the most dependable seamen in the west.

In 1270, about a year before Marco Polo started from Venice for China, Lancelot Malocello sailed from Genoa and out of the Mediterranean in search of the "Fortunate Isles," or Canaries (Isles of Dogs), that had been known to the Romans and from which, eastward, Ptolemy had marked the longitude on his map of the world. The details of Malocello's voyage, and its results, are shrouded in mystery, but it seems clear that it was followed by others like it. For Petrarch, who was twenty years of age when Marco Polo died, speaks of numerous voyages to the isles in the time of his father. Certainly it was not long before the isles were well known, for they appear on a Catalan map published in 1339. Five years later, in what was probably the first grant of non-European lands in the Atlantic to Europeans for colonizing purposes, Pope Clement VI, at Avignon, presented the islands to Don Luis de la Cerda, Admiral of France, whom the Pope dubbed "Prince of the Fortunate Isles." The Italians had been the first to rediscover the Canaries, but the Papal grant displeased not only the Italians, but the Portuguese as well; for they had claims to the new lands based upon voyages of exploration as recent as 1336. Even England protested, on the ground that the Canaries were part of the British Isles.

The ancients also had believed that Africa was an island. The Carthaginians were said to have attempted to circumnavigate it, and the Pharaoh Necho sent an expedition of Tyreans on the same errand. Now the idea was revived, and Tedirio Dorio, with the brothers Vivaldi, set out from Genoa in 1291, four years before Marco Polo's return from Cathay and two hundred years before Columbus, "to go by sea to the ports of India to trade there." They sailed down the coast of Africa, touching here and there as they went, but eventually disappeared. The voyage of the Vivaldi was

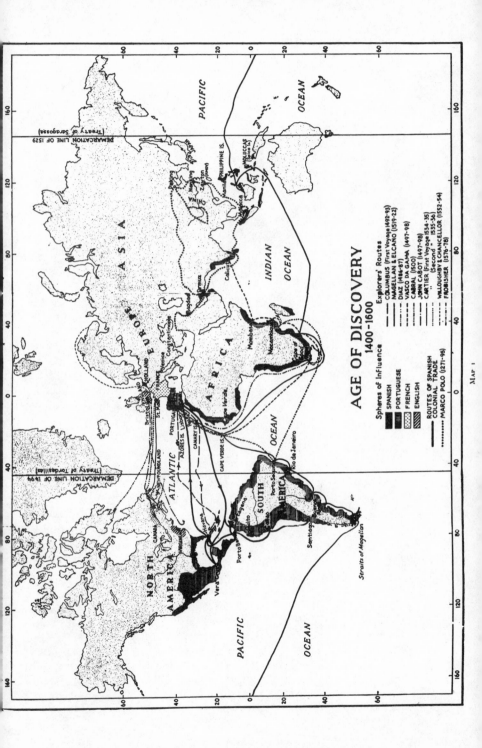

AGE OF DISCOVERY
1400-1600

Spheres of Influence

SPANISH
PORTUGUESE
FRENCH
ENGLISH

ROUTES OF SPANISH
COLONIAL TRADE

MARCO POLO (1271-95)

Explorers' Routes

COLUMBUS (First Voyage 1492-93)
MAGELLAN & ELCANO (1519-22)
DIAZ (1486-87)
VASCO DA GAMA (1497-98)
CABRAL (1500)
JOHN CABOT (1497-98)
CARTIER (First Voyage 1534-35)
CARTIER (Second Voyage 1535-36)
WILLOUGHBY & CHANCELLOR (1552-54)
FROBISHER (1576-78)

MAP I

apparently not soon repeated; but voyages down the coast of Africa became frequent during the fourteenth century, not only by the Italians, but also by Catalans, and, apparently, by the merchants of Dieppe and Rouen in France. In any case, Guinea, as a region on the southern shore of Africa producing gold, ivory and pepper, had become known to the Italians, the Marseillais and the Catalans, from the trans-Sahara traders who brought the products of Guinea overland to the shores of the Mediterranean for sale.

Thus the first impulse to exploration and an expansion of the bounds of commercial geographic knowledge was given by the Italians and followed the obvious path leading to the isles of the Atlantic and the west coast of Africa. But the greatest contribution of the Italians to the Age of Discovery, after their maps and instruments, was their service as officers and seamen in the navies and the merchant fleets of the western states. The king of Portugal appointed a Genoese admiral of the Portuguese navy, created in 1317; and for two centuries thereafter, among the crews and commanders of Portuguese, Castilian, English and French ships there were very many Italians. It was in this way that Cabot, Verrazano, and Columbus himself, all Italians, made discoveries in the name of England, France, and Spain. The Italians were indeed the teachers of the west in the science of geography, navigation, discovery and exploration.

THE PORTUGUESE PIONEERS

The Portuguese, too, had early taken to the sea. With the unification of the Portuguese state, the growth of Portuguese commerce, and the appearance of a Portuguese navy and merchant-marine, ships flying the Portuguese flag began to appear in the ports of northern Europe and the Mediterranean. And it has already been noted that the Portuguese were among the first to visit the northerly coasts of Africa and the Canaries.

But the true flowering of Portuguese discovery came as the result of the efforts of a prince of the royal house, Henry, called the Navigator. Henry, the son of John I of Portugal and the daughter of John of Gaunt, "half an Englishman by blood and more than half in character," was born March 4, 1394. He was educated in an atmosphere charged with commercial expansion and crusading zeal. Most important of all, Henry appeared at a time when all the necessary prerequisites for his career had been prepared: there was capital available for the financing of his explorations, together with the capitalistic spirit of speculation; Portugal had made such progress in its advancement toward national statehood as to provide a strong, permanent national backing and protection for his enterprise; and the sciences of geography and navigation had progressed so far as to make it possible for ships to sail for days, or even weeks, out of sight of familiar landmarks and return safely to their home ports. The Italians had already shown the way, and the Portuguese themselves had successfully begun a search for new lands to conquer and to convert. The world of western Europe was poised, as it were, for exploratory flights into the geographically unknown. Henry of Portugal was born at the proper moment, so to say, to become the pilot for those flights.

Henry was himself a man of austere mold. Deeply religious, he apparently had the crusader's desire to win a victory for Christianity by turning the flank of the Mohammedan hordes in Africa. At the same time, he was moved by the scientist's curiosity to explore new fields of knowledge, and as a patriot he hoped to add territory to the crown of Portugal. Most of all, he believed that the exploration of the coasts of Africa would bring him to Guinea and its wealth of gold, ivory and pepper, and finally, in all probability, "all the way to the Indians who are said to worship the name of Christ," with a consequent share in the lucrative trade in far-eastern commodities that was now a monopoly of the Italian cities.

Henry had probably learned of Guinea at Ceuta, which he helped his father conquer in 1415. He had read the ancient writers, and was convinced that Africa was an island. He was also familiar with the Italian voyages of the Vivaldi and their followers, and especially with Italian and Catalan maps. Then, when he was appointed governor of the Algarves, about 1419, he established his home on Cape St. Vincent, looking westward and southward over the ocean, and began to send his captains out from the little port of Sagres, on the Cape, to seek the southern lands. From 1422 onward, Henry sent out yearly expeditions down the African coast, and these expeditions visited the Canaries, the Madeiras, and eventually the Azores. But it took twelve years to pass Cape Bojador, beyond which toward the equator the ocean was thought to be boiling hot, or inhabited by great monsters—some said Satan himself—who devoured ships and men who ventured too far. Evidently, said some, this difficult cape was put there by God as a sign to men that they must go no farther, and to persist would be to fly in the face of God. But Henry commanded his men to go on, and finally, in 1434, Gil Eannes succeeded in passing beyond the cape and returning safely home. This was Prince Henry's greatest triumph, perhaps, for he had conquered the fears of his own men.

From then on, progress was fairly rapid. By 1436, they had passed the Rio de Oro. In 1441, they brought back some Negroes to tell of the country farther on, and in 1443 they began bringing back Negroes for sale as slaves; this was the beginning of the European-African slave trade. Now the merchants, who had held back while Henry financed his first expeditions out of his own funds, brought forward the capital for many voyages. And, while Henry continued to send out his explorers to show the way, the merchants followed to trade. They made good profits, too, of which the crown took its expected share. In 1444 Henry's explorers reached the Senegal River; in 1445 Dinis Diaz rounded Cape Verde. Henry had reached his goal, after twenty-five years or more of patient effort, and the Guinea trade at last was Portugal's: in 1445 twenty-five caravels sailed from Portugal to the trading stations on the African coast, and in 1446 there were fifty-six of them to sail.

Henry's fame spread all over Europe, and adventurers and explorers flocked to his standard. The merchants of Cadiz and Seville, hearing of it, began to trade on the African coast and in the islands, even advancing claims to both, on the grounds of prior discovery. But Henry appealed to the Pope, and he, as the umpire of all Christendom and the appointed disposer of all Heathendom, by a Bull of January 8, 1455, gave all the lands discovered and to be discovered by Henry southward and eastward toward India to Portugal. Interlopers in this Portuguese "sphere of influence" were to be thrown into the sea.

Henry continued his work until his death in 1460. The coast of Guinea was explored, and the Cape Verde Islands were discovered and explored in 1458. After Henry died his work was continued by his nephew, King Alfonso V and Alfonso's successor, John II. King John II, more nationalistic in his outlook even than Henry, threw all the influence and wealth of the crown into the business of exploration, using the gold from El Mina ("the mine"), amounting to some 170,000 gold doubloons annually, for the purpose. John II built up the informal *collegium* of navigators, astronomers and map-makers, that Prince Henry had begun, and this maritime organization was largely responsible for the brilliant climax of Portuguese exploration toward the end of the century. For with the aid of a commission of mathematicians, he was able to overcome the handicap to navigation beyond the equator inherent in the invisibility of the pole-star, by inventing a new method of finding latitude by the altitude of the sun at midday.

In 1482 he sent Diogo Cão to renew the search for the route to the Indies beyond the equator, which had been passed eleven years earlier. Cão found the mouth of the Congo River, and on a second voyage in 1485-86 he reached Cape Cross, almost at the southern end of Africa. In August of the next year Bartholomew Diaz sailed out to take up the work where Cão left off, and came to Walfisch Bay. After touching the coast again farther south, he ran before a northerly wind for thirteen days, then turned east to find the coast again. Not finding it, he turned north, and struck the shore to the eastward of the Cape of Good Hope. Success had crowned the Portuguese efforts at last, for they now knew they were on the route to India.

After a delay of ten years due to Portugal's domestic difficulties, the saga of Portuguese exploration reached its fitting climax in 1497, when Vasco da Gama, following the route of Bartholomew Diaz, rounded the Cape, picked up two Arab pilots at Mozambique, and sailed across the Indian Ocean into Calicut harbor, which he entered on May 22, 1498. On his return to Lisbon, completing the longest sea voyage yet made by man, and one much more difficult than that of Columbus, he brought home a cargo of East Indian wares that paid a handsome profit. More important still, he had opened a Portuguese route to the East, fulfilling the dreams of Henry the Navigator, and "Lisbon superseded Venice as the European mart for Eastern spices, then worth more than their weight in gold."

While da Gama was still in the east, the king of Portugal secretly sent Duarte Pachero westward to check up on the existence of lands reported by Columbus. Following upon his report, Pedro Alvarez Cabral, who sailed for India in 1500, was instructed to go far to the westward in making for the Cape of Good Hope. This he did, and fell upon the coast of Brazil. In the same year began a series of voyages by the Corte-Real brothers to the northwest to see whether the land touched by Cabot in 1497 was in the Portuguese sphere of influence under terms of the treaty of Tordesillas that had been signed by Spain and Portugal in the meantime in 1494. The Portuguese decided that it was; but what is more important is the fact that from these discoveries, the reports of Columbus, and the exploration of Brazil, the Portuguese quickly became convinced that the lands to the west constituted a new continent, and were not at all parts of the Indies, as Columbus claimed.

The Portuguese had explored the coasts of Africa and had found the true route to the Indies and, along with most contemporary cosmographers, they had found the right solution to the mystery of the western lands, "Antillia."

THE SPANISH PHASE: WESTWARD HO!

If the fifteenth century was Portugal's golden age of discovery, the early sixteenth was Spain's. Indeed, Castile already had its eyes fixed on the "new world," before Prince Henry died. The Catalans from Majorca and Barcelona had made voyages to the "isles" even before Henry was born. Castile contested Portugal's ownership of the Canaries, and even won Portugal's recognition to Spain's title to them as a Spanish sphere of interest in the treaty of Alcaçovas in 1479. But by the same treaty Spain had to recognize Portugal's right to Africa, and found itself shut out of expansion in that sphere. Thereafter, the crews of all Spanish ships found by Portuguese in African waters were thrown overboard. When, therefore, a Genoese navigator named Christopher Columbus appeared at the Spanish court with a scheme to discover an all-Spanish route to the Indies by sailing westward, Ferdinand and Isabella listened with interest, and submitted the scheme to a commission of "experts" for study. But the experts decided that his proposals were vain, impossible, and contrary to the teaching of the Bible. He was about to give up hope when his friends put him in touch with the Pinzon brothers, of Palos, who were interested themselves in westward exploration, and through their assistance Columbus again won the ear of Queen Isabella, and her financial support.

With his three small ships Columbus sailed from Palos on August 3, 1492. Taking the usual route to the Canaries, he fell into the trade winds, and, sailing straight before them westward, he sighted land—probably Watling's Island, in the Bahamas—on October 12. Naming it "San Salvador," he took possession of the new island in the name of the Catholic sovereigns of Spain. Then, after a rest of two days, he visited some of the other islands of the Bahamas. Turning southward, he came upon Cuba, which he told his crews was Japan. But Cuba did not answer to the description of Japan given by Marco Polo, so he continued his search. On December 5 he discovered Hispañola, and proceeded to build a small fort there—the first European colony in the western hemisphere. Leaving thirty-seven men in his fort, he fell into the northerly and easterly prevailing winds, and recrossed the Atlantic eastward.

Heavy weather drove him into the mouth of the Tagus, where, landing at Lisbon on March 4, 1493, he proclaimed that he had been to the Indies. The Portuguese were dumbfounded to hear that this man had done in one westward voyage what the Portuguese explorers had been trying to do by nearly a hundred years of systematic effort. (It was then only five years after Bartholomew Diaz' discovery of the Cape of Good Hope and still four years before the voyage of Vasco da Gama.) King John II immediately summoned Columbus to court. After courteously listening to Columbus' tale the king was suspicious that Columbus had been in the Portuguese sphere of influence, since the islands Columbus had discovered were thought to lie just a few leagues west of the Azores, and a Portuguese fleet was prepared to go and find out. At the request of King Ferdinand of Spain, however, the sailing of the Portuguese fleet was postponed until the ownership of the islands could be determined by negotiation. King John agreed, and negotiations began. But Ferdinand had already appealed to the Pope for confirmation of Spanish ownership, to which the Pope replied by a series of bulls (1493) that drew a line north and south one hundred leagues west of the Azores, and provided that all lands "discovered and to be discovered" to the west of that line should belong to Spain. Lands discovered to the east of the line were to be Portuguese. This principle was accepted by the Portuguese in the negotiations between the two states, but the line was moved 270 leagues to the westward in the treaty of Tordesillas (1494) that embodied it. Thus was the principle of "spheres of influence" established in the new world, following the pattern laid down in the treaty of Alcaçovas, already mentioned.

In 1493 Columbus made a second voyage to the western islands with a great fleet of seventeen ships. He arrived first at the Lesser Antilles, and, following the islands northward, came upon Puerto Rico, and finally landed once more at his colony on Hispañola. After reinforcing the colony he explored the southern coast of Cuba, then turned south to Jamaica. After some further disappointing voyages—for he still had not found any of the wealth described by Marco Polo—he returned to Spain again in 1496. He tried again in 1498, exploring the northern coast of South America, and a fourth time in 1502, when he explored the coasts of Central America, bitterly determined to prove, in the face of a growing skepticism at home, that he had actually discovered lands contingent upon Asia. He died in 1506, in bitterness, never having learned

that the lands he had discovered were really parts of a new continent lying between Europe and the east.

INTERNATIONAL RIVALRIES IN THE EXPLORATION OF THE "NEW WORLD"

After the second voyage of Columbus, other men quickly took up
the work of exploration. The news that he had discovered lands
to the westward which he reported to be the outposts of Asia excited the interest of the other commercial nations of the European
seaboard. There followed a century and a half of explorations made
by expeditions sent out by these competing nations for the purpose
of finding routes to the far east and of staking claims in the new
world as Portugal and Spain had done. These two nations thought
to set up closed spheres of interest for themselves by the presumptuous "line of demarcation." But the proclamation of this line was
not sufficient deterrent to prevent France and England from taking
immediate interest in the new lands to the west. In 1497 John
Cabot, an Italian living in Bristol, received from Henry VII permission to sail to the west and northwest in search of a passage to
India. Cabot, bearing a letter to the Great Khan, landed on the
northeast coast of America and returned with such glowing accounts of his exploits that King Henry VII awarded him a bonus
of ten pounds! Cabot thought he had reached Asia, but the king
of Portugal, hearing of Cabot's expedition, sent out two brothers,
Caspar and Miguel Corte-Real, to visit the land that Cabot had
discovered and to ascertain whether it were on the Portuguese side
of the line of demarcation. Both the Corte-Real brothers were lost,
but some of their ships returned, and Portugal claimed this north-
westerly land by virtue of the treaty of Tordesillas.

Spain also continued its explorations of the islands of the West
Indies and the mainland of America, and hearing of the British
"intrusions" in the Spanish sphere of influence, sent out Lucas
Vasquez de Ayllon in 1520 and Estevan Gomez in 1525 to explore
the lands that the British and the French had been visiting. Meanwhile, King Francis I of France, the personal rival of Charles I of
Spain, had sent out a Venetian by the name of Verrazano to do
some exploring for France. Verrazano visited the eastern coast of
North America and probably went as far north as the fiftieth degree of north latitude. In 1534 and 1535, Jacques Cartier of St.
Malo explored the gulf and river of the St. Lawrence for France,
and in the years 1541 and 1542, Cartier, with the Sieur de Roberval,

attempted unsuccessfully to establish a French colony on the river that Cartier had discovered. In Spain, meanwhile, Ferdinand Magellan, disgruntled at the treatment he had received in his native Portugal, convinced Charles I that he could reach the rich Spice Islands by sailing westward around the new continent of America and in 1519 proceeded to do so. Magellan himself was killed in a battle with the natives of the Philippine Islands, but one of his ships did succeed in circumnavigating the globe and returned in triumph to Cadiz in the year 1522.

The sixteenth century was thus marked by a succession of voyages of exploration, in the course of which the true nature of the land in the western hemisphere came to be known to Europeans, and most of the coastline of North and South America, with the exception of the northwestern coast of North America, was explored. Exploration had come to be a national enterprise, and the merchant princes of the commercial cities of England, France, Portugal, Spain and, later, Holland, backed by their wealth-seeking rulers, became the promoters of an era of geographic exploration that has never been equaled in intensity before or since. The century following the first voyage of Columbus was an era of great international rivalry for the establishment of spheres of influence in the new world. And this rivalry was the climax of a long period of commercial and capitalistic development within Europe itself. It was the trading nations of western Europe who were interested in discovery and exploration; and while they were more or less interested, also, in religious expansion, their chief concern was the discovery of new routes of trade with the old rich markets of the east, and the exploitation of the new lands, especially of those thought to be capable of producing gold and silver. It was this era of great competitive nationalistic and capitalistic enterprise that brought to the knowledge of Europeans new and exotic portions of the surface of the earth, demonstrated the attractiveness of the new world for scientists, for adventurers, for missionaries, and for investors, and led eventually to the spread of European civilization all round the shores of the Atlantic Ocean.

RECOMMENDED BOOKS FOR FURTHER READING

Contemporary Narratives

Henry P. Biggar, ed., *The Voyages of Jacques Cartier.*
Henry S. Burrage, ed., *Early English and French Voyages . . . 1543-1608.*

Richard Hakluyt, ed., *Principal Navigations . . . of the English Nation* (Everyman edition).
Frederick W. Hodge and Theodore H. Lewis, eds., *Spanish Explorers in the Southern United States, 1528-1543.*
Lionel C. Jane, ed., *Select Documents Illustrating the Four Voyages of Columbus.*
Richard H. Major, ed., *Select Letters of Christopher Columbus.*
Julius E. Olson and Edward G. Bourne, eds., *The Northmen, Columbus and Cabot.*
Edward J. Payne and Charles R. Beazley, eds., *Voyages of Elizabethan Seamen to America.*

MODERN ACCOUNTS

John N. L. Baker, *A History of Geographical Discovery and Exploration.*
Charles R. Beazley, *The Dawn of Modern Geography.*
Charles R. Beazley, *John and Sebastian Cabot.*
Charles R. Beazley, *Prince Henry the Navigator.*
John B. Brebner, *The Explorers of North America, 1492-1806,* Chapters 1-6.
Edward Channing, *A History of the United States,* I, Chapters 1-2.
Nellis M. Crouse, *In Quest of the Western Ocean.*
A. Grove Day, *Coronado's Quest.*
John Fiske, *The Discovery of America.*
William Foster, *England's Quest of Eastern Trade.*
James E. Gillespie, *A History of Geographical Discovery, 1400-1800.*
Henry Harrisse, *The Discovery of North America.*
Washington Irving, *The Life and Voyages of Christopher Columbus.*
Samuel E. Morison, *Admiral of the Ocean Sea.*
Samuel E. Morison, *Portuguese Voyages to America in the Fifteenth Century.*
Arthur P. Newton, ed., *The Great Age of Discovery.*
Edgar Prestage, *The Portuguese Pioneers.*
Irving B. Richman, *The Spanish Conquerors.*
Percy M. Sykes, *The Quest for Cathay.*
Henry Vignaud, *The Columbian Tradition on the Discovery of America.*
William C. H. Wood, *Elizabethan Sea-Dogs.*

4

The Earliest European Colonies
in America

THE AGE of exploration was also an age of colonization. For one of the essential teachniques of exploitation of the new world of discovery was the planting of agencies of conquest or commerce in the new lands just discovered, and these agencies tended quickly to become colonies. The Europeans were not content to come to a new land and trade with the natives and then return whence they came. They almost invariably left traders ashore, who had to be protected by fortresses and soldiers, and these posts, or forts, became the bases for further expansion of the areas of trade. Almost invariably, too, expansion meant conquest, and the subjection of the native peoples. This phenomenon followed similar patterns in Asia, in Africa, and in America.

It should be noted, however, that the colonization of Europeans in lands overseas in the sixteenth century was fundamentally different from the colonization of North America in the seventeenth century, since the first era of colonization was marked by conquest and the establishment of small, military colonies. The Europeans who went to the colonies in the seventeenth century, as a rule, went to the new world for the purposes of conquest or exploitation, but not to establish permanent homes there. Most of them expected to return "home" to Europe after a relatively short stay in the colonies. The colonization of North America in the seventeenth century, on the other hand, was marked by the migration of large numbers of people, and these men and women were intent, not upon conquest, a quick fortune, and a return to Europe, but upon acquiring land and establishing homes in the new world that would be permanent.

The earliest European colonies in America were of the former sort. Spain and Portugal began the process of planting European civilization on American shores, and for a century they had the field almost entirely to themselves. Several efforts to plant colonies in America were made by Frenchmen in the sixteenth century, all of which failed, and two or three efforts were made by Englishmen, with a similar result. The beginning of an era of successful

34

English, Dutch and French colonization in the seventeenth century is really the beginning of the second era of colonization, which was marked, as already suggested, by new characteristics of emigration, of colonial policy and of general outlook, which made this, as distinguished from the first century, an era of true colonization. These two centuries, in any case, saw the spread of European civilization to America, first as a foreign culture imposed upon the indigenous peoples, and then, in North America, as a movement of Europeans and their culture which gradually pushed the natives entirely out of the lands they had formerly occupied.

THE SPANISH EMPIRE

The first colony of Europeans in America was established by Christopher Columbus on the north side of the island of Santo Domingo in the course of his first voyage. The site he selected proved to be unsatisfactory and the colony was moved in 1496 to the south side of the island, and that settlement, the town of Santo Domingo, remains the oldest European city in the new world. Christopher Columbus and his brother Bartholomew, as governors of the new colony, failed to maintain order and to make the colony profitable. The king of Spain assumed control, therefore, in the year 1500, and sent over as governor Francisco de Bobadilla, who was succeeded in 1502 by Father Nicholas de Ovanda. Ovanda made the colony self-supporting by turning from a fruitless search for gold and silver to the cultivation of agriculture and the encouragement of the production of native plants and fruits. Meanwhile, from Santo Domingo as a base of operations other voyages of exploration were undertaken by the Spaniards, resulting in 1508 in the exploration of Cuba and in 1509 in the establishment of a colony on Puerto Rico. In the years from 1511 to 1514 Cuba was conquered and Santiago de Cuba and Havana were established. Juan Ponce de León, the governor of Puerto Rico, took an expedition to the coast of Florida in 1513.

During the same period other explorers had mapped the coastline of Mexico and the Isthmus of Panamá, and the Pacific had been discovered by Vasco Núñez de Balboa in the year 1513. The conquest of Mexico by Hernando Cortés in the years 1519-22 resulted in the expedition of great cargoes of wealth back to Spain and precipitated a gold rush from the island colonies to the mainland in the two decades following 1520. Peru was conquered by Francisco Pizarro between 1531 and 1534, and great quantities of the precious metals were shipped thence to Spain by way of Panamá. Buenos Aires was founded in 1536, Santiago de Chile in 1541. Mexico, Peru, the La Plata region, and Chile became the centers of a Spanish colonial empire on the mainland of America that extended from the Rio Grande practically to the southern tip of South America.

The work of exploration on the North American mainland which had been started by Ponce de León was carried forward by Alonzo de Pineda, who visited the coast of what is now the United States in 1519 and found trinkets of gold among the Indians. He was followed in 1528 by Pánfilo de Narváez, who set out to discover gold in the region of Florida but whose expedition met disaster on the western portion of the gulf of Mexico. One of his lieutenants, Alvar Nuñez Cabeza de Vaca, wandered across the plains of Texas and northern Mexico and eventually found his way to the Spanish settlements in 1536, after which he wrote an account of his wandering that constitutes one of the most thrilling narratives in all the literature of exploration. Narváez was followed in 1539 by Hernando de Soto, who died in the region west of the Mississippi River after four years of fruitless wanderings in the inhospitable swamps of the gulf coastal plains.

The Spanish explorations in the eastern parts of North America were without practical result. But the success of Spanish colonial establishments in Mexico and on the continent of South America led to the development of a great imperial system which in some ways provided a model for the colonial empires that were to follow. The first interest of Spain in the establishment of colonies, of course, had been the cultivation of trade relations with the Far East; but as the colonies began to prove their own worth, Spain more or less forgot its interest in the east and concentrated upon the exploitation of gold and silver mines in America. Gradually, as settlement progressed, the Spaniards turned to the development of agriculture and the raising of cattle for hides. Thus the production of gold and silver, coupled with the profits derived from the colonial trade, made Spain's empire an extremely profitable one and provided, indeed, a large part of the wealth by reason of which Charles I and his successors were able to make Spain one of the leading nations of Europe.

Even before Columbus died, control of the colonies had been placed under a special royal council called the Royal and Supreme Council of the Indies, of which the Archdeacon of Seville, Juan Rodriguez de Fonseca, was the head. From the first, too, trade and emigration to the Spanish colonies was limited to Spaniards, and the regulation of commerce under the Council of the Indies was placed in the hands of the *Casa de Contratación* (House of Trade) located at Seville and Cadiz. Colonial officials were appointed by recommendation of the Council of the Indies, laws for the colonies were made by the Council, and the regulation of commerce was left in the control of the merchants who made up the directors of the *Casa de Contratación*. The net result of all this organization was that the economic and political life of the colonies was controlled by men residing in Spain who had little or no familiarity with the actual situation in the colonies themselves.

The colonies were eventually organized in a number of vice-royalties; that of New Spain, the capital of which was Mexico City; the vice-royalty of Peru, centering at Lima; the vice-royalty of New Granada centering at Bogotá; and the vice-royalty of Rio de la Plata with its capital at Buenos Aires. Within each vice-royalty there were often a number of captaincies-general, such as the captaincy-general centering at Havana, Cuba, and within each captaincy-general there were a number of presidencies, each with its governor. As early as 1511 the governor of Santo Domingo was given a council called the *audiencia* composed of three members. This *audiencia* constituted both a court for the adjudication of crimes and disputes and a council for the advice of the governor. The power of the governor, on the other hand, who was appointed directly by the king, was theoretically unlimited; but his actions might be checked at any time by the so-called *residencia,* composed of specially appointed investigators. The only semblance of self-government in the Spanish colonies was the government of the towns, in which the *cabildo* or local town council was composed of merchants representative of the population and which had the right to petition the king directly.

The greatest single need of the Spanish conquerors in the administration of their new lands was for labor. But the Spaniards themselves were not sufficiently numerous—nor were they inclined—to perform all the needed labor in the mines and on their ranches. The most obvious supply of labor existed in the native population; but the natives were no more naturally disposed to hard labor than their conquerors—rather less so, in fact. It became necessary, therefore, for the Spaniards to devise some system for forcing the natives to work, and this need was supplied by the *repartimiento* and the *encomienda.* The significant feature of the *repartimiento* was its nature as the grant of a large area of land to some outstanding nobleman and his family, and in order to provide him with labor with which to work his grant, he was given an *encomienda* which gave him the authority to force the natives on his land to labor. Originally the *encomienda* was instituted not only to provide a supply of labor but also to place upon the landholder the responsibility for civilizing the natives; but its actual result was the practical enslavement of the native populations, which led to their great degradation and in some cases their practical annihilation. With the partial failure of the *encomienda* system, Negro slaves were introduced into the Spanish colonies to supply the need for cheap labor, and from the middle of the sixteenth century onward the Negroes constituted a large portion of the laboring population.

One of the major factors in the transit of Spanish civilization to Spain's empire in America was the work of the Spanish Catholic church. For of all the cultural influence of the Spaniards upon their subject peoples, the most powerful and lasting was that exercised in the field of religion. The bishops of Mexico and Lima were the heads of the hierarchy of the church as the viceroys were heads of the hierarchy of administration. The church, moreover, was not merely a religious body in the modern sense; it had its schools, its own laws, and its own economic activities. In the communal villages of the natives, it regulated practically every activity in the native's life—even to the limitation of the conjugal relationship to certain hours of the night, which were announced by the beating of a drum! It is probably not too much to say that, for the natives and the Spaniards not personally involved in politics, the church was the one agent of Spanish civilization which touched most closely and most universally the lives of the common people of Spanish America. Furthermore, it was the same church, with the same religion and the same church laws, from one end of the Spanish empire to another. Both as an agent for control and as a disseminator of European culture, the church, with its priests and its missionaries, played a role of enormous importance in the history of the Spanish colonies.

But no great number of Spaniards ever migrated to America. It is probable that at no time did the number of Spaniards in the Spanish colonies amount to more than five percent of the population. For Spain's chief interest in colonies was exploitation for the profit of the mother country, not the colonization of the new countries with people desirous of establishing homes there. The result was that while Spanish became the official language and Spanish civilization became ostensibly the civilization of these countries, its effect was superficial in most of the area under Spanish control. On the whole, what happened was the imposition of a European culture upon the native Indian culture in such a way that there resulted a mixture of the two. Recently there has taken place a strong, nationalistic resurgence of certain aspects of Latin-American civilization that were inherited from the Indians, rather than the Spanish.

PORTUGUESE BRAZIL

The colonial system established by Portugal in its colony of Brazil in some features differed markedly from that of Spain. Portuguese settlements were made along the coast of Brazil, but grew slowly until in 1530 Martim Affonso de Souza became governor. Shortly after Souza's appointment, and for the promotion of colonization, Portugal adopted the policy of granting *capitanias* along the coast to outstanding Portuguese noblemen who had the responsibility for establishing towns and transporting colonists to the new world. The relationship of these colonies to their aristocratic masters was a feudal one, based upon land tenure. From 1549 onward, sugar gradually came to be the greatest profit-making product of the country and the need for a labor supply led to brutal slave hunts among the natives and the importation of Negroes. The union of Portugal to Spain from 1580 to 1640 had little or no effect upon the Portuguese colonial system and presently there developed a semi-feudal plantation society governed by a governor-general appointed by the king of Portugal. Most of the functions of government, however, were performed by the holders of the *capitanias* along the coast.

FRENCH BEGINNINGS

For something over one hundred years after the successful establishment of the Spanish and Portuguese colonial empires, France and England were without colonies in the new world. Various attempts were made in the course of the sixteenth century, however, particularly by the French, to set up colonies in the lands discovered in the western hemisphere. In 1534 and 1535-36, as already noted, Francis I encouraged Jacques Cartier to search for a passage around America to the Far East, and Cartier's expeditions resulted in the exploration of the gulf and river of St. Lawrence. Then, in 1541, Jean Francois de la Roque, Sieur de Roberval, hoping to carve out for himself a great feudal landed estate in the new lands and to establish himself at a strategic point on the anticipated route to Cathay, and believing also that he might discover gold and silver in this part of the new world, took a colony of Frenchmen to Cap Rouge on the St. Lawrence River about twelve miles above the present city of Quebec. Cartier cooperated with Roberval in this venture and went ahead of him to build houses and a fort in anticipation of Roberval's coming. His settlers did discover some small but worthless diamonds in the sands of the river beaches, but the winter that Cartier and his men spent at Cap Rouge was disastrously cold, with the result that in the spring of 1542, before Roberval's arrival, Cartier decided to abandon the enterprise. He sailed out of the St. Lawrence and put into a harbor on the south shore of Newfoundland, only to meet Roberval on his way to Canada. Roberval ordered Cartier to turn back, but Cartier had had enough of this bitter climate and slipped his hawsers and sailed for France. Roberval went on to the settlement but he, too, found the bitter Canadian winter more than he could stand and returned to France in the spring of 1543.

The failure of Roberval's effort did not permanently discourage Frenchmen from colonial enterprises. It did apparently turn their attention to warmer climates, and with the spread of the Protestant doctrines in Catholic France, colonies came to be thought of as a suitable dumping ground for undesired Protestants. Thus it was that in 1555 Nicholas Durand de Villegagnon, supported by John Calvin and aided by Gaspard de Coligny, the Protestant Admiral of France, led a colony of Frenchmen to a small island off the coast of Brazil. He was not welcomed by the Portuguese, however, and partly because of the dissensions that sprang up in the colony itself, partly because of the Portuguese opposition, the enterprise was abandoned.

But the Protestants of France were not discouraged, and in the year 1562 Jean Ribaut led a motley group of sailors, soldiers, and nobles, most of whom were Protestants, to the River of May (St. John's River) in the Spanish-claimed territory of Florida. This was primarily a voyage of exploration, but some of the adventurers wished to stay in this pleasant country, so Ribaut left thirty of them and returned to France. The thirty who were left neglected to provide themselves with food and devoted their attention to a search for gold, with the result that they practically starved and eventually abandoned their post and set out for France. Having an inadequate food supply, they were reduced to the necessity of drawing lots to see which should be eaten by his fellows; but they came at last within sight of the shore of France—only to be taken captive by an English ship. In 1564 a second expedition went to Florida, this time under the command of René de Laudonnière. The men who composed this expedition were again, in name, Protestants, but they sought adventure and easy fortune rather than religious freedom or the establishment of homes. They built Fort Caroline on the River of May and devoted themselves to a search for gold, in the course of which they antagonized the Indians and came near to starvation. They, too, eventually decided to abandon the colony, but were relieved on the third of August, 1565, by the English adventurer John Hawkins, who sailed into the river on his way home from one of his slave-trading voyages to the Spanish Main. Hawkins sold Laudonnière a ship and the Frenchmen were awaiting a favorable wind to return home when, on August 28, a new fleet from Ribaut with 300 additional men appeared to reinforce the colony. Only a few days later, on September 4, 1565, a fleet of Spanish ships under Pedro Mendez de Aviles, sent to drive the Frenchmen out of Florida, appeared off the River of May. Having failed, for the moment, to destroy the French fleet, Aviles set to work to build the fortress of St. Augustine in preparation for a systematic campaign against the French post at Fort Caroline.

The appearance of the Mendez expedition was in conformity with a deep-rooted colonial policy of Philip II, now king of Spain. In the first place, Florida was located on the route followed by the Spanish treasure ships from Mexico and Havana on their way home, and any French colony that might be allowed to exist in Florida would be a constant threat to those ships. In the second place, this French colony had been established in defiance of Spanish rights, and Spain was determined to enforce what it considered to be its legitimate title to all the lands west of the line of demarcation. Finally, these Frenchmen were Protestants; and while religion was a secondary issue in the conflict, it at least made it easier for Mendez and his king to justify the slaughter that took place. The French colonists had determined to attack St. Augustine before it could be completed, and they set out in their ships to sail down the shore, but they were caught in a tropical hurricane and wrecked on the shore, where the survivors to the number of some three hundred were massacred in cold blood by the Spaniards. Thereupon, Mendez marched against Fort Caroline and destroyed it.

This was the end of the French colony in Florida, and for twenty years thereafter, during which time the attention of France was devoted to the religious and dynastic wars that divided the country, no serious effort was made to found any French colonies in the new world. In 1578 the Marquis de la Roche received a commission to occupy and settle the land in North America previously explored by Cartier. The first expedition went out in 1584 and was wrecked, but French interest in this northern country was revived and in 1588 a monopoly of the fur trade was issued to the nephews of Jacques Cartier, only to be withdrawn because of the protests of the fur merchants of St. Malo. In 1598 another expedition sent out by la Roche sailed for America. Sixty persons were landed on Sable Island while the ship went on to explore. The explorers were driven back to France by storms and the sixty persons left on Sable Island were forced for five years to subsist on cattle that had been left on the island by a previous expedition. In 1603 the twelve survivors were rescued by a special expedition sent out for the purpose by the king.

In 1599 a new monopoly of the fur trade was granted by King Henry IV to Pierre Chauvin on condition that he send fifty colonists to Canada, but Chauvin was interested only in the fur trade and again nothing came of this effort. Finally, on Chauvin's death in 1603, the Commander de Chastes was given the fur monopoly and de Chastes, in partnership with the fur merchants of Rouen and St. Malo, sent out an expedition in the year 1603 under the leadership of DuPont Gravé and Samuel de Champlain, which resulted in the establishment the next year, 1604, of Port Royal in Acadia, the first successful French colony in the new world. Four years later Champlain founded a more important post at Quebec.

It had taken a century, and a large number of disastrous experiments, to get the French flag firmly planted upon the shores of the new world. But the French colonizers showed the same desires for adventure, for land, for trade, and, most of all, for the quick road to fortune by the exploitation of gold and silver mines, that had inspired the Spaniards and the Portuguese before them. They also showed something of the same Catholic missionary zeal. But by the time the French efforts at colonization got seriously under way, the Protestant Revolt from Roman Catholicism had taken place in Europe, and to the motives already listed was added the impulse of Protestants to emigrate from the mother country to escape persecution—an impulse that was to have an enormous influence in the founding of the Anglo-Saxon colonies in North America.

ENGLISH BEGINNINGS OVERSEAS

During the first half of this century of colonial expansion, England had been only slightly interested in colonial enterprises. Its trade was rapidly expanding and it had devoted its attention chiefly to the affairs of commerce. Henry VIII had, indeed, been slightly interested in exploration, and in about 1527 seems to have sent out an expedition under the command of one John Rut; but Henry was more interested in building up English commerce with the continent and the countries of the Mediterranean, and in the promotion of an efficient and effective British navy. During the first half of the sixteenth century, however, English interest in trade with the far east became active and about 1555 there was formed the Muscovy Company, which grew out of an attempt to discover a route to China by way of the North Atlantic and the northeast. The northeast passage did not materialize, but the effort to find one opened the trade to Russia, which proved for a time to be very profitable. By 1560 Englishmen had again begun to consider the possibility of reaching the Pacific Ocean by way of a passage around America which was to be found by sailing northwestward, a passage which, they reasoned to their own satisfaction, must certainly exist. Martin Frobisher was commissioned by a group of English merchants to discover the northwest passage, but he succeeded, in three voyages (1576-78), only in bringing back a number of cargoes of what he thought was gold-bearing rock from Frobisher's Land which turned out to be worthless. He was followed by John Davis, who succeeded (1585-87), in discovering Davis Strait, but got no farther.

Leadership in English explorations to the northwestward was now assumed by Sir Humphrey Gilbert and his half-brother Sir Walter Raleigh. Gilbert had written a tract to prove the existence of the northwest passage and he now set out with Raleigh (1583) to found a colony on the island of Newfoundland. The expedition was popularized by Richard Hakluyt, who wrote a famous pamphlet, called *Discourse of Western Planting,* for the encouragement of English colonization in the new world. But the colony came to grief, and Gilbert lost his life on his way home. The interest in colonization was carried forward, however, by Sir Walter Raleigh, who now proposed to establish a colony farther to the southward. He petitioned Queen Elizabeth for permission to go and was granted a charter (1584) giving him title to the land of "Virginia."

He sent out a series of expeditions, which attempted to plant an English colony on the island of Roanoke, as will be noted in more detail later. These efforts, too, only resulted in failure.

Thus ended the first attempts of Englishmen to settle colonies in America. Their failure had demonstrated that the private fortune and interest of one man was hardly sufficient to sustain the losses necessary before any colony could achieve success. On the other hand, this first English attempt becomes very significant as indicating the lines that British colonial policy was to follow. It is significant also as illustrating the popular interest in colonial expansion that was now developing in England.

THE SIGNIFICANCE OF A CENTURY OF COLONIZATION

A brief review of the European efforts to found colonies in the American hemisphere in the sixteenth century presents a number of important factors in the movement. To begin with, most of the early foundations had their beginnings in the search for a passage to the far east. They thus grew out of an expanding world commerce, and the strongest motive behind them seems to have been the desire for commercial profits. There were other motives, however, notably the desire of some of the promoters of colonies to build up for themselves large feudal estates in America, and the desire to convert the natives to the Christian faith. No great number of Europeans actually migrated to America in the sixteenth century, and colonies were regarded merely as distant trading posts or military establishments in which men were on temporary duty. There was relatively little thought of establishing homes in the new world, although that motive was present, to be sure, in the minds of some of the colonists throughout the century. For the most part, colonization meant conquest, and the exploitation of the conquered by the conquerors. The true age of colonization opens at the end of the century, and was due chiefly to certain important developments during the century which brought considerable numbers of people to consider leaving their mother lands forever. The two most important of these factors were the development of an economic situation, particularly in England, which created a large body of people detached from the land who looked longingly to America toward the free land that might be had there, and the situation created by the Protestant Revolt, which split western Christendom into warring sects, one or another of which was constantly under persecution during two entire centuries—a situation which prompted many to seek escape to religious freedom in the new world. To these two developments must be added the political unrest that was developing in England as a result of the rising conflict between Parliament and the king. All three of these factors are visible in England during the reign of Queen Elizabeth, and must be kept in mind for an understanding of the appearance of a British empire in America.

The sixteenth century, then, was a century of tentative experiments in colonization and colonial policy on the part of Europeans in the new world. It was·also a century when the economic, social and political movements were taking place which were to change both the nature and the tempo of colonization, and were to make the seventeenth and eighteenth centuries the era of large-scale European emigration to America. The sixteenth was the century in which the transit of European civilization to America got under way.

RECOMMENDED BOOKS FOR FURTHER READING

CONTEMPORARY NARRATIVES

Edward G. Bourne, ed., *Narratives of the Career of Hernando de Soto.*
Henry S. Burrage, ed., *Early English and French Voyages . . . 1543-1608.*
Richard Hakluyt, *Discourse of Western Planting* (Hakluyt Society Publications, Second series, LXXVII).
Richard Hakluyt, ed., *Principal Navigations . . . of the English Nation* (Everyman edition).
Albert B. Hart, ed., *American History Told by Contemporaries,* I, Chapters, 2-5.
Alvar Nuñez Cabeza de Vaca, *The Journey of Alvar Nuñez Cabeza de Vaca and his Companions from Florida to the Pacific, 1528-1536,* edited by Adolph F. A. Bandelier.
Irene A. Wright, ed., *Documents Concerning English Voyages to the Spanish Main, 1569-1580* (Hakluyt Society Publications, Second series, LXXI).
Irene A. Wright, ed., *Spanish Documents Concerning English Voyages to the Caribbean, 1527-1568* (Hakluyt Society Publications, Second series, LXII).

MODERN ACCOUNTS

Wilbur C. Abbott, *The Expansion of Europe,* I, Chapters 12-16.
Edward G. Bourne, *Spain in America, 1450-1580.*
John B. Brebner, *The Explorers of North America, 1492-1806.*
The Cambridge History of the British Empire, I, Chapters 1-3.
The Cambridge Modern History, II, Chapter 16; III, Chapters 9-10.
Edward Channing, *A History of the United States,* I, Chapters 4-5.

Charles E. Chapman, *Colonial Hispanic America*, Chapters 1-4.

Edward K. Chatterton, *English Seamen and the Colonization of America*.

Julian S. Corbett, *Sir Francis Drake*.

Clarence H. Haring, *Trade and Navigation between Spain and the Indies*.

Frederick A. Kirkpatrick, *The Spanish Conquistadores*.

Roger B. Merriman, *The Rise of the Spanish Empire in the Old World and the New*.

Bernard Moses, *The Establishment of Spanish Rule in America*.

William B. Munro, *Crusaders of New France*.

Arthur P. Newton, *The European Nations in the West Indies, 1493-1688*, Introduction, Chapters 5-9.

Francis Parkman, *Pioneers of France in the New World*.

George B. Parks, *Richard Hakluyt and the English Voyages*.

Herbert I. Priestley, *The Coming of the White Man, 1492-1848*.

Percy M. Sykes, *The Quest for Cathay*.

Milton Waldman, *Sir Walter Raleigh*.

Clark Wissler [and others], *Adventures in the Wilderness*, Chapters 4-8.

Lowery Woodbury, *The Spanish Settlements in Florida*.

George M. Wrong, *The Rise and Fall of New France*, Volume I.

5

International Aspects of the Age of Discovery

THE DIPLOMACY OF THE COLONIZING NATIONS

THE DISCOVERY and exploitation of a new and hitherto unknown world outside the bounds of Europe had a profound effect upon the evolution of European diplomacy. For both the age of discovery and the appearance of a European diplomatic practice paralleled the emergence of the monarchic state and in a large sense sprang from it, and the new world became one of the great stakes in European diplomacy. Many times the colonies played important or even decisive roles in the making of European treaties or in the determining of national diplomatic policy, and at the same time many of the accepted principles of European diplomacy originated in the problems presented by international relations in the colonial world.

Modern diplomacy dates from the rise of the unified sovereign state. Diplomatic intercourse between peoples had of course always existed, but diplomacy defined as "the art of managed intercourse and adjusted relations between states by negotiations" dates from the appearance of permanent embassies among the states of Europe. Prior to the fifteenth century, business between states was carried on by means of special ambassadors sent on specific errands to accomplish specific purposes. Once the purposes of an embassy were accomplished, the ambassador returned home. But the rise of the sovereign state in the modern sense, and the problems of international commerce and colonial rivalry, produced a constant stream of correspondence between states and a series of problems arising between them that could only be solved by a permanent system of international correspondence. Each monarch felt himself under the necessity of setting up a permanent agent in the courts of his more important contemporaries to carry on this correspondence and to represent his interest in the negotiations pertinent to the settlement of these problems.

The small city states of Italy were the first to establish permanent embassies, and the city of Venice worked out a thoroughgoing set of rules to govern its ambassadors' conduct. Venetian ambassadors were required to surrender any gifts received while on mission to the government of the city; they were required also to furnish written accounts of their embassies upon their return; an ambassador was not allowed to take his wife with him on a mission for fear she might talk and divulge his secrets; he must take his own cook, lest he be poisoned. The implication in these rules was that the post of ambassador was secret and dangerous; that the ambassador was a man under suspicion and in danger of his life. This was, indeed, the case, for the ambassador was at the same time his master's agent for the promotion of his master's interest abroad and his master's eyes and ears for finding out the designs of his royal host. He was sent to reside "near" the court of some monarch, but the monarch actually kept him at as great a distance as politeness would allow.

The rules of ordinary morality did not apply to the conduct of an ambassador, for he represented the interests not of himself as an individual but of his state. The reason for this was that these adolescent European states based their diplomatic practice upon what has been called the Machiavellian system. This system was not invented by Nicholas Machiavelli, to be sure, but it was given his name because his book *The Prince* is a classic description of the actual practice of the states of Italy at the beginning of the sixteenth century. The essential idea in this system is that any measure whatever between states is justified if it promotes the selfish interest of the state in the direction of increasing the state's power or territorial extent. And an ambassador, as one English diplomat expressed it, was "an honest man sent to lie abroad for the good of his country."

The first permanent embassy was that established in Genoa in 1455 by the Duke of Milan, in the same year in which Pope Nicholas V issued the Bull giving the colonial world of Africa to Portugal. The practice was quickly adopted by other Italian city states and by 1494 Milan was represented in France by a permanent embassy and Venice had permanent ambassadors in England and the Holy Roman Empire. This practice was also taken up by the great states of western Europe—France, Spain, Portugal, and England—which emerged in the last half of the fifteenth century. In 1487 Spain established a permanent embassy in England—the oldest embassy with a continuous history existing in Europe today. In 1510 England established a permanent embassy in Spain and in 1519 another in France.

The appearance of a permanent European states system, then, coincides with the age of discovery, and some of its earliest and most troublesome problems were the problems that arose out of colonial expansion. It must be taken as a first principle that the policy underlying the colonial diplomacy of the great colonizing nations was truly and deeply Machiavellian. The aim of the colonizing states was to get and keep all they could; to keep others from getting anything if possible, and to use any policy which promoted their immediate interests, discarding it or violating it in favor of some other principle as soon as it ceased to serve their interests. Thus against a background of the emergent sovereign state and the colonial expansion of Europe, it should be noted that the relations of these states with each other, in dealing with the colonial problem, were based upon a monopolistic, mercantilist philosophy of state economy and a Machiavellian and utterly non-ethical system of international diplomacy.

FIRST RULES OF THE GAME

The first diplomatic rules governing the colonization of the new world were laid down long before the discovery of America. These principles were enunciated in connection with the exploring and colonizing work done by Henry the Navigator and his successors. For as early as 1435 Castile had begun to contest the Portuguese right to the Canaries and the coast of Africa, and by 1450 it had begun to send trading expeditions from Cadiz into the territories discovered by Henry's captains. Because of Castile's claim to the Canaries, based upon a Papal grant of 1402, the Pope issued a Bull in 1436 granting the Canaries to Castile. This grant was revised in the Bull of January 8, 1455, which grew out of Portugal's protest against Castilian interests in the Portuguese colonies of Africa.

Throughout the middle ages the Pope had been a sort of international umpire and the appeals of Spain and Portugal to the Holy See in their disputes over the colonial world were in accord with well-established practice. It was expected therefore that the rules laid down in the Bull of January 8, 1455, which gave Portugal the exclusive right to explore and convert the heathen beyond Cape Bojador southward and eastward might command the respect of both contestants. But the power of the Pope had greatly declined with the emergence of the national monarchies and Castile continued to claim Guinea as well as the Canaries. Therefore, when a dynastic war shortly broke out between Portugal and Spain, the war quickly became a colonial war also, and in the treaty of Alcaçovas, 1479, Castile gave up its claim to Guinea and the Azores, Madeira, and Cape Verde Islands in return for a clear recognition of its title to the Canaries. This treaty of Alcaçovas is of great interest because it not only recognized the Canaries as a Spanish sphere of influence and the coast of Africa as a Portuguese sphere, but it also recognized the right of both states to prohibit foreigners from trading in their respective spheres. Already, in these pre-Columbian rules of the game, it became an accepted principle that each state was to have its own sphere of colonial influence and that within that sphere its control was to be completely monopolistic.

When Columbus returned from his first voyage in 1493, he was forced by a storm to take refuge in the port of Lisbon. He was immediately summoned before the Portuguese king, who intimated that he had violated the treaty of Alcaçovas by going to lands recognized under that treaty as lying within the Portuguese sphere. When Columbus denied any violation of this treaty, the king of Portugal prepared an expedition to go out and investigate to make sure that Columbus was telling the truth.

THE LINE OF DEMARCATION

When news of the return of Columbus and the interference of the king of Portugal reached the ears of King Ferdinand and Queen Isabella, then residing in Barcelona, they made a hurried appeal to the Pope, Alexander VI, a Valencian, for a confirmation of the Spanish title to the lands Columbus had discovered, in order to forestall any Portuguese claim to them. The Pope complied with the Spanish request by issuing a series of Bulls in May and September, 1493, the most notable of which was the Bull *Inter Caetera* of May 4. This document confirmed the Spanish title to the lands that Columbus had discovered; it also proclaimed that all the lands discovered and to be discovered east of a line drawn from the north pole to the south pole 100 leagues west of the Azores should be Portuguese, and that all the lands discovered or to be discovered west of that line should be Spanish.

The Pope of course did not know how much of the earth's surface he was thus airily presenting to Spain and Portugal. The assumption of the right to do so, however, did not seem as preposterous then as it does to moдern minds. For the Pope was recognized as having the power to assign to any Christian king heathen lands for the purposes of civilization and conversion to Christianity. On the other hand, it was hardly to be expected that the other nations interested in commercial expansion overseas would long accept this presumptuous division of the entire new world between the two Hispanic kingdoms.

To Spain and Portugal, however, the arrangement was eminently satisfactory, except that Portugal complained that the Papal line of demarcation fell too close to the Azores and appealed to Spain for an agreement moving the line westward. Such an agreement was made in the treaty of Tordesillas in 1494 and established the line 370 leagues west of the Cape Verde Islands. The line as now established struck the continent of South America about the mouth of the Amazon River, and thereby gave eastern Brazil to Portugal. It is possible that Portugal's real reason for asking that the line be moved westward was based upon the knowledge that lands existed to the southeastward of those discovered by Columbus and a desire to save as much of those lands as possible for Portugal.

The treaty of Tordesillas was thus an international agreement confirming the general propositions laid down in the Papal Bulls of 1493. Portugal and Spain simply agreed that they would divide the new world between them; but they divided not only the land but the seas as well. The line, however, was for the time being not thought of as extending around the world into the Pacific. How could it be? The Europeans at the moment thought the lands discovered by Columbus were a part of Asia. They knew nothing of the Pacific Ocean until nearly twenty years later.

The treaty of Tordesillas was made three years before Vasco da Gama sailed to India. After he had demonstrated the practicability of water routes to the far east, and after the Portuguese under the leadership of Affonso de Albuquerque had set up their empire in India, and particularly after they had conquered Malacca and the Spice Islands (the Moluccas), they began to wonder* whether the line established by the treaty of Tordesillas extended round the world and, whether, if so, it would give them the possession of these new lands in the far east. There was some doubt in their minds and they appealed again to the Pope for a statement guaranteeing these far-eastern positions to Portugal. The Pope, now Leo X, issued a Bull in 1514 confirming Portugal's title to the lands discovered by going eastward and any other lands to be discovered by Portugal toward the east "wherever existing."

The Bull of 1514 thus ruled in effect that the line of Tordesillas did not extend round the world; but when Magellan offered to prove to Charles I that the Moluccas lay on the Spanish side of the line of demarcation, and when his expedition did actually prove that the Moluccas could be reached by sailing westward from Spain, Charles I claimed those islands for his country. It then became necessary to decide the question whether the line of Tordesillas did actually extend round the world, and, if so, where it would fall with regard to the Spice Islands and the Philippines. This negotiation resulted in an agreement in 1524 to establish the line on the other side of the world; but the location of the line was not actually agreed upon until the treaty of Saragossa of 1529, which provided that the line of demarcation should be drawn north and south seventeen degrees east of the Moluccas. As thus agreed upon, the eastern line of demarcation was not actually a continuation of the line of Tordesillas. Furthermore, it should have given both the Moluccas and the Philippines to Portugal, but Spain retained the latter group of islands until deprived of them by the United States in the Spanish-American War.

THE FRENCH CHALLENGE TO THE HISPANO-PORTUGUESE MONOPOLY

It was not to be expected that the other commercial nations of western Europe would accept the Hispano-Portuguese monopoly of the world. Almost immediately, as a matter of fact, France and England began to challenge the monopoly. Very soon after 1500 Frenchmen had begun to sail to Brazil, and as early as 1523 Spain was complaining that French pirates were making inroads upon the Spanish colonial trade, lying in wait for the Spanish treasure ships as they came eastward north of the Azores. Francis I, King of France, replied to the Spanish protest by proclaiming that the sea was the highroad of all and that Spain and Portugal had no right to claim an exclusive monopoly of the undiscovered parts of the earth. "The sun shines for me as for the others," he said. "I should like to see the clause of Adam's will which excludes me from a share of the world." This first pronouncement of the doctrine of the freedom of the seas was thus a defense mechanism against the enormous claims of Spain and Portugal.

French privateers under the leadership of Jean Ango continued to prey upon Spanish treasure ships returning from the colonies, and when war again broke out between France and Spain, France made a treaty with Portugal at Lyons in 1536 which provided for a benevolent neutrality on the part of Portugal that would allow French privateers to bring their prizes into Portuguese ports—a privilege which did inestimable damage to Spanish colonial trade. The inroads of the French privateers and Roberval's attempted colonization in Canada in 1541 and 1542 led Spain to consider a relaxation of its rigid claims to a monopoly of the commerce of the western colonial world, and Charles I went so far as to sign, in 1544, a treaty permitting Frenchmen to go to the Spanish colonies and trade, as long as they made no attempt at territorial settlement. The treaty was blocked, however, by the Spanish Council of the Indies, on the ground that trade would only be the opening wedge for settlement, and it was another century before Spain admitted any real modification of her claim to a monopoly of the western world.

Another attempt was made by the French in the treaty of Cateau-Cambrésis in 1559 to win a recognition of the French right to go into the new world, but the Spanish negotiators refused to budge. They preferred not even to mention the Indies in the treaty, and the result was an oral agreement to the effect that west of the first meridian might makes right; that is, that if Frenchmen should go into those waters they did so at their own risk and, if captured there, they might be punished by the Spaniards without having any such incident become a cause of war. This oral agreement was thus in effect an understanding that "there shall be no peace beyond the line"; that, as a matter of fact, Europe is one sphere for the operation of international law and America is another; and that treaties which apply between nations in Europe do not necessarily apply between those same nations in the American hemisphere. This was the famous "doctrine of the two spheres," which was an accepted doctrine during the first two centuries of colonial history and was revived in modified form by the United States after the winning of independence in the Monroe Doctrine of 1823.

THE BRITISH CHALLENGE THE MONOPOLY

The second nation to challenge the Hispano-Portuguese monopoly of the world was England. By 1559 England had definitely appeared on the scene as a naval and commercial and colonizing nation. Already her "channel pirates" had harried the French and Spanish ships moving in and out of the English channel, and already English diplomacy was looking in the direction of the colonial world. Up to the beginning of the sixteenth century English diplomacy had revolved around the Flanders wool trade, and the *Intercursus Magnus* for the protection and promotion of the wool trade, a famous treaty made in 1496 between Henry VII and the Duke of

Burgundy, was the cornerstone of British commercial and international policy. But with the expansion of British commerce in the first half of the sixteenth century, Englishmen had taken to the sea and English ships had sailed to the Baltic, to the Mediterranean, to Africa, and even to America. By the middle of the sixteenth century, England was in the midst of a great commercial expansion, but the dominion of the new trade areas of the world was held by Portugal and Spain, and English commercial expansion there had, perforce, to take place largely at their expense. As long as English diplomacy was concerned chiefly with the wool trade of Flanders, and until Charles I came into the ownership of both Spain and Flanders, English foreign policy was one of friendship with Spain; Henry VIII's marriage to Katherine of Aragon was in accord with this traditional British policy. But with the accession of Elizabeth there took place a fundamental shift in English foreign policy which brought England into a position of permanent opposition to Spain, a diplomatic revolution which is to be attributed in large measure to the worldwide expansion of British commerce.

The first conflict of England with the Hispano-Portuguese monopoly of the colonial world took place over Guinea, for as early as 1563 English traders began to go to the coast of Guinea, against which Portugal immediately and vigorously protested. For a time England bowed to Portuguese protests and Queen Mary prohibited English ships from going to Africa. But the trade went on, nevertheless, and with the accession of Queen Elizabeth the English government took the position that English traders would avoid territory actually occupied by the Portuguese but would maintain their right to go into countries which had not been actually colonized. This was a new principle in international relations with regard to the colonies and became known as the doctrine of effective occupation. The Portuguese were not satisfied, however, and there eventually broke out a war over the English incursions which was the first English colonial war. Peace between the two nations came in 1576, largely as the result of a Spanish threat at Portugal's independence; but the issue was not settled, because Queen Elizabeth refused to give in on the principle of effective occupation.

From this time on Spain became the most important enemy of England. For when English commercial interests abroad brought her into a conflict with the Hispano-Portuguese monopoly, her foreign policy changed and began to revolve around that conflict. The central theme in English diplomacy then became, and for many

decades remained, colonial rivalry with Spain. For Spain the appearance of England as a rival quite overshadowed the rivalry of
the French. The Spanish position in the world began to depend
largely upon the outcome of the Anglo-Spanish struggle. The conflict, which reached the stage of actual warfare in 1588, included
several elements. The first of these was religion. England was Protestant, Spain was Catholič. Philip II, King of Spain, had married
Mary Tudor and had attempted to make England Catholic. Upon
Elizabeth's accession to the throne he offered to marry her, but was
refused. From this point on there developed an increasing tension
between England and Spain over the question of the treatment that
Protestants were receiving in Spain and the treatment Catholics
were receiving in England. This tension eventually became almost
intolerable because of the presence of Mary Stuart, Elizabeth's chief
rival for the throne, in England. Philip II apparently encouraged
her and her Jesuit supporters to plot for Elizabeth's overthrow, and
these plots eventually led to Mary's execution in 1587.

Meanwhile, the Spanish Netherlands had begun their rebellion
against Spain, and Queen Elizabeth allowed and even encouraged
Englishmen to assist in that rebellion. In the colonies the religious
issue was important only as giving the English mariners a clear conscience in killing Spaniards. Led by Hawkins and Francis Drake,
English slave traders and adventurers persisted in visiting the
Spanish colonies and preying upon the Spanish colonial trade, and,
despite Philip's repeated protests to Elizabeth, this trade continued.
Sir Francis Drake was knighted by Queen Elizabeth, as well he
might have been, for the Queen was herself one of the great bene-
ficiaries of Drake's piracy. All of these things were intensifying the
antagonisms between England and Spain when Sir Walter Raleigh
embarked England in a program of actual colonization in America
in 1585. Against the Raleigh venture in Virginia Spain protested
vehemently, and Philip solemnly warned Elizabeth that if any Englishmen went to Florida—which in the Spanish mind included all
the Atlantic coast of North America—whether they were Protestant
or Catholic, they would be massacred as the French had been massacred at St. Augustine. Elizabeth paid no attention to Philip's protests except to assume the position that she had taken with regard
to the Portuguese, to the effect that Englishmen would not interfere with actual Spanish settlement but that they would not consent to their exclusion from the parts of the world not actually
occupied by the Spanish.

The execution of Mary Stuart brought a climax to Anglo-Spanish diplomatic conflict, and Philip II, having decided that diplomacy was useless against England, launched his great armada to cooperate with Alexander Farnese in the Netherlands in a conquest of England. But the great armada was broken up by a storm and its destruction was completed by the Elizabethan "sea dogs" yapping at its heels. The invasion of England did not take place. The war dragged on, however, until James I came to the throne in 1603. Because James considered the war "a personal quarrel" between Elizabeth and Philip, as well as for other reasons, he made peace with Spain in the treaty of London in 1604.

Now in the negotiations preceding this treaty, the colonial question was bitterly debated. Spain insisted upon a complete exclusion of the British from the Indies, whereas England insisted that it had a right to go to any territory where Spain had not actually planted colonies. The English claim to the right to go to the territories of the new world was based on old treaties allowing for reciprocal trade in the ports of each other, and specifically upon the *Intercursus Magnus* of 1496. Spain, on the other hand, contended that the *Intercursus Magnus* did not apply to the new world; that the new world constituted a separate sphere of international law and that treaties made to regulate problems in Europe did not apply in America. The final arrangement was an ambiguous compromise, a vague provision that there should be commerce between the two nations "where commerce existed before the war," which left both sides to interpret the treaty as they saw fit.

The immediate result was that when Jamestown was founded in Virginia in 1607, Spain protested that this enterprise was a violation of the treaty of London; but England proclaimed that under that same treaty Englishmen had a right to go to the new world. It is probable that Spain would have destroyed the settlement of Jamestown as she had destroyed Fort Caroline in 1465, but for the fact that by this time her power was waning and the vacillating Council of the Indies could not quite muster the determination and strength to equip and send out the necessary expedition.

The English challenge to the Spanish-Portuguese monopoly thus rested in an ambiguous provision of the treaty of London of 1604. The same ambiguous clause was renewed in the treaty of Madrid in 1630, and Spain continued to refuse the English the right to go to or settle in America until the treaty of Madrid of 1667, which must be discussed later.

THE DUTCH CHALLENGE TO THE MONOPOLY

By the end of the sixteenth century the people of the northern provinces in the Low Countries had thrown off their subjection to Spain and had set up the Dutch Republic. Hitherto they had enjoyed a trade with the Spanish Indies by way of Cadiz and Seville, and their ships had visited Lisbon to purchase the goods brought from the East Indies by the caravels. But when they declared their independence of Spain, and when Portugal was annexed by Spain in 1580, the Dutch found themselves excluded from both the Portuguese and the Spanish colonial empires, and adopted the practice of going directly to the Indies on their own account. As Holland was at war with Spain this was in entire accord with international practice. The Portuguese, however, attempted to prevent ships of the Dutch East India Company from going into the waters of the East Indies on the grounds that those were Portuguese waters prohibited to the Dutch. Conflict between Dutch ships and Portuguese ships resulted, and Hugo Grotius, to justify the Dutch practice, wrote his famous pamphlet on the freedom of the seas.

The seas, said Grotius, are common to all. They constitute the highway between nations and are essential to the conduct of international trade; therefore they are the common property of all. The Pope, who pretended to give the seas of the east to Portugal by the Bulls of 1493, had no right to do so, for how was he to give away something that he did not own? The seas, Grotius concluded, were and should be free to all nations; for every nation has a right to go wherever it pleases.

The Dutch challenge to the Spanish-Portuguese monopoly achieved its first success in the twelve years' truce of 1609, which recognized, in an obscure and ambiguous statement, the right of the Dutch to go to the Indies to trade. War was renewed between Spain and Holland in 1621 and lasted until 1648. It was then, in the treaty of Münster, that Spain at long last clearly and definitely recognized the right of the Dutch not only to go and trade in areas not settled by the Spaniards but also to own territory in the Indies. This was the first admitted breach in the Hispano-Portuguese monopoly of the new world, although as an actual fact France, England, and Holland all now had actual settlements both in the East Indies and in America.

CONCLUSION

Thus, out of the diplomatic history of the first two hundred years of European colonial expansion there came certain recognizable principles of international relations. First was the principle involved in the establishment of closed spheres of colonial interest—what might be called the principle of the "closed colonial door." Out of the protests chiefly of France and Holland against the doctrine of monopolistic ownership of land and sea in the colonial world arose the doctrine of the freedom of the seas, first enunciated in this connection by Francis I and given its classic expression by Hugo Grotius. Out of the colonial conflicts, also, arose the doctrine of the two spheres, which is the doctrine that Europe is one sphere for the operation of international law and the new world is another, and that international arrangements made with regard to one do not necessarily apply in the other. Finally, out of the international conflict over the new world arose the doctrine of effective occupation and the general acceptance of the idea that land not actually settled by any Christian prince was fair prey for another. The significance of these principles for the foundation and growth of the American colonies is very great; for these are the principles that governed the growth and regulation of empires in America, and their relationship to each other.

RECOMMENDED BOOKS FOR FURTHER READING

CONTEMPORARY DOCUMENTS

Frances G. Davenport, ed., *European Treaties bearing on the History of the United States and its Dependencies,* Volume I.

MODERN ACCOUNTS

George L. Beer, *Origins of the British Colonial System, 1578-1600,* Chapter 1.

Frances G. Davenport, "American and European Diplomacy to 1648," in American Historical Association, *Annual Report,* 1915, pp. 151-161.

Frances G. Davenport, ed., *European Treaties bearing on the History of the United States and its Dependencies,* Volume I, Introduction.

Hugh E. Egerton, *British Foreign Policy in Europe to the end of the 19th Century,* Chapter 1.

Philip A. Means, *The Spanish Main; Focus of Envy, 1492-1700.*

Arthur P. Newton, *The European Nations in the West Indies, 1493-1688.*

Edmund A. Walsh, ed., *The History and Nature of International Relations.*

6

Elizabethan England, Mother of British America

T HE MOST successful of the colonizing states of western Europe was England. English colonization, indeed, was more thoroughly a transfer of population and culture to America than was the case in any of the other great colonial empires; and because it was England from which the culture of British America sprang, some attention should be devoted to the economic, social, and political elements of English civilization.

ENGLAND'S COMMERCIAL EXPANSION

England in the sixteenth century was chiefly agricultural, but there was a growing commerce that had its origins in the wool trade with Flanders. This trade centered in the cities, and particularly the cities of London, Southampton, Plymouth, and Bristol. From the time of Henry VII, commerce had received an increasing support and encouragement from the English kings. It was chiefly the merchants of these towns, indeed, who furnished the capital for colonial enterprise. British capital was rapidly expanding in the sixteenth century, and this was a period in which Englishmen, as it were, took to the sea and discovered the true nature of British destiny. Prior to the sixteenth century the English carrying trade was monopolized by the Venetians on the one side and the Hanseatic League on the other. England was then the commercial outpost of Europe. But with the "discovery" of the Atlantic Ocean and the new world beyond, "the outpost of the old world became the emporium for the new." For of all the modern nations of western Europe, England is the one most dependent upon commerce for progress, the one which is most clearly the result of, and the one whose history is most clearly determined by, the insularity of the country and its position at the crossroads of world trade. Englishmen were aware of the sudden expansion of British commerce, and gloried in it. Richard Hakluyt gives expression to this enthusiasm for overseas commerce when he says:

Which of the kings of this land before her majesty [Elizabeth], had their banners ever seen in the Caspian Sea? Which of them hath ever dealt with the Emperor of Persia, as her Majesty hath done, and attained for her merchants large and loving privileges? Who ever saw, before this regiment, an English Ligier in the stately porch of the Grand Signor at Constantinople? Who ever found English consuls and agents at Tripolis in Syria, at Aleppo, at Babylon, at Balsara, and, which is more, who ever heard of Englishmen at Goa before now? What English ships did heretofore ever anchor in the mighty river of Plate?

An important element in this budding commercial adolescence of the Elizabethans which the patriot Hakluyt overlooked, however, was the fact that many of these vigorous English merchants were, to all intents and purposes, pirates. It is quite possible that he had Sir John Hawkins in mind when he wrote of the English ships that were anchoring "in the mighty river of Plate," and Hawkins had, indeed, carried British trade into distant places. But Hawkins had gone to the slave coasts of Africa in defiance of the Portuguese, and he had taken his cargoes of human freight, in 1562-63 and 1568, to the Spanish colonies in defiance of Spanish regulations excluding foreign traders, and he had sold his Negroes to the Spanish planters, when they were slow to buy, at the point of a gun. Spain had protested, but to no avail.

Quite the contrary, indeed; for Hawkins was only one of the best-known of the daredevil, swashbuckling English sailors, the "Elizabethan sea dogs," who drew no sharp distinction between piracy and legitimate trade, and who drew a certain unctious satisfaction from hoodwinking, robbing, or even murdering Spaniards—after all, were not the Spaniards Catholics, the disciples of the papal "antichrist," and the sworn enemies of England? No faith need be kept with Spaniards.

The greatest of the Elizabethan sea dogs was Francis Drake, who became "Sir" Francis Drake after he had "singed the king of Spain's beard" on both sides of the Atlantic. Drake was with Hawkins at San Juan de Ulloa, in 1568, when the expedition was trapped in the harbor by the great Spanish admiral Pedro Mendez de Aviles. Mendez violated the truce arranged between them, with the result that Hawkins lost all but two of his ships, his own and the one commanded by Drake. From that time on Drake became a terror to Spanish shipping and the Spanish colonies. His depredations reached their culmination in 1577-81 when he sailed boldly into the Pacific and robbed ship after ship of its gold and silver treasure, failed to find a passage back to England north of California (New Albion), and returned round the world in his own small ship, renamed the *Golden Hind,* having enriched himself and his queen with Spanish gold.

This was the more adventurous, more irresponsible side of Elizabethan expansion, and it was not without its significance for the founding of a British empire in America, for Humphrey Gilbert and Walter Raleigh were no less "Elizabethan sea dogs" than Hawkins and Drake, and these were the men who first colonized Newfoundland and Virginia for England.

But Elizabethan expansion had its more conservative, more methodical and businesslike side in the rapid but substantial growth of Britain's worldwide trade. In the course of this expansion of British commerce the merchants, in the interest of greater capital strength, devised several forms of commercial organization which had considerable effect upon the later establishment of the colonies. The first of these types was the so-called "regulated company." Such a company would customarily be organized for the purpose of exploiting some commercial market or undertaking some commercial enterprise and it would be composed of members who operated independently of each other under their own capital but who cooperated to the extent of obeying such regulations as were laid down by the company. The second general type of trading company was the so-called "semi-joint-stock company" which was customarily organized for a short period of time and usually for the purposes of one enterprise only. Under this type of organization a group of merchants would contribute a certain amount of capital each for the conduct of one trading expedition, say, to the coast of Africa, and that expedition would be conducted as a unit by the company; but the company would dissolve after the return of the expedition and the division of the profits. The third type, which is the more important of the three, was the permanent joint-stock company. Ordinarily such a company was composed of a permanent group of stockholders and was governed by a president or "treasurer," a board of directors called "assistants," and an assembly of the stockholders meeting periodically, usually every three months. There were other types of commercial companies, but it is this third type which is most important for the history of the British colonies in America; for this was the form eventually adopted by the Virginia Company and this commercial way of government was taken over in large measure by certain of the colonies for political purposes.

The first great overseas company in England was the Muscovy Company, founded in 1553 and chartered in 1555 with a capital of six thousand pounds, for a monopoly of the trade with Russia.

While it was of the regulated type, it was governed democratically by a governor, an elected council of twenty-eight, and an assembly of all the investors. In 1577 the Cathay Company was organized along similar lines to exploit the trade of China. This was the company whose object was to discover the northwest passage and which sent Martin Frobisher out to do so. In 1581 the Levant Company was organized to exploit the trade of Turkey and the eastern Mediterranean, and in 1588 another company called the African Company was organized to exploit the British trade on the coast of Guinea.

The classic example of these British trading and colonizing companies was the British East India Company, founded in the year 1600 to exploit the trade of the East Indies. The seizure of Portugal by Philip II of Spain in 1580 drove the English and Dutch merchants, who had hitherto bought far-eastern goods at Lisbon or Cadiz, into a direct trade with the east. And the first English expedition to the East Indies sailed under the command of Sir James Lancaster in 1591. This trade proved to be so profitable that companies were formed both in Holland and in England to promote it. The English company was formed under the leadership of Sir Thomas Smythe, perhaps the greatest capitalist of his day. Under its charter, this great company was both a corporation and a body politic, for it was given not only a monopoly of all the English trade in the lands between the Cape of Good Hope and the Straits of Magellan, but it was also empowered to license others to trade in this area, to buy land for the establishment of posts, and to make laws for the government of its trade and its lands. It could even fine and imprison offenders against the law and could maintain soldiers and armed fleets for its own protection. Not only was it empowered to carry on commerce, but it was practically sovereign within the areas defined by its charter. This company was governed by a president, a council of twenty-four assistants, and a general assembly of all the stockholders meeting annually. Within a very short time of its organization the East India Company began to pay fabulous profits and it served as both the inspiration and the model for the men who were responsible for the establishment of the colony of Virginia. It is to be noted also that the government of this company was democratic, in the sense that each stockholder in it was considered to have the same voice in its affairs as all the others.

These were the men, and such were the companies, who furnished the capital and the original impulse toward the founding of English colonies in America in the seventeenth century. Had it not been for the accumulation of capital in the hands of these merchant princes, surplus wealth which they were willing to risk in colonial enterprise, the settlement of British America could never have taken place.

ENGLISH POLITICAL INSTITUTIONS

The government of England itself was much less democratic than that of the commercial companies. Locally the unit of English government was the county and, indeed, the county was the only unit of government with which the common man ordinarily came into contact. The chief officer of the county was the sheriff, generally a nobleman, who was appointed by the king, who usually served for one year. It was his duty to call together the county court which met once a month and which at proper times elected representatives from the county to Parliament. The sheriff also entertained the judges who made up the semi-annual court of assizes, and performed other miscellaneous duties for the king. The sheriff, indeed, was in many ways the king's personal representative in the county. The Lord Lieutenant of the county was also generally a nobleman, whose powers were essentially military. It was he who was responsible for looking after the condition of the militia and who held the command of soldiers stationed within the county. Another important officer of the county was the coroner, whose duties included not only the inquiry into the deaths of persons who died for other than natural causes, but who also served as a sort of deputy for the sheriff in the service of writs and processes. His office was generally one of considerable honor and authority.

The local officers with whom the common people came most closely into contact, however, were the justices of the peace who conducted most of the everyday business of government. They presided over cases of small misdemeanors and composed the court of quarter-sessions which met every three months. Justices were also charged with certain administrative duties such as the maintenance of bridges, the collection of local taxes, the maintenance of local relief work, and so on, and they also administered marriages and funerals and miscellaneous functions connected with the general maintenance of the peace.

Within the county the parishes were the local governmental units. Ordinarily a town consisted of one church parish, which in medieval England was generally composed of a group of families residing around or near a church. The curate, of course, was the most distinguished resident of the town, and he had certain civil duties aside from his churchly office. Next to him stood the constable, usually elected by the vestry of the parish, who was charged with maintaining the peace in the town and executing sentences. Other local officers such as church wardens, vestry clerks, mole catchers, etc., were generally elected by the members of the parish.

A great many of these institutions of local government in England were carried bodily across the Atlantic and established there practically without change. The sheriff of our modern county, for example, is the institutional descendant in an unbroken line from the "shire-reeve" of medieval and Tudor England.

At the head of the national government of England stood the king, who from 1603 to 1625 was James I. James I and Charles I acted on the assumption that the king stood above the law; but the power of the king had always been limited by law, and as a matter of actual practice the parliamentary power of taxation provided additional checks upon the royal prerogative. The Tudors had practiced what amounted to absolute government by cooperating with Parliament while manipulating it to their own ends. But the Stuart kings were not as shrewd in getting along with Parliament as their predecessors had been; and in the face of the increasing amount of business the state was expected to perform, a bitter struggle ensued in the seventeenth century over the question of taxation which finally became a contest over the seat of sovereignty in the state itself. The outcome of the struggle was the final victory of Parliament in the "Glorious Revolution" of 1688-89. This struggle was just getting under way when the first colonies were founded, and it exerted a great influence upon many people otherwise disposed to emigrate, since it added to their other motives the desire to escape the insecurity that accompanied political strife and to avoid the dangers of what seemed to some of them a certainly approaching civil war.

The real center of government in seventeenth-century England was the Privy Council. In the time of James I it was composed of some eighteen members, the ministers and personal friends of the king. From time to time the king appointed committees of the Privy Council to handle problems arising in connection with the administration of the colonies, and after many different experiments this practice resulted in 1696 in the establishment of the so-called Board of Trade.

Parliament, which was the legislative body in England, was composed of two houses, the House of Lords and the House of Commons. The House of Lords was made up by the "lords temporal and spiritual," that is to say, the landed aristocracy and the high officials of the church. It constituted a sort of second council for the king for advice to him on important matters of state. In the seventeenth century it had a great deal of power, much more than the House of Commons at that time and much more, indeed, than the House of Lords in the twentieth century. Its members constituted the privileged class in British society. They could be tried only by juries of their peers, and they had the privilege of direct audience with the sovereign. The House of Lords constituted a high court for the trial of impeachments, and a final court of appeal from the lower courts of the realm. Thus its powers were very great, for in it were brought together certain powers in all three branches of the government, legislative, executive, and judicial.

The House of Commons was composed of two knights or gentlemen from each shire and one or two representatives from each important city. Theoretically they were representative of the counties and boroughs, but they could hardly be said to have been elected by the people. The seats in the House of Commons, as a matter of fact, were generally controlled by the great land owners and one member of the House of Lords might control anywhere from five to nine or ten seats in the House of Commons. On the other hand, the representatives of the boroughs were often elected by small groups of merchants who organized themselves into closed, self-perpetuating corporations for the purpose of controlling political affairs.

The House of Commons had originated in the desire of the kings of England to get the consent of the taxpayers to taxation, but its powers had steadily increased, until at the time of the Tudors it had come to constitute a real challenge to the power of the monarch. This challenge resulted in a struggle between James I and Parliament and eventually culminated in the civil war between Parliament and King Charles I. By this time England had become Protestant in religion and the struggle with the Crown revolved around questions of religion, the rights of Parliament to control taxation, and the conduct of foreign commercial and colonial affairs. The threat of civil war over the parliamentary struggle became very real in the period of the 1620's and 1630's, and was one of the important reasons why so many Englishmen decided to leave England to find new homes in a less disturbed country.

THE ENGLISH PROTESTANTS

The earliest English colonies were not founded chiefly as a result of religious motives, but rather because of the desire, on the one hand, of the merchants to exploit the new world of "Virginia," and the desire, on the other, of many of the common people to escape the economic and political disturbances of England and establish new homes in the plentiful expanse of free land that was to be had for the taking beyond the seas. Yet religious conditions in England contributed in considerable measure to the willingness of many Englishmen to emigrate, and this condition of religious unrest grew out of the progress in England of the Protestant Revolt.

Long before the Jamestown expedition of 1607, the lines of religious conflict in England were already being drawn. Henry VIII had achieved the separation of the English Catholic Church from Rome by about 1540, and the two decades following that date were in large measure taken up with a struggle to decide whether England was to be Catholic or Protestant. Gradually Lutheran and Calvinistic ideas crept into English religious life, and at the time of the accession of Queen Elizabeth in 1558 England had become predominantly Protestant. The adoption of the Thirty-nine Articles in 1563 established Anglican Protestantism in England, and this core of Anglican doctrine was reinforced by the adoption of a new prayer-book, the re-enactment of the Act of Supremacy, and the passage of the Act of Uniformity, all between 1559 and 1563.

Anglican Protestantism, as established in England by the "Elizabethan settlement," was governed by a hierarchy of archbishops, bishops, priests and deacons. The monarch was the supreme head of the church, but its active leader was the Archbishop of Canterbury, who was appointed by the king. It preserved a large portion of the Roman Catholic ritual, retaining a belief in the apostolic succession, the wearing of vestments by the clergy, the use of holy water, the sign of the cross and other ritualistic practices. In theology, however, it was Calvinistic; the Thirty-nine Articles proclaimed the Calvinistic doctrines of original sin, predestination, and salvation by faith.

But there were many men in England who were not satisfied with what they considered only a partial reformation of the English church by the Elizabethan settlement. They continued to agitate for a further purification, and for dispensing with the hierarchical organization of the church, the use of holy water, the sign of the cross and other vestiges of the "papish" ritual. These men had no quarrel with the doctrines of the church, but sought only to purify it of "popery." For this reason they were called "Puritans." The Puritans themselves, however, split into various groups; one group of the Puritans favored a central, presbyterian form of church government, and were called "Presbyterians." Another group of extremists, followers of Robert Browne, rejected all hierarchical or coercive church government, and insisted upon the independence or autonomy of every congregation of believers; they were called "Independents," or "Congregationalists," and split off entirely from Anglicanism. It was a group of these Independents who founded the colony of Plymouth, in New England. But for half a century or more most of the English Puritans still considered themselves Anglicans, and it was members of this group who settled the colony of Massachusetts Bay.

As time went on, the Puritans came to differ more and more widely from the Anglicans in matters other than church practice. As a reaction against the gaiety and the worldliness of Elizabethan England, for example, and as a part of their effort to live the sort of life prescribed by the Bible, they followed a rigorous code of morals, and Puritanism came also to mean a moral domination of one's self. Similarly, whereas Anglicanism allowed for a wide play of human reason in interpreting the Bible and other expressions of God's interest in men, the Puritans considered the Bible to be the literal word of God, the only clear and definite expression of the divine mind with regard to men. Puritanism thus came to be marked by its literalism and its disciplinarianism, whereas Anglicanism, while placing more emphasis upon ritual, was much more latitudinarian with regard to individual believers. Both these bodies of belief were of profound importance in the formation of an American colonial culture.

Thus by the time of the accession of James I there were four major groups of religious believers in England: there were still some Roman Catholics, following their religion more or less surreptitiously, and there was the great body of Anglican believers. More or less in revolt against Anglican Protestantism stood the Puritans who wished to purify Anglicanism, and the Separatists or Independents who had moved clear out of the established church institution. In 1604 about one thousand pastors of the Puritan persuasion presented the so-called "millenary petition" to King James I asking that they be allowed to worship in their churches according to their own Puritan way instead of according to the way laid down by the Elizabethan settlement. James is said to have heard their arguments until his patience was exhausted, and then, putting on his hat as though to leave, to have said "they will conform themselves or I will harry them out of the land."

That was the beginning of a new wave of official and semi-official persecution of the Puritans and Separatists. Those persecutions were not severe under King James I but became increasingly troublesome after the accession of Charles I and after Bishop William Laud of London became Archbishop of Canterbury in 1633. Laud attempted to force the Puritans to conform to the Anglican way. He even leaned somewhat toward Catholicism. But he probably made more Puritans by his reforms than he saved to the Anglican church. Thus, beginning about 1625 or a little earlier, there took place an era of religious persecution which brought sincere Puritans face to face with the necessity for deciding whether they would give up their Puritanism in Anglican conformity or seek for a haven of religious freedom elsewhere. To the motives for emigration springing from economic and political conditions, then, was added the desire to escape from religious persecution. All three of these sets of motives were important in the movement of men and women out of England into America in the first four decades of the seventeenth century.

THE GREAT MIGRATION

One more development in Elizabethan England contributed to the wave of emigration that took place in the thirty years following the accession of James I, and that was the appearance of a widespread popular interest in emigration. The people of England had become conscious of the new world through the exploits of Hawkins, Drake, and the other Elizabethan adventurers, as well as through the propaganda of such colonial promoters as Humphrey Gilbert, Walter Raleigh, Richard Hakluyt, and others. Elizabethan literature, indeed, is shot through with reflections of a widespread popular interest in the new world and the adventures to be had there. "The world's mine oyster, which I with sword will open!" exclaims one of the characters in The Merry Wives of Windsor, and Shakespeare's plays are full of the jargon of the sea and tales of far-off countries. The Tempest is said to have been inspired by the shipwreck of the Somers expedition on Bermuda in 1610. One of the most popular plays of the time was Eastward Ho, a play upon the popular craze for sailing, commerce, and exploration.

It took more, however, than a merely literary interest in adventures overseas to send thousands of common men away from their native land into the dangers and uncertainties of colonization in a distant wilderness. By the end of the sixteenth century England seemed to be overrun by beggars, vagrants, criminals, and the indigent poor. England seemed to be overpopulated. This condition was probably due to the social maladjustment brought about by the practice of enclosing agricultural land for sheep-raising purposes, which forced many agricultural workers off the land. England's total population, as a matter of fact, was hardly more than three million persons—considerably less than half the present population of the City of London—but near the end of Elizabeth's reign English leaders began to look toward colonies in the new world as a possible receptacle for the overflow of the burdensome "surplus" of population in England itself.

The flow of Englishmen overseas began with the founding of Virginia in 1607, and the first two decades of the seventeenth century constituted a period of English experimentation in colonization, not only in Virginia, but also in Newfoundland, along the shores of New England, in the islands of the West Indies, and on the mainland of South America. By 1620, however, the feasibility of colonies had been demonstrated, and in the next two decades, that is to say, between 1620 and 1640, the stream of emigration from England to America reached its flood.

In a period of about twenty years some seventy thousand people left England to establish homes in the new world. Of the total, some 12,000 went to Virginia, Bermuda, and the new colony of Maryland. About 18,000 went to New England, 14,000 of whom stopped in Massachusetts Bay, and about 37,000 went to the West Indies, where some 18,000 settled in Barbados, 4,000 in Nevis, 12,000 in St. Christopher's, and some 3,000 in the smaller English islands.

This is one of the most remarkable phenomena in all the history of English colonial expansion, and it is to be accounted for by several groups of facts. In the first place, the settlements in Virginia and Bermuda and elsewhere had by this time demonstrated that colonies were no longer experiments but could be made practicable. The risks involved in colonization were no longer insurmountable, a technique of colonization had been developed, and there had appeared an increased willingness among the common people to go to the colonies. This willingness was due in large measure to the abnormal conditions in England itself. Charles I's reign turned out to be a period of successive quarrels with Parliament over parliamentary rights and privileges which culminated in the dissolution of Parliament in 1629 and eventually the outbreak of the Great Rebellion in 1642. Beyond that, however, the Thirty Years War had broken out on the continent of Europe in 1618, and there was some fear of a Roman Catholic invasion of England. Many men

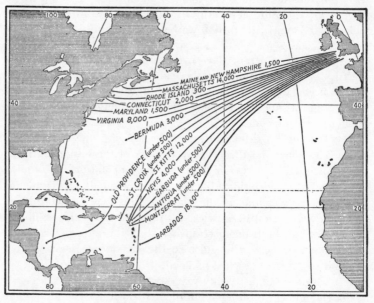

MAP 2. The English Migration to America, 1607-1640

feared the trend toward conflict and considered leaving England to escape the danger of civil or international war.

Further, it was a period of religious unrest. The persecution of non-conformists had increased. Roman Catholics were being tolerated, and in the minds of Puritans like John Winthrop there was the double threat of persecution on the one side and a revival of Roman Catholicism on the other. It should be remembered, however, that relatively few people actually left England on account of religion alone. The people who went to Virginia were largely Anglicans of the established church, and the people who went to the West Indies, which indeed absorbed by far the greater number of emigrants from England, were apparently inspired much more by economic interest than by political or religious considerations.

As a matter of fact, probably the vast majority of emigrants from England left because of economic considerations. The enclosure of lands for the production of wool, as already noted, had resulted in the existence in England of many unemployed poor. The rise in rents and land values, on the other hand, accompanying the agricultural prosperity dependent upon the wool industry made it more and more difficult for these people to subsist. But to make matters worse, between 1625 and 1630 there took place a severe depression in the wool business, owing to the partial collapse of the continental wool market during the Thirty Years War, then going on, and this depression increased the unemployment and the misery of the submerged classes. Thus it was that people of the poorer classes were in a mood to go to America for the sake of getting a new chance. For the middle classes, the standard of living was constantly rising without a corresponding increase in income. Men like John Winthrop, a gentleman of eastern England, found it more and more difficult to maintain their social position. On the other hand, there was much free land in the colonies; fortunes were to be made from land, and numbers of people with small amounts of capital became interested in the more speculative side of colonial development.

It was a combination of all these factors which led small clerks, merchants, and laboring men, attracted by the vision of free land or the speculative profits to be derived from business in the colonies, to decide to go to America. It was in the air. Roman Catholics, Puritans, Anglicans, Brownists, men of almost all conditions of life participated in this great English westward movement. The result was that by 1640 at least fifteen separate British communities had sprung up along the eastern shore of North America, stretching from the St. Lawrence to the Orinoco. It is not without reason that this has been called the Great Migration, or "the swarming of the English."

RECOMMENDED BOOKS FOR FURTHER READING

Contemporary Narratives

Alexander Brown, *The Genesis of the United States,* Volume I.

William Harrison, *Harrison's Description of England in Shakespeare's Youth,* edited by Frederick J. Furnivall.

Susan M. Kingsbury, ed., *The Records of the Virginia Company of London,* I, II.

William Stith, *The History of the First Discovery and Settlement of Virginia.*

MODERN ACCOUNTS

Charles M. Andrews, *The Colonial Period of American History,* I, Chapters 1-3.

Charles M. Andrews, *Our Earliest Colonial Settlements,* Chapter 1.

Charles A. and Mary R. Beard, *The Rise of American Civilization,* I, Chapter 1.

George L. Beer, *Origins of the British Colonial System, 1578-1660,* Chapter 1.

The Cambridge Modern History, II, Chapters 13-16.

Edward K. Chatterton, *English Seamen and the Colonization of America.*

Edward P. Cheyney, *European Background of American History, 1300-1600,* Chapters 8, 11-13.

Edward P. Cheyney, *A History of England,* I, pp. 309-459.

Edward P. Cheyney, *Social Changes in England in the Sixteenth Century.*

Julian S. Corbett, *Drake and the Tudor Navy.*

Mandell Creighton, *The Age of Elizabeth.*

William Cunningham, *The Progress of Capitalism in England.*

David Hannay, *The Great Chartered Companies.*

Ephraim Lipson, *The Economic History of England.*

Albert F. Pollard, *The History of England from the Accession of Edward VI to the Death of Elizabeth (1547-1603),* Chapters 10, 16, 24.

William R. Scott, *The Constitution and Finance of English, Scottish and Irish Joint Stock Companies to 1720.*

George M. Trevelyan, *England under the Stuarts.*

William C. H. Wood, *Elizabethan Sea-Dogs.*

PART II

The Beginnings of the British Empire in America, 1607-50

O NE OF the most dramatic events in the history of civilization took place in the first half of the seventeenth century when segments of British society and culture were transported almost bodily across the Atlantic and planted along the eastern fringe of the American wilderness from the Orinoco to the St. Lawrence. To the diverse soils and climates of this vast continent went groups of men of a common English nationality, inspired by common motives of economic hope and the desire to escape from the political, social, and religious uncertainties of life in England. In the course of a short half-century colonies were founded in the West Indies, in Virginia, in New England, and in Newfoundland. But already, at the end of that first half-century, these new communities had come to be rather sharply differentiated from their mother country and from one another. These were the nuclei around which were to form the later and greater communities of British Colonial America. In them English culture was transplanted to an American soil; but the plant, in a variety of new environments, by adaptation differentiated itself from the parent stock into several diverse forms of Anglo-American culture which, centuries later, emerged as the British West Indies, British Canada, and the United States of America.

7

The Geography of North America

THE LAND to which the emigrants from Europe came in the seventeenth and eighteenth centuries was very different from the land they had left behind. Most of these Europeans, it is true, settled in parts of America that lie within the North Temperate Zone, but they found a different climate, different soil conditions, peculiar situations by reason of the location of the mountain ranges, rivers, lakes, and other geographic features that inevitably forced them to reformulate their way of living. The geographic environment into which they went became, indeed, one of the major determinants in the history of these people after they settled. Their economic life, their political and social institutions, even their way of thinking, were in large measure determined by the geographic conditions into which they went.

THE ATLANTIC OCEAN AND ITS INFLUENCE

There are three major geographic divisions of the new world that profoundly influenced the history of British colonization in America. These are the Atlantic Ocean, the continent of North America itself, and the West Indies.

With regard to the Atlantic Ocean, the student should remember first that the North Atlantic presents an expanse of water three thousand miles wide between Europe and America. This great stretch of ocean presented in the beginning the most difficult obstacle to be overcome by Europeans in their search for new lands and new homes; but once having been crossed and the colonies once having established themselves on the American shore, the ocean seemed to present the most perfect guarantee of security for the Americans from involvement in the economic, social, and political distress of Europe. It is no accident that the American people, despite the fact that they have been involved somehow in most of the major European wars of the last three centuries, have clung to a belief in isolation from European distresses; for the ocean was an obvious and comforting barrier, their greatest wall of protection. The second feature that influenced the course of events in the history of America was the existence in the North Atlantic and the South Atlantic of two land bridges across the ocean which made it relatively easy at the beginning for Europeans to find their way to the western hemisphere. Across the North Atlantic it is only about 250 miles from the coast of Norway to the Faroe Islands and about 600 miles from the Faroes to Iceland, and a similar distance from Iceland to Greenland. It is another 600 miles, approximately, from Greenland to the coast of Labrador. While the Norsemen crossed by this route, however, the adverse winds and currents in the northern ocean were probably responsible for the fact that the navigators of southern Europe did not find the northern land bridge useful. Across the South Atlantic there is another land bridge along which the Madeira Islands are to be found some 600 miles from the coast of Portugal, with the Canary Islands and the Cape Verde Islands about 300 and 600 miles, respectively, beyond. The Cape Verde Islands are about 1,000 miles from the coast of South America. Thus it was that neither the Norsemen who made the first crossing of the North Atlantic, or Columbus who made the first crossing of the South Atlantic, had to travel any great distance out of sight of land.

The winds across the North Atlantic are predominantly eastward, as are the currents, but the winds across the South Atlantic along the route followed by Columbus, are the well-known trade winds blowing from northeast to southwest, north of the equator. As a matter of fact, the North Atlantic furnishes a sort of huge basin in which the Brazil current, flowing westward north of the equator, circles around through the Caribbean Sea and the Gulf of Mexico to issue from the gulf as the Gulf Stream crossing the North Atlantic at about the latitude of New England, and then part of it at least swinging southward down the coast from Portugal and westward across the Atlantic to join the Brazil current again off the coast of South America. It is no accident that as both currents and winds follow this circular motion in the North Atlantic, ships sailing from western Europe in the sixteenth century would bear southwards to catch the trade winds and touch at the West Indies before striking Central America or North America, and on their return bear northward through the Florida Strait, following the Gulf Stream and the North Atlantic winds across the ocean again to Europe. This situation in large measure determined the routes followed by Columbus on his four voyages and they determined to a considerable extent the routes followed by the Spanish flotas and galleons on their trips to and from Porto Bello and Vera Cruz.

Another geographic feature of the North Atlantic which has profoundly influenced the history of North America has been the existence of the so-called continental shelf, a submerged edge of the North American continent which is broad in the south off the coast of Florida and Georgia, narrow off the capes of North Carolina and Virginia, and very broad along the coast of New England and the mouth of the St. Lawrence River. The continental shelf, so-called, is widest opposite the gulf of the St. Lawrence, at a point where the cold Labrador current flowing southeastward brings a plentiful supply of cold water and the rivers from the continent bring abundance of organic matter from the land. The combination of these three facts is probably responsible for the presence in these regions of myriads of cod, mackerel, tuna, and other fish. The presence of these inexhaustible supplies of fish in this region led European fishermen to seek this part of America from the earliest times, perhaps even before Columbus published the news of his discovery of the West Indies. Every one of the colonizing nations of western Europe, as well as the United States and Canada, have at one time or another entered into diplomatic or even armed dispute over the sharing or the control of this great food supply. The first prosperity, indeed, of New England and of Canada sprang from the profits derived from the North Atlantic fisheries. To the southward it should be noted that the islands of the West Indies are closer to the old world by many leagues than the continent of North America. This fact, coupled with their location in the flow of the westward-moving ocean currents and trade winds is probably responsible for the fact that the West Indies were colonized a century before the Atlantic coast of the continent of North America. Located as they are between the two convex coasts of North and South America, the West Indies became almost inevitably the crucible of international conflict over American colonial possessions.

Thus the presence of convenient land bridges, the flow of ocean currents and the prevailing winds, the location of the West Indies in the ocean, relative to these other circumstances, the characteristics of the continental shelf, and the presence of the great supply of fish off Newfoundland—all these facts have profoundly influenced the history of the peoples who settled along the western shores of the Atlantic.

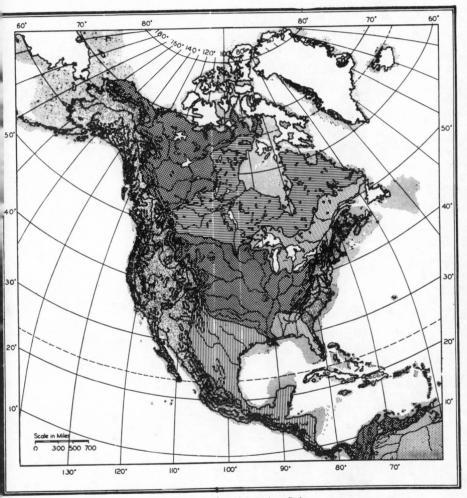

MAP 3. North America with its Drainage Basins

NORTH AMERICA AND ITS GEOGRAPHIC DIVISIONS

When we come to observe the continent of North America itself, we are impressed by the fact that this vast land area is divided rather obviously into four major divisions. The first of these is the Atlantic coastal plain, separated from the interior by the Appalachian highland which stretches from the Gulf of St. Lawrence in a southwesterly direction to within two hundred miles of the Gulf of Mexico. The second major division is the so-called Laurentian highland, a sort of geological shield depressed in the center toward Hudson Bay. This Laurentian highland or northern shield is composed of some of the oldest rock, geologically speaking, in the American hemisphere. Because of its climate and the barren nature of the soil, it has never been thickly populated by human beings, nor does it seem likely to be. The third major division is the great interior plain which may for the sake of convenience be divided into four great river basins, the largest of which is the basin drained by the Mississippi River and its branches; a second being the basin drained by the Great Lakes and the St. Lawrence River; a third being that part of the Great Plain drained by the Saskatchewan River and Lake Winnipeg and the Nelson River; and the fourth being the valley of the MacKenzie River which flows into the Arctic and along which are to be found Lake Athabaska, Great Slave Lake, and Great Bear Lake. This great interior plain extends almost north and south through the entire length of the continent and for many years presented, because of the desolate character of its western half, a barrier to the expansion of Europeans westward across the continent. The fourth major geographical division of the continent is the so-called Rocky Mountain highland stretching the entire length of the continent from the Arctic Ocean to the Isthmus of Panamá. Of relatively recent geological formation, these mountains present a great barrier between east and west, nor are the climatic and soil conditions along the highland as favorable to human life as conditions further eastward. Relatively speaking, the Rocky Mountain highland drops rather precipitously into the sea so that there is a narrow, almost nonexistent, continental shelf on the Pacific side of North America, except in the northern Pacific toward Alaska. There, as in the east, are to be found myriads of fish, particularly salmon and halibut, which have furnished a considerable supply of food to the peoples of eastern Asia and western America since before the dawn of history. South of the forty-ninth degree of north latitude the Pacific coast of North America offers practically no good harbors; the Bay of San Francisco and Puget Sound are the two notable exceptions. On the whole the coast is sharp and forbidding and offers a striking contrast to the low-lying and deeply indented coast along the Atlantic.

Mariners sailing from Europe to America found innumerable inlets, bays, and rivers into which they might sail along the Atlantic coast. The Gulf of St. Lawrence, the Bay of Fundy, Massachusetts Bay, Long Island Sound, Delaware Bay, Chesapeake Bay, Albemarle Sound, Pamlico Sound, Charleston harbor, and the St. John's River, are but the most notable of the numerous protected arms of the sea along this shore. From this point of view it was relatively easy for Europeans to find convenient sites for their settlements. Back of the shoreline the Atlantic coastal plain between the mountains and the sea is cut by numerous rivers, bringing the products of the hinterland down to the ships. The course of the rivers is broken, however, south of the Hudson, by a hard ledge of rock which is only a few miles from the ocean shore in the north but which runs back into the land as one moves toward the southward. In each of the rivers where this ledge is encountered there is a low waterfall, and this so-called "fall line," beyond which navigation is impossible, is several hundred miles from the ocean in Virginia and the south. The presence of the fall line was itself a determinant of considerable influence in the economic history of the southern English colonies. The soil to the eastward of the fall line varies in quality from a rich semi-glacial deposit in New Jersey to the relatively unfertile lands of the coastal plain in Georgia and Florida. West of the fall line, in the region called the piedmont, the land is high, rolling, fertile, and constitutes one of the most attractive agricultural regions in the entire continent. Northward of Long Island Sound, however, except in the river bottoms of the Connecticut, the soil is less favorable to cultivation. For in most of New England it consists largely of glacial deposit and is studded with large and heavy stones. It is said that in the early colonial period it ordinarily required sixty days of hard labor to clear one acre of land of glacial stones lying on the soil. One winter, however, was sufficient to force upward another "crop" of stones requiring another sixty days of labor before the field could again be planted. It is no wonder that the settlers in New England turned from the soil to reap the easier and more profitable harvests of the sea!

Climatic conditions also furnish a striking contrast between the lands of the north and those of the south. The climate of New England is relatively severe. The winters are long and cold. As one moves southward, however, the climate becomes more and more mild, so that in the middle region from the Hudson valley to the valley of the Potomac, one finds a climate which is very agreeable to human beings, with the seasons about equally balanced. Southward from the Potomac the climate becomes increasingly warm and humid, so much so that as one reaches Georgia and Florida, one arrives at a region in which it is difficult for white men to carry on heavy manual labor for long periods. Also, it should be noted that the Appalachian highland, standing, as it were, like a wall between the coastal plain and the great interior valley, tended to force the colonies settled along the Atlantic seaboard to be compactly filled before expanding farther west.

Within the Appalachian highland, however, there are great valleys, such as the Shenandoah, which present some of the most fertile soil and the most salubrious climate of the entire continent. In the wall of the mountains, moreover, there are to be found certain gateways, the location of which has profoundly affected the history of the continent. South of the Gulf of St. Lawrence, the St. John's River presents the most northerly gateway through the mountains. The Hudson River-Lake Champlain pass was a roadway for the Indians probably centuries before the white men came, and since the white men came it has been the scene of many a struggle between forces marching northward into Canada or southward from Canada into New York. The gateway to the west presented by the Mohawk River and Lake Ontario was the most important route of the Indian fur trade carried on by the English. Unfortunately for both French and English, it fell squarely across the Lake Ontario-St. Lawrence River route of the French fur trade with the great interior, and the rivalry for the control of this crossroads of trade with the western Indians became one of the major themes in American diplomatic and military history. Farther south the western branches of the Susquehanna and the headwaters of the Potomac, furnish roads through the mountains to the west. Still farther south the Kanawha River and the Cumberland Gap furnished other gateways to the valley of the Ohio and the headwaters of the Tennessee, and became strategic foci of the eventual movement of the English westward.

The most distinctive feature of the great interior valleys of North America is the system of great rivers that drain this area. The first of these rich valleys to be colonized was the St. Lawrence-Great Lakes drainage basin; and this long line of waterways became the line of communications between the settlements on the St. Lawrence and the widely scattered French settlements in the interior. After the exploration of the Mississippi this long thin line was extended down the Mississippi to its mouth, so that by the year 1700 the French had a string of settlements and trading posts from the mouth of the St. Lawrence to the mouth of the Mississippi. Commercial life and civilization followed these waterways, and eventually the presence of the French posts in the interior, blocking, as it were, the English along the seaboard east of the mountains, aroused their determination to break it and take for themselves the fertile, heavily forested lands of the great valleys. The Tennessee and Ohio rivers, the Great Lakes, and the Ottawa River, furnished the pathways for the first pioneers to penetrate the fur-bearing areas of the interior. Later on they became the pathways of moving parties of Indian warriors against the white men and columns of Europeans fighting against each other.

For the rest, the inhospitable western part of the great interior plain and the Rocky Mountain highland have little significance for the colonial period of American history, except in so far as the most intrepid of the colonial explorers, from the French settlements in Canada and the English settlements around Hudson Bay, found them to be the final heartbreaking barrier in the way of a passage across or around North America to the South Sea and the riches of the east.

THE CARIBBEAN AREA

The islands and mainlands in and about the Caribbean Sea and the Gulf of Mexico present geographic conditions that were of supreme importance in the determination of the history of America. For the colonial interests of the Spanish, Portuguese, French, Dutch, and English came into conflict here, and this region became the crucible, as it were, into which were poured the bitternesses and the economic rivalries of the seventeenth and eighteenth centuries of colonial imperialism. The mainland of America from the Rio Grande south to the Orinoco was settled by the Spaniards. After the conquest of Mexico by Cortés, Vera Cruz became the port through which the wealth of Mexico flowed back to Spain, and after the conquest of Peru by Pizarro, Porto Bello on the Atlantic side, and Panamá on the Pacific side of the isthmus joining the two continents became the gateway through which the silver bars of South America moved toward the coffers of the mother country.

All this region, indeed, became the rich prize of pirates and privateers and the wartime expeditions of all the other colonizing powers, with the possible exception of Portugal.

The islands, generally called the Antilles, stretching in a long line from Florida to the mouth of the Orinoco, may be divided into three groups. The largest and most important of the islands, Cuba, Santo Domingo, Puerto Rico, and Jamaica, which may be grouped together as the Greater Antilles, were the first to be settled by the Spaniards. The Lesser Antilles, lying to the eastward of the Caribbean and forming a sort of broken land bridge from Puerto Rico to the coast of South America, was settled, a hundred years after the Spanish had made their beginnings, by the French and English, who, coming late into this area, were forced to take the leftovers. The third group is composed of the small sandy islands lying east of Florida and north of Cuba, called the Bahamas. This group, however, furnishes little of interest in the history of the period covered by this study.

The climate of the West Indies is a warm subtropical climate tempered by the constant trade winds. The soil of the islands is generally fertile, suitable for the growth of cotton, tropical fruits, cocoa, and particularly sugar. Sugar, indeed, became the great staple product of the French and British islands, and much of the social history of the islands grew out of this industry.

The Atlantic shores of North America, where the English, French and Dutch colonies took root, may thus be divided into four regions —a northern, a middle, a southern, and a West Indian region. Owing in large measure to geographic conditions, the civilization founded in each of these areas differed from the others, as well as from that of the mother country. The influence of geography in the determination of history may not, to be sure, be considered the only determinant. But in the founding of civilization in America, the influence of geography was enormously important.

RECOMMENDED BOOKS FOR FURTHER READING

Albert P. Brigham, *Geographic Influences in American History.*
Albert P. Brigham, *The United States of America.*
Dixon R. Fox, *Harper's Atlas of American History.*
John P. Goode, *Goode's School Atlas.*
Emory R. Johnson [and others], *History of Domestic and Foreign Commerce of the United States,* Chapter 1.
Llewellyn R. Jones and Patrick W. Bryan, *North America.*
Alfred L. Kroeber, *Cultural and Natural Areas of Native North America.*

Charles P. Lucas, *A Historical Geography of the British Colonies*, Volume II, *The West Indies*.

Charles O. Paullin, *Atlas of the Historical Geography of the United States*, Part I, pp. 1-45; Part II, plates 1-5, 8-27, 33, 41-43.

Ulrich B. Phillips, *Life and Labor in the Old South*.

John W. Powell, *Physiographic Regions of the United States*.

Ellen C. Semple, *American History in its Geographic Conditions*, Chapters 1-3.

Thomas J. Wertenbaker, *The First Americans, 1607-1690*, Chapter 1.

8

The Planting of Virginia

THE CLASSIC expression of British interest in colonization in the age of Queen Elizabeth was written by Richard Hakluyt. His pamphlet, called *Discourse of Western Planting*, was issued probably for the purpose of winning the Queen's support for the enterprise of Walter Raleigh in the new world. In this pamphlet he gives many reasons why England should enter the game of actual colonization. First of all, a colony on the coast of North America would place Englishmen in a position to strike at Spanish power in America:

> If you touche him [the King of Spain] in the Indies, you touche the apple of his eye; for take away his treasure, which is *nervuus belli,* and which he hath almoste [all] oute of his West Indies, his old bandes of souldiers will soone be dissolved, his purposes defeated, his power and strengthe diminished, his pride abated, and his tyranie utterly suppressed.

Hakluyt's first reason for colonization, therefore, sprang from a warlike motive, a desire to make America a theater of international military rivalry and make the colonies pawns in the game of European international rivalries.

In the second place, America, says Hakluyt, would be a good location for trading stations on the way to the Indies. It was then fully expected that the South Sea would be found to lie only a short distance westward or southward from the Atlantic coastline, and that a passage to it would soon be discovered. A colony situated along that route would serve as a point of refreshment and further exploration for the ships moving to and from the opulent east.

As a third reason for colonization, Hakluyt expressed the contemporary craze for gold and silver. The cupidity of the British had been inflamed by the success of the Spaniards in Mexico and Peru, and the earliest colonists in Virginia, as elsewhere, were instructed to search for mines—which they did with the loss of a good deal of time needed for the cultivation of food and with a consequent period of instability and uncertainty. This get-rich-quick motive was not limited to the individual, indeed; it was also national, and it is to be noted that Hakluyt's pamphlet is only one of a long series of writings in England tending to show that the strength of the nation depended upon a favorable balance of trade and that a favorable balance of trade would be best promoted by the establishment of colonies.

In connection with this embryonic mercantilistic theory of national independence may be noted a fourth motive for colonization, which was the desire for nationalistic control of the sources of raw materials. If England controlled the fishing grounds of America, for example, England would therefore be freed of any dependence upon the Dutch or French fishermen for this part of her food supply. Similarly, if the forests of America could be made to provide masts and naval stores for the British fleets, then England would no longer be dependent upon Russia and the Baltic countries for these essential products, and the supply of gold flowing out of England to pay for these imports would be retained in England to promote the wealth and prosperity and military strength of that country.

The most important motives, perhaps, in the minds of the merchants were those growing out of the desire for profit on investments. It was thought that by colonies England's commerce would be increased by the opening of a great new market, for it was thought at first that the Indians were relatively civilized and would buy English textiles and other manufactured goods. This was in large measure a delusion, to be sure, for it was a long time before the half-naked savages came to buy any important amount of English manufactured goods or textiles. Eventually, however, they did buy quantities of pots and pans, tomahawks, rifles, shoes, and blankets, and this did eventually become a considerable part of the market for English goods in America. In any case the English colonists themselves were expected to buy quantities of English goods, and the growth of colonies would inevitably mean the multiplication of British exports and thereby a tremendous increase in the wealth of English merchants.

Still another motive for colonization may be found in the belief of some English leaders that the colonies would serve as a sort of overflow region for surplus or undesirable population. It has already been noted that by the end of the sixteenth century many thinkers had come to believe that England was overpopulated and that some place must be found to which this surplus population might be sent. Thus the unemployed, when sent to America, could find work. Criminals would be given a fresh start. Orphans and the indigent poor would be removed from the poorhouses and orphanages of England and given a chance to make good in a new English world overseas, to say nothing of the savings thus effected to the taxpayers who supported the poorhouses.

Finally, in the minds of some advocates of colonization there was the desire for missionary endeavor. The actual work carried on by the English missionaries in America was never very considerable as compared with the tremendous enterprises of the French and Spanish missionaries among the Indians of their colonies; and yet in every English colony there were men who endeavored to convert the Indians to the one true faith, Christianity, some of whom left England definitely for this purpose. Naturally enough, of course, the struggle for existence in America was more important to the people who settled there than was the missionary effort, with the result that missionary enterprises fell into the background.

RALEIGH'S VIRGINIA

In all these reasons for colonization, relatively little attention was given to the desires of the colonists themselves; rather, the greatest emphasis was placed upon the profits to be derived by the capitalistic entrepreneur and the nation as a whole. It was for motives such as these that Sir Humphrey Gilbert took out his ill-fated expedition to Newfoundland in 1583. It was for similar motives that Sir Walter Raleigh took up his half-brother's enterprises in 1584 and, after a preliminary exploring expedition, sent out a fleet to Virginia in 1585 with nearly two hundred colonists under the command of Sir Richard Grenville and Ralph Lane. The explorers, Arthur Barlow and Philip Amidas, had reported favorably upon the qualities of the new land, and Queen Elizabeth was so impressed that she suggested that the new colony be called Virginia, in honor of herself, the "virgin" queen.

By the patent under which this expedition went out, Raleigh was empowered (1) to hold heathen lands not possessed by any Christian prince or inhabited by a Christian people; (2) to exploit the gold and silver mines there to be discovered, on condition that he give one-fifth of the product to the Crown. A third provision was of great significance because it provided (3) that the colonists should "have all the privileges of free Denizens, and persons native of England . . . in such ample manner and fourme, as if they were borne and personally resident within our saide Realme of England." Further, (4) the colonies to be established were to be governed by such statutes as Raleigh might decree, provided they were "as neare as conveniently may be, agreeable to the forme of the lawes . . . of England."

Here is the beginning of British colonial policy. Raleigh had power to hold and to exploit the land and to make the laws; but the colonists who were to go to the new Virginia were to be guaranteed the rights and privileges of Englishmen and the laws must not be contrary to English law. For a time, during the history of the second and more successful attempt to colonize Virginia, this significant principle was abandoned; but it was re-established in 1619 and remained one of the most outstanding features of the British colonial system.

Grenville's fleet, sailing along the usual route from Europe to America, went first to the West Indies, arriving there in May of 1585. Then, after capturing goods and supplies from the Spaniards, it ran up the coast of Florida to the neighborhood of Cape Fear and finally settled upon Roanoke Island as a site for the colony. Grenville left Ralph Lane with one hundred men at Roanoke and sailed for home. Supplies were short, but Lane said the ravens would feed them! He did not wait for the ravens, however; instead, he commanded the Indians to bring food. The Indians replied by trying to massacre the colonists, which effort Lane forestalled; but the bad blood thus engendered between the whites and the Indians proved to be an unhappy omen for the future. Eight days after this skirmish, Sir Francis Drake, fresh from the sack of Cartagena, sailed up, having burned St. Augustine on the way, and offered to take the colonists back to England or leave them a relief ship. A sudden storm sank the relief ship to the bottom, so the colonists sailed home with Drake.

They had hardly left when a supply ship from Raleigh arrived, and fifteen days later three more ships under Grenville came; but finding the colony abandoned, they left fifteen men and returned to England. Meanwhile, the returned Lane with his colonists had taken with them the potato, which Raleigh planted on his estate in Ireland, and the tobacco plant, which Raleigh made popular at court. Raleigh was not daunted by the failure of his first two expeditions and sent out a third fleet under the command of John White, May 8, 1587, with instructions to go to Chesapeake Bay. But the pilot refused to direct them into the bay, so White settled again on Roanoke Island. The fifteen men left by Grenville had disappeared. Apparently they had been attacked by Indians and one of them killed. The rest had put to sea in a rowboat and disappeared. The colony settled down on Roanoke Island and a few days later,

Ellinor Dare, the wife of Ananias Dare and the daughter of White, gave birth to a child, Virginia Dare, the first English child born in America.

Ten days later White sailed to England, but he arrived there at a time when England was on the verge of war with Spain and it was not until 1591 that he returned to America. Arrived at Roanoke, he found only the word "Croatoan" carved on a tree, indicating that the colony had moved to an island of that name farther to the southward. No real evidence of the fate of the colony, however, was ever found and White returned to England.

Thus ended the first English attempt at colonization in Virginia. It had come to nothing, but it was significant as proving the difficulties that had to be met with in colonization and in indicating the inadequacy of private fortunes to support enterprises of such magnitude. Colonization, to be successful, must be backed up by strong corporate organization; with very few exceptions, the later English colonies in America were successful precisely by reason of their strong capitalistic support.

THE VIRGINIA COMPANY

Sir Thomas Smythe, already mentioned in connection with the British East India Company, with some of his business associates bought from Sir Walter Raleigh certain rights to trade and settle in Virginia about 1589. But England was at war with Spain and nothing could be done about colonizing America until peace was made. Peace came in 1604 after the accession of King James I, and according to the British interpretation of the treaty of London, Englishmen now had a recognized right to go to the Indies. It was, of course, well known that Spain still insisted Englishmen had no right to go to the new world and claimed that this exclusion was recognized by the treaty of London. It was known, also, that Spain might probably interfere with any new colony; but a number of merchants associated with the former enterprise were determined to take the risk. Thus it came about that Sir Ferdinando Gorges of Plymouth and Sir John Popham of London, along with Thomas Smythe, led a number of merchants in petitioning King James I for a charter for the colonization of Virginia.

There were two groups of merchants interested in this scheme, the so-called London group, composed of Smythe, Richard Hakluyt, and other merchants of London who had been interested in the Muscovy Company and the Levant Company and who held the rights of Sir Walter Raleigh, and the so-called Plymouth group, composed of investors and merchants in Plymouth and elsewhere in the west of England including Gorges, Raleigh Gilbert, and others, who were interested largely in the fishing business and who wanted new fishing grounds and fur-trade areas on the coast of America for exploitation. It should be added, perhaps, that a third group of people in England, led by Sir John Popham, were interested in the project because of their desire to provide relief for the poor of England. Thus it may be said that the people interested in this colony in large measure represented the national interests outlined by Hakluyt in his pamphlet of twenty years before. Certain it is that there was widespread public interest in this project, and the appeal for financial support received a gratifying response.

The government of King James I, instead of issuing separate charters to the two groups of merchants, issued a single charter in 1606. This charter, creating the London and Plymouth Companies, gave the Crown of England a very important part in the control of the affairs of the proposed colony and in this sense departed from the lines of policy laid down in the charters to early commercial companies as well as in the patent issued to Sir Walter Raleigh. It set up a royal council for Virginia, a sort of new privy council for the colonial domain, composed of thirteen or fourteen men, to sit in London and to have general administrative control in the name of the Crown over the whole area lying between the 34th and 45th degrees of north latitude. Recognizing the two groups of merchants interested, the charter provided that the two colonies to be established should be governed by instructions issued by this council for Virginia, and the instructions thus issued were to prescribe the judicial, administrative, and commercial institutions of the colonies.

The area for each colony was defined as follows: the London group was given the territory between the 34th and 38th degrees of north latitude, and the Plymouth group was given the territory between the 41st and 45th degrees of north latitude. The intervening space was to be open to both, but new settlements within this area must be at least fifty miles apart. In each colony there was to be a council of thirteen. This council would choose its own president and administer the economic affairs of the settlement in order to make it pay a dividend, and administer the laws or regulations provided for it by the council back in England. Land titles could be granted only by the Crown on petition by the local colonial council. Mines of gold and silver might be exploited, but one-fifth of the profits must be turned over to the Crown. Finally, the com-

bined Virginia Company was given the right to repel invasion by
force and for this purpose to maintain armed forces in its colony.
It will be seen that under this charter the new English colonies
were to be governed from England; but otherwise the colonists
were to be given the rights of Englishmen. Political responsibility

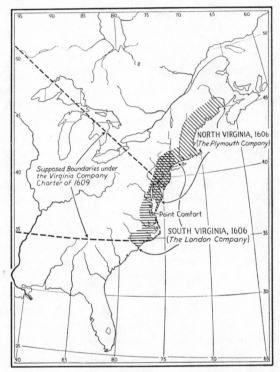

MAP 4. Virginia Boundaries, 1606 and 1609

for the colony was in the hands of the Crown and the supplementary Council for Virginia, but the economic administration of the
colony—or colonies—was in the hands of the companies of merchants. This separation of economic from political power turned
out to be the most disastrous feature of the charter and nearly
wrecked the venture right from the start.

However that may be, the charter of 1606 was an experiment in
colonial government and King James appointed as his Council for
Virginia Sir Thomas Smythe, the financier; Sir Ferdinando Gorges,
governor of Plymouth; Sir Francis Popham, Lord Chief Justice;

Thomas de la Warr, later Governor of Virginia; Sir William Wade, and others, men of great distinction in British economic and political life. This council worked out the first instructions for the government of the colonies after consultation with Hakluyt, legal advisers, and other theorists, as also the leaders of the company, and handed the instructions to the commanders of the two expeditions which set out from England early in 1607.

VIRGINIA SETTLEMENTS

The first of these expeditions actually sailed from London December 20, 1606, and headed for Chesapeake Bay, north of the site of Raleigh's old colony of Roanoke. The second, sent out by the Plymouth Company under George Popham and Raleigh Gilbert, went to the mouth of the Sagadahoc River in Maine where it arrived in August, 1607. There the emigrants built a settlement called Fort St. George. But the management was poor and the climate severe; and when Popham died and Gilbert fell heir to an estate in England the attempt was abandoned, in the summer of 1608. Thereafter, the Plymouth group of Virginia colonizers devoted themselves to the exploitation of the fisheries and the fur trade along the coast of North Virginia, going almost to the region in which the French had succeeded in founding their colony of Port Royal in 1605. Thus the western or "Plymouth" section of the Virginia Company resolved itself into a group of merchants interested in the exploitation of the fisheries and the fur trade of the coast of what later came to be called New England.

The other settlement, however, managed to stick. This famous expedition, which had left London December 20, 1606, was held up in the lower Thames by adverse winds. It finally got away early in 1607, and sailed along the trade winds to the West Indies in three ships, the *Susan Constant,* the *Goodspeed,* and the *Discovery,* carrying 120 colonists under the command of Captain Christopher Newport. They arrived at Dominica in April and then sailed northward. On April 26, 1607, they sighted the capes of Virginia, where, says George Percy, the chronicler of the expedition:

The same day we entered into the Bay of Chesupioc . . . There we landed and discovered a little way, but wee could find nothing worth the speaking of, but faire meddowes and goodly tall Trees, with such Freshwaters running through the woods, as I was almost ravished at the first sight thereof.

They were attacked by Indians, but the Indians were frightened away by the noise of the English guns. That night the sealed box containing the instructions was opened and the names of the new councilors were found to be Bartholomew Gosnold, Edwin-Maria Wingfield, John Smith, John Ratcliffe, John Martin, and George Kendall. Of these Wingfield was elected president, but Wingfield and Smith had quarreled on shipboard and the result was that from the first moment there was a factious division of the settlers which nearly ruined the colony.

The expedition having sailed into the bay, the colonists spent several days exploring, naming Capes Henry and Charles and Cape Comfort. They sailed up the James River (named, of course, for King James) and finally selected for their colony a spot some fifty miles up the river on the north shore. The location was not, as it turned out, a good one, but a low peninsula, half covered at high tide, selected contrary to instructions because there was a deep channel in the river alongside the land and because it seemed to be an easy place to defend against possible Spanish eradicatory expeditions.

"Now falleth every man to worke," says John Smith, "the Councell contrive the Fort, the rest cut downe trees to make place to pitch their Tents; some provide clapboard to relade the ships, some make gardens, some nets, etc. . . . Newport, with Smith, and 20 others, were sent to discover the head of the river: . . . in 6 daies they arrived at a towne called Powhatan. . . . To this place, the river is navigable, but higher within a mile, by reason of the Rockes and Iles, there is not passage for a smal boate: this they call The Falles."

In their search for a passage through the continent, they had reached the fall line of Virginia, and the fall line became the first western frontier.

In the colony, however, things were not going well. The site they selected was a poor one, and the fort was hardly finished before a malignant fever, probably malaria, struck them; and George Percy's journal becomes a long list of those who died day after day. The result was that when Newport returned with a new "supply" in January, 1608, only forty men were left of the original 104 who had come to the colony. Furthermore, they had wasted their time looking for gold and quarreling constantly among themselves. These men, indeed, were hardly suited for this work. Most of them were aristocrats who had come for adventure or an easy fortune, but not to build homes; and John Smith in desperation wrote back that he would rather have thirteen good laborers in the colony than one thousand of these incompetents.

Early in 1608 John Smith began to emerge as the real leader of the settlement. When Newport arrived in January, he had found Smith in jail under sentence of death because of the loss of two men on one of his exploring expeditions among the Indians, but the explorer was released and succeeded in getting corn from the Indians and in putting the settlers to work under his reputed rule that "he who works not, eats not." The second new supply of food and colonists arrived in October of 1608 and the little band of men managed to get over the hard winter of 1608-9. They attempted many and various ways to make the colony pay. They tried making glass, pitch, tar, potash, and lumber. They planted forty acres of Indian corn. They raised chickens and livestock. But still, after two years, the colony paid no profit.

Back in England popular interest had waned. Not only had the colony paid no profits, but a great proportion of those who went to the colony had died. Others had returned with depressing tales of misery and internecine strife. The company itself was hampered by the inefficiency of the dual control under the charter of 1606, and felt the need of a charter which would more effectively centralize control. As a result of these conditions and at the company's request, a new charter was issued in 1609. This charter was patterned after that of the East India Company and became the governing constitution of the company, with slight modification, for the rest of its history. The Virginia Company (it was now separated from the Plymouth group) was now set up as a joint-stock company, governed by a treasurer and an elected council, with power to appoint the governor of Virginia. The bounds of the colony were newly defined as extending two hundred miles north and south of Cape Comfort "up into the land, throughout from sea to sea, west and northwest." Colonists were offered stock in the company; they were expected to work for the general fund for a period of seven years, but after that time they would be given land in proportion to the stock that they held.

Under this charter the third new supply was sent out in the spring of 1609. It arrived in the colony only to find the men there starving. The supplies brought were not sufficient, with the result that the period from 1609 to 1610 has been called "the starving time." For the men were reduced to eating snails, snakes, Indians, "and other animals," and one man is even reported to have killed and partially consumed his wife in order that he himself might

live. Lord de la Warr was appointed governor under the new charter, but he was unable to go to America until the spring of 1610.
In the interim he sent out Sir Thomas Gates, Sir George Somers,
and others with a fleet of nine ships to relieve the suffering of the
colony. The ship carrying Gates and Somers was wrecked on the
Bermuda Islands, which thereby came to be known as the Somers
Islands. The shipwrecked colonists remained in Bermuda for some
ten months and eventually constructed from the wrecks of their
ships a pinnace in which they sailed to Jamestown, arriving on
May 23, 1610. But by the time Gates and Somers arrived in Virginia, conditions were so bad that it was decided to abandon the
colony. The returning ships, having bidden farewell to Jamestown,
sailed down the James, only to meet Lord de la Warr at last coming in. Then, on June 16, 1610, three years after the original founding of the colony, they all returned to Jamestown to try again.

   This was the low ebb of the colony's history. From that time on,
very slowly but surely, conditions got better. Men were put to
work and order was established; but sickness continued and Lord
de la Warr, himself unable to stand the climate, returned to England in the spring of 1611, to be succeeded by Sir Thomas Gates
and Sir Thomas Dale. The sixth new supply, which arrived in the
spring of 1611, found the colony, under the leadership of these two
men, on the up-grade, and from then on the success of the colony
was never again seriously in doubt. Gates and Dale are chiefly notable in the history of Virginia because they were the leaders who
established order and put the men to work. The colonists with
whom they had to deal were a hard lot; therefore the laws which
they set up, which have come to be known as "Dale's Laws," were
effectively severe. Swearing was punished by death, and all the colonists were required to attend religious service regularly; for the
first offense a man lost his rations, for a second offense he was
whipped, and for a third offense he was sent to the gallows. Unli-
censed trade with the Indians was punished by death. Avoidance
of labor was punished by imprisonment and, if repeated, by death.
Rebels were to be broken on the wheel, with bodkins stuck through
their tongues, and they were then to be chained to a tree until
they died.

   This severe set of laws brought order to the colony, but not contentment. As yet only a few women had come, and few of the men
had established themselves in Virginia with the idea of making it
their permanent home. Virginia was in bad repute in England. It
still had paid no profits and there were still coming from the colony

tales of suffering and misery which made it most unattractive to prospective settlers. Worst of all, the company now found it difficult to raise the capital necessary to carry forward the project and in 1612 it was granted a further modification of its charter extending the limits of the colony three hundred miles out to sea, in order to include the Somers Islands (Bermuda) and it was provided that the "generality" of the stockholders in the company should meet four times a year and make the regulations governing the company and its colony. The company was also given the power to punish offenders against its laws. Finally, the company was given the right to hold a lottery for the raising of capital and the publicity and popularity achieved for the new steps taken under the modified charter revived in some measure the company's prestige and power.

THE JAMESTOWN COLONY FINDS ITSELF

The lack of success in the infant colony of Virginia, however, lay in its failure to provide any commodity that would pay it or its backers a profit. The establishment of order and discipline among the workers in the wilderness was a prerequisite to any success, as was also the perfection of an efficient organization for the colony's sponsors, and these two negative prerequisites to success were satisfied by 1612. But the positive element of success was still missing, for the colony still lacked economic stability, or even promise. This was provided between 1612 and 1614 by the appearance of tobacco as a "pay crop." Once this factor appeared in the colony, its permanence became assured.

The cultivation of tobacco in Virginia had been begun by John Rolfe about the year 1612, who had apparently learned of its culture from the Indians and had managed to improve the quality of the native Indian product. It turned out to be a crop requiring little capital and very little skill. The tobacco that Rolfe shipped to England paid good profits, and it was not long before tobacco-raising became the colony's foremost industry. Tobacco provided the economic basis for the successful evolution of the colony of Virginia.

Unfortunately for the colony and its promoters, the Virginia Company had again fallen on evil days. It was torn by quarrels within the company over the question of subsidiary grants of the Bermuda Islands and of semi-independent colonies within Virginia itself. It was also torn by an attempt to grant the tobacco monopoly to a subsidiary company called "The Magazine," and by a quarrel over the control of the fur trade and the fisheries. The company was divided into factions, one faction led by Sir Thomas Smythe and the other by Sir Edwin Sandys. The Sandys faction had won control by about 1618, but, although Sandys himself was a great liberal, real harmony was never again restored within the company and this strife eventually led to its dissolution.

By this time, however, the economic success of the colony seemed assured and Sandys and his followers proceeded to revise its administration and government. As a philosopher, Sandys was far ahead of his time. He seems to have believed in the equality of men, the superiority of the law of reason over human law, and the social contract theory of government. It seemed to him that, contrary to the opinion of his sovereign, kings were not above the law, but that they held their power by consent of the people over whom they ruled. Partly because of his ideas, partly because of an increasing resentment in the colony against the dictatorial government of the officials sent out by the company, Thomas Yeardley was sent to the colony in 1619 with instructions to call an assembly modeled upon those of the company itself as organized under the charter of 1612.

This assembly, called by Yeardley and elected upon the basis of practically complete manhood suffrage, met in the church at Jamestown in the summer of 1619. It proceeded at once to the passage of laws regulating Sabbath observance, dress, the planting of food crops along with tobacco, and similar matters, and then acted as a court upon the case of one Thomas Garnet, a servant who had deserted his master, sentencing him to four days in the pillory. After the assembly had gone home, the governor and his appointed council proceeded to carry out the laws and judgment thus effected.

This was the first representative assembly held in the infant British empire. It is significant as being the first offspring of British parliamentary forms and as being the first representative government in a country that has ever since then been devoted to the representative principle. It is to be noted, however, that this assembly united in itself all three functions of government: the legislative, for it made laws; the judicial, because it acted as a court passing sentence upon a malefactor against the laws; and the executive, because the governor and council sat as members of the body that passed the laws, and then afterwards saw to their administration. This assembly is significant also because, in its elementary form though it was, it presented something of an advance beyond the parliamentary forms of England.

So it came about that by the year 1619 the colony of Virginia, small and fragile as it was, had arrived at the point where it could present the economic basis of permanence, established upon a native Indian weed, and the political institution for successful government, which was an adaptation of a European precedent to meet a local American need. In the success of the first English colony on the continent of North America, we see adaptation writ large: until that adaptation had been achieved the colony gave no promise of success; but after the economic and political adaptation of Englishmen and their institutions to the American environment, its permanent survival was never again seriously in doubt.

THE COMPANY LOSES ITS CHARTER

Sir Edwin Sandys and his associates in the Virginia Company had a program of reform which they believed would re-establish the financial strength of the company as well as the stability of its colony. They proposed, in the first place, to give the colony a "grand charter of liberty" which would result in the establishment of a large measure of self-government. This objective was accomplished in the Virginia assembly of 1619. Beyond that they planned to ask the Crown for a new charter which would grant the company greater privileges and make possible an expansion of the number of subscribers to the company's stock. If this were granted them, these leaders intended to devise more regular and systematic ways of meeting the needs of the colony; that is to say, the sending of ships, colonists, provisions, tools, etc., over a period of time long enough to get the colony well established. Finally, they hoped to take half of the production of tobacco, the staple product of the colony, and make it pay dividends by the creation of a monopoly in their own hands of all the tobacco imported into and sold in England.

It was in connection with the desire for a monopoly of tobacco that the company under Sandys' leadership asked the Crown for the so-called tobacco contract. The cultivation of tobacco in England had already been prohibited in 1619 for the benefit of Virginia, and high duties were placed upon competitive tobacco imported into England from Spain and Portugal. On the other hand, all the tobacco produced in Virginia was required to be sent to England. Under the terms of the contract arranged between the company and the Crown, the company was to have a monopoly of the tobacco business in England. The king on his side assumed one-third of the charges for the establishment and maintenance of the business and was to receive one-third of the receipts from sales. After a great debate in the company between the Sandys faction and its opponent the contract was accepted, but disputes immediately arose over the administration of the tobacco business; and because of the criticisms leveled at the tobacco monopoly, even by members of the company itself, the Crown instituted an inquiry into the affair which resulted in the cancellation of the contract.

This was a great blow to the company, but only one of a number of blows which it sustained during the years 1622-23. Because of the strife within the company, the colony was neglected, and as though to climax the series of troubles into which the Virginia enterprise had fallen, on Good Friday, March 22, 1622, the Indians of Virginia, under the leadership of Chief Opecancenough, fell upon the English settlements and destroyed houses, cattle, and crops and killed some 347 persons. Bitter complaint then went from Virginia to the mother country, and these complaints arrived in Europe just at the time when the company seemed to be breaking apart.

As a result of all these circumstances, a commission of inquiry was set up by the Crown in 1623 to investigate the conduct of the company in the colony. The result of this inquiry was a report to the effect that the affairs of the company and the colony were very badly managed. It pointed out that between 1606 and 1623 some 5,500 persons had gone to the colony but in the latter year only 1,200 persons were living there. Yet only 300 had returned to England from the colony, which meant that approximately 4,000 people had died out of 5,500 who had participated in the attempt to establish Englishmen upon American soil. Because of this unfavorable result the Privy Council suggested that the company accept a new charter, which, far from giving the company greater independence and privilege, was expected to establish a royal council in England which would have supervision of all colonial affairs and the appointment of a royal governor and council for Virginia by the Crown. This proposition was rejected by the company, and the Crown thereupon sued the company for a recovery of the charter of 1609. The verdict, handed down in the spring of 1624, was unfavorable to the company, and its charter was recalled.

This was to all intents and purposes an end of the Virginia Company. It had failed because it had had too little capital, because of mismanagement of its affairs, because of dissensions among its leaders, because it had been unable to make the colony pay dividends, and, finally, because the people of the colony itself were dissatisfied with company rule. The colony had been established, however. Regardless of the fate of the company, for the people living in Virginia and for those who followed, Virginia meant home; it was the first successful extension of British civilization overseas.

THE OLD DOMINION, 1625-50

The Virginia Company lost its charter in the year 1624. King Charles I, ascending the throne upon his father's death early in 1625, proclaimed the policy of maintaining "one uniforme course of Government in and through our whole Monarchie, [and] that the Government of The Colonie of Virginia shall immediately depend upon Ourselfe, and not be committed to any Company or Corporation." Thus Virginia became a royal province under the direct control of the Crown. At first a committee of the Privy Council was designated to have charge of colonial affairs, but it could not pay the necessary detailed attention to colonial business; so a special commission was appointed for the regulation of matters relating to Virginia. As a matter of actual practice, however, the conduct of Virginia affairs fell largely into the hands of the royal governor of the colony and his local council. Eventually, the governor and council came to be assisted by an elected assembly.

The first royal governor of Virginia was Sir Francis Wyatt, who returned to England in 1626. Wyatt had recognized the need of an elective assembly for the raising of taxes and the passing of laws in the colony, however, and, as a result, an assembly was held in 1628. Assemblies were held fairly regularly from that time on, but despite the fact that the king appointed a commission of his advisers in 1631 to study the Virginia situation and make recommendations with regard to the administration of the colony, it was not until 1638 that the Crown arrived at a clear-cut decision as to what the government of the colony should be like. It was only in 1639, therefore, that the governor of the colony was instructed to summon, once each year, "the burgesses of all and singular plantations there, which together with the governor and council shall have power to make acts and laws for the government of that plantation, correspondent as near as may be to the laws of England." These instructions formed a sort of constitution for the colony, and established the precedent whereby the freeholders in a royal colony were recognized as having a right to a voice in the making of the laws under which they were to be governed. The governor's powers included command of the military forces, and the position of head of the Anglican church, established in Virginia since the charter of 1609. The governor also appointed the colonial officials and the justices of the peace, and was responsible for the execution of the laws, in which function he was assisted by the council, the members of which were appointed by the Crown. The governor, indeed, was the personal representative of the king and had the power of vetoing all bills passed by the legislature.

The governor's council, composed of prominent Virginians, constituted an upper house of the legislature. It was expected to pass all bills and could initiate legislation on any matter except that dealing with money. As an advisory body to the governor, composed, indeed, of assistants to him, the council had certain executive powers; and by reason of its control over the judiciary and its function as a supreme court, it also had judicial powers. The lower house of the legislature, known as the House of Burgesses, was composed of representatives from the various counties elected by the freemen of the colony. This body had the power of legislation on all matters, and its peculiar prerogative lay in its exclusive right to initiate legislation with regard to money affairs.

The establishment of this, the royal form of government in Virginia, was an event of great significance in the history of political institutions in British America, for it meant that the British colonies were to be, in large measure, self-governing. This was in itself a recognition of the fact that the local affairs of these new overseas communities could most wisely be administered by the colonists themselves, rather than by a body of men, themselves unfamiliar with the conditions involved, sitting in London, three thousand miles away.

Meanwhile, Virginia had been growing in important ways other than political. In 1628 Sir John Harvey came to the colony as royal governor, but made many enemies by reason of his haughtiness and an exaggerated sense of his own importance. The antagonism of the colonists toward him came to a head over his refusal to transmit to the Crown a petition protesting the establishment of Maryland, in 1634, and he eventually resigned. Harvey was succeeded by Sir Francis Wyatt, who returned to Virginia in 1639 and remained its governor until 1642, when he was succeeded by Sir William Berkeley.

The Virginia to which Berkeley came was a very different community from that which the Virginia Company had lost in 1624. In the first place, the population of the colony had grown rapidly, and by the time of the new governor's arrival it amounted to some ten thousand souls. In 1634 eight new counties had been created. The banks of the James River were dotted with small settlements and the James River and Chesapeake Bay became the main highways, as it were, of this amphibian colony. There were no large settlements, but in the tiny villages which constituted the principal

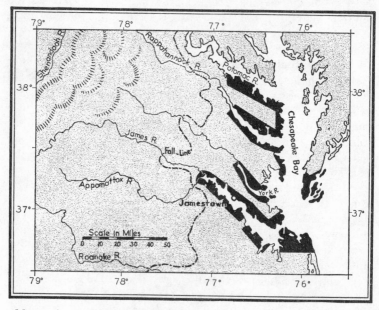

MAP 5. Approximate Extent of the Settlements in Virginia About 1650

towns, the houses were of brick and wood. Anglicanism was the established religion. A beginning had been made on the plantation system based upon the cultivation of tobacco; on any settler's plantation the settler himself lived in the "big house" surrounded by his lands and served by his servants and slaves. As yet slavery had not made great progress in the colony. The planters themselves did much of their own work, and they were assisted by white indentured servants who, upon the termination of their servitude, received land and were able thereby to set themselves up as planters. As a matter of fact, throughout practically the entire seventeenth century most of the planters of Virginia were proprietors of small areas and there were very few who had any considerable amount of wealth. Negro slavery, nevertheless, had appeared in the colony about 1619 and the number of slaves slowly but steadily increased throughout the century. It has been estimated that there were some 250 Negroes in Virginia in 1642; by 1680 the number had grown to 3,000.

The chief marketable product of the colony, of course, was tobacco; but other things, such as corn, hemp, leather, cattle and swine, were raised in considerable abundance. Experiments had been made with the cultivation of silk, vines, and figs, but these enterprises had not prospered. Commerce had grown immensely; Virginia was shipping goods back to England every year and paying a profit not only to the importers in the mother country but the planters of Virginia themselves. The ships from England would sail up one of the rivers of the colony and tie up at the wharf of some planter. There they would discharge packages of clothing, farming utensils, furniture, or other manufactured goods from England and take in return the great casks of tobacco. From one wharf a ship would sail to another, and commerce was conducted from the plantation, or from the small villages on the banks of the river, directly with the merchants of London. For this reason there was little need for large commercial towns for deposit and exchange of goods such as very early came to exist in New England.

Rivers were the principal highways, but trails were beginning to appear across the peninsulas and up and down the rivers and creeks; trails which were followed chiefly by men on horseback. Horsemanship, indeed, was coming to be one of the essential abilities of the planter because he was forced, in the supervision of the labor of his plantation, to traverse large stretches of land every day. Some class distinction was creeping in, but democracy was still a rule of Virginia society largely because every white man who came to the colony was given a minimum of fifty acres of land either upon his arrival or upon the termination of his contract or indenture with his master, and with energy and good sense almost any man might aspire to rise to the highest levels of Virginia economic wellbeing.

It was still a frontier society, nevertheless. The Indian menace was still present, and in 1644, two years after Berkeley arrived, the Indians under the now aged Opecancenough struck again and killed some three hundred people. But the effect of this second Indian war was relatively slight as compared with the effect of the massacre of 1622. William Claybourne led an expedition against the Indians and drove them out of the territory between the James and the York rivers, and Virginia continued to progress without any serious setback. This fact in itself was a demonstration of the stability and the permanence at which Virginia had arrived in the two decades since the revocation of the Virginia Company's charter.

Then came the Great Rebellion in England. The resentment of the English people at the arbitrary government of Charles I had had little chance to express itself in the years between 1629 and 1640 when Charles got along without Parliament. But when he was forced to call Parliament in 1640 to provide money for his wars in Scotland, Parliament gave expression to all the pent-up bitterness of a decade, and there ensued the bloody civil war, from 1642 to 1648, which culminated in the execution of Charles for treason in January, 1649. During the war a few of the king's friends fled to Virginia, and upon his execution, Sir William Berkeley, an ardent royalist, proclaimed his son, Charles II, king in Virginia. Meantime, while the English merchants were diverted by the civil war, Dutch traders found their way into Virginia and developed a flourishing trade, bringing slaves and manufactured goods and taking in return the tobacco of the Virginia planters. It was partly with the desire to drive the Dutch out of the Virginia trade and partly to punish the colony for its loyalty to Charles II that the Commonwealth government of England deposed Berkeley in 1652 and appointed a governor of a more republican turn of mind.

By mid-century the English colony of Virginia could present to the world a society that was well established: a society based upon the successful cultivation of the tobacco plant and the sale of that plant to merchants in England who resold part of it in the markets on the European continent. As yet democratic, it had in it the seeds of a more aristocratic social organism. Already, as a society it was different from anything that existed in England. Englishmen had come with their knowledge of agriculture, their ideas as to political institutions, their religious and social ideals and distinctions, and these had been planted in the American wilderness. But under the stress of the climate, the soil conditions, and the geographic conformation of the lands lying round about Chesapeake Bay they had had to readapt their old ways of living and their institutions to such a degree that the social and economic and political structure of the colony made it to all intents and purposes a new society.

RECOMMENDED BOOKS FOR FURTHER READING

CONTEMPORARY NARRATIVES

Alexander Brown, ed., *The Genesis of the United States.*

Richard Hakluyt, *Discourse of Western Planting* (Hakluyt Society Publications, Second series, LXXVII).

Albert B. Hart, ed., *American History Told by Contemporaries,* I, Chapters 9-12.

Susan M. Kingsbury, ed., *The Records of the Virginia Company of London.*

John Smith, *The General History of Virginia, New England and the Summer Isles.*

Lyon G. Tyler, ed., *Narratives of Early Virginia, 1606-1625.*

MODERN ACCOUNTS

Charles M. Andrews, *The Colonial Period of American History,* I, Chapters 5-10.

Charles M. Andrews, *Our Earliest Colonial Settlements,* Chapter 2.

Philip A. Bruce, *Institutional History of Virginia in the Seventeenth Century.*

Philip A. Bruce, *Social Life in Virginia in the Seventeenth Century.*

Philip A. Bruce, *The Virginia Plutarch,* I, Chapters 1-5.

Edward Channing, *A History of the United States,* I, Chapters 6-8.

Edward K. Chatterton, *Captain John Smith.*

John Fiske, *Old Virginia and Her Neighbors.*

Charles M. MacInnes, *The Early English Tobacco Trade.*

Herbert L. Osgood, *The American Colonies in the Seventeenth Century,* I, Chapters 2-4.

Ulrich B. Phillips, *Life and Labor in the Old South,* Chapters 1-3.

Mary M. P. Stanard, *The Story of Virginia's First Century.*

Thomas J. Wertenbaker, *The Planters of Colonial Virginia.*

Thomas J. Wertenbaker, *Virginia under the Stuarts, 1607-1688.*

Clark Wissler [and others], *Adventures in the Wilderness,* Chapter 9.

9

New Plymouth Plantation

AT THE time of the organization of the Virginia Company in 1606 the attention of the merchants of western England had been directed to the coast of North Virginia. The story of effective settlement of this coast between the first and fiftieth degrees of north latitude really begins with the French settlements that culminated with the colony of the Sieur de Monts and Samuel Champlain on the Ile Ste. Croix in the summer of 1604. During that summer and the next Samuel Champlain explored the coast southward as far as the island of Nantucket, looking for a better site for the settlement; but on account of the desire to remain close to the source of the fur trade, it was decided to keep the colony on the Bay of Fundy, and it was finally moved, in the summer of 1605, to Port Royal in the peninsula of Acadia.

The English, of course, had also made expeditions to this coast, dating from Humphrey Gilbert's ill-starred expedition to Newfoundland in 1583. In 1597 Charles Leigh had proposed to settle on the St. Lawrence River a colony of Separatists, but his plan was blocked by the opposition of French fishermen. Again, in 1602, Bartholomew Gosnold made a secret expedition to these coasts to trade and to study the possibilities of settlement—to the annoyance of Sir Walter Raleigh, who still held the patent for Virginia. Gosnold visited Massachusetts Bay and named Cape Cod. He also built a fort at Cuttyhunk and loaded his ship with sassafras, with which he returned to England. In 1603, the merchants of Bristol, with Raleigh's consent, sent another voyage under the command of Martin Pring, this time for trade. Pring explored Massachusetts Bay and Plymouth harbor. That year Queen Elizabeth died and Raleigh was imprisoned for treason, and it was shortly thereafter that the Gilbert interests and the mercantile and fishing interests of Plymouth combined with the Raleigh interests and the merchants of London to form the Virginia Company of 1606. Early the next spring, as already noted, the two ships *Gift of God* and *Mary and John* sailed from Plymouth under George Popham and Raleigh Gilbert to found the unsuccessful colony called St. George at the mouth of the Sagadahoc River on the coast of Maine, only to abandon it the next year, 1608.

After the abandonment of the attempt to settle northern Virginia, the Plymouth group in the Virginia Company settled down to a policy of sending shipping and trading voyages to the coasts of their land in North Virginia without making any effort to colonize it. In 1610, however, a group of merchants in Bristol formed a new organization called the London and Bristol Company, which succeeded in getting from the king a charter to the island of Newfoundland. Under the leadership of John Guy this company sent to that island an expedition composed of three ships, thirty-nine colonists, and a large supply of tools, seeds, livestock, and other supplies. The expedition landed in August, 1610, at Cupid's Cove, on Conception Bay, and there they built their settlement, after which they built fishing boats and engaged in fishing. But the winters were cold, the settlement was visited by pirates and disease, and the colony, while it managed to hang on, failed to prosper.

Yet this colony did demonstrate that Newfoundland was capable of permanent settlement by white men, and other Bristol adventurers purchased from the London and Bristol Company land a little to the north of Cupid's Cove, and there in 1617 founded the village of Harbour Grace. This settlement, too, devoted its efforts chiefly to fishing. Still another settlement was founded nearby in 1618 by Sir William Vaughan, who went to the island himself in 1622. Becoming bankrupt in the enterprise, Vaughan sold part of his tract to Sir George Calvert, who was so encouraged that he asked the king for a charter. His request was granted, and he was given a large tract of land facing on the ocean at Placentia to the south, at the town of Ferryland on the east, and at Conception Bay on the north, which he christened the colony of Avalon. His charter, similar to the one later given him for Maryland, made him proprietor and absolute ruler of the colony, but reserved to all Englishmen the right to fish offshore and to dry and sell their fish on the lands of the colony.

In the meantime, after the planting of Guy's colony, in 1614, two London merchants hired Captain John Smith, now returned to England from Jamestown, to go and hunt for whales on the coast of Northern Virginia. Smith was more keenly interested in colonization than in whaling, and he made use of his opportunity to search for likely places. His whaling efforts were unsuccessful; but he loaded his ships with a valuable cargo of fish from the Maine coast where he found a number of west English fishermen dry-curing their fish on the shore. He also did some valuable exploring work which he used as the basis for a map of the whole coast of North America. On his return to England he published a book about the country he had visited, with his map, which he called *A Description of New England,* thus coining the phrase "New England," paralleling the contemporary use of the phrase "New Spain," "New France," or "New Netherlands." His book was extremely popular and excited so much interest and was so widely circulated, especially among the west English merchants, that "New England" quickly came to supplant the earlier names of Norumbega and North Virginia. The book greatly encouraged the fishing industry and the cash from his voyage was so welcome to his employers that the old Plymouth group of merchants made him an admiral for life and engaged him to go out for them on other voyages. He never got back to America, however, for the one expedition in which he set out was captured by Spaniards.

By this time voyages to New England were frequent, and interest in New England had come to be widespread among Englishmen of all classes. One of the outstanding leaders of the interest in lands of New England was Sir Ferdinando Gorges, one of the original members of the Virginia Company. Many of the voyages sent to New England resulted unhappily, but Gorges and his friends were so interested that they applied to the king for a new patent for the Plymouth group of the old Virginia Company. This patent, creating the "Council established at Plymouth in the Country of Devon for the planting, ruling, and governing of New England in America," was issued in 1620; but because of the opposition of Sir Edwin Sandys it was not actually delivered until June, 1621. It was to this council that the merchants backing the "Pilgrims" from Leyden eventually applied for a confirmation of a grant for the land occupied by the Pilgrims when they settled at New Plymouth in 1620 without permission. It was to this council, also, that William Bradford and the Pilgrims themselves applied for a patent in 1629, when they were given a clear title to the land which they had occupied, upon the basis of which they then became the independent and self-governing colony of New Plymouth.

Shortly after the creation of the Council for New England, still another sector of this northern coast was parceled out to Sir William Alexander, an old Scotch friend of King James I. By this grant of 1621 Alexander was given all the land between the Atlantic and the St. Lawrence lying about the Bay of Fundy, under the name of Nova Scotia, thus cutting off the northern part of the area given the Council for New England, and, as in the case of the Council for New England, completely disregarding the settlements already established on the Bay of Fundy by the French. Alexander's patent was of a feudal character, patterned after the "baronetcies" created in 1611 to promote the colonization of Northern Island (Ulster), and gave him practical sovereignty within his domain—the first of the great feudal proprietary grants of land in America of which the charter of Maryland (1632) is the best known. Alexander issued a few patents and sent over a few colonists, and in the spring of 1627 he seized Port Royal from the French. But his colony languished despite all his efforts, and by the treaty of St. Germain (1632) all this area was recognized by England as belonging to France.

Meanwhile, a congregation of Separatists had migrated to the shores of Cape Cod Bay to found the town and colony of New Plymouth. This was the real beginning of permanent settlement in New England, and the movement must be traced back to its origin in England.

THE SCROOBY CONGREGATION

By the so-called Elizabethan settlement of 1559-63, as already noted, the Anglican form of Protestantism became the established religion in England. But this Anglican form failed to satisfy certain more radical Protestants, and there soon appeared within the ranks of the Anglican church numerous leaders, known as "Puritans," who hoped to purify the Anglican ritual of its remaining traces of Catholicism. Another group of Protestants who were dissatisfied with the Anglican way disagreed not only with the ritual but also with the doctrine of the Anglican church, to such a degree that they came to the conclusion that they could not remain within it. They refused to be governed by the church hierarchy, they refused to observe the Anglican ritual, and they refused to acknowledge all the points of doctrine laid down in the Thirty-nine Articles. Because of their determination to separate from the Anglican church, and because they believed that each congregation should be a separate, free, self-governing church unit, these people were called Separatists, or Congregationalists. Because their greatest leader was a man named Robert Browne, they were also called "Brownists." It is a group of these men who, about the time of the settlement of Virginia, were meeting, some fifty or sixty of them, in the chapel of the old manor house at Scrooby on the great north and south highway between London and Edinburgh. They were mostly small tenant farmers, and their leader was William Brewster, son of the bailiff of the manor. Brewster had apparently been a student at Cambridge, where Pembroke College was an intellectual center of Puritanism. He apparently did not graduate, but it was probably there that he became a religious radical, and when he eventually returned to Scrooby he gathered about him the small group which eventually became a church and finally moved to New Plymouth in New England.

Apparently this group of worshipers at first considered themselves Anglican, but by the fall of 1606 they had become a separate church, with Richard Clifton as their minister. Their faith was a simple one and their creed, in the words of William Perkins, one of the Separatist leaders of the time, was expressed as follows:

1st. There is one God, Creator and Governor of all things, distinguished into the Father, the Sonne, and the Holy Ghost.

2nd. All men are corrupted with sin through Adams fall, and so are become slaves of Satan, and guilty of eternal damnation.

3rd. Jesus Christ, the eternal Son of God, being made man, by his Death upon the Cross, and by his Righteousness hath perfectly, alone by himself, accomplished all things that are needful for the salvation of mankind.

4th. A man of contrite and humble spirit, by faith alone apprehending and applying Christ with all his merits unto himself, is justified before God, and sanctified.

5th. Faith commeth only by the preaching of the Word, and increaseth dayly by it; as also by the administration of the Sacraments, and Prayer.

6th. All men shall rise again with their own bodies; to the last Judgment: which being ended, the godly shall possesse the Kingdome of Heaven; but Unbeleevers and Reprobates shall be in Hell tormented with the Devil and his Angels for ever.

Thus the essential point in their religion was their belief in a trinitarian God, the fall of man and the inheritance of original sin, salvation by Jesus Christ, justification by faith which is promoted by preaching, the sacraments, and prayer, and a resurrection of the body after death with the reward to the saved of eternal bliss in heaven and the damnation of the condemned in hell. Such was the simple creed of the congregation at Scrooby. In it there was no place for ritualistic worship, no place for prayer-books, gowns, surplices, or the sign of the cross, nor was there any place for an hierarchical church government. They were simple folk, and theirs was a simple religion; but they took their religion very seriously.

In the group was a young lad named William Bradford, who walked ten miles from Austerfield, his home town, to attend the meetings of the Scrooby congregation. At about the time of their separation from Anglicanism the congregation was also joined by a brilliant young preacher with two degrees from Cambridge, named John Robinson, who became their pastor. These two men became the leaders who took the congregation out of England, and it was Bradford who led them to America. The new church came in for criticism by its neighbors, and early in 1607 a complaint was made to the ecclesiastical authorities at York, with the result that some of these worshipers were actually arrested and fined. Partly because of this persecution, but chiefly because they considered it a sin to remain in an unregenerate England, the worshipers of Scrooby decided to leave their native land in search of a more congenial environment.

They were not the first. Other small groups of Separatists had already left England, and it has already been noted that as early as 1597 a group of Brownists had asked to be allowed to go to America with Captain Charles Leigh. Others from the neighborhood of Scrooby had also emigrated. These had gone to Holland, where they had found spiritual comfort; and it was to Holland that the pastor of the Scrooby congregation, John Robinson, led his flock in the early summer of 1607. They were hampered by the authorities in their attempts to leave England, but they finally managed to get out of the country and went to Amsterdam, then one of the great metropolises of Europe. There they expected to find work, comfortable economic existence, and religious freedom. They did find freedom and work; but Holland was then the mecca of all the persecuted sects of Europe, and it was not long before the emigrants from Scrooby began to see their friends who had preceded them to Holland falling into the "errors" of other churches, especially the Reformed Church of Holland, or quarreling among themselves. So Robinson and his followers looked around for a more congenial spot where there were fewer sects, and settled upon Leyden, where economic opportunities seemed good, where they believed they would be relatively free from religious controversies, and where the Dutch church was the only competitor to be faced.

They moved to Leyden in the spring of 1609, and there they lived for eleven years. But they were not happy, and about 1617 they again took up the question of moving. William Bradford, in his *History of Plymouth Plantation,* gives several reasons for considering another move. First, they had to consider the international situation. They had come to Leyden in the year of the so-called "twelve-year truce" between Holland and Spain, who were then at war, but the truce would now soon terminate and it was expected that war would break out again. If Holland went to war, the Pilgrims might be caught in the sorrows and disaster of a conflict which was not of their making and they desired to escape from that possibility. They were also homesick. They thought of themselves as Englishmen and they preferred to live, if possible, under the English flag, although they did not desire to go back to England itself. Again, they found it very difficult to make a living in Leyden. That being the case, as Bradford noted in his *History*, others would be discouraged from coming to them and it would perhaps cause members of their flock to leave. They thus seemed actually to be in danger of disappearing as a body, "but it was thought that if a better and easier place of living could be had, it would draw many, and take away these discouragements." Further, the older members of the congregation were growing old and would soon die. Their children, because of the temptations and hardships in Leyden, seemed to be falling under the influence of the more worldly Dutch and drifting away from the old faith. Some of the young people became sailors or soldiers, others took up "worse courses" of life in the towns away from their parents. Finally, the Pilgrims hoped that by their migration they might carry the gospel into the remote parts of the world.

In all this there appears a variety of motives, patriotic, economic, moral, and religious. It is difficult to say that one motive was more powerful than the others, and it is probable that in the conscious thinking of the group all were equally important. In any case, when the question was put, a majority of the congregation decided that the hardships to be encountered were too great and they voted to stay. The others, a minority, preferred to go. Some of these proposed to go to Guiana where the fertile soil would make them wealthy, but it was objected that in such a hot climate Englishmen could not prosper. Not only that; the Spaniards would probably root them out as they had rooted out the French in Florida. With this unconscious tribute to geographic determinism, and on account of their fear, they thought of Virginia; and it was finally decided that they would ask the Virginia Company for a grant of land far enough away from Jamestown to permit them to worship according to their own way in peace.

Thus it happened that in the summer of 1617 Deacon John Carver and Robert Cushman went to London to open negotiations with the Virginia Company. The company, especially Sandys and his faction, welcomed Carver and Cushman, and broached their proposal to the king. James I was not willing to give formal consent to their proposed freedom of religion, but he is said to have agreed informally to "connive at them," so the Virginia Company issued them a patent. This patent, permitting them to settle in Virginia, was delayed by the quarrels in the Virginia Company itself, but was finally issued after the election of Edwin Sandys to the treasurership of the Virginia Company.

The Pilgrims still lacked capital, however, and while they were hesitating over their lack of means to make the move, they were tempted by a Dutch offer to convey them to America and support them there for a time if they would agree to go to a Dutch colony. But they still preferred to go to a spot under the English flag. Their hesitancy was ended by the appearance among them of one Thomas Weston, a merchant of London who came to offer them the backing of a group of London merchants who already had a patent from the Virginia Company and hoped to exploit the Pilgrims for their own financial gain.

After a series of negotiations that were not finally settled until 1622, the Pilgrims agreed to accept Weston's offer. Under the agreement they were to go and settle in America, where they would trade in furs, fish, lumber, sassafras, and other products. The majority of the Pilgrims were to work at these things while others were to till the ground for the production of food for the support of all. Goods and equipment were to be furnished by the capitalists in units of ten pounds, each of which would represent one share of stock, and every colonist was to receive one of these shares of stock in the enterprise. During seven years all the colonists would work for the common store and at the end there was to be a division of the profits according to shares and the property in America was to go to the colonists. The colonists themselves desired individual ownership of property, but the merchants refused to grant this, and threatened to abandon the enterprise if the joint-stock arrangement were not accepted. The Pilgrims finally gave in and made their plans to sail.

THE "MAYFLOWER" AND HER COMPANY

Under their agreement with the merchants the Pilgrims planned to sail from Leyden to Southampton, where they would meet a larger boat, the *Mayflower*, which was to bring emigrants from England. Only a minority of the Leyden congregation, about thirty-five of them, decided to go; the majority of the people in the expedition came from England, and many of them were neither Puritans nor Independents. At Southampton the Pilgrim leaders got into another quarrel with Weston and their merchant backers, but the two ships finally got under way. The *Speedwell* proved to be so leaky that she had to turn back, and the *Mayflower* went on from Plymouth alone on September 6, 1620.

The company on board the *Mayflower* was a mixed one. Thirty-five of them came from Leyden, sixty-seven from England. In addition there were some fifteen members of the crew. The emigrants were probably crowded, because while they had brought no cattle there were some swine, poultry, and goats. There was little furniture on board, and the Pilgrims had to provide their own food in the form of bacon, hardtack, salt beef, smoked herring, cheese, and beer, rations of which were issued daily and consumed uncooked. On November 9, after a somewhat troubled voyage, they arrived off Cape Cod and turned southward toward Virginia. Finding themselves in the shallow waters off the Cape, and fearful of the danger of shipwreck, they decided, after a conference, to turn into Cape Cod Bay. As the *Mayflower* made her way toward the Cape, a number of the ship's company, knowing themselves to be outside the legal jurisdiction of either England or Virginia, informed the leaders that they had no real authority and that, therefore, these Londoners would take the first opportunity to secure their freedom. This was in effect a mutiny against the Pilgrim leadership. To forestall any more of such rebellious action, the men of the group met together and signed a solemn compact among themselves on November 21, 1620, the day on which the ship came to anchor in Provincetown harbor.

This famous document, known as the "Mayflower compact," was an agreement among forty-one of the forty-four men in the company of emigrants that they would form a civil government:

We . . . doe by these presents . . . covenant and combine our selves together into a civill pody politick, for our better ordering and preservation & furtherance of the ends aforesaid; and by vertue hereof to enacte, constitute, and frame such just and equall lawes . . . as shall be thought most meete & convenient for the generall good of the Colonie, unto which we promise all due submission and obedience.

This was not a constitution, but rather a social compact in the seventeenth-century sense of the word; that is, it was merely an agreement between the members of a community to form a government and a promise to obey its laws when made.

The emigrants then set out to find a site for their colony. Taking a small boat, a party of men sailed along the shore of Cape Cod and finally came, on December 21, to Plymouth harbor. Feeling that this was the best harbor they could find, they decided that their settlement should be built there, and on December 26, the *Mayflower* arrived at that spot.

NEW PLYMOUTH

On the shores of Plymouth harbor, then, they began to build their town; first a common house and then separate houses for the members of the company. As the dwellings on shore were completed, the emigrants left the ship and took up their residence in the buildings that had been erected. There were ninety-eight persons in all. One hundred and two had sailed from Plymouth; one of the company had died, and one child, named Oceanus, had been born. Four of the company had died while the ship lay in Cape Cod Bay.

This was a good record, but the greatest hardships the settlers had to face were still before them. During the first winter the company was reduced to one-half its original size because of disease and exposure to cold. They managed to complete a few houses, cutting and dragging the logs across the winter snow by hand. These houses they had occupied before the *Mayflower* sailed away for England in April. During the spring they planted twenty acres of Indian corn under the direction of Squanto, a friendly Indian, putting small fish called alewives into the holes with the corn as fertilizer after the Indian fashion. In the summer they began their fur-trading expeditions and they also began to cut boards, which they carried to Plymouth and stored, against the time when another ship would be returning to England. All in all they performed a tremendous amount of labor; and in the autumn they reaped an abundant harvest of Indian corn, to celebrate which they held a thanksgiving feast, assisted by Chief Massasoit and his Indians. The feast lasted three days, with bountiful meals of wild fowl, deer, pudding, and brandy, with sports and drilling by the Pilgrims and native dances by the Indians.

Just after the feast the ship *Fortune* arrived from England and the Pilgrims were able to fill her hold with lumber and furs that they had gathered. This was a triumph of hard labor and boded well for the economic future of the colony; but, unhappily, the ship was taken at sea on her way home by a French privateer. Still more terrifying was the fact that the *Fortune* had brought thirty-five new colonists for the fifty-one old settlers to feed. The harvest that had been raised would have been adequate for the needs of the fifty-one over the winter, but with the addition of thirty-five men and the impossibility of raising more food before the winter set in, the colony again had to face starvation before a new food supply could arrive in the spring.

This problem of the food supply was a difficult one for the new and struggling colony to solve. Up to 1623 all things were held in common and all men worked for the common fund, but as the merchants back in England constantly failed to send out food, and as the colonists felt that they must do everything possible to stimulate the production of a food supply, the leaders decided to portion out the land to individuals instead of sticking to the old joint-stock system. So the land was now distributed for individual use, and while each man was to keep what he made, he had the responsibility for feeding himself. The result was an immense gain in production, and the harvest of 1623 ended for all time any doubt as to the ability of the colony to feed itself. This was not achieved, however, without one more period of grave discouragement, for during that summer there took place a long and severe drought. The corn began to wither and the Pilgrims set aside a day of prayer for rain. They prayed for nine hours and the next day the rain came, whereupon it rained for two weeks. They had an abundant harvest. But the greatest result was a psychological one; for they were now convinced that God approved of them and their work and that he would not desert them in their hour of need.

Thus the food problem was gradually and finally solved by the planting of Indian corn and a revision of their arrangement with the merchants. The solution of the problem of food supply, however, was far from relieving them of all their worries, for constantly, from 1620 to 1627, the Pilgrims had to face the unpleasantness of their relations with their merchant backers. When the merchants were informed where the Pilgrims had landed they turned to the Council for New England for a title to the land the Pilgrims had occupied. A patent was issued giving them the right to take up land around Plymouth, but without fixing any boundaries. But this patent, the so-called "Peirce patent," left the Pilgrims in a state of almost medieval vassalage to the merchants, on land belonging to the company rather than to the Pilgrims themselves. The Pilgrims accepted the situation, nevertheless, only to find that their relations with their sponsors were complicated by the greedy desire of the merchants for profit. Their backers were disgruntled with the bargain they had made with the Pilgrims, but the knowledge of the value of the *Fortune's* cargo revived their interest and they sent out more ships. The irregularity of the supplies furnished by the merchants led the Pilgrims to doubt whether they could depend

upon them for support, and because of this doubt the colonists proceeded to develop economic activities of their own, and particularly
an independent fur trade.

The merchants, on the other hand, did not trust the Pilgrims.
They were discouraged by their many failures and the apparent

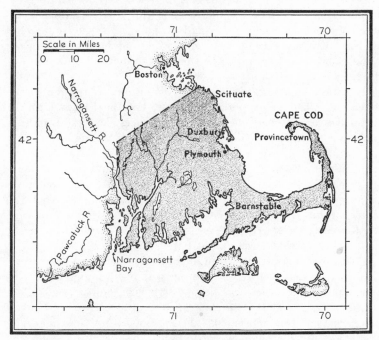

MAP 6. The Colony of Plymouth Under the So-called Bradford Patent
of 1630

NOTE: Because of the inaccuracy of geographic knowledge in the seventeenth century and
the vagueness of the language of the patent itself, the boundaries shown on this map must
be considered only approximately accurate.

inability of the colony to pay dividends. They sent out one ship to
aid the Pilgrims in their economic enterprises, but the crew mu-
tinied and the ship returned empty from a trading expedition to
Connecticut and Rhode Island. It was sent out to fish, but struck
a submerged rock and sank. It was raised, seized for debt, recovered
and sent out again for fish, only to be at last taken by the Spaniards.
The merchants sent out a salt maker and a shipwright. The shipwright died of fever and the salt maker built his fire too hot and
burned down his house and ruined his pans. About 1623 the merchant adventurers decided they could do no more and accordingly,

in 1624, declared the partnership dissolved. They made it clear, however, that they expected the Pilgrims to pay the indebtedness which remained for supplies and other services, and they still held the title to the land, which in 1622 had been renewed in the form of a "deed poll" which made the terms of their tenancy even more difficult for the Pilgrims than before. In view of these developments the Pilgrims undertook through their agent, Robert Cushman, a series of negotiations looking toward a complete freedom from their backers. The negotiations were successful, and in 1626 the merchants sold their title to the colonists for the sum of eighteen hundred pounds.

This was a huge sum, and it seemed impossible to pay the money. The colony had no corporate existence, but the leaders formed themselves into a company called "The Undertakers" and undertook to pay this sum, using for the purpose all the trading privileges of the colony. As a matter of fact, the business of the colony had actually prospered. The fur trade had grown and was now paying a handsome profit. By the terms of their purchase from the merchants the colonists found themselves in possession of a trading sloop, a fishing station at Cape Anne, and a fur-trading station on the Kennebec River. All these assets were turned to profit and their debt to the merchants was gradually but surely paid.

Meanwhile, land was issued to the individual settlers with a clear legal title, so that each family had one acre in town and a twenty-acre farm nearby, together with pasture rights on a large field which was reserved as a common. Finally, their "deliverance" was made complete by a new patent from the Council for New England which was issued in January, 1630. This, the so-called "Bradford patent," confirmed their title to the land and established understandable if somewhat vague boundaries—boundaries within which arose the towns of Plymouth, Bristol, Barnstable, Hingham, and Howe.

THE CONGREGATIONAL STATE

Back in Leyden the remainder of the original Pilgrim congregation heard with interest the news of the successful accomplishments of the colonists on the shores of Massachusetts Bay. In the year 1629 all those of the old congregation who wished were brought out to America, and the population of Plymouth was thereby greatly increased. As a matter of fact, considerable numbers of people had now begun to come to Plymouth from England, and some of these moved up or down the coast to form small settlements of their own, with the result that the colony of Plymouth became a congeries of small independent towns each grouped around its church.

Plymouth had never had a charter prescribing its form of government. As a matter of fact, when the Pilgrims first landed at Plymouth they were not a political body at all, but a church congregation. As such they elected their governor and an assistant, later some four to seven assistants, and the governor ruled as a sort of elected dictator. Yet the congregation met annually, as a general court of election and at certain other times when business seemed to demand it, and the members of the congregation gradually assumed the role of freemen or citizens of the commonwealth. Not all the residents of Plymouth, however, were freemen. There were "inhabitants" and "sojourners" more or less on probation, and there were also servants and some slaves who had no part in political life. As an inhabitant or sojourner came to be accepted in the community and in the church, however, he participated in the political life of the town.

Thus it was that a church congregation was gradually metamorphosed into a body politic. For a long time church and commonwealth were one and the same thing. As the population of the colony grew, however, and as other towns sprang up, it became increasingly difficult for all the freemen of the colony to go to Plymouth for the meetings of the general court, and almost without realizing the significance of what they were doing, the more remote congregations adopted the practice of sending representatives to Plymouth. Almost imperceptibly the government of Plymouth colony became a representative government. Here, as in Virginia, institutions appeared in response to local need, by a process of adaptation of the pure democracy of the church congregation to the exigencies of a new social and political scene.

By 1636, when the colony of Plymouth laid down its first code of laws in the so-called Great Fundamentals, this was a flourishing community, another outstanding example of the formative effects of environment and adaptation upon the ideas and the institutions of the people who had come from England. They had felt the necessity for government and they had signed a social compact on the basis of which they built out of a church congregation a civil government. They had been faced with the need for food in the absence of a supply from England and they had adapted to their uses the native Indian corn. They had been under the necessity of developing an economic life that would pay dividends, and they had turned to the sea for the profitable harvest of fish, and they had begun to trade with the native Indians for the furs that constituted the great harvest of the land. They had been faced with their uncomfortable and restrictive arrangement with the merchants and they had without precedent or experience formed themselves into a company to buy out the merchants' interest. They had no title to their lands, but they succeeded in getting a title from the Council for New England in 1630. Finally, not only did they make their congregation a civil government for the town of Plymouth, but they rebuilt the pure democracy of the congregational town meetings into a system of representative government sitting in the general court at Plymouth. Problem after problem had arisen; and for every problem, unlettered and untutored as most of them were, they were able to arrive at an adaptation of the resources that they found at hand to achieve their own peace and contentment in a successful civil society.

RECOMMENDED BOOKS FOR FURTHER READING

Contemporary Narratives

William Bradford, *Bradford's History of Plymouth Plantation, 1606-1646,* edited by William T. Davies.

Albert B. Hart, ed., *American History Told by Contemporaries,* I, 349-359.

Edward Johnson, *Johnson's Wonder-Working Providence, 1628-1651,* edited by John F. Jameson.

Charles H. Levermore, ed., *Forerunners & Competitors of the Pilgrims & Puritans.*

John Smith, *A Description of New England* (Peter Force *Tracts,* Volume II, no. 1).

George P. Winship, ed., *Sailors Narratives of Voyages along the New England Coast, 1524-1624.*

Alexander Young, ed., *Chronicles of the Pilgrim Fathers of the Colony of Plymouth, from 1602 to 1625.*

Modern Accounts

James T. Adams, *The Founding of New England,* Chapter 5.

Charles M. Andrews, *The Colonial Period of American History,* I, Chapters 13-16.

Charles M. Andrews, *Our Earliest Colonial Settlements,* Chapter 3.

James P. Baxter, ed., *Sir Ferdinando Gorges and His Province of Maine,* Volume I.

John Brown, *The Pilgrim Fathers of New England and Their Puritan Successors.*

The Cambridge History of the British Empire, I, Chapter 5.

Edward Channing, *A History of the United States,* I, Chapters 9-14.

John Fiske, *The Beginnings of New England,* Chapter 2.

John A. Goodwin, *The Pilgrim Republic.*

William E. Griffis, *The Pilgrims in Their Three Homes, England, Holland, America.*

Samuel E. Morison, *Builders of the Bay Colony,* Chapter 1.

Herbert L. Osgood, *The American Colonies in the Seventeenth Century,* I, Part I, Chapter 5.

Daniël Plooij, *The Pilgrim Fathers from a Dutch Point of View.*

Daniel W. Prowse, *A History of Newfoundland.*

Frances Rose-Troup, *John White, the Patriarch of Dorchester (Dorset) and the Founder of Massachusetts, 1575-1648.*

Roland G. Usher, *The Pilgrims and Their History.*

Justin Winsor, ed., *The Memorial History of Boston,* Volume I.

10

"The Caribbee Isles"

THE BEGINNINGS

THE "GREAT MIGRATION" of Englishmen to the new world sent its most numerous stream of emigrants to the small islands about the Caribbean Sea. The West Indies had caught the imagination of Englishmen more than any other part of the new world because of the fabulous riches that Spain had brought back from her own colonies there. Indeed, the chief interest of Englishmen in colonization during the sixteenth century, such as it was, had been in tapping that fabulous source of wealth. The treaty of London (1604) had brought an end to the long Anglo-Spanish war, and it opened the era of genuine colonization in America. For after that year English economic interest in colonization became an interest, not in tapping Spanish colonial wealth, but, rather, in raising new commodities for English commerce. Backers of colonization, as already noted in the case of Virginia, invested their money in colonizing expeditions to the West Indies largely with a view to reaping profits from the commodities that those islands might produce.

The West Indies had been, and remained, the cockpit of international rivalries in America; but by the beginning of the seventeenth century the nations of Europe had begun to give up hope of finding a passage to the east and to devote themselves to the cultivation of colonies for their own sake. Tobacco, first imported into Europe from Spanish and Portuguese colonies, had already become a valuable and profitable commodity in European commerce, and it was hoped that tobacco might also be grown in the lands around the Caribbean, for the benefit of English trade.

The first attempts of English, French and Dutch settlement in the region of the West Indies were directed toward Guiana on the northern coast of South America. The first English attempt was made by Charles Leigh, who attempted to plant a colony on the Wiapoco River about 1604, three years before the settling of Virginia. His objectives were the cultivation of trade with the Indians, the exploitation of gold mines and the planting of tobacco. He landed forty-six men, but in 1606 the colony was abandoned. In

1609 Robert Harcourt established a settlement on the Wiapoco, but as he had no royal sanction for his colony he applied in 1613 for a grant of all the land between the Amazon and the Essequibo. James I granted him the land, but the colony languished. Walter Raleigh led a marauding expedition to this region in 1617, but the expedition resulted in a fiasco, and Raleigh, for the appeasement of the Spanish king, lost his head.

About 1619 Roger North and other English merchants again took up the idea of creating an English Guiana where tobacco might be raised to compete with the tobacco now coming from Virginia. North formed the "Amazon Company" and, under a charter from James I, sent out an expedition in 1620. Because of the protests of Spain, however, the Amazon Company's charter was canceled and North's expedition was recalled. Still another company, called the "Guiana Company," was formed in 1626, but war soon broke out between England and Spain, and this company, like the others, failed.

Thus, while the Virginia Company was slowly getting its colony established upon the shores of Chesapeake Bay, other English merchants were attempting to establish colonies in the great area of vacant land between the Amazon and the Orinoco rivers in South America. But many circumstances combined to cause these enterprises to fail. The climate was not conducive to successful settlement; as already noted, it was for this reason that the Pilgrims, at Leyden, after considering Guiana, decided to go instead to Virginia. The early colonists, moreover, had been lured away from more prosaic, but more fundamental pursuits by the will-o'-the-wisp of gold seeking, and it was not until the middle of the century that the English succeeded in establishing a really stable colony in Guiana.

ST. CHRISTOPHER AND BARBADOS

Associated with Roger North in his efforts to plant a colony in Guiana had been one Thomas Warner. Warner was in Guiana until 1622, whence he returned home by way of the Lesser Antilles. He visited several of the islands with the idea of finding one suitable for colonization, and fixed upon the island of St. Christopher as the best for the purpose. On his arrival in London he succeeded in interesting Ralph Merrifield and a group of merchants in his project, and in 1624, the year in which the Virginia Company was losing its charter, he arrived back in the island with the financial backing of the merchants and with a group of colonists to aid in the settlement of the island. After a successful year of settlement and tobacco raising, Warner returned to England to get more colonists. At the same time he and his backers sought the approval of the new king, Charles I, who recognized the new colony and made Warner the king's lieutenant in the islands of St. Christopher, Nevis, Montserrat, and Barbados.[1]

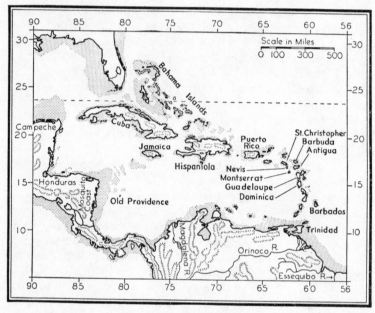

MAP 7. The Caribbee Isles

Meanwhile, another British colony was appearing far to windward of St. Christopher, on the island of Barbados. Here, in 1625, John Powell, captain of the ship *Olive,* sailing for the great Anglo-Dutch trading firm of Courteen Brothers, stopped on his way home from Brazil. Powell was greatly impressed by the attractiveness of the island, the soil, and its forests of dye-wood. He returned home by way of St. Christopher, where he told of his discovery, and, on his arrival in England, he convinced his employer that the island could be colonized with profit. William Courteen then formed a group of merchants, known as "Courteen and Associates," with the purpose of developing the island. The first expedition went out in 1627 with eighty colonists, and others followed. The colonists settled

[1] Probably originally intended to mean Barbuda.

along the western shore of the island, and founded the town of Bridgetown at its southwestern corner. Under their agreement with their backers the colonists were tenants of the merchants, and were maintained by them; in return for which the settlers turned over to the company the products of their labor, chiefly tobacco and dye-wood, as had been the case in the early history of Virginia and Plymouth. The colony prospered, and its population increased so rapidly that by 1629 it contained some 1,600 Englishmen—more, indeed, than Virginia had after a history of twenty years.

WEST INDIES GRANTS

It was not long before these two Caribbean colonies were at odds with each other. The two rival groups of merchants backing the two colonies realized the need of legal titles to their islands and turned to the Crown for confirmation. Both groups also knew the importance of having powerful friends at court. Merrifield and his associates, backers of Warner and the colony of St. Christopher, enlisted the support of the Earl of Carlisle, who succeeded in getting from King Charles I, on July 2, 1627, a charter for the colony of "Cariola," which made Carlisle the proprietor of all the islands of the West Indies between the tenth and twentieth degrees of north latitude. This area included not only the island of Barbados but also the Spanish islands of Santo Domingo and Puerto Rico, as well as a large slice of the mainland of South America. Under the terms of his charter Carlisle was the feudal proprietor of this area, for which he was to pay the king a rental of £100 per year and a white horse whenever His Majesty should come into those parts, which probably would not be often. Courteen, now on the defensive, himself looked for a patron at court, and found one in the person of the Earl of Montgomery. Montgomery appealed to the king for a charter covering the island of Barbados, and in February, 1628, was given proprietary title to all the land lying between the eighth and the thirteenth degrees of north latitude. This second grant would have included the settlements at the mouth of the Orinoco as well as the island of Barbados, and would have subtracted a number of uninhabited islands from those granted to Carlisle. The Earl of Carlisle thereupon appealed to the courts and obtained a ruling which set aside the Montgomery charter.

Unhappily for Barbados, the rivalry of the proprietors was carried into the island itself, and resulted in fighting that amounted to practically a civil war. Courteen was never able to recover his control of the islands, however, and Thomas Warner remained governor of all the British settlements in the West Indies under the Earl of Carlisle until his death in 1649.

In the course of the first fifteen years of their history, the English settlements in the West Indies expanded with phenomenal rapidity. From St. Christopher Englishmen went out and settled Nevis, Montserrat, Anguilla, and Barbuda, and the population of these islands increased so rapidly that by 1640 there were perhaps forty thousand Englishmen living in the Antilles, including Barbados. One of the curious offshoots of this rapid settlement of the islands of the Caribbean was the colonization of the island of Providence, off the coast of Central America on the route of the Spanish ships moving from Porto Bello to Havana on their way home to Spain. This island was settled by a company, formed at about the same time as the Massachusetts Bay Company under the leadership of the Earl of Warwick, John Pym, and other non-conformists and parliamentarians. This company, as it proclaimed, was formed to "plant the true and sincere Religion and worship of God" on the island of Providence, where they would establish a godly commonwealth as a base of operations in a holy war against the Catholic Anti-Christ of Spain. Incidentally, of course, they hoped that the holy war would make it possible for them to derive great profits from preying upon the Anti-Christ's West Indian and mainland trade. It thus fell out that the holy island of Providence became a base for privateers and pirates; so much so that it eventually lost its holy air entirely and became one of the great international scandals of the age. Spanish pride was piqued by this thorn in the side of Spain's American empire, and after several unsuccessful attempts the place was taken by the Spaniards and destroyed in 1641. Its only permanent result was the beginning of a logwood trade with the Indians who resided along the Mosquito shore of the mainland nearby, a trade which became the basis for England's claim to the territory later on.

In the older islands the rush of colonists was so great that Barbados and St. Kitt's (St. Christopher) became crowded. Every scrap of available territory was taken up and the population of Barbados alone in 1639 was estimated at 30,000. The struggle for existence was severe, and Barbados, which alone had a population of 37,000 in 1642 on an area of only 166 square miles, became, for the time being at least, one of the most crowded areas in the world with 220 persons per square mile. Clearly such conditions could not last, and after 1645 a great many people sought homes farther on, either in other islands or in the colonies of the mainland where there was more room.

POLITICAL INSTITUTIONS IN THE ISLAND COLONIES

Under the grants to the Earl of Carlisle, the West Indies had become proprietary colonies; that is to say, they were the property of Carlisle, and he had the power to appoint governors and arrange for the making of laws in his island possessions. Thomas Warner was made governor of St. Christopher for life in 1629 and it was under his administration that settlement spread to the other islands lying near St. Kitt's. Barbados was given a separate governor in the person of Sir William Tufton, who was succeeded by Henry Hawley. Under Hawley, in 1639, the first representative assembly met at Bridgetown. This assembly, however, was called merely to approve the government's acts; it had no power to initiate legislation. It was only after 1641 that the assembly was given the right to initiate laws. The Earl of Carlisle died in 1636, leaving his colony to his son, the second earl. But the second earl took little interest in the colony, and leased his proprietorship to Francis Lord Willoughby. Meanwhile the civil war had broken out in England, and the island of Barbados, left pretty much to its own devices, developed its government along lines which seemed to meet its needs without much outside interference. Thus by the time when Willoughby himself arrived in 1650 the pattern of government was not unlike that of Virginia, with a governor appointed by the proprietor, a council of two and an elected assembly composed of two burgesses from each parish. This legislature both made the laws "in the nature of the Parliament of England," and served as a supreme court of appeals.

Meanwhile, the Leeward Islands, under governor Thomas Warner, were developing separate institutions of their own. These little islands of Antigua, Nevis, and Montserrat, clustered about St. Christopher, looked to St. Christopher for leadership. Each, however, formed its own small legislature and had its own local governor. St. Christopher, the most important of this group of island settlements, assumed a sort of governmental oversight over the others in the name of the proprietor. The island itself was shared with the French, who had arrived in 1625 and had assisted the English in wiping out the native Caribs. A division of the island had taken place in 1627, under the terms of which the English took the central section with their villages of Old Road, Brimstone Hill and

Palmetto Point, and the French took the two ends, with the town of Basseterre and the salt works at the southern end.

During the Great Rebellion in England the people of the islands were divided in their loyalties. Willoughby in Barbados proclaimed Charles II king in that colony upon the execution of Charles I, as did also Virginia, Maryland and Bermuda, and this step was followed by Antigua. The other islands, however, wisely chose to remain neutral. For in 1651 the new Commonwealth government of England sent Sir George Ayscue with a fleet to the colonies to teach them a due sense of their obedience to the mother country, with the result that Willoughby was driven out of Barbados, and Daniel Searle was appointed governor in his place.

Theoretically, all the British islands in the Caribbean were the feudal possession of one man, the Earl of Carlisle, who had leased his rights to Lord Willoughby. Under the proprietary form of colonial administration the powers of government, sometimes exceeding locally even the powers of the king in England, were delegated to one man, who was thus empowered to govern his colony as he saw fit. In practically every colony of this type, however, the proprietor was compelled by the practical necessities of administration, often enough forcibly presented by the colonists themselves, to introduce representative institutions. Thus in all these island communities of the West Indies government had developed on the pattern of the English Parliament, often without the sanction, and, often indeed, almost without the knowledge of the proprietor. As a matter of fact, the tiny island assemblies were actually more representative of the people than was the Parliament in England, since they were composed of men elected by all the landowners in all the parishes. Here, as elsewhere, political institutions were the outgrowth of the adaptation of "self-government-minded" English people.

SUGAR AND SOCIETY

The first settlers in the British West Indies devoted themselves to the cultivation of tobacco, which they grew on small farms of from five to thirty acres. This was profitable for a time, but West Indies tobacco was coarse and rank, and when a depression in the world tobacco market took place in the sixteen-thirties, the islanders found it impossible to compete successfully with Virginia tobacco. The planters then began to experiment with other crops, such as indigo and cotton. These crops were only moderately successful. About 1640 Pieter Brower, a Dutchman, planted in Barbados some sugar cane brought from Brazil. After some experimentation it was found that sugar could be grown so successfully that one acre of sugar cane would pay higher profits than three acres of tobacco. The plant quickly spread through the islands, and by 1660 sugar had completely replaced tobacco as the staple crop of all the English island colonies.

The cultivation of sugar, however, brought about two fundamental changes in the island economy. For the business of raising sugar involved large outlays of capital, and large plantations. It was found, also, that the heavy labor involved could best be performed by Negro slaves. The result of these two facts was that the small planters were crowded out, and the islands, from being settlements made up of small farms, became communities made up, to a considerable degree, of large plantations. Thus there took place, hardly more than a generation after their founding, a social revolution in these islands. Not only did society change from one composed of small farmers to one dominated by large plantation owners, but the crowding out of the small planters resulted, in some of the islands, in an actual decline in population. Some of the planters thus forced out went to other islands, others went to the colonies on the mainland of North America. On the other hand, the large planters who remained became the nucleus of a planter aristocracy.

Thus sugar became the staple, profit-making commodity produced in the West Indies as the cultivation of tobacco was coming to be the economic foundation of society in colonial Virginia. Moreover, when the West Indies began to specialize in the cultivation of sugar, it became necessary for them to purchase their supplies of food, horses, lumber, and manufactured goods abroad. This in turn opened a great market, not only for British manufactured goods, but, also, for the fish and lumber and horses of the northern continental colonies. Almost from the first decade of their history New England ships were to be found in the ports of the British West Indies. The New Englanders, taking their commodities to the West Indies, received in return sugar which they took to England to pay for manufactured goods which they themselves needed, or they returned with the sugar to New England where it was made into rum; and this rum became a great staple in the fishing trade—where it was used "for heating purposes."

While the civil war was going on in England, the trade of the British West Indies fell largely into the hands of the Dutch, as was the case also in Virginia. It was partly to bring the islands under the control of Parliament and partly to exclude the Dutch from the island trade that the British passed the act of October 3, 1650, which closed Barbados, Bermuda, and Virginia to all trade and prohibited foreigners from entering into trade with any of the English colonies in America. This act was followed by the Navigation Act of 1651, which will be noted later, and in the same year the Ayscue expedition called at Barbados and deposed Lord Willoughby, as already related, and set up instead Daniel Searle, who was expected to govern in the name of the Commonwealth and in accord with its colonial policy.

From this time on, because of the successful cultivation of sugar and the great market that they provided for English manufactured goods, the West Indies became the most profitable of all the English colonies and an important exemplification of the idea of a "self-sufficient empire" which soon came to dominate English colonial policy.

RECOMMENDED BOOKS FOR FURTHER READING

Contemporary Narratives

Robert Harcourt, *A Relation of a Voyage to Guiana . . . 1613*, edited by Charles A. Harris (Hakluyt Society Publications, Second series, LX).
Vincent T. Harlow, ed., *Colonising Expeditions to the West Indies and Guiana, 1623-1667* (Hakluyt Society Publications, Second series, LVI).
Walter Raleigh, *The Discoverie of the large and bewtiful Empire of Guiana*, edited by Vincent T. Harlow.
Irene A. Wright, ed., *Documents Concerning English Voyages to the Spanish Main, 1569-1580* (Hakluyt Society Publications, Second series, LXXI).

Modern Accounts

Charles M. Andrews, *The Colonial Period of American History*, II, Chapter 7.
The Cambridge History of the British Empire, I, Chapter 5.
Julian S. Corbett, *Drake and the Tudor Navy*.
Nellis M. Crouse, *French Pioneers in the West Indies, 1624-1664*.
Nicholas D. Davis, *The Cavaliers & Roundheads of Barbados, 1650-1652*.
Clarence H. Haring, *The Buccaneers in the West Indies in the XVIIth Century*.
Vincent T. Harlow, *A History of Barbados, 1625-1685*.
Philip A. Means, *The Spanish Main; Focus of Envy, 1492-1700*.
Arthur P. Newton, *The Colonising Activities of the English Puritans*.
Arthur P. Newton, *The European Nations in the West Indies, 1493-1688*, Chapters 9-14.
James A. Williamson, *The Caribbee Islands under the Proprietary Patents*.
James A. Williamson, *A Short History of British Expansion*, Part I.
William C. H. Wood, *Elizabethan Sea-Dogs*.

11

Massachusetts Bay

A$_T$ ABOUT the time when the Pilgrims were completing their plans to emigrate to America, Sir Ferdinando Gorges, one of the outstanding English colonizers of the reign of King James I, undertook to reorganize the defunct Plymouth branch of the old Virginia Company. In contrast with Edwin Sandys, however, Gorges was no democrat, nor even a liberal. He was, rather, an aristocrat; and his interest in establishing colonies in America was based chiefly upon his desire to build for himself a profitable manorial estate. Thus it was that the patent for the Council for New England, issued on November 3, 1620, provided that the Council should be composed of forty members, among whom there were at first no merchants. The Council was given the sole ownership of all the land between the fortieth degree and the forty-eighth degree of north latitude, with the power to make grants and establish governments in this territory. They were also given a monopoly of the trade and fishing along this coast and an immunity from customs duties for seven years. Gorges, it seems, had the idea of establishing in New England a great composite feudal principality with one governor-general and a council of those to whom lands were granted by the Council for New England. According to his scheme there would be a bishop, chancellors, and other high officials, and an assembly of delegates from the local divisions or colonies.

Organized at the moment when the great migration was beginning to get under way, the Council for New England was soon called upon to issue grants of land to various colonial promoters. The grant to John Peirce in 1621 for the land upon which the Pilgrims had settled has already been noted. Very soon after the Pierce patent came others. In the spring of 1622, Thomas Weston, the former backer of the Pilgrims, who had now separated from his merchant associates, sent a large party of "rude and profane fellows" to Plymouth, apparently with the idea of having them go from there to some convenient spot to found a fishing colony, although it is probable that he had no authority from the Council for New England. This "lusty crew" were certainly not welcome at Plymouth, so they moved over to Wessagussett, now Weymouth, where they built their houses. They neglected the all-important precaution of planting crops and providing a food supply by fishing, with the result that they suffered much from hunger during the ensuing winter. Because of their distresses they abandoned the colony the next year, some of them going home to England and others to other points along the coast.

Another settlement, similar to Weston's and only a few miles away, at a place near the site of the modern town of Braintree, furnished one of the most diverting episodes in early New England history. For here one Captain Wollaston tried his hand at colonizing about the year 1624, only to abandon the place in favor of Virginia shortly thereafter. One of his lieutenants, Thomas Morton by name, remained with a number of the settlers, many of whom were indentured servants. Morton freed the servants from their indentures and changed the name of the place from Mount Wollaston to Merriemount. The whole company then engaged in trade with the Indians and made the settlement a center of merry Elizabethan living—so riotous and so merry, indeed, that it soon scandalized the "unspotted lambs of the Lord" down at Plymouth.

Thomas Morton was a gay, convivial spirit who had brought to the colony among his "equipment" a plentiful supply of hard waters. On the departure of Wollaston from the settlement and the renaming of Merriemount, Morton and his colonists proceeded to live up to the new name. He made friends with the Indians as he traded with them. He hunted in the woods and fished in the waters of the bay. White men and Indians mingled at the Mount, and in the spring of 1627 Morton and his comrades erected a maypole, as Bradford says in his *History of Plymouth Plantation,* "drinking and dancing aboute it many days togeather, inviting the Indean women for their consorts, dancing and frisking togither, (like so many fairies, or furies rather), and worse practices." The maypole was eighty feet high, with a deer's antlers fixed to the top; and on it was nailed a poem celebrating the occasion. A song was also made which, according to the record, "was sung with a Corus, every man bearing his part; which they performed in a daunce, hand in hand about the Maypole, whiles one of the Company sung and filled out the good Liquor, like Gammedes and Jupiter." The song they sang went thus:

Refrain:
>   Drinke and be merry, merry, merry, boyes,
>   Let all your delight be in Hymen's joyes;
>   Io! to Hymen, now the day is come,
>   About the merry Maypole take a Roome.

>   Make greene garlons, bring bottles out
>   And fill sweet Nectar freely about,
>   Uncover thy head and feare no harme,
>   For here's good liquor to keepe it warme;

>   Nectar is a thing assign'd
>   By the Deities owne minde
>   To cure the hart opprest with griefe,
>   And of good liquors is the cheife.

Here was a breath of the old world Renaissance come to America. Naturally, it stank in the nostrils of the Pilgrims. Even so, Morton and his crew might have been tolerated had they not committed a much graver sin, for they sold the Indians firearms. This was far more serious than anything else that they had done, for all the young settlements along the coast were endangered by placing in the hands of the Indians weapons that would make them the equals of Europeans in battle. The scattered settlers, therefore, led by Plymouth, protested to Morton against this practice; but without result. Twice did the governor of Plymouth complain against Morton's methods of trade, only to receive flippant answers. Finally, in June, 1628, Captain Miles Standish—"Captaine Shrimpe," as Morton called him—was sent to Merriemount and ordered Morton to surrender. Morton and his men resisted, according to Bradford, and

if they had not been over armed with drinke, more hurt might have been done. They [Standish's men] sommaned him to yeeld, but he kept his house, and they could gett nothing but scofes and scornes from him; but at length, fearing they [Standish's men] would doe some violence to the house, he [Morton] and some of his crue came out, but not to yeeld, but to shoote; but they were so steeld with drinke as their peeces were too heavie for them; him selfe [Morton] with a carbine (over charged and allmost halfe fild with powder and shote, . . .) had thought to have shot Captaine Standish; but he [Standish] stept to him, and put by his peece, and tooke him. Neither was ther any hurte done to any of either side, save that one was so drunke that he rane his own nose upon the pointe of a sword that one held before him as he entered the house; but he lost but a little of his hott blood. Morton they brought away to Plimoth.

They shipped Morton back to England. He was soon again in New England, however, with more liquor and more defiance. But now the Puritans had begun to come to Massachusetts Bay, and stern, godly Governor John Endicott came over from Salem and chopped down the maypole, arrested Morton and put him in the bilboes, burned his house, and shipped him home to England. There, of course, he naturally joined the ranks of the enemies of the Massachusetts Bay colony, of which more later .

Meanwhile, settlements of a more legal sort were appearing around the shores of Massachusetts Bay. In March, 1622, Captain John Mason had been granted the land between the Naumkeag River and the Merrimac, extending inland to the sources of these two rivers. Shortly thereafter Sir Ferdinando Gorges and Captain Mason jointly were granted the lands between the Merrimac and the Kennebec, which they later divided between them at the Piscataqua River. On December 30, 1622, Robert Gorges was given a grant of the the lands along the shore of Massachusetts Bay from the Charles River to the Saugus, and was made governor-general of all New England. Late in June, 1623, the Council for New England declared a "divident" of part of its land, which was distributed by lot among its land-hungry members, and shortly thereafter Robert Gorges set sail for the province of New England, taking with him a large number of colonists for the founding of a town. He attempted to make a settlement at Weston's old place at Wessagussett. But young Gorges, along with many others, was unable to adapt himself to the hardships of a New England winter in the wilderness, and early in the spring of 1624 he abandoned his colony and went home. The colonists had quarreled among themselves, and most of them dispersed, some going back to England, some finding more congenial surroundings in other colonies—or in solitude. The distinguished Reverend William Blackstone moved to the Shawmut peninsula, where the town of Boston was later to appear, and Samuel Maverick moved to Noddles Island, in Massachusetts Bay. Both these men played important roles in later Massachusetts history. A few survivors stayed on at Wessagussett, and this little town, later named Weymouth, thus became the second permanent English colony on the shores of Massachusetts Bay.

THE MASSACHUSETTS BAY COMPANY

In the summer of 1623 another little settlement had been founded on the shores of Cape Ann, at the northerly limit of Massachusetts Bay. This enterprise had had its beginning in a party of fourteen men who had been left on the Cape by the ship *Fellowship,* which had brought them to America from Dorchester, a fishing and merchant town on the southwest coast of England. For there, in Dorchester, a number of merchants, led by one Richard Bushrod, had caught the fever of colonization for the purposes of fishing and trade, and had obtained from the Council for New England a license to fish on the New England coast. Early in 1623 they had received a patent for a permanent settlement, and had sent out the *Fellowship* to make a beginning. Despite the fact that the results of the voyage of the *Fellowship* were not very promising, they organized themselves into a company, and enlarged the scale of their enterprise, sending out two ships and more colonists in 1624.

The moving spirit in this company was the Reverend John White, Anglican rector of the Church of the Holy Trinity in Dorchester. White recognized the economic advantage of having men on the fishing banks early in the season; but he also hoped to make the new settlement a religious center for the settlers and the fishermen along the New England coast. The grim, inhospitable character of Cape Ann itself was not conducive to success, and after the partial failure of the expeditions of 1623 and 1625 the company decided to send out Roger Conant, brother of one of the promoters, to try to make the colony prosper. Conant, however, could do little better than his predecessors, and in 1626 the Dorchester Company, having expended its capital with no return, collapsed. Most of the colonists returned home.

Conant was one of those who stayed, confident in the belief that a colony in this region, if not on the Cape itself, could be made a success. In the fall of 1626, therefore, he led his little group along the coast to the mouth of the Naumkeag River, where they settled, thus founding the town of Salem. Conant communicated his confidence to some of the promoters at home, and suggested that the new colony might become a "receptacle" for many people who were dissatisfied with the religious situation in England. This idea coincided exactly with those of the Reverend John White, who, as an Anglican, did not wish to separate from the Anglican church as the Pilgrims had done, but, rather, to purify it from within. White was thus a Puritan, in the original sense of the word; his appeal for support, in his renewed efforts to found a colony, were henceforth to be made chiefly to Puritans.

White now began to negotiate with certain businessmen of London and some interested Puritans of eastern England. The businessmen saw the opportunities in the proposal for a colony, as well as the popular appeal that an emphasis upon the Puritan way of worship would have to this persecuted religious group. The result was the formation of the New England Company to take over the enterprise of the Dorchester Company and to found a colony which would make a special appeal to English Puritans. The New England Company turned to the Earl of Warwick, president of the Council for New England, and in March, 1628, obtained from him a patent granting them the land lying along the New England coast from a point three miles south of the Charles River to another point three miles north of the Merrimac, and extending from the Atlantic Ocean to the South Sea. Obviously, however, this grant overlapped those already made to Robert Gorges, John Mason, and Sir Ferdinando Gorges; and it was a foregone conclusion that it would be opposed by these men or their heirs.

In the summer of 1628 the New England Company sent over its first contingent of colonists and supplies. They sent John Endicott to replace Roger Conant as the local director of the enterprise; it was he who crossed the bay to Merriemount and chopped down Thomas Morton's maypole. But as the uncertainty of the title to its lands became more apparent to the company, and as legal attack upon it seemed to be a certainty, the stockholders decided to go over the heads of the Council for New England to the king himself, and get a charter which would both make them independent of this threat and give them the power to set up a separate government of their own. In this appeal they were successful, and the new charter was issued in March, 1629.

Under this new charter the name of the company was changed to "The Governor and Company of the Massachusetts Bay in Newe England,". or the Massachusetts Bay Company. The bounds of its grant remained the same as in the grant to the New England Company. Its powers and prerogatives were greatly enlarged, however, by this grant from the king which, indeed, effectively effaced the claims of those holding grants in the area from the Council for New England. The Massachusetts Bay Company was incorporated as "one body corporate and politique," with a governor, an executive board of eighteen "assistants" to be elected by the "freemen" or stockholders, who were to meet as a body in a general assembly once every quarter. This government of the company was empowered to make laws and regulations for the administration of their colony, appoint officials, grant lands, punish, fine, or imprison evil doers, and "all other matters" useful for good and orderly government. Thus reorganized, the Massachusetts Bay Company dispatched, in the summer of 1629, a fleet of five ships loaded with cattle, supplies, tools, goods for the Indian trade, and between two and three hundred colonists. They confirmed the appointment

of John Endicott as governor, and changed the name of their settlement on the Naumkeag to "Salem"—the house of peace. It is to
be noted that the men who made up this commercial company were

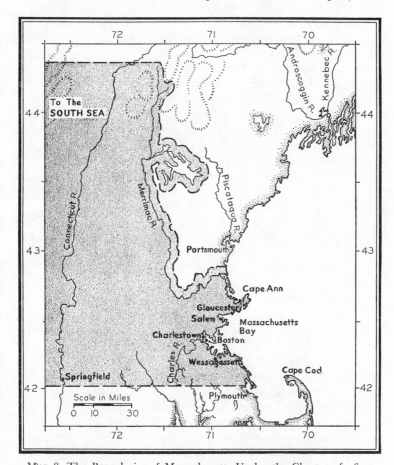

MAP 8. The Boundaries of Massachusetts Under the Charter of 1629

NOTE: Because of the inaccuracy of geographic knowledge in the seventeenth century and
the vagueness of the language in the charter itself, the boundaries shown on this map must
be considered only approximately accurate.

of three groups, the Dorchester group of merchants and fishing
magnates, certain merchants of London, and a number of well-to-
do Puritans of eastern England. The Dorchester group and many
of the London merchants were Anglicans in religion, and interested in the profits they hoped to derive from the company. But

the Puritan group were also interested in setting up a religious commonwealth fashioned according to Puritan ideas. Gradually this group got control of the company and transformed it from a trading corporation to a colonizing society with religious objectives.

It was a group of these Puritans who seem to have conceived the idea of moving the company, with its charter, to the colony on Massachusetts Bay. Since their desire was to set up a religious community, and as the company, under the charter, was an open corporation, liable to fall under the control of non-Puritans, these men felt that the only way to achieve their ideal would be to transport the government of the company to America, where they might see to it that only those with like ideals to their own could become freemen, and where they might feel reasonably free from interference, either by the government of England or by their enemies. Many of the Puritan leaders were even considering going to America themselves, since their positions in England, political, economic, and religious, seemed to be becoming increasingly insecure.

Typical of this group was John Winthrop, a Puritan squire living at Groton, in eastern England. Winthrop was finding it difficult to maintain the standard of living of his social class, and, as a result, he was heavily in debt. Life among the young people seemed to him to be frivolous and dissolute in the extreme, and he feared for the souls of his children should they be caught in the general corruption. His own position as an attorney in the court of wards and liveries at London seemed to be jeopardized by the general political situation and the fact that he was a Puritan. He was convinced that God would soon bring a great disaster upon England, from which He might save a few by taking them across the sea to found a new and better civilization. Perhaps, thought Winthrop, emigration might be the solution of all his problems. The idea of emigration was in the air, and Winthrop was only one of many who were now considering the step seriously.

On August 26, 1629, a group of Puritans met at Cambridge and debated the possibility of going to the colony as a group. The chief obstacle seemed to be the insecurity of their colony under a company resident in England. They, therefore, agreed that could the charter and the government of the company be transported to America—which meant it must be placed in their hands—they would themselves be prepared to go. When this proposal was presented to the company, there took place a famous debate, with the merchants and the religious moderates opposing the transfer and the "radicals"—the Puritans—favoring it. The general assembly, with only a minority of the stockholders present, voted to move the patent to New England; which was equivalent, in effect, to voting the company out of existence as an English corporation. Then, as Mathew Cradock found he could not go to America, the company elected John Winthrop its president with the responsibility for effecting the transfer.

FROM COMPANY TO COMMONWEALTH

In the spring of 1630 the Massachusetts Bay Company transferred itself to its colony. Between February and June of that year no less than seventeen ships, loaded with more than a thousand colonists, made their way across the ocean to Salem, Charlestown, and other parts of the Massachusetts Bay area. With this migration went the government of the colony, carried by what was the most distinguished group of men to cross the ocean at one time in the entire colonial period. For Winthrop and his associates were well-educated leaders of English life, moved by the determination to set up in the wilderness a society built according to the Puritan plan—which, they were convinced, was a plan laid down by God.

The first problem confronting the Massachusetts Bay Colony was the problem of government. The Massachusetts Bay Company was a commercial company; under its charter it had a governor, a council of eighteen "assistants," and a "general court" meeting quarterly. But most of the assistants had resigned and there were very few of the freemen of the company now in the colony to constitute a general court. Winthrop called a meeting of the assistants on August 23, 1630, at Charlestown. There were eight assistants present, and this group proceeded to appoint justices of the peace for the regulation of local affairs after the fashion of the justices of the peace in England. The first general court was called for October 19, but as there were so few stockholders, or freemen, in the colony, this meeting amounted to hardly more than another meeting of the assistants. It did not hesitate, however, to vote power to the assistants to elect the governor, to make laws, and to appoint officers.

This was done in an attempt to keep the control of the colony in the hands of the small group of Puritan leaders. For these men were no democrats. "Democracy," said the minister, John Cotton, in a much-quoted phrase, "I do not conceyve that ever God did ordeyne as a fitt government eyther for church or commonwealth. If the people be governors, who shall be governed?" Quite the contrary. The leaders of the mass emigration were Puritans who had left England in large measure to escape the danger of religious persecution. It did not matter that the mass of people came not for religious purposes but to escape economic depression and to make new homes for themselves in a more promising economic environment. The leaders had come to set up a commonwealth after their own fashion; and if they allowed the common people to get control of the Massachusetts Bay Company, the whole point of their emigration would be lost and they would be forced to see their ideal of a Puritan commonwealth disappear.

At the second meeting of the general court, in May, 1631, there were over one hundred applications for admission to the company as freemen. How were these men to be admitted and yet preserve the ideal of the Puritan leaders? It was decided that new freemen of the company must be members of the churches, thereby insuring that all freemen would share the ideals of the founders. This was a violation of the company's charter because it placed a religious qualification upon citizenship. But with the provision for the admission of new citizens, the company ceased to be a commercial organization and became a political commonwealth; and the ruling of May, 1631, became the basis for the selection of an electorate for the continuance of government. As time went on the freemen, the voting citizens, constituted only a minority in any town. Only the freemen voted, and thus it came about that the Commonwealth of Massachusetts became a commonwealth whose political life was effectively controlled by a religious minority.

There were about three other classes of people in the population. A few of the colonists were members of the churches but had not been accepted into the freemanship of the company. On the other hand, there were a great many residents of Massachusetts who were not church members but who had taken the oath of fidelity to the commonwealth and who were in general sympathy with its ideals. This group, taken together with the freemen, probably constituted a majority of the population. Finally, there were a considerable number of people who were neither freemen nor church members: Anglicans, Presbyterians, some indentured servants, and, eventually, a few slaves. They were in the colony but not of it.

At the meeting of the general court in the spring of 1632 the freemen from Watertown entered a protest against the arbitrary assessment of taxes by the assistants. Winthrop replied that the court of assistants represented the body of the freemen; but his answer was unsatisfactory to his critics and there developed an agitation for, a greater share in government on the part of the freemen. The result of the agitation was that the governor and assistants were henceforth elected by the generality of freemen, and election day came to be the day on which the general court met in the spring.

Another step in the evolution of Massachusetts government was taken in 1634 when the freemen from the towns again protested against the arbitrary assessment of taxes. There ensued a stormy meeting and the protestors demanded to see the terms of the charter covering taxation. As a result of this appeal to their constitution, the session finally came to the decision, first, that only the general court could levy taxes; second, that assessment of taxes should be by estate and not by the size of a man's family, and, third, that the freemen of the towns might choose delegates to serve as their representatives in the meetings of the general court. This decision was of extreme importance because it vested the power of taxation in the general court and it made the general court a representative body instead of an assembly consisting of all the freemen of the colony. The charter was no longer the charter of a commercial company but the written constitution of the Massachusetts Bay commonwealth. Out of the geographic necessity inherent in the wide distribution of the Massachusetts towns had grown, as in the case of Plymouth, an American representative government.

The next stage in the evolution of the Massachusetts government took place in the division of the legislature into two houses. The question appeared as early as 1635 when the Reverend Thomas Hooker proposed to take his flock to Connecticut. The magistrates or assistants opposed his plan to leave the colony, but the deputies from the towns favored it. If the general court voted as one house, the majority would carry Hooker's proposal; but the magistrates claimed the right to veto action by the deputies. In this case the magistrates had their way; but the question came up again and again, and reached a climax when, in 1642, the council of assistants, acting in its capacity as a court, acquitted Robert Kayne of the charges of the widow Sherman relative to the widow's pig. For the widow appealed from the council of assistants to the general court as a whole. The deputies were for the widow but the magistrates again raised the contention that they had the "negative voice" over action by the deputies and their veto was effective. Out of this and other cases there came in 1644 the separation of the general court into two houses, the house of deputies and the council of assistants, each to have a veto power over the action of the other. From that time on, for any law or action to be effective it had to be approved by both houses.

A problem paralleling the evolution of government was presented by the need for a code of laws for the governance and the protection of the people. At the beginning, the magistrates had taken the Bible as their law and judgments had been harsh and often enough manifestly unjust, according to the individual magistrate's interpretation of the Bible text that seemed to cover the case. It should be added, however, that the magistrates were themselves raised in reverence of the common law in England, so that in the earliest stage in its evolution the law of Massachusetts was in practice a mixture of the Bible with the common law.

As early as 1635 discontent over this uncertainty began to appear among the people, and there developed a move for a written code of laws. Grand and petit juries were established after the English fashion and local courts were established, with the council of assistants acting as the highest court of appeals. In 1636 the Reverend John Cotton proposed a written code of laws which was a mixture of Bible precept and English common law. But this code was not adopted. In 1639 Nathaniel Ward and John Cotton presented a code which, two years later, was adopted as the Massachusetts Body of Liberties. It was soon found, however, that this code was too conservative, giving too much power to the magistrates, and there took place a revision, published in 1648 as the Laws and Liberties of Massachusetts, which became the basic code of Massachusetts law. This law was a combination of Mosaic or Bible law, English common law, and the laws passed by the legislature of the colony. Needless to say, from the point of view of the twentieth century, it was harsh and inhuman. From the point of view of the men who made it, however, it seemed to provide the sort of legal groundwork for society that would protect and maintain the social ideals of the founders of the colony. As such it remained the guiding basis of law in Massachusetts for at least two generations.

THE NEW ENGLAND TOWN

With the growth of population in the commonwealth, as a result of the great migration of England, more and more people passed through the towns on the seaboard to locations farther inland, or citizens of old towns moved westward to establish new locations farther on. As the general court was the sovereign body in Massachusetts, any group of freemen proposing to set up a new town must first get a grant of land from that body. When they arrived at the location for their town, the settlers generally laid out the town plan with great care. In the center they left a lot, perhaps two or three to five acres in extent, to be used as a common, and the main street of the town ran around this rectangular common. At the most appropriate place facing the common they built their church and set aside lots for the residence of the minister and a school. The other land facing upon the common was also divided into lots; each of the original proprietors was given one lot and any remaining lots were reserved for newcomers. These were called the home lots. In the nearby lands outside the village, each freeman was assigned to a strip of land for cultivation. Another part of the land was reserved for common pasturage and still other parts were reserved for a common woods. Thus any freeman possessed his home lot and his plot of arable land not far away, plus the right to enjoy the village common or pasturage in the common pasture, and the privilege of cutting wood in the common woods.

Ordinarily, each of the original freemen was also a member of the church and, therefore, could participate in the political affairs of the village conducted in town meeting. This meeting, in which the voters were also the members of the church congregation, was generally held in the "meeting house." Every freeman of the town could speak and could vote, and the meeting elected both the "select men" who were charged with the administration of the town business, such as road building, maintenance of schools, etc., and the delegates from the town to the general court of the commonwealth. The town meeting was thus dominated by the freemen of the town; as new people came into the town, while they might buy land and establish their residence there, unless they became members of the local church they could not vote in the town meeting. The non-church members might attend, to be sure, and, indeed, were sometimes even required to attend, and they might even speak; but they could not vote. It has been estimated that not more than twenty percent of the population of Massachusetts Bay were actually members of the churches. This estimate may be too conservative, but in any case it is probably true that even if the majority of the residents were not church members, they were in sympathy with the ideals, both of local and the provincial government, and were satisfied with the sort of government they got. It is of considerable interest to contrast the indigenous combination of representative and democratic institutions that sprang up in

Massachusetts with the royal form of representative government
that developed in Virginia. It should be noted, also, that the town
government here described—and somewhat oversimplified, be it
noted—spread all over New England. The religious qualification
for citizenship, however, was not everywhere insisted upon.

THE MASSACHUSETTS "THEOCRACY"

Political life in Massachusetts was in the hands of the members
of the church, and the leadership of the church members was in
the hands of the Puritan ministers. At first, the Puritan leaders who
came to Massachusetts Bay thought of themselves as being Anglicans, and there were among the Massachusetts churches certain
ones which were more radical than others; but as time went on
the leaders of the church gradually moved in the direction of
greater and greater uniformity. As early as 1631, as already noted,
the franchise was limited to the members of the churches. In 1635
church attendance was made compulsory for all, whether members
of the church or not. From 1636 onward the organization of new
churches had to be approved by the magistrates and the church
elders. Everyone was taxed to support the ministry in the towns
whether they were church members or not, and in 1637 was held
the first synod of Massachusetts churches, which drew up a list of
heretical opinions to be condemned and expurgated with the assistance of the civil authorities. The church was apparently moving in the direction both of Presbyterianism within the church
and of a close alliance between the ministry and the government.
But the movement toward genuine Presbyterian government was
checked by the opposition of those of a more congregational turn
of mind.

Because of the close alliance between church and state and the
discrimination against non-church members, Robert Child and
others presented a petition in 1645 which called attention to the
evils resident in the theocratic nature of the Massachusetts government. The Child petition protested against the taxation of
non-church members without representation in political affairs
and asked that members of other churches, such as the Anglicans,
might be given political rights. But Child's petition was denied
and Child himself was prosecuted for criticism of and resistance
to the established government. Soon after this, some of the elders
presented to the general court a bill asking for a synod to consider
the problems of church organization and the standardization of

church membership. The bill was blocked by the deputies; but a request nevertheless was made to the pastors to this effect, and the synod that met from 1646 to 1648 worked out the famous "Cambridge platform" which became both a statement of faith for the Massachusetts churches and a framework for religious and political cooperation.

The Cambridge platform adopted the Westminster confession of faith, first adopted in 1643 by a group of British Puritans called together by the British Parliament, as the basis of religious belief in the Massachusetts churches. It proposed that the full power of the state should be used to enforce the rules of the clergy and that religious offenses should be punished by civil authority. Finally, it proposed that the magistrates engage themselves to adopt a method of coercion for the prevention of the "separation" of individual churches from the general church association.

In the general court the Cambridge platform met with the approval of the magistrates but the opposition of the deputies. The deputies, who constituted the more popular element in government and represented the feelings of the lay members of the churches, were jealous of the already great power of the pastors over government. But the Cambridge platform was eventually passed by the court in October, 1651. This was the greatest triumph of the so-called Protestant priesthood in Massachusetts, for by placing the power of the state largely under the control of the ministry it made Massachusetts more than ever a complete political theocracy. It remained so with slight modification until the revocation of the Massachusetts charter in 1684 and the establishment of the dominion of New England in 1686.

COLONY AND MOTHER COUNTRY

One more feature of the political evolution of Massachusetts should be considered, and that is the relationship between the colony of Massachusetts and the mother country. The Massachusetts Bay Company had made many enemies. Ferdinando Gorges, particularly, had seen a large part of his own lands given away by the king to this group of Puritans. He was jealous of their success and he took steps to recover control of the colony established on what he considered his own lands. The Puritans had, indeed, in large measure escaped from the control of the crown. It was partly with this purpose in mind that they had emigrated in the first place. Gorges was of course interested to notice their tendency toward independence, and made much of this tendency in his appeals for a recovery of his estates. In 1632 he appealed to the Privy Council for action in his behalf, but his appeal was dismissed. A little later, because not only of the efforts of Gorges, but also of other opponents of the company such as Thomas Morton, John Mason, and others, a new inquiry was set on foot with regard to Massachusetts.

In 1633 a commission called the Commission for Foreign Plantations, a sort of standing committee of the Privy Council under the presidency of Archbishop Laud of Canterbury, was designated by the Crown to administer colonial affairs. The colony feared this commission, and justly so; for this new body soon demanded a return of the Massachusetts charter to England. The governor and assembly in the colony evaded the issue, and the Crown brought in a suit of *quo warranto* in the Court of Kings Bench which entered judgment against the company. But the company was three thousand miles away in America and there was little or no way of enforcing the judgment. King Charles appointed Gorges governor-general of Massachusetts, nevertheless, with John Mason vice-admiral, and the two of them proceeded to make plans to put down this "first American rebellion." But the ship in which they were planning to take their coercive expedition to Massachusetts broke on launching. Mason had died, and Gorges was without the necessary funds to establish himself in America. His efforts, therefore, failed; and when resistance to the Crown in England took active form in 1640 and eventuated in armed rebellion in 1642, the Massachusetts issue was lost from sight.

This was in effect a victory for Massachusetts and it confirmed that colony in its tendency toward independent action. The result was that for the first fifty years of its history, Massachusetts acted very much as though it were an independent sovereign state. It was not until after the Restoration and the adoption of a vigorous mercantilist colonial policy in Great Britain that Massachusetts was successfully disciplined and brought to a sense of its dependency upon the Crown.

ECONOMIC AND SOCIAL LIFE IN THE BIBLE COMMONWEALTH

The society that developed in the province of Massachusetts Bay was as different from the society of Virginia or the West Indies as it was from that of England. From the one thousand people who moved to Massachusetts in 1629 the population had grown to some 14,000 by 1640. These people had come to America partly to escape religious persecution in the mother country, but many of them were land-hungry peasants who hoped to get land for themselves in New England. Others came because they had heard of the prosperity of the fishing industry and the fur trade. The first comers engaged in a variety of pursuits. Some engaged in agriculture, but agriculture was not an encouraging business in this cold climate and rocky soil. Others plunged into fishing and the cod became the great symbol of Massachusetts prosperity. Others developed the fur trade and still others began to exploit the abundant forest resources to lay the foundations for a great shipbuilding industry.

The New England towns were for the most part self-sufficing, and for the newcomer there was a fair assurance of a modest competence. His land was free and labor was free. In general, every man cultivated his own lands with his own hands. It was hard work and it turned out to be a rigorously selective process. The poorer workers accepted the status of indentured servitude or of journeymen laborers, but the more ambitious were able to sustain themselves, and a great many began to accumulate small estates. Many of those who, by reason of physical dislike or inability with regard to the hard labor involved in wringing a living from the soil or the sea, became the shopkeepers of the towns, and a given town might present a society in which there was something of a balance in the population between farmers and merchants, or, along the shore, between farmers and fishermen; in every case the town produced almost everything that it needed. Such things as furniture, clothing, tools, and hardware, to be sure, were imported from England. On the whole, however, their economic sufficiency made them considerably less dependent on the mother country for supplies than were the colonies farther south. This economic fact had a tendency to encourage in them a more independent spirit.

Within a very few years Massachusetts had begun to sell its products to the other colonies. By 1634 it was sending wheat to the colonies of Maryland and the West Indies. It had begun to ship fish, cattle, and hides to Virginia and the Caribbean colonies, and in these colonies the ships of the New England "yankees" took on local products which they either carried to England, which they exchanged, in turn, for British manufactures or far-eastern goods or brought back to the continental colonies for sale. Their furs, lumber, masts, and hides, and their better fish they sent directly to England and took in return manufactured goods. But the best fish they soon began to send to Spain and Portugal, taking in exchange salt, lemons and wine. Thus the people of New England took the product of their agriculture, of their forests, of their Indian trade, and of their fishing enterprises, to the southern colonies, the West Indies, and southern Europe, whence they obtained commodities or letters of credit with which to build up a credit in England which made it possible for them to buy the goods necessary for their own existence. Gradually they even became distributors of English manufactured goods to the colonies farther south along the coast, and out of all this they developed business practices and an active commerce which made them the merchants *par excellence* of the colonial world. Almost unconsciously they had used the resources which they found at hand in their new country and turned those resources to a comfortable profit which eventually accumulated in the form of substantial wealth. Naturally, it was in the commercial towns that this wealth accumulated, and Boston became the metropolis of a commercial New England.

Upon these economic foundations Puritan New England built its society. In contrast to Virginia, where the typical unit of social organization was the tobacco plantation, the characteristic social institution here was the New England town. In contrast to Virginia, too, New England society, while it recognized and accepted the stratification of classes it had inherited from the old country, did not develop the wide cleavages which were to mark the social structure of the "old dominion." Negro slavery, while it existed, did not flourish; on the other hand, a high premium was placed upon industry and thrift, and the foundations of many a New England fortune of a later day were laid by industrious youths who by dint of hard work and judicious investments were able to raise themselves from the status of "servant" to that of "master." Out of their experiences arose a faith in economic individualism and free enterprise which justified and supported that tendency toward independence of the mother country which marked the settlers of New England from the beginning of their history. Here, as elsewhere in America, Englishmen were forging a new culture out of the culture they had brought with them, hammering it out, as it were, upon the hard anvil of experience in a new and strange environment.

RECOMMENDED BOOKS FOR FURTHER READING

CONTEMPORARY NARRATIVES

James P. Baxter, ed., *Sir Ferdinando Gorges and his Province of Maine,* II, III.

William Bradford, *Bradford's History of Plymouth Plantation, 1606-1646,* edited by William T. Davis.

Alexander Brown, *The First Republic in America.*

Thomas Hutchinson, *The History of the Colony and Province of Massachusetts-bay,* edited by Lawrence S. Mayo.

Edward Johnson, *Johnson's Wonder-Working Providence, 1628-1651,* edited by John F. Jameson.

Perry Miller and Thomas H. Johnson, eds., *The Puritans.*

Thomas Morton, *The New English Canaan of Thomas Morton,* edited by Charles F. Adams.

John White [supposed author], *John White's Planters Plea, 1630.*

John Winthrop, *Winthrop's Journal, "History of New England," 1630-1649,* edited by James K. Hosmer.

Alexander Young, *Chronicles of the First Planters of the Colony of Massachusetts Bay, from 1623 to 1636.*

MODERN ACCOUNTS

Charles F. Adams, *Three Episodes of Massachusetts History,* pp. 1-208.

James T. Adams, *The Founding of New England,* Chapters 6-7.

Roy H. Akagi, *The Town Proprietors of the New England Colonies.*

Charles M. Andrews, *The Colonial Period of American History,* I, Chapters 15-22.

Charles M. Andrews, *Our Earliest Colonial Settlements,* Chapter 3.

James P. Baxter, ed., *Sir Ferdinando Gorges and his Province of Maine,* Volume I.

Henry S. Burrage, *The Beginnings of Colonial Maine, 1602-1658.*

The Cambridge History of the British Empire, I, Chapter 5.

Edward Channing, *A History of the United States,* I, Chapters 10, 12.

John Fiske, *The Beginnings of New England.*

Perry Miller, *The New England Mind.*

Perry Miller, *Orthodoxy in Massachusetts, 1630-1650.*

Samuel E. Morison, *Builders of the Bay Colony.*

Samuel E. Morison, *The Founding of Harvard College.*

Herbert L. Osgood, *The American Colonies in the Seventeenth Century,* I, Part II, Chapters 1-3.

Vernon L. Parrington, *The Colonial Mind, 1620-1800,* Book I, Part I.

Frances Rose-Troup, *John White, the Patriarch of Dorchester (Dorset) and the Founder of Massachusetts, 1575-1648.*

Herbert W. Schneider, *The Puritan Mind.*

William B. Weeden, *Economic and Social History of New England, 1620-1789.*

Justin Winsor, ed., *The Memorial History of Boston,* Volume I.

12

Roger Williams and the Founding of Rhode Island

ROGER WILLIAMS

THE COLONY of Rhode Island was a dissident offshoot of Massachusetts. As it ultimately developed, it was a congeries of settlements formed by men and women who dissented from the Massachusetts way of life and fled to escape its intolerance as the founders of the bay colony had sought to escape the intolerance of England. As the Reverend William Blackstone put it when he departed from Boston for the shores of Narragansett Bay, "I came from England because I did not like the Lord Bishops, but I cannot join with you because I would not be under the Lord Brethren." The great impetus to the movement of dissenters to the region of Narragansett Bay, however, came from Roger Williams, one of the most inspiring figures ever to come to America from England.

Roger Williams was probably the most original thinker and certainly one of the most consistently noble characters to appear on the shores of America before the Revolution. He was born in London in 1603. There he came into contact with all the sordid as well as the stimulating features of city life. He taught himself shorthand and became secretary to the great Sir Edward Coke, the classic commentator on English law. In that capacity he found his way into the Court of the Star Chamber where he saw the inside of royal injustice, the unequal operations of the law, and the passions and unrighteousness of men. Through his contacts there he met practically all the great figures in that period of English history, so that judging him either by the products of his own mind or by his acquaintanceship with Oliver Cromwell, John Milton, the Earl of Warwick, Sir Henry Vane, and many others, he may be considered as one of the great men of seventeenth-century England.

He started life as an Anglican, but at the age of eleven was converted to the Puritan point of view. He was devoutly religious and studied theology in Pembroke Hall at Cambridge, after which he became private chaplain in a distinguished Protestant family, that of Sir William Masham. In 1629 King Charles dismissed Parliament and began his period of autocratic rule. William Laud, then Bishop of London, preaching High Anglicanism and the divine right of kings in support of Charles, heard of Roger Williams, who was just then attacking the prayer-book and Laud's High Anglicanism, and began to "pursue him [Williams] out of the land."

Now Roger Williams was well acquainted with both John Cotton and Thomas Hooker, who later became leading ministers in Massachusetts Bay. Known also to other members of the Massachusetts Bay Company, he was invited to go to the church at Salem, and finally accepted the invitation. He arrived in Boston on February 5, 1631. He was welcomed, of course, as a very distinguished personage and the Boston church immediately invited him to become the teacher there. But he refused this call. For by this time Williams had become a Separatist, and he found that the Boston church was still "unseparated"; that is, it still claimed membership in the Anglican church. Moreover, it appeared to him that the Boston church was too active in civil affairs. Thus in refusing the Boston call, he expressed three principles which were later to appear in his controversies with the authorities of the Bay: his rigid separatism, the principle of absolute soul liberty, and the complete separation of church and state.

Naturally this gratuitous criticism of the Boston church created a dilemma among the leaders. His doctrine, if admitted, would threaten the society of the Bible commonwealth. Yet he was a very distinguished man, and to oppose him would make enemies for the commonwealth among the Puritan leaders of England. They therefore contented themselves with a warning to the Salem church not to take him. They did not feel strong enough to coerce the Salem congregation. That church, as a matter of fact, had accepted the Plymouth or Separatist way and paid no attention to the Boston warning. Williams went to Salem and took up his work there. But the opposition to him grew, and the breach between him and the Puritan leaders gradually widened, and he decided to move again, this time to Plymouth. While he was in Salem, he had begun a fur trade with the Indians which was proving profitable, and in Plymouth he continued this trade and even went into the villages of the Narragansetts, where he studied them and their habits and achieved a considerable command of the Algonquin language.

His contacts with the Indians and his ability to see the Indians' point of view not only made him a friend of the savages, but brought him to the conviction that the king of England had no right to give away the Indian lands. So he wrote a pamphlet attacking the Massachusetts Bay title, a pamphlet which the cautious Pilgrims prevented him from publishing on the ground that it would only stir up a disagreeable situation between Williams and the leaders of Massachusetts Bay. He did, however, send a copy of his paper to John Winthrop, who in turn indiscreetly showed it to the magistrates of the Bay. This was a tactical blunder, and increased the feeling of distrust already existing in the minds of the Massachusetts magistrates against Williams.

Shortly after this incident the Salem church recalled Williams, and it was not long before the conflict between him and Massachusetts broke out in all its bitterness. It began in 1634 in a dispute over the law requiring all residents of the Bay colony to take an oath of allegiance, whether they were freemen or not. For Williams opposed this law, on the ground that an oath is a religious act and the state has no right to require any religious act of any of its citizens. The residents indeed were not even freemen and Williams eloquently resisted the implication in the law that these people must support a government in which they had no voice. The result of his opposition was to make him the champion of the unrepresented classes in the colony and opposition to the oath became so strong that in large measure it failed of effect. This made Williams popular, but it impressed upon the Puritan leaders the tragic necessity of silencing him if the purity of the ideals of the commonwealth was to be preserved. He was in effect a rebel threatening to overthrow the state.

Then in 1635 came the laws requiring church attendance and the payment of a tax for church support. Williams opposed both these measures on the ground that they were, in effect, interference by the civil authorities in private religious matters. This was more than the magistrates and the elders could stand, and they warned the Salem church against him; but as yet they did not dare attempt to force the Salem church to get rid of him. They received the supreme rebuff on April 12, 1635, when the Salem church elected him its pastor. Thereupon the general court sent for Williams to attempt to correct his errors and Williams went to the general court to hear what the magistrates had to say. But he would not be corrected. Unfortunately for the cause of tolerance in Massachusetts, Salem at this moment made an appeal to the general court for confirmation of its title to certain lands on Cape Ann, and the general court, under the dominance of the pastors, seized upon this economic leverage to pry Williams loose from his anchorage in that town. The general court refused Salem's request; and this attempt at coercion caused Williams to call upon the other churches to rebuke the general court. This was outright rebellion and Williams was called to trial. He called upon his church to support him, but the Salem congregation did not feel willing to do so, whereupon Williams resigned. He was tried in the church of Thomas Hooker at Newtown, where were gathered the fifty most prominent members of the oligarchy to judge him. He was accused on three points: he had attacked the law of the commonwealth in his strictures upon the laws requiring the oath of allegiance and church attendance; he had attacked the charter of the commonwealth and the validity of titles to property in his manuscript on titles to Indian lands; and he had incited the churches of the commonwealth to rebellion. It was a foregone conclusion that the court would condemn him, for it was realized that if he were allowed to proceed with his attacks upon the theocracy, the Bible commonwealth would come to a quick and ignominious end.

He was sentenced to banishment, but as the autumn had now come and as Williams was in poor health, he was allowed to reside in the commonwealth until the spring, on the condition that he keep quiet. He was not the sort of man who could keep quiet, however, and he continued to hold meetings of his friends, where he preached to them and enlarged upon his criticism of the administration of the colony. The magistrates determined to arrest him; but he, having been warned by John Winthrop, escaped secretly and made his way overland to his old friends the Narragansett Indians, on Narragansett Bay, just outside the jurisdiction of Massachusetts. There he was joined by sympathizers and others who were discontented under the rule of the "Lord Brethren," and there he began his colony.

PROVIDENCE PLANTATION

Roger Williams had clashed with the church and the province of Massachusetts Bay on three major issues. It seemed to him that the Bay church was not sufficiently separated from the Church of England. He himself was an extreme Separatist and he could not be comfortable in a scheme of things in which the pastors acting together had such great power over the individual churches. It seemed to him that this was in effect Presbyterianism, a sort of church organization that he could not abide. In the second place, it seemed to him that the quasi-union of church and state in Massachusetts was entirely pernicious. He believed in the complete separation of church and state because he was deeply convinced that religion is the private affair of the individual and must not be interfered with by the civil authorities. Finally, it had seemed to him that the government of Massachusetts Bay was a sort of theocratic oligarchy, whereas Williams was himself a believer in the sovereignty of the people exercised under the dictates of right reason or the operation of natural law in the human mind. It was upon these three points, complete religious toleration, the separation of church and state, and a relatively democratic principle of civil government, that his colony of Providence Plantation was founded.

During his trading and traveling among the Indians, Williams had bought a strip of land around the head of Narragansett Bay. It was to this land that he went in the dead of winter in January, 1636, and for some weeks he lived with the Indians. Apparently he had at first no intention of founding a colony, but there seemed to have come to him a number of outcasts from Massachusetts Bay. Joining themselves to him they lived for a time on the bank of the Seekonk River, but finding that that region was claimed by Plymouth, Williams and his friends moved around to the Great Salt River, where Williams built his house and laid out his town. The town they called Providence Plantation; and as others came, Williams assigned them land. The heads of families he called together fortnightly to discuss the town's affairs. In effect the new town of Providence Plantation had become another New England town regulating its affairs in the typical New England town meeting, except that here there was no religious qualification for voting.

Beyond this, however, they had no government; Williams believed that the less government they had the better it would be for everyone. Yet they had no patent or charter for the land on which they built their town, and as the town grew they realized the necessity for some sort of a government. They therefore formulated and signed a compact in which they agreed that they would "from time to time subject ourselves in active and passive obedience to all such orders and agreements as shall be made . . . by the major consent of the present inhabitants . . . and others whom they shall hereafter admit unto them, [but] only in civil things." Here was another social compact; but it was different from the Mayflower compact in that the older document was the agreement of a church congregation which constituted itself a community, whereas this was merely a miscellaneous group of settlers. The compact made by Williams and his friends was a social compact, to be sure, for the establishment of a civil government, but the power of this civil government was clearly limited to civil things. In it are to be found the outstanding ideas then appearing among the political philosophers of the time: the idea of the conscious institution of government, the political equality of men—or at least of householders in the community, a recognition of the principle of natural rights, the principle of majority rule, the separation of church and state, and, finally, freedom of conscience. Clearly, if these ideals were carried into practice in the government of Providence Plantation, they would constitute the most enlightened political institution in the world at that time. In all these things Williams went far beyond any government then in existence, and his significance lies in the establishment of a free, secular, relatively democratic republic in the midst of an area of dictatorships and oligarchies of one sort or another.

Williams owned the land upon which Providence Plantation was built and he was recognized as the real head of the community. His position was in a sense feudal, and by 1637 he was one of the most powerful men in New England. He carried on his trade with the Indians and began a commerce with the Dutch at New Amsterdam. He sent his goods to old England and established for himself a comfortable fortune. He had welcomed to his plantation all sects and creeds; but not only that, he insisted that every individual allow every other individual to worship God as he would. The only thing, apparently, that he would not tolerate was intolerance. But Williams did not like the business of government, and the Providence compact was not adequate to meet the detailed problems of political administration. Therefore, on October 8, 1638, he deeded his land to a group of thirteen associates, of which he was a member, and from that time on the land was administered by this group. These men thus assumed a position comparable to that of the selectmen of the typical New England town. In 1640 the town adopted a sort of constitution called the "twelve articles," in which it was provided that the town should be governed by five "Disposers" acting under the compact of 1636, an assembly or town meeting of all the voters, that is to say, heads of families who owned land. Practically, this meant that only bachelors were excluded from the franchise in Providence Plantation.

THE RHODE ISLAND AND NARRAGANSETT BAY SETTLEMENTS

In 1638 another group of exiles, among them Mrs. Anne Hutchinson, settled at Aquidneck on Rhode Island, a settlement which later came to be known as Portsmouth. A year later, 1639, William Coddington, one of the founders of Portsmouth, founded the town of Newport at the southern end of Rhode Island. In 1643 Samuel Gorton, another rebel against the theocracy of the Bay, settled the town of Warwick on the west side of Narragansett Bay.

Mrs. Hutchinson was a religious enthusiast who had come to Massachusetts as a follower of the Reverend John Cotton. So interested was she in Cotton and his sermons that she formed the habit of holding meetings at her house on Tuesdays for the women who had been unable to attend church on Sunday. At these meetings she explained the sermons to her friends, and had, it seems, Cotton's approval. It was not long, however, before she was reading into the sermons ideas of her own, in which she departed somewhat from Cotton's teachings. For Mrs. Hutchinson emphasized the "covenant of grace" and the individual experience of the worshiper, which gradually led away from the cold rational Puritanism and the doctrine of predestination toward a warmer, more emotional religion which suggested that the divine grace might be won by the piety and the devotion of the believer. She even went so far as to preach a direct revelation. This, of course, brought her into open conflict with the elders, whom she did not hesitate to criticize for what she called their "covenant of works." She was winning followers and dividing the people of the commonwealth against their leaders. Thus she, too, quickly came to be regarded as a threat to the life of the godly experiment, and was tried and banished. It was then, just a few months after Williams had settled at Providence Plantation, that Mrs. Hutchinson led a band of her followers to Portsmouth, on the island known as Rhode Island. William Coddington, who took Mrs. Hutchinson's side in her "antinomian controversy" with the elders, had left Massachusetts in 1638 and preceded Mrs. Hutchinson to Aquidneck (Rhode Island), in Narragansett Bay, where he and his associates founded the town of Portsmouth. But when Mrs. Hutchinson arrived, Coddington quarreled with her and moved on down the island to found the town of Newport, in 1639.

Along with Mrs. Hutchinson had come another stormy petrel of religion, Samuel Gorton. Gorton had ideas of his own at variance

with the accepted doctrine in Massachusetts, but he had gone to
Boston from England in 1637 in the mistaken notion that Massachusetts practiced religious toleration. He was soon at odds with
the authorities, and was banished from Massachusetts. He went
first to Plymouth, but finding that colony hardly less intolerant
than Massachusetts, he went over to Aquidneck. But there he got
into trouble with Coddington, was whipped, and fled to the protection of Roger Williams at Providence Plantation. Still unable
to get along, he moved down the western shore of Narragansett
Bay in 1643 and settled at Warwick, where he was joined by others
of like mind. His troubles were not over, by any means, but this
settlement slowly grew, and formed one of the four communities
ringing the waters of Narragansett Bay.

THE RHODE ISLAND CHARTER OF 1644

With four such communities of vigorous individualists and dissenters settled in close proximity to each other, it was hardly to
be expected that relations between them would be cordial. Nor
were they. It was only their weakness, and the dangers pressing
upon them from without that led them slowly, but with stubborn
resistance, to unite. For, bound together only by their common
enmity to authoritarianism, they were brought to a sense of their
danger by the formation, in 1643, of the New England Confederation, one of the purposes of which was thought to be to annex the
lands round about Narragansett Bay to the colonies of Plymouth,
Massachusetts Bay, and Connecticut. In the face of this threat, and
with the desire of getting a legal title to the lands occupied by the
four dissident settlements, Roger Williams went to London to
try to get a charter from Parliament. He stayed in London about
a year and returned with a charter dated March 24, 1644, which
he had won from Parliament in the face of the opposition of Massachusetts Bay.

This charter of 1644 became the legal basis for the organization
of the new colony of Rhode Island. It granted to the "Incorporation of Providence Plantations" the power to settle and dispose
of land around Narragansett Bay. Further, it granted them the
right to rule themselves in such a form and by such constitutions
as they by voluntary consent of the majority might adopt, and to
make laws not contrary to the laws of England. Their title to the
land, they felt, had derived from the Indians, but they now had
recognition of their title from the Crown of England, and with it

the right to govern themselves and to set up such institutions for self-government as they might see fit to establish.

Under this charter, in 1647, the four towns united in one government. They feared a strongly centralized government after their observation of the experiences of Massachusetts Bay, but in the face of the danger from their neighbors and from the Indians, and because some, indeed, of their citizens proposed to unite these settlements with Plymouth or Massachusetts Bay, representatives of the four towns met in a representative convention at Portsmouth on May 18, 1647. This convention adopted a sort of constitution under which the colony of Rhode Island was to be governed by an assembly composed of representatives of the towns. Because of their fear of a strongly centralized government, however, they were careful to provide that all laws passed by the assembly must be ratified by the towns in a sort of referendum. On the other hand, it was provided that the assembly could not initiate legislation, but that it could only be initiated by one of the towns themselves, who must submit it to discussion by all the other towns before it was brought into the assembly for passage. Thus Rhode Island, while hardly more than a loose federation of four separate towns, presented a relatively democratic political organization, with complete freedom of conscience, the separation of church and state, and a government composed of the president, four assistants elected by the assembly annually, and an assembly composed of four representatives from each of the towns in the colony. In the constitution were embodied the ideas of Roger Williams that civil government is concerned only with civil things, that all civil authority rests upon the consent of the people; that all men are equal in their liberty and their political privileges, and that they are to be governed, in the last analysis, in accord with the principle of natural rights.

The adoption of this constitution is not to be taken as the end of uncertainties for the colony of Rhode Island. William Coddington opposed the union of the four towns and sought to destroy it. He went to England and succeeded, in 1651, in securing a charter to the island of Aquidneck which effectively withdrew the island from the group. But Williams was able the next year to secure a revocation of Coddington's grant. The period from 1651 to 1658 was marked by continued internal political conflict and squabble over the ownership of lands, but after the restoration of the Stuarts in 1660 and the successful acquisition of a new charter from King Charles II in 1663 Rhode Island settled down to a period of comparative rest and order and was perhaps the most liberal—for a time at least—of all the English colonies in America.

RECOMMENDED BOOKS FOR FURTHER READING

CONTEMPORARY NARRATIVES

John R. Bartlett, ed., *Records of the Colony [and of the state] of Rhode Island, and Providence Plantations*, Volume I.

John Cotton, *Master John Cotton's Answer to Master Roger Williams*, edited by Jeremiah L. Diman.

Samuel Gorton, *Simplicities Defence against Seven-headed Policy* (Peter Force *Tracts*, IV, no. 6).

Albert B. Hart, ed., *American History Told by Contemporaries*, I, 397-407.

Roger Williams, *The Bloody Tenet of Persecution*, edited by Samuel L. Caldwell.

Roger Williams, *The Bloody Tenet of Persecution yet More Bloody*, edited by Samuel L. Caldwell.

MODERN ACCOUNTS

James T. Adams, *The Founding of New England*, Chapter 8.

Charles M. Andrews, *The Colonial Period of American History*, II, Chapters 1-2.

Charles M. Andrews, *Our Earliest Colonial Settlements*, Chapter 4.

Charles M. Andrews, *The Fathers of New England*.

Samuel G. Arnold, *History of the State of Rhode Island and Providence Plantations*.

Samuel H. Brockunier, *The Irrepressible Democrat, Roger Williams*.

Edward Channing, *A History of the United States*, I, Chapters 13-14.

Edward Channing, *The Narragansett Planters*.

James E. Ernst, *The Political Thought of Roger Williams*.

James E. Ernst, *Roger Williams, New England Firebrand*.

Herbert L. Osgood, *The American Colonies in the Seventeenth Century*, I, Part II, Chapters 4, 8.

Vernon L. Parrington, *The Colonial Mind, 1620-1800*, pp. 62-75.

Irving B. Richman, *Rhode Island, its Making and its Meaning*.

Oscar S. Straus, *Roger Williams, The Pioneer of Religious Liberty*.

Arthur B. Strickland, *Roger Williams, Prophet and Pioneer of Soul-liberty*.

William B. Weeden, *Early Rhode Island*.

13

The Expansion of New England

RHODE ISLAND was founded by dissenters from the Puritan ways of Massachusetts who had fled that colony's intolerance. Connecticut was similarly founded by emigrants from Massachusetts; but these emigrants were mostly Puritans, moved chiefly by the economic attractiveness of the land in the Connecticut valley.

The penetration of the Connecticut valley by the older colonies of New England had begun with a trip made by Edward Winslow of Plymouth into that region in search of trade in 1632. Other trading expeditions to this territory followed, made by New Englanders, the most notable of whom was John Oldham. The Dutch from New Amsterdam had already been trading in this area, and, to forestall the English, they built in the year 1633 a small trading post at the site of the present city of Hartford. The Pilgrims, not to be outdone, built another post a few miles farther up the river, at Windsor. Meanwhile, reports of the fertility and general attractiveness of the lands along the Connecticut had reached the ears of the settlers along the shores of Massachusetts Bay. These reports aroused the interest of many of the less fortunate settlers, and a group of people moved from Dorchester to the Connecticut valley in the summer of 1635. These pioneers of the "westward movement" settled on the lands adjoining the Plymouth post at Windsor, much to the embarrassment of the Plymouth colonists who had seized that land from the Dutch. Soon others came, and the trickle of newcomers quickly grew to a steady stream.

In England, meanwhile, the Earl of Warwick, friend of the Puritans, backer of the Puritan colony of New Providence in the Caribbean, and member of the Council for New England, had deeded to a group of Puritan noblemen the land about the mouth of the Connecticut River which he had received from the Council. These men, most prominent of whom were Lord Saye and Sele, Lord Brooke, and Sir Richard Saltonstall of the Massachusetts Bay Company, sent John Winthrop, Jr., to the mouth of the Connecticut with instructions to build there a post and a settlement, both to protect the English claim from the Dutch and to maintain their rightful authority over the settlements that were springing up along the Connecticut River. Winthrop stopped at Boston and negotiated an agreement with Thomas Hooker of Newtown (Cambridge), who was preparing to move to the Connecticut, and then went on to found the town of Saybrook, at the mouth of the river. This was in 1635.

Thomas Hooker was pastor of the church at Newtown. This town had been laid out in close proximity to Watertown, also on the Charles, and the people of these two villages, together with those of Roxbury and Dorchester, lying close to Boston on the south, already felt themselves crowded by the great influx of new settlers and the consequent expansive growth of all of them. Their lands were poor and unprofitable, moreover, and their appetite for better lands farther west was whetted by the reports now coming from the Connecticut region. Hooker and his congregation, therefore, petitioned the general court for permission to remove with some of the residents of the other towns to the Connecticut, a petition which, after some hesitation, was granted. Thus in the summer and fall of 1635 two groups of emigrants, one from Dorchester and one from Newtown, made their way overland to the Connecticut. Hooker himself did not go until the spring of 1636.

Hooker was not moved by economic considerations alone in thus transferring himself and his people out of the Massachusetts jurisdiction. He had arrived in the colony in 1633, and had become one of the leaders in the commonwealth, but he was probably uncomfortably conscious of being overshadowed by John Cotton. He soon found much to criticize in the godly commonwealth, too, for Hooker had ideas of his own as to how a colony ought to be governed. To begin with, Hooker, like Roger Williams, criticized the close connection between church and state in Massachusetts. Too much, he thought, was left to the discretion of the magistrates; and the religious qualifications for full citizenship placed the control of the government in the hands of too small a minority of the people. Rather than remain under such a government Hooker preferred to move into a new land and found there a government with a broader popular base and a more stable foundation of law.

Thus the government erected in Connecticut stood on a somewhat broader franchise than that in Massachusetts, although in its underlying philosophy it was hardly more popular than that of the older commonwealth. In the migration of the people to the new colony, several towns were founded—Hartford and Windsor, already mentioned, Wethersfield, and Springfield, the latter of which later separated from the other river towns and joined itself to Massachusetts. These settlements, under the agreement made between John Winthrop, Jr., the general court of Massachusetts, and Hooker, were at first administered by commissioners appointed by Massachusetts. Shortly after the arrival of Hooker, however, steps were taken which eventually led to the erection of an autonomous government of their own.

The first step was taken in May, 1637, when a "general court," made up of representatives of the towns, met to devise ways and means of meeting the danger of war with the Pequot Indians living between the Connecticut and Narragansett Bay. In 1639 the general court drew up the famous "Fundamental Orders of Connecticut," which provided a legal base upon which to build a government.

The preamble of the Fundamental Orders is a social compact, in which there was nothing particularly new. The settlements in the Connecticut valley had no charter, and they formulated their compact in response to the necessity for some sort of government which they could all obey. The body of the Fundamental Orders is devoted to the elaboration of a frame of government. It provided for a general assembly to be composed of four representatives from each town, which was to meet twice yearly whether called by the governor or not. It provided also that electors or freemen in any town should be merely those who were accepted by a majority of the householders of the town. There was no prescribed religious basis of citizenship. Theoretically, at least, citizenship was based upon acceptability to the other citizens of a town rather than upon religious considerations. In effect, however, since the original settlers were of a strongly Puritan turn of mind, only those newcomers were "acceptable" who were themselves of the religious mold. The General Assembly was to have power of legislation upon all matters pertinent to the welfare of the settlements, and all the towns were to be bound by its laws. The Fundamental Orders provided also for a group of magistrates to be elected by the deputies. This group of magistrates constituted both an upper house of the assembly and an executive body for the administration of the law. Their duties were not clearly defined, but at this moment their status was at least clearer than that of the magistrates in Massachusetts. The governor was to be elected by the general court for one year, and, to avoid the possibility of arbitrary abuse of his power, it was provided that he should hold office continuously for no more than one year at a time.

Under this government Connecticut lived until the English Restoration of 1660. On the surface it appears considerably more liberal than that of Massachusetts; but it must be remembered that these men were Puritans, hardly less exclusive and intolerant than the leaders of Massachusetts Bay. In its operation, therefore, the government of Connecticut was in most essentials like that of the parent colony. Be that as it may, under this government the Connecticut towns steadily expanded their jurisdiction up and down the river until it included the town of Saybrook, at the mouth of the river, and two new towns on Long Island. Eventually, in 1662, the colony was given a charter by King Charles II which included in it not only all the towns in the valley but the Puritan colony of New Haven as well.

NEW HAVEN

While the Connecticut River towns were being established, still another Puritan colony was being built a little farther west on Long Island Sound. This settlement, called New Haven, together with the towns that soon sprang up around it, brought the English to the very borders of New Netherland. The founders of New Haven were the Reverend John Davenport, former pastor of the Nonconformist Church of St. Stephen, in London, and Theophilus Eaton, one of his parishioners there. These men, fleeing the persecution of Archbishop Laud, decided to emigrate to New England, and went to Boston in the spring of 1637. But they arrived in the midst of the antinomian controversy, and Davenport and Eaton were unwilling to submit themselves to the Massachusetts government. They therefore looked around for a new territory that they might call their own, and, having found a site on the shore of Long Island Sound, sailed around Cape Cod in the spring of 1638 and began their settlement at the town of New Haven. Thus, though without legal authority to do so, they established themselves upon the land. In June, 1638, the "freemen" of the town met in a barn to establish a government. With David Brown presiding, this meeting of the freemen decided that in the first place their law was to be no other law than the word of God. The freemen might be only those who were members of the church in good standing. These freemen were to choose seven magistrates and the governor. In October, 1638, the second court elected Theophilus Eaton gov-

ernor. Thus the holy society of New Haven became another theocracy, with a general court of freemen meeting every year.

It was not long before other towns sprang up around New Haven and in 1643 these towns united with New Haven for the
purposes of protection and better government. Because of the dis-

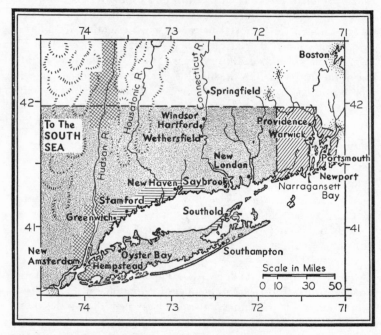

MAP 9. The Boundaries of Connecticut and Rhode Island Under the
Charters of 1662 and 1663

NOTE: Because of the inaccuracy of geographic knowledge in the seventeenth century and
the vagueness of the language in the charters themselves, the boundaries shown on this map
must be considered only approximately accurate.

tances between towns and the difficulties of travel the colony now
found itself faced, as were the older colonies, with the necessity for formulating some sort of a representative government. As
a result it adopted in 1643 a sort of constitution providing for a
governor, magistrates, and a general court composed of two representatives from each town, but the basis of citizenship was still
church membership and the basic law was still the Bible. Trial by
jury, the old "citadel of English Liberty" was dispensed with because it was not found in the Mosaic law. As settlement spread
over to Long Island and further westward along the Sound, these

regions were included in the New Haven Colony, Southold on Long Island being admitted in 1649, and Greenwich in 1656.

As the men who settled New Haven were merchants, as well as Puritans, they envisaged the expansion of their commerce in all directions. As they were hemmed in by the Connecticut towns on one side and the Dutch on the other, they sought to extend their "empire" southward, into the waters of Delaware Bay. Some of the New Haven merchants, therefore, organized a "Delaware Company," and sent a settlement to Varkenskill, on the east side of Delaware Bay, which, though it did not flourish, managed to survive despite the opposition of the Dutch and Swedish settlements that had preceded it.

Thus, the colony of New Haven included, besides the town of New Haven, a number of towns along the Sound, several settlements on Long Island, and the little colony on the Delaware. This federation of towns, governed by strict Puritan rule and depending for a livelihood upon agriculture and Indian trade, continued as an independent, unauthorized colony until 1662 when it was absorbed into the colony of Connecticut by the charter of 1662.

NEW HAMPSHIRE AND MAINE

Another offshoot of Massachusetts was the colony of New Hampshire. The land between the Merrimac and the Kennebec had been granted to Mason and Gorges by the Council for New England, but they had done little or nothing to populate their colony. They had divided the land between them, Mason taking the area between the Merrimac and the Piscataqua, and Gorges taking the land between the Piscataqua and the Kennebec. Straggling settlements had appeared at Dover and at Portsmouth, but these towns languished under the neglect of their proprietors and, as their population was fed largely by emigrants from Massachusetts, they looked more and more to Massachusetts for their government.

In 1641 they sent delegates to the general court of Massachusetts for help in their government, and the theocracy sent a deputation there to restore order. Mason had sold his patent to Lord Saye and Sele and Lord Brooke, and these men now turned the land over to the colony of Massachusetts. About 1644 it was taken over by the Bay colony and remained practically a part of Massachusetts until 1679, when it was separated from the older colony and set up as a royal province by King Charles II.

In the region assigned to Gorges, a similar development took place. Technically, the land between the Piscataqua and the Kennebec belonged to Gorges and his heirs, but the land was settled in large measure by emigrants from Massachusetts, and that colony assumed practical control of the northern region. Massachusetts absorbed the district of Maine in 1658 and that region continued to be a part of Massachusetts Bay until 1820, except in the period between 1664 and 1691 when it was a part of the personal colony of the Duke of York.

THE NEW ENGLAND CONFEDERATION

About the time of the penetration of the Connecticut valley, there took place a series of Indian murders of white men who had settled on Indian lands in that neighborhood. One thing led to another until, about 1636, the whole frontier was in an uproar. Either the Indians must be subdued or the settlements of the white men would be restricted to the shoreline and perhaps permanently ejected from New England. The safety of the new social and political experiments then going on in that part of the world seemed to be at stake, and, as was their practice, the leaders of New England interpreted the course of events to mean that God desired them to take the Indian lands. This of course was no unique phenomenon in history. It is much the same thing as happens whenever a conquering, expanding race comes in contact with a weaker established race. Either the weaker race is destroyed or absorbed, or the expansion has to cease, and in the case of New England it was almost a foregone conclusion that it must be the Indians who must be destroyed to make way for the stronger—not to say superior—civilization.

In 1637 Captain John Mason (not the John Mason of the New England grants) was sent against the Indian towns of eastern Connecticut to bring an end to the series of Indian raids and murders against the whites. The campaign was successful and Mason's greatest achievement took place in the summer, when he succeeded in surrounding and burning an Indian town whose normal population was about three hundred but which, by special dispensation of God, as the Puritans believed, had been raised by the war to over five hundred Indians. Needless to say, most of the Indians were killed and the Pequot war came to a speedy end, to the great jubilation of the people of New England and the almost immediate occupation of the Pequot lands. The great Indian menace had for a time at least been scotched. Once again forty years later the

Indians under King Philip raised the tomahawk against the expanding whites, only to be finally and forever driven from their lands by the conquering race.

Out of the Pequot war came a realization of the necessity for a common front against an Indian danger and out of the possibility of war with the French settlements on the north and with the Dutch on the southwest came a consciousness of the desirability of union in the face of the threat of international war. The lands occupied by the religious radicals in the settlements around Narragansett Bay were claimed by Plymouth, Massachusetts, and Connecticut, and it seemed desirable to take concerted action to annex those lands and wipe out the "sink of iniquity." It was in response to these three motives—the possibility of Indian war, the fear of war with their European neighbors, and the desire to wipe out Rhode Island—that the four colonies of Massachusetts, New Haven, Plymouth, and Connecticut organized, in the year 1643, the so-called New England Confederation. Each of the four colonies sent two delegates to Boston and there was formulated what they called "a firme and perpetual league of friendship and amytie for offense and defense, mutual advice and succor upon all just occasions. . . ." Rhode Island and Maine both asked to be admitted to the Confederation but Rhode Island was far outside the bounds of respectability and the people of Maine had tolerated exiles from Massachusetts and had even shown dangerous tendencies toward popular government, so both were refused admission.

In any case, the Confederation organized in 1643 was the first federation of colonies in North America. Its constitution or articles of confederation tacitly recognized the independence of these four colonies, both of each other and of England. It provided that the member provinces should jointly pay the costs of any wars and furnish men for fighting them in proportions that were fixed according to the size of the colony. The management of the Confederation was to be entrusted to a directorate of eight men, two from each colony, who must be church members, and it was agreed that a vote of six of the eight would be sufficient to carry a decision. The articles provided, further, for cooperation in the maintenance of justice and the return of escaped prisoners, runaway servants, and other fugitives. They provided for a joint management of Indian affairs, and that the Confederation should make no treaties with foreign powers without ratification by the directorate. Finally, it was agreed that quarrels between members of the confederation were to be settled by arbitration.

The formation of the New England Confederation is a significant development in American colonial history, because it is the first of several attempts at cooperation or confederation for common purposes. The Confederation assumed its own practical independence of England and mutually recognized the principle of self-determination for each member colony except in matters of common interest. On this point the Confederation assumed the right to make war and treaties, two of the most essential attributes of sovereignty. Its history, however, was typical of the history of most of the other similar attempts, because it was not long before certain of the members, notably Massachusetts, began to nullify its provisions by engaging upon activities contrary to the desires of the Confederation as a whole. Nevertheless, it was successful in avoiding entanglements with the French in Nova Scotia by the treaty of Boston in 1644 and in postponing the inevitable conflict with the Dutch by the treaty of Hartford in 1650.

The history of these relations between the English colonies in New England and their French and Dutch neighbors presents an interesting example of the indigenous growth of native American diplomatic policy and practice. The first serious international problem to arise in the history of New England was that which emerged from the civil war between the forces of Charles de la Tour and the Sieur d'Aulnay-Charnisay in Acadia. Port Royal had been seized by an English expedition sent out by Sir William Alexander in January, 1627, and had been returned to the French by the treaty of St. Germain of 1632. The French government had sent out the Sieur de Razilly as governor and on Razilly's death in 1635 French Acadia was divided between Charles de la Tour and the Sieur d'Aulnay-Charnisay. But la Tour and d'Aulnay fell to quarreling between themselves and both appealed to the "Bostonnais" for help. La Tour got there first and made several requests for aid. He finally succeeded in hiring ships belonging to Boston merchants and in engaging soldiers to aid in his war. There immediately took place a vigorous protest on the part of Richard Saltonstall and other leaders of the Bay colony, on the ground that this was tantamount to intervention in a civil war going on within the territory of a friendly nation and might involve Massachusetts in a war with d'Aulnay. Governor Winthrop, placed on the defensive by this protest, assumed the position that the Boston ships had never been hired by la Tour and that as neutral carriers Boston ships were not committed to actual participation in the war. On the other hand, he claimed, the New England ships were entitled to the rights and privileges of neutrals on the high seas. The responsibility for the action of the soldiers was disclaimed, and Governor Winthrop took care to reassure d'Aulnay that permission to la Tour to engage ships and men did not in any way indicate a hostile attitude on the part of Massachusetts Bay. Shortly thereafter d'Aulnay himself, armed with a commission from the king of France constituting him the rightful governor of Acadia, began a series of negotiations which culminated in the treaty of Boston of October 8, 1644. In this treaty it was provided that the English and French in Massachusetts and Acadia should have the right to trade with each other and with any other people whatsoever, a provision aimed particularly at the Indian trade of Boston merchants in territory claimed by Acadia. The treaty further provided that disputes between the government of Massachusetts Bay and d'Aulnay should be settled by peaceful means.

Out of these close contacts with the French, then, had come expressions of principles which were later to be very important to the people living in the United States. The protest of the leaders against Governor Winthrop's actions laid down the principle of non-intervention. Winthrop himself expressed the principle of the freedom of the seas and the rights of neutrals; and the treaty between Massachusetts and d'Aulnay established an arrangement guaranteeing to both the principle of free trade and the peaceful settlement of disputes.

A similar development appeared out of the contact between the English along Long Island Sound and the Dutch in New Netherland. A conflict had arisen between the Dutch and the merchants of New Haven over the seizure of New Haven ships in Delaware Bay, and friction had arisen over the boundaries between New Haven and New Netherland. After numerous quarrels on these two subjects, old Peter Stuyvesant journeyed from New Amsterdam to Hartford in Connecticut where he negotiated with the commissioners of the New England Confederation an agreement to appoint a joint commission to study the quarrels between the Dutch and the English. Four commissioners were appointed and their report recommended that the claims of New Haven against the Dutch be referred to the Dutch and English governments in Europe, and that the boundaries between the English and the Dutch be designated as a line running across Long Island from Oyster Bay southward and by a line on the mainland which was to begin at Greenwich Bay and run northward into the country. Stuyvesant's agreement had thus resulted in the effective arbitration of the boundary dispute; this arbitration resulted, for the time, at least, in a peaceful settlement of the quarrels between the English and the Dutch. His agreement, however, was never ratified by the British government and therefore had no permanent effect.

Both the treaty of Boston, 1644, and the treaty of Hartford of 1650, were ratified by the New England Confederation. Out of the problems arising from their contacts with their neighbors the New England colonists had formed a confederation which had practically all the attributes of a sovereign state, and in the course of the brief history of this Confederation they arrived at solutions to the problems of diplomacy which seemed to have been implicit in their geographic situation. In formulating the principles of their conduct with their neighbors they arrived at doctrines which curiously forecast those adopted by the United States a century and a half later.

RECOMMENDED BOOKS FOR FURTHER READING

CONTEMPORARY NARRATIVES

James P. Baxter, ed., *Sir Ferdinando Gorges and his Province of Maine,* II, III.
Frances G. Davenport, ed., *European Treaties bearing on the History of the United States and its Dependencies,* I, 347-352, II, 1-6.
George M. Dutcher, ed., *The Fundamental Orders of Connecticut.*
Albert B. Hart, ed., *American History Told by Contemporaries,* I, Chapter 18.

MODERN ACCOUNTS

James T. Adams, *The Founding of New England,* Chapters 8-11.
Charles M. Andrews, *The Beginnings of Connecticut, 1632-1662.*
Charles M. Andrews, *The Colonial Period of American History,* II, Chapters 3-5.
Charles M. Andrews, *Our Earliest Colonial Settlements,* Chapter 5.
Charles M. Andrews, *The Rise and Fall of the New Haven Colony.*
Charles M. Andrews, *The River Towns of Connecticut.*
Warren S. Archibald, *Thomas Hooker.*
Howard Bradstreet, *The Story of the War with the Pequots, Re-Told.*
Henry S. Burrage, *The Beginnings of Colonial Maine, 1602-1658.*
Isobel M. Calder, *The New Haven Colony.*
Edward Channing, *A History of the United States,* I, Chapters 14-15.
Dorothy Deming, *The Settlement of the Connecticut Towns.*
John Fiske, *New France and New England.*
Alexander Johnston, *Connecticut,* Chapters 3-8.
Andrew C. McLaughlin, *The Foundations of American Constitutionalism,* Chapters 1-3.
Herbert L. Osgood, *The American Colonies in the Seventeenth Century,* I, Part II, Chapters 7, 9-10.

14

Proprietary Maryland

IN CONTRAST to the composite nature of the proprietary colony of the West Indies, the proprietary province of Maryland was the creation of one man. In the Caribbean isles the initiative had come from rival groups of merchants interested chiefly in the profits to be derived from the colonies, who promoted the issuance of proprietary charters only in order to have high-placed patrons at court to protect them from the vicissitudes of politics. In the case of Maryland, the initiative came from George Calvert, first Lord Baltimore.

It should be remembered that most of the people who left England during the great migration did not do so for religious reasons alone. It is probably true, indeed, that most of them went to the new world mainly for economic reasons. Yet certain it is that religion did play an important part in the thinking both of the emigrants and of the entrepreneurs of the new British colonies. In the case of George Calvert, this mixture of motives was probably as real as in other colonizers. He had been raised in the era of great popular interest in overseas expansion. He was a member both of the Virginia Company and of the Council for New England. In 1622 he had received a grant of a part of Newfoundland and had established there a colony which he had named Avalon, as already noted. About 1624 he was converted to Roman Catholicism, and in 1625, probably because of his religion, retired from public life. He now devoted his attention entirely to colonization, and actually went to Newfoundland in 1627. But he found the climate too cold and bitter and wrote to Charles I that he would like to move his colony somewhere farther south. About 1629 he visited Virginia, and was well received there, but because he was a Roman Catholic he found it impossible for him to stay in that Anglican colony. He was tendered the oath of supremacy and when he could not take it, it was intimated that he should leave. Calvert was greatly impressed, however, by the attractiveness of the country round about Chesapeake Bay, and he petitioned for a grant of land in northern Virginia. There was, of course, great opposition from the Virginians; but that colony was now a royal province and the king could do what he would with his own. As Calvert was a friend of the king, he practically wrote his own charter, which was issued in June, 1632.

George Calvert died while his charter was being prepared, and it was issued in the name of his son Cecilius. Under its terms the second Lord Baltimore was given all the land between the fortieth degree of north latitude on the north and the south bank of the

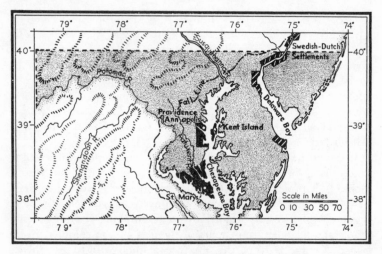

MAP 10. The Boundaries of Maryland Under Lord Baltimore's Charter of 1632

NOTE: Because of the inaccuracy of geographic knowledge in the seventeenth century and the vagueness of the language of the charter itself, the boundaries shown on this map must be considered only approximately accurate.

Potomac River on the south, including that part of the peninsula east of the Chesapeake lying between the fortieth degree and Watkins Point, opposite the mouth of the Potomac. The colony was to be named Maryland. Baltimore was given this land, amounting to some ten million acres, "in free and common soccage," with all the powers of government enjoyed by the Bishop of Durham. As the Bishop of Durham was practically an absolute king within his "palatinate," this clause made Baltimore an absolute lord in Maryland. His answerability to the king of England was that represented by the vague, if picturesque feudal recognition of the king's suzerainty symbolized by the payment of two Indian arrows each year, together with one-fifth of the gold and silver to be found within the colony. The proprietor was empowered to sub-infeudate his lands, causing them to be held of himself instead of the king, and

to set up manors, with their manorial courts, on the lands thus sub-
infeudated. He was given the power to make laws, with the advice
and consent of the freeholders, provided the laws made were not
repugnant to the laws of England, and to set up courts and appoint
judges and officials. He could collect rents and taxes from the land
and make regulations governing the commerce of the colony, including the laying and collecting of duties. Maryland was a feudal
seigniory in the wilderness of North America.

Lord Baltimore's first interest in setting up a colony in America
was probably to provide himself and his family with an income-
paying estate, but he was a generous and tolerant man, affected by
the religious and political struggles of his day, and he hoped that
his colony might prove a haven of refuge, particularly to the Roman
Catholics whose position in England was at this moment one of
great uncertainty, even of actual persecution. It was for this reason
that the first settlements were led and dominated by Catholics; but
Maryland was by no means entirely settled by people of that religion. Many, indeed, if not an actual majority of the first comers
to Maryland, were Protestants.

The first expedition of emigrants sailed in two ships, the *Ark*
and the *Dove,* which left Southampton on November 22, 1633.
They took the West Indian route, stopping on their way at
Barbados, and arrived in the Chesapeake Bay on February 27,
1634. On board the ships were two Jesuits, seventeen Roman
Catholic gentlemen with their wives, and some two hundred
others, the majority of whom were Anglicans. On their arrival
in the Chesapeake they selected St. Mary's, near the mouth of the
Potomac, as the site for their first settlement. They landed, bartered
with the friendly Yoacomaco Indians for land, and even occupied
fields already cultivated by the savages. This happy circumstance,
coupled with the fact that they had wisely chosen high, well-situated
land for their settlement, probably accounts for the absence, in the
history of this colony, of a long period of scarcity and illness comparable to the "starving times" in Virginia and Plymouth. Leonard
Calvert, the young Lord Baltimore's brother, now twenty-eight years
of age, was the governor of the colony, instructed to establish a community which would be free from religious animosity and contention. He was instructed, further, to distribute the land, which he
did according to a feudal system which set up manorial lords who
held their lands directly from the proprietor and from whom the
"freeholders" or small planters held their farms in feudal relationship. In the course of the seventeenth century there were set up

about sixty manors in Maryland, generally containing from one thousand to three thousand acres, with manorial courts, leet and baron. The small planters rented their land and paid the rent in kind. There were, as a matter of fact, certain freeholders outside the manors who held their land directly from the proprietor; all, however, were required to pay a permanent quit-rent to the proprietor. Right from the first Maryland was a colony organized along feudal lines, with a land system that was feudal to a degree found nowhere else in the colonies—except, perhaps, in the patroon system of Dutch New Netherland along the Hudson River. In no other colony were the feudal institutions of landholding and society transplanted so completely to the soil of America. Maryland was a country of actual manors, freeholders, and quit-rents.

ECONOMIC AND SOCIAL DEVELOPMENT OF THE COLONY

Economically, the colony was fairly prosperous from the beginning. The first colonists planted corn, or acquired it from the Indians immediately after their arrival, and in 1634 were able to send the *Dove* to Boston to exchange Indian corn for fish. A few people in the colonies found it profitable to engage in a fur trade with the Indians. But by far the greater number engaged in the cultivation of tobacco, which became the staple crop of Maryland as it had already become the staple crop of Virginia.

Socially, there was a gulf fixed between the landed aristocracy and the common people. Most of the landed aristocracy were Roman Catholics, and the common people were of other sects. But so hierarchical a social scheme could not be maintained in a frontier country where there was a plenitude of land and an expanding commerce, a rapidly increasing population, and definite social and religious opposition to the system. Gradually the legal features of the feudalistic regime in early Maryland sloughed off and practically disappeared; the quit-rents remained a permanent feature of the system, however, as did the social stratification that was a part of it.

It was in connection with its economic life that the colony came into conflict with William Claiborne. Claiborne was a Virginian who had established a fur-trading station on Kent Island, lying in Chesapeake Bay within the limits of the Maryland grant, before Lord Baltimore's charter was issued. He had bought the island from the Indians, and had gotten the support of a group of merchants in London for whom he acted as agent in the fur trade, together with a license from King Charles for carrying on the business in the back country beyond the upper ends of Chesapeake and Delaware bays. On Kent Island itself he had built a fort, several houses, a church and a mill, and had brought over a considerable body of settlers, who had made of the island a prosperous, happy community. When Lord Baltimore claimed the island, therefore, as a part of Maryland, Claiborne resented it as an intrusion upon his prior rights; furthermore, he was an ardent, conscientious Protestant, utterly unwilling to place himself under the government of a Roman Catholic.

Baltimore was willing to recognize Claiborne's property rights in the island, provided only that Claiborne admit it to be a part of Maryland and accept it as a fief from the proprietor. But this Claiborne was unwilling to do. When Claiborne rejected the friendly overtures of Leonard Calvert and went on with his trading contrary to Calvert's orders, the governor resorted to force. He seized one of Claiborne's sloops, whereupon Claiborne attacked ships belonging to the proprietor. Claiborne had already appealed to the courts in England, but as he had never had an actual patent from the king for his colony, Baltimore's title seemed better, and he lost his case. This judgment was borne out by a report of the Commission for Foreign Plantations, on April 4, 1638, to the effect that Kent Island lay in Maryland and that Claiborne might trade there only under license from Lord Baltimore. Thus deprived of his enterprise, Claiborne returned to Virginia. But he was not soon to forget the treatment he had received, and he returned to plague the colony of Maryland later on.

THE EXPERIMENT IN RELIGIOUS TOLERATION

Cecilius Calvert ardently desired to make his colony a community in which there would be no religious conflict. In the first instructions to his brother he particularly charged him to preserve good relations with the Protestants in the colony, and to see that the other Roman Catholics did likewise. It was his great desire to provide a place where the Catholics themselves might worship in peace, but he seems to have realized the uselessness of religious bickering and bitterness, from any point of view. But it was not easy to control the ardor of his co-religionists, just escaping from the repression under which they had suffered in England, and this was especially true of the Jesuit priests who accompanied the colonists. For the priests set out to convert, not only the Indians, but the Protestants as well. This inevitably aroused complaint and bitterness in the minds of the Protestants, and was the beginning of religious faction. It is only the more significant, therefore, that Protestants and Catholics succeeded as well as they did in living together, in that age of religious absolutism.

With the outbreak of the civil war in England, in 1642, the cause of Protestant Puritanism became identified with parliamentarianism, both in England and in the infant colony of Maryland. William Claiborne, now the inveterate enemy of the proprietor, took advantage of Leonard Calvert's absence in England to seize Kent Island again by force, while another Protestant parliamentarian, Richard Ingle, seized St. Mary's. Calvert, on his return to Maryland in 1644, was forced to flee to Virginia, and it was only with the help of Governor Berkeley that he succeeded in recovering control of the province of Maryland. Ingle then went to England to accuse the proprietor of enmity to the new Commonwealth government of the mother country and the Catholics of tyranny in the control of society, economic life, and government in the province.

To make matters worse for the proprietor, there was now taking place a large influx of Puritans into Maryland, many of whom came from Virginia, where they had not been happy under Anglican rule, to enjoy the peace of religious toleration under the Catholics. The numerical superiority of the Protestants in the colony was thus increased, and, with the increase in numbers, an increase in their demand for a larger share in the government. Most of the newcomers went to the town of Providence (later Annapolis), where they established a self-governing community much like a New England town. The influx of Puritans increased the strain between the two sects. The situation was greatly aggravated, on the other side, by the aggressive attitude of the ·Jesuits, who seemed to be determined to acquire great areas of land and to set up an independent spiritual dominion, with the separate canon law and great temporal power under the suzerainty, not of Baltimore, but of the Pope.

It was in these circumstances, therefore—partly to protect the Catholics from persecution by the Protestants, partly from the genuine desire to preserve religious peace in the colony—that Lord Baltimore instructed Governor Stone to have passed a law guaranteeing religious liberty to all Christians. Public opinion in England was definitely against tolerating Catholics there; but there was growing in England—indeed, among Englishmen everywhere—the idea of "liberty of conscience," and Baltimore merely took advantage of this sentiment to put into the form of law a principle he had

expressed in the instructions to his governor at the very first settlement of the colony.

The "Act concerning Religion" enacted in 1649, however, actually
established only a very limited sort of religious toleration. It provided that "noe person or persons whatsoever within this Province
. . . professing to believe in Jesus Christ, shall from henceforth bee
any waies troubled, Molested or discountenanced for or in respect
of his or her religion nor in the free exercise thereof. . . ." Severe
penalties were provided for those who violated this provision, or
who even called another such approbrious names as "heretick,"
"scismatick," "idolator," "puritan," "popish prest," "Jesuite," etc.
But that was as far as toleration was to go. For the Puritan-
controlled assembly which passed the bill saw to it that a clause—
not suggested by Baltimore—was inserted providing the death pen-
alty for those who denied the divinity of Christ.

The Maryland Toleration Act, so-called, was thus not a true
measure of the tolerance of the founder of the colony. Such as it
was, it provided a negative sort of toleration between Catholics and
Protestants, and no more. Yet, negative and partial though it was,
it was nonetheless a significant milestone on the road toward the
tolerance which slowly and painfully became one of the characteristics of American society.

THE EMERGENCE OF POLITICAL INSTITUTIONS

For the first fourteen years of its history the colony of Maryland
was governed by Leonard Calvert. As his brother's agent and vice-
regent, the governor was the feudal head of a feudal political organization. For he was the military commander of the palatinate,
both on land and at sea; he appointed all officials, and governed
their work. He was the head of the judicial system, as the supreme
judge in the colony, with power to appoint officers for the administration of justice. He was also commissioned to regulate commerce
under the proprietor's monopoly, to issue commissions, collect the
monies due the proprietor, and otherwise to govern for the proprietor's benefit. In him were centralized every branch of government; and there was no one in the colony to oppose him.

It was not the intent of Cecilius Calvert to govern his colony permanently without consulting the people, however. Some sort of an
assembly seems to have been held in 1635, and in 1637 the proprietor instructed his brother Leonard to call an assembly of the
freemen early in the next year. This assembly duly met, composed

of nineteen or twenty men, most of whom were office-holders appointed by the governor or the proprietor. These men held proxies for three times their own number, and on one question nineteen members cast sixty-nine votes. Furthermore, this assembly was no true law-making body, since it had no power to initiate legislation, but could only appraise or reject laws presented by the governor. This assembly, as those which followed it from time to time for several years, was hardly more than a rubber stamp for the governor.

As time went on, however, the colonists began to demand more and more power. In 1642 the assembly passed resolutions to the effect that it could be prorogued, like the Parliament in England, only by its own consent. Gradually, representation came to be placed upon a territorial basis, with the delegates elected from the local "hundreds," or townships, and the councilors summoned by writ. For many years this legislature, such as it was, met as one house, but in 1650 it was divided into two houses, and laws, to be effective, henceforth had to be approved by majority votes in both houses. Since a majority of the people were Protestants, and since the Parliament in England seemed to be assuming complete control of the English government, the proprietor was faced with a growing body of political discontent, and a whittling away of his own political power. He had, perforce, to accept these reforms and to grant to the legislature the right to initiate legislation. When news of the execution of Charles I arrived in Maryland, Thomas Greene, the deputy governor, on November 15, 1649, proclaimed Charles II king in Maryland. He did this apparently without the knowledge of the proprietor, and it was only the influence of Lord Baltimore in England that prevented Maryland from being disciplined by the Commonwealth government of England as were Barbados and Virginia in 1651 and 1652. Nevertheless, the expedition sent to Virginia was used by William Claiborne to even up his old grudge against Maryland, for Claiborne prevailed upon its leaders to allow him to go to Maryland, drive out Baltimore's Governor Stone, and to set up a new council and a Protestant, William Fuller, to conduct the business of the colony in the name of the Commonwealth of England. The result was civil war, which resulted in a victory for the Puritan-Parliamentary group, the persecution of Catholics, and the repeal of the famous Toleration Act (the "Act concerning Religion") of 1649.

Thus Maryland had now been rent by civil war, and the populace was split into two factions—one Protestant, favoring direct control by the government of England and more representative government in the colony, the other favoring the proprietor, more conservative government, and greater toleration for the Catholics. The proprietor's charter was restored in 1658, and with it the Act of Religion of 1649; but only after far-reaching concessions to the parliamentary faction. The history of Maryland for the next half-century is dominated by the strife between these two factions.

MARYLAND'S CONTRIBUTION

The foundation and growth of Maryland introduced several new and peculiar streams into the forming of American colonial society. The proprietary form of colonial promotion and administration was not new with Lord Baltimore, since the charter of the Council for New England, Sir William Alexander's charter for Nova Scotia in 1621, the Earl of Carlisle's charter for the West Indies in 1628, and even Baltimore's own charter for the colony of Avalon, had all been of this type. The patent for Maryland, however, was the most extreme grant of this kind, and had the effect of practically separating that part of the embryonic British empire from the Crown and turning it over to a private individual to do with almost as he pleased. This local absolutism had the effect of retarding the growth of indigenous political institutions, an effect that was aggravated by the political institutions of feudalism that was imposed upon the colony by the proprietor. Yet the institutions of self-government grew, despite these handicaps, out of the inadequacies of feudalism on the frontier and the demand, arising both from the need for more effective government and from the parliamentary ideas inherited from England, for a more representative political institution.

In its society Maryland was peculiar in the distinctly feudal forms imposed upon it. On the American frontier, where land was to be had for the taking, it was hardly to be expected that feudalism, either political or social, could last. Yet the introduction of the cultivation of tobacco, with its resultant tendency toward the formation of large plantations operated by slave labor, probably operated in the contrary direction to reinforce and preserve the feudal lines of social organization longer than otherwise might have been the case. It is probably for this reason that Maryland society preserved certain relics of feudalism as long as it did.

But the most notable contribution of Maryland to the rising American culture was in the field of religious toleration. Had Baltimore had his way that contribution might have been greater than it actually was. For in this realm of life the very heterogeneity of the frontier in Maryland operated to limit and hedge about with Puritan intolerance the broader principles of its founder.

RECOMMENDED BOOKS FOR FURTHER READING

CONTEMPORARY NARRATIVES

Albert B. Hart, *American History Told by Contemporaries,* Chapter 11.
Andrew White, "An Account of the Colony of the Lord Baron of Baltimore, 1633," in *Narratives of Early Maryland, 1633-1684,* edited by Clayton C. Hall, pp. 1-10.

MODERN ACCOUNTS

Charles M. Andrews, *The Colonial Period of American History,* II, Chapter 8.
Charles M. Andrews, *Our Earliest Colonial Settlements,* Chapter 6.
Matthew P. Andrews, *The Founding of Maryland.*
Matthew P. Andrews, *History of Maryland: Province and State.*
William H. Browne, *George Calvert and Cecilius Calvert, Barons Baltimore of Baltimore.*
William H. Browne, *Maryland; the History of a Palatinate,* pp. 1-50.
Edward Channing, *A History of the United States,* I, Chapter 9.
John Fiske, *Old Virginia and her Neighbors,* I, Chapters 8-9.
Clayton C. Hall, *The Lords Baltimore and the Maryland Palatinate.*
John H. Latané, *Early Relations between Maryland and Virginia.*
Newton D. Mereness, *Maryland as a Proprietary Province.*
Herbert L. Osgood, *The American Colonies in the Seventeenth Century,* II, Part III, Chapters 1, 3-4.
Bernard C. Steiner, *Beginnings of Maryland, 1631-1639.*

15

New Netherland and New Sweden

DUTCH EXPANSION OVERSEAS

WHILE Englishmen were busy founding English-speaking communities on the shores of North America in the first half of the seventeenth century, the other commercial nations of western Europe had become interested in the same sort of activity. Of greatest significance for the future history of the young English colonies was the appearance, along the St. Lawrence valley in the north and among the islands of the West Indies to the south, of the French colonies which were to be the nuclei of a "New France." For these were the colonies which were to be the strong competitors of the English, and more must be said of them later.

Of more immediate significance for the English settlements than the French, however, were those beginnings of colonies that were being made by the Dutch. For just at the time when the Virginia Company was approaching its end, when Thomas Warner was beginning the English settlement on St. Christopher, and when the Pilgrims were conquering the problem of a food supply at Plymouth, Dutchmen were settling about the mouth of the Hudson River, between Plymouth and Virginia. The colonization of America by both Frenchmen and Dutchmen was a manifestation of the continuing expansion of the commercial life of France and Holland, which paralleled, in many ways, the expansion of England. The growth of Dutch commerce is a part of the story of the development of Holland as a nation and its challenge to the Hispano-Portuguese monopoly of the commerce of the colonial world.

The Spanish Low Countries had begun their war of independence against Spain in 1565. This war had had its origin in resistance to Philip II's arbitrary regulation of commerce and his attempt to inflict upon the Protestant people of the Low Countries a restoration of the Catholic religion. During the course of the war, in 1579, the seven northern provinces (Holland) separated from the southern provinces, and in 1581 declared themselves independent of Spain. The southern provinces (Belgium) compromised their quarrel with Spain and remained under Spanish control. The war of Holland alone with Spain then continued until 1609, when a twelve-year truce was arranged, at the expiration of which period the war was resumed and became a part of the Thirty Years War. Dutch independence was finally recognized by the treaty of Münster, in 1648.

As dependencies of Spain, the Low Countries had enjoyed rich profits from the Spanish and Portuguese colonial trade, for Cadiz and Lisbon were the terminal points for the overseas trade routes, and Dutch vessels went to these ports with cargoes of manufactured goods and other products of the north to take in exchange the spices of the far east and the tobacco or hides or gold and silver from America. With their separation from Spain, however, and with the annexation of Portugal by Spain in 1580, the Dutch merchants found their vessels excluded from Portuguese and Spanish ports. Partly for this reason, and partly because of the high profits to be derived from direct trade, Dutchmen began to sail directly to the Indies, east and west, where they traded in the markets of the colonies and preyed upon Spanish and Portuguese ships. These activities on both sides of the world were very profitable and in 1602 the Dutch East India Company was formed for trade and warfare against Spain and Portugal.

It was this company that engaged Henry Hudson, an Englishman, to go out in 1609 to search for a passage round America toward the far east. He eventually came to a river which he called the Mauritius after Prince Maurice, but which later came to be known as the Hudson River in honor of himself, and sailed up that river to the head of navigation. In the course of his journey he traded up and down the river with the Indians, and the skins that he took back to Holland paid good profits. This was the beginning of the Dutch fur trade on the Hudson.

Following the expedition of Henry Hudson, other ships went to the river of Mauritius almost every year; and in 1614 Adriaen Block went on a voyage in which he not only engaged in trade, but in exploration as well. On this voyage he sailed along the shores of Long Island Sound, probably as far as Block Island, and he probably entered the Connecticut River. As a result of his voyage, which was a profitable one, there was organized a group of merchants in Amsterdam called the New Netherland Company, who petitioned the Dutch Estates General for a patent which, when granted, gave them the right to send out four trading voyages in a period not exceeding three years. They built a fort on the river somewhat above the site of the present city of Albany, but their monopoly ran out in 1618 and was not renewed; whereupon the trade along the river was opened to anyone who cared to engage in it.

It was at this time that the twelve-year truce made in 1609 was approaching its end and the English Pilgrims in Leyden were beginning to think of emigrating from Holland to America. The merchants interested in trade, led by William Usselinx, looking forward to the renewal of the war which was a foregone conclusion, proposed to organize a great trading company which would have the threefold objective of carrying on a profitable privateering warfare against the Spaniards in America, the establishment of colonies in the new world, and trade with the North American Indians. Their greatest interest was in war and commerce rather than in colonies; but it was expected that colonies would be useful bases of operations in the carrying on of their other activities. In 1621 the Estates General issued a charter to the Dutch West India Company. The company was composed of merchants in the various parts of the Netherlands, and each regional group had its own board of directors. These regional boards sent representatives to Amsterdam to form a council of nineteen men, eighteen of whom were representatives of the regional directorates and one of whom was appointed by the Estates General. This council of nineteen became the governing agency of the Dutch West India Company and worked out most of the policies that were carried out in the company's colony of New Netherland. The company was given a monopoly of all the commerce along the shores of America and in the Atlantic generally south of the tropic of Cancer. It was also given the right to maintain armies, make laws, punish offenders, make war and treaties with native princes or foreign powers. It was practically a state within a state.

The Dutch West India Company was chiefly interested in privateering against Spain in the West Indies, and turned its first attention to that profitable business. Thus, in December, 1623, the company sent a powerful expedition against the Portuguese part of Bahia. This expedition was successful; Bahia fell in the spring of 1624, and the company reaped an enormous profit in the form of booty. But the Dutch were driven out of Bahia in 1625, after which the Spaniards turned against the Dutch and their English allies in their newly founded colonies of the West Indies. Meanwhile, in 1624, the Dutch West India Company had turned to the second and third of its objectives, the planting of a colony on the continent of North America and the fur trade with the Indians.

NEW NETHERLAND

The Dutch West India Company's first colonizing expedition, under the command of Cornelius Jacobsen May, was composed chiefly of French-speaking Protestants from the southern provinces of the Low Countries that had compromised their differences with Philip II. The settlers went first to Manhattan Island, on which the heart of New York City now stands. But since the company's intent in founding a colony revolved chiefly about the anticipated profits from the fur trade, they were divided into small groups, one of which went up the Hudson and established the trading post of Fort Orange, while another went over into the Delaware valley and built Fort Nassau. A third small party went to the mouth of the Connecticut, and a few stayed at the mouth of the Mauritius (Hudson) River. This place, because of its location, became the economic and political center of the colony. Of the other settlements, Fort Orange became the most important, by reason of its strategic position relative to the fur trade.

The first settlement of the Dutch at the mouth of the Hudson was on what is now known as Governors Island. But as other ships followed the *New Netherland,* with more colonists and livestock, this island was found to be too small, and a permanent fort was built in 1625 at the lower end of Manhattan Island, with the town, called New Amsterdam, stretching eastward along the shore of the East River. Within the fort was the office of the Dutch West India Company, a market place, the residence of the governor, barracks, and the church. Outside, the land was laid out in "bouweries," or farms, where the settlers built their first permanent houses of bark. By the time Peter Minuit took charge as "director general," in 1626, the colony already had taken on a certain air of bustle and prosperity. It was Minuit who purchased the island of Manhattan from the Indians, buying it for goods valued at about sixty guilders—or some forty dollars in modern American money.

In sending out its colonists, the Dutch West India Company laid down a set of rules which had a profound effect upon the development of the colony. In the first place, the settlers were considered servants of the company, and were required to give the director of the colony absolute obedience. They were expected to be members of the Dutch Reformed (Calvinist) church, and they were expected to bring the savages to Christianity by their example; but it was specifically provided that no one was to be persecuted for his reli-

gious beliefs—a religious toleration that reflected the broad tolerance
of the mother country. With some exceptions the colonists, as servants of the company, were subject to call for work for the company,
for which they were paid, and were liable to be sent to the places
where they were expected to live, at least during the first six years.
They were brought to the colony at the expense of the company,
and were given the land they were to cultivate. During the first two
years the company furnished them with tools, livestock, and supplies, for which the colonist was expected to pay only after he had
begun to make a profit on his land. Each settler might produce
what he could, or engage in trade, but he was required to sell only
to the company any products he might have for export. Handicraft
industry, however, was prohibited, since the company hoped to
derive some of its profits from its monopoly of the sale of manufactured goods to the colonists and the Indians.

ECONOMIC AND SOCIAL GROWTH

The colony of New Netherland was never a very profitable venture for the Dutch West India Company. But as a community it
grew, slowly but surely, and laid the foundations for later prosperity. The farmers near the fort at New Amsterdam found that
wheat and rye flourished in the good soil and equable climate of
Manhattan Island, with the result that 45,000 guilders' worth of
grain was exported in 1626, and by 1632 this amount rose to 125,000
guilders. As the country was heavily forested, lumbering and shipbuilding became important parts of the colony's economy. The company had a monopoly of the export of furs and for a time the fur
trade proved to be the most important single economic activity of
the colony.

The population of the colony was composed of Walloons, Frenchmen, Negro slaves, and Dutchmen, but there was no great interest
among the people of Holland to emigrate to the new world. In
order to encourage emigration, therefore, the company hit upon the
plan, about 1629, of creating patroonships under the terms of which
responsibility for encouraging emigration to the colony would be
assumed by distinguished members of the Dutch West India Company. Under the arrangement the company undertook to grant a
strip of land along the river to any member who would bring over
fifty persons for settlement. The land would extend four leagues
along the river if on one side only, and two leagues if on both sides
of the river, and as far back into the country as desired. To this

land the patroon had a feudal title and over his settlers he had complete feudal control. For they were attached to the land, for which they had to pay him feudal dues, and they had to take their disputes to his courts. This arrangement bade fair to establish in New Netherland the same sort of feudal society that had been established in Maryland and in the French colony of Canada along the St. Lawrence. As a matter of fact, however, few if any of these patroonships were in the long run successful. The most famous of them was Rennselaerwick on the Hudson south of Fort Orange.

The patroons were semi-independent feudal lords who might govern their people in almost complete independence of the company. This led to complications, but the most annoying feature of the patroon system was that the patroons began to engage in commerce on their own initiative and it became necessary about 1633 to pass a law requiring that all goods shipped in and out of the colony must stop and pay duties at New Amsterdam. Under this requirement the patroons could engage in commerce only with a license from the company. In 1633 Walter Van Twiller came to the colony as its governor to succeed Peter Minuit and his five-year tenure of the governorship is notable for the growth of the liquor traffic. Under him the brewery business expanded rapidly and the commerce in drink came to be second only to the fur trade in its economic importance to the colony. Drunkenness had come to be so bad by 1638 that the residents in the town of New Amsterdam began to lose their rest by reason of the caroling of drunken sailors and it became necessary to regulate the sale of liquor and to require that "sea faring persons" be aboard their ships before dark. It also became necessary to prohibit the sale of liquor to the Indians because of the Indian tendency to become rough and disorderly when under the influence of drink; but this regulation failed.

Van Twiller was succeeded in 1638 by William Kieft. Kieft managed to get along with one councilor instead of three and made himself notorious on account of his unpleasant relations with the Indians. He tried to tax them and took their lands without their consent. He distrusted them and they distrusted him. By 1641 there was a serious danger of war with the natives so Governor Kieft called a council of twelve men to advise him on the situation. This gave the twelve men an opportunity to demand a democratic government for the colony but Kieft dismissed them and nothing was done about it. In 1643 actual war broke out with the Indians and Kieft again called a group of men, this time eight, to advise him. They took advantage of the opportunity and protested against the taxes, demanded a more democratic form of government and sent a request home to the Dutch West India Company for a new governor. On the other hand, they did organize a campaign against the Indians, and, with the aid of the English from New Haven, defeated them. In 1647 their request for a new governor was granted in the person of Peter Stuyvesant.

THE STRUGGLE FOR A GOVERNMENT

The colonists had no share in the administration of the colony. The customary laws of Holland were extended to New Netherland, but Cornelius Jacobsen May, the first governor, had been the captain of the ship which brought the colonists, and ruled the colony as a sea-captain rules his ship. Thereafter, the director-general was an official of the company, but his councilors were sea-captains, and the "ship's company" model of government was retained. Gradually, however, the government lost its most obvious "amphibian" characteristics. The director-general was assisted by a commis, or "super-cago," a secretary who also supervised the fur trade, and a "schout-fiscal," a prosecuting officer who maintained order. The director-general also had an appointed council of four men, who advised with him and voted on local questions of policy. Thus the governor and council were both court and legislature, responsible only to the company back in Holland. Laws made by the council had to be approved by the company, and appeals might be made to it from the council's judgments.

The further evolution of government was slow. As the government of Massachusetts Bay resulted from a metamorphosis of a company into a civil state, the government of New Netherland appears to have the result of a metamorphosis of a ship's company into a body politic. It has been called an "amphibian" colony, with half its activity on land and half at sea; its governor has been compared to a ship's captain and the governor's council to the ship's mates who assist the captain but do not control him. There was no thought of representative government. The people were under contract to the company and they were governed by the company's representative, the governor. They had no voice in their own political destiny; but they did manage, on occasion, to protest against their arbitrary governors, as already noted.

Peter Stuyvesant, who became governor in 1647, was an ex-soldier who had brought his military habits to his duties as governor of New Netherland. He hesitated to lay more taxes on the colonists without their approval and called together a group of nine prominent colonists to aid him in government. These men quarreled with him on many issues but this body is to be distinguished from the two groups called together by William Kieft, since it was a semi-permanent group of advisors constituting a loose sort of council rather than a legislature. On account of their quarrels with Stuyvesant the nine men petitioned the government of Holland for direct control. This was not granted them, but certain reforms in their local government did take place. In 1652 the government of New Amsterdam was revised and a "schout" or sheriff was appointed to govern with the aid of two burgomasters and five aldermen appointed by the governor. As for the colony as a whole, in 1653 Stuyvesant called a meeting of representatives from the towns which sent in a remonstrance against the arbitrary appointment of magistrates by the governor, the promulgation of laws without their consent and against the interests of the people, and the manipulation of the lands of the colony for the benefit of the governor's friends. This meeting petitioned for a larger share in the control of their political affairs. The only result, however, was that the schout of each town and those appointed to assist him in government were thereafter generally appointed from the residents of the town concerned; thus, while the governor still did all the appointing, the local officials represented in large measure the desires of the people. In addition to this each town was allowed to have a local excise or tax for its own local purposes. This was as near as New Netherland ever came to self-government under the Dutch regime.

NEW NETHERLAND AND ITS NEIGHBORS

The colony of New Netherland had been founded along the Hudson and Delaware rivers between the English colonies of Connecticut and New Haven on the east and Maryland on the south. To make matters worse, about 1638 the Swedish West India Company was formed for the purpose of settling colonies in America and fixed upon the Delaware River as a convenient place for its settlement. The result was that the Swedes built Fort Christina on the Delaware and began to cultivate a prosperous trade with the Indians. It was not long before the Dutch and Swedes came into conflict; and after the Peace of Westphalia in 1648, which brought an end to the Thirty Years War in Europe, Governor Stuyvesant determined, under instructions from the Dutch West India Company, to drive out the Swedes, which he did in 1655.

On the other hand, the relations between the Dutch and the English were still more serious. Ships from New Haven had been seized in Delaware Bay under Governor Kieft, and the expansion of the English westward along Long Island Sound both on the mainland and on Long Island, had brought the New England villages face to face with the settlements of the Dutch. Because of the resulting conflict, Stuyvesant was instructed to negotiate a boundary line with the English which he succeeded in doing in the treaty of Hartford of 1650. As this treaty was not ratified by the English government, however, the danger of absorption by the English continued to hang over the Dutch colony until it actually took place in 1664.

LIFE IN NEW NETHERLAND

The colony established by the Dutch along the Hudson and Delaware rivers is one of the most interesting of all the early European settlements in America. It was composed of people from a variety of nations, and as early as 1664 it was reported that eighteen different languages were spoken in the town of New Amsterdam. The population was chiefly Dutch, but there were Walloons, Swedes, Englishmen from New England, Frenchmen, Germans, and many others who had straggled into the colony from one place or another and who gave this settlement from the earliest decade of its history the cosmopolitan character that it has retained ever since. Naturally these emigrants brought with them various religions and various social customs, and except for one or two sporadic bursts of religious persecution, the general atmosphere of the colony was one of religious toleration.

There was little or no life that could be called cultural. The Dutch West India Company was not particularly interested in education, although it did send over a school teacher about 1637. That poor man, however, was forced to take in washing to supplement the meager income that he received from his scholarly activities. In 1649 the nine men complained that there was still no school building and in 1652 Governor Stuyvesant received authority from the company to use the funds derived from the city tavern for the purpose of erecting a school. A school building appeared in 1655, and in 1658 there was established a Latin School.

The progress of New Amsterdam nevertheless is marked by certain notable civic improvements, and by 1657 there had been established a fire patrol that was maintained appropriately enough by a tax on chimneys, and in 1658 there was organized a police force. Certain of the streets of this little Dutch town had been paved, the first of which, we are told, was the street of the breweries. In general, this was a frontier village of a stolid, satisfied Dutch people, without self-government, to be sure, but enjoying a large measure of religious and social tolerance. In many ways it was a more urbane, cosmopolitan, and secular society than had appeared in any of the European establishments thus far located on the shores of the new world.

RECOMMENDED BOOKS FOR FURTHER READING

CONTEMPORARY NARRATIVES

John F. Jameson, ed., *Narratives of New Netherland, 1609-1664.*
Amandus Johnson, ed., *The Instruction for Johan Printz.*

MODERN ACCOUNTS

Charles M. Andrews, *The Colonial Period of American History,* III, Chapter 3.

John R. Brodhead, *History of the State of New York,* Volume I.

Edward Channing, *A History of the United States,* I, Chapters 16-17.

John Fiske, *The Dutch and Quaker Colonies,* Volume I.

Alexander C. Flick, ed., *History of the State of New York,* Volume I.

Maud W. Goodwin, *The Dutch and English on the Hudson,* Chapters 1-9.

John H. Innes, *New Amsterdam and Its People.*

John F. Jameson, *William Usselinx, Founder of the Dutch and Swedish West India Companies.*

Amandus Johnson, *The Swedish Settlements on the Delaware.*

Edmund B. O'Callaghan, *History of New Netherland.*

Herbert L. Osgood, *The American Colonies in the Seventeenth Century,* II, Part III, Chapter 5.

Llewelyn Powys, *Henry Hudson.*

Theodore Roosevelt, *New York,* Chapters 1-3.

William R. Shepherd, *The Story of New Amsterdam.*

Bayard Tuckerman, *Peter Stuyvesant, Director-General for the West India Company in New Netherland.*

Mariana G. Van Rensselaer, *History of the City of New York in the Seventeenth Century,* Volume I.

Christopher Ward, *The Dutch & Swedes on the Delaware, 1609-64.*

James G. Wilson, ed., *The Memorial History of the City of New-York,* Volume I.

PART III

England Discovers Her Colonies, 1650-89

B
Y THE time when Charles II re-ascended the throne of his fathers in England in 1660, at the end of twenty years of civil war and republican experimentation, probably two hundred thousand of his subjects were residing in America. They were scattered along the coast from Newfoundland to Cape Fear, in Bermuda, and in half a dozen or more of the islands of the West Indies. By this time these settlements had conclusively demonstrated their value, both to the private capitalists who had invested in them and to the government, as well as to the colonists who had succeeded in planting themselves in the new world. Colonial commerce was becoming a profitable item in English trade, of prime importance to the merchants of England, particularly of London; colonial lands offered a rich promise to aristocratic land speculators; and the customs duties that might be levied upon imports and exports to and from the colonies promised a handsome income for the royal exchequer. The major theme in the development of the policy of England toward the colonies under Charles II and James II, therefore, is furnished by the desire of these three groups to make money out of the American colonial establishment. The merchants and the Crown found their interests to coincide in the policies that led to the regulation of colonial commerce and the establishment of a fairly effective institution of imperial administration in the committee of the Privy Council called the Lords of Trade; the aristocratic land-speculators found what they hoped might provide them with profitable feudal estates in the colonies in the schemes for new proprietary colonies on the old pattern of Nova Scotia, the West Indies, and Maryland.

These three tendencies were not altogether consistent with each other, however; nor was there, for the time being, any serious effort to co-ordinate them. This explains why, even within a single decade, England with one hand enacted laws which fixed a large measure of imperial control upon colonial commerce and sent out royal commissions to investigate the independent tendencies of the old New

England colonies, while with the other it donated to the king's favorites princely domains in America under terms which made them, legally at least, more independent than New England had ever been. The evolving colonial policy of England was still in a formative stage, in which various aspects of it were determined by these three separate groups of interests—the merchants, working through Parliament, the courtiers, working through the king, and the official imperial interests, working through the Privy Council and the administrative agencies of the Crown. It was not until the end of the century that a serious effort was made to co-ordinate all these interests in a single consistent colonial policy. Even then, it was not entirely successful.

From the point of view of the colonies, this period was marked by two major developments. One was the founding of new colonies in Jamaica, Carolina, New Jersey, New York, Pennsylvania, and Hudson Bay, all of them, except Jamaica, on the proprietary model. The other was an increasing amount of control by England, chiefly in the form of the stricter regulation of colonial commerce, but also, later, in the form of an effort by the mother country to reduce the extent of the political autonomy assumed by the colonies in the first decades of their existence.

Thus, from the points of view both of the mother country and of the colonies, the major theme of this period of American history is the tightening of the imperial relationships. At the same time it should be noted that the old colonies continued to grow and expand, and to consolidate the economic and social institutions laid down in the years of their first beginnings. Finally, it should also be noted that during this period the English colonies, by their growth, began to rub elbows with an expanding French empire. Slowly but steadily, the lines of competitive expansion were laid down that were to bring English colonies and French colonies almost inevitably into conflict; and in the minds of the English-Americans and French-Americans were engendered the mutual distrust and hatred that were to color their relations with each other for a century.

16

England's Colonial Policy

EARLY COMMITTEES AND COMMISSIONS

THE FIRST English colonies in America were settled, as it were, in a fit of absent-mindedness. England had no policy with regard to colonies. King James I did, it is true, call into consultation such colonial "experts" as Hakluyt, Popham, and others when the Virginia Company was organized, and the creation of the Council for Virginia in the charter of 1606 was the result of the deliberations of these experts. It was soon found, however, that the council had little active interest in the colony and less facility for the administration of practical problems. The result of the failure of the council was a new charter to the Virginia Company in 1609 and its revision in 1612, which placed the management of the colony completely in the hands of the company. From that time on the Crown took little interest in the Virginia colony until it was forcèd to do so by the complaints arising against the company's administration. Similarly, when the Council for New England was created in 1620 the affairs of the New England colonists were left in the hands of the council or in the hands of the leaders of the colonists themselves, until in 1628 the Massachusetts Bay Company appealed for a charter directly from the king, which was expected to obviate any interference by the Council for New England.

With the accession of King Charles I, the Crown was compelled to take a more active interest in colonial affairs, for the revocation of the charter of the Virginia Company made it necessary for the king to do something about the administration of that colony. The result of this was the designation of a committee of the Privy Council charged with the Virginia administration. At about the same time the interests of rival groups of merchants in the West Indies led to appeals for royal charters for the Windward Islands and these appeals resulted in the Carlisle grants of 1627-28. It will be noted that this was the same year in which the Massachusetts Bay Company appealed for a charter, and about the time when Lord Baltimore was beginning to cast about for a location for a colony in a climate more salubrious than that of Newfoundland. There were thus a good many reasons why, in the years from 1625 to 1633, the British Crown should have been increasingly interested in the colonial problem.

In 1634 the king appointed a standing committee of the Privy Council as a board of "Commissioners for Plantations in General" charged with the consideration of all colonial problems, at the head of which was Archbishop Laud. It was to this commission that Ferdinando Gorges and John Mason took their case in their effort to recover the land occupied by the Massachusetts Bay Company. But colonial affairs were in large measure lost sight of in the rising storm of parliamentary antagonism to the king, and it was not until 1643 that any further steps were taken in the evolution of administrative institutions for the colonies. In that year Parliament, having assumed the dominant place in the English government, appointed a committee of its own members, assisted by a group of experts in colonial matters, to serve as a permanent executive body to deal with the colonies. This was the so-called Warwick Commission under the leadership of the Earl of Warwick. But with the establishment of the Commonwealth in 1649 and the creation of the Council of State, colonial affairs fell into the hands of committees of this great council, which was essentially analogous to the Privy Council under the king. Under the Council of State there was created in 1650 the so-called Council for Trade, an advisory body composed of merchants and colonial experts which handled colonial affairs for about a year and then turned its responsibilities back again to the committee of the Council of State. A permanent committee of the Council of State assumed the colonial responsibility in 1652, but after the next year, when the Protector's Council was set up by Oliver Cromwell, colonial problems were handled by special committees appointed for special problems as they arose. In 1656 the Protector again named a permanent standing committee, fashioned after the original committee of 1634.

In these changes there appears what is effectively a series of experiments in ways and means of administering the colonial problem. In general, it is to be observed that the series seemed to be moving in the direction of the establishment of a permanent committee of the Privy Council or Council of State. It appears also that there was a growing realization that the English government had no agency established for the administration of colonial affairs and that some such machinery should be created as a permanent and recognizable part of the machinery of the government in England. For by this time the colonies had begun to demonstrate their importance to the mother country. They presented a distinct problem of administration that some institution of government must be created to meet. The problem was not yet solved, however, for the permanent committee of the Protector's Council was not an effective instrument for the purpose; England had to go through another forty years of experimentation before an effective administrative institution was produced in the form of the Board of Trade.

THE FIRST NAVIGATION ACT, 1651

The question of colonial administration was only one side of the problem presented to England by the colonies. Of far greater importance to the average Englishman was the question of the economic relationships between the colonies and the mother country, for by 1650 the colonies had demonstrated their value; the West Indies had discovered the profitable nature of sugar, Virginia had demonstrated the value of tobacco, and New England had not only produced a swarm of fishing vessels and fishermen to man them, but New England merchant ships were already finding their way down the coast of the southern colonies and into the West Indies and even into the slave trade of the coast of Africa. On the other hand, little or no manufactured goods were being produced in the colonies, and these goods had to be furnished by England. The result of all this was that the English merchants, located as they were at the economic center of the empire, shipped out to the colonies quantities of manufactured goods every year and took in return the products of New England or Virginia or the West Indies, which they sold again in England or exported to the continent at great profit to themselves. Moreover, they reaped a considerable profit from their function as bankers and financiers for the colonial industry and trade. England, as it were, suddenly awoke to a realization that its colonial empire was—or might be—extremely profitable, and from about 1650 on there was a steady rise in the interest of the English government in the economic life of the colonists which resulted in an increasingly vigorous effort to control colonial economic life in the interest of the merchants of England.

King James I had attempted to favor the colony of Virginia and the Virginia Company by prohibiting the cultivation of tobacco in England and by closely regulating the importation of foreign tobacco. Beyond this, however, little or no attempt had been made to control colonial commerce; and with the coming of the Great Rebellion the attention of English merchants and entrepreneurs was temporarily diverted to the situation created by the war. At the end of the war it was discovered that the Dutch had taken advantage of their opportunities to enter actively into the trade of the British colonies, with the result that a large portion of the tobacco trade of Virginia and the sugar trade of the West Indies was carried in Dutch ships and a large proportion of the products of these colonies was sent directly to Holland. Evidently the normal economic self-interest of the colonies tended to lead them in the direction of free trade with all nations and into the habit of shipping their goods on the vessels which gave them the best terms and took their goods to the best markets. The colonies realized more or less clearly that Parliament represented the mercantile interests of England and that, once they were in control of the British government, the tendency of parliamentary leaders probably would be in the direction of a close regulation of colonial economic life for their own benefit. It is no accident, therefore, that colonial sympathies in the civil war were in large measure on the side of the king, whose attitude was thought to be one of a more complete *laissez faire,* or that, when Charles I was executed by Parliament, certain of the colonies, such as Virginia, Maryland, Antigua, Bermuda, and Barbados, should have proclaimed Charles II king. It is true, of course, that there were men in these colonies whose sympathies were genuinely on the side of the king; but it is equally true that in proclaiming Charles II they hoped for greater economic freedom than they expected to receive at the hands of Parliament. The New England colonies, although they carefully refrained from proclaiming the king and although their sympathies were in general with the Puritan and Presbyterian parties in the civil war, also made it very clear that they would not accept commercial regulation at the hands of the Puritan government of England.

To the new Commonwealth government of England the proclamation of Charles II in a number of the colonies meant economic rebellion as well as political disloyalty, and Parliament took immediate steps to suppress what was in effect the first colonial revolt. Parliamentarians insisted upon the principle of parliamentary supremacy over all the affairs of the empire; the merchants of London, piqued by the successful inroads of the Dutch, insisted upon the principle of a national monopoly of imperial economic life. Parliament therefore passed, on October 3, 1650, a coercive act which was both political and economic in its implications.

First of all, the act stated clearly and decisively the principle of parliamentary supremacy over colonial affairs; for, as the preamble puts it, the colonies in America, "which were planted at the cost

and settled by the people and by authority of this nation . . . are
and ought to be subordinate to and dependent upon England, and
hath ever since the planting thereof been, and ought to be, subject
to such laws, orders and regulations as are or shall be made by the
parliament of England." The act then laid down certain regulations
concerning colonial commerce. In the first place, all trade with the
rebellious colonies of Barbados, Bermuda, Virginia, Antigua, and
Maryland, was prohibited until further notice. In addition to that,
however, trade to all the colonies was prohibited to all foreign ships
not holding special licenses from the British government; and it
was expressly stated that the Council of State in England had the
power to regulate colonial affairs on all matters, the colonial charters "to the contrary notwithstanding."

Here was a significant pronouncement of colonial policy. Evidently the colonies were no longer to regulate their own affairs
as practically sovereign states. Parliament had asserted its supreme
power over colonial matters: it had closed certain of the colonies
to all trade whatsoever, and it had prohibited trade in the colonies
by foreign ships. The act was disregarded, of course, until 1652
when the Council of State sent Sir George Ayscue to the West Indies
and to Virginia to bring the rebellious colonies to a sense of their
responsibilities. The expedition was successful because the colonies
were in no position to offer any serious resistance by force. Governors more amenable to the imperial ideas of the Commonwealth
were placed in office, and the Navigation Act of 1651, which followed the coercive act of 1650, was applied to the trade of all the
colonies.

This Navigation Act of 1651 was a milestone in the evolution of
the English policy of regulation of colonial commerce. According
to its preamble this act was passed "for the Increase of the Shipping and the encouragement of the Navigation of this Nation
[England], which under the good Providence and protection of
God, is so great a means of the Welfare and Safety of this Commonwealth." But while the chief objective was, indeed, the building up of a great British merchant marine, that objective was to
be attained by a close regulation of the business of carrying imperial commerce over the high seas; and this inevitably called for
control of the commerce of the colonies.

The act of 1651 provided, first, that goods brought from Asia,
Africa, or America to England or the English colonies must be
brought only in English ships, of which the captain and a majority
of the crew should be English. It required that goods from Europe

to England or the colonies must be brought in English ships or the ships of the country producing the goods, with the exception of a few specified articles. Foreign goods from other countries must be brought in English ships and they must be brought only from the place of their origin; an exception was made only for the goods produced in Spanish and Portuguese colonies which were closed to English shipping: these goods must be brought from Spain or Portugal. Certain goods such as salt fish, fish oil, whale bone, and other products of the fisheries could be imported into England only in English ships, and could be exported from England only in English ships, for it was felt that the fishery was the greatest of all schools for seamen, the breeding ground of ships and men to man them. Finally, this famous act provided that the coastwise trade of England and the trade between one part of the empire and another—that is to say, between the mother country and the colonies—must be carried only in English ships.

This act was passed with the desire to build up a great British (English and colonial) merchant marine by creating a monopoly of the carrying trade of the British empire in the hands of British ships and seamen. It was felt that a great merchant marine supplementary to the armed fleet would be a great asset in the defense of England and the empire. Obviously enough, the effect of such a policy must inevitably be a close regulation of colonial commerce that would run counter to the free-trade tendencies of the colonies themselves. It was only natural, therefore, that in all the colonies there was a failure to observe the act. As yet England had created no machinery for the enforcement of commercial regulations, and the colonists themselves took active steps to nullify it. Governor Willoughby of Barbados refused in 1651 to accept the provisions of the act on the grounds that it not only prejudiced the economic prosperity of the colonies but infringed the inalienable rights of Englishmen to govern themselves. Sir George Ayscue's expedition, therefore, was in large measure calculated to impress upon Barbados and Virginia the fact that Parliament and the Navigation Act meant business. Nevertheless, the act was difficult to enforce. There was frank opposition in practically all the colonies, and the colony of Virginia went so far, in 1660, as to make a commercial treaty with New Netherland providing for mutual free trade. The seizure of Dutch vessels by the English navy in Massachusetts was declared by the legislature to be illegal and contrary to the liberties of Massachusetts. The Rhode Island assembly two years later openly declared that the Dutch might trade in their colony without interference, and in 1658 it went further and declared that no one might seize ships in Rhode Island unless expressly authorized to do so by the English Parliament or the Rhode Island assembly. The governor of Connecticut in 1660 assured Peter Stuyvesant that Dutch ships would not be molested in Connecticut waters.

Thus it was that in the decade following the passage of the first navigation act, the act was in very large measure nullified by the colonies, chiefly because of the fact that the government of England had no agents or agencies for its effective administration in the colonies themselves. It was only natural that when Charles II returned to the throne in 1660 he should have made the regulation of colonial commerce one of the first matters calling for his attention.

ORGANS OF ADMINISTRATION: THE LORDS OF TRADE

The period between 1660 and 1696 is one marked by rapid increase in the value of the English colonies to the mother country. It has been estimated that in the decade between 1660 and 1670 the colonial trade accounted for one-tenth of the total trade of the empire, with a value of some eight hundred thousand pounds sterling per annum. In the second decade of this period, between 1670 and 1680, the value of the colonial trade amounted to one million three hundred thousand pounds, and by 1690 it had risen to one million seven hundred fifty thousand pounds, or about one-seventh of the value of the entire imperial trade. This consistent rise continued into the eighteenth century and in its report of 1721 the board of trade estimated that the mother country imported goods to the value of one million five hundred thousand pounds from the colonies and exported to them goods to the value of slightly over one million. The board concluded that about one-third of all the shipping employed in the commerce of the British empire at that time was maintained by the plantation trade.

In view of the rapid increase of the economic value of the colonies to England, and an increasing realization of this fact among the merchants and statesmen of the mother country, it was only natural that this period should witness a rapid crystallization of British colonial policy. This tendency, indeed, was perhaps accelerated by the fact that King Charles II and his courtiers were gentlemen of somewhat diminished fortunes and sought every means, including the exploitation of the colonies, to recoup their fortunes. As already noted, the evolution of British colonial policy followed two lines. One was the establishment of governmental institutions charged with the administration of colonial problems—an evolution which resulted in certain remarkable modifications of the British constitution; the second was a series of laws calculated more effectively to control the navigation and the commerce of the empire according to the mercantilistic philosophy.

The series of experiments in colonial administration that had been carried on under the first two Stuarts and the Commonwealth was continued in the time of Charles II. This indigent king returned to the throne in 1660, and one of his first acts was the creation of two councils, a Council for Trade and a Council for Foreign Plantations. As their names indicate, these were advisory councils, one charged with a study of imperial commerce, the other with consideration of colonial problems. They were advisory only, and were composed partly of members of the Privy Council and partly of merchants and others, "experts" in colonial affairs. The Council for Plantations was instructed to carry on investigations of colonial matters and make recommendations for rendering the colonies more useful to England. It was also to consider the problem of bringing about a more uniform type of government in the colonies and to study ways and means for the enforcement of the acts of navigation and of trade. The Council for Trade, on the other hand, was not so directly responsible for colonial matters, but as the colonies were, first and foremost, commercial enterprises, this council had also to concern itself with colonial affairs, and particularly with colonial commerce. As they had no power, these two councils could do nothing more than debate the questions that came before them; with the result that interest in them languished and they ceased to function about 1665. In 1667 a shake-up of the Privy Council attendant upon the dismissal of the Earl of Clarendon shifted the control of colonial affairs again to a permanent committee of the Privy Council, called the Committee on Trade and Plantations. Again, however, it was found that these politicians were not familiar with the problems of the colonies and that there was a genuine and pressing need for expert assistance. In 1668, therefore, a new advisory council called the Council for Trade was organized with instructions to take over a large share of colonial and commercial matters. This council was composed of experts only, and served as an advisory body to the committee of the Privy Council. The similar Council for Plantations was revived in 1670 with instructions also to pay particular attention to colonial matters. In 1672 these two councils were merged into one

Council for Trade and Plantations under the presidency of Anthony Ashley Cooper, Earl of Shaftsbury, and with a paid staff, among whom was John Locke, who, in 1673, became the secretary. This Council of 1672 considered colonial affairs and made reports and recommendations to the Privy Council, and wrote instructions for colonial governors and other officers appointed by the Crown. In this activity the influence of Shaftsbury and Locke became noticeable, and these two men had a considerable influence upon the determination of colonial policy.

The Council of 1672 still lacked executive power, however, and there still existed the anomalous dual situation created by the existence of an advisory council and a more or less executive committee of the Privy Council operating side by side. This arrangement was abandoned in 1674, and the work of the Council of 1672 was turned over to an enlarged committee of the Privy Council, henceforth called The Lords of Trade, which remained fairly permanent and had a paid staff of clerks and office assistants with its own archive. In effect, while the Council of 1672 was abandoned in form, yet the clerks and executive officers of that council continued to influence colonial affairs as employees of the Lords of Trade. It was this committee of the Privy Council which controlled colonial affairs from 1675 to 1696, when it was finally reorganized into the Board of Trade and Plantations, an organization which dominated the colonial administration for almost a century.

The administration of the colonies under the regime of the Lords of Trade was handled through four agencies. In the first place, this body appointed its own agents in the colonies and instructed those agents by letters directly from itself. At the same time, the Lords of Trade wrote instructions for colonial governors and from time to time instructed the colonial governors directly. On the other hand, the Lords of Trade often made its recommendations to the Secretary of State, and this official then used the authority of his office to instruct the governors and other representatives of the Crown. A third agency concerned with colonial matters was the admiralty, for the admiralty controlled matters pertaining to commercial ships and seamen and the navy; if the Lords of Trade desired some action taken with regard to the disposition of naval vessels or naval officers, that body made its recommendations to the admiralty and the latter, if it agreed with the desirability of the recommendations, sent out the desired order. In many instances, of course, the admiralty acted on its own responsibility. Similarly, the Lords of Trade often made recommendations to the treasury;

because the treasury was concerned with the collection of customs duties in the colonies and the administration of those funds. Throughout this period all four of these agencies, the Lords of Trade, the secretary of state, the admiralty, and the treasury, had representatives in America.

The most important agent of the British government in America was the colonial governor. In the royal provinces, such as Virginia or Jamaica, he was appointed by the Crown, but in the corporate colonies, such as Massachusetts or Connecticut, he was elected, and in the proprietary colonies such as Maryland, he was appointed by the proprietor. Nevertheless, in all cases the Crown attempted to make the colonial governor, regardless of the status of his colony, responsible to the Crown; and the provision embodying this policy was incorporated in the great Navigation Act of 1696.

The chief duty of the governor, from England's point of view, was the enforcement of the acts of trade. This was relatively easy in the royal colonies because there the governor was directly responsible to the king. It was less easy, however, in the proprietary colonies where the governor was responsible to the proprietor, and it was almost impossible in the corporate colonies where the governor was responsible to the electorate and might evade with considerable impunity instructions that he received from England.

The men who examined ships' papers and took bonds for delivery of goods in England and otherwise enforced the navigation acts were called naval officers. At first they were appointed by the colonial governors, but as time went on they came to be appointed by the Privy Council; and they were responsible, along with the governor, to the council, acting through the secretary of state. Customs duties during the first part of this period were collected by representatives of the farmers of the customs, that is, private individuals in England who for a lump payment to the Crown were given the privilege of collecting the customs in the colonies with as much profit to themselves as they might make. These agents were, of course, responsible directly to their employers in England, but they often complained of the evasions of the navigation acts and their employers went to the Lords of Trade or to the secretary of state with these complaints. Because of its inefficiency and irregularity the farming system was abandoned in 1671 and collection of customs in America was delegated to commissioners paid by and responsible to the Board of Customs in England. Of these agents the most notable was Edward Randolph, appointed in 1678 as customs commissioner for New England. In 1683 William Dyre was appointed surveyor general of the customs for all the colonies.

Thus it was that, aside from the Lords of Trade themselves, there were three governmental departments in England concerned with the administration of colonial problems, the secretary of state, the treasury, and the admiralty. At the beginning violations of the navigation acts might be tried in admiralty courts in which the governor or his deputy, serving as vice-admiral, presided; in these courts there were no juries. Or the case might be tried in common law courts where jury trial was the rule. In such cases it was difficult to get convictions under the law, because of the widespread sympathy among the people, particularly of New England, for the violators. Cases involving customs offenses in England were often tried in courts of exchequer; this method was sometimes followed in the West Indies.

Thus it appears that in the colonies themselves there was a triple system—one might say triply confused—of colonial administration. There were three different kinds of colonies; there were three different departments of the British government involved in colonial administration; these three departments sent three different kinds of colonial agents to America; and cases involving the administration of the imperial law were tried in three or more different kinds of courts. It is no wonder that the result was an amazingly inefficient sort of colonial administration.

There was nevertheless inherent in this system of administration a certain clear and progressively clearer set of ideas as to what the relationship between colonies and the mother country should be. In the instructions to the various councils charged with an investigation of colonial affairs the most constant question was how best might the colonies be made useful and beneficial to the mother country. Little thought was given to making colonial administration useful and beneficial to the colonies. And to the end that the benefit of the mother country might most effectively be served, the councils and commissions studying colonial affairs were instructed to inform themselves of the conditions of the colonies, administrative, economic, social, and so on; they were to provide instructions for new governors; they were to scrutinize laws passed by the colonies and determine their "constitutionality." These bodies were, indeed, charged to inquire as to the best methods for promoting the defense of the colonies, the welfare of the inhabitants and the status of such subdued classes as servants, slaves, and Indians. But on these questions the councils wasted little or their time; it must be remembered, however, that this imperial administration did seek to promote the welfare of the people of the colonies insofar as that would benefit the mother country. And the fact that the mother country engaged itself to protect the colonies as well as to provide for them a protected English market for their products redounded in considerable measure to the benefit of the colonies themselves.

The underlying philosophy in this system, seen in the instructions to the councils and to the governors and agents in the colonies themselves was that of mercantilism, a philosophy of national and imperial welfare that will be discussed in detail in another place. Its fundamental objectives, so far as the colonies were concerned, were the supervision and regulation of imperial and foreign commerce, the encouragement of English manufactures, the production in the colonies of commodities which England itself was unable to produce, and the advancement of fishing and the merchant marine of Englishmen.

COMMERCIAL REGULATION: THE NAVIGATION ACTS OF 1660, 1663, AND 1673

The philosophy underlying British colonial policy was carried out in legislation even before the organs of administration were developed. As a rule colonial administration was not considered a part of the functions of Parliament, but the regulation of imperial trade and, particularly, the protection of British home manufactures and merchants was. Thus while King Charles II was setting up his Councils of Trade and of Plantations in 1660, the new Parliament busied itself with tightening up the legislative control of imperial commerce established in the Navigation Act of 1651. This legislation had failed to oust the Dutch from the British imperial trade. There was a desire to restate the principle of that law and to tighten up its provisions in such a way as more effectively to exclude foreign competitors and to establish a British monopoly of the imperial carrying business. At the same time Parliament represented a growing desire to use the colonies as sources of materials which the English needed and thus rectify an unfavorable balance of trade with certain parts of Europe and the east, notably Sweden. Finally, the navigation laws represent an effort to make England the depot through which all the manufactured goods shipped to the outlying parts of the empire must pass.

It was with these three objectives in mind that a series of acts was passed in 1660, 1663, and 1673 which sought to regulate British imperial commerce. The fundamental law in this system of laws was the Navigation Act of 1660, which sought to accomplish two of these three objectives: it attacked, first, the problem of navigation and the building up of the British merchant marine, and then the problem of establishing a monopoly of the colonial market and colonial products in the hands of British merchants.

In many of its provisions the act merely restated those of the Navigation Act of 1651. It provided that no goods might be shipped to or from the colonies except in English ships, that is to say, ships owned in England and of which the master and three-fourths of the crew must be Englishmen. This was a reaffirmation of one of the provisions of the act of 1651, but it went further than that act in totally excluding foreign ships from the colonial trade and in making more stringent the regulation defining the status of ships permitted to indulge in it. Like the act of 1651 this act provided that goods from Africa, Asia, and America might be brought to England only in English ships. Further, it provided that goods produced in foreign countries with certain exceptions must be brought from the place of production; this provision was aimed at such middlemen as the Dutch merchants of Holland. The act provided, also, that European goods might be brought to England in the ships of the nation producing the goods or in English ships, but not in the ships of any third power. This repeats a provision of the act of 1651 and was also aimed at middlemen carriers such as the Dutch.

In the above provisions the act was calculated to promote and develop the British merchant marine by placing the control of British imperial trade in the hands of Englishmen residing either in England or in the colonies. In its second aspect the act listed the major products of the colonies in what came to be called the "enumerated articles," and required that these articles be shipped from the colony producing them either to England or to some other colony. On this list appeared sugar, tobacco, cotton, indigo, ginger and dye-woods. This was a new provision which had not appeared in the act of 1651, although the principle was not particularly new. The list, moreover, did not enumerate all the colonial products, but only those intended eventually for the use of the household and textile industries, plus the tobacco trade. It included the staple products of the southern and West Indian colonies, but it affected the northern colonies relatively little.

The list of enumerated articles was later extended to include rice, molasses, naval stores, and furs, and in the reformulation of British legislation with regard to colonial commerce that took place after the French and Indian wars, a law was passed in 1766 which provided that even though not on the enumerated list, articles shipped from a colony had to be landed in England before going on to its destination except in cases where the destination lay in countries south of Cape Finisterre. This was the final peak of the mercantilistic attempts by England to control colonial commerce for the benefit of English merchants.

The act of 1660 thus attempted to establish in the hands of the English shippers a real monopoly of the carrying trade of the British empire and in the hands of English merchants a monopoly of the staple products of the colonies. The third objective in English economic policy with regard to the colonies was to make England the "staple" or depot for goods going to the colonies, and this objective was responsible for the so-called Staple Act of 1663. This act provided that all European goods intended for the colonies must first be landed in England, with the exception of salt coming from the Cape Verde Islands, servants, horses, provisions from Scotland and Ireland, and wines coming from Madeira and the Azores. This act was clearly calculated to promote the interests of English merchants and factors as against the interests of the colonists, for it was to the interest of the colonial merchants to buy directly from the country producing the goods, and, indeed, to sell directly to those countries without having the major items of their import and export forced to pass through the English depot and pay the charges of handling and of resale at that point. The colonies could buy woolens, tools, and other manufactured goods more cheaply in Holland than they could in England; but direct trade between the colonies and Holland, it was thought, would be ruinous to the commerce of England itself because England would be forced to compete with the cheaper prices—and the greater cleverness, it may be—of the Dutch.

With the passage of these laws and other minor acts related to them, steps were taken to enforce them. Colonial governors were required to take an oath to enforce the act of 1660, to keep lists of ships coming in and out, and to see to it that foreign ships did not enter the colonial ports. Later on, the governors were even expected to furnish bond guaranteeing enforcement of the navigation acts. It was soon found very difficult to enforce these acts, however, partly because the economic interests of the colonists encouraged nullification, partly because of the presence of Dutchmen and Frenchmen on the borders of the English colonies, and partly because of the inefficiency of the British administration itself. A great deal of smuggling took place despite the acts, and clever Yankee skippers devised ways and means of fulfilling the letter while evading the spirit and intention of the law. The act of 1660, for example, required that the enumerated articles be landed either in England or another colony; but it became fairly easy for a ship captain to take on board a load of sugar in Barbados, carry it to Charlestown, and then sail directly to Holland, thus escaping the necessity of landing his goods in England and paying duties on them there.

In order to put a stop to these and similar practices, Parliament passed in 1673 the explanatory act or Plantations Duties Act, which required that duties on enumerated goods shipped from one colony to another be paid at the point of shipment, if going to another colony. It provided also that ship captains must post bonds to take the goods either to England or to another colony for actual use in that colony. Naturally this law greatly affected the coastwise or inter-colonial trade by imposing customs duties on the enumerated articles shipped from one colony to another, and it necessitated the creation of numerous customs officials. The object of the act was not in the first place revenue, but rather the control of the trade; that is, to prevent evasions of the act of 1660, and to keep the inter-colonial trade in the hands of English merchants.

Such was the system by which England sought to capture the profits of her empire. While shortsighted and selfish to a remarkable degree, it yet sought to build the empire into an orderly unity. It almost completely ignored the natural tendencies in the economic development of the colonies; yet judged by the standards of administration and control in the colonial empires of Spain, Portugal, and France, it seems singularly broad and progressive. For, while the colonies remained essentially in economic subjection to the mother country, they also derived the benefits of protection, a certain market for their goods in the mother country, and more free, direct trade with foreign countries than the colonies of any other European state. Nevertheless, the restrictions placed upon the economic life of the colonies by the system reveals the essential economic cleavage between the mother country and the colonies. This phenomenon, already observed in the events of 1650-52, was one of the deepest of the roots of eventual American independence.

RECOMMENDED BOOKS FOR FURTHER READING

CONTEMPORARY NARRATIVES AND DOCUMENTS

William Macdonald, ed., *Select Charters and Other Documents Illustrative of American History, 1606-1775*, pp. 106-115, 133-136, 168-170.

Edward Randolph, *Edward Randolph; including his Letters and Official Papers, 1676-1703*, edited by Robert N. Toppan and Alfred T. S. Goodrick.

MODERN ACCOUNTS

Charles M. Andrews, *British Committees, Commissions, and Councils of Trade and Plantations, 1622-1675.*

George L. Beer, *The Commercial Policy of England Toward the American Colonies*, Chapters 4-7.

George L. Beer, *The Old Colonial System, 1660-1754*, I, II.

George L. Beer, *The Origins of the British Colonial System, 1578-1660.*

Ralph P. Bieber, *The Lords of Trade and Plantations, 1675-1696.*

The Cambridge History of the British Empire, I, Chapters 7, 9.

Edward Channing, *A History of the United States*, I, Chapter 19; II, Chapter 1.

William Cunningham, *The Growth of English Industry and Commerce*, Volume I.

George Edmundson, *Anglo-Dutch Rivalry during the First Half of the Seventeenth Century.*

Hugh E. Egerton, *A Short History of British Colonial Policy*, Book I; Book II, Chapters 1-3.

Charles H. Firth, *Oliver Cromwell and the Rule of the Puritans in England.*

James E. Gillespie, *The Influence of Oversea Expansion on England to 1700.*

Lawrence A. Harper, *The English Navigation Laws.*

Gertrude A. Jacobsen, *William Blathwayt.*

Emory R. Johnson [and others], *History of Domestic and Foreign Commerce of the United States*, I, Chapters 3-4.

Herbert L. Osgood, *The American Colonies in the Seventeenth Century*, III, Chapters 6-7.

John R. Seeley, *The Growth of British Policy*, II, Parts 2-3.

17

The Old Colonies Under the Restoration: The West Indies, 1660-89

JAMAICA

THE British West Indies underwent, during the middle and the latter half of the seventeenth century, a series of mild revolutions. In the first place, Jamaica, subsequently the most important of the British islands, was added to the British empire by Oliver Cromwell in 1655. At the same time, certain economic and social changes were taking place which profoundly affected the subsequent history of all the islands. Finally, it was during this period that the West Indies ceased to be proprietary provinces and became royal colonies under the direct control of the Crown, an event, indeed, which illustrates a tendency to be noted throughout the British empire during this period.

After the restoration of Charles II to the throne of England in 1660, and as population progressively increased, the military nature of the Jamaica colony was gradually sloughed off and in 1662 the island was given a legal constitution as a royal province with a royally appointed governor and council and an elected assembly. The assembly met for the first time in 1664 and immediately fell to wrangling with the governor over the administration of finances. Political relations between the population and the royal arm of government remained strained for a number of years and in 1678 a Jamaica version of Poynings' Law was passed by the English Parliament which required that legislation for Jamaica must originate in the English Privy Council. This removal of legislative initiative from the island created an impossible situation, however, and it was not long before the colony regained its autonomy and continued its progress as a royal province.

The economic and social growth of Jamaica was slow; but because of its strategic position as the nearest British colony to the Spanish mainland, it gradually came to enjoy an economic life which distinguished it from the other British West Indies. By 1673 the population of the island had grown to include some eight thousand whites and ten thousand Negroes. These people devoted their energies largely to the cultivation of sugar, indigo, cotton, tobacco, and ginger; but they soon found that Port Royal was in a position in large measure to monopolize the illicit trade with the Spanish colonies. Finally, during the series of wars, formal and informal, that took place between 1665 and 1670, Jamaica was found to be a splendid base of operations for privateers who preyed upon French, Dutch, and Spanish shipping in time of war and who, as "buccaneers," reaped golden harvests from preying upon the commerce of friendly nations, particularly Spain, in time of peace. The most famous of these buccaneers was Sir Henry Morgan, who openly used the harbors of Jamaica for his licit and illicit operations, and even went so far as to carry on an armed private warfare with the Spaniards on the mainland, which reached its famous climax in the sack of Panamá on the isthmus early in the year 1671. With the recognition of English ownership of the island by Spain in the treaty of Madrid in 1670, however, this buccaneering went into a decline and slowly but surely was suppressed and finally came to a practical end when Morgan himself was appointed lieutenant-governor of Jamaica.

THE OLDER ISLAND COLONIES

Of the older British West Indies, both Barbados and the Leeward Islands were undergoing a profound social and economic change. The concentration of land in the hands of large landowners that had continued steadily since the introduction of sugar into these islands had forced out many of the small landowners, who were now going to Jamaica or to the southern colonies on the mainland. Barbados had suffered an actual decline. The population of this island in 1643 had been some twenty thousand whites and a few Negroes; but by 1666 the white population had decreased to eight thousand, while the Negro population had increased to some forty thousand.

As in the case of Virginia and its tobacco, the islands suffered much from the enumeration of sugar in the Navigation Act of 1660, which compelled the sugar producers to send their product to England before it could be shipped to a foreign market. After the surrender of Barbados to Sir George Ayscue in January, 1652, the Barbadian sugar exporters, interpreting the terms of their surrender as permitting them freedom of trade, practically nullified the Navigation Act of 1651 by reopening their profitable, Dutch-carried commerce with Holland and Hamburg. But war broke out between Holland and England that same year, and this, the first Dutch war, put a more effective stop to this free trade than any law could do.

In its political life, Barbados had much reason to complain over the renewal of the Carlisle patent upon the restoration of Charles II. For under the old patent land was still held in feudal tenure, and Francis Lord Willoughby, who had leased the islands from the Carlisle heirs and now returned to Barbados as governor, engaged in a campaign to reassert the power of the proprietor's prerogative against the autonomous tendencies of the island's legislature. As a result of the complaints of the planters and their request that Barbados be given the status of a royal province, the colonists in 1663 were given the right to purchase outright their lands from the proprietors, thus instituting an era of freehold tenure. In return for this concession, however, Barbados had to accept the permanent imposition of a duty of four-and-one-half percent upon all "dead" exports from the colony, the funds from which were supposed to be used to support the administration of government. In 1671 the proprietary charter was completely canceled, and Barbados became a royal province after the fashion of Jamaica.

Up to this time, Barbados and the Leeward Islands had been under the same proprietary administration, under the Carlisle charter of 1628 and the lease of the islands to Lord Willoughby; and the inhabitants of St. Christopher, Nevis, Antigua, and Montserrat were subject to the same distressing conditions as those of Barbados. Their distance from Barbados and their particularistic interests led them, in 1667, to ask that they be separated from the government of Barbados with a government of their own, and this was done in 1672. Sir William Stapleton was sent over as the first royal governor-general of the colony of the Leeward Islands, with a residence at St. John's, Antigua. The new government was thus of the "royal" type, but it was peculiar in that each of the four islands had its own lieutenant-governor and its own legislature—a sort of miniature colonial federation.

THE INTERNATIONAL COCKPIT OF THE AMERICAS

The West Indies and the lands lying around the Caribbean Sea and the Gulf of Mexico constituted in the seventeenth century the cockpit of international colonial rivalries in America. Ever since the discovery of America the nations on the western seaboard of Europe had fought for the possession of these lands and for the right to exploit the mineral and other wealth of this area. Geography itself, indeed, seemed to make of this area a sort of funnel into which poured all the religious, political, economic, and social conflicts in the new world. The stakes of international rivalry were high, and for a century after the foundation of the Spanish and Portuguese empires, the French, English, and Dutch had contented themselves with preying upon the Spanish treasure fleets and occasional raids upon Spanish towns.

With the foundation of French, Dutch, and English settlements in the islands at the beginning of the seventeenth century, the international rivalries in this area became intensified; and Spain protested every step that her rivals took in the way of territorial expansion. It was not until 1648—and then only after a long and disastrous series of wars—that Spain reluctantly admitted the right of the Dutch to own territory in the new world or even to go there for trade. Thereafter, it was one of the major objectives of British and French diplomacy to win the same recognition of their right to settle unoccupied territories in the new world. All the British settlements, indeed, from Virginia to Barbados, had been made in territory Spain claimed under the treaty of Tordesillas of 1494, and practically every settlement that was made was followed not only by diplomatic protest from Madrid but even by the threat of military destruction. The English settlements had been seriously challenged only once or twice, however, and with the restoration of Charles II to the English throne in 1660, England could present a formidable line of long-established colonies along the Atlantic shores of America from the forty-fifth degree of north latitude southward to the tenth. Charles, to be sure, had been well received at the Spanish court and the king of Spain had actually made an agreement with him in 1656 by which he promised to support Charles's claim to the British throne in return for a promise by Charles that he would return to his Catholic Majesty the island of Jamaica. Shortly after returning tó England, however, Charles fell under the domination of the mercantilistic theory and began to see that both personal and national profit lay in the policies advocated by the merchants, particularly those in the city of London. He soon forgot his promises to return Jamaica and instead he made a treaty with Portugal, which had been struggling for twenty years for independence of Spain, in return for a Portuguese wife who brought him a large dowry and certain territorial and commercial concessions in the Portuguese empire. Spain was disgusted by this reversal of Charles's policy, but in the face of a threatened renewal of the old war with France the Spanish king did not feel in a position to do more than protest. As a matter of fact, in an effort to keep England neutral in the threatening war with France, Spain conceded both Portuguese independence and the right of the British to go to America. Thus, in 1667, Spain, for the first time, recognized the right of the British to own and occupy lands in the new world and to go to non-Spanish territories there for trade. Three years later, in 1670, Spain and England made another treaty in which they mutually recognized each other's possessions in the new world generally.

More must be said about the international history of the West Indies during this period in another place. Suffice it to say, for the moment, that their position in the crucible of international rivalries in America, coupled with their natural defenselessness, emphasized their dependence upon the mother country and discouraged the growth of such strong tendencies toward independence as were observable, for example, during the same period in New England.

The end of the seventeenth century, then, found the British West Indies organized in three separate colonies: Barbados, the Leeward Islands, and Jamaica. Each of these colonies was now a royal province. All of them had become sugar-producing colonies which at the same time cultivated cotton and indigo with profit. Jamaica, moreover, had already begun to exploit the profit-making possibilities of the logwood forests on the shores of Yucatan and Honduras and had begun to engage in an illicit slave trade with the Spanish colonies that was to make Jamaica in the eighteenth century the great slave emporium of the new world. Jamaica, indeed, soon became the most profitable of all the colonies, as the West Indies as a whole had already become the most profitable section of the British empire. Significantly for all the British colonies in America, the West Indies colonies were now closely bound to those on the mainland, and particularly those of New England, by the ties of a flourishing intercolonial trade in sugar, molasses and rum on the one side and fish, lumber, and slaves on the other. Both areas were now integral and interdependent parts of the same empire. Because of their now demonstrated capacity to produce a profit, as well as because of their strategic position with regard to international colonial rivalries, the West Indies—French, British, and Spanish—became the focus of intense and protracted diplomatic attention. For almost a century the West Indies were to be the pivot upon which the history of the British empire in America was to turn.

RECOMMENDED BOOKS FOR FURTHER READING

CONTEMPORARY NARRATIVES

Alexandre O. Exquemelin, *The Buccaneers of America*, edited by William S. Sonnenschein, Parts II, III.

Thomas Gage, *The English-American, a New Survey*, edited by Arthur P. Newton.

Richard Ligon, *The True & Exact History of the Island of Barbados*.

Hans Sloane, *A Voyage to the Islands Madera, Barbados, Nieves, S. Christophers and Jamaica*.

Dalby Thomas, *An Historical Account of the Rise and Growth of the West India Colonies*.

MODERN ACCOUNTS

Charles M. Andrews, *The Colonial Period of American History*, II, Chapter 7; III, Chapter 1.

Violet Barbour, "Privateers and Pirates of the West Indies" in *American Historical Review*, XVI, 529-566.

The Cambridge History of the British Empire, I, Chapter 8.

Clarence H. Haring, *The Buccaneers in the West Indies in the Seventeenth Century*.

Vincent T. Harlow, *A History of Barbados, 1625-1685*.

Charles S. S. Higham, *The Development of the Leeward Islands under the Restoration, 1660-1688*.

Charles S. S. Higham, "The General Assembly of the Leeward Islands" in *English Historical Review*, XLI, 190-209, 366-388.

Philip A. Means, *The Spanish Main; Focus of Envy, 1492-1700*, Chapters 8-10.

Stewart L. Mims, *Colbert's West India Policy*.

Arthur P. Newton, *The European Nations in the West Indies, 1493-1688*, Chapters 14-23.

James A. Williamson, *The Caribbee Islands under the Proprietary Patents*.

James A. Williamson, *A Short History of British Expansion*, Part III, Chapter 11.

18

Virginia and Maryland Under
the Restoration

DEPRESSION AND REBELLION IN VIRGINIA

THE HISTORY of Virginia during the thirty years following the restoration of Charles II revolves chiefly about the problem of tobacco. At the beginning of this period the population of the colony was about forty thousand souls, of whom some two thousand were slaves. Most of these people were engaged, directly or indirectly, in the business of raising this staple product. The Navigation Act of 1660 had made tobacco one of the enumerated articles that had to be shipped to England before being sold abroad, with the result that the market for the colony's staple product was greatly limited. Prior to this time Virginia had enjoyed a large measure of freedom of trade, and had only recently, in 1660, made a treaty of commerce with Governor Peter Stuyvesant and the Dutch at New Amsterdam. Governor Berkeley protested vehemently to the Crown against the navigation acts, claiming that the requirements of the acts would impoverish a whole people for the benefit of some forty merchants in London. The acts of 1660 and 1663, he said, restricted the market for the Virginia product, forced down the price, and brought poverty upon the colony. He and the colony were helpless, however, for their complaints fell upon deaf ears. Nevertheless, Virginia continued to produce tobacco more rapidly than it could be used, and this fact, coupled with a world surplus, caused the price of tobacco to go down to levels which made it very difficult for the small planters to live. All these factors combined resulted in a concentration of the tobacco business in the hands of those planters who had sufficient capital to weather the depression. Numbers of the small planters were forced out of business and moved on to the frontier. An effort was made, in cooperation with Maryland, to "stint" or reduce the amount of tobacco produced, but this effort failed. The same result was produced, however, by a great hurricane late in August, 1667, which destroyed much of the unharvested tobacco crop in both colonies. Prices rose immediately, only to be forced down again by the over-planting of tobacco the next year. Depression came again as a result, and was intensified by the partial paralysis of commerce incident to the second Dutch war from 1672 to 1674.

Beginning about 1670, there were several years when harvests in Virginia were poor, and the immediate effect of this was to force prices of foodstuffs upward, while the price of tobacco stayed down. This placed an additional burden upon the poorer classes, whose distress was already acute; but the complaints of the people when they reached the ears of the colonial assembly or the aristocratic governor and his council went unheeded. Meanwhile the conditions of life along the frontier were demanding governmental attention; for as the frontiers pushed farther and farther into the lands of the Indians living in the Piedmont, the relations between the Indians and the whites went from bad to worse, a condition which broke out into active warfare early in 1676.

In January of that year, the Susquehannocks fell upon the settlements, killing thirty or forty Virginians, among them the overseer of one Nathaniel Bacon, a planter who had recently arrived in the province and established himself near the falls of the James River. The frontiersmen had repeatedly appealed to Berkeley for aid against the Indians, but Berkeley and his council had been opposed to any vigorous action against the red men because certain of the tidewater planters were interested in the profitable fur trade with the Indians and did not wish to antagonize them. Upon the outbreak of January, 1676, therefore, the planters in Charles City County rose against the Indians and elected Bacon as their leader. Bacon led his frontiersmen into the wilderness against the Indians, but he was immediately declared a rebel by the governor on the ground that he had marched without a commission. The governor ordered Bacon's men to return to their homes, but sixty of the frontiersmen stuck with him and they succeeded in administering a thorough beating to the troublesome savages.

Meanwhile, the discontent over the arbitrary and stupid government of old Sir William Berkeley was coming to a head. The people who could make themselves heard were demanding a new assembly and a better distribution of the benefits of political office. Berkeley was compelled to give in and held an election, and Nathaniel Bacon himself became one of the members of the House of Burgesses. The new assembly promptly passed a series of reforms called "Bacon's Laws," but all of them were just as promptly disallowed by the king.

Bacon, however, had been declared a rebel by the governor, who had sworn to destroy him. Consequently, when he came down the James River to the meeting of the legislature in an armed sloop, Berkeley had him arrested. But because of the popular sentiment in his favor, the crotchety old governor was compelled to pardon him. It was not long before trouble again broke out between the two men, and Bacon returned to Jamestown, this time with a body of armed men, demanding a regular commission for war against the Indians. Berkeley was forced to give in and sign the commission, and Bacon marched to the Indian war; whereupon the governor again declared him a rebel and raised the militia against him. Thus a conflict which had begun as a war against the Indians along the frontier became a civil war between the governor and the rebellious frontiersmen. Bacon returned and succeeded in taking and burning the town of Jamestown, and Governor Berkeley fled across the bay to Accomac County. Bacon died, however, in October, 1676, while preparing to go to Accomac, and the irascible old governor returned. The rebellion then collapsed, and thirteen leaders of the rebellion were hunted down and executed. The king eventually heard about all these goings-on, recalled Berkeley, and asked him for an explanation. The old man was severely censured for his arbitrary attitude toward demands for reform in the colony, and soon afterwards died.

The problems that had brought on the rebellion, however, were still unsolved.

CHANGING VIRGINIA GOVERNMENTS AND SOCIETY

Berkeley was succeeded in 1679 by Thomas Lord Culpeper, who declared an amnesty to all the rebels and succeeded in restoring peace. None of the issues of the rebellion, however, was settled. Fundamentally, the outbreak had been a protest against arbitrary and oligarchical government, induced by economic depression and a conflict of interests between the frontier and the tidewater. The issues were not settled, indeed, for many years; and Culpeper went out of office without having made any effective effort to solve them. He was succeeded in 1684 by Lord Howard of Effingham. The distress of the people continued, and Lord Howard's period of office was one in which there took place a series of riots and attempts to limit the amount of tobacco produced, with the view of increasing its price, but all without success. The governor insisted upon large tobacco crops because that would mean more customs duties paid in England; but this position brought him into direct opposition with the interests of the planters, and when the governor blocked crop restriction by the legislature, the poorer planters took matters into their own hands and destroyed the growing plants, whereupon he punished them as rebels.

Lord Howard succeeded in making himself additionally unpopular in Virginia by removing from the assembly its power of hearing appeals from the lower courts. Up to this time, the assembly had acted as the highest court of appeals in the colony, but after the denial of its power by the governor this function was taken over by the governor himself, leaving the final appeal to the king. This development is significant because it meant the separation of the judiciary in Virginia from the legislative branch of government and took out of the hands of the assembly the control that it had hitherto exercised over the colony's courts. From now on the justices of the peace and the judges of the general court, appointed as they were by the governor and responsible to him, came effectively under the governor's control and served in a fairly effective manner as a check upon the legislative power. As might have been expected, the assembly and many of the leading citizens of Virginia protested to the king for restoration of the judicial power of the assembly, but the power of hearing appeals was never restored.

At about the same time, still another check upon the power of the legislature was established by the demand of the governor for a permanent income for the Crown. Hitherto the governor's salary and the expenses of government had been voted annually by the legislature. Now, about 1680, the governor demanded the right to lay a permanent tax to provide for these expenses, and thereby take control of the officials out of the hands of the legislature. The legislature demurred, but the governor threatened to raise the quit-rents and to demand their payment in specie; the result was that a compromise arrangement was arrived at whereby a permanent support was granted to the governor and his officials out of the money derived from the export duty of two shillings per hogshead levied on tobacco. This compromise made it forever impossible for the Virginia assembly to exercise such a check upon the governor of that colony as those to which the governors of Massachusetts and New York, for example, were subjected by their legislatures during the eighteenth century. The net result of these two measures was the establishment in Virginia of a system of checks and balances which left the greater measure of political power in the hands of the executive and judicial agents of the Crown, and thus made of Virginia an ideal royal province—from the point of view of British colonial administration.

Perhaps the most remarkable development in the social structure of Virginia in this period was the differentiation that was taking place between the tidewater and the Piedmont. As population increased, the newcomers to Virginia were compelled by the scarcity of lands in the tidewater to go beyond the fall line into the highlands lying between the falls and the mountains. Many of these settlers carried on the tradition of tobacco planting, but a great many others devoted their attention to the raising of livestock and the cultivation of wheat. As these were economic activities demanding intelligence and consistent effort, the settlers in the Piedmont found that slavery was somewhat less adapted to their needs than it had been in the lands of the tidewater. There resulted from this situation a society in which the farmers were owners and operators of relatively small areas of land as compared with the great tobacco plantations. In order to ship out of the country such goods as they had to sell abroad, however, it was necessary for these Piedmont planters to send their products down to the fall line where they could be placed on board sea-going ships. Thus it became necessary for them to use the wharves and the warehouses of the great planters who owned the lands along the rivers, and this circumstance placed them in a certain economic subjection to the tidewater aristocrats.

Their frontier conditions probably contributed a good deal to the democratic turn of mind of the planters in the Piedmont, and it was only natural that they should demand, as their settlements expanded, more adequate representation in the colonial legislature; but the government of Berkeley and his successors was in the hands of the great planters, and little or no reform took place until the time of Nathaniel Bacon. Even his reforms were soon nullified and forgotten. Thus it was that the men of the Piedmont found themselves at odds with the people of the tidewater on social, economic, and political grounds, and by the end of the seventeenth century Virginia was a divided province containing within its boundaries what were essentially two separate societies. But it was not until the great influx of the next century that the differentiation between frontier and tidewater reached its full effect, and it was not until the eighteenth century that the Piedmont won an adequate voice in the colony's affairs.

The second half of the seventeenth century had thus been one of economic distress, social change, and demand for political reform. None of the deep-reaching social problems involved had been settled; yet Bacon's Rebellion had demonstrated that the authority of England could be successfully resisted, and it had set a precedent of rebellion which was to be an influence in the minds of the generation of men who were to appear in Virginia after the turn of the century. The British Crown had succeeded in establishing in Virginia a government of checks and balances against the will of the Virginians; but in the struggle of political issues the Virginians had formulated a set of political principles which they passed on to the succeeding generation—the generation of George Washington, Thomas Jefferson, and James Madison.

POLITICAL CONFLICT IN MARYLAND

In the local "civil war" in Maryland in 1655 Lord Baltimore's governor William Stone had been driven from office, and a Puritan government, with William Fuller as its governor, had been inaugurated. Lord Baltimore of course protested to the government of Oliver Cromwell in England against this violation of his charter by the Puritan faction in the colony, with the result that his charter and powers were restored to him in 1658. From this time onward to the end of the century he remained the owner of the colony. But the resistance to his authority that had manifested itself in the civil war simmered on, and resulted in a long struggle of the Protestant majority of the settlers for a greater share in their government.

The restoration of Charles II to the throne of England strengthened the position of the proprietor in the colony. In 1661 he appointed his son Charles Calvert, afterward third Lord Baltimore, governor of Maryland. Charles was given almost absolute power, although he was instructed to call the assembly from time to time for advice and consent to new laws. His executive council, composed of eight men, was made up of lords of manors in Maryland, who were appointed to the council by the proprietor; these eight, supplemented by seven others, also constituted the legislative council, the upper house of the legislature. Since these barons were usually friends or relatives of the governor, and mostly, if not all, Roman Catholics, this body bore more than passing resemblance to the English House of Lords. For Maryland it was, in effect, a Roman Catholic House of Lords.

The assembly or lower house, on the other hand, was elected by the freemen of the colony, of whom the vast majority were Protestants. The lower house, therefore, found itself in almost constant opposition to the upper house, both on the grounds of religion and on the basis of political principle. For the assembly looked upon itself as a sort of House of Commons in Maryland, and about 1670 it won the recognition of its privileges and prerogatives as such. The assembly did recognize Lord Baltimore's charter as a sort of written constitution for the province, however, and generally carried its differences with the upper house no farther than debate.

The discontent with the proprietary regime reached a climax about 1676, when, after having placed a fifty-acre land-holding qualification upon the franchise, Baltimore reduced the number of members of the assembly by half. In 1681 the lower house demanded that a larger number of deputies be elected, but the demand was refused, and there ensued a deadlock. In the face of a threatened Indian war, however, the assembly gave in. But the discontent was still great and ill-contained, for the common people of the province were restless under what seemed very high taxes, their exclusion from government, and the oligarchical control exercised by the proprietary faction. The first open protest had been made in 1676, at the time of Bacon's Rebellion in Virginia, but the leaders of the protest were hanged. Another violent protest, amounting to an attempt to overthrow the proprietor's authority entirely, was made under the leadership of Josiah Fendall about 1681, but this failed, and Fendall was banished.

In 1684 Charles Calvert, now Lord Baltimore, went to England, whence he never returned to the colony. His deputy governor fell into disgrace, and for four years the colony was without an effective head. When, in 1688, Baltimore sent over William Joseph as his governor and Joseph adopted an attitude reflecting the "divine right" ideas of James II in England, the long-smoldering resistance to the proprietary came to a head. A heated and bitter controversy broke out between the governor and council on one side and the assembly on the other. Then came news of the "glorious revolution" in England, the flight of James II, and the accession of William and Mary to the English throne. The neglect of Lord Baltimore in not promptly proclaiming the new sovereigns only added to the already inflamed state of public feeling against him and his government. During the summer of 1689 the so-called Protestant Association, under the leadership of John Coode, rose in rebellion against the proprietor, seized St. Mary's and called a new assembly, one of the first acts of which was an appeal to the new rulers of England to make Maryland a royal province.

This successful rebellion was the culmination of a long period of dissatisfaction with the feudal regime of the proprietor which had its earliest expressions in the period of the Great Rebellion and the Commonwealth in England. It was in effect a protest against feudal land-holding, favoritism in government, social inequalities, inadequate protection against the Indians, and the control of politics and society by a Roman Catholic, aristocratic minority. It was not in any direct way a movement for democracy. On the contrary, it was a movement for the full rights of Englishmen which were considerably reduced by the proprietary regime. Insofar as it was a manifestation of the demand of the people of a frontier community for a share in their government and a more suitable political institution than feudalism could offer them, it did demonstrate the inadequacy of the feudal organization of society and government in the American wilderness.

The Lords of Trade, indeed, had long been considering the cancellation of Baltimore's charter, because of the troubles in the colony and the difficulty of compelling the proprietor to enforce the navigation acts. Now the appeal from the "rebels" of Maryland fell on willing ears, and the Lords recommended that the government of Maryland be taken out of the hands of the proprietor, which was done in 1691. The proprietor retained his title to the soil, but the government was taken over by the Crown, and Maryland became a royal province. The proprietary rights were, indeed, restored in 1716; but only in modified form, and the feudal system of government and society of the seventeenth century in Maryland were never again restored.

ECONOMIC AND SOCIAL PROGRESS

Despite its troubles in the political side of life, Maryland, during the second half of the seventeenth century, continued to grow. Tobacco continued to be the staple crop of the province, and the plantations multiplied along the shores of the lower Potomac and Chesapeake Bay. Foreigners were now coming in, and provision had to be made for their naturalization. Negroes were coming into the colony in increasing numbers, too, as the expanding plantations called for more and more cheap labor. By 1692 the population was probably about 30,000 souls, of whom perhaps 8,000 were Negroes.

By the end of the century, a few roads, ferries and bridges had been built. The legislature frequently passed legislation for the encouragement of commerce, and efforts were made to encourage the building of towns for the purpose of collecting the export duties on tobacco. So long as the ships could sail right up to the plantations along the shore, however, no great need for towns was felt, and St. Mary's, the capital, and the Puritan settlement at Providence (the name was changed to Annapolis in 1696) remained the only towns worthy of the name. The plantations were raising 50,000 hogsheads of tobacco per year, which meant an income of perhaps £100,000 per annum for the colony. The proprietor, too, was beginning to reap the profits anticipated by Sir George Calvert. For he was receiving some £5,000 per year from his tax on tobacco, port dues from the ships entering and leaving the colony, quit-rents of two shillings for each hundred acres of land, and fees received from the execution of legal documents. In all, the proprietor probably received some £12,000 per year from his palatinate, out of which he had to pay his governor and certain other officers, which left him perhaps £5,000 per year—with the value of perhaps ten times as much in modern money.

In Maryland, as in Virginia and the West Indies, there was some grumbling over the effect of the navigation acts. For Maryland, like these other colonies, had enjoyed a considerable measure of free trade, especially in the period of the English civil war. After the passage of the act of 1660, whether because of the effect of the act or because of a glutting of the world market, there was a serious decline in the price of tobacco, and the legislature was asked to pass a law to prohibit the planting of tobacco for one year in the hope of raising prices. The legislature, representing the lesser planters, refused to pass the desired legislation and the proprietor disapproved the project, much to the chagrin of Virginia, which had hoped for the effective cooperation of Maryland in a similar move. More important for the subsequent history of the colony, perhaps, was the conflict of jurisdictions arising from the fact that the Maryland charter had given the proprietor of the colony so much power. For the question arose as to whether the customs collectors for the Crown or those employed by the proprietor should collect the duties on trade imposed by the navigation acts. The proprietor claimed the collection should be made by his officials; but his insistence on the point showed a lack of realization of the importance the colonial revenues were coming to have to the Crown, and resulted in a move to deprive him of his charter. The same fatal error had been made by Massachusetts, with the same fatal result.

RECOMMENDED BOOKS FOR FURTHER READING

CONTEMPORARY NARRATIVES

Charles M. Andrews, ed., *Narratives of the Insurrections, 1675-1690,* pp. 3-164, 301-401.

Charles Deane, ed., *The History of Bacon's . . . Rebellion.*

Peter Force, ed., "The Beginning, Progress, and Conclusion of Bacon's Rebellion in Virginia . . . 1675 and 1676" in *Tracts and Other Papers,* I, No. 8.

Charles H. Lincoln, ed., *Narratives of the Indian Wars, 1675-1699,* pp. 1-168.

MODERN ACCOUNTS

Matthew P. Andrews, *The Founding of Maryland,* Chapters 13-15.

James C. Ballagh, *White Servitude in the Colony of Virginia.*

Philip A. Bruce, *The Institutional History of Virginia in the Seventeenth Century.*

Philip A. Bruce, *Social Life of Virginia in the Seventeenth Century.*

Philip A. Bruce, *The Virginia Plutarch.*

Edward Channing, *A History of.the United States,* II, Chapter 3.

William E. Dodd, *The Old South.* Volume I: *Struggles for Democracy,* Chapters 9-10, 12.

John Johnson, *Old Maryland Manors.*

Eugene I. McCormac, *White Servitude in Maryand, 1634-1820.*

Newton D. Mereness, *Maryland as a Proprietary Province.*

Herbert L. Osgood, *The American Colonies in the Seventeenth Century,* II, Part III, Chapters 3-4.

Mary N. Stanard, *The Story of Bacon's Rebellion.*

Thomas J. Wertenbaker, *Patrician and Plebeian in Virginia.*

Thomas J. Wertenbaker, *The Planters of Colonial Virginia.*

Thomas J. Wertenbaker, *Torchbearer of the Revolution.*

Thomas J. Wertenbaker, *Virginia under the Stuarts, 1607-1688.*

19

The Breaking of Rebellious New England

CHARTERS FOR CONNECTICUT AND RHODE ISLAND

UPON the accession of Charles II, Connecticut and Rhode Island, the first of which held no charter and the second of which held a charter only from the parliamentary government of England, had to secure royal confirmation of their legal existence. As a result of its application for royal approval, Connecticut was granted in 1662 a charter which established the colonial boundaries of Connecticut as the southern line of Massachusetts and Narragansett Bay, and included in the colony all the land to the westward as far as the South Sea. This charter obviously included the Dutch colony of New Netherland, but was superseded a year later by the grant to the Duke of York which included all the territory from the Connecticut River to the Delaware. Thus the Connecticut charter of 1662 included the old colony of New Haven, part of the land claimed by Rhode Island, and all the land claimed by the Dutch; it was soon to involve the colony of Connecticut in a quarrel with the Duke of York over the land between the Connecticut and the Hudson. With the granting of this charter, the colony of New Haven ceased to exist as a separate colonial establishment.

Under Connecticut's new charter the Crown recognized the existing Connecticut government. That is, the government of Connecticut was recognized as being composed of a governor and council elected by the assembly, and an assembly elected by the freemen. In thus recognizing the established form of government in Connecticut, King Charles II gave official sanction to a set of political institutions which were perhaps the furthest of all those among the colonies in America from the British ideal of royal control; for no single official in this colony was more than technically responsible to the king; they were responsible, rather, to the governor or to the assembly, and it was not long before England came to realize that it had made a mistake in granting the colony so much freedom.

Early in 1663 a charter was issued to the colony of Rhode Island which gave official confirmation to the political organization of that colony that had been evolved under the charter of 1644. The

boundaries of Rhode Island were defined as including the land between a line drawn three miles east of Narragansett Bay, the
southern boundary of Massachusetts and the "Narragansett" River.
There immediately ensued a dispute with Connecticut as to what
the boundaries between Rhode Island and that colony should be,
but it was finally agreed that the Pawcatuck River should be considered the Narragansett for the purposes of the two charters. The
most significant provision of the new charter, however, was the official recognition and confirmation, by the Anglican government of
Charles II, of the colony's "livelie experiment" in religious tolerance. For the charter excused Rhode Island from any responsibility
to Anglicanism and embodied what amounted to a constitutional
guarantee of "full libertie in religious concernements."

REFRACTORY MASSACHUSETTS

The granting of these charters to Connecticut and Rhode Island
is a surprising exhibition of liberalism on the part of the Restoration government, at a time when the general tendency of colonial
policy was in the opposite direction. For the advisers of Charles II
were gradually coming to the conviction that the American colonies
should be given not more self-government, but less. This tendency
has already been noted in the establishment of royal provinces in
the West Indies during this period. It is true that in the same year
in which the charter to Rhode Island was issued, Carolina was
granted to eight proprietors, and New York was granted to the
Duke of York, under terms which did not differ essentially from
those of the grant of Maryland to Lord Baltimore. When the charter
to William Penn was issued, however, only some seventeen years
later, many conditions and restrictions upon his authority were
written into the document in such a way that the control of the
Crown over Pennsylvania was potentially much greater than was
the case in either Maryland, Carolina, or New York.

It was as a part of this gradually evolving policy of control that
the Crown sent to New England in 1664 a commission to investigate complaints that had been received in England relative to the
independent tendencies of the New England colonies, and particularly the province of Massachusetts Bay. These commissioners were
well received in Rhode Island and Connecticut because those colonies thought it prudent; but they were badly received in Massachusetts, and every obstacle was placed in the way of their getting
the information that they desired.

Massachusetts, indeed, had long been a thorn in the side of British colonial administration. The colony had successfully refused to surrender its charter upon demand in 1637; and during the civil war and the Commonwealth period, while its sympathies were clearly on the side of the parliamentary party, the colony had coolly stood aloof from the civil war and from the European entanglements of England. It had even gone so far as to pass a law practically nullifying the Navigation Act of 1651 so far as Massachusetts was concerned. Now, after the Restoration, the independent attitude of the colony continued, and complaints began to come in to the colonial administration that the colony was not obeying the Navigation Act of 1660. Further, the dissidents in the colony seized upon the Restoration as an occasion to complain about the arbitrary administration of justice, the religious persecution of Quakers and others not in sympathy with the New England way, and the exclusion of Anglicans and others from participation in political affairs. It was largely because of these complaints, and particularly because of the reported refusal of the colony to obey the Navigation Act of 1660, that the royal commission of 1664 was sent to Massachusetts. As might have been expected, their report was unfavorable to the colony. It concluded that Massachusetts had assumed an attitude of practical independence of the British government, that it had violated the rights of Englishmen in refusing participation in politics on religious grounds, that it was violating and actually defying the navigation acts, and that in general it had become an economic competitor with old England. The colony was summoned to send agents to England to explain its apparent independence, but the demand was evaded. After the creation of the Lords of Trade in 1675, Edward Randolph was sent to Massachusetts as the agent of that body, and he proceeded to send in a series of reports that steadily increased the antagonism between the mother country and her erring Massachusetts daughter.

KING PHILIP'S WAR

Randolph arrived in New England just about the time when Massachusetts—as, indeed, all New England—was entering one of the greatest crises in its history. For it was in 1675 that the greatest of all New England wars, known as King Philip's War, broke out along the New England frontier from Maine to Connecticut.

From the vantage point of the twentieth century, this conflict appears to have been inevitable. The English had settled all along the coast from the Kennebec to the Hudson and they had slowly pushed their way back inland up the rivers and into the forests until in many places they completely surrounded the remaining Indians and in other places they had pushed them back far inland. In this process they had taken the Indian lands. In many cases they had "bought" those lands, to be sure; but the Indians had hardly realized that they had signed contracts to surrender to the white men the hunting grounds upon which their very existence depended, for wherever the white men went and settled, the wild animals disappeared and it was upon these animals that the Indian depended both for his food supply and for the skins that were his chief commodity in trade. But the English added insult to injury, for they were arrogant and domineering and treated the Indians as inferiors; they attempted to rule the savages and even, on occasion, to tax them. The old chief Massasoit, who had supplied food to Plymouth and made peace with the Pilgrims in 1621, died in 1661 and was succeeded as king of the Wampanoags by his son Philip. King Philip was a friend of the colonists, but he could not stand the arrogance of the English; when he was forced to acknowledge himself an English subject by the government of Plymouth, and when, finally, in 1671 he was required to pay tribute to that colony, his patience with the white men came to an end. From this time on, relations with the Indians went from bad to worse, but the Englishmen failed to see the danger inherent in the Indian situation and when the final outbreak came it found them unprepared. Even then, many of their leaders failed to see that this was the result of their own economic expansion, and attributed the disaster to the wrath of God over their having allowed Quakers to remain among them, or because they had indulged in the "conceit" of wearing wigs.

In June, 1675, the Indians fell upon the town of Swansea; then the Puritans of Boston and Plymouth marched against them. There followed several years of ghastly warfare. Towns along the frontier were attacked, and such places as Deerfield, Northfield, and Springfield were ravaged and burned. Practically all the Indians of New England took part in King Philip's War, from the hitherto friendly Narragansetts of Rhode Island to the bloody and ardently antagonistic Abenaki Indians of Maine. All along the frontier, houses and towns were burned and the settlers were killed. In Massachusetts and Maine, whole towns were wiped out and abandoned, and the frontier of settlement retreated in some cases many miles back toward the older and more easily defensible English establishments.

The real end of the conflict came in Massachusetts with the death of Philip in 1676, although the fighting continued for two years longer along the frontier in Maine. In the meantime, several Indian strongholds, as well as many of the towns of the whites, had been wiped out with men, women, and children. One man out of every sixteen in the white population was said to have been killed in the course of the war.

It was of course inevitable that the white men should win, because they outnumbered the Indians by about four to one. Further, they had the advantage of the more effective organization and greater consistency of purpose, and they had the tremendous backing of a now well-established community along the seaboard. In the face of the irrepressible expansiveness of the superior civilization of the whites, the Indians could not hope for long to maintain their hold upon their lands. The phenomenon that was manifesting itself in King Philip's War, as in the earlier Pequot War, was simply the triumph of a stronger, more closely knit, and more efficient and more advanced culture over a more primitive civilization that stood in its way. The Puritans interpreted their victory as a manifestation of the favor of God toward their enterprises. In a more objective view, the victory of the English is to be taken more or less as a matter of course in the history of British expansion.

MASSACHUSETTS LOSES HER CHARTER

In June, 1676, two months before the death of King Philip, Edward Randolph—agent extraordinary of the Lords of Trade, collector of customs, searcher of records, and investigator generally of New England affairs—landed at the port of Boston. The old complaints against Massachusetts Bay still existed, but two things had happened to increase the purpose of the king and council to bring Massachusetts Bay to a sense of its responsibilities. In the first place, the law offices of the Crown, in May, 1675, had given an opinion that the claims of the heirs of George Mason to New Hampshire and those of Ferdinando Gorges to Maine were valid and that, therefore, the assumption of government over these territories by the province of Massachusetts was illegal and unfounded. The other and more important event had been the passage of the so-called Plantations Duties Act of 1673. Massachusetts disobeyed this law, as it had disobeyed the navigation acts that had preceded it. The act had been passed, indeed, to close the legal gaps which permitted sea captains to evade the provisions of the act of 1660 with regard to the enumerated articles, and in these evasions the Massachusetts shippers were perhaps the worst offenders. New England produced none of the enumerated articles itself, but New Englanders did carry them directly to the continent of Europe from the other colonies, and the New England vessels returned directly to the colonies without stopping in England, which was a violation of the Staple Act of 1663.

Randolph came to Massachusetts already prejudiced against that province, and Massachusetts cordially hated him. The council received him coldly, and when he called the attention of the governor to several ships that had arrived direct from Europe in violation of the Staple Act, the governor coolly replied that laws made by the king and Parliament did not apply to New England. Randolph made a tour of New England and returned to England, where he handed in a report that was very unfavorable to Massachusetts. The king then again summoned the colony to appoint agents to present the colony's case in the face of Randolph's charges, but Massachusetts merely wrote an answer to the king's letter without appointing any agents.

Randolph's report pointed out the insubordination of New England and the danger of Massachusetts' consistent violation of the navigation acts to the whole imperial structure; for evidently, if Massachusetts were to go on nullifying the navigation acts at will, their whole purpose would be defeated and England would have in one of its own colonies a competitor that would be more dangerous to English economic life than even the Dutch or the Spanish had been.

The conflict between mother country and colony was rapidly approaching a climax and Massachusetts finally decided to send two agents, William Stoughton and Peter Bulkeley, who arrived in England in January, 1677. There they were confronted by the charges of Randolph, who directly recommended that the Massachusetts charter be annulled and that Massachusetts be made into a royal province. The Massachusetts agents, on their side, limited by their instructions, were unable to do more than attempt an evasion of the issue, and Massachusetts was condemned and rebuked for its spirit of independence and the passage of laws by the colony which were repugnant to the laws of England. But the colony continued to quibble and evade the issue, again asserting that laws made in England did not apply in Massachusetts and that, as the province was not represented in Parliament, it could not be held subject to the navigation acts. The Massachusetts general court did, however, condescend to re-enact the navigation acts in Massachusetts so so as to make them applicable to Massachusetts citizens. Obviously, to have accepted this argument of the province would have been tantamount to a recognition of complete legislative autonomy in the province of Massachusetts Bay. It would have been the acceptance of a situation in the empire which did not become a reality for another two hundred years. Naturally enough, the Massachusetts attitude only goaded the Lords of Trade into a further determination to reduce the province to a position of due obedience.

The colony persisted in its resistance, and Randolph, back in Massachusetts now as a revenue officer, continued to send in reports of Puritan intransigency and nullification of the navigation system. His complaint was threefold—Massachusetts continued to trade directly with foreign countries; the magistrates and the people connived in this illicit trade, making it impossible to get judgments in the courts because the juries always favored the accused; and, finally, the colony had taken matters under its own control by the erection in 1681 of a naval and customs office of its own, taking the revenue for itself instead of sending this revenue to the Crown.

Thus it came about that in 1683, in complete disgust, the Lords of Trade started legal proceedings against the Massachusetts Bay charter, and on October 23, 1684, the Court of Chancery declared the Massachusetts charter forfeit. At the same time, and for similar reasons, proceedings were begun against the charters of Connecticut and Rhode Island, and they, too, were annulled in 1686 and 1687 respectively.

THE DOMINION OF NEW ENGLAND

In the meantime, New Hampshire had been separated from Massachusetts in 1679 and set up as a royal province on the plan of the colony of Virginia. Now, Massachusetts had lost its own charter and a large part of the land it had formerly controlled. It seemed to be a foregone conclusion that Massachusetts itself would become a royal province. Charles II died, however, in 1685, and was succeeded by his brother, James, who had ideas of his own as to what the relationship between the colonies and the mother country should be. In its contest with the mother country Massachusetts, and along with it the other New England colonies, had fought a losing battle, but it should be remembered that there was more to the struggle than merely the desire of these colonies to be free; for New England more than any other section of the British empire had developed along lines of economic interest which brought it into conflict with the mother country. New England had no important staple commodity for export except fish. It did, indeed, export many other things, but the great economic progress of the New Englanders was derived from their business as carriers of the products of other parts of the empire. By the end of the seventeenth century, New Englanders were carrying fish to the West Indies and sugar to England. They carried tobacco and rice from the southern continental colonies to England and to Europe, and in return for all these commodities they brought back to America cargoes of manufactured goods. They sold their fish to the Catholic countries of southern Europe and took in return fruits and wines which they distributed along with manufactured goods to the southern and middle colonies, and even to the planters of the West Indies. Some of their sugar they brought to New England and manufactured it into rum, which they then used as a medium of exchange which they gave in return for the "black ivory" from the Slave Coasts of Africa, which they in turn sold to the sugar planters of the Caribbean. The New Englanders, in short, were building their wealth and their civilization upon commerce. As carriers they were the competitors of the English merchant marine, and Boston, the great metropolis of New England, was becoming a rival, so far as the empire was concerned, of London itself, and the merchants of Boston were in a large degree the competitors of the merchants of London.

As merchants and as carriers of imperial commerce, it was to the interest of the New Englanders to insist upon complete freedom of trade. It was to their interest, more than to that, perhaps, of any other part of the empire, to be able to take their cargoes to the most profitable markets, and to buy the commodities that they peddled along the Atlantic seaboard where they could be most cheaply had. It was no accident, therefore, that they were prepared to go to almost any length in their opposition to a series of navigation laws passed by the British Parliament that was calculated to restrain and limit rather than to promote the economic prosperity of New England. Conflict over the navigation acts was thus basically an economic conflict, and the loss by Massachusetts of her charter is in a sense one of the political evidences that England and its merchants were now determined that every penny of profit that could be wrung out of the colonies should be directed into the coffers of the London counting-houses.

King James II ascended the throne of England with pretty definite ideas about the position of the Crown in England as well as in the empire. He was already the proprietor of Maine and New York under his charter of 1664, and he was intrigued by the idea that the provinces of New England, for better administration and control, might be united into one great "dominion." It was for this reason, therefore, that in 1686 Sir Edmund Andros, erstwhile governor of the province of New York, was sent to Boston as its governor. The Dominion of New England was to include New York and New Jersey, Connecticut, Rhode Island, Massachusetts, New Hampshire, and the territory of Maine. They were all united under one governor, but a lieutenant-governor, Francis Nicholson, was sent to New York to govern there as the representative of the governor of the Dominion.

For the time being Andros was empowered to govern the dominion without a representative legislature. He was given an appointed council, and this council assumed the right not only to make laws but to impose taxes. As might have been expected, the people of New England, and particularly Massachusetts, resisted—unsuccessfully—the attempt of Andros to tax them without the consent of their representatives. An opposition to this arbitrary establishment smoldered throughout the New England colonies.

Fire was heaped upon the heads of the Puritan oligarchy, too, when the royal governor insisted not only upon the establishment of an Anglican church in Boston but in actually using the building of the Boston church for the conduct of Anglican services. Further, the Anglicans who came to New England with Andros began to celebrate Christmas, a holiday which had been discarded by the Puritans as smacking of popery, and even went so far as to erect a maypole, hated symbol of a happy, worldly England, upon the Boston common!

It was on many grounds, therefore, that the New Englanders felt themselves aggrieved at the government of Sir Edmund Andros, and it is not surprising that, when news arrived in Boston of the successful consummation of the Glorious Revolution of 1688, the Massachusetts leaders arrested Andros and packed him off to England, or that they established in the province an assembly which governed it temporarily until the pleasure of the new king, William III, should be known. At the same time, Connecticut and Rhode Island quietly resumed their old institutions as though their charters had never been annulled, and New Hampshire proceeded as though the Dominion of New England had never been. A new charter for Massachusetts was issued in 1691, but this new frame of government opens a new era in Massachusetts history, and that era must be left for a later story.

RECOMMENDED BOOKS FOR FURTHER READING

CONTEMPORARY NARRATIVES

Charles M. Andrews, ed., *Narratives of the Insurrections, 1675-1690*, pp. 167-297.

Benjamin Church, *The Entertaining History of King Philip's War.*

Charles H. Lincoln, ed., *Narratives of the Indian Wars, 1675-1699*, pp. 1-168.

Edward Randolph, *Edward Randolph; including his Letters and Official Papers, 1676-1703*, edited by Robert N. Toppan and Alfred T. S. Goodrick.

Mary W. Rowlandson, *Narrative of the Captivity and Restoration of Mrs. Mary Rowlandson.*

MODERN ACCOUNTS

James T. Adams, *The Founding of New England*, Chapters 11-17.

Viola F. Barnes, *The Dominion of New England.*

Edward Channing, *A History of the United States*, II, Chapters 3, 5-6.

George W. Ellis and John E. Morris, *King Philip's War.*

Everett Kimball, *The Public Life of Joseph Dudley*, Chapters 1-3.

Kenneth B. Murdock, *Increase Mather, the Foremost American Puritan.*

Herbert L. Osgood, *The American Colonies in the Seventeenth Century*, II, Chapters 3-4; III, Chapters 10-12.

Ralph D. Paine, *The Ships and Sailors of Old Salem*, Chapters 1-3.

James D. Phillips, *Salem in the Seventeenth Century*, Chapters 18-24.

William B. Weeden, *Economic and Social History of New England*, Volume I.

Justin Winsor, ed., *The Memorial History of Boston*, II, Chapter 1.

20

The Founding of Carolina

IN APRIL, 1663, King Charles II issued a charter to eight of his land-hungry courtiers which gave them the princely domain of Carolina. Two years earlier he had taken over Jamaica as a royal province, and the preceding year he had approved a charter for Connecticut. Three months after the charter for Carolina he approved a new charter for Rhode Island, and one year later he gave the conquered New Netherland to his brother, the Duke of York, as a proprietary province, and sent a royal commission to New England to attempt to bring that wayward region to a greater subservience to England's motherly control. In 1670 the Hudson's Bay Company was organized to exploit the Hudson Bay fur trade, and Charles granted the Bahamas to a group of proprietors who were closely associated with the proprietors of Carolina. In 1672 and 1673 Barbados and the Leeward Islands became royal provinces.

The creation of Carolina was thus no isolated event. It came, rather, in the midst of a decade or more of great colonial activity, in which the expansion of the British empire included not only the formulation of policy in the form of imperial constitutions and imperial commercial regulation already reviewed, but also the annexation of such foreign territories as Jamaica, Acadia (returned to France in 1670) and New Netherland and the colonization of the remaining unoccupied areas along the coast of the continent.

CAROLINA

The greatest single unoccupied space on the continent was that lying between the English settlements in Virginia and Spanish Florida. As early as 1629 the attention of British colonizers had turned to this area and Sir Robert Heath had been given a grant to this territory under the name of Carolina. But Heath had done nothing to settle his grant, and, aside from the few people who had moved into the country from Virginia, the area between Virginia and Florida remained vacant.

To this land, as a matter of fact, Spain had a much better claim than England. For the Spaniards, after having chased out the French heretics in 1665, had extended a line of missions along the coast, which they called Guale, as far north at least as St. Elena. Spain had protested the settlement of Roanoke Island by Sir Walter Raleigh in 1685-87, and the Virginia Company's colony at Jamestown in 1607. But her protests were ignored, and her threats of annihilation were never carried out. Nevertheless, the Spanish claim to the territory, at least south of Cape Fear, was based on actual occupation, and it was only in 1661, just two years before Charles II's first grant to the Carolina proprietors, that the Spanish missions of St. Elena and Port Royal were raided by a fierce northern tribe of Indians and the Spanish mission frontier retreated southward to the mouth of the Santa Ana River. The Spanish occupation, when the first colonists came to Charleston in 1670, was then actually effective only south of the Savannah; nevertheless, on the basis of the principle of effective occupation, the Spanish title to the whole region south of Cape Fear was obviously much better than that of England. The Spaniards regarded the English occupation of Carolina, therefore, as a trespass upon Spanish soil, and it was only in the face of the threat of war with France that Spain was willing, in 1670, to sign the treaty of Madrid which recognized for the first time on the part of Spain all the existing English settlements in the new world and conceded to England the ownership of the coast even as far south as Charleston and the island of Jamaica.

THE CAROLINA PROPRIETORS AND THEIR TWO INFANT COLONIES

The moving spirits in the settlement of Carolina were John Colleton, a former Barbados planter who realized the social revolution then going on in that colony and the possibilities of populating a new colony with emigres from the West Indies, Anthony Ashley Cooper, and Sir William Berkeley, governor of Virginia. These men and their associates hoped to found in the vacant territory south of Virginia a colony in which they would hold large and remunerative landed estates and from which they would derive quantities of silks, wine, and fruit, which would not only be profitable to themselves, but would relieve England from the necessity of buying these commodities in the countries of southern Europe. Realizing the need of influence at court, these promoters invited a number of distinguished men to share with them in their project; with the result that the Earl of Clarendon, the Earl of Albemarle, Sir John Berkeley, Sir George Carteret, and the Earl of Craven, together with the three mentioned above, formed a group of eight proprietors who received from the king on March 24, 1663, a feudal grant to the land south of Virginia, henceforth, in honor of the king, to be known as Carolina.

This charter was fashioned after that of Maryland, using the Bishopric of Durham as the pattern for the new "palatinate." To begin with, the proprietors were given all the land lying between the thirty-first degree and the line of 36° 30' north latitude, and stretching across the continent from sea to sea. The Spanish claims to this area were ignored, and in 1665 the charter was revised to move the southern boundary southward to the twenty-ninth degree, thus taking in the Spanish town of St. Augustine. Within this vast area the proprietors were given the power to erect churches, and to make laws, "with the advice, assent and approbation of the Freemen of the said Province," or their representatives, whom the proprietors were required to call together as occasion might demand. The proprietors were encouraged to produce in their colony wines, silks, olives, and other semi-tropical products, by an exemption of such commodities produced in the colony from the usual customs duties in England for a period of seven years. Since monarchy and aristocracy were again in style in England, the proprietors were given the power to create an aristocracy in the colony—so long as they created no title of nobility which would be the same as any in England. As governors they were empowered to erect forts, maintain armies, appoint officials and incorporate towns. Finally, they were authorized to grant to their colonists such religious toleration as they might see fit to do—and for all this domain and these princely powers they were merely to pay to the king twenty marks yearly, at the Feast of All Saints, plus one-fourth of all the gold and silver to be mined in the colony.

The first expedition to Carolina was organized in New England, and went to the mouth of the Cape Fear River in 1663. This group, however, discouraged by the hardships of colonizing a new country and by the apparent barrenness of the soil, gave up the effort and returned to New England and others of the older colonies. Another group of migrants was organized in Barbados. This expedition, composed largely of victims of the social revolution going on in Barbados by reasons of the growth of large sugar plantations, left Barbados in October, 1665, under Sir John Yeamans. It, too, went to the mouth of the Cape Fear River, where the colonists made a settlement they called "Charles Town." But they were disturbed by fierce storms that destroyed much of their equipment, and discontent arose over the barrenness of the soil. A number of the settlers deserted the settlement and went overland to Virginia, after which

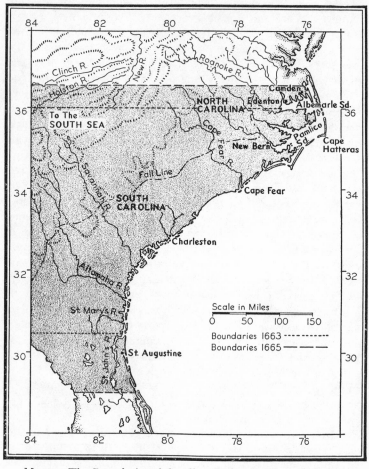

MAP 11. The Boundaries of Carolina Under the Charter of 1665

NOTE: Because of the inaccuracy of geographic knowledge in the seventeenth century and the vagueness of the language of the charter itself, the boundaries shown on this map must be considered only approximately accurate.

the movement became general. Some of the settlers went to New England, some to Virginia, some to the settlements that had appeared along the shores of Albemarle Sound, and others went to Barbados. By the end of 1667 the Cape Fear settlement was again deserted.

It was at this juncture, after four years of discouragement, that

Anthony Cooper began to assume the leadership of the proprietors, aided by his friend John Locke. A new effort was determined upon, and this time the nucleus of the colonists came from England itself, although others came from Barbados and Bermuda. This expedition arrived, after much delay and exploration, at the mouth of the Kiawah or Ashley River in the spring of 1670. Here, on the south side of the river some sixty-five miles from its mouth, they began their new settlement, which they, also, called Charles Town (Charleston).

Meanwhile, along the shores of Albemarle Sound, in the northern part of the Carolina grant, a number of settlements and scattered farms had already appeared. The movement of population into this area from Virginia had begun, indeed, before the issuance of the Carolina charter, and probably as early as 1653. These people, "squatters" on the land, had begun to raise tobacco, following the example of Virginia; but they also found it profitable to grow Indian corn and livestock, which they sold to their neighbors to the northward. Thus it came about that Sir William Berkeley, returning to Virginia in the year 1664 after participating in the business of launching the Carolina project, received instructions to take charge of the Albemarle settlements. This he did by appointing William Drummond governor of the area, which was called the province of Albemarle. This region, the nucleus of the later North Carolina, was thus already permanently established five years before the settlement of Charleston on the shore of the Ashley River. It was never to be as prosperous, however, as its southern sister.

JOHN LOCKE'S FUNDAMENTAL CONSTITUTIONS OF CAROLINA

Upon receipt of their charter, the proprietors set about finding ways and means of attracting colonists. One means employed was that of promising a liberal government, and to this end a document known as the "Concession and Agreement" was worked out for publication. Although this document had little effect upon the history of Carolina, it was actually used in New Jersey, as noted later. When John Locke and Anthony Cooper became the dominating spirits in the Carolina enterprise, they formulated a new political frame for the colony, known as the "Fundamental Constitutions of Carolina"—one of the most fantastic constitutions in the entire history of British colonization.

The "Fundamental Constitutions of Carolina" are notable for

their ideas with regard to society and government in a frontier country. To begin with, it was expected that the society of Carolina would be an aristocratic society based upon land ownership, "since all power and dominion is most naturally founded on property." The authors of the document, therefore, sought to balance the ownership of the land between the hereditary nobility and the lesser freeholders; thus two-fifths of the land was assigned to the nobility and three-fifths to the manorial lords and the commoners. These theorizers were afraid both of a top-heavy aristocracy and a "numerous democracy."

In elaborating their proposed scheme of things they provided that the eight proprietors should have the rank of "seignors" with an estate of twelve thousand acres each in every county. Next to them in rank were to stand the "landgraves," and each landgrave was to have four baronies each, or a total of forty-eight thousand acres. The "caciques" were to have twenty-four thousand acres of land each. The "commoners" were divided into two groups, first the lords of the manors who were expected to have from three thousand to twelve thousand acres of land, and the freeholders who were expected to own at least fifty acres each, on the principle that "every man who is Empowered to dispose of Property and Estate of others, should have a Property of his owne."

The highest organ of government for the colony was to consist of the eight proprietors themselves, who were expected to act as a body in the government of the colony. Each proprietor was to have a resounding title, the eldest was to be known as the Lord Palatine. Others were to be called the Lord High Admiral, the Lord High Chamberlain, the Lord Chancellor, the Lord Constable, the Lord Chief Justice, and the Lord Steward; acting together, this body was to be known as the Palatine Court and might disallow laws made in the colony as well as hear appeals from the colonial courts. In the colony itself there was to be a governor appointed by the Palatine Court. He was to be assisted by an assembly, a single legislative house, and a grand council of fifty which was expected to propose laws to the assembly for acceptance or rejection. The assembly was to be composed of the governor, eight deputies of the proprietors, all the landgraves and caciques in the province, and the elected deputies of the freemen. As originally conceived, the assembly was not expected to formulate legislation but only to accept or reject laws proposed to it by the Grand Council.

Under the fundamental constitutions, finally, there was provided a system of local courts with grand and petit juries. But it was provided, curiously enough, that no man could plead before any court for money—a provision that reflects the current prejudice among the proprietors against members of the legal fraternity. This constitution never became a working part of the colony, for the colony was a frontier society and hardly to be expected to accept any such fantastic arrangements for its government. Yet certain parts of it were actually put into operation. The Palatine Court was established and actually interfered in the legislative history of the colony; delegates of the proprietors did actually sit in the colonial assembly, and titles of "landgrave" and "cacique" were granted in the colony, constituting a hereditary nobility with the right to sit in the council of the governor. A few seignories were also granted; but the practical effect of the creation of the landed aristocracy was merely the creation of large plantations in the hands of a favored few. The fundamental constitutions are important, also, not only because of the effect of this particular brand of political theory upon the colonial history of America but also because it became the basis of a series of attempts to impose this form of government upon an unwilling colony. As such, its chief effect was to stir up the colonists to demand an increasing share in the management of their government, and, eventually, to ask that Carolina be taken out of the hands of the proprietors and made a royal province.

SOUTH CAROLINA

The colonists sent to Carolina by the proprietors in 1669 arrived, after various vicissitudes of fortune, in Charleston harbor at the mouth of the Ashley River (so named for Lord Shaftesbury) in April, 1670. The first settlement was located on the south side of the river but was eventually moved over to the peninsula between the two rivers and this place later became the city of Charleston. The climate was salubrious, the harbor was good, and the confluence of the two rivers made the little peninsula on which this village was located the natural market for the produce of the farms established along the rivers. The town grew from the very first, although not without hunger and hard work, so that in two years its population was estimated at 400. It was in 1679 that a town was laid out on the peninsula and the colony moved over to that place. It was about the same time that a number of Huguenots, driven out of France by the persecutions of Louis XIV, came to Charleston, where they were encouraged to try their hand at the cultivation of silk. Charleston, as a matter of fact, very early took on a rather cosmopolitan character, with settlers from New England, Barbados, and France. By 1683 a number of Scotsmen had come to Port Royal, farther down the coast, and numerous Germans had settled at points along the rivers inland.

Very few people, indeed, came from England to the new colony; for by this time interest in emigration from England had practically ceased and mercantilist thinking with regard to colonization had now veered round to a point where it was considered undesirable for the inhabitants of England to emigrate because to do so would weaken the manpower and the economic productiveness of the mother country. It was desired, rather, that inhabitants of the new colony might be drawn either from foreign countries or from the older colonies in America. Despite this fact, however, the population of the colony grew fairly rapidly, so that by 1690 there were settlements up and down the coast from Cape Fear to Port Royal and inland as far as the trading post which later came to be known as Augusta.

Economically, the colonists were not long in finding the bases for success. They early turned their attention to the production of corn, dairy products, livestock, and naval stores. About 1690 rice made its appearance in the colony, particularly along the tidal streams and marshes of the coast lands, and it was not long thereafter before rice came to be the chief staple commodity of South Carolina as tobacco had become the staple of Virginia. At the same time the Indian traders from Charleston had made their way into the Piedmont and beyond, and there had sprung up a flourishing trade in deerskins which gave the colony another important commodity for commercial exchange.

It was in the pursuit of this Indian trade that the Carolinas came into contact with the French; for Robert Cavelier de la Salle had reached the mouth of the Mississippi from Canada in 1682, twelve years after the founding of Charleston, and shortly thereafter the French had begun to trade in the regions along the lower Mississippi and in the valleys of the Alabama River system. The more active conflicts growing out of this rivalry for the Indian trade of the gulf coastal plain belong to a later story, but already, within two decades of its founding, southern Carolina had become a frontier outpost threatened by the Spaniards from St. Augustine and rapidly coming into irritating contact with the French of the Mississippi valley.

The colony was governed by an arrangement that was something of a compromise between the scheme laid down in the Fundamental

Constitutions and the customary plan of representative government existing in such colonies as Maryland. Very soon after the founding of Charleston, indeed, the people had demanded an assembly. The first governor was William Sayle, who came to the colony from Bermuda, and he was at first aided by a council of whom five were appointed and five elected; but the demand for an assembly would not be hushed, and in the summer of 1671 the first "parliament" was held and thereafter met biennially. Legislation, however, originated in the "Grand Council" and the assembly simply approved or rejected laws which were suggested to it. The assembly, as a matter of fact, was in almost constant conflict with the proprietors, who repeatedly attempted to institute a regime more in accord with the fundamental constitutions. The result was that the end of the century found an increasing demand for the overthrow of the proprietary regime entirely.

NORTH CAROLINA

By the turn of the century the two parts of Carolina, north and south, had become rather clearly differentiated from each other. The original settlers of North Carolina had been stragglers from Virginia in search of free land who settled along the waters of Albemarle Sound during the governorship of Sir William Berkeley. When Carolina was granted to the proprietors in 1663, William sent William Drummond into this Carolina settlement to institute a government, which he did in the form of a council composed of eight deputies appointed by the eight proprietors and an assembly made up of sixteen representatives elected by the colonists. Right from the first, however, society in North Carolina was of a radical, experimental sort. The people were extremely poor and demanded entire freedom from taxation and from proceedings against inhabitants of the colony for debts that they owed outside the colony.

This was an easy-going society composed in large measure of broken and troublesome men. Piracy and illicit trade flourished; and in 1676 when an attempt was made to enforce order there took place a small rebellion which forced the governor and the officials into an effective compromise with the customary social institutions of the people. Under Governor Seth Sothel, graft, iniquity, and disorder were largely banished after 1688 and the colony gradually became more orderly. Its separate status was effectively recognized in 1691 with the appointment of a separate governor for "North Carolina."

In their economic life the settlers along Albemarle and Pamlico sounds turned their attention to the raising of foodstuffs, the manufacture of naval stores, the raising of tobacco and livestock, and the conduct of illicit trade and piracy. But the most remarkable thing, perhaps, about the history of the two Carolinas in the seventeenth century is the marked differentiation which took place between these two groups of settlements which were so close together. The southern colony became, almost from the first, a society based upon commerce and the cultivation of rice. It became an orderly, conservative, aristocratic, but cosmopolitan society. The northern settlements, by contrast, were composed of poor men, small landowners who were fiercely attached to the principles of individualism and liberty—because, it may be, of the nature of their economic pursuits. Of considerable significance, also, is the fact that, as already noted, these two colonies were not settled by Englishmen from England but rather from the older colonies and from foreign countries; they were, in a very real sense, "the first fruit of the expansion of colonial America."

RECOMMENDED BOOKS FOR FURTHER READING

Contemporary Narratives

Albert B. Hart, ed., *American History Told by Contemporaries,* I, Chapter 12.

Alexander S. Salley, ed., *Narratives of Early Carolina, 1650-1708.*

Modern Accounts

Charles M. Andrews, *The Colonial Period of American History,* III, Chapters 5-6.

Samuel A. Ashe, *History of North Carolina,* Chapters 5-12.

John S. Bassett, *The Constitutional Beginnings of North Carolina (1663-1729).*

Edward Channing, *A History of the United States,* II, Chapters 1, 12.

Robert D. W. Connor, *Studies in the History of North Carolina.*

Verner N. Crane, *The Southern Frontier, 1670-1732,* Chapters 1-3.

Arthur H. Hirsch, *The Huguenots of Colonial South Carolina.*

Edward McCrady, *The History of South Carolina under the Proprietary Government, 1670-1719,* Chapters 1-10.

Herbert L. Osgood, *American Colonies in the Seventeenth Century,* II, Part III, Chapters 9, 11.

Charles L. Raper, *North Carolina, A Study in English Colonial Government.*

Harriott H. R. Ravenel, *Charleston, The Place and the People,* Chapters 1-3.

21

New Netherland Becomes New York

THE RESTORATION AND THE DUTCH

WHEN Charles II returned to his throne in 1660 he was in great need of money. He had passed twelve years in exile, and his fortune had been practically exhausted. Yet a number of his aristocratic supporters had been loyal to him, and had even depleted their own fortunes in their long, discouraging struggle to hold the monarchy together against a day when they all might return to a happier England. Now that they had returned, they hoped and expected the king would reward them for their loyalty and recompense them for their losses. The king, for his part, though he was unable to repay them in money, was in a position to offer them offices of honor and perquisites, favors, titles, and commissions. Most of all, he was able to give away large areas of still unoccupied lands in America, even some that were already occupied. He was also ravenously interested in the expansion of commerce in every way that would be of profit to the people of England and the state, as already noted. In both the extension of the territorial status of the empire and the promotion of British commerce he was urged on by the merchants of London, who had only recently, since the Civil War, discovered the value of colonies to the expansion of British and imperial trade. The new movement to found colonies, therefore, should not be understood as merely the acts of generosity of a grateful king to his followers. On the contrary, the movement had its source and moving spirit in two groups of men in England who were interested chiefly, almost solely, in the profits that were to be derived from colonization. One of these groups was composed of imperialistic merchants, mostly resident in London, who hoped to expand their commerce by the expansion of Britain's empire. The other group was made up of such aristocratic promoters as the Duke of York, Prince Rupert, the Earl of Clarendon, and Anthony Ashley Cooper (later the Earl of Shaftesbury), who founded the Hudson's Bay Company and the Royal African Company and promoted great landed estates for themselves, upon the Maryland pattern, in New York, New Jersey and Carolina.

The area of the new world which most obviously attracted the interest of these two groups of promoters was the Dutch colony of New Netherland. For the Dutch had become the carriers of the world's trade, including that of some of the British American colonies. It was in an effort to exclude the Dutch from the colonies that the Navigation Act of 1651 had been enacted, and it was in large measure to enforce the determination to monopolize the trade of the British empire that the first Dutch War had been fought in 1652-54. New Netherland was recognized as a focus of Dutch trade in America at the time of that war, and Major Robert Sedgwick had led an expedition to America in 1654 with the object of annexing it to the British Crown; but he arrived in New England after peace had been made.

The Dutch trade with the colonies continued, and New Netherland remained a "nest of interlopers" in British colonial commerce. Now, with the restoration of Charles II and the passage of the Navigation Act of 1660, it seemed even more imperative than before that the Dutch settlements be brought under the British Crown. Many Englishmen had filtered into the Dutch colony from New England and were urging their government to take over the province. The Duke of York, as Lord High Admiral of the British Navy, closely associated both with the mercantile interests and the land-hungry courtiers, became convinced of both the desirability and the feasibility of wiping out the prosperous Dutch colony.

It was almost inevitable, therefore, that the newly created Council for Foreign Plantations should be asked to prepare a report upon the question, which it presented in January, 1664. In its report the council stated that the Dutch colony was a serious encroachment upon British territory and trade, that the people were discontented under the arbitrary rule of Peter Stuyvesant, and that the province was only poorly defended. At the request of the Duke of York, therefore, the king made a grant of all this land, in March, 1664, to the Duke as a proprietary estate. All the Duke had to do was to conquer it.

THE DUKE OF YORK AND HIS COLONY

By the terms of his charter the Duke of York was given all the land lying between the Connecticut and the Delaware rivers, including Long Island. He was also given the land of Maine between the Kennebec and the Ste. Croix, and the islands of Nantucket and Martha's Vineyard. Within these lands he was to be sole proprietor and ruler, symbolically recognizing the suzerainty of the king by the payment each year of forty beaver skins. No provision was made for representative government; the only limitations upon the pro-

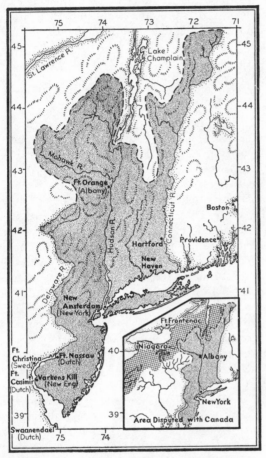

MAP 12. New York as Granted to the Duke of York, 1664

NOTE: Because of the inaccuracy of geographic knowledge in the seventeenth century and the vagueness of the language in the charter itself, the boundaries shown on this map must be considered only approximately accurate.

prietor's power were that his laws must conform, as nearly as possible, to the laws of England and that the inhabitants might appeal from the judgments of his courts to the king. It was probably the most extreme example of the creation of an absolute proprietorship in the entire history of the colonies.

Having received his charter, James appointed Richard Nichols as his deputy governor. Nichols was given four ships and four hundred soldiers, with which he went first to Boston, where he got some recruits, and then to the entrance of the harbor of New Amsterdam. Here he issued a proclamation announcing his coming to the inhabitants and promising them favorable treatment, and then wrote to Peter Stuyvesant, demanding the surrender of the colony. Stuyvesant had long since warned the Dutch West India Company of the danger the colony was in, but the company had now fallen on evil days, and had done nothing for New Netherland's protection. The place was therefore indefensible, and Stuyvesant knew it. He played for time, nevertheless, and Nichols agreed to a delay of three days, during which the English troops were put ashore and began their march toward Breucklyn (now Brooklyn). The warships then took up positions in the bay and river in preparation for a fight, should Stuyvesant decide to fight. Two of the frigates sailed right past the fort itself to take up a position in Hudson River opposite the town. The council of burghers realized the hopelessness of the situation and urged Stuyvesant to surrender; the old man, after much storming and show of resistance, finally gave in and surrendered the place on September 8, 1664. With this act New Amsterdam fell to the British, and the same day the name of the city was changed to New York. Within a month the British had taken possession of Fort Orange on the Hudson and Fort Casimir (which had replaced the old Fort Nassau in 1651) on the Delaware. With the conquest of the Dutch on the Delaware the formerly Swedish Fort Christina, whose name the Dutch had changed to New Amstel (it was changed again, later, by the English to Newcastle), came under the jurisdiction of the Duke of York. This land, on the west side of the Delaware, was not within the boundaries provided in his charter; it was now his simply by right of conquest.

Very soon after receiving his own charter the Duke of York made over to John Lord Berkeley and Sir George Carteret, two of the eight proprietors of Carolina, the land between the Hudson and the Delaware. This land the new proprietors erected into the colony of New Jersey. Nearly twenty years later the Duke made over the formerly Swedish lands on the west side of the Delaware to William Penn; later still, these, the "three lower counties," became the province of Delaware.

THE TRANSITION TO BRITISH INSTITUTIONS

The government of the Duke of York in the former province of New Netherland has been called the most absolute and arbitrary of all the colonial governments. For the proprietor was not required to ask the "advice and consent" of the freemen to the laws, or to call an assembly for any other reason. He was empowered to make laws and ordinances, and to establish courts and officials for their administration. He had complete control of commerce, with the power to lay and collect tolls or customs duties; and he could grant lands and levy taxes. But there was no "palatinate clause," such as appeared in the charter of Maryland, and there was a specific reservation of the right of appeal to the inhabitants from the proprietor and his courts to the king.

In actual practice, however, the Duke's government was both liberal and "benevolent." By the terms of the surrender the Dutch inhabitants were allowed to retain their Dutch citizenship, although provision was made for naturalization as Englishmen of those who might so desire. Their titles to property were recognized, and quarrels over contracts were to be adjudicated according to Dutch law. The city of New York was given an elective city government, and the Dutch merchants were even permitted to continue their trade with Holland; but this was a manifest exception from the navigation acts that was cancelled in 1668. Complete religious freedom was guaranteed.

Beginning with Nichols, the Duke's governors were instructed to govern liberally, and to promote immigration, commerce, and trade. The proprietor's interest in the colony was first and always financial; yet since it was good business to do so, the liberal terms of the surrender were faithfully adhered to. In general, the governor's councilors were chosen from among the most distinguished colonists themselves, as were the local magistrates and officials. In the distribution of land a liberal policy was followed in order to compete successfully with other colonies seeking to attract new colonists.

As a first governor, Richard Nichols was a peculiarly happy choice. For his task was a very difficult one, and he met his exacting and complex problems with tact, intelligence, and success. One of his first responsibilities was to settle the boundary with Connecticut. The charter to the Duke of York had given all the land west of the Connecticut River to New York, a fact much resented by the Puritan colony, and Nichols negotiated a boundary agree-

ment with that province by which all Long Island was acknowledged to belong to New York and which laid out a boundary between the two on the mainland. The boundary line was so vague,
however, that the agreement was not ratified by the Duke, and the
line was not settled until much later.

In his dealings with the Dutch, Nichols was entirely successful.
He permitted their trade with Holland, as provided in the capitu-
lations, until the practice was ended by order from England in 1668,
and his revision of the government of New Amsterdam was, if anything, an improvement over the old Dutch institution. Among the
towns on Long Island, however, which had been founded by immigrants from New England, there was a demand for local self-
government on the New England plan, which Nichols could not
grant. For there was no provision in the charter or in his instructions that would allow him to call a representative assembly and
give it control over taxation, as the towns were demanding.

He did call a meeting of deputies from the towns of the province
at Hempstead, on Long Island, on March 1, 1665, at which he
promulgated the basic laws of the province in what was called the
"Duke's Laws." This body of laws was intended chiefly for the English towns on Long Island, and was based chiefly upon the codes
of the older New England colonies. These laws provided for freedom of worship, guaranteed existing titles to land, and provided
for town government. Each town, under these laws, was to be governed by eight overseers or selectmen and a constable to be elected
by the freemen. Locally, justice was to be administered by appointed justices of the peace, and as England was soon at war with
France and Holland, Nichols created at New York a court of admiralty to hear prize cases. A high "Court of Assizes," meeting
annually, was set up at New York to hear appeals. This high court
was composed of the governor and his council, with the high sheriff
and the justices of Yorkshire (New York County). This court, indeed, the members of which were all appointed by the governor,
was also a sort of quasi-legislature for the province—the nearest
approach to a legislature that New York was to have until 1683.

Nichols was succeeded in 1668 by Colonel Francis Lovelace, who
continued Nichols' policy of conciliation. His administration was
troubled, however, by continued boundary disputes with Connecticut, Massachusetts, Maryland and New Jersey, and by a
Swedish revolt at Newcastle on the Delaware. He even managed
to get into a quarrel with Rhode Island over the ownership of certain islands in Narragansett Bay and jurisdiction over Martha's

Vineyard and Nantucket. His most troublesome problem, however, was the continued clamor of the towns of Long Island for a larger share in the government. Some of the towns even refused to pay the taxes, on the ground that they were laid without the consent of the freemen or their representatives, and that they were, therefore, violations of the rights of Englishmen. He was unable to do more than remind them that they must accept whatever rule the Duke gave them, and the conflict went on, to be brought to a temporary suspension by the reconquest of New York by the Dutch in 1673.

THE STRUGGLE FOR REPRESENTATIVE GOVERNMENT

Unfortunately, Nichols' successors did not have his ability. Francis Lovelace was inferior to him in every way. The third Dutch war broke out in 1672 and when, in the second year of the war, a Dutch fleet came to New York and captured it Lovelace of course returned to England. The Dutch held New York for some sixteen months, and many features of the old Dutch regime were revived in the colony itself. But New York was returned to the English at the end of the war by the treaty of Westminster (1674), and the patent to James was renewed.

Thereupon the Duke appointed Sir Edmund Andros governor. The Andros regime, which lasted until 1683, is notable chiefly for the continued growth of a sentiment demanding representative government. This increasingly urgent demand culminated in 1681 when merchants refused to pay certain duties placed upon the commerce of the colony by the Duke, on the ground that as Englishmen they could not be taxed except by their own representatives. Andros was in England at the time, and Thomas Dongan, who came to New York as governor in 1683, was given instructions to call an assembly. This was a great concession by the Duke of York, who had consistently opposed the move for representative government, and on October 17, 1683, a body of representatives of the landholders of the province met in the city of New York. This assembly consisted of two deputies from each court district, the five members of the legislative council, and Governor Dongan. It met for three weeks and passed a "Charter of Libertyes and priviledges," and fourteen laws.

The most important of these enactments was the "Charter of Libertyes and priviledges." For it proposed to establish in the colony a representative government in form, with "a Governour,

Councell, and the people Mett in Generall Assembly." It provided that all freeholders and freemen should have the franchise and that there should be free elections, and it outlined a new system of courts, taxation, and land tenure; it also provided for freedom of religion, the naturalization of aliens, and the support of the poor. In short, it was a sort of constitution for this province formulated by the assembly; all it lacked was the approval of the Duke of York.

All these measures, indeed, were approved by Dongan, and it appeared that New York was on the verge of achieving an extremely liberal form of government. But before the work of the assembly could reach the Duke, Charles II died and James became king of England. The demand of the province for representative government was placed in abeyance. Dongan did give charters of incorporation to New York City and Albany; but the province was incorporated into the Dominion of New England in 1686, and it was not until 1692 that New York province received a really representative government of its own.

ECONOMIC PROGRESS

Meanwhile in the period from 1660 to 1685 the province of New York had developed rapidly. The English continued the custom of granting large landed estates, and there appeared along the shores of the Hudson and elsewhere in the province a number of estates comparable to those then appearing in Virginia; but the majority of the landowners in New York were holders of relatively small grants. Agriculture flourished, and by the end of the century some sixty thousand bushels of wheat annually were produced. In addition to this, New York was rapidly becoming an exporter of beef, pork, and other foodstuffs, most of which were shipped to the West Indies. But the greatest element in the economic life of New York was still the fur trade.

During the Dutch period, Fort Orange (Albany) had become a great depot for the skins brought in by the Iroquois, and a center for the trading of manufactured goods in exchange. After the English conquest this trade went on in the hands of the Dutchmen who remained and the English traders who now began to share in it, and great fortunes were made from this business. The English were successful in maintaining the friendship of the Indians, largely because they could sell goods more cheaply than the French in Canada. This fact came to be of great importance in the period of rivalry between the English and the French for the control of the fur trade which was just getting under way in Dongan's time, and this great economic stake became the basic element in a diplomatic conflict between the British and the French over the possession of the lands lying around the Great Lakes—a conflict which lasted well nigh one hundred years.

In its social aspects the city and the colony of New York presented a thoroughly cosmopolitan aspect. There was a large measure of religious toleration, with Catholics, Dutch and English Protestants, Quakers and Jews worshiping in perfect freedom. Its population was composed of men of many nationalities, English, Dutch, Swedish, Danish, Germans, Frenchmen, and Indians, each group with its own peculiar language and customs. It was rapidly becoming a commercial colony, giving its foodstuffs and its furs in exchange for the manufactured wares of Europe and the semitropical products of southwestern Europe and the West Indies; and the city of New York, located at the crossroads of this ocean commerce and at the gateway to the interior of the continent, began to give evidence of its great future as the chief market of exchange on the continent of North America.

LEISLER'S REVOLT

Upon the fall of James II in 1688, the people of New York split into warring factions. Francis Nicholson, lieutenant-governor of New York under Sir Edmund Andros, had to face a revolt of the militia demanding the recognition of William and Mary and protection against the French who were thought to be at the colony's doors. Nicholson, unable to quell the disorder, decided to abandon his post and return to England. The leader of the revolted militia, Jacob Leisler, now proclaimed William and Mary sovereign in New York, and assumed the leadership of government until the desires of the new sovereigns might be known. But Leisler's assumption of authority by force enraged the rival group of entrenched politicians, and there ensued a bitter civil strife which did not end until the rival faction, having gotten the ear of the new king, succeeded in having Leisler arrested, tried for treason, and executed.

In the meantime, however, Leisler had vigorously undertaken the defense of the province, and had called an intercolonial congress, which met at New York on May 1, 1690, to plan cooperative measures in the conduct of the war with France that had now begun. With the arrival of Colonel Henry Sloughter as the new royal governor in 1691, New York was given its first regularly established representative government, and took its place among the other royal provinces.

RECOMMENDED BOOKS FOR FURTHER READING

CONTEMPORARY NARRATIVES

Jasper Danckaerts, *Journal of Jasper Danckaerts, 1679-1680*, edited by Bartlett B. James and John F. Jameson.

Edmund B. O'Callaghan, *The Documentary History of the State of New York*, I, Chapter 6.

MODERN ACCOUNTS

Charles M. Andrews, *The Colonial Period of American History*, III, Chapters 2-4.

John R. Brodhead, *History of the State of New York*, Volume II.

Edward Channing, *A History of the United States*, II, Chapter 2.

Alexander C. Flick, ed., *History of the State of New York*, II, Chapter 3.

Francis W. Halsey, *The Old New York Frontier*, Part I, Chapters 1-3; Part II, Chapters 1-4.

Martha J. R. N. Lamb, *History of the City of New York*.

Herbert L. Osgood, *The American Colonies in the Seventeenth Century*, II, Part III, Chapters 6-8; III, Chapters 12, 15.

Francis Parkman, *Count Frontenac and New France under Louis XIV*.

Ellis H. Roberts, *New York*, I, Chapters 6, 9-12.

Edwin P. Tanner, *The Province of New Jersey, 1664-1738*.

Mariana G. Van Rensselaer, *History of the City of New York in the Seventeenth Century*.

George M. Wrong, *The Rise and Fall of New France*, I, Chapters 19-20.

22

The Founding of Pennsylvania

THE VALLEY of the Delaware River and Delaware Bay had been the scene of European colonization from 1624, the year of the building of Fort Nassau by the Dutch, onward. Swedes and Danes had tried their hands at colonization there, and the Puritan colony of New Haven had planted there an offshoot of itself at Salem Creek (Varkenskill). The Swedish settlements had been taken over by the Dutch in 1655, and the whole area had fallen to the Duke of York in the conquest of 1664. The territory between the Delaware and the Hudson had been made over by the Duke to Sir George Carteret and John Lord Berkeley at the time of the conquest, as already noted, and this area became the colony of New Jersey. Upon the reconquest of New Netherland by the Dutch in 1673 and its restoration to England in 1674, the Duke of York's charter was reissued, and it became necessary for the Duke to reaffirm his grant of New Jersey to Berkeley and Carteret. Berkeley, however, had in the meantime sold his share of New Jersey to the Quaker John Fenwick, as agent for Edward Byllinge. The Duke's grant was renewed, therefore, only to Carteret, and a line was drawn across the province from Barnegat Creek, on the Atlantic side, to Rankokus Kill on the Delaware, thus dividing it into East New Jersey and West New Jersey. Byllinge then transferred his title to three other Quakers, William Penn, Gawan Lawrie, and Nicholas Lucas.

West New Jersey thus became a Quaker colony, the title to which was confirmed to its Quaker owners by the Duke of York in 1680. But Sir George Carteret died in that same year, whereupon his province of East New Jersey was also sold, to another group of Quakers which included the proprietors of West New Jersey. Curiously enough, men of other faiths added their capital to that of the Quakers, and the Jersey proprietors came to include Catholic and Presbyterian lords as well as Quaker merchants. This group finally surrendered its political authority to the Crown in 1702, and New Jersey became, in government, a royal province.

The Quaker infiltration into West New Jersey had begun at

about the time of its transfer from Berkeley to Byllinge, shortly after its restoration to England by the Dutch. When the other Quaker proprietors took over the colony, a new constitution, called the "Laws, Concessions, and Agreements," probably the work of William Penn, was set up in 1677, for its government. This was perhaps the most liberal colonial constitution of its times; it provided complete liberty of conscience, jury trial, guarantee against arbitrary arrest, security of property, and a liberal policy in the granting of land. It provided also a representative government having complete control of taxation (but not including the quit-rents to be paid to the proprietors). Members of the assembly were to be elected by the freemen and inhabitants, were to be paid, and were guaranteed freedom of speech while in the assembly. The assembly was to elect ten "Commissioners of State" for the executive administration of the province, and was empowered to erect courts for the administration of the law. Justices and judges, however, were to be elected by the people; other officials were to be chosen by the assembly. This remarkable constitution, and the remarkable government created under it, remained in force until West New Jersey was reunited to East New Jersey in 1692 and lost its peculiarly Quaker individuality.

Meanwhile, however, the colony had prospered in its economic life, and its success as a haven for the persecuted Quakers of England probably inspired William Penn, one of its proprietors, to his great effort to found a colony of his own on even more generous lines.

WILLIAM PENN AND HIS CHARTER

William Penn was born in the year 1644, in the midst of the Great Rebellion. At the age of twelve he was taken to Ireland, where he fell under the influence of the Quakers, who made a profound impression upon his adolescent mind. When he was sixteen he went to Oxford, and stayed there for two years; but he was disgusted with the formalized religion that he found there and he was expelled for refusing the obey regulations. His father, old Admiral Penn, somewhat disturbed over the religious leanings of his son, sent the boy on a grand tour of Europe, in the company of a rather worldly young man, Robert Spencer, Earl of Sunderland, apparently in the hope that contact with the pleasures and the excitements of the great world would cure him of his Quakerism. While abroad he studied at the Huguenot college at Samur in Anjou, and on his return he took up the study of law at Lincoln's Inn.

His trip abroad did apparently cure him for a time, but he again fell under the spell of the Quakers about 1667 or 1668 and he definitely announced his adhesion to that despised sect; upon which the Admiral beat him and turned him out of his house. Reconciliation was later affected between father and son, but in the meantime young Penn had a number of personal experiences with the persecution of the Quakers then going on in England, and it is probably out of these experiences that there grew in his mind his ideas upon the subject of religious toleration which he expressed in his pamphlet, "The Great Case of Liberty of Conscience."

The Quakers were a group of religious dissenters, followers of George Fox, who carried the doctrine of individual inspiration and interpretation much farther than any other sect. Quakerism had probably originated among the Quietists or Pietists of Germany. In doctrine and in practice they sought to get back to the simple, pure religion of the Apostles. Led by Fox, they rejected all forms and ceremonies. They had no ordained priesthood, nor did they consecrate temples built by human hands. They rejected all the sacraments, including that of the Lord's Supper, or the Mass, and they discarded the practice of formal preaching in the churches. They looked upon themselves as being all preachers. Every man preached—whenever moved by the spirit, but only then.

As to doctrine, they believed in a God who speaks directly to the human heart. As William Penn said: "They by this ministry found *within* . . ." the "right way to peace with God," which "others had been vainly seeking *without.*" The most essential thought in their doctrine was that the voice of God speaks within every individual, that in this respect all men are equal, and that all should be encouraged to speak. To them it was by listening to the voice of God that man was to be saved, not by any form or predestined arrangement. The voice of God they believed to be universal. It is heard by every man, Christian or heathen, and all that the missionary can do is to point it out to others who do not recognize it when they hear.

In their religious and social practices the Quakers were equalitarians. They refused to recognize any differences of rank, and in order to emphasize the ideas of social equality they addressed everybody as "thee" or "thou," including the king himself. Because of these ideas, the Quakers were considered extreme social radicals, dangerous to society and to the state. They refused to pay tithes to support an Anglican ministry; they claimed exemption from military service because they were opposed to war; they refused to take oaths in court, as contrary to Christian doctrine. They were persecuted largely because of the fear that, if permitted to grow, their doctrines would bring about the dissolution of society and the English state. It was this persecution that probably first moved Penn to plan a commonwealth where the Quakers might be free to worship God as they chose.

Penn himself was no democrat. He was from an aristocratic family, and had an aristocratic training; yet his religion prompted him to a faith in the common man which he found it difficult to put into actual personal practice. He was a close friend of many of the most distinguished and aristocratic men of his time, including King Charles II and James, Duke of York. He lived for many years at court and moved in the circle of people interested in colonial development. When his father died in 1670, leaving him a large estate and an unpaid debt of some sixteen thousand pounds due the admiral from the Crown, it occurred to him that the Crown might be willing to pay the debt by a grant of land in America. Thus it was that he presented his petition to this effect in 1680, and he found King Charles agreeable. There was some opposition to giving a proprietary grant to a Quaker, both in the Privy Council and among the Lords of Trade. Moreover, the governor of New York claimed that the land requested by Penn already belonged to the Duke of York; but the Duke waived any rights he might have, reserving only the lands around Newcastle, and the charter eventually went through bearing the date of March 4, 1681. The next year the Duke of York turned over to Penn the three Delaware counties of Newcastle, Kent, and Sussex which he had acquired from the Dutch by conquest in 1664 (they were not a part of his original grant from Charles II), as a feudal fief, in return for which the Duke was to receive a rent of five shillings for Newcastle and "for the rest, a rose to be paid on the Feast of St. Michael the Archangel, if demanded, and a moiety of the profits."

Under this charter, the eastern boundary of William Penn's territory was to be the Delaware River from a point twelve miles north of Newcastle to the forty-third degree of north latitude. The northern boundary, the line of the forty-third degree, was to extend westward from the river five degrees of longitude, and the boundary on the south was to be an arc drawn from a point from the Delaware twelve miles north of Newcastle and using that town as its center to the fortieth degree of latitude and then along the fortieth degree of latitude to the western boundary. All this land, which included an area about the size of England, was to be held in feudal tenure from the king, "yeelding and paying therefore into us . . . two Beaver skins . . . on the first day of January in every year," together with one-fifth of all the gold and silver that should happen to be mined within the province. Penn was the seigneur and ruler of Pennsylvania, so named in honor of his father the admiral, with power to make laws and impose taxes by and with the advice and consent of the freemen of the province.

It was provided in his charter, however, that the laws to be made in Pennsylvania should not be repugnant to the laws of England, and that there must always be the right of appeal from Pennsylvania to the mother country. It was required that all products of the province be shipped to England, and the proprietor was compelled to promise to enforce the navigation acts. The proprietor was granted the right to erect ports, but he was expected to accept the customs imposed upon the province by act of Parliament. Moreover, Penn was required to maintain an agent in London to answer for violations of the navigation acts and for the proper administration of the colony generally. The proprietor, finally, was given the right to lay taxes upon the people, and the king on his part promised not to tax the Pennsylvanians except with the consent of the proprietor or their own assembly or by act of the Parliament in England. This last provision is of peculiar interest because its acceptance by Penn apparently meant an acceptance for the province of the principle of parliamentary taxation.

This charter is of considerable significance in the general history of the colonies during this period, for it emphasizes and illustrates the progress of British colonial policy toward an increasing amount of control over the colonies. Coming at the moment of the culmination of the struggle between Massachusetts and the mother country, it not only envisaged a representative government but also provided that there should be the right of appeal from Pennsylvania courts to the British Privy Council. This is a far cry from the absolute and unlimited power of the proprietor of Maryland, as granted in the charter to Lord Baltimore, or from the power granted to the Duke of York in the charter of 1664. The same centralizing tendency is to be seen in the requirement that products of the colony be shipped to England, that the administration of the colony cooperate with the Crown officers of the customs, by the inclusion of the principle of parliamentary taxation, and by the requirement that the proprietor assume responsibility for the effective administration of the navigation acts. The charter embodies, in a word, the now emerging British desire to limit the autonomy of individual colonies, whether corporate or proprietary.

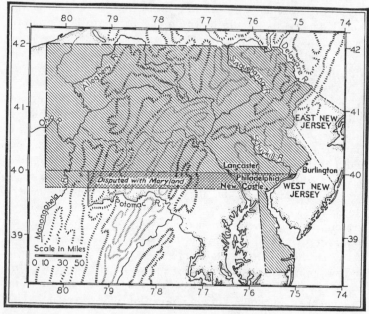

MAP 13. The Boundaries of Pennsylvania Under William Penn's Charter of 1681 and the Three "Lower Counties of Delaware"

NOTE: Because of the inaccuracy of geographic knowledge in the seventeenth century and the vagueness of the language in the charter itself, the boundaries shown on this map must be considered only approximately accurate.

PENN'S GOVERNMENT AND LAW

Having received his charter, and while making preparations for the settlement of the colony, Penn wrote a constitution for his new commonwealth which he called "the frame of the government." In it he gave expression to a philosophy of government that is interesting as coming out of an age when the scientific study of government was just beginning, and it shows him to be something of a political philosopher in his own right. To begin with, he quotes St. Paul to the effect that "the powers that be are ordained of God: whosoever therefore resisteth the power, resisteth the ordinance of God." To him, then, government is of divine origin and it has two chief ends: first, to terrify evildoers, and second, to cherish and protect those who do well. The philosophers are divided, said Penn, as to the best form of government. Some advocate monarchy, others aristocracy, and others democracy, but they are all agreed, as he himself thought, that the end of government is the happiness of men. As for himself, he professed never to have seen a form of government which had never been altered by time or circumstance; and, therefore, it seemed to him that it is impossible to find any government that will serve all nations alike. Men dispute monarchy, aristocracy, and democracy, but it seemed to him that "any government is free to the people under it (whatever be the frame) where the laws rule, and the people are a party to those laws, and more than this is tyranny, oligarchy, or confusion." There is no frame of government in the world, he said, "so ill designed by its first founders, that, in good hands, will not do well enough . . . Wherefore governments rather depend upon men, than men upon governments. Let men be good, and the government cannot be bad; if it be ill, they will cure it. But, if men be bad, let the government be never so good, they will endeavor to warp and spoil it to their turn."

Under his frame of government Penn proposed that there should be established in the colony a parliament composed of two houses: the upper house, or council, should contain 72 members who would be elected by the freemen of the province, which would prepare all bills; and the assembly, to be composed of 100 elected members who would merely vote upon the bills presented to them by the council, establish courts, and nominate judges. Voting was to be by ballot, and the constitution or frame of government might be amended by a six-sevenths vote of the council and assembly.

Obviously, such an unwieldy governmental machinery was hardly appropriate for a small and struggling community of settlers; but Penn, still in England, was not yet aware of this. On the contrary, he was in a fever of organization and preparation, and he desired that every possible provision be made to guarantee to his colonists the rights and the privileges that he thought they ought to have. Thus as soon as he had written his constitution he turned his attention to the formulation of a set of laws for his colony. Among other things, Penn's laws provided that a freeman in the colony should be (a) any man who buys or rents 100 acres of land and cultivates at least 10 acres, or (b) any servant who, upon being freed from servitude, should take up his 50 acres of land and cultivate 20 acres, or (c) any artificer or other inhabitant of the colony who paid taxes. This was probably the most liberal franchise in all the English colonies in America. It came nearer to universal manhood suffrage than the franchise arrangement in any other colony except perhaps Rhode Island. Penn's code of laws provided, further, that there should be no taxation in the colonies except by law—that is to say, no taxation except by representatives of the people. All freemen were equal before the law, and all trials were to be trials by jury. Prisons were to be workhouses, and were to furnish free board and lodging to the prisoners instead of forcing the prisoners to pay these expenses, as had been the older English custom. Under the law there were to be only two capital offenses— and this at a time when there were over two hundred capital offenses in England—treason and murder. All children were to be taught some useful art or skill "to the end that none may be idle, but the poor may work to live, and the rich, if they become poor, may not want." Servants were to be kindly treated, and "all persons . . . who confess and acknowledge the one Almighty and eternal God . . . and that hold themselves obliged in conscience to live peacefully and justly in civil society, shall, in no ways, be molested or prejudiced for their religious persuasion, or practice, in matters of faith and worship, nor shall they be compelled, at any time, to frequent or maintain any religious worship." There was still no place for atheists, but under this law Penn would apparently admit Jews and Unitarians.

The similarity of these documents to the "concessions" of West New Jersey is evident. It is to be noted that Penn proposed that his government should be relatively democratic and that the laws should be enlightened. As a matter of fact, this code of laws laid down by Penn for the regulation of his colony was perhaps the most enlightened in the world at the time. It was approved by the first assembly that met in the colony and became for a time the actual law of the province of Pennsylvania. It was not long, however, before it was modified in a conservative direction and became decidedly less enlightened than Penn himself would have made it.

THE COLONY

William Penn sailed for America on September 1, 1682, and arrived at Newcastle on the Delaware on October 27. After stopping to go through the form of taking possession, he went on up the Delaware River to a spot four miles above the mouth of the

Schuylkill River, where his engineers had already laid out Philadelphia, the City of Brotherly Love. The plan for the city is notable,
and Penn may be called the first city-planner in America. Thomas
Holme, who supervised the work, laid out the two main streets at
right angles, and he was farsighted enough to place their inter-
section approximately halfway between the Delaware River and
the Schuylkill, so far, indeed, that the site of the city hall is still
the approximate geographic center of the city. Market Street he
laid out at right angles to the river and 100 feet wide, in order to
accommodate the market which was expected to be held there.
Broad Street, equally wide, was laid out roughly parallel to the
river. The other streets of the city were 50 feet wide; trees were
planted along the streets, a parkway was reserved along the river-
front, and at regular intervals squares were reserved as public parks.
As the city began to grow, the houses were built with plenty of
space between them, and as good clay was plentiful, it was not
long before brick houses appeared and came to be typical of the
city.

With the founding of his town thus in motion, Penn turned to
the Indians and had the semi-legendary meeting with them, at which
he bought the land included in his grant from the king (or at least
the part of it lying along the river). Report has it that Penn entered
into the spirit of the occasion, ate hominy and acorns with the
Indians, and then entered running and jumping contests with
them in which he performed better than any of the Indians. However, as Penn was a man already almost forty years of age and of
"a noble portliness of figure," it is doubtful whether his exploits
surpassed those of the Indians, whose actual livelihood depended
upon their physical activities and skill. In any case, this conference was the first of a series of meetings which cemented the good
relations already established by the Dutch and Swedes, and which
instituted a long period of peace between the Indians and the
whites. The Quakers bought food, game, and furs from the Indians,
paying for them in trinkets, blankets, guns, shoes, wampum, and
the like. The good relations thus established between the Indians
and Penn's settlers lasted for over 70 years.

On December 14, 1682, Penn held his first assembly. This assembly was not elected according to the frame of government, but
consisted of seven men from each community, or a total of 42, and
they sat and acted as one house. The chief accomplishment of this
meeting was the adoption of the set of laws drawn up by Penn
in England. Interestingly enough, this was done expeditiously by

the adoption of the parliamentary rule that "none speak but once before the question is put, nor after but once, and that none fall from the matter to the person, and tedious and superfluous speeches may be stopped by the speaker." This assembly also passed the so-called "Act of Union" which united the three lower counties of the Delaware, called the "territories," with the province of Pennsylvania. It also suggested to the proprietor that the frame of government or constitution be modified in such a way as to reduce the numbers of council and assembly to 72 in all, with 18 members of the council and 54 in the assembly. These suggestions were accepted and when the second assembly met early in 1683 Penn called the members on the basis of this plan, and this second assembly adopted a new frame of government embodying it.

The assembly of 1683 passed several other laws dealing with land and appointments which limited the powers given the proprietor in the charter. This was a distinct pulling away from the proprietary control envisaged in the charter and an assertion of that reaction against restraint and the drive toward self-government which was to be observed in all the colonies during this period. In the case of Pennsylvania, this tendency was to a large part due to the non-Quaker elements in the colony, who had no confidence either in Penn or in the Quakers, and who began immediately to complain in England against the proprietor and to agitate for a change of the colony from a proprietary to a royal status.

Penn was thus pulled from both sides from the very beginning of his experiment. The British government had placed several restrictions upon his proprietary autonomy, and the settlers, despite his extreme liberalism in political matters, were demanding a greater amount of self-government than he had planned to give them. Penn was wise enough to adapt himself to the dissident element while he was in the colony, but when he was forced to return to England to attempt a settlement of the dispute with Lord Baltimore over the boundary of Pennsylvania and Maryland, the complainers gave him no end of trouble and almost succeeded in making him lose his charter.

The boundary dispute with Baltimore grew out of the uncertainty as to where the line of 40 degrees north latitude was. Under the patent to the first Lord Baltimore the province of Maryland was defined as extending north from Watkins Point in Chesapeake Bay to the line of the 40th degree of north latitude, and this line, as the southern boundary of the province of Pennsylvania, was expected to strike a circle drawn around Newcastle at a distance of twelve miles from the city. As a matter of fact, however, the line of 40 degrees did not strike this circle. It actually lay to the north of the site of Philadelphia, and when the line was surveyed it was found that the city lay within territory legally belonging to the province of Maryland. Penn, however, believing that the line lay farther south, occupied and settled land belonging to Maryland, and Lord Baltimore was technically right in claiming that Penn had trespassed. Thus it came about that Baltimore attacked Penn in England at about the same time that Thomas Dongan, governor of New York, began to dispute Penn's claim to the land in the neighborhood of the northern boundary of Pennsylvania, the line of 43 degrees north latitude, on the ground that this territory lay within lands purchased from the Iroquois Indians by the Duke of York.

It was for these reasons, but chiefly on account of the dispute with Lord Baltimore, that Penn returned to England to defend his title. The dispute with New York was settled by the deeding of any lands lying south of the 43rd degree of latitude to William Penn by the Duke of York, but the dispute with Baltimore dragged on, and it was not until 1760, when Charles Mason and Jeremiah Dixon surveyed the famous Mason and Dixon Line, that the quarrel was finally brought to an end. This line actually fell some nineteen miles south of the line of 40 degrees north latitude.

While Penn was in England, internal affairs in the province continued to give him trouble. When he had left Pennsylvania he had made the council as a whole his deputy to govern for him, but when the assembly met in the spring of 1685 it fell to wrangling with the council, whose president was Thomas Lloyd, over the respective powers of the two houses under the frame of government. Both sides violated the frame and the assembly took unto itself much more power than it was supposed to have. The charter rights of the proprietor mattered little. What the assembly wanted was a more complete control of government, a desire which was prophetic of the line of development that the political history of the province was to take. Penn, to bring order to the province, appointed an executive commission of five in 1686, but the quarreling went on and he finally appointed a governor, Captain John Blackwell, whom in his disgust he instructed to rule with authority. Blackwell failed, however, and Penn again turned the reins of government over to the council under the leadership of Thomas Lloyd. Thus it was that by 1688 the government of the province was practically in the hands of the settlers, leaving the proprietor merely the owner of the land, to whom customs duties and quit-rents must be paid. In 1692, Penn's enemies accused him of sympathizing with the exiled James II and his charter was suspended for four years, during which Pennsylvania was administered by the governor of New York. His province was restored to him, however, in 1696, and it remained in the hands of Penn and his descendants until the time of the American Revolution. Penn himself returned to the colony in 1699, and once more he attempted to adapt his government to the desires of his critics in the colony. As a result of the suggestions of the assembly, he worked out "A New Charter of Privileges" which was put into effect in 1701 and which remained the constitution of Pennsylvania through the rest of the colonial period.

SOCIAL AND ECONOMIC GROWTH

Meanwhile, Penn's colony was rapidly growing into one of the most important and one of the most cosmopolitan of all the colonies. Penn had widely advertised the religious freedom and attractive land to be had in Pennsylvania. His pamphlets were translated into Dutch, German, and French, and, as it happened, this propaganda began to circulate in central Europe at a very opportune time. For this was the moment when Louis XIV had begun a new program of persecution of the Huguenots in France and the attempts at religious uniformity which led in 1685 to the revocation of the Edict of Nantes. Already many Huguenots were going over to England, whence considerable numbers of them went on to Pennsylvania. Germany had been devastated repeatedly through the Thirty Years War and on several occasions since, and now Louis XIV was proposing once more to overrun the Rhineland. He had seized the city of Strasbourg in 1681, which led to the formation of the League of Augsburg against him, and his invasion of the Palatinate in 1688 precipitated a series of invasions and devastations which were not to cease for another twenty-five years. The conditions of the poor people of the Rhineland were almost desperate. Germany had not yet recovered from the effects of the Thirty Years War, to say nothing of the earlier wars of Louis XIV; and there was a considerable amount of religious persecution going on in the Rhineland countries, by Protestants and Catholics alike. There had arisen a number of new sects of a Pietist sort, and these sects hailed Penn's advertisements as messages sent from heaven; with the result that numbers of them decided to migrate to the new land of promise. Many of these religious radicals emigrated to Pennsylvania, but the best-known group, probably, were the Mennonites, similar to the Quakers, of whom the best known was Francis Daniel Pastorius. It was a group of these people, with Pastorius, who founded Germantown in 1683. This German migration, beginning thus early in the history of the province, was later on to grow to striking proportions. Eventually it resulted in the peopling of the counties back of Germantown and Philadelphia with Germans who came to be known as the "Pennsylvania Dutch." Meanwhile, also, considerable numbers of Welshmen, Irishmen, and Dutchmen came into the province, with the result that by about 1700 Philadelphia and the surrounding country presented a cosmopolitan character which could be matched only by the city and colony of New York.

The result of the attractive combination of religious freedom, economic opportunity, and good advertising was a rapid increase in population. It has been estimated that in 1682 there were about one thousand people in Pennsylvania; by 1683 this number had grown to four thousand, and six years later, in 1689, it probably amounted to as many as twelve thousand souls. It was not long before Pennsylvania became the most populous colony on the Atlantic seaboard. Penn profited from the experience of other colonies; the land was healthy and amazingly fertile, and he had made adequate preparations for his settlement, promising prospective immigrants almost complete religious toleration. He had initiated an intelligent and liberal Indian policy; and he was wise enough to adapt the political institutions of his colony to the desires and the needs of his people. Economically, the province was almost immediately self-supporting, and very soon it began to export wheat, pork, beef, and flour to the West Indies; Philadelphia, almost from the first, became a thriving commercial center. Because of all these things, Pennsylvania began to pay profits to its owner; indeed, it was probably the most profitable of all the proprietary provinces.

Pennsylvania was the last of the English provinces to be settled in the seventeenth century. By the end of that century the work of founding a new empire in America had been done. Thereafter, the colonies entered into a new phase of their history, a period marked by internal development and the perfection of institutions the foundations of which had now been laid. The expansion of England for the time being had come to an end. Colonies that were founded later were founded under very special circumstances and for special reasons, and cannot be considered as having been the result of the peculiar social and economic expansion that had resulted in the foundation of some sixteen separate British communities along the eastern seaboard of America.

Each of these communities presents to the historian certain peculiarities. Each diverged in one way or another from all the rest, as well as from the mother country. Virginia differed widely from Massachusetts, New York from South Carolina, Pennsylvania from Jamaica or Barbados. In every case the men and women who had come to the colony had brought with them the ideas, institutions, and customs along which they had been reared, but they had found it convenient, if not absolutely necessary, to modify this cultural inheritance under the compelling influence of the new environment, weather, soil conditions, climate, waterways, or even the presence of a strange and unfriendly native population with whom they might trade but who had to be overcome and driven out before the Englishmen could call the land their own. Thus as the result of an adaptation of themselves and their customs to new environments, they had produced in America a number of new and peculiar societies which were the embryos, as it were, from which their modern counterparts have grown. They were different from each other and they were different from the mother country. The problems of life, society, and government in a land three thousand miles from England could not be adequately understood by English colonial statesmen; and yet, by the end of the seventeenth century, England had adopted a policy which made directly for an increasing amount of economic and political control. Already, in many of the colonies, the colonists had expressed their resentment of this control in an unmistakable fashion. And from the point of vantage of the twentieth century it is easy to see that if the process of control were continued and intensified in the mother country's relationship to communities which were growing increasingly strong and independent in their own right, and increasingly away from the mother country in their normal economic, cultural, and social development, conflict was inevitable. Sooner or later the time must come when the colonies, grown to maturity, would even more vigorously resent and reject the tutelage which seemed to bind them to the mother's apronstrings.

The story of that conflict belongs, of course, to a later chapter;

but at this point it may be wise to notice that four major events had taken place in the history of the American British empire. The colonies had been founded and had begun to grow toward a maturity of economic and social life peculiar to themselves. The mother country, discovering late in the seventeenth century the actual and potential value of the empire that had been founded, as it were, by Englishmen in a fit of absentmindedness, had made the beginning of a colonial policy which sought to organize the relationships of the colonies with the mother country on an imperial plan. As the colonies grew, they developed in the direction of not one but many new civilizations in the new world; and the differences between themselves and the mother country, appearing almost unconsciously at a moment when the mother country was establishing her control over them, contained within themselves the roots of inevitable conflict and, almost equally, inevitable independence.

RECOMMENDED BOOKS FOR FURTHER READING

CONTEMPORARY NARRATIVES

George Fox, *The Journal of George Fox* (Everyman's Library).
Albert C. Myers, ed., *Narratives of Early Pennsylvania, West New Jersey and Delaware, 1630-1707.*
William Penn, *The Peace of Europe; The Fruits of Solitude and Other Writings* (Everyman's Library).

MODERN ACCOUNTS

Charles M. Andrews, *The Colonial Period of American History,* III, Chapter 7.
Mary R. Brailsford, *The Making of William Penn.*
Bonamy Dobrée, *William Penn, Quaker and Pioneer.*
Edward Channing, *A History of the United States,* II, Chapter 4.
Sidney G. Fisher, *The Making of Pennsylvania.*
Sidney G. Fisher, *The Quaker Colonies.*
Sidney G. Fisher, *The True William Penn.*
William I. Hull, *William Penn and the Dutch and Quaker Migration to Pennsylvania.*
Herbert L. Osgood, *American Colonies in the Seventeenth Century,* II, Part III, Chapter 11.
Isaac Sharpless, *A Quaker Experiment in Government.*
Isaac Sharpless, *Two Centuries of Pennsylvania History,* Chapters 1-3.
William R. Shepherd, *History of Proprietary Government in Pennsylvania.*
Clifford Smyth, *William Penn, Quaker Courtier and Founder of Colonies.*
Colwyn E. Vulliamy, *William Penn.*

23

The Rise of New France

SANGLO-FRENCH COLONIAL RIVALRY IN ACADIA

ENGLAND had three rivals in the colonization of North America: the Spanish, the Dutch, and the French. The rivalry between the British and the Spanish peoples for colonial power lay chiefly in the West Indies and along the frontier of Florida and Georgia; but by the treaty of Madrid of 1670 that rivalry came at least to a temporary end with the recognition of England's possession of certain former Spanish islands in the West Indies and the British settlement in Carolina. The Dutch had settled in the valleys of the Hudson and Delaware Rivers, but they had been eliminated in 1664 by the seizure of New Netherland.

With the French, however, England was to engage in two centuries of struggle for the mastery of the interior parts of the continent. The beginning of this rivalry may be dated from the very first years of colonization, for three years before Jamestown was settled in Virginia, the French under Champlain and De Monts had founded a colony on the Ile Ste. Croix, which was moved in the summer of 1605 to Port Royal in Acadia. Three years after the founding of Jamestown, a French ship was taken by a British ship off the coast of New England on the ground that the Frenchman was trespassing in English territorial waters, and three years later still, in 1613, Captain Samuel Argall sailed up from that same Jamestown to destroy Port Royal and the Jesuit colony on Mount Desert Island.

This was the beginning. From this time on there was constant and unrelenting conflict between Frenchmen and Englishmen and their respective Indian allies over the control of territory and resources in the forests of North America. As more colonies were founded and as the older colonies expanded, there appeared more points of contact, more friction, and a more and more intense hatred of each other, until in the middle of the eighteenth century it became a life-and-death struggle for survival which eventuated in the elimination of the French empire from North America.

The rivalry between these two great colonial powers was inherent both in the geography of North America and in the mutually antagonistic systems of colonial administration and control. For an understanding of this rivalry, therefore, it becomes necessary to devote some attention to the settlement and growth of the French colonies in Acadia and the valley of the St. Lawrence. It has already been noted that Port Royal was founded in June, 1605. It was abandoned in 1607 and rebuilt in 1611, after which it struggled through an uncertain and precarious existence until it was seized by a British expedition sent out by Sir William Alexander, after which it was restored to France by the treaty of St. Germain in 1632. All of Acadia, known to the English as Nova Scotia, had been granted to Sir William Alexander in 1621, and Alexander had made a few grants of land along the coasts of Nova Scotia and on the River St. John and had sent over a few colonists. His title to the land was consistently denied by the French, but the seizure of Port Royal gave Alexander clear possession, so that Charles I felt it necessary to reimburse him for his loss when the territory was handed back to France in 1632. Alexander's ownership of Acadia had meant little or nothing, however, for most of the new colonists he sent over either died or abandoned the effort, leaving the field to their more hardy French competitors.

After the treaty of St. Germain, Claude de Razilly became governor of Acadia in the name of France, and upon his death soon after his arrival his two lieutenants, Charles de la Tour and Charles de Menou d'Aulnay-Charnisay, fell to quarreling between themselves over the governorship of Acadia and the profits of the fur trade with the Indians. This colonial civil war was ended only by the death of d'Aulnay in 1650 and the peace that ensued was doubly cemented by the marriage of d'Aulnay's widow by La Tour in 1653. Acadia fell into the hands of the British again in 1654 and was returned to the French by the treaty of Breda of 1667. It changed hands twice more, once at the end of King William's War and again after it was seized by the British in 1710 and left in their hands by the Peace of Utrecht in 1713.

During all the vicissitudes of its early history, Acadia was a colony of only slight importance, peopled by a scattered, ignorant, and poverty-stricken peasantry, valuable only for the profits derived from the fur trade with the Norumbega Indians and from the fisheries along its coasts. It was a thorn in the side of the British, nevertheless, for the coasts of Norumbega, which later came to be known as Maine, were peopled with Indians, and the fur trade with these Indians was a source of considerable profit to the Englishmen from Plymouth and Boston—the "Bostonnais." Throughout the seventeenth century, in time of peace as well as in time of war, both sides had seized each other's trading posts, vessels, and furs, and each group had incited its Indian friends against the other. At the latter game of intrigue the French turned out to be somewhat more effective than the British, and the seizure of Boston ships and trading posts by Frenchmen along these coasts was a healthy reminder of the need of British protection. This needed protection, indeed, was probably one of the chief reasons why Massachusetts felt itself obliged to acquiesce in the revocation of its charter in 1684.

CANADA: THE ERA OF CHAMPLAIN AND THE COMPANY OF ONE HUNDRED

Meanwhile, three years after the founding of Port Royal, Samuel Champlain had built a post at Quebec; and during the remainder of his life, from 1608 to 1634, he devoted himself to the development of his colony and the exploration of the rivers and lakes that poured their waters into the St. Lawrence. In the summer of 1609 he joined an Indian expedition against the Iroquois Indians which took him to the shores of the lake that bears his name. In 1611 he explored the waters of the St. Lawrence as far as the La Chine Rapids above Montreal, and in 1613 he explored a considerable part of the Ottawa River. Two years later, after a visit to France, he was back in Quebec and accompanied a party of Hurons up the Ottawa and across Lake Nipissing to Lake Huron, the eastern shores of which he carefully examined before returning to the settlements. In all these explorations Champlain had been moved by a desire to find a route across the continent to the South Sea, but he was also a French patriot seeking to add to the greatness of France's empire, and he saw the value of the fur trade, which he did everything he could to encourage.

During Champlain's governorship, the fur trade was controlled by a series of companies organized by the merchants of Rouen, St. Malo, and other French towns, but the trade did not prosper. Cardinal Richelieu, when he came into power in France about 1623, took it upon himself to reorganize both the colony and the trade in such a way as to place it under the control of a group of men who would be more responsible to the Crown than the former holders of the fur-trade monopoly. The Cardinal was anxious also to build up the population of the colony and extend the bounds of the French colonial empire. He therefore organized, in the year 1627, the Company of New France, the so-called "Company of the One Hundred Associates," which was composed of a hundred handpicked leaders of French economic and civil life.

In the charter that Richelieu issued to the Company of New France, the company was granted the territory of North America from Florida to the Arctic Circle, and from the Atlantic Ocean to the great inland seas that Champlain had discovered. It was given the power to issue grants of land under a feudal tenure and to issue titles to the grantees. It was given, moreover, a permanent monopoly of the fur trade and a monopoly of all trade with the colony for a period of fifteen years. The fisheries, however, were left open to any French citizen. In return for this huge gift, the company on its part promised to take out four thousand colonists before the year 1643. No foreigners could be taken, and no Protestants. Only good French Catholics were to be allowed to go, and special encouragement was to be given to tradesmen and artisans, in order to promote the economic welfare of the colony. The company promised, furthermore, to send out priests and establish missions, and to maintain them, either by direct subsidy or by grants of land.

The charter granted to the Company of New France was liberal for its time, for it placed an emphasis upon emigration and provided inducements to the best sort of emigrants to go. It granted citizenship to the inhabitants of Canada, even to the Indians who should become Roman Catholics. On the other hand, however, it had certain fatal weaknesses. It limited emigration to those who did not wish to go. It is probable that many French Huguenots would have welcomed a chance to escape persecution by emigration to the new world, but these were prohibited from doing so by the terms of this charter. Further, the charter had a tendency to throttle the normal economic development of the colony by placing all the power in the hands of one company. It resulted in the planting in Canada of a feudalistic tenure of land. Finally, for better or for worse, it fixed upon the colony the Roman Catholic hierarchy, which made French Canada completely Roman Catholic for a hundred and fifty years.

The company started with enthusiasm and immediately equipped a fleet of four ships and four hundred colonists, together with necessary supplies, which it directed to Canada; but unhappily for the colony and for the company, it entered upon its project in the very year when England declared war upon France in the name of the Protestants of La Rochelle, and this first company fleet sailed for America just in time to meet a British fleet under the command of David Kirke in the mouth of the St. Lawrence River. The French fleet was taken by the British, and the expedition turned out to be a complete loss for the company. The next year, 1629, the company again sent a fleet of ships and many colonists. This time there was to be a convoy furnished by the king; but the treaty of Susa, which made peace between France and England, was signed on April 24, so the convoy was withdrawn and this fleet, unprotected, sailed to Canada, only to meet another British fleet. One of the French ships was captured, one escaped, and one sank. Champlain, without supplies for two years, was starving in the fort at Quebec, and was forced to surrender to the English expedition in July, 1629. This first British conquest of Quebec resulted in a British occupation that lasted for three years, but Canada was returned to France along with Acadia by the treaty of St. Germain (1632) and Champlain returned to the colony for which he had spent his life early in 1633.

By this time the company had fallen upon evil days. So much of its capital had been invested in the first two disastrous expeditions that it was unable to continue and was forced to sub-lease its monopoly of the Canadian trade. This event marks the beginning of the second era of Canadian settlement, for the sub-company did send out colonists and missionaries, and the colony at last began to grow. Colonists were still difficult to obtain, however, and the company resorted to the plan of granting seigneurial tracts to persons who would undertake to take a certain number of colonists to Canada. The first of these feudal grants was made in 1634; by 1640 there were about fifteen of them in Canada facing on the St. Lawrence River and running back to the hills. Perhaps the most important of all the feudal grants made for lands in Canada was that of the island of Montreal, granted to the Sulpician Order of Paris in the year 1640. The colonization of Canada thus took on a distinctly feudal aspect, with peasants living on the land and cultivating it, and a class of landed aristocrats who owned the land and, in a local way, governed the peasants.

In this manner the population in the colony slowly but steadily increased, and the towns of Three Rivers and Quebec became the village centers of a rural feudal society.

The grant to the Sulpicians resulted in the founding of the town of Montreal in the year 1642 as an outpost in the work of evangelizing the Indians. The Sulpicians were aided by other charitable people who built a hospital, schools, a nunnery, and other institutions, with the result that the town of Montreal quickly became a strong outpost of French civilization and an important trading depot for the canoeloads of skins and furs brought down the Ottawa and St. Lawrence Rivers by the Indians of the west.

One more aspect of Canadian life in this period should be noted, and that was the strong hold that religion had upon the colonists and their relations with the Indians. The most important of the missionary organizations was the Society of Jesus, or the Jesuits, who, not content to wait for the Indians to come down from the villages, established their missions in the Indian towns themselves. Thus they became not only missionaries but representatives of French civilization and government and, in a way, diplomatic agents to cultivate good relations' between the Indians and their French neighbors. The influence of the Jesuits upon the history of Canada was enormous, both in the colony and at home. Year by year the missionaries wrote reports of their missions, and these reports, the famous *Jesuit Relations,* were printed and circulated among the intellectuals and the wealthy of France, with the result that an extraordinary popular interest in the colony was developed in the mother country. In the colony itself the Jesuits and the Franciscans were not merely missionaries. Very early in the history of the colony they established schools, the first of which was set up in Quebec in the year 1634; and they made every attempt to bring the Indians into the orbit of the French settlements and prepare them for absorption into French civilization.

Thus, in the period between 1632 and 1663, when the Company of New France finally lost its charter, the chief lines of French colonization were laid down. Government was to all intents and purposes in the hands of the company in France. Socially the colony was distinctly feudal in aspect, and in its religious life it was so permeated with the Roman Catholic religion that practically every important event that took place in the colony had a distinctly religious tinge. In one aspect, however, the colony developed in a way that was purely American, for the only profitable enterprise in Canada, aside from the fisheries, was the fur trade, and upon the success of this business depended the very life of the colony itself. The importance of the fur trade is shown by the fact that when the Iroquois took the warpath against their kinsmen the Hurons living to the northward of the Great Lakes late in the 1640's, the paralysis of the fur trade that followed upon the extermination of the Hurons threatened to destroy the colony. Partly because of the economic distress that resulted from this paralysis of the fur trade and partly because of the contentions that had arisen over economic and political questions under the government of the Company of New France, Louis XIV, on his accession to the ~~throne~~ of France in 1661, decided to take control of the colony out of the hands of the company and administer it directly in his own way.

THE OLD REGIME

The accession of Louis XIV to the throne of France marks the beginning of the era of French Canada's greatest prosperity. Louis XIV was interested in the expansion of the French empire, and he was assisted by the great mercantilistic minister Jean-Baptiste Colbert. Louis and his minister were determined to develop New France, and one of the first things they did was to revoke the charter of the Company of the One Hundred Associates. The king created the office of intendant for the assistance of the governor and sent to New France a bishop to take charge of religious life. He named as his governor of New France the Sieur de Tracy and sent him to Canada with instructions to chastise the Iroquois and restore the economic prosperity of the colony. This Tracy succeeded in doing in the year 1667. He marched into the country of the Mohawks, one of the Iroquois tribes, burned their villages, and forced them to make a peace which lasted for almost twenty years. Tracy, having restored peace, retired, leaving the government in the hands of a series of governors, the greatest of whom was the Comte de Frontenac.

Meanwhile, the king and his minister had adopted a policy of paternalistic encouragement of social and economic development. The king had sent as the first intendant Jean Talon, a man of great ability, who contributed a great deal to the economic and social progress of the settlements. At the same time Colbert proceeded to send out more settlers, shiploads of girls to be wives for the soldiers whose regiments were disbanded in Canada after the Tracy expedition, tools and animals for the farmers, nets for the fishermen, and other aids for the development of a self-supporting economic life. The population of the colony grew rapidly from some four thousand in 1665 to about fifteen thousand in 1690. Little by little the colony turned its attention to the raising of foodstuffs and livestock, so that by the end of the century Canada was producing practically all its supplies except the manufactured goods that had to come from France. Its government was almost purely paternalistic. At the head of the civil government stood the governor, who was the personal representative of the king, military commander and recipient of the honor and ceremony due the king. At his side stood the intendant, charged with the administration of civil affairs such as the building of roads and bridges, the promotion of agriculture, the regulation of commerce, the hearing of disputes between colonists, and even the regulation of marital affairs. The intendant was, as a matter of fact, probably the most powerful member of the government because of his close contact with so many of the everyday affairs of the inhabitants. The third member of the trilogy of government was the bishop, charged with the administration of religious matters. Religion, however, was interpreted to include a great many things now relegated to civil life. Swearing, drunkenness, divorce, marriage itself, as well as missionary enterprise and the moral welfare of the Indians, all fell within the purview of the bishop and his agents, and offenses in these fields, as in many others, had to be brought to the bishop's court rather than to the court of the feudal lord or the court of the governor. As might have been expected, there were many bitter quarrels among the three heads of government over their respective spheres of influence and authority. Throughout its history, indeed, French Canada was the scene of long and bitter political feuds among these three branches of government.

There was nothing even remotely suggestive of representative government. The governor, the bishop, and the intendant, together with a number of councilors that varied from three to twelve, constituted the council of the colony. This council, however, did not make laws; the most it could do was to issue ordinances relative to local and comparatively unimportant problems. The important laws and recommendations for the colony were made by Colbert or the king in France, with the result that the government of Canada was a sort of remote control conducted on the basis of lengthy reports written to their superiors by the governor and the intendant or other royal agents in the colony and without particular regard for the wishes of the colonists themselves.

Canada, then, was in its external aspects a feudal society ruled over by governor, intendant, and bishop. But its most significant occupation was the exploitation of the fur trade with the Indians, and this fur trade exerted a deep and permanent influence upon the development of the colony. Year by year, every spring, fleets of canoes would come down the rivers to Montreal, Three Rivers, or Quebec, and there the Indians would barter their furs for the pots and pans, guns, lead, scalping knives, shoes, and blankets offered in trade by the Frenchmen. The most important of the trading towns was Montreal, and the "Montreal Fair," as it was called, came to be the high point in the annual round of life of the people of that city, for to the fair the Indians would come to sell their furs and there would ensue days or even weeks of haggling and trading, after which the Indians would get gloriously drunk before their return to their native haunts. The use of liquor was extremely demoralizing to the Indians, and one of the bitterest controversies between the bishop and the governor was over the question whether the trade in spirits should be prohibited. But it was generally recognized that the life of the fur trade depended in large measure upon the continuance of the liquor traffic, with the result that no really effectual effort was ever made to stop it.

Another significant outgrowth of the fur trade in Canada was the appearance of a new social group among the people. This group was composed of young men who, not content to wait for the Indians to bring their pelts down to the settlements, went into the Indian towns themselves and there traded with the Indians on their own grounds. They went far into the Indian country and stayed there—sometimes for years—moving about with the Indians, consorting with Indian women and producing a race of halfbreeds, following the Indians in their hunting, accumulating cargoes of skins, and returning to the settlements only long enough to dispose of their cargoes, spend the money that they had taken as profit on their ventures, then to go again into the forest. So attractive was this wild, semi-savage life and so great were the numbers of young French-Canadians that entered into it, that it became a serious social problem for the colony, and many attempts were made to prevent Frenchmen from leaving the villages to go for trade into the Indian country. All such attempts failed, however, and the result was the appearance in French Canada of a considerable body of men who were of a bold, lawless, semi-savage type who provided an element of trouble for the colony, but who also rendered invaluable service to France in the long series of wars with the English because of their friendship with the Indians and their understanding of the Indian manners and customs.

THE EXPANSION OF FRENCH CANADA

The aspect of the development of New France that was of most importance to the English colonies, however, was the expansion of Canada to the westward. The exploration of the west had been suspended during the period of the Huron-Iroquois wars, but late in the 1650's two young men, Pierre Esprit Radisson and Médard Grosseilliers went up the rivers and the lakes and returned after two years with an extremely valuable cargo of furs. They went again to the country to the westward, whence they returned in 1663 with some 360 canoeloads of skins. But they were ill-treated by the governor, and the profits from their journey were practically wiped out by confiscation by the agents of the Company of New France on the ground that they had traded with the Indians without a license. They then turned in disgust from New France to the English, and led an expedition of Englishmen to the shores of Hudson Bay in 1669 which resulted in the formation of the Hudson's Bay Company in 1670. The significance of their early voyages for New France, however, lay in the fact that they called attention to the existence of a great rich land lying about the Great Lakes which offered limitless possibilities for expansion, missionary enterprise, and exploitation.

There followed an era of rapid penetration in the lands about the upper lakes. Already the Jesuits had begun to take an interest in the country; Père René Ménard established the first Jesuit mission on Lake Superior in 1661. Three years later Père Claude Allouez founded a mission at Chequemegon Bay. Allouez heard of and reported the existence of a great river to the westward that was said to fall into the sea. Allouez was followed in 1668 by Père Jacques Marquette and, in 1669, with the aid of Père Claude Dablon, Marquette built the mission at Sault Ste. Marie, at the outlet of Lake Superior. Allouez then went on to found a mission at Green Bay on the western side of Lake Michigan, whence he explored the rivers flowing into Lake Michigan and into Green Bay and found the route to the Mississippi which lay only six days distant in travel from the lake.

In Quebec, meanwhile, the great intendant Jean Talon, anxious to get possession of this western land for France and to build up trade, sent Daumont de St. Lusson to the Lake Superior country to take possession in the name of France. Talon had dreams of a great French empire in the inland parts of the continent and at about the same time that he sent Lusson up the lakes he was sending Louis Joliet to search for the copper mines on Lake Superior and to ascertain their value and, if possible, to find a cheap and direct route for the transfer of the copper to the port at Montreal. Joliet found the copper mines, but he reported that they were too far away for exploitation for the present. About three years later he was sent out again, this time in the company of Père Marquette, to discover the great river reported to flow westward. Joliet and Marquette started on their voyage in May of 1673, ascended Green Bay and the Fox River flowing into it, crossed Lake Winnebago, and descended the Wisconsin River, whence they entered the Mississippi on June 17. They traveled down the Mississippi as far as the Arkansas, but there, having satisfied themselves that the great river flowed not into the Atlantic at Virginia nor into the Pacific at Lower California but into the Gulf of Mexico, and fearing to fall into the hands of the Spaniards who ruled that gulf, they turned back and returned to Canada, where they reported their discovery.

Marquette and Joliet were followed in the exploration of the western waters by Robert Cavelier de la Salle. La Salle had come to Canada, where he had settled at the western end of the island of Montreal, in 1667, but he had heard of rivers flowing westward, and he was consumed with a desire to discover a route to the Pacific. So interested was he in finding the route to the South Sea, indeed, that his settlement was in derision called "La Chine." His interest never wavered, however, and in 1673 he accompanied Governor Frontenac to Lake Ontario, where, at the outlet to the lake the governor caused to be built a fort which he proceeded to turn over to La Salle as a fief. This fort, named after the governor, was the first of a series of forts built by the French toward the west, and became the base of La Salle's later western explorations. In 1680-82 La Salle succeeded in descending to its mouth the river that Joliet and Marquette had explored, and took possession of all the valley drained by the Mississippi and its tributaries in the name of France, calling it Louisiana in honor of his king. In the years that followed, the French extended their line of posts from Fort Frontenac to Niagara, Detroit, Michillimackinac, St. Louis on the Illinois, Kaskaskia in the Illinois country, Natchez on the Mississippi, and eventually New Orleans and Biloxi on the shores of the Gulf. Biloxi was founded in 1699, Mobile in 1711, and the town of New Orleans in 1718.

Thus it came about that by the end of the seventeenth century the French had established a long line of forts and settlements from Quebec to the mouth of the Mississippi. France had staked its claim to the great interior valley of the continent and the English suddenly awoke to a realization that they were hemmed in on the seaboard and that if they were to expand it must be by breaking the French line of settlements.

INEVITABLE CONFLICT

The rising conflict between Frenchmen and Englishmen in America was focused by the end of the seventeenth century in a number of widely separated areas of the new world. In the Hudson Bay region, Englishmen and Frenchmen were fighting over the control of the fur trade of that region, for Radisson, dissatisfied with the treatment he had received from the Hudson's Bay Company, had returned to Canada to form the *Compagnie du Nord* for the exploitation of the fur trade of that northern region. He had taken a group of traders to the western shore of the Bay, where he had founded Fort Bourbon and where he had come into bloody conflict with the agents of the Hudson's Bay Company. But that was just the beginning, for "Company Men" and "Canada Men" fought each other for the possession of the forts around the southern end of James Bay, and these forts changed hands rapidly in the decade following 1686. In Newfoundland, settled by the English in 1610, English fishermen and French fishermen were contending for the control of the fishing banks and the ownership of the lands of the shores on which to dry their fish. The English had a settlement at St. Johns and the French had a settlement at Placencia, and both nations claimed title to the island, England on the ground of prior discovery by John Cabot and settlement by John Guy, France on the ground that Newfoundland had been occupied and exploited by Breton fishermen since long before the expedition of Cabot. The checkered history of Acadia has already been noted; but elsewhere, too, even in time of peace, Frenchmen and Englishmen seized each others' goods and ships and neither scrupled at murder in the effort to control the fur trade with the Indians or the fisheries off the coasts.

A fourth area of conflict lay in the lands to the south of the Great Lakes. These were the lands of the Iroquois Indians, but when the Sieur de Tracy invaded the Mohawk country in 1666, Governor Nichols of New York had protested on the ground that this area lay within the territory formerly occupied by the Dutch and now granted to the Duke of York. Later on, when the Iroquois again began to make trouble for the French, Governor Denonville invaded the Iroquois country and began building a fort on the south or east side of the Niagara River. Governor Dongan of New York vigorously protested both the invasion and the building of the fort, on the ground that this land had always been a part of New York, and he now bolstered his claim with what he called a deed from the Iroquois Indians to the British Crown, by which he claimed the Iroquois had subjected themselves and their lands to British rule. The French immediately rejected any such argument on the ground that the territory belonged to France by right of exploration; all the land drained by the waters that flowed into the rivers traversed by the French explorers, they claimed, belonged to France. In any case, the governors of New York and New France glared at each other across the frontier, each waiting for an opportunity to seize what he considered to be the property of his sovereign. Far to the southward, in the plains drained by the Alabama and Appalachicola river systems, Englishmen were beginning to penetrate the interior in the prosecution of their rapidly growing deerskin trade with the southern Indians, and soon after the turn of the century their penetration of those regions also was challenged by the French, who were entering the same valleys by way of Biloxi and Mobile.

In the islands about the Caribbean Sea, the colonial rivalry of the two powers was just as vigorous as on the continent. France and England had jointly occupied St. Christopher early in the century, and as their settlements had expanded the French islands were soon sprinkled among British islands, and here and there nationals of both contested for the same lands. St. Lucia was one such island. The English and French inhabitants of St. Christopher attempted to avoid becoming entangled in Anglo-French wars by the treaty of Sandys Point of 1678, but it was impossible for the islands and the two countries not to be drawn into the conflict when their mother countries went to war.

Such was the situation in America when James II came to the throne of England in 1685. Englishmen and Frenchmen were fighting each other in time of peace all along the frontier from Hudson Bay to Guiana. The stakes in the conflict were great—the fur trade in Hudson Bay, the fisheries of Newfoundland and Acadia, the control of the Great Lakes route to the fur trade of the west, the possession of the Gulf coastal plain and the exploitation of the deerskin trade, and the possession of the sugar-producing islands of the Lesser Antilles. The American colonies were not the pawns of European diplomacy; far from it—they were anxious for war, for successful war meant empire, and empire meant profit. Sooner or later the trial by war must come.

RECOMMENDED BOOKS FOR FURTHER READING

CONTEMPORARY NARRATIVES

Isaac J. Cox, ed., *The Journeys of René Robert Cavelier, Sieur de La Salle.*

William L. Grant, ed., *Voyages of Samuel de Champlain, 1604-1618.*

Harold A. Innis, *Select Documents in Canadian Economic History, 1497-1783.*

Louise P. Kellogg, ed., *Early Narratives of the Northwest, 1634-1699.*

William B. Munro, ed., *Documents Relating to the Seigniorial Tenure in Canada, 1598-1856.*

Edmund B. O'Callaghan, ed., *Documents Relative to the Colonial History of the State of New York*, Volume III.

Reuben G. Thwaites, ed., *The Jesuit Relations and Allied Documents,* XXXIV, pp. 71-231; LXIII, pp. 269-293.

MODERN ACCOUNTS

The Cambridge History of the British Empire, I, Chapter 10; VI, Chapters 1-2.

Charles W. Colby, *Canadian Types of the Old Régime, 1608-1698.*

Charles W. Colby, *The Fighting Governor.*

Charles W. Colby, *The Founder of New France.*

James Douglas, *Old France in the New World.*

Frances O. J. Gaither, *The Fatal River: the Life and Death of La Salle.*

François X. Garneau, *History of Canada,* Volume I.

Harold A. Innis, *The Cod Fisheries,* Chapters 1-5.

Harold A. Innis, *The Fur Trade in Canada.*

Louise P. Kellogg, *The French Régime in Wisconsin and the Northwest.*

Thomas G. Marquis, *The Jesuit Missions.*

Stewart L. Mims, *Colbert's West India Policy.*

William B. Munro, *Crusaders of New France.*

William B. Munro, *The Seigneurs of Old Canada.*

William B. Munro, *The Seigniorial System in Canada.*

Francis Parkman, *Count Frontenac and New France under Louis XIV.*

Francis Parkman, *The Jesuits in North America in the Seventeenth Century.*

Francis Parkman, *La Salle and the Discovery of the Great West.*

Francis Parkman, *The Old Régime in Canada.*

Francis Parkman, *Pioneers of France in the New World,* Part II.

Adam Shortt and Arthur G. Doughty, eds., *Canada and its Provinces,* Volumes I, II, *New France.*

Reuben G. Thwaites, *Father Marquette.*

James A. Williamson, *A Short History of British Expansion,* Part IV, Chapter 3.

Justin Winsor, *Cartier to Frontenac.*

George M. Wrong, *A Canadian Manor and its Seigneur.*

George M. Wrong, *The Rise and Fall of New France,* Volume I.

24

The British Empire and European Diplomacy, 1648-1713

THE RISE in the economic value of colonial empires in the second half of the seventeenth century greatly enhanced the importance of their role in the evolution of European diplomacy in the sixty-odd years following the Peace of Westphalia. Colonies were not yet dominant considerations in the calculations of the chancelleries of Europe, but their weight in the balance of international affairs steadily increased. The appearance of French, British and Dutch colonial empires in America had brought about new rivalries. The common hostility of France, Holland and England to the Hispano-Portuguese monopoly of the new world ceased to be the chief theme in international relations with regard to it, and gave place to a complex set of new contests between these younger colonizing powers themselves, and from competition for maritime power these rivalries went on to what was in its broadest aspects a competition between methods of colonization, exploitation and government of colonial empires. So far as the British colonies were concerned, three general diplomatic developments are to be noted during the era of Louis XIV which were of profound importance for the later history both of the colonies and of Europe. First of these was the international rivalry of the British with the Dutch for colonial commerce, in which the British were the ultimate victors. The second was the growing rivalry in America between the British and French commercial and colonial empires, the effort to neutralize Anglo-French colonial conflicts as a cause for European war, and the American counterparts of the Anglo-French wars that reached their dramatic dénouement in the Peace of Utrecht. The third was made up of the sordid rivalries and diplomatic bickerings that grew out of the question of the Spanish Succession, involving, as it did, all the wealth, colonial and commercial, of the Spanish Indies.

ANGLO-DUTCH COLONIAL AND COMMERCIAL RIVALRY

From the opening of the era of colonization in North America, the Dutch began to be serious competitors of the English for the profits of empire. With a growing establishment at the mouth of the Hudson and with bases in St. Eustatius and Guiana in the Caribbean area, the Dutch were in a fine position to trade with the English colonies. This they did, to the profit of both parties, and during the decade of the English civil war, when English merchants were preoccupied with events at home, the Dutch built up such a commerce with the English colonies as to threaten to exclude the English from it altogether. It was to recover the lost ground by the exclusion of the Dutch as carriers of colonial commerce that the first navigation act was passed in 1651. The government of the United Provinces immediately sought to neutralize the effects of this British law by the channel of negotiation. It is interesting to note that the Dutch proposed a mutual recognition of the principle of the freedom of the seas as against the British claim to sovereignty over all the waters surrounding the British Isles, the suspension of the navigation act insofar as it affected Dutch shipping, and an agreement upon a boundary between Dutch New Netherland and the English colonies on each side of it. All of these propositions the British rejected, and a refusal of the Dutch fleet to recognize British sovereignty over the English Channel led to war in 1652. New Netherland attempted to maintain its neutrality, but it was only the neutrality of Massachusetts that prevented New Haven and Connecticut from forcing the New England Confederation into the war. As it was, Connecticut seized the Dutch fort at Hartford; England sent over an expedition under Major Robert Sedgwick, and Massachusetts was won over to the cause of the war; New Netherland was saved from British attack only by the signature of the Anglo-Dutch treaty of Westminster of 1654. This treaty was a diplomatic victory for England, for the Dutch tacitly recognized the validity of the British Navigation Act of 1651. Disputes over commerce, seizures, etc., were to be submitted to an Anglo-Dutch joint commission, and, in case the commission should fail to agree, to the arbitration of Switzerland.

From that time on the Dutch recognized the British navigation law, but continued to trade with the English colonies much as before. It was partly to tighten the enforcement of this law against the Dutch that it was re-enacted with certain additions in 1660. But it was still impossible to enforce the exclusion of the Dutch from the colonial trade so long as they remained in New Netherland, and it was resolved, for this and other reasons, to drive them out. This was done in 1664, as already noted. In the war that followed, Louis XIV attempted to mediate between England and the Netherlands but failed, whereupon France entered the war on the side of the Dutch. In the West Indies the French succeeded in taking the British part of Antigua and Montserrat, together with St. Eustatius and Tobago that the British had already taken from the Dutch. In the Peace of Breda (1667) that followed, both sides kept what they had taken, which meant that Britain retained New Netherland, now New York, and the Dutch kept Surinam (Guiana). So far as the colonial trade was concerned, the Dutch again recognized the British navigation act and the principle of monopoly in intra-imperial commerce.

In 1670 King Charles II of England made a secret treaty of alliance with France against the Dutch, by which Charles also promised to aid Louis XIV to acquire a part, if not all, of the possessions of Spain upon the expected death of Spain's invalid king. Soon after, France went to war with the Dutch, and in the course of the fighting that broke out between the Dutch and the English, the Dutch retook New York, on August 9, 1673. But the English people and Parliament were not in sympathy with this war, and Charles II was practically forced to make a separate peace with the Dutch early in 1674. By this treaty the Anglo-Dutch treaty of Breda was renewed, and New York was restored to the British.

This peace, forced upon Charles II by his people, was a turning point in Anglo-Dutch relations. For William of Orange, now leading the Dutch state, saw in Louis XIV, rather than England, the great enemy of his people, and he was prepared to go to considerable lengths to win England's support. Later in 1674, therefore, he made a marine treaty with England which recognized British mastery of the seas, and in 1678 made an alliance with Charles II which made the Dutch the economic and diplomatic satellites of England for a century. William's marriage to Mary, the daughter of James, Duke of York (later James II of England) and niece of Charles II, prepared the way for his own accession to the throne of England and the active belligerency of that country at the side of the United Provinces against the great dictator, Louis XIV.

ENGLAND AND THE HISPANIC MONOPOLY

Until the middle of the seventeenth century, Spain obstinately maintained her claim to the new world divided between herself and Portugal by the Papal Bulls of 1493 and the treaty of Tordesillas (1494). The two claims had been united by Spain's annexation of Portugal, which gave Spain a shadowy claim to all of the American hemisphere, most of Africa, and a large portion of Asia. But the long rebellion of Portugal that began in 1640 eventually separated the Portuguese colonial empire from the Spanish, and the defeat of the Hapsburgs in the Thirty Years War forced Spain for the first time to admit, in the treaty of Münster (1648) with the Dutch, the right of another nation to sail to the West Indies and to trade and acquire territory there.

So far as England was concerned, Spain still maintained her claim to a monopolistic ownership of all the lands and the seas of America. Portugal, on the other hand, to win England's support for her struggle for independence, opened the trade of Brazil to British ships in the Anglo-Portuguese treaty of Westminster in 1654, which also indirectly recognized the British navigation act excluding the Portuguese, along with the Dutch, from a profitable trade with the British colonies. Upon the return of Charles II to the throne of England, Portugal cemented this budding friendship by arranging a marriage between Charles and the Portuguese princess, Katherine of Braganza (successfully out-bidding the Spanish candidate for Charles' hand), and by giving England Tangier and a predominant role in the commerce of the Portuguese East Indies, in return for further English aid in winning Spanish recognition of Portuguese independence. The Portuguese share of the monopoly of the East and West Indies was thus liquidated, and Portugal became, in effect, the commercial vassal of England.

Charles II then turned to the task of winning Spanish recognition of Portuguese independence, and with the secret aid of France he succeeded. But he was even more interested in breaking down the exclusiveness of Spain in its own American colonies. Spain, finding itself isolated and in danger of attack by France, welcomed British overtures with regard to Portugal and European commerce, but balked at acknowledging the right of Englishmen even to sail the waters of the West Indies. After a long and tedious negotiation, however, Spain promised to recognize Portuguese independence, and a treaty was finally signed at Madrid, in 1667, which recognized the same rights with regard to Englishmen in the Indies as had been recognized as pertaining to the Dutch in the treaty of Münster—that is, Spain at last recognized the right of the English to sail to the Indies, east and west, and to trade and acquire territory there, provided always that they stay strictly away from the territories owned and occupied by Spain.

Spain hoped, by this treaty, to bring an end to the piracy and plundering then practiced upon Spanish commerce and colonies in America by Englishmen, but her hopes were not realized. Piracy continued, under color of a fictitious legality given by letters of marque and reprisal, and such buccaneers as the notorious Henry Morgan of Jamaica continued to fatten at Spain's expense. When the latter raided and burned Porto Bello on the Isthmus of Panamá, one of the richest towns in Spanish America, in June, 1668, Spain protested to England that this raid was a flagrant violation of the treaty of 1667. England, reversing the position it had maintained at the beginning of the century, now argued that the treaty of 1667 did not apply to America; that, in accord with the ancient doctrine of the two spheres—according to which Europe was one sphere of law and America was another, in which European law and treaties did not apply—"might made right beyond the Line"; that, in other words, if Spain desired peace in America, she would have to make a special treaty dealing specifically with American questions. Spain's desire for English friendship in the face of the expansion of France in Europe led Spain to acquiesce, and in 1670 a new treaty, dealing solely with America, was signed.

This significant instrument, giving documentary witness, as it were, to the doctrine of the two spheres, sought to settle the Anglo-Spanish disputes in America. Its most important clause was one giving mutual recognition to the possessions of the two signatories, and providing that Great Britain should retain for the future all the territory in America then occupied by British settlements. This meant that Jamaica, seized from Spain in 1655, was now recognized as a British possession, and that the settlements at Charleston and elsewhere in "Florida," were to be left unmolested by Spain. But England also promised that its subjects should not interfere with Spanish colonial commerce or visit the Spanish colonies for trade or any other purpose except in case of distress from storms or pirates.

It was in 1671, shortly after the signature of this treaty—before news of it arrived in America, according to his report—that Henry Morgan carried out his most famous exploit, the sack of the city of Panamá. But that was the last of the great buccaneering expeditions, for Great Britain made a serious effort to stop them. On the other side, the Spanish claim to a monopoly of the hemisphere was clearly broken, and Spain and England entered a period of relatively good relations, drawn together by their common fear of the expansiveness and the rising commercial and colonial power of France—against which they became allied in the war of the Palatinate, which broke out in Europe in 1688.

THE GROWING RIVALRY OF GREAT BRITAIN AND FRANCE

The imperial competition of Great Britain and France in the world of commerce and colonies was much more far-reaching and of far more profound significance for America than the relatively short-lived conflict between the English and the Dutch. This competition had gotten under way in the first decade of successful English and French colonization in America, with the settlement of Port Royal in Acadia and of Jamestown in Virginia, as already noted. In the short war of 1627-29 the English had taken Acadia and Canada from the French, but had returned them under the terms of the treaty of St. Germain-en-Laye (1632). Again, in 1654, Oliver Cromwell sent Major Robert Sedgwick to seize Acadia, where he succeeded in taking Port Royal, Fort St. John, and the post at the mouth of the Penobscot. But at this moment France was still in a life-and-death conflict with Spain, and Cardinal Mazarin, at the head of the French state, overlooked the "insult" and signed the Anglo-French treaty of Westminster (1654) which provided for a joint commission to adjust reciprocal claims for ship seizures and the question of the restoration of Acadia. But the commissioners were never appointed, and England retained possession of Acadia until after the treaty of Breda (1667).

It was, indeed, only after the accession of Louis XIV to power and the aggressive commercial and colonial policies of his minister, Jean-Baptiste Colbert, that the British began really to awaken to the threat of French rivalry in the imperial world. The rapid development and expansion of New France, the brawls of French and British fur traders on the shores of Hudson Bay and of fishermen on the banks of Newfoundland, and the raids and counter-raids in the islands of the West Indies, became matters of intense concern to Englishmen, both in the colonies and at home. The support of the Dutch by France in the second Anglo-Dutch War (1664-67) was hardly the beginning of serious conflict between the two empires, however, since Louis XIV and Charles II were more interested in promoting their own dynastic interests in Europe by cooperation than in extending their imperial territories in America by war.

As a matter of fact, the most striking feature of Anglo-French diplomacy with regard to America in the three decades between 1660 and 1689 was the policy of the two crowns which sought to separate the affairs of the two continents by a revival of the old doctrine of the two spheres. Louis XIV declared war on England in support of the Dutch in 1666 only after having attempted to confine the Anglo-Dutch War to America in order to avoid antagonizing Britain and driving her into an alliance with Spain just when he was about to seize a part of the Spanish Netherlands. Then, when he found himself engaged in the war, he instructed his governors in the West Indies and Canada to remain neutral. But the British governors attacked the French colonies, and fighting ensued all along the line. In the West Indies the French succeeded in conquering the English part of St. Christopher and the islands of Antigua and Montserrat, and recaptured several places already taken by the English from the Dutch. The French expedition into New York to chastise the Iroquois in 1666 threw that colony on the defensive, but no actual fighting took place there between the French and the English. Both Louis XIV and Charles II were anxious to end the war in 1667; at Breda, while the Dutch and the English were agreeing to keep what they had taken from each other, England and France agreed to restore the conquests they had made, including the restoration of Acadia to France by England. This transfer was made in 1670.

The idea of colonial neutrality in European wars was not new. As early as 1627 the French and English residents of their respective parts of St. Christopher had agreed that in case of war between France and England they would not fight unless commanded to do so, and this agreement had been renewed at various times thereafter. Similarly, Peter Stuyvesant, under instruction from the Dutch West India Company, proposed to the Confederation of New England that the Confederation and the colony of New Netherland remain neutral in the first Dutch War in 1652, and it was the isolationist sentiment of Massachusetts which gave Stuyvesant's proposal effect. The inhabitants of St. Christopher had renewed their treaty of neutrality at the beginning of the war in 1666; but it had failed to save them from hostilities. In 1678, however, when war between France and England again seemed imminent, it was renewed again, and this time it was made to include the other Leeward Islands.

Thus the treaty of Sandys Point, as it was called, provided that, should war break out between England and France in Europe, the inhabitants of the English Leeward Islands and the French islands would abstain from attacking each other, and, should disputes arise between them, they were to be settled by peaceful means. Hostages were to be given on both sides, and an appeal was to be made to the home governments for a ratification of the agreement. When the treaty was submitted to the mother countries, both approved in principle, but France asked that the treaty be extended to include Barbados and Jamaica, since it still left the French islands open to attack from these two, the strongest of the British West Indies.

The treaty failed of ratification; but the idea was again taken up in the negotiations between the two countries which followed the accession of James II to the throne of England in 1685. Louis XIV was in the midst of his expansion of the French frontiers toward the Rhine, and desired nothing so much as to keep England neutral; and James II was just embarking upon his three-year campaign to reform the government of England upon the model of absolutist, Roman Catholic France. Neither monarch thought the colonies and their frictions important enough to warrant allowing them to embroil the two countries in a European war. The policy of James II was a personal one, and contrary both to the commercial interests of Englishmen and to the commercial and territorial interests of the Americans; but its essential element—the idea of isolating America from Europe's conflicts, was native both to European diplomacy and to the American mind.

Be that as it may, Frenchmen and Englishmen were killing and robbing each other along the frontiers of America from Hudson Bay to Guiana. In 1683 a group of French Canadians had raided the Hudson's Bay Company port at the mouth of the Nelson River, and the company had retaliated in kind; on the coasts of Acadia and the Bay of Fundy Frenchmen seized New England ships on the ground that they were fishing and trading in French territory; friction was occurring in Newfoundland, where the French were reported to be encroaching upon the English; in the region south of the Great Lakes the Iroquois were again stirring up trouble against the French, and Thomas Dongan, James II's governor of New York, encouraged them while extending over them his "protection"; in the West Indies Anglo-French relations had deteriorated, both sides encouraging the native Caribs to make trouble.

It was in these circumstances in Europe and America that Louis XIV sounded out James II on the subject of a treaty of neutrality for all the colonies in America. As James was anxious to make just such a treaty, it was easy to formulate the treaty of Whitehall (1686), which is probably one of the most peculiar documents in American colonial history. For this treaty provided, in the first place, that there should be a firm peace between the colonies of the two countries in America, and that, even though hostilities should arise between England and France in Europe, that should not be considered a cause for war between them in America; and, conversely, that, should hostilities arise between the colonies of the two powers in America, such hostilities should not be considered a cause for war in Europe. On the contrary, disputes arising in America were to be settled in a peaceful manner by the French and English governors in the regions involved; or, failing settlement, the disputes were to be referred for peaceful settlement to the two sovereigns. In order to reduce possible friction to a minimum, each nation recognized the American possessions of the other, and each agreed not to permit its ships to enter the colonies of the other for the purpose of fishing or for trade.

It was thus hoped to isolate the future troubles of America from those of Europe. But the treaty made no provision for the adjustment of disputes already existing, and for this purpose commissioners were appointed on both sides in 1687. These commissioners were also charged with agreeing upon boundaries between the English colonies and the French; and in December, 1687, they took the first step in the form of an agreement to order strictly the suspension of all fighting in America until the commissioners should complete their work.

It should be noted that neither of these Anglo-French agreements had any possibility of success. The colonists in America, both English and French, hated each other with a cordial hatred; and there were always enough men in almost every colony who had a sufficient financial interest in war, or at least a sufficient recklessness of the results of their own conduct, to keep the bitter fires of conflict burning, and in this, on both sides, the colonists were encouraged by powerful private commercial interests at home. The conflict in America was not an addendum to some conflict in Europe, but a first-class rivalry in its own right that was to become more and more intense as the two empires, in their expansion, developed more and more points of contact and friction; nor was it to end, nationalism and diplomacy being what they were in the eighteenth century, until one of the protagonists had completely driven the other out of the hemisphere.

KING WILLIAM'S WAR

William III, stadholder of Holland, who ascended the throne of England when James II was driven out in the "Glorious Revolution" of 1688-89, read the commercial and colonial aspirations of his new subjects more accurately than James had done. For this was the same William of Orange who had been struggling to protect his native Netherlands against the ambitions of Louis XIV. He was a Protestant, and England was Protestant; he knew and understood the interests of a commercial people as James had not, and the English were a commercial people; he hated and feared Louis XIV, and most of the English people shared his feeling. It was not very difficult, therefore, for William to bring England into the war of the Palatinate against Louis XIV, just then breaking out in the Rhineland, under the terms of the Anglo-Dutch alliance of 1678. England now found itself allied with Holland, Sweden, the Holy Roman Empire, and Spain to maintain the balance of power in Europe. Significantly, however, in issuing his declaration of war, William took cognizance of the offenses of Louis' subjects in America against the English colonies there—in Newfoundland, in Hudson Bay, in the West Indies, in New York, and in Nova Scotia. By doing so William had not only the support of such powerful interests as Hudson's Bay Company in England, but also the enthusiastic cooperation of his subjects in America—or at least all, and there were many, who felt they had interests at stake in the war.

Fighting broke out immediately around the shores of Hudson Bay, and French and British posts changed hands over and over in dizzying sequence; most of them, at the end of the war, were in the hands of the French. Newfoundland, too, was the scene of bitter fighting, but it finally fell to the Canadian Pierre le Moyne, Sieur d'Iberville. Bitter Indian warfare took place all along the New England-New York frontier. Count Frontenac, upon the outbreak of war, quickly organized mixed expeditions of Indians and Frenchmen to strike at the English settlements, one of which fell upon Schenectady, in the winter of 1690, surprised it, and destroyed it. The American English, on their side, sent Captain William Phips against Acadia in that same year, and the expedition was a complete success. Meanwhile, the raid on Schenectady had emphasized the perilous position in which Albany and other frontier positions stood, and Jacob Leisler, then at the head of the government of New York, issued a call to the other colonies for a congress to meet at New York and plan a joint campaign against the French. This congress met in May, 1690, and was attended by representatives of Massachusetts, Plymouth, Connecticut, and New York. Rhode Island, Maryland, and Virginia, although not represented, pledged their cooperation and support. This first attempt at joint action by all the continental colonies—a sort of descendent of the now defunct New England Confederation—agreed upon a double attack upon Canada. One expedition was to go by sea, and the other by land over the Lake Champlain route. William Phips was given command of the expedition to the St. Lawrence, and actually appeared before Quebec; but he failed miserably in his effort to accomplish its capture. The land expedition collapsed before it got under way, largely because of the failure of the various colonies to send the required quotas of men; and the Iroquois, who were expected to assist in great numbers, hearing of an outbreak of smallpox at Albany, refused to move, on the ground that God had blocked their road. Thereafter, the war in this area degenerated into a series of frontier raids. The Iroquois, disgruntled because, as they said, their English allies left them to do all the fighting, entered into negotiations with Frontenac for a separate peace.

In the Caribbean area the war became a contest for the control of the sea. In the first year, before the arrival of British naval forces, the French again conquered the British section of St. Christopher, but upon the arrival of the fleet in 1690 the French were driven out and the English then recaptured St. Eustatius for the Dutch, and seized the French islands of St. Martin and St. Bartholomew. Fighting took place between French and Spanish forces in Santo Domingo, and in 1697 a French fleet sacked the rich Spanish port of Cartagena.

The fighting in America was thus indecisive, and Louis XIV was able with some success to divide his enemies in Europe. The result was the indecisive treaty of Ryswick (1697), by which it was agreed that all territories conquered during the war should be returned. Commissioners were to be appointed, however, to determine the ownership of the posts in Hudson Bay. Thus came to an end the first phase of the long contest between England and France in America. Nothing was settled; in fact, fighting hardly ceased in the forests and the islands of America. But when open war broke out again, five years later, alignments of forces had shifted; and added to the causes for war between France and England was their competition for one of the richest prizes of colonial war, perhaps, in all history, which was nothing less than control of the wealth of the Spanish empire in America.

AMERICA AND THE SPANISH SUCCESSION

One of the principal objects of Louis XIV's greedy ambition was the acquisition of part or all of the fabulously wealthy Spanish empire in Europe and America. His activities in that direction began immediately after the death of Philip IV of Spain in 1665, when, by a bit of legal trumpery called the principle of "devolution," he seized certain Spanish possessions in the Rhineland in the name of his wife, Maria Theresa, who was a daughter of Philip. But his appetite was only whetted by this success, and the fact that Charles II of Spain, Philip's heir, was a sickly weakling who was not expected to live more than a few months inspired Louis to make certain arrangements against the day when Charles would die.

Now Spain's empire was still one of the most extensive and profitable that history had ever known. For, besides continental Spain, it included holdings in Italy and in the Germanies, the Spanish Low Countries (Belgium), and the vast, rich empire of the colonies in America. Louis XIV knew that if Charles died without issue, as he was expected to do, there would be a great international scramble for the succession to the Spanish throne and for parts of the Spanish inheritance. But he also knew that if he could bargain with the possible heirs beforehand he might both avoid a war and get a larger portion for himself. It thus fell out that Louis passed a considerable portion of the waking hours of his lifetime studying ways and means of dividing up the Spanish inheritance; and the result of his scheming was a series of treaties that are of interest for the history of America.

The first of these was made by Louis with Leopold of Austria, Holy Roman Emperor, who had married another daughter of Philip IV by a second wife. In this very secret treaty of Vienna (1668) the two brothers-in-law piously divided the Spanish inheritance between them.

"Although no thought [they said] and still more, no event could ever in the world be more painful and grievous to their Majesties than that the Most Serene Catholic King of Spain, their well-beloved relative, . . . should die prematurely without children of a lawful marriage, and although they will earnestly beseech the Divine Goodness in their prayers that this may not happen," nevertheless, they felt it incumbent upon them to "prevent the fires of a new war" by dividing their kinsman's property between them. Leopold and his heirs were to have Spain, the West Indies, the Canary Islands, and certain territories and places in Italy; Louis and his heirs were to receive the Spanish Netherlands, Naples, Sicily, and the Philippine Islands. This treaty, had it been carried out, would have made Spanish America a German empire, and would have left the Philippines in the hands of France instead of Spain.

But Charles II of Spain surprised everybody in Europe by clinging to life for thirty-odd years longer. Besides, there were other claimants to shares in the Spanish estate; nor was it to be expected that the other powers of Europe would sit idly by and allow the balance of power to be upset by the addition of Spain to France or the Holy Roman Empire. Although the treaty of Vienna was unknown to them, Holland, Great Britain, and Sweden agreed that they would stand together to prevent France and Spain from making any bargain with regard to the Spanish inheritance that would be prejudicial to the interests of the three allies. When France and Spain ended the War of Devolution by the treaty of Aix-la-Chapelle (1668) the same three allies, at the request of Spain, agreed by treaty (1669) to guarantee Spain and its possessions from attack by France, either in Europe or in America.

But Louis started right in to nullify this guarantee by winning away from the alliance his good friend Charles II of England. Thus, in the negotiations preceding the secret treaty of Dover (1670) in which he won the promise of Charles' support against the Dutch, Louis asked also for Charles' aid in securing any "new rights" in the Spanish inheritance that might fall to him by reason of the death of the king of Spain. Charles II of England asked for the American colonies of Spain as his part of the bargain, but as Louis had just promised this part of the Spanish empire to Austria in the treaty of Vienna, he had to content Charles with an evasive provision that the exact division would be made by agreement at the time of Charles of Spain's death.

While Louis was carrying on his war against the Dutch, and making the seizures of Rhineland territories that led eventually to the war of the Palatinate in 1688, the question of the division of the Spanish estate remained in abeyance. But after the Peace of Ryswick Louis again took up the problem of the Spanish inheritance. He now realized it would be impossible to carry out the treaty of Vienna in the face of a united European opposition; and he hoped, by letting England and Holland into the plot, to win their support. William III of England and Holland was interested above all things in blocking the further expansion of France in the colonial world, and was glad, therefore, of an opportunity to avoid war over the question by entering into a treaty of partition. The treaty of 1698 between France, Great Britain and the Netherlands, called the "First Partition Treaty," divided the Spanish inheritance among the Dauphin of France, the infant electoral prince of Bavaria, and the Archduke Charles of Austria. The throne of Spain, with the Spanish empire in America, was assigned to the electoral prince of Bavaria.

But the young prince died on February 6, 1699, and a new partition treaty had to be made. This, after much squabbling, was done at London in 1700, and the throne of Spain, with the Indies, was assigned to the Archduke Charles of Austria. But Charles II of Spain, now dying, decided to make a new will keeping his possessions intact. Then, after considering all the possible heirs, Charles finally decided to leave his entire "estate" to Philip of Anjou, the second son of the Dauphin of France, and grandson of Louis XIV. The death of Charles II on November 1, 1700, placed Louis XIV in the position of having to make the most fateful decision he was ever called upon to make; for he now had to choose between the partition treaty of 1700, dividing the empire of Spain, or accepting the deceased king's will, by which his own grandson would become king of all the Spanish possessions, and might, some day, by also becoming King of France, unite those possessions to those of France. It was too much for a poor, ambitious Louis XIV to resist. He decided for "legality"—that is, the will—though he knew that by doing so he would again plunge Europe—and America—into war.

The War of the Spanish Succession, in which France supported the candidacy of Philip Anjou (Philip V of Spain) for the Spanish Crown and the allies of the partition treaties supported that of the Archduke Charles of Austria in the so-called Grand Alliance, lasted from 1702 to 1713. It was a world war, in the sense that nearly all the nations were involved and that fighting took place in Europe, America, Africa, and Asia. For the allies, aside from what each hoped to gain from it, the war was a war to prevent Louis XIV from growing any more powerful than he was; it was a war for the maintenance of the European balance of power—but it was also a war, in the language of the Grand Alliance, fought "especially in order that the French shall never come into possession of the Spanish Indies nor be permitted, directly or indirectly . . . to navigate there for the purpose of carrying on trade." For Holland and England, it was a war over colonies and trade. These two countries were determined to prevent a union of the French and Spanish crowns; but they were above all determined to prevent France from getting into a position to block their own commercial and territorial ambitions in America. Fearful for their own safety and for the success of their own colonial expansion, they applied the doctrine of the balance of power to America as a means of forestalling the expansion of their great rival.

The most important and decisive campaigns of the war were carried out in Europe, and may not detain us here. But some of the incidents and campaigns of Queen Anne's War—its American counterpart—were of considerable significance for the future history of the continent. One of the most significant aspects of the war in America was the development of foreign trade with the Spanish colonies. England abstained at first, but French merchants had received the Assiento for supplying Spanish America with Negroes in 1702, and used it as a covering pretext for trade of all kinds, and it was not long before English traders, "in self-defense," were swarming into Spanish colonial ports. Another development was a rapid and profitable extension of privateering, all along the coast of America. In the actual fighting in the West Indies the French were driven from St. Christopher forever, and the English devastated Guadeloupe; French and Spanish forces captured the Bahamas and used them as a base for privateering; and Commodore Sir Charles Wager took most of a fleet of galleons worth £15,000,000 and destroyed the rest. In the long run, however, the war was an exhausting setback for all the colonies, English, French, and Spanish alike. In the northern British colonies an alliance with the Iroquois protected the frontier of New York from raids by hostile Indians, but Maine and New Hampshire suffered heavily. In western Massachusetts, in the winter of 1704, the village of Deerfield was surprised by a party of French and Indians, and there ensued one of the most horrible massacres in all the annals of America. The New England fisheries suffered heavily at the hands of French privateers, and the French successfully raided St. John's on the island of Newfoundland. But the British again captured Port Royal in Acadia, which this time they were to keep, and sent an imposing expedition against Quebec. This expedition, the only military operation of first-class importance in this area, consisted of fifteen warships and forty-six transports carrying five thousand troops, sent into the St. Lawrence under the command of Admiral Sir Hovenden Walker and General John Hill to take Quebec. But by carelessness or stupidity eight transports were run on the reefs of Egg Island and lost, and the expedition was abandoned. None of these American actions had any effect upon the outcome of the war, for that was decided in Europe.

It should be noted, however, that many colonists had participated in the war with interest and vigor, both at sea and land. That the Americans hoped for a reduction of French power in America is shown by their suggestions for the conditions of peace. Jamaica merchants urged that the French be removed from Santo Domingo; other West Indians urged the annexation by Britain of the islands of St. Lucia, Dominica and Tobago—later called the "neutral islands"—and the retention of the entire island of St. Christopher; New Englanders urged the retention of Nova Scotia. The colonists hoped to gain much from a decisive British victory.

THE PEACE OF UTRECHT

The Peace Congress held at Utrecht in 1712 and 1713 was one of the four great international congresses that have sought to rearrange the affairs of Europe in modern times. Each of these congresses has followed a long and devastating war; and with each of them America has had an important, though secondary, connection. The peace made at Utrecht, which brought to an end the War of the Spanish Succession, was a triumph for the defenders of the balance of power, and particularly, so far as America was concerned, for the then champion of the balance of maritime and colonial power, Great Britain. Of the European aspects of this complex nexus of treaties and agreements, no note need be made here of anything except the "eternal" separation of the thrones of France and Spain. Philip of Anjou was recognized as Philip V, King of Spain, but he had to sign a solemn renunciation of every possibility that he might some day also become the King of France, and so, by uniting the two crowns, overweight the balance of European power to the advantage of the Bourbon dynasty. Not only that, all the possible heirs to the French throne had also to sign a renunciation of every chance they might ever have to succeed to the throne of Spain. The concert of Europe—to use a later phrase—was determined never to let the legendary and still protentially terrifying power of Spain become united with the presently terrifying power of the world-conquering Louis XIV.

In its American aspects the Peace of Utrecht sought to establish in the new world an equilibrium similar to that in Europe. It was for this reason that in the treaties of peace France was made to renounce any intention "to try to obtain or even accept in the future" special commercial privileges in either Spanish America or the Portuguese colony of Brazil. Spain, on the other hand, was required to promise never to alienate any of its territories in America "to the French or to any other nations whatever." On the contrary, "that the Spanish dominions in America may be preserved whole and entire," Great Britain undertook to guarantee "that the ancient limits of [Spain's] dominions in America be restored and settled as they stood in the time of Charles the Second." A similar pledge of guarantee was given by Britain with regard to the Portuguese arrangement. Thus did Great Britain fix in European international law the principle of the maintenance of the American status quo—a sort of British Monroe Doctrine—at the beginning of the eighteenth century.

The areas of America where friction had occurred between Frenchmen and Englishmen were all ceded to Great Britain. Hudson Bay and Newfoundland were recognized as British possessions, but France was given the privilege of fishing and drying fish along the uninhabited northern coasts of Newfoundland. Acadia, "with its old boundaries," was ceded to Britain, and the Iroquois Indians were recognized as being under British sovereignty. France gave up forever the parts of St. Christopher formerly occupied by Frenchmen. Commissioners were to be appointed to decide upon a boundary between Hudson Bay and Canada and to decide which tribes of Indians, other than the Iroquois, should be considered allies of the French and which allies of the British. In general, these recognitions of British ownership, given in the name of establishing peace and good relations along the frontiers of North America did bring to an end some of the Anglo-French disputes—notably in Hudson Bay and St. Christopher. But their general effect was also to increase British power; and many questions were left, through ignorance and lack of foresight, undecided. The Anglo-French peace was a genuine effort at a permanent arrangement, and was so regarded through three decades; but it failed to provide more than a long pause in the developing world conflict of the French and British empires.

But it was in the realm of colonial commerce that Great Britain made its greatest gains at Utrecht. For it made several commercial treaties with France and Spain which left little doubt of the supremacy of England upon the sea and in the realm of overseas commerce. Into the Anglo-French commercial treaty was written the principle of the freedom of commerce and the doctrine that "free

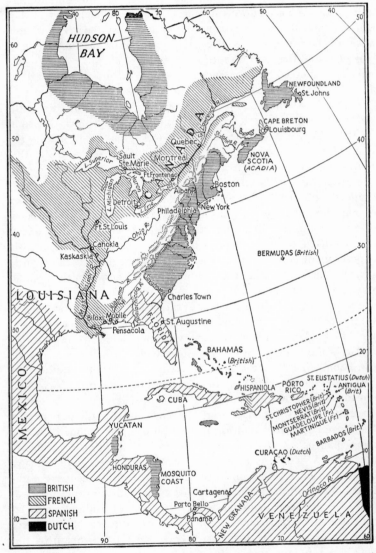

MAP 14. European Possessions in North America After the Peace of
Utrecht (1713)

ships make free goods" in time of war. This treaty was defeated in England for political and commercial reasons, and, therefore, never ratified. But it has a curious significance for the later history of the United States because it became the basis—in some parts word for word—of the first commercial treaty ever made by the independent United States, that with France in 1778.

The commercial arrangements made with Spain were a good deal more important, for Spain agreed to take away from France the "Assiento," or contract for supplying the Spanish colonies with Negro slaves, and give it to an English company. Under this contract the English South Sea Company was given the profitable responsibility of importing 4,800 *piezas de India* (Negroes) into the Spanish colonies in America each year for thirty years, and it was also given the privilege of sending one ship laden with general merchandise each year to the great fair at Porto Bello for the purposes of general trade. This was an extraordinary exception to the laws of Spain requiring all foreign trade with the Spanish colonies to be conducted through agencies at Cadiz, and it gave the British a position of considerable advantage over the French merchants, say, who carried on their trade with Spanish America in the regular way. Both these major provisions, moreover, opened wide doors to the smuggling of British goods into the Spanish colonies—an opportunity which the promoters of an expanding British commerce, both in England and in America, were not liable to overlook.

Out of the Congress of Utrecht, then, Great Britain emerged with the "lion's share" of the imperial spoils. A threefold equilibrium had been established to keep the peace in Europe and America. The crowns of France and Spain were forever separated, the American territorial status quo had been "frozen," and British traders had been given a favored position in Spanish colonial commerce which more than balanced the favored position of the French merchants at Cadiz. When it is considered that British merchants already enjoyed a favored position in the commerce of Brazil, to say nothing of their own flourishing imperial trade and the rapid penetration of even French colonial markets in the West Indies, it may be concluded that the commerce of the entire American hemisphere, with the exception of that carried back and forth to Spain by the *flota*, was very largely in British hands. It is no wonder that British colonial and diplomatic policy in the eighteenth century concerned themselves chiefly with the improvement of that happy situation. So far as America was concerned, the equilibrium established at Utrecht was a British equilibrium, and Britain was its guardian.

But the rapid expansion of the British empire made Britain, also, the first nation to disturb it on a serious scale.

RECOMMENDED BOOKS FOR FURTHER READING

CONTEMPORARY DOCUMENTS

Frances G. Davenport, ed., *European Treaties bearing on the History of the United States and its Dependencies*, II, III[1]

MODERN ACCOUNTS

The Cambridge History of the British Empire, I, Chapter 10.

George N. Clark, *The Dutch Alliance and the War Against French Trade, 1688-1697*.

Samuel A. Drake, *The Border Wars of New England*.

Charles B. Judah, *The North American Fisheries and British Policy to 1713*.

Philip A. Means, *The Spanish Main; Focus of Envy, 1492-1700*, Chapters 8-10.

Stewart L. Mims, *Colbert's West India Policy*.

Arthur P. Newton, *The European Nations in the West Indies, 1493-1688*, Chapters 16-23.

David Ogg, *Europe in the Seventeenth Century*, Chapters 6-7, 10.

Francis Parkman, *A Half-Century of Conflict*, Volume I.

George M. Wrong, *The Rise and Fall of New France*, II, Chapters 21-23.

25

The First Americans

A T THE end of the seventeenth century the work of planting European civilization in North America and the West Indies was practically completed. For about a century Europeans had been coming to North America, in a "westward movement" that drew emigrants from England, Holland, France, Denmark, and Sweden, and, to a lesser degree as yet, from Germany, Ireland, and Scotland, to say nothing of the Spaniards and the Portuguese already established in Florida, Mexico, the Caribbean, and South America. The Dutch had been eliminated as serious competitors of the British in the field of colonization, and the Spanish and Portuguese colonial empires were sufficiently distant from the "sphere of influence" the British had laid out for themselves to avoid impinging upon it. But the French, in their colonies in Canada, Louisiana, and the West Indies remained, to constitute an increasingly strong rival empire; one, indeed, which inspired the English, both at home and in America, with a growing hate and dread.

The western hemisphere had thus, by the end of the seventeenth century, been divided up into four great empires, Spanish, Portuguese, French and English, with the Dutch maintaining a few small holdings in the West Indies. Each of these empires had its own system of settlement and of administration, its own social institutions, its own language and its own culture; and in all these things each empire naturally followed the instruction it received from the mother country. Under the influence of the new world environment, however, each had in many ways already been differentiated from the mother country; the seeds of European civilization, sown in a new soil, were growing into cultures which were new and different from the old.

The British American empire was scattered from the chilly fur-trading posts on the shores of Hudson Bay to the fever-ridden swamps of Guiana. In about twenty separate communities along the shores of America under the rule of Great Britain, there lived about 350,000 souls of non-American ancestry. Perhaps 100,000 of these were Negroes, while the rest were of European, chiefly English, stock. The settlements were grouped in regions, following geographic differences. Thus New England constituted one regional unit; the middle colonies of New York, New Jersey, Pennsylvania and Delaware together formed another; Maryland, Virginia and the Carolinas constituted a third, and the West Indies a fourth. The Newfoundland settlements were unique in that they were devoted almost entirely to fishing; the Hudson Bay posts were trading stations dealing in Indian goods and furs.

The American colonies as a whole were sharply differentiated from the mother country. The section that most nearly resembled England was, perhaps, New England; but there were in New England many features of economic life, of social and political organization, and of religion and manners, that had no exact counterpart in old England. The same is true of the middle colonies, while the economic and social scenes in the southern colonies and in the West Indies were radically different from those "back home." Not only that, the sections of the empire were widely separated from each other, and differed from each other as widely as they differed from the mother country. In the natural circumstances provided by climate, soil conditions, geographic conformation, and natural resources, the colonists, in their struggle to succeed and grow, had followed the line of least resistance, with the result that there had taken place a certain amount of regional economic specialization. Social organization, manners, and intellectual life tended to follow the economic lead, so that the regions differed in culture and society as widely as they differed economically. The founders of the colonies had been English; but the colonists of 1700 were, strictly speaking, no longer English. Under the influence of "the first frontier" they had lost much of their English character, and had taken on much that was new. Now they were "New England Yankees," or "Virginians" or "West Indian planters"; in a word, they had ceased to be Englishmen; they were beginning to be "Americans." As T. J. Wertenbaker puts it:

England after all had not been extended to the shores of the New World, but . . . her settlements there were things apart, with separate economic and, therefore, with separate political and social interests. . . . [This separateness] was based upon conditions beyond the power of man to change, upon the broad expanse of the Atlantic, upon soil, climate and geography.

THE BUSINESS OF MAKING A LIVING

A. *Agriculture*

The first and most vital problem that confronted the earliest settlers in North America was the problem of making a living. Most of them had begun by agriculture, and agriculture remained, in 1700, the source of a livelihood for the vast majority of the American population. But agriculture varied widely in its forms— as widely as the climate and soil conditions varied between geographic regions. Thus the farmers of New England found it difficult to produce surplus crops for export, so that agriculture in New England took the form chiefly of subsistence farming, which raised just enough to provide a food supply for the population. Some exceptions to the rule, of course, existed; for exports to the West Indies now included beef, pork, and horses raised on New England farms as well as fish from the banks off-shore and lumber from the New England forest.

Further south, from Long Island Sound to Delaware Bay, agriculture was a profitable business. Already the soil of Long Island, New Jersey and Pennsylvania, as well as the southern counties of the Hudson valley, had proved its fertility; and already, in 1700, these regions were producing a surplus of agricultural products, chiefly wheat, flax, Indian corn, and livestock, for export. It is no accident that these colonies were coming to be called the "food colonies."

Still farther south, in Maryland and Virginia, tobacco was now almost exclusively the staple commodity of export. Here, in contrast to the small farms of New England, agriculture was on a larger scale; plantations were becoming increasingly large, owned by a slaveholding farmer-aristocracy that dominated southern society. North Carolina was still a frontier community. But South Carolina had now found its great, profitable staple of export in rice; and that colony was just embarking upon the "rice era" in its history—an era marked by large, slave-operated plantations and all the social phenomena that went with them.

In the British West Indies, agriculture was now devoted chiefly to the production of sugar-cane, from which derived sugar and molasses, and in a lesser degree indigo and cotton as well. Large plantations operated by slave labor had practically driven out the small farms. The plantations were, in effect, large capitalistic enterprises, owned and operated by the planter-capitalists in an impersonal, coldly profit-making way—planter-capitalists who, when they could, moved back to England to live and left the management of their plantations to overseers.

Thus agriculture remained the basic industry of the greater number of the people in this new Anglo-American society. All the colonies raised their own agricultural food supply, with the exception of the West Indies, which imported cereals and meats from the northern farms; but the important fact was that in all of the four sections agriculture was now producing surplus commodities for export, and with the exception of New England, where the fisheries were all-important, agriculture was the basis of trade.

B. *The Fisheries and Shipbuilding*

Even before the English colonists had begun to come to America, the myriads of edible fish in the seas off the shores of New England had been the object of exploitation by Englishmen. The earliest colonies, indeed, were founded with the deliberate intention of making them bases for this richly profitable business. It is no accident, therefore, that, from the founding of Plymouth onward, the New Englanders along the Atlantic shore made fishing their great staple industry.

In view of the difficulty of wresting a food supply from the rocky New England soil in the short growing season between the long, cold New England winters, the settler was forced with the choice, as it were, between farming and going fishing; if he chose the latter he merely followed the line of least resistance. Be that as it may, by the end of the century the New England fishermen were competing successfully with the English fishermen as well as with those from France. It is estimated that New England exported some fifty thousand quintals (a quintal is roughly one hundred pounds) in the year 1700. Estimated at above 18 shillings a quintal, the value of this export totaled some £47,000, or nearly $300,000 in gold. Fish was thus easily the greatest item of export in New England commerce.

The presence of an untouched forest along the shore and in close proximity to water-power provided an easy answer to the problem of a supply of boats and ships for the fisheries and for commerce. The industry began with the launching of John Winthrop's *Blessing of the Bay,* in July, 1631, hardly a year after his arrival in the colony, and it increased rapidly. By the end of the century New England ships had acquired a reputation for excellence and were competing favorably in price and quality with English ships, even in England itself. Edward Randolph estimated, in 1676, that up to that year 730 ships had been built in Massachusetts alone. By that time the shipbuilding industry in New England was giving employment to thousands of men, and paying handsome profits to the builders.

Farther south, in New York and Pennsylvania, shipbuilding was an active industry, but of somewhat less value and importance than it was in New England.

C. *The Fur Trade*

The fur trade was second only to the fisheries in importance as a source of profit and favorable commerce for the early American colonists along the North American seaboard. The exchange of European trinkets and manufactured goods for the skins of fur-bearing animals had been a business attractive and profitable to Europeans from their earliest visits to the northerly coasts of the continent, and from the time of the settlements of Virginia and Plymouth onward, this trade had played an important part in the economic development of all the colonies on the continent. Virginia had begun a fur trade with the Indians soon after its settlement, and this trade constituted a fairly important element in the economy of the colony for a century or more. Plymouth had been quick to exploit the possibilities of this profitable business, and made their first fur-trading voyage, guided by the friendly Squanto, to the shores of Massachusetts Bay in the fall of their first year. By 1628 they had built a trading post on the Kennebec, in Maine. From that time on the fur trade was of considerable importance to New England, where it reached its peak just before the end of the century.

The luxurious courts and fashions of Europe still provided a lively market for North American furs, and the organization of the Hudson's Bay Company in 1670 had come at a time when this market was rapidly expanding. Thus the North American fur trade had grown, and had reached an enormous volume by the beginning of the French Wars in 1689. Thousands of packs of furs were taken to Europe from the shores of Hudson Bay annually by the ships of rival French and British companies. Many more thousands were sent every year from French Canada, and in the year 1699, 15,000 skins were exported from New York alone. England was importing about £90,000 worth of furs annually; France was importing about £135,000 worth.

Of the British colonies on the continent, New York was the fur-

emporium *par excellence*. For the skin traffic initiated by the
Dutch had continued to grow, and the merchants of this province
were now beginning to tap, by way of Albany and the Iroquois
"middlemen," the great fur-producing regions of the Great Lakes
basin. Many New York traders and trappers, like the Canadian
coureurs de bois and other traders engaged in this rough traffic,
even began to go themselves into the distant parts of the wilderness. These men constituted a distinct class in provincial society,
while at the other end of the social scale several of the great merchants became quite wealthy from the profits of the fur trade; the
fortunes of some of the great New York families, such as the Liv-
ingstons and the Schuylers, date from this era and this business.

In Pennsylvania, more recently founded, the fur trade was just
beginning, and was destined to enjoy an important growth. Even
in Virginia and Maryland the fur trade was still a fairly important
business, and provided occupations and profit for many individuals.
Still farther south, centered at Charleston, South Carolina, there
existed a flourishing trade in deerskins with the Cherokee and Creek
Indians of the southern mountains and the Gulf Coastal Plain.
Some £2,000 worth of deerskins were exported from Charleston
in 1687, and until superseded by rice, skins remained the chief
item of South Carolina export. Even after rice became the staple,
the trade in deerskins remained an important economic and social
factor in the life of that colony.

Thus, for the British colonies on the continent, the fur trade
was a business of enormous importance. With slight variations it
extended from the Arctic Circle to the shores of the Gulf of Mexico. Thousands of Americans, in nearly all the colonies, gained
their livelihood by it. But not only that, the manners and the
outlook on life of the men engaged in this great industry were
inevitably affected by their contact with the vast wilderness and
with the Indians, and by the conditions of life and adventure beyond the frontiers of civilization.

D. *Manufacturing Industries*

With the exception of shipbuilding, there was as yet no manufacturing industry in the British American colonies that fabri-
cated articles for export. There was very little capital for such enterprises, to begin with; but the market for manufactured goods
was as yet too small and too uncertain to make manufactures
profitable. Even had these other conditions been more propitious,
however, it would still have been relatively easy to get better Eng-

lish goods. As a matter of fact, the British government was already deliberately discouraging American industries that tended to compete with those of England. There were, nevertheless, a few colonial manufacturing industries of a substantial sort serving the colonial market.

One of these was the manufacture of iron. The extraction and foundering of bog-iron had been a fairly profitable business in New England since the early days of settlement. John Winthrop, Jr., had been a pioneer in this industry, and had a foundry at East Haven, established in 1660. Lynn was, perhaps, its most important center in Massachusetts. Farther south, the iron deposits in Virginia had been discovered early in the colony's history, and Governor Spotswood founded, early in the eighteenth century, an extensive iron works on his land at Spotsylvania. Similarly, the iron deposits in New Jersey and Pennsylvania soon attracted attention, and eventually became a fairly important element in the economic life of those two colonies.

A very important industry, especially in New England, was that concerned with the tanning of hides for leather. For leather was an important item of apparel both for working clothes and in the manufacture of shoes. There were many tanneries in New England, and the local supply of hides was supplemented by skins imported from South Carolina.

Another industry of universal importance was milling. Flour mills and grist mills were built in all the colonies, and they were operated, generally, by water power. The miller was usually a farmer, who first built the mill for his own use and then extended its facilities to his neighbors in return for a share of the finished product. As a rule the operation of the mills was seasonal, for the milling of flour or corn was generally done in the fall, after the harvest. A little flour was being exported at the turn of the century; but it was not long before the milling of flour and meal became a year-round activity, and flour became an important item of export, especially from the "food colonies." This was particularly true of New York, whence large quantities of flour were exported to the West Indies. Two thirds of the people of New York City, "the growingest town in America," were said, about 1698, to gain their livelihood by milling, baking, or coopering.

By far the greater part of the manufactured goods used by these first Americans, however, was made in the home. Money and credit were scarce, and such of both as the American settler might have had, had to be used for the purchase of tools, furniture, a few luxury goods, and other products of English manufacture that were difficult or impossible to manufacture at home. But the Americans were men of great adaptability: success on a New England or Pennsylvania farm or early Virginia plantation depended upon the settler's ability to make the things he needed immediately and on the spot.

The "homespun" industries thus included everything from the making of shoes to the brewing of beer. The farmer slaughtered his own beef and pork; he cut his own wood, and in many cases hewed out the timbers for his house; he was a stone-mason, a blacksmith, a tanner, and a carpenter; and he added to the family larder by hunting in the nearby forest. In the summer he was busy from dawn to dusk in the fields; but in the winters, particularly in the north, he turned his time to the making of rough furniture, harness, or shoes, or to the weaving of cloth.

The women were as industrious as the men. They cooked for their families—usually large ones—baking their own bread, even milling the flour when a mill was too distant, and preserving fruit and other perishable foods. They spun thread from the wool or the flax raised on the farm, and wove it into "homespun" cloth from which the clothes of the family were made. They sewed, made quilts and other bedding, wove rugs of various kinds, and in their "spare time" dipped candles for the long winter evenings.

Life was fully occupied, in this first century of colonial life in America. Men—and women and children, too—worked hard and long at the business of making a living. Homes had literally to be carved out of the wilderness, and they had to be furnished and stocked with food. On the frontier each man and his family were dependent upon themselves alone, and this meant that they had little time or money for luxuries, or even intellectual pursuits. The business of making a living was a grim, all-absorbing business.

E. *Early Colonial Commerce*

And yet, a little surplus of wealth and leisure had begun to accumulate along the seaboard, a surplus that was in large measure the profit from a successful and growing commerce. It had been by the sale of tobacco in England that Virginia had first acquired the economic sinews of success; and it was by the sale of furs, clapboard, and fish that Plymouth had been able to pay off its mortgage. In the West Indies it was first tobacco, then sugar; in the middle colonies it was furs and wheat.

Very early in the history of New England its ships were visiting the colonies to the southward—Maryland, Virginia, the West Indies, and, later, Charleston and Philadelphia. To the southern colonies they took fish, and manufactured goods from England. In the West Indies they took sugar in exchange for the goods they brought, and sold the sugar in England in return for more manufactured goods. Similarly, in Virginia they took on tobacco which they carried to England, and in Charleston they took on skins or rice. The ships of New England, aided by those of New York and Philadelphia, became the carriers of the British colonies in America—in competition, be it said, with the ships of old England.

Thus, as the seventeenth century neared its end, the colonies were developing a prosperous commerce. New England had little to export to England, the source of the more highly manufactured goods used in America, but by this three-cornered system of exchange, based originally upon fish and furs, and, later, upon lumber, horses and other miscellaneous products, the New Englanders had made money. Boston became the greatest market town in North America, and many of its merchants were modestly wealthy from the profits of buying and selling and carrying for the rest of the colonies.

New York and Pennsylvania were in a case similar to that of New England. But New York and Pennsylvania had a few staple products, such as furs, for which there was a steady market in England, with the result that there was somewhat more direct trade between these colonies and the mother country. Farther south, in Virginia and Maryland, practically all the tobacco produced went directly to England, and was there exchanged for manufactured goods—furniture, books, dresses, and the like—that came back to the plantations, either directly or by way of Boston. South Carolina deerskins followed much the same route; the rice, on the other hand, sought its natural market in southern Europe, and was there sold for bills of exchange on London, which were used, in turn, for the purchase of British goods. West Indies sugar went, for the most part, directly to England, carried there in English or New England ships, which again took British manufactures in return. But the West Indies were the least able, of all the colonies, to provide their own food supply, which was brought to them in the form of fish and flour by the New Englanders and New Yorkers. Much of the sugar of the West Indies, therefore, went to the "continental" market of North America to pay for this food supply, and most of the molasses went along with it, to be made into the rum which was the staple of exchange in the now rapidly growing African slave trade.

All in all, by 1700, the commerce of the British colonies in America had settled into the pattern it was to follow for the remainder of the colonial period. The colonies had found the products they could sell at a profit, and the profits derived from buying and selling were making the colonial merchants modestly wealthy. The total value of colonial commerce, including that with England, trade with foreign countries, and the intercolonial trade, was probably £1,000,000 a year.

Most of the trade was carried on by barter. There was little hard money—or, indeed, money of any kind. For the balance of trade with England was generally unfavorable. High profits were made in the roundabout trades already described, but the money and the credits derived from them went to pay off this balance owing to the mother country. The Americans were slowly, but surely, accumulating wealth from commerce, almost without money. No wonder the Yankee trader developed a reputation for shrewdness!

F. *The Economic Bases of Society*

Out of this brief review of the economic life of the Americans at the end of the first century two facts emerge with striking clarity. First, it is clear that basic economic occupations were regional, and followed the lines of least resistance indicated by the climate, the soil conditions and the natural endowments of the four different regions. This fact had a profound effect upon social and political institutions and intellectual life; for cultural differences tended to follow economic differences.

The second striking fact with regard to the economic activities of the four major regions was the observable difference between the economic life of America and that of the old country. Neither of the regions was an economic extension of old England. All of them were different: the West Indies with their great plantations presented an economy which could not be duplicated in the old world; no more could the rice plantations of Carolina nor the tobacco plantations of Virginia and Maryland. The combination of food production and fur trade in the middle colonies or the fishing-and-commerce economy of New England were more similar to the economy of old England, to be sure, than those of the southern colonies or the West Indies, yet the absence of industry, and the relatively greater importance of agriculture, fisheries and fur trade in the commercial life of these colonies differentiated them sharply from the mother country.

What had happened was a large-scale adaptation of Englishmen to the climate and other conditions of the new world. But adaptation meant differentiation, and these first Americans were no longer Englishmen. Their ways of making a living had been changed from the original English model, and with their economies, their societies. They were Americans; and they had laid the foundation stones of an American civilization.

SOCIAL INSTITUTIONS

In the founding of civilization in Anglo-Saxon America, social institutions tended to follow the lines laid down by economic practices. As the British colonies in North America were differentiated into four regions by their economies, so also were they to be distinguished from each other and from the mother country by their differing social systems.

A. *New England*

The unit of social life in New England was the town, which was actually the center of social and political life, as well as of religion. Nearly all men did their own work; but that did not make this a democratic society. Far from it. Nothing was further from the minds of the founders than the idea of the equality of men, as such a conception of society was utterly contrary to their understanding of God's ways with the world. "God almightie," wrote John Winthrop, "in his most holy and wise providence hath soe disposed of the Condicion of mankinde, as in all times some must be rich and some poore, some highe and eminent in power and dignitie; others meane and in subieccion." Society, for the founders of New England, was a unit, organized in a sort of hierarchy in which each man was given his place by God. Thus there took shape an aristocratic arrangement in which the ministers and the magistrates, at the head of the church membership, occupied the upper levels of society. In this group should be included the wealthy merchants and the "gentlemen" from England. Below them stood the artisans and freehold farmers, most of whom were church members, and who were generally in sympathy with the ideals of the Puritan commonwealth. These folk enjoyed the titles of "goodman" and "goodwife," and may be said to have been the backbone of New England society. On the third level of society stood the unskilled laborers, while the indentured servants constituted a fourth class; the slaves stood at the bottom of the social scale.

Social life was thus dominated by the religious minority; and, since this same minority also controlled the state, the political power stood behind the churches in the prescription of social custom. Naturally enough, social life was fairly drab, as judged by twentieth-century standards. Men dressed according to class; such fineries as lace, embroidery or ruffs were prohibited to the lower classes. The people were allotted places in the church according to rank, and a man was liable to be fined if he sat in the pew of an individual who was deemed superior to him in social station. Yet, since economic opportunity was free and equal to all, or nearly all, men tended to pass from one of these classes to the other, and this artificial stratification of society was already, at the beginning of the eighteenth century, showing a tendency, if not to break down, at last to re-form along lines more in accord with the flexible conditions of economic life.

Nor is it to be assumed that the people of New England were unhappy in their social experience. New England, to be sure, and especially Connecticut, was the original home of the "blue laws." Conduct on the Sabbath was severely regulated by law; unnecessary work was prohibited; women were even prohibited from kissing their children on the Sabbath. Card-playing, dancing, stage plays, and mince pies were prohibited, as were musical instruments not mentioned in the Bible—which left one free to choose trumpet, drum or jew's-harp! Liquor-drinking and tobacco-smoking were severely regulated. Boys were not allowed to go swimming, and even shuffle-board was looked upon as a dangerous diversion conducive to wasteful idleness.

Yet on the other side of the account may be placed many genuine and healthful diversions. Thanksgiving Day was a fairly regular feast throughout New England. "Training days," for the training of the militia, offered occasions for sober sport, with target practice and athletic competition. Election day was another pleasant day for the New Englanders, and even the mid-week lecture, with its occasions for gossip, the announcement of marriages, and the punishment of certain offenses, provided so much excitement that it threatened to become a positive dissipation. Commencement day at Harvard was also an occasion for gaiety, with orations, the presentation of degrees, a great commencement feast, and almost unlimited robust drinking. Sports, too, such as hunting and fishing, bear-baiting, and the like for boys and men, or sewing-parties for the girls and women, were naturally popular. Life was not all darkness in New England.

With the coming of the Anglicans to New England with Governor Andros, things changed rather markedly. The king's birthday, Christmas, and May-day were added to the list of days for merrymaking—maypoles were to be seen in New England once more—and the attitude toward dancing, stage plays, and other diversions began gradually to unbend. It should be noted, however, that this was a time when life generally was beginning to be less dominated by religion and becoming more secular in outlook; the gradual weakening of Puritanism was part of a phenomenon that is to be observed all over the western world.

B. *The Middle Colonies*

The social situation that had crystallized in New York by the end of the seventeenth century was quite different from that of New England. Here was an aristocracy of a different sort, built squarely upon the ownership of land. Wealthy merchants, especially those engaged in the fur trade, were appearing among the ranks of the landed aristocracy, but even these generally acquired large estates as a sign of their wealth and social position.

The formation of a landed aristocracy in New York really had its beginning with the establishment of the patroonships by the Dutch. For, although only a very few of these patroonships succeeded, yet they served as a model for the English, who, in a rough way, continued the system.

Pennsylvania, still less than two decades old at the end of the century, was, probably, the most democratic of all the colonies with the exception of Rhode Island. William Penn and those associated with him were Quakers, to begin with, with the Quaker faith in the equality of men in the eyes of God. But not only that, Pennsylvania and central New Jersey could boast some of the most fertile soil and one of the most equable climates in the entire coastal region. There was plenty of land, so that a premium was placed upon the industry of the individual farmer. Thus both the economic and the ideological bases of social equality were present in Pennsylvania right from the beginning.

Outside of the raw young towns of Philadelphia and Germantown, the settlers of Pennsylvania were almost without exception farmers. This was also true of New Jersey and Delaware, which formed with Pennsylvania a single societal and economic unit. This region along the Delaware was populated, already, by an extraordinary mixture of peoples—the descendants of the original Swedes and Dutch, English Quakers, German pietists, French Huguenots, and, shortly after the beginning of the new century, the first arrivals among the Scotch-Irish.

C. *The Plantation Colonies*

In Maryland, Virginia, and South Carolina society had begun to shape itself in an aristocratic mold, while North Carolina was still hardly more than a crude frontier—"Lubberland," as William Byrd II called it. In these "plantation colonies," aristocracy was built upon land tenure. Maryland's system of landholding had been feudal from the first. Feudalism itself did not take root, but the plantation system, demanding, as it did, large capitalization and a plentiful supply of cheap labor, made for the emergence of an aristocratic landowning class. This happened in Maryland, Virginia, South Carolina, and the West Indies in the seventeenth century. By the end of the century, the small yeomen had all but disappeared from the tidewater areas of the south and from the West Indies, and the aristocratic cast of society had become fairly fixed in the form it was to retain for more than a century longer.

Below the landed aristocrats in the social scale were the "poor whites"—landless workers and servants—and at the bottom of the scale were the Negro slaves. These were the three major classes in all the plantation colonies; and it was now becoming increasingly difficult to pass from one to another. The general trend in these colonies, at the end of the century, was toward an ever-increasing proportion of Negroes. This trend may be seen from the fact that Virginia, which had a population of some 15,000 people in 1648, only 300 of whom were Negroes, in 1700 had a population of 70,000 people, of whom perhaps 20,000 were Negroes. The same trend is to be noted in Maryland and South Carolina; but nowhere did it reach such an extreme development as in the West Indies, where, as already noted, the Negro populations greatly outnumbered the whites.

There were few towns in the tobacco colonies. Towns, indeed, were not necessary, since the ships that took the tobacco to England could sail right up to the plantation that produced it, or to one near by. This was not true of the rice plantations in South Carolina. On the contrary, the Carolina rivers did not lend themselves so well to navigation by ocean-going ships, and it was necessary to have a depot for the assembling of the plantation product for export. This was true, too, of the deerskins that were brought from the foothills and the mountains far inland. Charleston, with its harbor, supplied the need for an entrepôt, and became a flourishing commercial city, the metropolis of a gay and urbane society.

This was true, similarly, of the West Indies, where there were practically no rivers at all. Bridgetown in Barbados was at once the shipping center for the great sugar staple and the metropolis for the social life of that island. Port Royal performed the same role for Jamaica. Similarly, each of the other islands had its chief town, which was both a shipping and a social center. The most striking social fact about all the British islands was the "absentee-landlord" system of plantation administration, which was just beginning, with all its degrading effects upon society in general. As already noted, the planters who could afford it were beginning to set up their residences in England, leaving their plantations under the care of overseers. This had a particularly vicious effect upon West Indies society, since it at once deprived the islands of some of their best leaders and left the administration of economic life in the hands of employed managers who were generally moved by anything but humane motives.

Society of the islands was already formed in an aristocratic mold, with a resultant stratification of society similar to that in the southern continental colonies; with this difference, however, that the proportion of Negroes was much greater, and that the absentee-landlord system tended to encourage an "absentee" patriotism and a loyalty to England, rather than to the islands—an attitude which seemed to look upon the islands as factories to be exploited rather than as homes. The climax of the evils of this system was reached later, however, and properly belongs to a later chapter of West Indian history.

THE RELIGIONS OF THE FIRST AMERICANS

Religion, at the end of the seventeenth century, was still a much more vital matter to most Americans than it has been at any time since. As a matter of fact, the period at the turn of the eighteenth witnessed the true end of medieval religious orthodoxy and the beginning of modern secularization, both in America and in Europe. Most of the men who settled English America "believed" with a deadly earnestness not easily understood by the enlightened, tolerant twentieth-century mind. And until well into the eighteenth century there were relatively few dissident religious groups in these colonies.

New England, despite the influx of Anglicans that came with the assumption of royal control by James II, was pretty solidly Puritan in faith. New York was officially Anglican, but there were still many adherents of the Dutch Reformed Church, and there were a few members of numerous other denominations. East New Jersey was largely Puritan, having been settled in large measure by settlers moving "westward" from New England; the people of West New Jersey were largely Quakers. Pennsylvania was, as yet, predominantly Quaker, although the other sects were numerously represented, and the Germans, centering in Germantown, were mostly Lutherans and Mennonites. Virginia, Maryland, the Carolinas and the West Indies were officially Anglican. Here, too, however, allowance must be made for the presence, as in South Carolina, of groups of French Huguenots, Scotch Presbyterians, and German pietists; in Maryland there were still a great many Roman Catholics.

Roughly, then, there were at this time four major religions in British America: Puritans, Anglicans, pietists (Quakers, Mennonites, and others), and Catholics. The first of these, Puritanism, had established its stronghold in New England. Puritanism had begun, as already noted, as an effort to purify the Anglican Church of the vestiges of "popery," in ritual and in doctrine. But as New England Puritans had come to realize the deep cleavage between their beliefs and Anglicanism, they gradually began to look upon themselves as an entirely separate sect. At the same time, the differences between Puritanism and the Congregationalism of the Separatists at Plymouth became less and less sharp, while both adopted many of the tenets of Calvinism.

Puritanism, as in the case of most of the Protestant sects, was based upon the conviction that the Bible, as the word of God, was the ultimate authority in questions bearing upon man's relationship to his maker. This meant the rejection of all churchly authority in matters of doctrine, such as was claimed by the Catholic Church and the Pope. The Puritan believed that human reason was capable of understanding the word of God, as found in the Bible, though it might not understand the whole of God's plan, and this naturally implied a certain amount of education. But the chief doctrinal conflict with Anglicanism arose over the mode of application of reason to the Scriptures, and the relative importance of reason and the Scriptures in determining belief. Thus the Puritan looked upon the Bible as the literal word of God, to be taken exactly as it was; and the part of reason was to understand it exactly. For the Puritan, God had spoken in the Bible, and had said no more; this was as much of God's thought as man needed to know. The Anglican, on the other hand, thought of the Bible as being God's word, to be sure, but only one of many ways in which God has revealed himself to man. Even the Bible, said the Anglicans, is not to be taken literally in all its parts and in every word; is it possible that God really cares whether or not men wear wigs? Furthermore, the Anglican believed that reason had been given men to guide them in situations where the Scriptures might not apply. The Puritan refused to believe that any such situation could even arise; the Bible was intended by God to cover every conceivable situation, and there were no exceptions.

Thus the Puritan was a literalist, the Anglican more of a latitudinarian, in matters involving interpretation of the Bible; and this difference lay at the basis of the differences between their practices. Since the Puritan was a literalist, he sought to follow the Bible literally in his faith, in his morals and in his politics. For a time, at the beginning, the Bible was his only code of laws; but he gradually compromised with the English common law and statute law to form codes which were curious mixtures of all three. He made sure that the righteous should determine the way of political life by limiting the franchise to church members; and in order to be eligible for church membership the prospective communicant had to furnish ample evidence that his reason had been enlightened and quickened by the infusion, in him, of the divine grace of God. This was the phenomenon known as regeneration, and was thought to come to a man only by the free and generous act of God himself. But only a few had their eyes thus opened and their souls thus inspired by a knowledge of the true nature of goodness; those who were thus to be saved had been known to God—since God is omniscient—forever.

As a practical matter, however, since few men were absolutely sure they had received God's grace, and since fewer still could demonstrate it to the scrutinizing elders, the number of church members tended to fall short of that required for the maintenance of the church's strength. This practical difficulty of keeping up the church-membership led, about 1662, to the adoption of what was known as the "Half-Way Covenant," which permitted persons not yet full communicants in the church to make a confession of faith which would give them such "half-way" membership as to entitle their children to be baptized and entitle them to vote. This was a beginning of compromise, however faint, for it was essentially a recognition that a man might be of a deep piety, yet never experience a sense of the visitation of God's grace. Life on the New England frontier was not, indeed, conducive to this essential part of the Puritan experience; and under the frontier influence Puritanism was already, despite all its convictions to the contrary, moderating its vigor.

Similarly, since the Puritan was a literalist in his interpretation of the Bible, he tried to follow the Bible exactly in his moral life. Men are by nature sinful, according to the Puritan doctrine, incapable of doing good until regenerated by divine grace. But the regenerate Puritan was also a perfectionist. A relative good did not satisfy him; he was constantly striving to achieve the highest perfection in his life and conduct and, since the continuance of his ideal of life and society depended upon the practice of perfection, and since he was convinced that this perfectionism was in accord with the intent of God with men, he insisted that all men, even the unregenerate, live up to the Puritan moral standards, or depart.

Such was the Puritanism and "puritan conscience" that pervaded the religious life of New England in the seventeenth century. Not exactly to be duplicated elsewhere, it was peculiar in its own century—a vigorous attempt to get back to the primitive Christian life with God. But it was of the most profound significance for the later history of American civilization; for the Puritan outlook on life has colored, if it has not actually determined, much of American culture from the seventeenth century to the twentieth.

Puritan perfectionism was impossible to enforce. It was unnatural, to begin with. But the conditions of the frontier, which tended to make men impatient of restraint, coupled with the influence of the general secularization of society that was already beginning in Europe, brought about a gradual weakening of Puritanism, both as a doctrine and as a morality. This weakening, or "watering-down," of Puritanism was already, in the year 1720, an important reality in New England life.

In parts of New York, in Maryland, Virginia, South Carolina and the West Indies, Anglicanism was the official religion. It was only in Virginia, however, and possibly the West Indies, that a majority of the population were adherents of that church. In New York there were many dissenters, members of the Dutch Reformed Church, Puritans, and others. In Maryland there were many Catholics and a great number of Puritans. In South Carolina there were Puritans, French Huguenots, Lutherans, and others, with the result that the Anglicans numbered probably only about one-third of the population.

The Anglican doctrine was still the doctrine of the Thirty-nine Articles. But under the influence of American conditions the form of the church had changed. In Virginia, where it was strongest, the widely scattered settlements produced parishes that were large and relatively independent of each other. As there was no American bishop, American Anglicans were included in the diocese of the Bishop of London, who occasionally appointed commissaries to act for him. But the influence of the Bishop was weakened by distance, and the American parishes tended to govern themselves as small, oligarchic groups without the guidance or the discipline of the hierarchy.

The low pay and general unattractiveness of the American parishes discouraged the best ministers from coming, with the result that the pastors in the Anglican colonies were often men of a worldly, hard-riding, hard-drinking and sporty type, lacking the qualities of religious inspiration. There were some able, earnest men among them, to be sure; but these found the distances between plantations, the all-but-impassable roads that had to be traveled on horseback, and the uncertainties of the weather almost insuperable obstacles to successful religious work. Furthermore, the great distances made for laxness in the liturgy. The dead were buried in family burial plots instead of the consecrated ground of the churchyard. Services, even the sacraments, were often administered without the proper vestments and vessels, and marriages were often performed at home instead of in the church. All in all, the Anglican Church in America was fairly demoralized.

The Bishop of London in 1690 finally appointed James Blair as his commissary to Virginia with instructions to see what could be done. The result was a series of reforms calculated to improve the position of the pastor and reinvigorate church discipline. At the same time a seminary, the College of William and Mary, was founded in 1693 for the training of ministers—the second institution of higher learning in British America. The movement for reform was only partially successful, however. The American frontier was simply not congenial for this highly ecclesiastical form of worship.

Another effort to bolster the failing Anglican way was made in the organization of the Society for the Propagation of the Gospel in Foreign Parts. This society, chartered in 1701, had as its objective the sending of missionaries to the colonies to work among the Indians, slaves, white servants, and others not already Anglicans. But it was not successful. The few missionaries sent to the Indians failed to make any considerable number of converts and generally returned to the settlements; the plantation owners objected to the conversion of the slaves, for fear that a common religion might be conducive to the organization of slave rebellions.

Anglicanism, like Puritanism, was thus modified in organization and in point of view by the influence of the American frontier. In this, as in other religions, the end of the seventeenth century saw a gradual turn toward a more secular outlook on life, with a consequent lessening of the influence of religion in human affairs.

In Pennsylvania, West New Jersey, and Delaware, the religious outlook at the end of the seventeenth century was dominated by the doctrines and practices of the Quakers, already described.

One of the features of colonial life that was most typically American was the wide prevalence, at the end of the seventeenth century, of religious toleration. It is probably safe to say that no country in the world, at that time, presented either such a variety of religious sects or such a large measure of tolerance. Tolerance was not peculiar to America, for many men in England were advocating more liberal religious attitudes throughout the seventeenth century. Yet the multiplicity of sects in the colonies, living in close juxtaposition to each other, made mutual tolerance almost an absolute practical necessity. Furthermore, the entrepreneurs of colonization, such as William Penn and the Carolina proprietors, found it to be simply good business to offer religious toleration as one of the inducements offered prospective immigrants. In the case of Maryland, toleration was the outgrowth largely of a desire to protect a specific persecuted sect, the Catholics. Throughout the growth of tolerance, however, the positive intellectual justification of it accompanied the more utilitarian reasons for the practice, and this intellectual justification was coming to be notable throughout the colonies by the end of the seventeenth century.

THE INTELLECTUAL OUTLOOK

The level of intellectual attainment among the Americans at the end of the seventeenth century was undoubtedly lower than that of the first-comers. Many of the leaders of the first colonies were university-bred, especially in New England. Others had come from the upper middle classes, and were men of great intellectual ability and refinement. But this high intellectual quality had not been maintained. The business of establishing homes in the wilderness was all-absorbing; men had little time or money for the luxuries of education, reading, and general culture. Thus it came about that the second generation of settlers had less intellectual training than their fathers who had come from England, and the third generation had still less.

This does not mean, however, that education, literature, and the arts disappeared. All these refinements of life persisted, and in very interesting forms. For the Puritans, some education was essential to every citizen, if the Puritan commonwealth was to be preserved. The whole Puritan system was built upon the presumption of the ability in every man to read and understand his own Bible. It was no accident, therefore, that the Massachusetts General Court, in 1642, passed a law (very imperfectly carried out, be it said) requiring schools. In New Amsterdam, schools under the Dutch had barely managed to exist.

In the Quaker colonies, education was neither a matter of state-concern, as in New England, nor yet a matter of purely private concern, as in the Anglican colonies. For the Quakers, as for the other pietist sects of Pennsylvania, New Jersey and Delaware, education was a matter of grave concern, closely bound up with the very survival of the group concerned. Lacking state support, however, the religious groups undertook the education of their children as a matter of group interest. The result was that in this region, more than elsewhere, education followed denominational or sectarian lines.

In the Anglican colonies of the south and the West Indies, education, as a private matter, was left almost entirely in the hands of the parents. If the father cared to educate his child, he might; if not, that was his own concern. Those who cared to have their children educated, and who could afford it, hired tutors or engaged the parish parson to give the parish children lessons in the three R's. At the end of the century it had become a popular custom among the wealthy to send their sons to England for their education, both in Virginia and in the West Indies. There was little money, as yet, for such expensive education; and there was even some sentiment against it. Crotchety old Governor Sir William Berkeley was probably not entirely alone when he enunciated his famous dictum: "I thank God we have no free schools." Conditions in education were, if anything, worse in the West Indies than in the southern continental colonies.

The year 1700 saw two colleges in British colonial America, Harvard in Massachusetts and William and Mary in Virginia. Yale was founded in 1701. These three colleges are typical of the seventeenth century. For, as noted, this was a century of deep religious convictions, when the intellectual and religious leadership of the people was in the hands of the ministers. Yet the turn of the century saw the end of the old, dominant position that religion had held in the lives of men and the beginning of a new intellectual era in which the frontier, science, and the influence of European philosophies all contributed to an increasing secularization of the outlook on life—a secularization that must be discussed in another place.

Literature, in seventeenth-century America, was of a fairly primitive sort. The first-comers, to be sure, were Elizabethans, of a productive literary age, and they produced, after their arrival in this country, some writings that merit the name of literature. The second and third generations were singularly unproductive, however, for literature, even more than education, found it difficult to flourish in a world where men's minds were dulled by days of back-breaking toil in the forest and in the field. Literature demands, for its flowering, leisure and wealth; in America at the end of the seventeenth century, there was precious little of either.

And yet, these first Americans were not without a native literature. Naturally enough, as the seventeenth was a century in which men's minds were dominated by religion, individuals of great intellectual endowment were drawn into the ministry, and literature was predominantly religious. This was particularly true in New England, the most literate of the colonial regions. Thus, from the establishment of the first printing press in 1639, the literary product of the New England press was overwhelmingly religious in character One of the first, and one of the most famous books to be produced by the press at Cambridge, was the Bay Psalm Book, containing a metrical translation of the psalter and selections from other favorite parts of the Bible. This book passed through edition after edition, and must have been the preferred reading of many. Moreover, as these psalms were the only songs sung by the people, the influence of this book must have been much more than merely literary. Sermons, especially election sermons, constituted a large part of the literary diet of the people. There were also many poems of a religious nature; the most popular of these was the grim "Day of Doom," by Michael Wigglesworth (1631-1705) which remained one of the most popular readings in New England for a century.

But there were also writings of a more secular nature. Historians there were, such as Cotton Mather, who, to be sure, wrote history with a religious bias; diarists, such as Samuel Sewall, whose journal gives a striking insight into Puritan character and customs, and a few describers of the frontier experience, such as Mary Rolandson, whose narrative of her captivity among the Indians is one of the classic testimonials of Indian war and Puritan fortitude. There were secular writers in a lighter vein, too, of whom by far the most genuinely gifted was Anne Bradstreet, whose poems express the mind and emotions of the Puritan woman planted, somewhat against her will, in the wilderness.

Toward the south, there were far fewer writers from whom to choose. Daniel Denton's description of the province of New York, and the Dutch Jasper Danckaerts' description of his voyage to New York and New England in 1679-80 were about as much as New York could offer in the way of literature, and Pennsylvania was as yet too young to have produced any notable writings. Both Maryland and Virginia had felt the stirrings of the literary impulse, however. Ebenezer Cook's *Sot-Weed Factor* is a sprightly poetic description of life and manners in Maryland. In Virginia, James Blair, the dour Scotch founder of the College of William and Mary, made his contribution to southern intellectual life as an educator, as a describer of life in the colony, and as a writer of religious essays. Robert Beverley, a native Virginian, published his *History of Virginia* in 1705. But the greatest native wit of this generation of Virginians was Richard Byrd, II, whose *History of the Dividing Line,* an entertaining description of life on the Carolina frontier published in his old age belongs, perhaps, among the literary products of the eighteenth century, rather than the seventeenth.

In general, it may be said that the literature produced by these "first Americans" was rather of a rough, primitive sort. It was usually marked by two major interests, the still prevalent concern with religious things, and the frontier. This early literature was doubtless influenced by English literature, especially that of the Elizabethan first-comers; but the genuineness of these first-fruits of American literature resides in their having arisen out of the living experience of the pioneers in the new world of America. These men were sons of Englishmen, but they had never seen England. They spoke and wrote the English language, but their emotions and their intellectual, literary urge rose from what they saw about them, from what they believed was their contact with God, and from the epic struggle with the frontier that was their very life.

Much the same thing may be said of art. The artistic heritage the first settlers brought with them, in the folk arts, in architecture, and in painting, was the heritage of Elizabethan England. By the end of the first century of colonization much of that heritage had worn away, and the art that rose in America was Elizabethan in form but American in its directness and its honesty, in its very bluntness and candidness—characteristics which grew, one way and another, out of the actual colonial experience in this new world. The beginnings of art in North America were made in the folk arts, probably when glass-blowers in Massachusetts began to make ornamental glass beads for sale to the Indians. The artistic impulse made itself felt in every branch of the household crafts. English silversmiths had begun their craft in Massachusetts as early as 1650, and Jeremiah Dummer, "the first native silversmith," was born in 1645. Both glassware and silverware became famous as items in the artistic output of seventeenth-century New England.

Painting doubtless had its beginning with the signboard painters. As street numbering had not yet been invented, these signboards were used as identification of houses, and the streets of the colonial towns were filled with them. Boston finally had to take steps to limit the number of sign-posts in the streets. The gifted painter did not hesitate to paint signs, fences, houses, carriages, and the like. Indeed, art in New England, as was only natural under the Puritans, had a distinctly utilitarian flavor—and art that was merely to give pleasure was discouraged. Religious subjects were taboo, as smacking of idolatry, and as yet New England had no great historical themes to portray.

This does not rule out portrait painting, however; on the contrary, there are in existence today four hundred portraits from New England and New Netherland that derive from the period prior to the year 1700; there is not a single painting of any other kind. Evidently, the perpetuation of the likenesses of distinguished or beloved persons was considered worth while. In any case, in a frontier country as poor as America, the business of being an artist was not very profitable. The "limners," for thus were they called, went out into the country and traveled from farm to farm to dispose of their product. This practice became common somewhat later; but at no time or place was it ever very profitable. Art in America at the end of the seventeenth century had, in short, barely been born; it was still in the veriest swaddling clothes.

THE END OF A CENTURY

The end of the seventeenth century brought with it the end of active colonization by the British in North America—with the exception of Georgia, founded in 1733. The first labor, that of laying the foundations, had been done. British civilization had been brought to the shores of this continent and planted here. This civilization had grown; but it had grown along lines which diverged from the European pattern. For the Americans had developed customs, institutions, and ideals that already differed widely from those of the mother country. Their ways of making a living, their economic institutions, their social divisions and customs, their political institutions, their religion, their literature, art and science—all were European in background, but American in form and expression. The American civilization of the year 1700 was one of history's clearest and most dramatic examples of the metamorphosis of an old civilization, under the pressure of a new environment, into a civilization that was new. Thus, in the emerging American way of life, there are to be observed two characteristics. The first is the European heritage. The other is made up of those features which are distinctly American—which have their roots, as it were, and which grew up, in an American soil. The result of this synthesis, this amalgam, was something new: a new world had made new men.

RECOMMENDED BOOKS FOR FURTHER READING

CONTEMPORARY NARRATIVES

William Byrd, *William Byrd's Histories of the Dividing Line betwixt Virginia and South Carolina*, edited by William K. Boyd.

Ebenezer Cook, "The Sot-Weed Factor" in *The Maryland Muse*, edited by Lawrence C. Wroth.

Albert B. Hart, ed., *American History Told by Contemporaries*, II, 35-52, 65-77, 90-99.

Cotton Mather, *Diary of Cotton Mather, 1681-1724*.

Cotton Mather, *Magnalia Christi Americana*.

Perry Miller and Thomas H. Johnson, eds., *The Puritans*.

Samuel Sewall, *Diary of Samuel Sewall, 1674-1729*.

MODERN ACCOUNTS

Roy H. Akagi, *The Town Proprietors of the New England Colonies*.

Charles M. Andrews, *The River Towns of Connecticut*.

Charles A. and Mary R. Beard, *The Rise of American Civilization*, Chapters 1-3.

Philip A. Bruce, *Economic History of Virginia in the Seventeenth Century*.

Philip A. Bruce, *Institutional History of Virginia in the Seventeenth Century*.

Arthur W. Calhoun, *A Social History of the American Family from Colonial Times to the Present*.

Lyman Carrier, *The Beginnings of Agriculture in America.*

Frank S. Child, *The Colonial Parson of New England.*

Victor S. Clark, *History of Manufactures in the United States,* Volume I.

Ellwood P. Cubberley, *Public Education in the United States.*

Alice M. Earle, *Curious Punishments of By-gone Days.*

Alice M. Earle, *Home Life in Colonial Days.*

Alice M. Earle, *The Sabbath in Puritan New England.*

Ralph H. Gabriel, *The Lure of the Frontier,* Chapter 1.

Ralph H. Gabriel, *Toilers of Land and Sea,* Chapters 1-3.

Edward L. Goodwin, *The Colonial Church in Virginia.*

Oskar F. L. Hagen, *The Birth of the American Tradition in Art,* Chapters 1-4.

Talbot F. Hamlin, *The American Spirit in Architecture,* Chapters 1-4.

Edward R. Johnson [and others], *History of Domestic and Foreign Commerce of the United States,* I, Chapter 5.

Robert M. Keir, *The Epic of Industry,* Chapter 1.

John A. Krout, *Annals of American Sport,* Chapter 1.

Perry Miller, *The New England Mind.*

Perry Miller, *Orthodoxy in Massachusetts, 1630-1650.*

Samuel E. Morison, *Harvard College in the Seventeenth Century.*

Samuel E. Morison, *The Puritan Pronaos.*

Herbert L. Osgood, *American Colonies in the Seventeenth Century,* II, 433-442; III, 507-521.

Ulrich B. Phillips, *American Negro Slavery.*

Rolla M. Tryon, *Household Manufactures in the United States, 1640-1860.*

Moses C. Tyler, *A History of American Literature,* Volume I.

Williston Walker, *A History of the Congregational Churches in the United States.*

William B. Weeden, *Economic and Social History of New England, 1620-1789,* Volume I.

Luther A. Weigle, *American Idealism,* Chapters 1-4.

Thomas J. Wertenbaker, *The First Americans, 1607-1690.*

Thomas J. Wertenbaker, *The Planters of Colonial Virginia.*

Stanley T. Williams, *The American Spirit in Letters,* Chapter 1.

Clark Wissler [and others], *Adventures in the Wilderness,* Chapters 9-14, 16-17.

PART IV

The Theory and Practice of Empire

THE EMPIRE and the civilization that rose in America upon the foundations laid in the seventeenth century had a three-fold nature. Looked upon as a whole, the British empire was a single organism, with its nucleus in England. The appearance of this phenomenon in the world was itself an event of major importance in human history. In its English brain and nerve-centers were elaborated the policies governing the growth and the co-ordination of the whole; and the later history of Anglo-America was profoundly influenced by the fact that it was for nearly two centuries an organic part of the larger imperial unity. Certain problems, such as that involved in the relationships of the parts of the empire to each other, the growth of an economic life in the colonies that was clearly differentiated from that of the mother country, and the gradual evolution of institutions of government in the colonies which were the offshoot of, but clearly to be distinguished from, those of the mother country, were common to all the empire, and must be treated as such. The phenomenal growth of population and the corresponding expansion of economic activity were also factors in the growth of this new civilization that overlapped colonial boundaries. In the second place, however, it should be noted that the growth of the empire was in large measure sectional, and the various sections were as different from each other as—perhaps even more than—they were from the mother country. Thus the British colonies in America may be said, roughly, to have been divided into about four distinct sections—the West Indies, the southern continental colonies and the northern continental colonies, and the fishing and fur-trading colonies of Nova Scotia, Newfoundland, and Hudson Bay. Each of these sections had a way of life peculiarly its own; it was only two of the four sections whose way of life was leading them toward a complete separation from the imperial organism of which they were a part.

The third aspect of imperial and colonial development in the eighteenth century is that presented by the development of the individual provinces. Each province had its own economic, social,

329

and political peculiarities; each was a sort of laboratory in which were worked out the experiments which eventuated in the present states and provinces. But this third aspect of American colonial history is more properly the matter for a later section of this review. The emphasis here is upon the development of the colonies as a whole, and the problems and the interests that were common to all of them.

26

The British Imperial System

ALTHOUGH founded as private enterprises and left to govern themselves for a century with relatively little interference from the mother country, the British colonies were, nevertheless, not isolated and independent communities. They were, on the contrary, units in a larger system. British settlements or trading stations in America, Africa, or Asia were but outlying nuclei of a political and economic entity which had its center at London. Ultimate decisions as to their economic life, their laws, their political institutions, and their relations with each other, the mother country, and the outside world were there made and co-ordinated into a common—if variegated—pattern, on the basis of a common general policy. The most fundamental problem, therefore, in the history of the colonies prior to 1776 was probably this problem of external relationships—with the mother country, first of all, with foreign nations, and with other colonies. Slowly but surely, in the course of the seventeenth and eighteenth centuries, England built up a set of institutions, laws, regulations, and precedents governing these relationships that together made up the British imperial system—or, rather, an imperial constitution, as distinguished from the constitution of England itself or that of any single colony. The formulation of this imperial constitution, like the growth of the English constitution, was not a deliberate act, but was slow, cumulative, and hardly even self-conscious. Like the constitution of England, it "just grew." But running through it, giving it consistency and form, was a body of ideas and practices which, taken together, are known as mercantilism.

THE UNDERLYING PRINCIPLE

Britain was not alone in following out a mercantilistic policy with regard to its colonies. All the colonizing powers did the same. Indeed, mercantilism was both a political and an economic doctrine which had as its chief and fundamental objective the promotion of the welfare of the nation; and it was practiced, in one form or another, by all the integrated states that had risen from the ruins of medieval feudalism. It was a philosophy of national political economy embodying the twin ideals of a supreme political authority of the state within its own borders and the economic self-sufficiency of the nation among the nations.

No systematic presentation of the mercantilist theory of the state was ever formulated. Its doctrines were worked out piecemeal, in scattered writings, in laws, and in institutions. Pieced together from these various sources, the theory appears about as follows:

| The existence and prosperity of the state depend upon its power, and its power depends upon its wealth. Some of the early mercantilists made the mistake of identifying wealth with money; but by the eighteenth century most mercantilist thinkers spoke of wealth as a surplus of goods of one sort or another, most important among which was money, or gold and silver bullion. The state could accumulate a surplus, according to this theory, only by selling more than it bought; therefore, exports must exceed imports. This principle did not, however, rule out an unfavorable balance of trade such as existed in the case of India, since the imports from India were re-exported at a profit, just as the unfavorable balance of trade with the British West Indies was offset by the re-export of West Indian sugar. Thus a state accumulating a surplus of wealth could maintain an army and a navy of such strength as to command the respect of other nations and maintain, or even expand, its economic and political power. Colonies, according to the theory, served as constantly expanding markets for the products of the mother country that would not be closed in war. Such a market, buying much from the mother country and selling her little, would thus contribute to the accumulating surplus of the mother country's wealth. But if the state were dependent upon other countries for vital raw materials, such as iron or naval stores, its power was to that degree weakened, and it became an integral part of the mercantilist doctrine that, wherever possible, the state should acquire sources of raw materials over which it would have control and which would not be shut off in time of war. Thus it was expected that colonies would supply such raw materials, whenever possible, and thereby contribute to the self-sufficiency of the mother country and itself. It was for this reason, for example, that England made such persistent efforts to encourage its American colonies to produce naval stores.

In its political aspect, the state was regarded as having supreme power over the individual. It sought to promote his interest by its policies, to be sure; if the state were prosperous, commerce and industry would prosper; profits would flow into the coffers of the proprietor, and steady employment and high wages would be the happy lot of the laborer. But the merchant must obey the law; he must ship his goods on British ships, even though the freight might be less on Dutch ships, in order that the profits of freighting might stay in England, Similarly, the colonies must ship their products to England, if England willed it for the good of the empire, even though they might receive a higher price elsewhere.

Naturally, too, in its international relations each state sought to improve its markets and weaken the markets of its rivals, and to expand its colonial empire at the expense of rival empires. As a general rule, the colonial empire was regarded as a closed commercial sphere, with the subjects of that empire holding a monopoly of its commerce and shipping, since to admit foreigners would introduce rivals for the profits of the colonial market and correspondingly weaken the economic and military power of the mother state. It was, of course, to the interest of the mother state to protect its colonies, both by its arms and by diplomacy. At the same time it became an accepted principle in international diplomacy in the eighteenth century that no one colonial empire should be allowed to become too great, since the wealth derived from an overwhelmingly large colonial empire might enable the mother state to lord it over the other states in Europe. Thus the principle of a balance of power among colonial empires was adopted as a colonial corollary of the then prevailing international doctrine of the balance of power in Europe.

As far as the colonies were concerned, they were subordinate in importance to the interest of the state or the empire as a whole, and were considered valuable and justifiable only insofar as they contributed to its welfare. For most English merchants, of course, and many English lawyers and statesmen, that meant that the colonies existed for the profit of England. But the more thoughtful British mercantilists saw the imperial relationship in terms of a self-sufficient empire in which each unit performed, for the benefit of the rest, the functions best suited to itself, receiving in return the services or the products of the others. Thus, according to this way of thinking, the Crown, in the form of a government resident in England, furnished a co-ordinating and defensive leadership, and England itself, peculiarly well equipped for it, was considered the part of the empire best prepared to furnish the colonies with manufactured goods. The colonies, on their side, were expected to buy the mother country's manufactured goods and to send her, in return, raw materials for which she might otherwise be dependent upon other countries—sugar, tobacco, rice, furs, iron, dye-woods, and naval stores, for example.

Such, in brief, were the fundamental tenets of mercantilism; and mercantilism was the underlying ideological basis of British colonial policy.

THE NAVIGATION ACT OF 1696

It was during the reign of King William III that British imperial policy took the form that it was to follow during the eighteenth century. In less than five years, between 1695 and 1700, the lessons that had been learned in the first century of the empire were crystallized. For within this period the great Navigation Act of 1696 was passed, the new Board of Trade was created, vice-admiralty courts were set up in the colonies for the better enforcement of the laws regulating shipping, and a beginning was made upon a new series of laws regulating colonial commerce and industry called the Acts of Trade.

The Navigation Act, which became law on April 10, 1696, was at once a supplement to earlier navigation laws, particularly those of 1660 and 1673, and a new effort to make the whole system of regulations for colonial trade more effective. Ever since the passage of the first colonial navigation act in 1651, enforcement had been difficult, and even after the creation of the Privy Council committee known as the Lords of Trade in 1675 the system still failed to achieve the desired effect. French and Dutch ships still found a welcome in the British West Indies; great quantities of enumerated articles still found their way into Ireland and the markets on the European continent; and New England continued to disregard the laws to the great annoyance of Edward Randolph, surveyor-general of the customs. But the greatest interlopers upon colonial trade were now the Scotch. For these "foreigners" sent their ships to the Chesapeake and Delaware Bays, or to New England, where they found it easy to circumvent the intention of the navigation system by selling Scotch manufactured goods and taking tobacco directly back to Scotland. Then, in 1695, the Scottish Parliament passed a law creating a great company called the Company of Scotland trading to Africa and the Indies, for the purpose of planting Scotch colonies in the new world and developing Scotch foreign trade. This company was given a monopoly of trade from Scotland in Asia, Africa, and America, in direct competition with the English merchants, particularly the English East India Company and the Royal African Company. The English merchants were alarmed, and the move of Randolph and others for a tightening of the old navigation system was given a powerful impetus by the fear of the English traders of the effect of the Scotch competition. The Navigation Act was thus the result of a twofold effort to make effective the navigation system and to forestall possible competition by the Scotch company.

The act as passed provided that no goods of whatever nature might be imported into or exported out of the British colonies in America, Asia, or Africa except in ships built in England, Ireland, or the colonies and owned by Englishmen of these places, of which at least three-quarters of the crews must be Englishmen. All English ships must register with the customs officials, thus providing for the first time an effective ship-registry for English ships; ships not so registered would not be considered English under the terms of the law. The governors of all the colonies were required to take oath and post a bond for the conscientious enforcement of the law, and the customs officers in America were made directly responsible to the Commissioners of the Customs in England. A very significant provision was that which provided that customs officers might secure "writs of assistance," or search warrants, from a judge or a justice of the peace and enter ships and warehouses, by force if necessary, to see that the law was not being violated. The colonies were to pass no laws contrary to the act, and cases of violation of the act might be tried in vice-admiralty courts, which were non-jury courts. In trials before juries, the act specified that the juries must be composed entirely of native-born Englishmen, Irishmen, or Americans—a provision aimed at Scotchmen.

The Navigation Act of 1696 provided little that was new in the way of regulation; it did, however, introduce new and more stringent provisions for enforcement. And therein lies its significance. For it was a serious and—while not entirely effective, even so—the most effective effort yet made to regulate the colonial trade for the benefit of England. Shortly after its passage, in 1697, vice-admiralty courts were set up in America for the more effective administration of the law itself; and these courts proved to be much more successful than the common-law courts, since, as Randolph had complained, American juries were generally in sympathy with the violators of the navigation laws. As often as not, he said, the jurymen were themselves violators of the laws! Be that as it may, the Navigation Act of 1696 lay the legal basis for the effective enforcement of the laws governing the economic relationships of the various parts of the empire with each other and the outside world.

THE BOARD OF TRADE AND OTHER AGENCIES
OF IMPERIAL ADMINISTRATION

In the field of imperial administration, there took place, in the spring of 1696, a reorganization that was as profound and as significant for the future history of America as the passage of the Navigation Act. For on May 15, just a few weeks after the passage of that law, King William III created the "Lords Commissioners of Trade and Plantation," generally known as the Board of Trade. An advisory body, entirely without executive power in its own right, the Board was, nevertheless, the mercantilist policy-making body for the British imperial administration, and formulated most of the important decisions made by the Crown with regard to the colonies for nearly a century.

The conditions leading to the creation of the Board of Trade were similar to those which had led to the passage of the Navigation Act. The Lords of Trade, the committee of the Privy Council charged with the administration of commercial and colonial affairs since 1675, had been again merged with the entire Privy Council as "a standing committee for Trade and Plantations" by James II in 1688, and as a result had lost its initiative and much of its interest in colonial affairs. English commerce was demoralized by the war with France which began in 1689, and the British navy was proving itself incompetent to offer it protection. Trade seemed to be decaying for the lack of government interest in it, and such great mercantilists as Sir Charles Davenant and John Evelyn were urging that Parliament set up a council of some sort for the protection and the promotion of the nation's commerce. Parliament took the matter in hand early in 1696, but failed to pass the proposed law setting up a council, whereupon the king established the Board of Trade by executive action the following May.

As organized in 1696 the Board of Trade was composed of two groups of members; the Lord Chancellor, the President of the Privy Council, the First Lord of the Treasury, the First Lord of the Admiralty, the Lord High Admiral, the two Secretaries of State, and the Chancellor of the Exchequer were *ex-officio* members of the Board by reason of their membership in what was gradually emerging as the British Cabinet. But for the purposes of the regular work involved and in order to command the constant services of men familiar with colonial problems, eight commissioners or "experts" were named as permanent members. Thus the Board, as set up in

1696, was composed of sixteen members, eight of whom were nominally members of the Privy Council and in close contact with the government of England, while eight were not members of the Privy Council, but, rather, experts capable of understanding and solving problems presented by the colonial situation. It was the latter group who did most of the work, although the *ex-officio* members occasionally attended the meetings and contributed what they could to the deliberations and decisions of the body.

The instructions of the Board of Trade are expressive of the British attitude toward the colonies throughout the eighteenth century. According to these instructions,

> We . . . require you . . . to inform your selves what Navall Stores may be furnished from Our Plantations, and in what Quantities, and by what methods Our Royall purpose of having our Kingdom supplied with Navall Stores from thence may be made practicable and promoted; And also to . . . inform your selves of the best and most proper methods of settling and improving in Our Plantations, such other Staples and other Manufactures as Our subjects of England are now obliged to . . . supply themselves withall from other Princes and States; . . . and what Trades are taken up and exercised there, which . . . may prove prejudiciall to England, by furnishing themselves or other Our Colonies with what has been usually supplied from England; And to finde out proper means of diverting them from such Trades, and whatsoever else may turne to the hurt of Our Kingdom of England.

Here is the classic example of the philosophy underlying British colonial policy. The Board was to study the problem of finding in the colonies a supply of naval stores and other products for which England was dependent upon other nations, such, for example, as Sweden, whence most of the naval stores used in England were coming. The colonies were to be studiously cultivated as markets for English commerce and manufactures. Those markets are not to be free markets; they are to be limited for the sake of English merchants interested in that field of trade. On the other hand, the products and the commerce of the colonies were to be limited, as much as possible, to those products and trade which were impossible or impracticable in England itself. The Board was to examine colonial legislation and to recommend a veto for any colonial law according to "the Usefulness or Mischeif thereof . . . to Our said Kingdom of England." It had also to prevent colonial competition with England. Finally, it is to be noted that throughout these instructions it seemed to be taken for granted that the colonies existed for the benefit of England. Any wishes or needs the colonies may have had were completely ignored or deliberately opposed wherever and whenever they might come into conflict with the interests of England. This point of view was not malicious; it was simply an expression of the economic philosophy of the day comparable to the neo-mercantilistic philosophies of national protectionism so common in the twentieth century.

In its day-to-day work, the Board of Trade studied all sorts of problems relating to the colonies and submitted its reports to the Privy Council, that is, to the king. The execution of the Board's recommendations, however, might be assigned to the Secretary of State, the Treasury, or the Admiralty. On special occasions the Board reported directly to the House of Commons or the House of Lords. It prepared instructions for the colonial governors, which had to be officially approved by the Privy Council before being transmitted to the recipient by the Secretary of State; it reviewed colonial legislation to see whether it conformed to the laws of England or ran counter to England's economic interests. On the basis of its own mercantilist ideas it often formulated suggestions as to policy. Under the leadership of William Blathwayt, Martin Bladen, and, later, the Earl of Halifax and the Earl of Shelburne, the Board of Trade made numerous reports and many suggestions, including proposed laws, for the better administration of the colonies, and so exercised a profound influence upon the history of British America throughout the course of the eighteenth century.

One of the Board's favorite projects was the move for a unification of all, or part, of the American colonies under one government. Such an effort had been tried out in the form of the Dominion of New England under Andros from 1686 to 1689, but the Dominion had broken up with the fall of James II and the dismissal of his governors. But the idea was revived by the Board, and it repeatedly suggested such action, if only for the purposes of defense. One such suggestion was made in a famous report of the Board in 1721. Another of the Board's projects, inherited from the era of James II, was the effort to bring the "private" colonies, whether corporate or proprietary, more closely under the control of the Crown. The flourishing condition of piracy in the proprietary colonies and the prevalence of illegal trade in both the proprietary and the corporate colonies led the Board to recommend to Parliament that the charters of these colonies be recalled and that they be given the status of royal provinces. It was hoped that direct royal control would bring about a greater effectiveness in the enforcement of the navigation system, and a bill for recalling the charters of the private colonies was introduced in Parliament in 1701. But William Penn, the Carolina proprietors and the agents of Rhode Island and Connecticut were able to muster so much opposition that the bill failed of passage. The attack was renewed in 1704 and 1705, but failed again. The Board then made an effort to have the Crown purchase Pennsylvania, and all but succeeded; a few years later it had the satisfaction of bringing South Carolina and North Carolina under royal control. Its plan had a setback, however, when Maryland, the administration of which had been taken on by the Crown in 1689, was restored to Charles Calvert, fifth (and Protestant) Lord Baltimore, in 1715. All in all, however, the mid-century saw all the American colonies brought to the status of royal provinces except the two proprietary provinces, Pennsylvania and Maryland, and the two corporate colonies, Connecticut and Rhode Island.

Of the other administrative agencies concerned with colonial affairs, it should be noted that the Privy Council was the most important. For that body, receiving its pertinent data from the Board of Trade, instructed the appropriate officials as to how to carry out its desires. The most important executive concerned was the Secretary of State for the Southern Department ("one of His Majesty's [two] Principal Secretaries of State"), who was charged, among other things, with the administration of colonial affairs. It was the Secretary of State, for example, who usually presented his instructions to a royal governor. Similarly, the Lords of the Treasury administered affairs arising out of the collections of customs duties; the Lords of the Admiralty administered naval affairs concerning the colonies, the Lord Chancellor, acting for the Privy Council, heard appeals from colonial courts, and so on.

It is to be noted that all these agencies were of an executive sort. But the evolution of a responsible cabinet system of government in England drew the executive and legislative branches steadily closer together; and, in most cases, parliamentary action, where necessary, followed upon executive, or cabinet, leadership. Thus, when a law affecting the colonies was desired, a report to that effect, sometimes even embodying a proposed text for the desired law, was prepared by the Board of Trade and submitted to the Privy Council, who then, through the appropriate cabinet member, had the proposed law introduced into Parliament. As the working members of the Board of Trade were merchants, in sympathy with the mercantile interests of their class, it is no wonder that British colonial legislation and colonial policy in general, as carried out through these agencies, should have had, throughout the eighteenth century, a strongly mercantilist trend.

It is no wonder, either, that the Board of Trade and the executive agencies should have followed a philosophy of the imperial constitution which held the prerogative of the Crown to be an integral—and superior—element in the constitution of every colony. For to have admitted any other position would have been to surrender the right of the Crown to interfere in the affairs of the colonies, political or economic, for the benefit of England. No other concept of the empire was to them possible, indeed, than that which gave the Crown the right to pass in review every act, however small, of a colonial legislature or a colonial official. This was the political side of a mercantilist philosophy of imperial administration without which economic mercantilism would not have been possible. Like the economic program, however, this philosophy of the imperial constitution failed to take into account the growing autonomy of the colonial constitutions; and the struggle between this "prerogative of the Crown," on the one hand, and the constitutional ideals of the colonists, on the other, became the major theme in the history of the political relationship of the colonies to the mother country throughout the century. It was this question of interpretations of the imperial constitution, indeed, which, when the showdown came in 1774-76, lay at the heart of the political conflict within the American Revolution.

THE ACTS OF TRADE

It was as a result of this same basic policy of exploitation that England passed in the eighteenth century a series of laws to prevent the growth of colonial manufactures which might be competitive with British manufactures and to encourage the colonies, on the other hand, to produce goods that England needed. About 1698, just after its organization, the Board of Trade made an inquiry into the condition of the British wool trade and in its report called attention to the growth of woolen manufactures in the home industries of the colonies and concluded that "notwithstanding it was the intent in settling our Plantations in America that the people there should be only employed in such things as are not the product of this kingdom . . . yet New England and other Northern Colonies have applied themselves too much, besides other things, to the improvement of woollen manufactures amongst themselves, which in its proportion is as prejudicial to this kingdom as the working of those manufactures in Ireland; wherefore it is submitted the like prohibition be made with relation to them."

It was for this reason that the Woolens Act passed by Parliament in 1699 prohibited the export of wool and woolens from the colonies to the British Isles, to foreign countries, and from one colony to another. These provisions evidently meant that while woolens might be produced for sale within, say, Massachusetts, the Massachusetts woolens makers might not be permitted to take advantage of a market for their goods in Virginia. That market was reserved, under the terms of the act, for the manufacturers of England. The next year a further attempt was made to discourage colonial woolen manufacturers by removing the heavy export duties on wool shipped from England to America. This was done to keep the price of British wool in America down and make it possible for British woolens to compete with the home manufactured goods of the colonies, particularly of New England.

While all this obviously worked against the interest of the colonies, the Board of Trade realized that, if the colonies were to pay for the goods they bought from England, they must be encouraged to produce staple products that would have a market in England. It was upon the basis of this reasoning that the Board took up the old suggestion of encouraging the production of naval stores in the colonies, and in 1705, on the recommendation of the Board, an act was passed placing naval stores on the list of enumerated articles and offering bounties on naval stores produced in the colonies. A little later (1710) a colony of three thousand Germans was sent to New York at the expense of the government, where they were settled on the Hudson River, in an attempt to promote the production of naval stores in that colony. The attempt was a failure, but it is significant as showing that the Board of Trade was considering seriously the needs both of England to become independent of the Baltic countries with regard to this product and the needs of the colonies, and particularly the northern colonies, for a product that they could sell to the mother country to even up the adverse balance of trade. Unfortunately, the colonists found the naval stores business less profitable, even with the bounty, than other forms of industry and the policy of encouragement adopted by the Board achieved, for the time being, only a moderate success.

These attempts at the regulation of colonial manufactures reflect the sort of thinking along economic lines that was going on in the minds of British statesmen. In general, they conceived of the British empire as constituting a self-sufficient whole, each part of which might make its contribution to the development of all the other parts. According to this way of thinking, it might be expected that New England would produce naval stores and fish; New York and Pennsylvania, foodstuffs; Virginia, tobacco; the West Indies, sugar; the mother country, manufactured goods; and so on. Thus, the empire would become more and more nearly self-sufficient in an economic way and the national wealth and power would be correspondingly increased. Obviously, any section of the empire that failed to place imperial interest above its own local interest would be guilty of disloyalty and might on occasion have to be coerced. This theory of the unified, self-sufficient empire seemed to be demonstrated and justified by the position occupied by the West Indies, and it was largely because of this theoretical justification that the "West Indian lobby" was able to prevail upon Parliament to take a series of steps in the early eighteenth century to promote the interests of the sugar-producing islands, even at the expense of the continental colonies.

It will be recalled that, in the latter part of the seventeenth century and now, in the first half of the eighteenth century, the Yankee traders from New England and the middle colonies had developed a thriving trade in provisions and lumber with the French West Indies. In return for their northern products, they took French sugar and molasses, which they delivered in the continental colonies for consumption or for manufacture into rum; on occasion, they even smuggled French sugar into the British islands, whence it was sent to England as British sugar. The sugar planters of the British West Indies looked upon this trade with the French islands as disastrous to their own interests and they entered complaint after complaint with the Board of Trade. Their complaints were strengthened by the increasing difficulty which they found in competing with French and Dutch sugar in the world market, and in order to meet the two problems at once, they requested the Board to adopt a policy of exclusion of French sugar from the empire.

The problem presented to the Board by this situation was an extremely difficult one. If the Board allowed the northern colonies to continue their trade with the French West Indies, French sugar would compete with British sugar even within the British empire. In effect, it would mean that British ships and British money were assisting in building up the French empire in general, and the French islands in particular, as competitors of the British. On the other hand, should the Board of Trade recommend the prohibition of this trade, it might have two or three results, the first of which would be the violation of the law by the northern traders. But more important still, it would obviously have an adverse effect upon the trade and prosperity of the northern continental colonies: it would, in fact, be a deliberate discrimination against the northern colonies in favor of the islands. The total exclusion of French sugar from the imperial market, moreover, would force it to go elsewhere, which probably would have the effect of lowering the world price of sugar with an indirectly depressive effect upon the prosperity of the British sugar islands. A third possible solution of the problem might be the removal of sugar from the list of enumerated articles. This would mean a direct trade in sugar between the British islands and the Dutch and French sugar markets on the continent. It would tend to make possible a lower price for British sugar in the continental market because of the saving effected by eliminating the handling of the commodity in England, and this would be an advantage; but such a step would almost certainly result in a direct sale of Dutch and French manufactured goods to the British West Indies colonies and would adversely affect the interests of British manufacturers. Finally, as a compromise, the trade might be discouraged without prohibiting it, so as to neutralize the advantage enjoyed by French sugar in the continental colonies, for example, because of its lower costs of production.

The Board of Trade evaded the issue presented to it by the West Indian sugar planters. But the "West Indian lobby" turned to Parliament and succeeded in getting that body to pass the Molasses Act of 1733. This act was based upon the fourth alternative suggested above; that is to say, it was an attempt to discourage the trade with the French islands and the importation of French sugar into the continental colonies by making it unprofitable. Thus it was that the act, while not prohibiting the importation of French sugar, placed high import duties upon sugar, molasses and rum imported into the British colonies from foreign plantations. In effect, it was a discrimination against the northern colonies in favor of the islands, and it is significant as showing the importance of the West Indies in the empire because of their greater value to the mother country. Its greatest significance, perhaps, lies in the way in which it illustrates the gradual divergence of economic interests taking place between the British West Indies and the continental colonies. For it marks the appearance of an economic separation which resulted in a complete parting of the ways as between the two sections when, at last, there was presented to them the question of independence.

Another illustration of the developing conflict of economic interest between the colonies and the mother country is the attempt of England to regulate the colonial iron industry. Iron works of some importance had gradually developed in Virginia, Maryland, Pennsylvania, and New England. On the surface it would appear that England might well have welcomed such a development, for England was in need of crude iron and was under the necessity of importing iron from Sweden. The importers of crude iron in England did, indeed, favor encouraging colonial production. But the British hardware manufacturers frowned upon the development of the industry in the colonies because they feared to lose the colonial market for hardware, of which they enjoyed a monopoly. The question came up repeatedly in governmental circles but the iron masters always opposed attempts to extend encouragement of the industry to the colonies. Finally, in 1750, a compromise was arrived at in the famous Iron Act of that year. According to this act, colonial bar iron might be imported into London free of duty, but Parliament took care to forbid the colonies from setting up mills, forges, or furnaces, and from manufacturing hardware. Thus England attempted to profit by the raw materials produced in the colonies, but to maintain its own monopoly of the colonial market for the finished product; colonial crude iron was to be shipped to the mother country, manufactured into hardware, and returned, as hardware, to the colonies! Similarly, the mother country attempted to control the colonial hat industry. In 1732 Parliament passed a law limiting the number of apprentices who might be employed by colonial hat manufacturers and later prohibited the shipment of hats from one colony to another.

Of still greater importance in the story of British control of colonial economic life is that revolving about the question of paper currency. Partly because of their dependence upon the mother country for manufactured goods, and partly because of the limiting effect of the Acts of Trade, the colonial balance of payments with England (except in the West Indies) was permanently in favor of the mother country. This balance amounted, in 1700, to about fifty thousand pounds a year, and in 1760 to about two million pounds. A serious problem was presented by the question how the colonies might pay this unfavorable balance. As a new country and a poor one, it had no invisible exports to redress the balance, but must depend on money payments. The northern colonies, where the unfavorable balance was heaviest, depended upon gold and silver coin which could only be derived from trading with the West Indies, both British and foreign, and by money collected as freight charges on goods shipped from one part of the empire to another. But the colonies were constantly drained of specie, and this at a time when, because of the growth of the population, the opening of new areas to settlement, the expansion of trade, and the expense of the intercolonial wars, the colonies all along the seaboard were in dire need of an expanding rather than a contracting currency. The demand for an available currency was so great and so intense, and the values of foreign coins fluctuated so rapidly, that every imaginable remedy for this financial ill was attempted.

Because of the premium placed upon hard money in the colonies, and because the value of foreign coins varied from colony to colony, the Board of Trade prevailed upon Parliament in 1708 to pass a law regulating the value of foreign monies in the colonies. But the law was a dead letter from the day of its passage, for the colonial merchants, and even colonial legislatures, openly defied it. The economic law of supply and demand was very much stronger than parliamentary legislation could be. But Parliament kept on trying. As the use of paper money increased throughout the colonies, the Board of Trade tried every conceivable means of discouraging it. Governors were instructed to discourage it; and in 1740 the old Bubble Act was applied by Parliament to the colonies in order to destroy the Massachusetts land bank, as will be related later. In 1751, Parliament passed a currency act severely restricting the issuance of paper money by the colonies in New England; this law was applied to all the colonies in 1764.

One more law affecting trade and intercourse among the colonies of America was the Post Office Act of 1710. Originally, the colonies had made their own postal arrangements. Then, about 1692, a private monopoly of the transport of mail had been given to one Thomas Niel of Boston; but this arrangement had proved unsatisfactory and the Act of 1710 took control of postal communications out of the hands of private individuals and placed it in the hands of the government. The act provided for the establishment of post offices in New York and certain other towns. It fixed the rates of postage and laid down rules for the carrying of the mail. The object of the act was both the raising of revenue and the better regulation of postal intercourse; but it was in effect taxation of the colonists. There was some slight opposition to it on this ground, but it marked an improvement in the situation and the opposition soon disappeared.

THE INHERENT CONFLICT

In all the laws just reviewed, as well as in the British system of imperial administration, there is to be observed one consistent motive, the desire to make the colonies profitable to Great Britain. With one exception these laws were recommended by the Board of Trade in order to fulfill its original instructions to improve the colonial markets for English manufactures, to discourage the colonies from engaging in industries that would compete with those of England, but to encourage the colonies to produce raw materials that might be useful to England in her manufactures or in her profitable re-export trade with Europe. Many of the merchants, as already suggested, acted from shortsighted and purely selfish motives; but in the minds of the more statesmanlike of the English imperial administrators, there was always the broad idea of the unified empire, involving not only the centralized control of imperial economic life of London, but also the reciprocal services of co-ordinated administration, defense, and economic encouragement within certain desired lines rendered by the empire to its composite colonies. In the administration of the imperial program, certain groups in England were pitted against each other—the crude-iron merchants against the hardware manufacturers, for example—and the favorable treatment of the West Indies, as the most valuable of the colonial groups, involved an inevitable discrimination in favor of one section of the colonial empire against another. Taken all together, however, the developing English system of laws and institutions for the regulation of colonial economic and political life, despite the high-minded philosophy of the integrated empire, brings into clear relief the profound fact that there was a wide divergence between the economic interests of England, on the one side, and the developing colonial economy on the other. The tragic weakness of the English mercantilist program of colonial control was its inflexibility, its complete inability to adapt itself to the needs of the expanding economic life of the colonies. Logical though it seemed to be, England's mercantilist colonial program was shortsighted, selfish, and inflexible; under such conditions, and given a continuation of the economic expansion of the continental colonies, as contrasted with the West Indies, the more developed colonies were bound, sooner or later, to demand a greater measure of economic autonomy and of freedom from English economic control. Unfortunately for England, it decided upon a tightening of its mercantile system of control at the precise moment when, after the expulsion of the French, the continental colonies found themselves upon the threshold of a new era of expansion. At that moment it would have been too much to expect British mercantilists to see that the only way they could retain the loyalty of the colonies was to give them more economic freedom, rather than less. Thus it was that inherent in the British system of imperial control lay the very forces that were to bring about the destruction of the empire.

RECOMMENDED BOOKS FOR FURTHER READING

CONTEMPORARY NARRATIVES

Josiah Child. *A New Discourse of Trade.*
Charles Davenant, *Discourses on the Publick Revenues and on the Trade of England.*
Joshua Gee. *The Trade and Navigation of Britain Considered.*
Thomas Mun. *England's Treasure by Forraine Trade.*
Dudley North, *Sir Dudley North on Discourses upon Trade, 1691.*
Leo F. Stock, ed., *Proceeding and Debates of the British Parliaments respecting North America,* IV. 805-817.
Dalby Thomas, *An Historical Account of the Rise and Growth of the West-India Colonies.*
William Wood, *A Survey of Trade.*

MODERN ACCOUNTS

Charles M. Andrews, *The Colonial Background of the American Revolution,* Chapter 1.
Charles M. Andrews. *The Colonial Period of American History,* IV, Chapters 6-11.
Charles M. Andrews. *The Royal Disallowance.*
Arthur H. Basye, *The Lords Commissioners of Trade and Plantations.*
George L. Beer, *The Old Colonial System, 1660-1754,* Volume II.
Arthur C. Bining, *British Regulation of the Colonial Iron Industry.*
The Cambridge History of the British Empire, I, Chapters 14, 21-22.
William R. Carlton, "New England Masts and the King's Navy," *New England Quarterly,* XII. 4-18.
Helen J. Crump, *Colonial Admiralty Jurisdiction in the Seventeenth Century.*
Oliver M. Dickerson, *American Colonial Government, 1696-1765.*
Lawrence H. Gipson, *The British Empire before the American Revolution,* I, Chapters 1-3, 5.

George H. Guttridge, *The Colonial Policy of William III in America and the West Indies.*

Eli F. Heckscher, *Mercantilism.*

Arthur B. Keith, *Constitutional History of the First British Empire.*

Ephraim Lipson, *The Economic History of England.*

Ephraim Lipson, "England in the Age of Mercantilism" in *Journal of Economic and Business History,* IV, 691-707.

Winfred T. Root, *The Relations of Pennsylvania with the British Government, 1696-1765.*

Elmer B. Russell, *The Review of American Colonial Legislation by the King in Council.*

George R. S. Taylor, *Robert Walpole and His Age.*

27

The Colonial Constitution

THE GOVERNMENT of the British colonies in America was a curious mixture of imperial, or federal, and local, or provincial, elements. For the colonial constitution, like the British constitution of which it was an offshoot, "just grew"—out of the experience of the colonists in their slow progress toward the perfection of a governmental machine that would work. It is true, of course, that in the middle of the eighteenth century there were several different types of colonial government in America. Without mentioning the company government still in vogue in the Hudson Bay trading posts, the military government of Newfoundland, or the trusteeship of Georgia, which became a royal province in 1752, three types of colonial government may be noted —the royal type, established in the royal provinces, the proprietary type, in Maryland and Pennsylvania, and the corporate type, still operating vigorously in Connecticut and Rhode Island. Despite the superficial differences between them, however, they had much in common; and most of the comments that may be made about one of them would apply to all. In any case, since the greater part of the provinces had royal governments, it is that type which is taken as the basis of the present discussion.

THE IMPERIAL CONNECTION

At the head of the government in every colony stood the provincial governor.

The governor had a double function; for he was at once the agent and symbol of the sovereignty of the Crown in the empire and the executive head of the provincial government within the colony. He was at once a cog in the great wheel of the empire and the hub of the smaller wheel of the province. As the personal representative of the king he was the repository and the agent of the "prerogative," that vague, ill-defined authority of the Crown, as the symbol of the nation as a whole, over the individuals, groups, or communities within the nation. But as the executive head of a constitutional government in the colonial province he was also the responsible servant of the voters of the provincial common-

349

wealth. Every citizen of a self-governing British colony had a two-fold loyalty to his province and to the Crown; but the governor was an active agent in the service of both, and in a very real sense responsible to both. His responsibility to the Crown took precedence over his responsibility to the province over which he was governor; but when the two came into conflict, as they often did, he had to face the displeasure, even the discipline, of the people of the province, and his position became a very uncomfortable one indeed.

The governor was thus an imperial agent in each of the colonies. Even in the two corporate colonies, where the governors were elected, the governor was subject to the limitations placed upon him by the Navigation Act of 1696, and was in general answerable to the Crown for his behavior. In the proprietary colonies, where the governors were appointed by the proprietors, they were subject to Crown approval, and, though one step removed from direct royal control, they were always liable to interference by the Crown whenever it considered its interests endangered. The instructions to the governors, particularly those of the royal provinces, were expressions of the thought and will of the mother country with regard to its dependencies. Formulated, as a rule, by the Board of Trade and transmitted by the Secretary of State for the Southern Department, the instructions became a part of the fabric of the imperial constitution; as such they were expected to have the force of law in the provinces and to be considered a part of the provincial constitution. Both these assumptions, however, were successfully rejected by the provincial assemblies. The governors' instructions nevertheless constituted a check upon the liberal tendencies of the assemblies and a persistently conservative influence upon the growth of the colonies toward self-government. Inevitably there took place between the conservative influence of the "prerogative" and the liberal tendencies inherent in colonial political growth a conflict which was the major theme in colonial political history. More must be said of this conflict at a later time.

The governor, then, was the personal representative of the king and the symbol of the empire in the colony, "endowed with vice-regal powers, analogous though inferior in degree to those of the monarch." As such he was the commander-in-chief of the military forces in the colony and the chief among the agents of the Crown. He had the power to appoint judges in the vice-admiralty court, where there was such a court in his colony, and judges, justices of the peace, and sheriffs in the administration of civil justice. He also had the power to nominate members of the executive council chosen by the Crown from among the distinguished men of his province, and the power to veto acts passed by the legislature which he considered contrary to the king's interest. He appointed the members of the legislative council, the upper house of the legislature (usually identical with the executive council), and as a part of the legislative arm of government signed all laws passed by the two houses. Generally the council either served as the supreme court of appeals or, where there was a separate court, the judges were also members of the council, over which the governor presided.

The governor's powers were thus fourfold; for he was at once a Crown agent and the effective head of the executive, the legislative, and the judicial arms of government. He was the point at which the provincial constitution impinged upon the imperial constitution. His influence, therefore, usually exercised as a conservative force, was enormous. The governors were generally men of honor, distinction, and ability and they generally did their best to govern well. But they were in an impossible situation, standing as they did for the British idea of what the colonial government should be like, whereas the idea of government that was gradually shaping itself in America was something very different indeed. The governor represented the principle of government by royal grace and favor, whereas the evolving American idea was grounded upon the principle of government by consent of the governed. From the point of view of the British Crown, the participation in government enjoyed by the colonials was a favor granted to them by the king which might be retracted at any time. From the point of view of the colonials, representative government was theirs by natural right and by right of the long struggles for self-government and the limitation of royal power that had been won step by step through generations of their English ancestors.

The royal governor came to America as the executive head of a colonial government with instructions made out by men, three thousand miles away, who had never been in America, who understood American conditions only partially if at all, and who, even if they had understood the problems, would not have sympathized with the American way of solving them. Nevertheless, there was a strong bond of emotional attachment between the people of the colonies and the mother country and the arrival of a governor in a colony was always a time of celebration. He was usually greeted by a committee of distinguished citizens who escorted him to the town hall or government building in which was the council chamber. There he read his commission, took the necessary oaths, and swore in his council. Then he issued a proclamation stating his inauguration, which was read to the assembled multitude, after which the meeting adjourned to a near-by tavern where entertainment was provided at public expense. Speeches and fireworks followed the celebration, sometimes lasting for several days.

The governor was assisted in his imperial duties by a set of officials who were appointed directly by the Crown and who were also responsible to the imperial government rather than to the colony. Thus the "naval officers," in charge of ship-registries and inspections, and vice-admiralty officials, to say nothing of the commanders of warships in the American stations, were appointed by, and responsible to, the Admiralty. Military officers, and officials concerned with military supply, were appointed and paid by the War Office. Collectors of the imperial customs in the colonies were responsible to the Board of Customs Commissioners in England, and this Board, in turn, was responsible to the Lords of the Treasury. These men were of great importance, since it was they who collected the duties under the navigation act, the so-called "plantations duties" under the act of 1673, and others. Their work was supervised by the Surveyor of the Customs, of whom there were two in the colonies after 1720, one for the northern colonies and the other for the colonies south of Pennsylvania, including the West Indies. Within the royal colonies the quit-rents, small taxes paid the Crown in perpetuity from the time of the original grant of the land, were assessed and collected under the supervision of the Surveyor-General of the royal revenues in America—which, incidentally, also included fines and certain other incomes as well as quit-rents.

Thus the imperial authority and functions constituted a very real and active part of the political institutions in all the colonies, even the most autonomous of them. The role of the imperial government in colonial affairs has often—and rightly—been compared with that of the federal government in the affairs of the United States under the Constitution of 1789. As a matter of fact, however, there never was a clear line drawn between the imperial authority and colonial authority, and this overlapping of the two is clearly illustrated in the realm of law. For clearly such parliamentary laws as the Navigation Act of 1696, the Coin Act of 1708, the Hat Act, and the Iron Act, already discussed, and many others, had complete legal validity in every province. Parliament was legislating upon intra-colonial or imperial matters, and colonial resentment toward the assumption of this power by Parliament was negligible; it was accepted as a matter of course.

Similarly, the English common law—as much a part of the cultural heritage of every English subject as the English language itself—was regarded as having full force in all the colonies. But the peculiar conditions affecting social and legal developments in the colonies were, nevertheless, gradually bringing about a divergence between the statutory law of the provinces and the common law, and raised the question of which should take precedence over the other. In the Connecticut case of Winthrop *versus* Lechmere, for example, one John Winthrop claimed, under the common law, the entire estate of his father, Wait Winthrop, who had died intestate; his sister, wife of Thomas Lechmere, claimed a share of the estate under a Connecticut statute. The Connecticut courts ruled in favor of Mrs. Lechmere and the Connecticut statute; but on appeal the Privy Council in England in 1728 declared the Connecticut statute null and void, as "contrary to the laws of England." In a similar Massachusetts case a few years later, however, the Privy Council was compelled to reverse itself, since the Massachusetts law had not been disallowed by the Privy Council within the legally provided period. The more liberal statutory laws of the colonies were encroaching upon the conservative common law, and appeals from colonial courts to the Privy Council were a necessary device for defining the boundary between imperial law and provincial law. Of deep significance, too, was the principle of judicial review of colonial legislation that emerged from these appeals as well as from the practice of submitting colonial laws to the Privy Council for approval.

Through all these institutions, then—the governor and the "prerogative," the other Crown agencies, and English parliamentary and common law—the imperial constitution performed its very important function in the provinces of the empire. But there were many points at which the imperial and provincial constitutions came into conflict—over the governor's salary, in the provincial encroachments upon the collection of customs, in the interference or competition of civil courts with the admiralty courts, and in many other ways. As in the conflict over "states' rights" in a later era, the line between the authority of the imperial constitution and that of the provincial government was not clearly drawn. Nor was it, during the colonial period; indeed, the American Revolution was, at the beginning at least, a fight over this very question.

THE EXECUTIVE

If the colonial governor was the agent of the Crown and the embodiment of the prerogative in his province, he was also the executive head of the provincial government. As such it was his function to carry out the will of the people of his province or their representatives; this he could do, of course, only so long as their will did not conflict with the wishes of the Crown or the laws of the empire as a whole. He was assisted in his work as chief executive by an executive council (generally identical with the legislative council), the members of which were appointed by the Crown on his recommendation from among the most able and distinguished citizens of the colony. He was also assisted by the surveyor-general and the receiver-general, the attorney-general, and the chief justice, all of whom were appointed. This little group, with their clerks, carried on the everyday business of government; at times one even gets a glimpse of something rather closely resembling a "cabinet." As the appointees of the Crown, however, these officials often found themselves at issue, if not in actual conflict, with the group of officials appointed by the assembly, such as the assembly's treasurer or the colonial agent in London—a group of "legislative-executives" of whom more must be said later. The governor also generally appointed local administrative officers such as sheriffs and justices of the peace.

It was thus the business of the governor, as the executive, to carry out the business of governing. For this purpose his powers were very broad. In the first place, he was the commander-in-chief of the armed forces of the province, both military and naval. As such he might raise a militia, when provided by the assembly, and he appointed its officers. He organized the defense of his province, and built forts and other military works when authorized to do so by the assembly. His naval duties were light, since no province had a navy; yet he might issue letters of marque and reprisal, and he appointed the officials in the admiralty courts.

The governor also conducted the relations of his province with its neighbors. Thus the governor was generally charged with negotiating with the Indians, when necessary. The purchase of land from the Indians was generally in his hands, as was also the regulation of Indian trade. Private individuals continued to buy lands, however, and to violate the governors' regulations. This caused much confusion, and tended especially to make the Indians discontented, with the result that, after the Albany Congress of 1754, a part of these powers was taken out of the hands of the governors and placed in the hands of two Indian agents with powers that were continental in scope. On questions of common interest the governor of one colony often corresponded with another—sometimes, as in cases of defense, for the purposes of cooperation; at other times in a very angry, even belligerent mood, when the correspondence was concerned with, say, a disputed boundary between the two. Diplomatic relations between Britain and foreign states with regard to a colony like Georgia, for example, were carried on by the two mother countries; yet the colonial governors on numerous occasions negotiated agreements between themselves subject to the approval of the home governments. The governor was also in a very real way a negotiator for the colony with the mother country; but because the governor came to be distrusted by the assemblies, those bodies developed the practice of sending their own agents to represent them in London.

The governor's power of appointment, his powers to grant lands, determine fees, issue licenses, and pardon criminals and his position as the military commander of his province placed a great deal of patronage at his disposal and gave him an enormous political influence. But many of the colonial governors used their powers corruptly for their own personal profit at the expense of the province. The result was a steady tendency on the part of the assembly to limit the governor's power of appointment. Thus the assemblies passed laws placing residence requirements upon appointed office holders; in numerous cases terms of tenure were fixed by law. The assemblies contended, and to a large degree won their point, that appointments by the governor should be made with the advice, at least, of the Council, and the lower houses were able to exert a very effective check upon appointments by the simple device of controlling—or withholding, when necessary—the salaries of appointed officials. The assemblies, indeed, even went so far as to assume certain powers of appointment to themselves. The general tendency, throughout the colonies, was in the direction of weakening the power of the executive as a defense against corruption, and in the direction of a general encroachment by the assemblies upon the governor's power with the more or less deliberate objective of increasing the power of the legislature.

THE COLONIAL LEGISLATURE

The colonial governor, as the apex of the pyramid of provincial government, was technically also a part of the legislature. As a matter of fact, the legislature could not meet unless he called it together; but several of the provinces succeeded, despite the opposition of the mother country, in getting on the statute-books "triennial acts" requiring that the legislature meet at least once every three years whether the governor called it or not—thus making it impossible for the governor to ignore it. Also, no law could become effective without the governor's signature. Thus he had the veto power, and there was no way of passing a law over his veto. He might also decline to act upon a law "until His Majesty's pleasure thereon" might be known. The Crown, acting in the Privy Council, might disallow any provincial law within a specified period of time; laws received under the "suspending clause" usually did not become effective until the Privy Council had made its wishes known. The governor was almost certain to veto any law he considered inimical to the interests of the Crown or of the empire as a whole; he "suspended" laws with regard to which he was in doubt.

The legislative council, composed, with a few exceptions, of the same men who made up the executive council, was the upper house of the law-making body—except in Pennsylvania, where, although the governor had the usual executive council, there was no upper house of the legislature. The members of the council were appointed, except in Massachusetts, where they were elected by the general court, from among the wealthy and distinguished citizens of the province, and their outlook was generally conservative and loyal to the interests of the Crown. As the upper house, the council voted upon all bills, and might reject any of which it disapproved. It did not have the power to initiate bills dealing with financial matters, however, and it gradually became an established principle that the council could not even amend a money bill. In general, the council stood with the governor as a check upon the radical tendencies of the assembly; not having the popular support of the citizens, its influence was probably less than an elective council might have had—although, curiously enough, the Massachusetts council, which was elected, was just as conservatively minded as its fellows.

But the most active and powerful branch of the legislature was the assembly, variously called, made up of representatives elected by the property-owners of the province. The property qualification for voting varied from province to province, but the lowest was probably that of Pennsylvania, where the voter must own fifty acres of land, twelve of which were under cultivation, or have fifty pounds in cash. These bodies, representing the "popular" interests in the provinces, claimed the same rights and privileges as the House of Commons in England, and, like their maternal prototype, succeeded, in the course of the eighteenth century, in winning a position of predominant importance in provincial government.

By the beginning of the century the colonial assemblies had won recognition of their exclusive right to initiate legislation affecting provincial finances. Following parliamentary precedents, they continued to extend their privileges to include freedom of debate in their sessions, the right of the assembly to judge the qualifications of its own members, the exclusion from the assembly of officers appointed by the Crown, regular meetings of the assembly, and the right of the assembly to decide upon its own adjournment or dissolution. There were exceptions to the universal acceptance of these parliamentary privileges, to be sure, but by the end of the colonial period a good many of these precedents had been accepted by the Crown in most of the colonies. By these privileges, along with its control of finance, the assembly had practically excluded the executive, at the mid-century, from any effective control of legislation.

At the beginning the assemblies had imposed taxes and appropriated money at the request of the governor. But as the money was appropriated in lump sums, without any requirement of strict accounting, the governors often found it easy to divert much of the money to their own corrupt purposes. It was for this reason that the assemblies adopted the device of appropriating only specific sums for specific purposes and for specified periods of time—usually one year. As a further device for checking any corrupt or disloyal tendencies the governor might have, the assemblies fell into the habit of appropriating the governor's salary only for one year at a time, and at the end instead of the beginning. Thus, if the governor had acted in a manner pleasing to the assembly, he might expect a large salary, promptly paid; if he had displeased that body, he might expect to have his salary unexpectedly reduced, and even, on occasion, to have trouble in collecting it.

This was humiliating in the extreme to the governors, particularly those of the royal provinces. But it was still more important to the Crown because it interfered with the effectiveness with which the governors might carry out their instructions. The question of the governor's salary, therefore, became one of the perennial disputes in the struggle between the assemblies and the prerogative. And this battle was particularly keen in Massachusetts, New York, and Jamaica. Governor Belcher finally had to surrender to the assembly in Massachusetts in 1730, and New York won its battle in 1755. In Jamaica alone of all the colonies, the assembly lost the battle for control of the governor's salary and was compelled to make a permanent appropriation which made the governor independent of the assembly's control. In Virginia also the governor was financially independent of the assembly; but this was because the civil list had been permanently provided for, by an arrangement of 1682, out of the money raised by the provincial export duty of two shillings per hogshead levied on tobacco.

While the assemblies were thus reducing the governors to dependence upon themselves through their control of the provincial purse, they were steadily extending their own powers along other lines which even encroached upon the powers of the executive. Thus, on the ground that the people's money, appropriated by the people's representatives, should be disbursed under the supervision of an agent responsible to the assembly, the assemblies advanced the claim that they should appoint the provincial treasurer. They succeeded in a majority of the provinces; and the effect of their success was to remove practically all control over finances from the governor's hands, and to place this executive function—the disbursement of moneys—under the strict control of the legislature.

But the tendency of the legislatures to encroach upon the executive powers was not limited to affairs concerning money. For collectors of provincial customs and taxes were in some colonies also appointed by the assemblies. Similarly, when a military expedition was to be organized or forts to be built, they had to be authorized by the assembly, which often enough appointed commissioners responsible to itself to see that its wishes were properly carried out. Similarly, too, in some colonies, such as South Carolina, the assembly appointed Indian commissioners responsible to itself. Even in the field of military organization the assembly assumed the right to appoint officers responsible to itself, or to bring about the discharge of officers who had the misfortune to arouse its displeasure. This tendency became most clearly marked during the Seven Years' War.

Finally, the provincial assemblies gradually asserted their right to appoint agents to represent the colonies at the court in London. This functionary, a sort of provincial representative at the Court of St. James, had had his origin in the middle of the seventeenth century in connection with the occupation and administration of the island of Jamaica by Cromwell. By the middle of the eighteenth century he had come to be a very important institution, indeed, in the imperial constitution. Thus the colonial agent was expected to inform the colony of impending action or legislation that might be of interest to it, to appear before the Board of Trade in defense of the actions or laws of his province, to plead his colony's cause in boundary disputes, and so on, in addition to which political functions he was something of a commercial agent as well. The question arose whether the agent should be appointed by the provincial governor or by the assembly, and to whom he should be responsible. Obviously, if he were appointed by and responsible to the governor, his attitude in London would be liable to be very different from that of a man responsible to the assembly. Since the welfare of the province was so vitally affected by this office, the assemblies generally insisted that the colonial agents should represent them. The quarrel over appointment and control of the colonial agents was long and bitter; but gradually the assemblies had their way. By 1750 the colonial agents, representing the popular arm of government in the colonies, were recognized as an established mechanism in imperial administration.

It would be a mistake to suppose that the colonial assemblies had their way in all the conflicts between the prerogative and the representatives of the people that have been here briefly reviewed. On the contrary, there were many exceptions to the rule, many defeats for the assembly along the route of its progress. But one thing is clear: there was a fundamental conflict between the prerogative of a distant Crown and a branch of government that sprang from the needs and the experience of the people. Slowly but surely the assemblies were moving toward autonomy, and the prerogative was in retreat. By the checks they succeeded in placing upon the executive, but especially by their own encroachments upon the executive's power, the colonial "parliaments" seem to have been moving clearly in the direction of a type of parliamentary government having an executive cabinet responsible to the legislature. The Crown, on the other hand, took every conceivable means to establish a system of checks upon the "democratical" tendencies of the assemblies. Thus the governors were consistently instructed to refuse to sign triennial acts, acts for placing the power of dissolution exclusively in the assembly itself, laws creating an independent judiciary, and any others tending to increase the power of the legislature at the expense of the executive.

But all to no avail. The trend in the development of the colonial constitution was clearly toward autonomous, parliamentary government. This trend was seen by many of the colonial governors, as by many British statesmen. And it frightened them; for they found it impossible to envisage colonial legislative autonomy within the empire. The achievement of complete legislative autonomy in the colonies, to them, could only mean independence; and independence meant the dissolution of the empire itself.

COLONIAL LAW AND THE ADMINISTRATION OF JUSTICE

There were some five sorts of law that had to be administered in the American colonies of England. The most fundamental and most widespread was the English common law, which had come to America as an invisible item in the cultural baggage of the very first settlers. But the common law, under the influence of a new environment, became modified and changed; and there appeared in America something that might well be called an American common law—an offshoot of its English original, to be sure, but distinguishable from it at many points. Parliamentary law pertaining to England alone did not apply to the colonies, as a rule; but where specifically applied to them such laws as the navigation acts and the acts of trade did apply in the colonies, as already noted, and took precedence over contrary colonial statutes. These two sets of law were general, and applied to the empire as a whole. But the statutes of any colony, and the instructions to the governor—the status of which as law the colonists themselves generally denied—pertained to one colony alone. Finally, in the corporate colonies, the colonial charter itself, which had the character of a treaty or a contract between the colony and the Crown, affected only the relations between that one colony and the mother country.

For the administration and interpretation of this complex body of law, each colony had its own system of courts. The vice-admiralty courts, to be sure, were parts of an imperial system analogous to the federal district courts of a later day in America. But they concerned themselves almost entirely with the consideration of maritime cases, and rarely touched the life of the average citizen. For the normal daily conduct of judicial activity, the following generalized system of courts—allowing, of course, for local variation—was the usual pattern within nearly all the colonies.

The lowest judicial officers in the colony were the justices of the peace. These men, who generally had no legal training, were appointed by the governor, and had jurisdiction, without juries, over small breaches of the peace or quarrels involving trifling sums of money. More important cases went to the county courts, which might have, as some did, both civil and criminal jurisdiction, or which might be divided into two parts, one for civil cases and the other for criminal cases. Above the county court stood the supreme court, which heard appeals from the lower courts and had original jurisdiction in very important cases. In some colonies there were also chancery courts to hear cases in equity, as distinguished from the others, which were courts of fixed common or statute law. In certain colonies, too, such as Virginia, the governor's council was the supreme court of appeals within the province—thus uniting in itself, since it was also an executive council and the upper house of the legislature, all three of the arms of government. The governor, too, as the presiding officer of the council, had a judicial function added to those already noted. But for every colony the truly supreme court was the Privy Council back in England; for every British subject theoretically had the right of appeal to the king. Not many cases were actually appealed to the Privy Council, because of the expense, time, and other obstacles involved. But the principle of appeal to an imperial supreme court was well established, and, along with it, the principle of review of colonial legislation, as already explained.

Originally, the governor had had certain judicial powers, and still, in the eighteenth century, retained a shadowy jurisdiction in probate and other testamentary matters. But his judicial functions had dwindled away, and now amounted only to the power to create certain special courts and to appoint judges in all courts with the concurrence of the council. By contrast, and as a counterpart to the expanding legislative powers of the assembly, that body was also attempting to extend its powers over the judiciary, both by contesting the provincial governor's power to create courts and by attempting to remove the courts from the governor's power to use them corruptly by insisting that judges be appointed during good behavior, instead of during the pleasure of the king, which was the common practice.

Thus, another long-drawn battle arose between the assemblies and the prerogative over the control of the courts. The governor, by his commission, was authorized to establish courts of justice in his province with the advice and consent of his council, and this he did when occasion demanded, particularly at the beginning of the eighteenth century. But the assembly also took it upon itself to erect courts and define their powers. This method gradually superseded the creation of courts by the governor, and there developed a feeling, indeed, that the governor had no right to set up courts without an act of the legislature. It was on just this point, for example, that Lewis Morris quarreled with Governor William Cosby prior to the famous trial of John Peter Zenger in New York. By the end of the colonial period the principle that courts could be erected only by the assembly had come to be pretty generally recognized.

The assemblies did not gain so complete a victory, however, in the contest with the prerogative over the tenure of the judges in the courts. The governors' commissions empowered them to appoint judges, but it soon grew evident that the governors were liable to use this power for corrupt purposes, and that the fear of removal was liable to constrain the judges themselves to interpret the law in the governor's favor. The assemblies, therefore, began to pass laws requiring that judges be appointed during good behavior. This seemed all the more logical since, in England, the Act of Settlement of 1701 provided that all judges should hold office during good behavior—a provision that was made precisely for the purpose of preventing the judges from being browbeaten by the king. But the acts of the colonial legislatures for the purpose of making the colonial judiciary independent of the governors were consistently disallowed by the home government. Thus, an act of this sort passed by the Jamaica Assembly in 1751 was disallowed on the ground that it was an unwarranted interference with the prerogative and contrary to the interests both of the colonies and of the mother country. The Board of Trade probably gave the real reason, however, when it said that appointment of judges during good behavior tended "to lessen that just Dependence which the Colonies ought to have upon the Government of the Mother Country."

But the assemblies continued the battle, and in New Jersey and New York the assemblies declared they would pay no salaries to judges not appointed for good behavior. In New York, upon the death of King George II in 1760, the judges refused to accept the customary renewal of their appointments unless made for the duration of their good behavior. This amounted to a strike, and New York was left without courts for an alarmingly long period. One of the judges finally accepted his appointment, however, after which they all returned to their posts. This was another victory for the prerogative; but the last word had not been said, since this became one of the grievances that found their way into the Declaration of Independence.

In summary, then, it may be noted that in the struggle over the courts and the judiciary may be observed the same general forces that were struggling over the control of the executive and that were bringing about a steady expansion of the legislative arm. The colonial assemblies wished to check both the corruption and the over-powerful influence of the governor by establishing its own right to erect courts and by making the judiciary independent of executive influence. The governors, with the Crown behind them, were seeking to stem the tide of colonial autonomy by fixing upon the colonies a judicial system that they had long since discarded in England itself. Here, as in the struggles over the executive and the legislative branches of government, the actual day-to-day conflicts were of less significance than the profound ideological disagreement that existed between the colonies and the mother country over the real nature of the colonial constitution.

THE ORIGINS OF POLITICAL PARTIES

In the course of the struggles just reviewed, there appeared certain natural political groupings which may be taken as the seeds from which later political parties were to grow. The most common division of political sympathies was one between those who tended to support the governor and his claims for the prerogative, and those who favored more or less conscious encouragement of colonial autonomy. Out of such a division appeared, in the royal provinces, at least, the "governor's" or "court" party and the "colony party." In the proprietary provinces, a similar division produced the "proprietary party" and the "colony party."

But that did not mean that the people of the province were united in their opposition to the governors. Far from it, indeed, for the largest and bitterest factions were formed over issues that were confined within the province itself. Thus there appeared a "gentlemen's party" and a "country party" in almost every province. So far as politics were concerned, the country party generally favored increased representation in the assembly for the western counties, more adequate defense for the frontiers, and a more liberal franchise, whereas the "gentlemen's party" was almost always more conservative, opposing any change in the political *status quo* that might lessen its hold upon the government. But these political divisions were economic and social, too—as, indeed, all political parties tend to be—and the "gentlemen's party" almost always was made up of the well-to-do landowners and merchants, the aristocratic creditor classes, whereas the "country" or "popular" party was made up of farmers, small shopkeepers, and frontiersmen. It was the latter who favored a plentiful supply of paper money, and who generally supported the land banks. The "gentlemen's party," however, was more conservative, standing for a stabilized currency, distrust of the "popular" elements, and all the political encouragement possible to land-speculation and business generally.

It would be a mistake to suppose that these general statements applied in every case. But it is probably safe to say that in nearly all the colonies there was a three-way division of public opinion into those who adhered to the prerogative philosophy of colonial government, those who were well-to-do and conservative, and those who were less well-to-do and of more progressive, even democratic, mind. Political parties tend to form themselves upon the basis of economic interest; but there is always a sincere intellectual reasoning to justify the party actions.

It would also be a mistake to think of these groups as being the highly organized political machines of a later day. On the contrary, they could hardly be called more than factions. At the beginning, these factions grouped themselves about the personalities of individual men—as in the case of the "Leislerians" in New York. But as time went on they adopted programs, as in New York, and then selected the men who best might succeed in putting their political programs into effect. When a faction adopted a fairly permanent program and formed a fairly permanent organization, as they did in New York and Massachusetts and elsewhere, and chose their candidates in conformity with their programs, rather than the opposite, they had arrived at the stage where they may correctly be called political parties.

The "gentlemen's party" often stood with the "governor's" party on most issues; but the provincials were pretty consistently united in the checks they put upon the prerogative. The reason for this is to be found only in the profound cleavage between the rising American philosophy of autonomous government and the mercantilist philosophy of imperial administration held by English statesmen and the Board of Trade.

BRITISH THEORY VERSUS AMERICAN EXPERIENCE

In all that has been said thus far upon the imperial, the executive, the legislative and the judicial aspects of colonial government, certain general developments stand out clearly. In the first place, it is clear that neither the imperial constitution nor the provincial constitution was every clearly thought out and formulated in precise terms; on the contrary, both were emerging, in the eighteenth century, from the fumbling experiences of the Crown, on the one side, and the colonials on the other in their efforts to find legal mechanisms for the adjustment of their respective problems. They both, like Topsy, "just grew." Both also—at least as far as ideas were concerned—sprang from the heritage that derived from the constitutional history of England. But they diverged broadly as a result of their historical experience. The imperial constitution was hardly more than a sincere, if muddling, effort to adapt and apply the English constitution to possessions overseas—an effort that failed at many points, as has already been observed. The colonial constitution, on the other hand, grew, as it were, from the new soil in which English constitutional ideas had been sown. Here, with few of the outworn modes of feudalism to retard progress, but with a new situation demanding new modes, the colonial constitution of the eighteenth century was probably the most progressive in the world, with a broader base of popular representation in government, with a more simplified system of law, and a clearer conception than elsewhere of the idea that government springs from the needs and the rights of the people rather than from the grace of a monarch.

The most striking fact in the political history of all the British colonies prior to 1776 is the growth of the power of the assembly as the popular arm of government, expressing this same popularizing ideal. But there was an ineluctible conflict between the colonial concept of autonomous and popular provincial government and the imperial concept of government by the grace of the king. The assembly, as the agent of the former, found itself in almost irreconcilable conflict with the governor, as the agent of the latter. The result was a reciprocal set of checks and balances devised, on the imperial side, to check the march of the assemblies toward autonomy and popular government, and calculated, on the colonial side, not only to check the arbitrary and corrupt influence of the executive, but also to extend the assembly's influence over the executive itself. It thus seems clear that the "checks and balances" that the Crown sought to impose upon the colonies was, in fact, contrary not only to the trend of political evolution in England itself but also to the natural trend in the colonies. It seems probable, indeed, that, had the American Revolution and the conservative reaction that followed it not intervened, the colonial constitution must have eventuated in a system of responsible cabinet government, just as it did in England. In any case, the state constitutions set up in the early stages of the Revolution, embodying as they did the idea of an all-powerful legislature and a weak executive, seem to have been the clear culmination of almost two centuries of constitutional evolution.

For the English theorist of colonial government, the provincial governments were hardly more than mere corporations, created by the grace and free will of the monarch; and what the monarch had thus freely bestowed, he might as freely take away. If he did not interfere more frequently in the internal affairs of the colonies, it was because of distance, inconvenience, or preoccupation with other things, not because of a lack of any right to do so. But most of the rights of the monarch had been assumed by Parliament, in the course of the eighteenth century, and that body had effectively captured control of the Cabinet, the Board of Trade, the Privy Council, and even the king himself, so that, in effect, the wish of "the Crown" or "His Majesty's prerogative" was almost tantamount to the will of Parliament itself. And this development, so far as the colonies were concerned, would have brought them more and more effectively under the control of Parliament had it not been for the growth of an opposing colonial theory.

John Locke, the apologist of the parliamentary resolution of 1688 in England, had been practically forgotten in that country by 1750. Not so in America, however, where his theory was found to be a perfect rationalization of the colonial political experience. For, to begin with, the Americans had been led by their experience to believe strongly in the doctrine of natural rights. They had inherited "the rights of Englishmen," and these they had identified with the laws of nature. In certain cases, such as Connecticut, Rhode Island, and Plymouth, "social compacts" of a sort had been actually made long before Locke rationalized them. The colonial charters, where they still existed, were regarded as contracts, in the Lockean sense, between the people of the chartered provinces and the Crown. But even in the royal provinces, where there were no charters, the royal instructions to the governors, instead of creating government by the grace of the sovereign, according to the colonial view, merely recognized the natural rights of Englishmen to representative government. In every case, according to the colonial theory, government springs from the people themselves upward, not from the sovereign downward; and this conviction was borne out, not only by the social compacts and the charters of the seventeenth century, but, also, by the long-established and accepted custom of granting the franchise to every man who accumulated a sufficient amount of property and representation to every new district that could present a sufficient number of these freemen. Thus emerged two ideas that were foreign to the British system. One was the growing belief in written constitutions, and the other was a belief in the direct representation of the citizens upon a territorial basis, as against the "virtual" representation, by the privileged classes, of Englishmen at home.

In the course of the forging of a colonial governmental mechanism, there emerged a sort of double system of checks and balances. But the checks imposed upon the executive by the colonial assemblies and the assemblies' struggle for a free judiciary were perhaps less calculated to produce a permanent system of balanced powers than to lead to a supremacy of the legislature such as actually occurred in the Revolutionary constitutions already noted. If this be true, it is only another indication that government in America was moving in the direction of popular government—a greater degree of which it had, as a matter of fact, achieved, at the middle of the eighteenth century, than any other section of the civilized world.

But political thinking is never entirely static. As some of the Americans became wealthy and comfortable, they became satisfied with the degree of popular government that they had. These were the conservatives of the "gentlemen's party." The smaller property-owners, the farmers, the settlers on the frontier, and the more affluent of the unfranchised artisans, were not satisfied, and demanded a continual extension of the base of popular control. These were the "radicals" of the "country," or "popular" party. Thus, political theory and political action were divided two ways. American theory, as a whole, now stood fundamentally at odds with British theory, and this conflict of ideas was perhaps the most profound ideological conflict involved in the American Revolution, when it came. But the American political mind was divided within itself between conservative and progressive, and it was this division, among other things, which was to make the war for American Independence a revolution as well as an imperial civil war.

RECOMMENDED BOOKS FOR FURTHER READING

Contemporary Narratives

Albert B. Hart, ed., *American History Told by Contemporaries,* II, Part III, 127-223.

Thomas Pownall, *The Administration of the Colonies.*

Modern Accounts

Charles M. Andrews, *The Royal Disallowance.*

Alice M. Baldwin, *The New England Clergy and the American Revolution,* Chapters 3-6.

James J. Burns, *The Colonial Agents of New England.*

Oliver M. Dickerson, *American Colonial Government, 1696-1765.*

Beverley W. Bond, Jr., "The Colonial Agent as a Popular Representative" in *Political Science Quarterly,* XXXV, 372-392.

Homer C. Hockett, *The Constitutional History of the United States, 1776-1826,* Volume I.

Leonard W. Labaree, *Royal Government in America.*

Andrew C. McLaughlin, *A Constitutional History of the United States.*

Andrew C. McLaughlin, *The Foundations of American Constitutionalism,* Chapters 1-3.

Richard B. Morris, *Studies in the History of American Law.*

Lillian M. Penson, *The Colonial Agents of the British West Indies.*

Elmer B. Russell, *The Review of American Colonial Legislation by the King in Council.*

Edwin P. Tanner, "Colonial Agencies in England During the Eighteenth Century," in *Political Science Quarterly,* XVI, 24-49.

Edson L. Whitney, *The Government of the Colony of South Carolina.*

Benjamin F. Wright, Jr., *American Interpretations of Natural Law.*

28

The Expansion of the Colonial Economy

THE MOST striking feature of economic life in the British American colonies in the eighteenth century is its expansiveness. The seventeenth century, the century of economic beginnings, was past, with all its hazards overcome. The Americans had found products which they could produce at a profit, and they had found markets in which to sell them. The returns from internal trade and foreign commerce had first stabilized the American economy upon a fairly fixed pattern, and had then begun to accumulate, providing a fund of capital in the hands of American businessmen which demanded investment in the rapidly growing colonial agriculture, commerce, and industry. This capitalistic expansion would probably have taken place with only a normal increase of the population; but the enormous influx of immigrants, particularly to the continental colonies, gave an impetus to the growth of these basic industries that was little short of phenomenal, and added land-speculation to the list of highly promising fields for the investment of surplus funds.

THE EXPANSION OF AMERICAN AGRICULTURE

Agriculture was the basic economic activity of the citizens of the British colonies in America in the eighteenth century and the industry which had, in the first instance, been responsible for the earliest modest accumulations of capital and the beginnings of capitalistic enterprise. The first permanent settlers upon the shores of America, almost without exception, had turned first for a livelihood to the cultivation of the soil. They had invested their labor in the soil, their homes, and the improvements they had built upon the land. Their returns in the form of money had been negligible, if they existed at all. But they won their subsistence from the soil and they were able, by their own labor, to build new barns, new roads, wagons, or other equipment, and to plant new fields for harvest. Their return was thus in the form of capital goods; and every time a farmer planted a new field of corn he was literally "plowing his profits into the soil." This was the expansion of his capital; and this was the sort of capitalistic agricultural expansion that was going on apace nearly everywhere in the British colonies in the eighteenth century. But it is especially characteristic of the continental colonies, where the supply of new land was inexhaustible and where there was a phenomenal influx of new farmers from abroad to cultivate it.

From the small subsistence farms of New England to the great capitalistic plantations of the West Indies, probably more than 95 per cent of the people of the British colonies in America derived their livelihood from the land. There were, in fact, three distinct agricultural areas in the British American colonies. The first was an area of small farms, which included all the colonies from Pennsylvania and Delaware northward and a broad strip of land extending along the Appalachian valley and the upper Piedmont southward. The second region was made up of those parts of Virginia and the Carolinas devoted to the raising of tobacco, rice, and indigo on plantations operated by slave labor, and the third was the sugar-empire made up of the great slave-operated plantations of the West Indies colonies. Each of these agricultural areas presented certain general characteristics peculiar to itself.

In the small-farms region the size of the farms averaged from 100 to 200 acres each, with somewhat larger farms on the frontier and somewhat smaller ones in the older parts of the settlements. The farmer worked his own land, with such help as he could get; but agricultural laborers were scarce, for the presence of cheap or free land on the frontier was an ever-present inducement to the farm laborer to take up land of his own. The most dependable source of farm labor was the system of indentured servitude under which an incoming immigrant contracted to labor for a period of years in return for his expenses in coming to this country. This system was in vogue in all the colonies and, although it caused much hardship, it served a useful purpose in providing a needed supply of agricultural labor and in giving the laborer himself a start in the new world.

The farm itself was almost a self-sufficient economic unit. For on it were raised the food supply for the family and servants, wool which was manufactured into clothes, and hides which were manufactured into shoes. The women cooked for the family, and made soap, candles and preserves; they spun the wool into thread, wove it into cloth, and then made clothes of it; or they wove linen from flax and made it into sheets, pillow-cases, towels, and table-cloths. The men, in addition to the actual cultivation of the fields, hunted for food in the forest, tended the livestock, built furniture and crude-iron objects, and made harness and shoes from the hides from the cattle raised and slaughtered on the farm. Trade was of little importance at the beginning, but as the farm began to produce a surplus, the farmer would haul his wheat or his salt pork to market at Boston, New York, Philadelphia, or Baltimore or drive in his livestock for shipment or slaughter, and would receive manufactured goods in the form of hardware, guns and ammunition, and such luxuries as he could afford, in return.

There was little to export from the farms of New England. In fact, that region was importing a considerable part of its bread-stuffs from farther south. But even that region, in which perhaps as much as one-fourth of the population depended upon the non-agricultural pursuits of fishing and commerce, was still able, with this exception, to raise enough farm products to feed its own towns. Cattle were occasionally driven to New York and Boston, and horses, beef, pork, apples and dairy products were exported in fairly large quantities to the West Indies. The middle colonies, on the other hand, had a huge exportable surplus, especially of wheat, flour, and other breadstuffs—for which reason they came to be known as the "bread colonies." Thus quantities of flour and baked bread were shipped from New York and Philadelphia to the West Indies, and wheat was sent to southern Europe by the ship-load. Three-quarters of a million bushels of wheat and some twenty thousands tons of bread and flour were shipped to Europe in the year 1770 alone. But in addition to grain and flour, these farming colonies also exported great quantities of flaxseed, Indian corn, beef and pork, horses, sheep and hogs. Here, as nowhere else in the colonies, the basis of a flourishing commerce was farm produce brought from the agricultural hinterlands of New York, Philadelphia, and Baltimore.

Farming then, in the northern colonies, was the basic enterprise. The farmer was a small capitalist, and the bulk of the population was made up of small farmers. The farmers were prosperous, and every man who had a modicum of intelligence and a congenial feeling for hard work could make a living—even a competence—by his own individual efforts. It is no wonder the Americans became economic individualists; nor is it any wonder that, with the equality of economic opportunity represented by the presence of an uncounted amount of free or nearly free land, the American farmers should have tended to discard their old-world ideas of social inequality in favor of a belief in the equality of men. But be that as it may, the farmers of the eighteenth century saw their capital expanding in the form of new and better houses, bigger barns, more livestock, and a higher standard of living. But not only that. The number of farmers in the small-farms area multiplied enormously in the course of the century, as thousands upon thousands of immigrants from Europe swarmed into the colonies, many of them to find their way, eventually, to the frontier, where they started farms of their own to increase the total of American agricultural capital and to push the bounds of civilization ever westward.

Of the plantation colonies to the southward there is a different story to tell. For there, in contrast with the small-farm agriculture of the north, a favorable soil and climate producing staple subtropical commodities for which there was a constant and profitable market in Europe made for the concentration of large parcels of land operated by cheap labor in the hands of wealthy and powerful individuals. At the beginning, here as elsewhere, farms were small. But after the Navigation Act of 1660 placed a premium upon mass production of tobacco in Virginia, for example, the yeoman farmers were crowded out; land accumulated in the hands of those with enough capital to buy; cheap slave labor now rapidly replaced the more costly white labor, and a gulf was fixed between the capitalist—the plantation owner—on the one side, and the laborer—the slave—on the other.

After 1694, when rice culture was introduced into Carolina, the plantation system took root there; and after the prohibition of slavery in Georgia was removed in 1750 it moved into that new colony too. The introduction of indigo into South Carolina from the West Indies about 1742 only extended the plantation belt farther inland, and South Carolina became, in the course of the century, a colony of which the population in 1750 was about two-thirds Negro.

As an economic unit, the southern plantation was rather less self-sufficient than the small farm of the north. The central feature of the plantation was the great house, where the "master" lived with his family, with the kitchen, carriage house and gardens attached to it in the rear. At some distance were barns, tool shops, stables, drying sheds and other buildings, and still farther away were the one-room cabins of the slaves. The chief business of the plantation, if it was in Virginia or Maryland, was to raise tobacco, and the labor involved was performed by the Negroes under the eyes of a white overseer. Seeds were sown in beds and allowed to sprout, then the tender plants were transplanted to the prepared fields. After about a month's growth they were "topped" in order to force the growth of the seven or eight leaves left on the stalk. Thereafter they were weeded, and after six weeks, when the leaves turned a ripe brownish color, the plants were cut and hung in the drying sheds for another six weeks to dry. For one week they were piled up for sweating, and then the leaves were stripped off the stalks and sorted according to quality. The leaves were packed into hogsheads, the weight of which, filled, was between eight hundred and one thousand pounds. The hogsheads were rolled to warehouses, inspected, and stamped, and the tobacco was ready for shipment.

During the eighteenth century the size of the plantations expanded as the plantation owners acquired more land and more slaves to work it, thus increasing their capital goods. The average size of a plantation was from one thousand to six thousand acres, but there were many which were much larger than this. At the same time the rapid increase in population expanded the area of tobacco cultivation well up into the Piedmont. The result was a rapid increase in the amount of tobacco produced—an increase which the market often found it difficult to absorb, thus precipitating painful depressions and efforts by both Virginia and Maryland to control production. Despite these efforts, however, production continued to increase; the volume of the tobacco annually exported from Virginia increased over seven million pounds between 1745 and 1754; in the latter year it amounted to over forty-five million pounds.

The planter, as a businessman, was generally heavily in debt. He shipped his crop to his factor or a merchant in London, who sold it for him, charging a commission (usually two and one-half per cent) for the service. But freight charges, insurance, and commissions raised the price far above what the planter got for it. When the tobacco was sold the factor or merchant would purchase and ship to the planter such clothes, furniture, books, luxuries, or other manufactured goods as he needed, and then, after deducting a commission for this service and the charges for the purchases, he would credit the planter with the balance—if there was any. In times of depression the planter remained in debt to the factor, trusting to pay him after the next good year—with interest. But all too often the depressions lasted for years at a time, and the debts would never be completely paid; often enough they were passed on from father to son for generations. There was a particularly bad depression from 1756 to 1765, which left the planters of Virginia hopelessly in debt to their English merchant-factors just at the moment when, after the Seven Years War, England began to alarm the colonies with an irritating series of coercive acts. The planters had come to resent the debtor-creditor relationship in which they found themselves, and their resentment was heightened by their belief that the London merchants acted in collusion to keep the price of tobacco down and the price of necessary commodities up. An attempt to break the deadlock in 1749 by a law making all debts payable in depreciated Virginia currency at a fixed rate of exchange was blocked by the Crown, and the planters began to feel themselves caught in an economic subjection to England which was slowly driving them all toward bankruptcy. Some of them turned to more diversified crops, others abandoned old, exhausted fields and planted fresh, more productive ones; still others took advantage of the increase in population to indulge in land speculation. On the eve of the revolution the tobacco planters had been made to feel a conflict of economic interest between themselves and the merchants of the mother country; tobacco was beginning to decline as the staple crop of the province; and the great planters had taken up a new and exciting form of capitalistic enterprise: speculation in the lands of the west.

The economy of the rice and indigo plantations was similar, in its broad outlines, to that of the tobacco plantations of the Chesapeake. Rice, grown in the fresh-water swamps along the rivers, involved even greater labor cost than tobacco. First the swamps had to be cleared of trees and underbrush; then rice was planted in rows where it could be flooded. Then it must be weeded regularly. At the end of the season, usually in September, it was harvested by hand-sickle and threshed with a hand-flail. It was then winnowed with a fan, ground in a hand-mill in order to remove the husk, and pounded in a mortar to remove the skin of the grain. Finally, it was barreled, and it was ready for shipment. The size of a rice plantation was usually small, worked by about thirty slaves with an overseer; but one planter might own a number of plantations. The expansion of the area of rice culture was limited by the extent of the swamp lands; but in 1748 some fifty-five thousand barrels of rice were exported, with a value of £618,750, South Carolina currency.

Happily for the planter-capitalists of this colony, another avenue of expansion was found in the cultivation of indigo. Introduced into the colony about 1740 by Mrs. Eliza Pinckney, indigo quickly became a second staple for the plantations, using, conveniently enough, the better drained land just beyond the swamps. The most disagreeable stage in the process of preparing this dye was that in which the plants were allowed to ferment in great vats and then, after having been agitated for a sufficient period by the slaves, allowed to curdle, after which it was pressed into cubes, dried, and shipped in casks. After Parliament offered a bounty on indigo in 1748, the cultivation of the plant rapidly expanded, and on the eve of the Revolution South Carolina was exporting half a million pounds of the stuff annually.

The life of the planters of South Carolina was somewhat different from that of Virginia, for they generally had houses in Charleston, and spent a good deal of their time in the city. They also had the advantage of a more diversified market for their products, less foreign competition, and a more favorable balance of trade. The South Carolina planters thus escaped the burden of debt that oppressed their neighbors around the Chesapeake, and Charleston, their metropolis, because of these facts as well as because of a prosperous trade in hides from the Indian country, became a center of wealth, luxury and refinement which rivaled, if it did not surpass, the cities of the commercial colonies to the north.

In the West Indies, again, there existed a type of plantation economy that differed in several essential ways from that of the southern continental colonies. In the first place, the cultivation of sugar required a larger capital investment than that of tobacco or rice; it was also exposed to greater risks from fire, drought, and hurricane. Heavy equipment in the form of cane-presses, containers, boilers and evaporators, and coolers had to be purchased and housed, and this outlay suggested the advantages of mass production involving large numbers of slaves and a constantly increasing amount of land—the more land the better. Thus at the center of the sugar plantation stood the houses of the owner and the overseer. Near by would be located the cane-press or mill, a boiling house, a curing house, and a distillery. In addition to the equipment involved in these processes the owner must have mules and wagons for hauling the cane, stables to house them, and cooperage and carpenter shops to keep all in repair. A little farther away were the cabins for the slaves. No plantation with less than three or four hundred acres of cane could hope to pay a profit upon such a capital outlay, and there had to be, in addition to the cane land, several hundred acres for firewood, grazing for the livestock, and food supplies. Thus the plantation could hardly be less than one thousand acres, and a unit of this size could be worked most efficiently by not less than fifty or sixty slaves.

The process of sugar production was a tedious one, stretching over a period of two years. The cane was planted late in the year in broad holes; after sprouting it had to be cultivated and weeded almost constantly through about a year and a half, and then it was cut and hauled to the mill. At the mill, which was driven by oxen— or by water power, where available—the juice was pressed out of the cane and boiled. When as much of the water had been evaporated out of the juice as was possible, the thick liquid was allowed to stand until the sugar settled, and the molasses was drained off. The sugar thus obtained was a thick, brown stuff called muscovado, which had to be refined before it could be sold to the public. Much of the refining, however, was done in England or the continental colonies.

It is easy to see that large-scale operations in such a business were more efficient than could possibly be the smaller farms which were dependent upon their larger neighbors for the use of their equipment. As distress came upon the sugar business in the first half of the eighteenth century many of the smaller proprietors sold out to the large operators; and there took place a marked tendency, in all the islands, toward larger and larger plantations. Since there were no navigable rivers in the islands, the planters had to haul their product to the nearest port, and these ports became busy markets for this staple of export and a variety of imports. For the sugar planters made no pretense of raising enough food for their slaves. On the contrary, great quantities of third-rate fish were imported from the northern colonies. At the same time the planter also had to import his lumber and barrels from the north, and his slaves from Africa. Lucky for him that he could depend upon a monopoly of the English market for his product!

Despite the difficulties inherent in soil exhaustion, loss of the world market, and foreign competition, the intensification of culture and the use of fresh lands actually resulted in the doubling of the planters' output of muscovado in the eighteenth century. This was because they had a monopoly of the British market, and the British people evidently doubled their consumption of sugar. For, whereas in 1708 England consumed some 300,000 hundredweight of sugar, in 1730 it consumed probably 800,000 hundredweight, and in 1770 over 1,500,000. The significance of this is that the West India planters, on the eve of the American Revolution, were almost completely dependent upon the British market for their existence. At the same time the trade of the northern colonists with the foreign islands had both greatly weakened the position of British sugar in the northern colonial market and roused the resentment of the West Indies planters toward their New England compatriots. The

West Indies planters were thus becoming increasingly dependent upon the mother country and resentful toward the continentals at a moment when the planters and the farmers of the north were finding more and more reason to complain against the mother country—a set of facts which played no small part in determining the attitude of the West Indies, when the time came, toward the American Revolution.

COLONIAL COMMERCE WITHIN THE EMPIRE

In 1721 the Board of Trade reported that the commerce of England with its colonies totaled £2,375,179, of which £1,495,499 were in imports of colonial products into England and £879,680 were in exports of English goods to the colonies. To the latter figure, however, must be added at least £100,000 as the value of slaves introduced into the colonies by English slave-traders who brought their living wares from Africa. Thus England was importing from the colonies roughly £500,000 worth of goods in excess of the value of the goods she sold to them. But of the colonial goods imported, such great quantities of sugar, tobacco, rice, furs, dyewoods and other products were re-exported from England to continental Europe and elsewhere as to exceed the unfavorable colonial balance and show a handsome profit for England from her colonial empire. Thus the Board reported that about one-third of the tobacco brought into England from the colonies was re-exported; an even greater proportion of the sugar was re-shipped to markets abroad—although it should be noted that British sugar was beginning to find it increasingly difficult to compete in the world market with French, Dutch and Portuguese sugar, for reasons that will appear presently—and about three-fourths of the rice imported from Carolina was re-exported to northern and southern Europe. The Board of Trade estimated that about one-third of all the ships engaged in English foreign trade were maintained by England's trade with her colonies. It was a profitable empire, indeed!

So far as the colonies themselves are concerned, to be properly understood this report of the Board of Trade must be considered with regard to the three major sections of the American "plantations." Thus New England and the middle colonies imported roughly £209,760 worth of goods from England, and sent the mother country only £92,675 in return. This "commercial" section of the colonies thus showed an unfavorable balance of some £117,085, which was increased to perhaps £130,000 by services and commissions. The Board reported that the southern colonies on the continent sold the mother country £289,901 worth of tobacco, rice, hides, naval stores, etc., and bought from her goods worth £221,264. But these colonies imported probably £50,000 worth of Negro slaves brought in by English traders, and this item, coupled with invisible items in the form of freight charges, interest, and commissions paid in England more than balanced the account, and placed the southern planters generally in debt to their English factors; and as the century advanced this debt steadily increased. The West Indies, in contrast with the other two sections, showed an enormous favorable balance of trade with the mother country, selling her £1,102,219 in colonial products, chiefly re-exportable sugar, and buying from her only £348,318 worth of English goods—to which should be added, however, probably £100,000 worth of Negroes brought from Africa.

Thus, of the three major sections of the American empire, the commercial colonies showed a heavy unfavorable balance in their trade with the mother country; the plantation colonies on the continent were not quite able to balance accounts, and the West Indies showed a favorable balance of perhaps £500,000—much of which stayed in England, and was spent there by absentee West Indian landlords. This pattern of the colonial trade with the mother country was followed fairly closely throughout the century; but the figures for the close of the colonial period showed a striking expansion in the trade itself. Thus in 1768, which was perhaps the last normal year before the Revolution, the trade of the continental colonies with the mother country totaled £3,408,702, of which £2,157,248 were in imports from her and £1,251,451 were in exports to her. The unfavorable balance of £905,794 that appears here was probably increased to about £1,000,000 by interest charges and commission. Thus the total trade of the continental colonies with the mother country had increased from an estimated £813,604 in 1721 to well over £3,400,000 in 1768, and the adverse balance had risen from an estimated £125,000 (the Board of Trade's figure of £200,000 appears to have been too high) to £1,000,000. In approximately half a century the trade with the mother country had multiplied fourfold; but the adverse balance—if the estimates are even approximately correct—had apparently multiplied eight times.

Even if the amounts and rates of these increases are exaggerated, as they may be, two profoundly significant facts remain: the phenomenal increase in the trade itself, and the growing adverse balance against the colonies. The adverse balance had the effect of draining the colonies of hard money and contributed to the widespread use of paper money. But the steadily increasing indebtedness of the colonies to the mother country, particularly in the south, made for resentment, discontent and conflicts, of which the disputes over paper money furnish only one example. The commercial colonies managed to pay off their indebtedness to the mother country—or most of it—with the profits from other trades; but this was not true of the south. The two sections tended to be drawn together by their common debtor-creditor relationship to England and by their resentment against British interference in such questions as those pertaining to colonial paper money. This community of interest was galvanized into active joint resistance to the mother country by the tightening of her regulations of colonial commerce following the end of the Seven Years War.

The British West Indies, during the fifty years that preceded the American Revolution, passed through an economic experience that was very different from the phenomenal expansion of the continental colonies. These island communities were regarded as by far the most valuable portion of the British empire, since they produced such products as sugar, coffee, pimento, cotton, dyewoods, etc., for which England would otherwise have been dependent upon foreign supplies, and which could be re-exported from England at a profit to swell the favorable balance of England's foreign trade. But in the years following the Peace of Utrecht the British sugar islands began to fall on evil days; and in the three decades from 1720 to about 1750 they passed through a temporary but none the less severe economic decline.

Many causes contributed to the economic distress of the island colonies. To begin with, the soil in the islands had lost much of its productivity by a century of wasteful, unscientific use. Thus the Board of Trade reported in 1735 that the soil of Barbados was "almost worn out," and "many more hands and much more manure are requisite than in the fresh lands lately planted by the French in Hispaniola and other Parts of the West Indies." This additional labor and manure made the cost of production of the Barbados product higher than that of the "fresh" French islands, and the higher cost of production made it almost impossible for English sugar to compete with French sugar in the world market. So expensive had production become in Barbados and elsewhere in the West Indies, indeed, that much of the land formerly used for sugar cultivation was now turned back to pasture, and it was estimated that the island's production of sugar declined from

22,769 hogsheads in 1736 to 13,948 as an average between 1740 and 1748, and to 9,554 hogsheads in 1784.

But that was not all. The islanders and the English sugar merchants complained that the retention of sugar upon the list of enumerated articles, with the consequent payment of import duties in England, raised the selling price of British sugar in the world market, and that the duties imposed upon sugar shipped from one colony to another under the Plantations Duties Act of 1673 encouraged the traders of the commercial colonies on the continent to import French sugar into the colonial market to compete with the British products. Both these claims were true, and matters were made worse by the fact that the New England traders not only encouraged foreign (French) sugar producers at the expense of the British sugar planters—in scandalous contravention of the mercantilist theories—but actually imported French sugar into England itself, by way of New England, declaring it to be British sugar upon which the "plantation duties" had been paid!

The West Indian planters and their sympathizers in England made many efforts to check the trade of the northern colonists with the French sugar islands, but to no avail. The Board of Trade refused to discriminate against one section of the empire in favor of another. But the "West Indian lobby" won the ear of Parliament, and succeeded in getting that body to pass the Molasses Act of 1733, already noted, which was a dead letter practically from the day of its passage. At the same time the West India planters and the sugar merchants of England sought to have sugar removed from the list of enumerated articles. They had their way in 1739. But the effect in the world market was negligible; for it proved to be simply impossible to recapture the European markets in the face of the cheaper French, Dutch and Portuguese sugars. This act did have the effect of raising the price of sugar in England, however, and this fact, coupled with the partial strangulation of the supply of French sugar in the wars following 1744 and the occupation of "fresh" sugar islands after the wars, gradually restored a measure of West Indian prosperity. The turn in the trend did not become noticeable until after 1740, however.

In the meantime, the island colonies had lost the European market and a large portion of the market in the continental colonies. They had become dependent upon the English market, which took, indeed, the greater part of their produce. The aid extended to them in the form of legislation by the British Parliament tended to increase their sense of dependence upon the mother country

Thus, while the continental colonies were developing with the mother country a commercial debtor-creditor relationship that made for resentment, competition, and antagonism, the West Indies were becoming more and more dependent upon the mother country, both for a market and for legislative protection. From the point of view of the empire as a whole, the trade of the northern colonies with the French islands—upon which, indeed, they were heavily dependent for a large part of their prosperity—illustrates a rapidly growing rift in the economic fabric of the empire: the West Indies needed and received such protection as could be afforded it under the mercantilist system; the commercial colonies of the north appear to have been moving directly toward freedom of trade.

INTERCOLONIAL AND FOREIGN TRADE

Coastwise Commerce

While the trade of the colonies with the mother country was the largest single item in their external commerce, yet it was far from being the only one. For all the British "plantations" in America had commercial relations with each other, and most of them had economic intercourse, illicit or otherwise, with the neighboring foreign colonies of France, Spain, Holland, and Portugal.

From the first the English colonies had traded with each other, and a flourishing and mutually advantageous exchange between New England and the British West Indies had reached a high stage of development before the end of the seventeenth century. In the eighteenth century this coastwise and intercolonial commerce steadily expanded. Boston and other New England ports had almost a monopoly of the trade with the other continental colonies to the southward, and small New England sailing vessels of shallow draft peddled fish, rum, iron, and British manufactures in the harbors and rivers of the southern colonies, taking in return the tobacco of Virginia, the pitch and turpentine of North Carolina, and the rice and indigo of South Carolina and Georgia. Boston also received foodstuffs such as wheat, Indian corn, flour, pork and beef from the colonies farther south, and for these she exchanged fish, sugar and rum, and British manufactures. Along with this legitimate coastwise trade, too, went a good deal that was illegitimate; for enumerated articles, such as tobacco, would often be brought to a New England port and then carried directly to a

Dutch or German market without landing it in England—thus violating the Navigation Act of 1660—and manufactured goods from Europe would be taken in return, which would then be smuggled into New England to compete with English manufactures—thus violating the letter and the spirit of the Staple Act of 1663. It was to stamp out such practices as these that the Navigation Act of 1696 had been passed, but it had been only moderately successful.

Another coastwise activity was the piracy that flourished in the coastal waters from New England southward to Florida, as well as in the West Indies. For the long series of wars in the last half of the seventeenth century had placed a premium upon privateering, and after the Peace of Utrecht (1713) the ease of seizing unarmed merchant vessels encouraged numerous fortune-hunters to continue the practice in time of peace. The pirates were encouraged to bring in their ill-gotten cargoes by the merchants and others who were accustomed to smuggling in violation of the navigation acts, and the collusion between smugglers and pirates became very difficult to suppress. The years from 1713 to 1725 saw piracy at its height. English warships were sent over to stop the reign of terror along the coast of New England, and energetic action by the governors of Virginia and South Carolina succeeded, about 1720, in stamping out the nest of pirates who infested the shallow and difficult waters of the coast of North Carolina. The most famous of these was Edward Teach (or Thatch), widely known as "Blackbeard," about whom it was said that he had sixteen wives of whom he personally strangled only three! "Blackbeard" operated under the protection of no less a person than Governor Eden himself; but he was finally destroyed by an expedition sent out for that purpose in 1718 by Governor Alexander Spotswood of Virginia. Similarly, in the West Indies piracy was a constant menace, many pirates using the Virgin Islands as their base; and the use of the British navy was required to stamp out this danger to the shipping of New Englander and Britisher alike. It had been effectively eradicated by the middle of the eighteenth century.

The West Indies

But much more vital to the commercial colonies than the coastwise trade along the continent was the intersectional exchange between the northern colonies on the one side and the West Indies on the other. For this exchange had become the most important and profitable departments of the trade of New England, and it was only a little less important to the middle colonies. Thus, in 1770, at the end of the colonial period, the exports from the continental (chiefly northern) colonies to the West Indies totaled £844,178, and imports amounted to £949,656, or an excess over exports of £105,478. These figures include the trade with the foreign West Indies; but it is to be noted that half of the imports are accounted for by "Jamaica" rum—from the British islands; nearly all the raw molasses imported came from the French islands. More than two-thirds of the sugar imported still came from the British islands, but the proportion of the total exchange that was carried on with the foreign colonies was of very great importance, for another reason.

Superficially it might appear from the figures just given that this trade with the islands was unprofitable for the northern colonies; but the case is just the reverse. In the first place, the sugar and rum imported into the continental colonies were sold at high profits. But it should be noted that a New England ship, bearing fish, staves, horses and lumber to Barbados might—and quite often did—take on a load of sugar products that it transported to England, thus helping to pay New England's debt to the mother country. In England this same ship would take on a load of English manufactures and return to her home port in New England, having made, at the end, three profits for her owners—one on the cargo to Barbados, a second on the cargo to England, and a third on the manufactured goods to be sold in America. But a third importance of the West Indies trade which does not appear in the figures cited derived from the fact that the molasses, imported mostly from the French islands, was made into rum at Newport or Providence or elsewhere in New England, and this rum was sent to the coast of Africa, where it would be exchanged for "black ivory." The Negroes would then be taken to the islands on the southern continental colonies, where cargoes might be taken on for New England, as before.

From the point of view of the British West Indies, this commerce was just as vitally important as it was to New England. For the British sugar islands depended upon the continental colonies for the foodstuffs with which to feed their teeming slave populations, for barrel-staves and hoops, lumber, horses, naval stores, and oil. Had the imports from the north been cut off, it is difficult to see how the island colonies could have survived. Yet the commerce of the northern colonies was growing more rapidly than that of the British islands. The islands were finding it increasingly difficult to supply all the sugar and molasses needed by the New England traders for their home market and for the trade to Africa, because, chiefly, of the exhaustion of their soil. The French islands, on the other hand, could produce sugar and molasses more cheaply than they, and offering a standing invitation (despite the half-hearted protests of France) to the New Englanders to trade with them on very favorable terms. It was for reasons such as these that the West Indies planters prevailed upon Parliament to pass the Molasses Act of 1733 which sought to discourage the importation of foreign molasses into the English colonies. But had that act been enforced it is probable that the entire economy of New England, and, to a less degree, of the middle colonies, would have suffered irreparable injury thereby, since the greatest natural market for the products of the northern colonies would thus have been largely paralyzed.

But this trade with the West Indies, both English and foreign, was important to the northern colonies for another reason, and that was that it furnished them with specie with which to pay their indebtedness to England. Of the English islands, Barbados and Jamaica were bases of a trade with the Spanish colonies that was partly legal, carried on under the Assiento Treaty of 1713, and partly illegal, carried on by smugglers. In return for the slaves and English products sold the Spaniards the English received Spanish doubloons (worth about £1 sterling) and pieces of eight, or dollars (worth about 4½ shillings sterling). These coins returned to the English islands; but the Yankee traders fell increasingly into the habit of demanding coin in payment for their northern commodities—after which they sailed around the corner to St. Eustatius or a French island and bought sugar and molasses from them at a lower price than the English planter could afford to charge. The English planters were furious, but they had to have the Yankee products; and, by the practice, the English islands were practically drained of specie. But the New England trader did not stop there; he took cash wherever he could get it—French pistoles (worth about £1 sterling) and French crowns (five shillings sterling) in the French islands and a certain amount of Dutch guilders and stivers in Curaçao, Dutch Guiana, or St. Eustatius.

Southern Europe

It would be difficult to exaggerate the importance of these interlocking trades to the empire as a whole. England and Englishmen had a tendency to think of the commercial colonies in America as competitors, and of the West Indies and Virginia as the perfect examples, under mercantilism, of the role that colonies ought to play. Yet the prosperity of the West Indies depended upon that of the northern continental colonies, and the prosperity of the latter depended upon the trade with the foreign West Indies. The prosperity of a mercantilist empire seems to have depended, in the last analysis, upon a practice of free trade which contradicted the main tenets of mercantilism itself.

Those tenets were also contradicted, at least by implication, by the trade of the commercial colonies with the countries of southern Europe and the isles of the ocean. For Italy, Spain, Portugal, the Azores and Madeira provided a steady market for the first grade of New England fish, lumber, and rum, South Carolina rice, and wheat, Indian corn and flour from the middle colonies. In return the American traders took silks, fruits, and wine; port and madeira wines were the favorite drinks of the colonial "gentlemen"—as distinguished from the poorer workers, who drank rum—throughout the eighteenth century. Very often, however, a captain, after unloading his cargo in one of the southern countries, would take in payment a bill of exchange drawn on London and sail to England in ballast, if he could not get a cargo for the mother country; and there he would take on a cargo of English goods for America, thus completing another commercial triangle and a series of profitable turnovers of his capital.

The African Slave Trade

Still another trade of great significance for the English colonial world was the African slave trade. This business had gotten under way, so far as the English were concerned, when interloping slave traders like John Hawkins poached for slaves in Portuguese Africa and sold them at the point of a gun in Spanish America. During the seventeenth century a series of companies had been formed for the traffic, and in 1663 Charles II created "The Company of Royal Adventurers of England Trading into Africa," with a monopoly of the African Negro trade, which was soon surrendered to the "Royal African Company of England." It was this company which was supplying the British West Indies, at the end of the seventeenth century, with some five thousand slaves a year and the southern continental colonies with their proportionate numbers. But about the turn of the century the company had to face the competition of free traders, whose activities it was unable to check, and among these were a number of merchants in the northern colonies, especially Rhode Island.

The flourishing of the institution of slavery in the eighteenth century in America is a part of the expansion of American economic life; with cheap land available for most of the free men who came to the colonies, white labor was prohibitively expensive for the sort of work that had to be done in the plantation colonies. Moreover, climatic conditions made it impossible for white men to perform the labor required. Yet without a plentiful supply of cheap labor, large-scale plantation economy would have been impossible. The situation, as it existed, created a market for slaves which the American traders were not likely to overlook, since it was intimately associated with the West Indies markets for continental foodstuffs and the like. Thus, when the African trade was thrown open to free traders in 1698, the New Englanders began to take part, and Rhode Island became the principal center of the trade in the colonies, with the exception of Jamaica.

The New England trader would set out from Providence or Newport with a cargo composed chiefly of rum to Africa where the captain would remain, moving from point to point, until he had completed his cargo of slaves. From Africa his ship would then make the infamous "middle passage" to the West Indies. With each Negro allowed just enough deck space to permit him to lie down between his fellows, between decks that were only sufficiently separated from each other to allow the Negroes to crawl out for exercise at stated intervals and for meals, the slave-ship carried the greatest possible cargo of stinking humanity and misery. The conditions on these ships, by all accounts, and especially in rough weather when the Negroes were liable to be seasick, stagger the imagination. Once arrived in the colonies the slaves were sold—those who had survived the voyage—and a slave who cost £3 in Africa would bring from £15 to £25 in the colonies. These were good profits, and the Rhode Islander would then take on a cargo of sugar or molasses and proceed back to Rhode Island to begin the triangle again.

One other feature of the slave trade may be mentioned briefly. In 1713, as part of the general pacification of that year, Spain agreed to grant to an English company the privilege of bringing Negroes into the Spanish colonies in America—The South Sea Company was also granted the privilege of sending one ship each year to the great fair at Porto Bello for the purposes of trade. The history of this contract, called the Assiento, is long and sordid; but so far as the English colonies are concerned it was important because the company made Jamaica an entrepôt for its African product, purchased from the Royal African Company, thereby making Jamaica the greatest slave-market in British America. But it was still more important because of the good, hard Spanish money that the company brought back to the West Indies from their dealings on the Spanish Main. This coin, as already noted, in large part found its way to the northern continental colonies, whence it flowed to England to pay North America's unfavorable balance of trade. Thus human misery played a large part in the building of American prosperity and many of the early American fortunes.

THE GROWTH OF COLONIAL MANUFACTURING

The basic industry in British America was agriculture, but the increasing wealth of the colonies was derived from internal trade and an external commerce involving the exchange of colonial agricultural products, fish, and furs for commodities imported from abroad. As yet there was but little industrial production of consumers' goods manufactured for sale, in any of the colonies. Such goods were mostly imported from England. This was due partly to the British legislation discouraging colonial manufactures already noted, but chiefly to the simple fact that, for the newcomers to America, agriculture and commerce, requiring less capital and less technical skill than manufacturing, offered a quicker, easier, and more dependable way of making a living.

There were, nevertheless, certain extractive and manufacturing industries in the colonies which were already important in the eighteenth century; and there were others which gave promise of soon becoming more so. In the former category were the fishing industry, the fur trade, lumbering, naval stores manufacturing, and ship-building, and the extraction and partial manufacture of iron; in the latter group fall such seedling industries as the manufacture of woolens, hats, shoes, and glass. As might be expected, industrial developments were much farther advanced and much more diversified in the north than in the plantation colonies, where capital was largely employed in the large-scale production of staple crops.

Fishing, which was almost peculiar to New England, will be discussed in some detail in connection with the eighteenth-century progress of that region. Suffice it to say here that this industry enjoyed an expansion in the eighteenth century comparable to the expansion that was taking place in almost all other lines of economic activity in the colonies; in 1731 the fishing industry was said to support some 6,000 men; in 1765 it had expanded to 665 ships and 10,000 men, producing a "harvest" worth nearly £2,000,000.

The closely related industries of lumbering, naval stores manufacturing, and shipbuilding were probably the most highly developed group of intercolonial industries of a non-agricultural sort, and also, probably, the most profitable. All along the Atlantic seaboard there were abundant forests. In New England, magnificent stands of spruce, pine, and oak, closely contiguous to rivers flowing to waterfalls near the sea, provided a set of circumstances inviting the New Englanders to set up sawmills at the falls for cutting the lumber for their houses, and shipyards below the falls for building their fishing boats and the ships to carry their commerce overseas. Lumbering, particularly in New England, was carried on largely by farmers as a winter-time industry, to be carried on while the frozen ground made farming impossible and logging easy. In the spring the logs would be floated to the mills at the waterfalls, and the lumber shipped to the towns for distribution or for export to England, the West Indies and the countries of southern Europe. Over 42,000,000 board feet of sawed lumber were exported from the colonies in 1770, and along with it went some 15,000 tons of timber, 20,000,000 barrel-staves, and 3,000,000 hoops!

But shipbuilding was a full-time industry in all the colonies, although its chief centers were in the provinces north of Maryland. Nowhere in the world, probably, were such fine ships built as were built in America in the eighteenth century. So rapidly did this industry grow, indeed, and so successful was the American competition with the British builders, even in England itself, that in 1724 certain master shipbuilders of London begged the Board of Trade to curb it. But the Board refused to discourage the building of ships, upon which the prosperity of England so heavily depended, either in America or elsewhere in the empire. Thus shipyards dotted the coasts of New England, and flourished at New York, Albany, Philadelphia and Wilmington, turning out three-masted ships and barks for ocean-borne freights, brigs and brigantines for the islands commerce, and sloops and schooners for fishing and the coastwise trade nearer home. Most of these ships were small, of from twenty-five to fifty tons burden for fishing and intercolonial commerce, and from one hundred to three hundred tons burden for ocean voyages. Ships could be built in America thirty per cent more cheaply than in England; and in 1774 it was reported that about one-third of the ships engaged in the commerce of Britain itself were of American construction.

Closely allied with shipbuilding was the production of naval stores, an industry of great military as well as monetary value to the empire, since tar, pitch, turpentine, rope, and the like were so essential to the maintenance of both the navy and the merchant marine. The importance of this business in the eyes of British statesmen is shown by the many encouragements offered the colonists to engage in it, and, in particular, by the Naval Stores Act of 1705 which placed bounties upon naval stores, masts, yards and hemp shipped from America to England. The manufacture of these forest products in America never reached the proportions desired and expected by the mother country, but there was, nevertheless, a substantial growth in the industry in New England and in North and South Carolina. About 140,000 barrels of pitch, tar and turpentine were exported in 1768; but this does not present a true picture of the industry, since the expansion of shipbuilding during the century in the colonies themselves absorbed much of the increase in the output of naval stores.

One of the picturesque elements in the forest industries grew out of the need of masts for the ships of the royal navy, and the age-old prerogative of the Crown to have first choice of all trees suitable for masts for the king's ships. It thus transpired that in 1692 Edward Randolph was named "Surveyor-General of His Majesty's Woods in North America," and laws were passed forbidding the cutting of any white pine trees that were over two feet in diameter twelve inches above the base. The agents of the surveyor-general of the king's woods went through the forests and placed the broad arrow, the king's mark, upon all such trees as were thus reserved for the navy, and no one was permitted to cut them except for that express purpose. In a day of sailing ships masts were perhaps the most precious and costly part of any vessel; and the American forests proved to be a veritable storehouse of these great "sticks," extending from Maine to the Delaware. The forests farther south were not suitable for this kingly industry. The great trees were felled in the winter, dragged over the snow to a river by teams of oxen, and floated down the rivers to the sea, where they were loaded on board ship for carriage abroad. Three thousand tons of masts were shipped from the colonies in 1770.

Another "forest industry"—of a very different sort—was the fur trade, which concerned practically all the colonies from Maine to Georgia. The North American forests abounded in fur-bearing animals, and the sale of these skins in the markets of Europe had been a profitable business from the beginning of colonization. But as civilization had advanced steadily westward the animals retired—with the Indians—before it, and the traders had to go farther and farther afield to find an adequate supply. By the middle of the eighteenth century the fur trade had sunk to relative insignificance in New England; but it was still flourishing in New York and Pennsylvania. Deer skins bought from the Indians continued to be a very important commodity of export farther south. Augusta, founded on the frontier of Georgia in 1736, rivaled Albany as one of the most important centers of the trade on the continent.

The methods of the traders were pretty much the same everywhere. Pack-trains of horses or heavily burdened canoes set out into the wilderness from the "settlements" laden with blankets, shirts, shoes, hardware, arms and ammunition, the inevitable "firewater," and other "Indian goods," and went into the Indian country. There, in the Indian villages, the trader would haggle with the natives over the price of the skins taken by the Indians in their hunts during the preceding winter. The trader might stay in the Indian country several seasons hunting, playing, and mating with them until his supply of "Indian goods" was exhausted. Then he would return to civilization and dispose of his pelts to the merchant who backed his expedition, either on the basis of shares or by outright sale. As the traders were usually entirely unscrupulous in their dealings with the Indians, much trickery took place and much Indian resentment was the result—especially when the traders got the Indians drunk and then took advantage of them. Efforts were made to control the traders by regulation, but without much success.

The great center of the fur trade was the Great Lakes; but, as this region was claimed by France, the English traders operating out of Albany through the Iroquois Indians had to compete with the French fur traders from Montreal. Both England and France claimed the strategic Iroquois country which controlled the inland fur trade, and their disputes over this area, along with other similar disputes, brought them into a fateful conflict which finally ended with France being driven out of North America. As for the English fur trade, it steadily declined, until only £91,000 worth of furs were exported from the continental colonies in 1770. By that time, however, England had taken over Canada, with its fur trade, and this, together with the business of the Hudson's Bay Company, more than made up the loss to the mother country.

The colonial iron industry, on the other hand, was distinctly expanding. Small beginnings at the production of hog-iron had been made in the seventeenth century; but the real beginning of efforts to exploit commercially the deposits of iron in the hills of

America was made after the turn of the century. One of the early efforts of this sort was made by Governor Alexander Spotswood of Virginia, who set up smelting works on his estate at Germanna, in Spotsylvania County, whence he exported twenty tons of pig-iron to Bristol, in England, in 1723. Elsewhere, mines and smelters were appearing in Maryland, Massachusetts, Connecticut, New Jersey and Pennsylvania. The colonies, indeed, were encouraging this development. Virginia freed iron-workers from the duty of labor on the provincial roads and permitted them the free use of timber for their roads and bridges; Massachusetts actually paid bounties upon bar iron, rod iron (used for nails) and articles made of cast-iron. Massachusetts was soon exporting iron articles—axes, for example— to some of the southern colonies; in 1733 there were six furnaces and nineteen forges in New England. The most rapid development was in Pennsylvania, however, and by 1750 this province was producing more iron than any other colony.

The development of the colonial iron industry was a matter of considerable concern to the iron manufacturers of England. For it tended to diminish the colonial market for British iron products, particularly crude objects like nails, axes and rough iron-ware, which the colonists were beginning to make. The British iron industry actually declined, in the first half of the century, and the British manufacturers attributed the decline to the rapidly increasing quantity of iron made in the colonies, which was, indeed, at least partially true. Efforts had been made to meet this colonial competition and in 1721 all export duties on iron shipped from England to the colonies were removed in order to make it possible to compete with the American product in price. But the situation presented a curious dilemma to the British mercantilists. For England was importing most of its crude iron from Sweden and Russia, and the mercantilists realized that this fact would be embarrassing, if not actually disastrous, in time of war with either of these powers. It had been demonstrated that American iron was of a very high quality, and importation of iron from the colonies would make England self-sufficient with regard to this commodity. But the encouragement of the iron industry in America would almost certainly reduce still further the colonial market for British hardware. An effort was made, therefore, in 1738, to draft legislation encouraging the production of crude iron in America while prohibiting the manufacture of hardware. The effort was dropped because of the approach of war with Spain, but was taken up again in 1749, and in 1750 the famous iron act was passed. This law provided for the free import of unwrought iron into London (later extended to include all England), but it prohibited the erection of any new slitting or plating mills or steel furnaces in the colonies. Colonial governors were required to enforce the law on pain of forfeiting £500 sterling and the loss of their jobs.

This act has often been cited as one of the most glaring examples of British selfishness with regard to the colonies and the obtuseness of the British legislators and statesmen who failed to see the inevitability of a native American economy. And it was in line with the same sort of policy that Governor Hopson of Nova Scotia was instructed, in 1752, to discourage the development of the coal mines of Nova Scotia, since that might prevent the clearing of lands and "as the use of Coals in America would furnish the people with the means of carrying on a variety of manufactures, the raw materials of which we now receive from them and afterwards return manufactured." The fact is that the iron act, like the Molasses Act of 1733, remained practically a dead letter. The Americans did welcome the British market, however, and exports of iron to England rose from about three thousand tons in 1750 to nearly eight thousand tons in 1770. At the same time the domestic market and supply were both expanding; and more American capital was going into this business. The significance of this colonial industry is thus twofold; for it illustrates at once the growth of a great native industry and the fundamental cleavage between the developing American economy and the basic principles of British colonial policy.

Of other American manufactures it may be noted only that every American farm was itself a factory of sorts, manufacturing everything possible in order to avoid the outlay of money. Thus home manufactures included clothes, furniture, tools, and food products. Few of these articles were manufactured on a large commercial scale during the colonial period; but the makers of certain commodities, especially when they were shopkeepers in the towns, gradually tended to specialize, and woolen cloth, hats, shoes, and leather goods found an increasing intraprovincial market. Intercolonial trade in woolens and hats was prohibited by English law, as already noted; but these laws were not effectively enforced. There was no prohibition placed on shoes and leather goods; three thousand pairs of shoes were shipped from the continental colonies to the West Indies in 1770.

From this review of the expansion of American industry in the eighteenth century, certain things seem clear. The colonies were slow in developing manufactures on a large scale, perhaps chiefly because of a lack of capital; but this seems also to have been due in part to British legislation and in part to the inexhaustible supply of cheap or free agricultural lands. In the northern colonies, nevertheless, certain native colonial industries enjoyed a dramatic development in the course of the century. These industries, with certain notable examples such as the production of naval stores, brought American industry into competition with British industry, with the result that England, true to the policies laid down in 1696 and earlier, sought to protect its own—at the expense of the colonies. The Americans were growing industrially, as in other lines of economic activity. American capital was competing with British capital. Sooner or later American industry would demand the right to expand freely, along its own natural lines.

THE PROBLEM OF AN EXPANDING CURRENCY

From what has gone before, it seems clear that the American colonies of England were enjoying, in the eighteenth century, one of the greatest periods of economic expansion in the history of this continent. The growth of agriculture, commerce and industry was multiplied and intensified by the constant influx of new population whose most apparent effect was to push the frontiers of settlement deeper and deeper into the American forest. But such phenomenal expansion could not take place without some sort of money. The settler must pay for his land; the merchant must pay the farmer for the products the merchant sold abroad; and the merchant must pay for the goods imported from overseas. As already noted, the colonies of the continent were constantly in debt to the mother country, and had to find a means to pay that debt. The West Indies had a favorable balance of trade with the mother country, but their balance of payments with the continental colonies was unfavorable. Thus the continental colonies used their balance from the West Indies to pay their debt to the mother country; and as Barbados and Jamaica had a favorable commerce with the Spanish colonies that paid them in Spanish money, the continental colonies took their payments from the West Indies, whenever possible, in the form of Spanish dollars or pieces of eight. It thus happened that the chief form of hard money in all the colonies was Spanish; but it drifted steadily away to England to pay for the unfavorable balance of trade. Thus were the parts of the British empire bound together by the golden and silver threads of Spanish coin.

The scarcity of coin in the colonies brought about by the flight of hard money to England inspired many experiments designed to furnish the colonies with the necessary medium of exchange. In the seventeenth century, many suggestions were made for the establishment of mints in the colonies, and Massachusetts actually set up a mint in 1652, from whence issued the famous pine-tree shilling. This coin was made to contain less silver than the sterling English shilling, in the hope that this debasement would tend to keep the coins in Massachusetts. But the English treasury discountenanced the issuance of special colonial coins, and the Massachusetts mint was closed when that colony lost its charter in 1684.

Another, and more successful, method of carrying on exchange was by the use of commodity money. In the absence of any other workable form, the West Indies early adopted sugar as a legal currency, and both accepted it in payment of taxes and used it for the payment of salaries. Similarly, all the other colonies adopted commodity money, or "country pay," as a regular part of their financial and monetary systems. Thus, rice was acceptable in South Carolina, naval stores in North Carolina, tobacco in Virginia, wheat in Pennsylvania and the other middle colonies, and a variety of products, including livestock, in New England. But commodity money offered certain great disadvantages. It was bulky, and caused much trouble in the mere course of its use; it might depreciate or appreciate in value before a transaction could be completed; or it might lose value by reason of the transportation charges in hauling it from place to place. Nevertheless, commodity money offered a very real part of a solution for the money problems through the colonial period.

Still, commodity money was ill-calculated to meet the needs of a rapidly expanding economy. Some medium of exchange must be found that would be easy to handle, flexible, and acceptable to debtors and creditors in the everyday conduct of business, large or small. The needed medium was found in paper currency; and it is probably no exaggeration to say that American civilization of the eighteenth century was built with paper money.

The origin of paper money in the colonies is probably to be found in the early use of bills of exchange and bills of credit offered by private persons. The captain of a warship in American waters needing supplies might pay for them with a draught, or bill of exchange, drawn upon the Admiralty in England. As the credit of the Admiralty was generally thought to be good, the bill of exchange might be endorsed by the recipient to someone else, who, in turn, might pay with it his debt to a third. Similarly, a merchant, in paying another merchant for imported goods, might give him a bill of exchange drawn upon a factor or a merchant in London, and these bills of exchange might pass through several hands before being finally paid by the firm upon which they were drawn. A simpler device was a personal note made by a wealthy person promising to pay at a certain time; the recipient of the note could endorse it over to another, and the note might thus travel far before its final payment by the original maker. It was not very long before proposals began to be made that "banks" be formed to issue such bills of credit, or that they be issued by the provincial governments.

It was just such bills of credit as these that were issued by the Massachusetts government in 1690 to pay for the expedition against the French in Canada. South Carolina issued similar bills in 1703, and Barbados tried it in 1706. Thereafter, the other colonies followed, issuing bills to pay for war debts for which there was no cash in the provincial treasuries, but conscious, at the same time, that a supply of money would greatly stimulate business. The success of the Massachusetts bills led that colony to continue the practice for peacetime purposes; bills were issued against future tax receipts, and were used to pay public debts as well as for carrying on the war. Usually, when such bills were issued, the taxes to be used for their redemption were specified, or were actually imposed to cover a specific issue of bills. This was not always the case, however, and some of the colonies printed bills without any provision whatever for their redemption. Some of the colonies, too, found it impossible to collect taxes in amounts sufficient to pay off the bills issued. On the other hand, since the bills issued constituted a sort of forced loan from the public, much of the colonial paper money bore interest, usually at five per cent.

With the end of Queen Anne's War in 1713, the use of bills of credit for peacetime purposes spread rapidly. Massachusetts issued £50,000 in new bills in 1714; New York issued £27,000 in the same year; and Rhode Island issued £40,000 in 1715. The amounts of the bills issued were far in excess of the taxes collected, which led to the issuance of new bills. But not only did provincial governments issue currency; groups of private individuals began to form "banks" to issue bills of credit of their own against mortgages on land. And because the security behind these bills was inadequate or even non-existent, they, too, had a very uncertain value. As a result of these two developments—governmental issuance of bills in excess of tax receipts, and private or semi-private bills of credit issued by land banks—confidence in this paper began to decline. British merchants refused to accept colonial currency in payment of sterling accounts; and when colonial legislatures passed laws making the colonial currency legal tender, the laws were disallowed by the Privy Council. As confidence in the bills declined, prices went up, and there ensued an era of monetary depreciation which affected most of the colonies and produced a bitter social cleavage between debtors and creditors within the colonies.

For the farmers, frontiersmen, and debtors generally were not slow in noticing that as the supply of money increased prices for their commodities increased, and that as the value of the money declined their debts to their creditors were automatically scaled down by a corresponding amount. The result was that creditors began to oppose the issuance of more paper money, and that debtors generally favored it. In colonies such as Rhode Island, where the legislature was controlled by the rural or debtor classes, paper money was issued in great quantities; in colonies where the creditors were in control, the paper-money policy tended to be much more conservative. Thus the planters of Barbados found themselves arrayed against the merchants of that colony as early as 1706 over a law creating a land bank which would lend the planters bills of credit on their plantations. The law was also opposed by the British merchants interested in the island, and it was disallowed.

This was the beginning of an active interest of the Crown in colonial currency questions. Governors were instructed to veto legal-tender laws, to discourage the formation of land banks, and to make sure that public bills of credit were covered by adequate taxation. When the debtors of Massachusetts formed the famous land bank of 1740, the merchants of the colony allied themselves with British merchants in an appeal to Parliament, which responded by applying to the colonies the old Bubble Act of 1720—which effectively destroyed the Massachusetts land bank. A similar conflict took place between debtors and creditors in Rhode Island, where the colonial paper money was worth only one-eighth of sterling in 1750. When the Rhode Island legislature proposed to create yet another land bank, the merchants appealed to England. Parliament responded this time by passing the Currency Act of 1751, applicable to all the New England colonies, which prohibited the creation of land banks as well as laws making bills of credit legal tender. It also required that new bills of

credit be adequately covered by tax receipts and that they be retired promptly. This law was extended to all the colonies in 1764.

The intervention of Parliament in the colonial currency situation doubtless had a salutary effect in the direction of stabilization.
It was well known, however, that this intervention was carried out
in the interest of English and American creditors against the interests of American debtors. That there was a need for an expanding
currency in the expanding economy of the colonies, however, is
clear. The Americans were experimenting in their search for a solution to this problem. But they were divided, according to their interests, in their ideas as to what the solution should be. The intervention of England, while it stabilized the situation, also intensified the bitterness of the rural and debtor classes, not only against
the colonial merchants, but also—and even more, perhaps—against
the mother country itself. Samuel Adams, the younger, whose father
was ruined by the destruction of the Massachusetts land bank in
1741, was only one of a number of Americans whose bitterness
against the mother country may be traced back to her intervention in a problem which might, perhaps, have been left to be
worked out by the colonists themselves.

TRENDS IN AMERICAN ECONOMIC THOUGHT

From this review of the economic life of the colonies of England
in America, the most striking characteristic of the colonial economy
in the eighteenth century appears to have been its expansiveness.
Colonial agriculture, colonial commerce, both domestic and foreign, and colonial industry were all growing at a pace that was
greatly accelerated by the rapid increase in population. But economic sectionalism was at work to split the empire apart. The
economic development of the West Indies tended to increase and
to emphasize the economic dependence of those colonies upon the
mother country. The economic development of the continental
colonies, on the other hand, while it did multiply the gross economic exchange between those colonies and the mother country,
seemed, nevertheless, to be of a nature eventually to make those
colonies economically independent and resentful of British economic control. The efforts of the imperial government to control
the colonial economy, with a very few exceptions, were calculated
to restrict the normal economic growth of the continental colonies
in the interest of the mother country. Happily for the colonies,

these efforts at remote legislative control of economic forces were, almost without exception, ineffectual.

The normal economic evolution of the continental colonies seemed to be toward a freedom to trade in every market in the world that was open to them. It is no surprise, therefore, to notice, despite their own local mercantilistic regulations of commerce, a clear trend in American economic thought toward a free trade philosophy. Yet such a trend inevitably ran counter to British thought and British policy. Sooner or later the conflict in interests and ideas was to bear fruit in a readjustment of the economic relations between the colonies and the mother country.

RECOMMENDED BOOKS FOR FURTHER READING

CONTEMPORARY NARRATIVES

Ernest L. Bogart and Charles M. Thompson, eds., *Readings in the Economic History of the United States,* Chapters 1-3.

Harry J. Carman, ed., *American Husbandry.*

Andrew M. Davis, ed., *Colonial Currency Reprints, 1682-1751.*

Elizabeth Donnan, ed., *Documents Illustrative of the Slave Trade to America.*

Albert B. Hart, ed., *American History Told by Contemporaries,* II, Chapters 13, 18.

John F. Jameson, ed., *Privateering and Piracy in the Colonial Period.*

Thomas Jefferson, *Notes on the State of Virginia.*

Thomas Jefferson, *A Summary View of the Rights of British America.*

Ulrich B. Phillips, ed., *Plantation and Frontier Documents, 1649-1863.*

MODERN ACCOUNTS

Charles M. Andrews, "Colonial Commerce," *American Historical Review,* XX, 43-65.

Herbert C. Bell, "The West India Trade before the American Revolution," *American Historical Review,* XXII, 272-287.

Arthur C. Bining, *British Regulation of the Colonial Iron Industry.*

Charles J. Bullock, *Essays on the Monetary History of the United States,* Part I, Chapter 4; Part II, Chapters 1-2; Part III, Chapters 1-2.

Lewis J. Carey, *Franklin's Economic Views.*

Harry J. Carman, *Social and Economic History of the United States,* Volume I.

Victor S. Clark, *History of Manufactures in the United States,* Volume I.

John R. Commons [and others], *History of Labour in the United States,* Volume I.

Andrew M. Davis, *Currency and Banking in the Province of Massachusetts Bay.*

Joseph S. Davis, *Essays in the Earlier History of American Corporations.*

Clive Day, *History of Commerce of the United States.*

Ralph H. Gabriel, *Toilers of Land and Sea,* Chapters 1-4.

Lawrence H. Gipson, *The British Empire before the American Revolution,* II, Chapters 3, 5, 9-10; III, Chapters 8-10.

Lewis C. Gray, *The Genesis and Expansion of the Plantation System.*

Lewis C. Gray, *History of Agriculture in the Southern United States to 1860.*

Evarts B. Greene, *The Provincial Governor in the English Colonies of North America.*

Louis M. Hacker, *The Triumph of American Capitalism,* Chapters 1-11.

Harold A. Innis, *The Cod Fisheries,* Chapters 1-6.

Elmo P. Hohman, *The American Whaleman.*

Emory R. Johnson [and others], *History of the Domestic and Foreign Commerce of the United States,* Volume I.

Robert M. Keir, *The Epic of Industry,* Chapters 1-2.

Robert M. Keir, *The March of Commerce,* Chapter 1.

Ralph G. Lounsbury, *The British Fishery at Newfoundland, 1634-1763.*

William S. McClellan, *Smuggling in the American Colonies at the Outbreak of the Revolution.*

Raymond McFarland, *A History of the New England Fisheries.*

Curtis P. Nettels, *The Money Supply in the American Colonies before 1720.*

Curtis P. Nettels, *The Roots of American Civilization,* Chapters 9-10, 16, 19.

Robert E. Peabody, *Merchant Venturers of Old Salem.*

Frank W. Pitman, *The Development of the British West Indies, 1700-1763.*

William G. Sumner, "The Spanish Dollar and the Colonial Shilling," *American Historical Review,* III, 607-619.

William B. Weeden, *Economic and Social History of New England, 1620-1789,* Volume II.

29

Immigration and the Old West

AN EXPANDING POPULATION

ANGLO-SAXON America was the product of a series of waves of emigration from Europe. The first of these waves started from England, in the first four decades of the seventeenth century, and among the thousands of men who came to the shores of this continent in that movement two distinct groups of motives are to be observed. It is probably true that the great majority of these people came to better their economic condition. Not, that is, because they were particularly distressed, economically, but simply because they had heard of a great new area of vacant land that had become available for those who would go and take it. In this sense the "great migration" was merely a land-rush from England into America. On the other hand, a considerable minority of these emigrants left England to escape actual distress of one sort or another. Some were in poverty, and sought a new chance in the new world. Others were suffering from political conditions in one way or another, and sought a larger measure of political security. Still others were suffering under religious persecution, and sought on these shores a haven of religious freedom.

The same mixture of motives is to be observed, in varying degrees, among the people who built New Netherland, New Sweden, and New France. While it is probably true that the economic motive was the predominant one among all these groups, yet it is equally true that many French Protestants came to New Netherland by way of Holland and to New France directly, despite the prohibition of such emigration.

The second great wave of immigration into Anglo-Saxon America did not come from England. During the second half of the seventeenth century the number of Englishmen who emigrated to America relatively declined. Such new colonies as were founded during the period of the Restoration were peopled in large measure by emigrants from the older colonies, driven out by distress of one sort or another such as debt, a harsh climate, or such an economic and social revolution as was taking place in the West Indies. At the same time, this was the period when immigrants

400

from other lands began to enter the English colonies in ever-increasing numbers. Huguenots from France, Germans from the Rhineland, Scotch-Irish from the northern counties of Ireland, people of many tongues and many cultures, seeking economic betterment or fleeing from religious persecution, the devastation of war, or an unjust economic system, found on American shores a home and a haven of escape from the distress and misery of their motherlands.

It was during the first half of the eighteenth century and especially after the Peace of Utrecht, that this stream of immigrants reached its flood. But it was already getting well under way by the time when William Penn founded his colony of Pennsylvania. These people, coming late and finding the choice spots along the coast pre-empted by the earlier comers, moved inland to fill up the spaces back from the coast, along the Piedmont and the Appalachian Highland, to form the second frontier, the "old west."

This wave of immigration was one of the major factors in the history of the continental colonies in the eighteenth century. This was an age of rapid expansion in the colonies, in commerce, in population, and in the area of actual settlement westward. But this extraordinary influx gave an added impetus to the normal growth of population, and resulted in an almost phenomenal expansion, which, in turn, stimulated a greater expansion of commerce and of capital, and the westward movement. During this period the population of the continental colonies rose from about 300,000 in 1700 to some 2,500,000 in 1775—almost a ten-fold increase; the population approximately doubled every twenty-five years.

THE CONDITIONS OF EMIGRATION: THE VOYAGE AND THE LANDING

It was not without encouragement that so many Europeans left their homes and emigrated to America. The liberal land policies, political concessions, and broad religious toleration offered newcomers by the proprietors of Carolina, Maryland, the Jerseys, New York and Pennsylvania were offered deliberately, as an inducement to colonists. For the proprietors realized that growth and profits depended upon a rapidly expanding population. William Penn, when he began to seek for colonists for Pennsylvania, wrote pamphlets setting forth the advantages of Pennsylvania, called "Quackerthal" by the Germans, and these pamphlets were translated into Dutch, German, and French and distributed widely on the continent.

The news that America was a land of political and religious freedom, where land was free, reached the poor of Europe by other means, also, such as letters from those who had already gone, by the reports of ship captains and merchants, and by the printed narratives of travelers in America, and it was mostly the poor who emigrated. Those who could raise the necessary £6 or £8 for a passage paid their own way. But many of the emigrants could not pay their passage money. In such cases the ship captains might agree to carry the emigrant and his family to America, on the condition that the emigrant sign an indenture, or contract, by which the emigrant agreed to labor for a period of years, three, five, or sometimes seven, to pay for his passage. The emigrant thus became the "servant" of the ship captain for the term of his contract, and on his arrival in America his "master" could sell his labor to someone needing a servant in the colony for whatever it would bring. This business of buying and selling human labor became profitable, and agents called "newlanders," working on commission for Dutch "man-stealers" induced many emigrants to leave their homes in the Rhineland. Similar practices took place among the Irish; even in England men, women and children were "spirited" aboard ships and their labor sold in the colonies.

The conditions the emigrants had to face on the voyage were discouraging, at best; often enough they were terrible. The voyage from a European port to an American port generally lasted from five to eight weeks, and sometimes took as much as six months. The emigrants were often crowded together below decks with little privacy and less sanitation, and it is no wonder that emigrant ships were often swept by disease. As one of them described existence on shipboard, "betwixt decks, there can hardlie a man fetch his breath by reason there ariseth such a funke in the night that it causeth putrefaction of the blood and breedeth disease much like the plague." Generally the emigrants furnished their own food, which often became exhausted before the voyage was many days old, or became spoiled and uneatable; emigrants sometimes fought for the bodies of the ship's rats. Disease was more terrible than hunger; scurvy, smallpox, and worse scourges would sweep away great numbers of a ship's passengers, and their bodies would be thrown into the sea. Women who were so unfortunate as to give birth to children on shipboard very seldom survived the voyage.

On the arrival in an American port, the business of disposing

of the indentured servants would begin. Merchants might purchase "parcels" of servants, who would then be advertised for sale.
Individuals in need of servants might come on shipboard and
purchase the servants directly from the captain; any "left-overs"
might be bought at a low price and then led, or peddled, about the
countryside by "soul-drivers" in search of purchasers. At its worst
the system resulted in much misery arising from the exploitation
of human beings; husband might be separated from wife, or mother
from child. If husband or wife died, the other might be required
to work out the term of servitude provided in the contract. Such
cases, however, were relatively rare.

At its best this system provided a real opportunity for the newcomers. For in all the colonies there were laws requiring that the
servants be well treated. Indeed, it was to the interest of the master
to treat his servants well, since such treatment would result in
better service. At the end of his term of servitude, the servant
would receive a small sum of money, or clothes and tools from
his master, and, generally, fifty acres of land for every member of
his family from the province in which he lived. If a foreigner, he
might be naturalized as a citizen, either under British law (1740),
which required that he be a Protestant and reside in British territory seven years, or under the law of the colony where he lived.
The laws of the separate colonies, indeed, who were seeking to
increase their population, were often much more liberal than the
imperial law; Massachusetts, for example, required a residence
period of only one year. Citizenship and the possession of land
in most colonies entitled the former servant to the privilege of
voting. As a general thing, once his servitude was past opportunity
was open to him; and multitudes of these "self-made" men became
distinguished, useful citizens of the new world.

NEWCOMERS AND NEW HOMES

A. The French

Who were these people?

The first large group of foreign immigrants to the British colonies, after the Dutch and the Swedes, were, perhaps, the French
Huguenots, Protestants of the Calvinist faith. These industrious,
thrifty people, given a large measure of religious freedom and
political autonomy by good King Henry IV in the Edict of Nantes
in 1598, had seen their privileges and autonomy whittled away

by Cardinal Richelieu and others, in the course of the seventeenth century, in the name of national unity. When Louis XIV came to the throne of France he began a program of persecution, inspired by both religious zeal and nationalism, which reached its climax in the revocation of the Edict of Nantes in 1685. The Huguenots were forbidden to hold meetings for worship, either public or private; their political autonomy was completely abolished; and they were forbidden to leave the country. When the Huguenots adopted a policy of passive resistance, soldiers were quartered in Huguenot towns and even in their homes. Meetings were broken up, and the people mistreated; those who resisted were sent to the galleys or sold as slaves to the planters of the West Indies. This policy of intimidation, which had as its motive national and religious unity, simply forced many of the bolder spirits to flee France to seek religious freedom elsewhere. They were aided in this by the "newlanders," and made their way to Holland, England, and Denmark, where many of them made their homes and whence others proceeded to the colonies.

Some of these French emigrants went to New England, where the New England brand of Calvinism offered them a congenial atmosphere. About one hundred and fifty families are said to have arrived in Massachusetts alone in the two years following the revocation of the Edict of Nantes; others went to Newport and other towns in Rhode Island; others went to Maine. Already, in 1685, there was a French Protestant Church organization in Boston, although it had no building until some years later. This group was looked upon with some misgivings by the people of Boston, however, who felt sure all Frenchmen were Catholics, who deplored the French gaiety which saw no harm in celebrating such feasts as Christmas which the Puritans did not observe, and who looked askance at the other amenities of life that the Frenchmen brought with them. At Oxford, near Worcester, in Massachusetts, a Huguenot community was founded in 1687, but it did not flourish; the Huguenots were mostly townspeople, and they were most successful in America in the growing American cities. Despite their little success as frontiersmen, however, probably 7,000 French Huguenots had settled in New England by 1700. Paul Revere, Peter Faneuil, Peter Bowdoin, and other famous New England personages of the Revolutionary era, were descendants of the Huguenots.

Numerous French Huguenots went to New York and Philadelphia. They had begun to enter this section with the Dutch; it has already been noted that most of the first settlers at Manhattan in 1624 were probably French Protestant refugees. By 1688 there were two hundred French families in New York, and an active French press appeared in the city about the end of the century. New Rochelle, founded in 1689, was a French community noted for its schools and cultural life. A great many Huguenots went to Pennsylvania, beginning with those attracted by Penn's propaganda, the majority of whom lived in or near Philadelphia. John Jay, the DeLanceys, as well as many other prominent families of New York and Pennsylvania, were descendants of these original Huguenot refugees. In the south, a considerable number of Huguenots went to Virginia, where they became tobacco planters. It was Charleston, South Carolina, however, which became the greatest center of French Huguenots in the colonies. The Huguenots had been encouraged to come by the Carolina proprietors, as already noted, in the hope that they might establish the production of wine, silk, olives, and other sub-tropical commodities. The center of the early French settlements in Carolina was the Santee River, where there were many French plantation owners. There were other foci of Huguenot settlements in South Carolina, such as St. Denis, St. Stevens, Orange Quarter, and elsewhere; but here, as elsewhere, the city was more attractive to them than the country, and Charleston society was largely leavened by French customs, dress and manners. Similarly, the architecture of the town was strongly influenced by French styles. There were several French churches in Charleston, but most of them were gradually assimilated into the established Anglican church. One of them, however, the French Huguenot Church, remains to this day. French planters and merchants took an active and important part in South Carolina politics and economic life, and furnished some of the leaders of the American Revolution.

In all, probably not more than 15,000 Huguenots came to America prior to the Revolution. Nor did they conform to the general rule that the newcomers were of the poorer classes. For the Huguenots who came to America did so, for the most part, after first stopping in Holland and England, where the poorer ones among them remained. Those who came to the colonies were generally fairly well-to-do, and were well-educated and highly cultivated people. They contributed an extremely important stream of culture to the emerging culture of the colonies.

B. *The Germans*

One of the largest and most significant of the streams of foreigners flowing into British America in the eighteenth century was that made up of Germans. And not without reason; for in the unhappy lands of the Germanies conditions, economic, social, political, and religious, were "ripe" for a wave of emigration. Ever since the outbreak of the Thirty Years War in 1618 the lands lying along the Rhine had been overrun again and again by foreign armies. At the end of the Thirty Years War the German countryside lay waste and bankrupt; recovery had hardly begun when Louis XIV started a new series of wars with his "War of Devolution" in 1667. This war was followed by the Franco-Dutch War from 1672-78, the seizure of Strasbourg in 1681, with fighting that lasted until the Truce of Ratisbon in 1684, the War of the League of Augsburg from 1688 to 1697 and the War of the Spanish Succession from 1701 to 1713. Thus, about sixty-three years of the period between 1618 and 1713, or roughly two-thirds, were years of active warfare, involving marching and counter-marching across the soil of the Netherlands and the lower Rhineland by the armies of France, England, Holland, Sweden, Prussia and Austria. Often enough these armies took their subsistence from the countries over which they marched, sweeping the farmlands clean of grain, hay, and livestock, and leaving the peasants with no hope of payment. Not only that, land in these areas of Europe was generally held in feudal tenure. The peasant operating the land could not even call the land his own, but must pay certain dues and services to his feudal overlord. He must obey the commands of his overlord, both as to the land and, in many cases, to the extent of giving military service when called upon. At the same time the petty South-German princes, aping the magnificence and luxury of the French court at Versailles, laid exorbitant taxes upon their subjects to pay for their own folly. It is no wonder that the prospect of owning outright their own lands in America, without feudal ties and relatively free of taxes, was an irresistible attraction to many of the German peasants.

Still another strong motive force behind the wave of German emigration was religion. For southern Germany was the home of many sects of a "pietist" type which were seeking a haven of escape from religious persecution. Germany had been the cradle of the Protestant Revolt from Roman Catholicism led by Martin Luther, and the Peace of Augsburg, of 1555, ending, for the time being, the religious wars, had recognized the right of a prince to determine the religion of his subjects. The Catholic "counter-reformation," especially in the first half of the seventeenth century, had recovered some of Catholicism's lost ground, however, and had reinvigorated Catholicism itself. South Germany remained largely Roman Catholic, and a number of the South-German princes, such as the fanatical elector of the Palatinate, sought to maintain Catholicism within their dominions. In the effort at religious uniformity both Catholic and Lutheran princes resorted to persecution.

Protestantism, meanwhile, had broken up into many sects, and other forms, particularly that of Calvinism, had spread into southern Germany and the Netherlands. In the course of the seventeenth century this "breaking-up" process continued, and many Germans of humble station, dissatisfied with the ritualism of the Catholic way, the cold rationalism of Calvinism and the aristocratic tendencies of Lutheranism, turned for solace and escape from their earthly woes to religious sects of a more personal and emotional kind. Of these sects there were many—Moravians, Mennonites, Schwenkfelders, Quakers, and others—but nearly all were efforts to get back to the simple, pious religion of Jesus. Most of them were pacifists, and most of them rejected any priesthood, emphasizing, on the contrary, a warm personal relationship between the individual and his God. The princes, in an instinctive fear of the political effects of such beliefs and in their desire for religious uniformity, persecuted these simple people. Their property might be confiscated, their churches were seized or destroyed, and many of the worshipers themselves were expelled. To these people, in the midst of their persecution, the news that America was a land of religious freedom came like a call from God.

The first considerable band of German emigrants to come to America as a result of William Penn's propaganda arrived in Pennsylvania under the leadership of Francis Daniel Pastorius on the ship *Concord* in 1683. This group founded the town of Germantown, a few miles to the north of Philadelphia. A few years later another group, under Johann Kelpius, settled at Wissahickon on Wissahickon Creek, not far away.

It was not until after the turn of the century, however, that the tide of German emigration reached its flood, beginning with the great movement of peasants out of the Palatinate. This small principality had been devastated in 1707, in the course of the War of the Spanish Succession, and many of the peasants had had their homes destroyed. Beginning in 1708 numbers of Palatines had begun to go to England, whence they hoped to go to the colonies, and in 1709 some thirteen thousand families entered England. In England the problem of caring for such a crowd of refugees was turned over to the Board of Trade, which proposed that they be sent to America to make naval stores. It thus fell out that some three thousand Palatines were naturalized as British citizens and in 1710 were sent to New York. Here they were given land on the Hudson, and founded the town of Newburg. They had to be supported by the colony, however, and as neither the naval stores business nor their farming prospered, the support was withdrawn and most of them left the settlement and went to the richer lands of the Schoharie valley or to Pennsylvania.

The failure of the attempt to settle the Palatines in New York did not deter others from coming to America. At about the same time when that effort was being made, one Baron Graffenried took a group of families to North Carolina where they founded the town of New Bern. Other Germans went to Pennsylvania; it was to this colony, indeed, that by far the greater number of German immigrants found their way. For this was the heyday of German pietism, and the pietist sects found in Pennsylvania the rich, free land, the political freedom and the religious toleration which made this colony the "new world paradise of the sects." Among the first to arrive were the Mennonites, following Menno Simon, who came to the colony about 1710 from German Switzerland, where they had refused to take the oath to bear arms. These pious people, not unlike the Quakers in their belief, settled to the southwestward of Philadelphia, in Lancaster County, where they were joined by many of their brethren from southern Germany and Holland. Another important German group were the Dunkers, or Baptists, who also went to Lancaster County. Of more importance than the Mennonites or the Dunkers were the Moravians, the followers of Count Zinzendorf. These men, who were also closely similar to the Quakers in their beliefs, were moved by a missionary zeal, and were responsible for the establishment of many schools and the sending of a number of missionaries to the Indians. It was this sect, too, which founded the town of Bethlehem in Pennsylvania, and Berks County became the center of its influence.

As time went on, and German immigrants continued to flow into the colony, the newcomers pushed farther westward and southward, following the Great Valley of the Alleghenies to mingle with the Scotch-Irish who were building the new frontier. By 1727 they had begun to establish themselves on the Shenandoah, whence they moved on southward, some to the upper branches of the Tennessee, and others southeastward through the passes of the Blue Ridge into the Piedmont of Virginia and North Carolina.

Meanwhile, other Germans were coming into the southern colonies by way of Charleston and Savannah. These Germans moved out to the frontier along the Piedmont. The movement into these colonies, which began about 1731 to South Carolina, was encouraged by the colonial governments in the hope that the newcomers might cultivate silk and wines. After the establishment of Georgia in 1733 a group of Germans founded New Ebenezer, up the river from Savannah.

The center of the German settlement, however, remained Pennsylvania. Probably as many as one hundred thousand Germans came to the colonies in the course of this movement, and the greater part of them came to Pennsylvania, where they settled the area between Philadelphia and the Susquehanna. While the vast majority of these people were simple folk, farmers and artisans, a very large proportion of whom came over as indentured servants and "redemptioners," yet their leaders and pastors were often enough men of university training. Of a deeply religious nature, they established religious communities, schools, printing presses and other institutions of a cultural character. Christopher Sauer, a German printer of Germantown, was hardly less influential among the Germans than was Benjamin Franklin among the English. Many another important name in American cultural history sprang from this group, and the Germans as a whole exercised a profound influence upon the developing American culture.

C. *The Scotch-Irish*

Of no less importance than the Germans in the eighteenth-century expansion of the population of the American colonies were the Scotch-Irish. These immigrants, like the Germans, were driven to America by the desperate political and economic conditions at home; like the Germans, too, religious persecution had a considerable influence upon their coming. The Scotch-Irish were the descendants of Scotchmen who had been moved from Scotland to Ulster in Northern Ireland by the British government early in the seventeenth century, with the idea of bringing order to that troubled island and of preventing it from being used as a military base by the enemies of England. This movement, which had its beginning at about the time of the founding of Virginia, was part of the widespread British interest in colonization, and was inspired by the same economic impulses that moved the members of the Virginia Company. As a matter of fact, some of the financial backers of Virginia were also backers of the colonization of Ulster, but the most important promoters were the fifty-nine Scottish "undertakers" who were given grants of land in Ulster on condition that they settle Scotchmen there, which they did.

A great many Scotchmen and numerous Englishmen went to Ulster, and its population grew rapidly. These people were Protestants, chiefly Scotch Presbyterians, and this part of Ireland became distinctly Presbyterian in religion. Life in the "colony" was difficult, however, and event after event took place to lead the inhabitants to look elsewhere for escape. To begin with, Archbishop Laud extended to Ulster his effort to force dissenters to conform to the Anglican way of worship, and this policy was vigorously carried forward by Thomas Wentworth, Lord Stafford, Governor of Ireland. The result was an era of religious persecution which sought to establish the Anglican Church and the power of an absolute king. The outbreak of the English civil war took Wentworth back to England, where he was executed by the Parliamentary party; but it also brought a Catholic Irish uprising which struck at Ulster and wiped out many of the Protestants of the "Northern Counties."

It was to escape from conditions such as these that some of the "Scotch-Irish" in Ulster began to emigrate to America about the middle of the seventeenth century, going largely to the shores of the Chesapeake in Maryland. But the movement was greatly accelerated by the mercantile policies of England with regard to the Ulster colony, which almost paralyzed its economic life altogether. For Parliament, after the Restoration, prohibited the importation into England or the colonies of cattle, sheep, beef, pork, butter and cheese from Ireland, in the hope of thus protecting English farmers from Ulster competition. But since these were the principal export products of the colony, and as England was its principal market, its economic life was seriously crippled. Many of the Ulsterites turned to the raising of sheep and the manufacture of woolens; but then Parliament prohibited the importation of wool and woolens, and the community was again crushed. The people of Ulster were reduced to complete despair about 1718 by the increased rents imposed by the absentee English landlords upon the Ulster lands. But already the inhabitants of this colony, having no limitless expanse of free land upon their frontiers to which to escape, had begun to sail away to America. Now the stream of emigrants reached its flood and continued to flow until the Revolution.

One of the earliest groups of these Scotch-Irish Presbyterians was that which went in five shiploads to Boston late in 1718. There they split up, some of them going westward to the frontiers of Massachusetts, others going northward and eastward into New Hampshire and Maine. It was one of these groups that founded the town of Londonderry, in New Hampshire, whence some of them, or their children, continued their migration out into the frontier forests of New Hampshire and across the Connecticut River into the Green Mountains to found the settlements that later were to become the state of Vermont. Other emigrants from Ulster went to New Jersey and New York; the names of Orange and Ulster counties in New York are surviving witnesses of this movement. From these bases they moved on into the upper Susquehanna Valley or up the Hudson and eastward into Vermont to meet their westward-moving kinsmen from Londonderry. Grants to them from the governor of New York conflicted with grants to their kinsmen by the governor of New Hampshire, and brought on one of the bitterest and most persistent boundary quarrels of the colonial period and after.

But it was to Pennsylvania that the greatest numbers of Scotch-Irish immigrants went, entering the province by way of Philadelphia or Newcastle or by going up Chesapeake Bay and the Susquehanna River. In the southern counties of Pennsylvania they mingled with the Germans already there; but many of them went on out beyond the band of German settlements and found new places for themselves in the untouched wilderness. As often as not they squatted on the land, with little or no regard for the property rights of king, proprietor, province, or private owner. As they continued to come in, in an apparently never-ending stream, some went up the branches of the Susquehanna and over the mountains into the lands along the upper branches of the Ohio, which they reached about the eve of the Seven Years War. Others, following the line of least resistance along the southward-bending valleys, flowed along with the Germans moving into western Maryland and into the Shenandoah Valley of Virginia, which they reached about 1732. In the Valley, and in the Piedmont just east of the Blue Ridge, they met another stream of their kinsmen moving into the western country by way of the Chesapeake and the rivers of Virginia. Still farther south the southward-rolling stream met others moving into the Piedmont from the coast. Thus, by the mid-century there had been settled—thinly, to be sure, and unevenly—a band of Scotch-Irish frontiersmen stretching from the Kennebec in Maine to Augusta, on the Savannah, in Georgia. Mixed here and there with Germans, especially in Pennsylvania, Maryland, and Virginia, these tough and hardy people became the greatest Indian fighters in the colonies, the source at once of protection to the older colonies and much trouble to colonial governments because of their fiery and undisciplined ways of life.

D. *Other Foreign Newcomers*

Less important numerically than the Germans and the Scotch-Irish, but of considerable importance for the developing civilization of America none-the-less, were certain other small groups of newcomers from Europe. Among these should be mentioned, first, the Swiss who came to America—as did so many others—to escape landlordism and the consequent poverty in their homeland. At first encouraged to emigrate and then prohibited from leaving the country, many Swiss men and women escaped down the Rhine and came to America. A few of them had come to Carolina with Baron Graffenried's New Bern colony in 1710, and others followed to both North and South Carolina, where inducements were offered them in the form of land, money, houses, and tax exemptions because of their reputation as sober and industrious workers.

Another group of interest were the Roman Catholic Irish immigrants from southern Ireland. These drifted chiefly into Maryland and Pennsylvania, because of the greater tolerance there of their Catholic faith. A few Scotchmen from Scotland, too, found their way to Barbados, Virginia, and Massachusetts, and it was Scotchmen who founded the town of Port Royal, in South Carolina. Still another group whose importance was probably out of proportion to their numbers, was made up of Jews from Spain and Portugal who came to escape the religious persecution of those Catholic countries and to share in the abounding prosperity of the new land. The Jews went chiefly to the cities, although a few were farmers, and were to be found in Bridgetown, Barbados, in Kingston, Jamaica, and in Charleston, Philadelphia, New York, and Newport on the mainland. Everywhere they went the Jews came to be noted for their culture as well as for their success in business.

NATURALIZATION

The swarm of newcomers into the colonies raised the very difficult question of citizenship. How were these foreigners to be treated? Should they retain their foreign status, or should they be given a means of becoming British citizens? Up to this time in the evolution of the modern states system the question of naturalization had not presented much difficulty, because very few people had ever thought of changing their allegiance from one king to another, even if it could be done. A man was born a Frenchman or an Englishman, and it was popularly no more expected that a man could change his allegiance than that he could change the color of his skin. The process had been provided for, nevertheless, and was beginning to be recognized by international law. Thus in England a man might be made a citizen by the act of the king—a process called "denization"—who might also withdraw the privilege, or it might be done by act of Parliament—a process called "naturalization." In both cases, however, citizenship was limited, and the new citizen was liable to continue to be looked upon as an alien, a "foreigner."

When it was proposed in 1709 to bring a number of Germans from the Palatinate to New York to make naval stores, it was also proposed that the new immigrants be promised full citizenship. There followed the naturalization law of 1709, the first of its kind, which promised immigrants all the rights of native-born Englishmen if they would take an oath of allegiance to the king, abjure their old allegiance, and partake of the sacrament according to the Anglican form. The law was repealed in 1711, but was reenacted in 1714 with certain additional limitations. But thousands of foreigners had already found their way into the colonies, and their status had to be considered by the colonial legislatures. Generally speaking, the colonies welcomed the newcomers, because they provided labor and a market for the rapidly expanding colonial economy. Naturalization laws had already been passed in the seventeenth century by Maryland, Pennsylvania, New York, Virginia, and South Carolina; these laws were improved in the course of the eighteenth century, and were imitated by other colonies. Usually the conditions of naturalization were quite liberal, and in some cases, as in South Carolina, actually offered the immigrant tax exemption for a period of years in order to induce him to become a citizen of that colony. As the laws of any colony ap-

plied only within its own boundaries, an immigrant thus naturalized was a citizen only of that particular province. Parliament
took steps to end this anomaly in 1740, when it passed the naturalization law of that year. This law provided that foreign-born residents who had lived in any of the colonies for seven years might
become British citizens upon taking the necessary oaths and par-
taking of the sacrament (except by Quakers and Jews) in some
Protestant church. This law was limited to the colonies, however,
and citizens naturalized under this law did not have full citizenship rights in England. Thus was created a sort of dual citizenship
in the empire—of one sort for Britain itself and another and inferior sort for the colonies. The children of such naturalized citizens, however, had the same rights and privileges of native-born
British subjects.

"THE OLD WEST"

By the middle of the eighteenth century the rapid increase in
the population of the continental colonies had pushed the frontiers
of settlement to a line running, roughly, along the crest of the
Allegheny divide from the Penobscot River in Maine to the Altamaha River in Georgia. But it had also created a new phenomenon, the "west," as distinguished from the older, more settled
communities along the seaboard. Roughly defined, the "west" consisted of the band of frontier settlements lying just east of the
divide and along the Appalachian Valley. But its greatest significance lay not in its geographic definition but rather in the fact
that, as a society, it showed certain characteristics of its own which
distinguished it from the seaboard society.

In the first place, it was of a very mixed population, largely
foreign in makeup; and in the mixture the English, German, and
Scotch-Irish strains predominated. But in addition to this it was
in general made up of pioneering small farmers, who literally
carved their small farms out of the wilderness with their own
hands. In their religion they were for the most part Presbyterians,
German Pietists, Quakers or Baptists, all with "a high emotional
voltage," as distinguished from the more sedate and aristocratic
Anglicanism or Congregationalism or Quakerism of the older settlements. Their lives were rough; their standard of living was low,
and their existence was constantly overshadowed by the danger
of enemies, animal or human, in the forest. All had fled from
Europe to escape economic, political or religious distress, and
their feeling toward Europe was generally one of indifference and

relief, if not of downright hatred. Many of them had borrowed tools, livestock, capital, or all of them, from the merchants of the seaboard towns, and many owed money for their lands to absentee landlords living in the settlements. When they marketed their

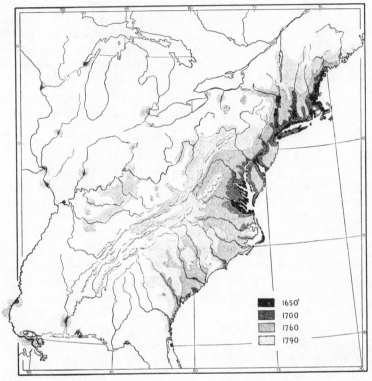

MAP 15. Expansion of Population

wheat or their cattle—when they had any to market—they had to accept the merchant's price for their goods and pay him his price for the tools or gunpowder or other necessaries they purchased from him. They constituted a debtor community, many of them standing in a relationship to the merchants and landlords of the seaboard that was not unlike the relationship of the planters of Virginia to the merchants of London, and their suspicion and distrust of the merchant was not liable to be any less strong. Further, their feeling of distrust was increased and intensified by the control which these very merchants and landlords exercised over the colonial legislatures to prevent redistributions of representation that would give the frontiersmen a stronger voice in government or to prevent the organization of courts in the frontier counties to provide for the administration of justice. The "frontier" of the "old west" was a new society, or at least a new section, distinct from and suspicious of the "east." Its interests were merged with those of the east during the Revolution; but the divergence of interest and thoughts as between east and west that thus appeared in the eighteenth century became, nevertheless, one of the most persistent themes in American history.

AMERICA, THE MELTING POT

Enough has now been said to show to what an extent the British Colonies in America, but particularly those on the continent, became, in the eighteenth century, a refuge for the distressed and oppressed of Europe. Thousands upon thousands of non-English Europeans came to America in the course of the century, and the inevitable result was that into the cultural crucible of America, in which the chief ingredient was the English heritage of the seventeenth century, were thrown the new, imported cultures of Scottish, German, French, Irish and Jewish-Latin homelands. That these importations should have had an influence upon the economy, the politics, the religion, the thought, the art, and the language of the colonies was inevitable; the curious thing is that their effects were relatively as slight as they were.

America had already become the melting pot. On the eve of the Revolution Hector St. John Crèvecœur, noting this amazing and encouraging phenomenon, described "the American" in the following terms:

What then is the American, this new man? He is either an European, or the descendant of an European, hence that strange mixture of blood, which you will find in no other country. . . . *He* is an American, who, leaving behind him all his ancient prejudices and manners, receives new ones from the new mode of life he has embraced, the new government he obeys, and the new rank he holds. . . . Here individuals of all nations are melted into a new race of men, whose labors and posterity will one day cause great changes in the world. . . . The American is a new man, who acts upon new principles; he must therefore entertain new ideas, and form new opinions. From involuntary idleness, servile dependence, penury, and useless labor, he has passed to toils of a very different nature, rewarded by ample subsistence. This is an American.

RECOMMENDED BOOKS FOR FURTHER READING

CONTEMPORARY NARRATIVES

John Bartram, *Observations on the Inhabitants, Climate, Soil, Rivers . . . and Other Matters.*

Andrew Burnaby, *Travels through the Middle Settlements in North America, in the Years 1759 and 1760.*

Michel G. St. John de Crevècœur, *Letters from an American Farmer.*

Christoph von Graffenried, *Christoph von Graffenried's Account of the Founding of New Bern,* edited by Vincent H. Todd.

Albert B. Hart, ed., *American History Told by Contemporaries,* II, Chapter 16.

Pehr Kalm, *Travels into North America.*

Newton D. Mereness, ed., *Travels in the American Colonies.*

Gottlieb Mittelberger, *Gottlieb Mittelberger's Journey to Pennsylvania in the Year 1750.*

Janet Schaw, *Journal of a Lady of Quality,* edited by Evangeline W. and Charles M. Andrews.

William Smith, *A Brief State of the Province of Pennsylvania.*

MODERN ACCOUNTS

Charles M. Andrews, "Immigration and Population of the South to 1783," *The South in the Building of the Nation,* Volume V.

Charles W. Baird, *History of the Huguenot Emigration to America.*

Lucy F. Bittinger, *The Germans in Colonial Times.*

Beverley W. Bond, *The Quit-Rent System in the American Colonies.*

Allen H. Carpenter, "Naturalization in England and The American Colonies," *American Historical Review,* IX, 288-303.

Edward Channing, *A History of the United States,* II, Chapter 14.

Frank R. Diffenderffer, *The German Immigration into Pennsylvania.*

Albert B. Faust, *The German Element in the United States.*

Albert B. Faust, "Swiss Emigration to the American Colonies in the Eighteenth Century," *American Historical Review,* XXII, 98-132.

Henry J. Ford, *The Scotch-Irish in America.*

Lawrence H. Gipson, *The British Empire before the American Revolution,* III, Chapter 7.

Maude Glasgow, *The Scotch-Irish in Northern Ireland and in the American Colonies.*

Evarts B. Greene and Virginia D. Harrington, *American Population before the Federal Census of 1790.*

Evarts B. Greene, *Provincial America, 1690-1740,* Chapter 14.

Charles H. Hanna, *The Scotch-Irish.*

Marcus L. Hansen, *The Atlantic Migration, 1607-1860.*

Marcus L. Hansen, *The Immigrant in American History.*

Cheesman A. Herrick, *White Servitude in Pennsylvania.*

Arthur H. Hirsch, *The Huguenots of Colonial South Carolina.*

Marcus W. Jernegan, *Laboring and Dependent Classes in Colonial America.*

Walter A. Knittle, *Early Eighteenth Century Palatine Emigration.*

Levi O. Kuhns, *The German and' Swiss Settlements of Colonial Pennsylvania.*

Herbert L. Osgood, *The American Colonies in the Eighteenth Century,* II, Part II, Chapter 6.

Emberson E. Proper, *Colonial Immigration Laws.*

Frederick J. Turner, *The Frontier in American History,* Chapters 1-3.

Carl F. Wittke, *We Who Built America,* Chapters 1-6.

30

British America in International Relations, 1713-63

THE Peace of Utrecht left the colonies of the European powers in America in a condition of unstable peace. England had participated in the War of the Spanish Succession largely to prevent the further colonial and commercial expansion of France in the new world, and the peace had been a monument to the achievement of this objective. For not only did it recognize England's unquestioned title to certain disputed territories in America, but it also gave England a key to the commerce of Spanish America and a guarantee that no Spanish territory in the new world would ever be joined to the colonies of France. The general principle written into the peace was thus the principle of the balance of power, in America as well as in Europe, and by the Anglo-Spanish Treaty of Utrecht England was made guarantor of the balance in the new world. Yet the diplomatic history of the colonies during the half century following the peace is not so much the story of the maintenance of the American balance of power as of the expansion of the British colonies and British commerce to such a degree as to upset the balance, and of the efforts of the two other great colonial powers, France and Spain, to preserve it.

THE EXPANSION OF THE BRITISH COLONIES

The expansion of the British empire in America took three forms. In the first place, the British continued to seize and occupy territory claimed by other nations and to extend, by their own arbitrary action, the territorial holdings recognized as British by the Peace of Utrecht. In the second place, British commerce, both that of England and that of the colonies, increased at a surprising rate, and penetrated even the closed colonial possessions of both France and Spain, to say nothing of Brazil and the remaining Dutch colonies of Surinam, Curaçao and St. Eustatius; finally, the phenomenal growth of the population of the British colonies caused them to push against the frontiers of the thinly populated colonies of France and Spain.

The territorial settlement at Utrecht had left England in possession of Hudson Bay, Newfoundland, Acadia "with its old boundaries," the old continental colonies from Maine to South Carolina, Bermuda, the Bahamas, Jamaica, the Leeward Islands, and Barbados. But there was one significant omission from the territorial Treaty of Utrecht between England and France: There was no clear statement of the boundary line between the colonies of the two crowns in North America. Similarly, no boundary was specified in the Anglo-Spanish treaty as existing between the English and Spanish colonies; it was merely provided that England and Spain recognized each other's possessions as they had existed in the time of Charles II and as recognized by the Treaty of Madrid (1670). In the Anglo-French treaty there was, however, a provision that a joint Anglo-French commission should be appointed to determine the boundaries between Hudson Bay and Canada, and to decide which of the Indians of the interior—other than the Iroquois, who were recognized as being under British sovereignty—should be regarded as "friends" of France and which "friends" of England. France, in the balance of power thus vaguely defined, retained Canada, Louisiana and the islands of Martinique and Guadeloupe in the West Indies, together with half of the island of Santo Domingo, of which Spain still retained the other half. Spain's colonial empire was still intact, including Florida, Cuba, Puerto Rico, and half of Santo Domingo, and all the mainland of the continent from Mexico to Cape Horn, with the exception of Portuguese Brazil and Surinam (Guiana). The omission of any effort to fix the boundaries between these vast empires except that of Hudson Bay was probably not due to any intention on the part of the makers of the treaties, but, rather, simply to the vagueness of geographic knowledge of the continent. Nor, indeed, did there seem to be any pressing need for fixing the boundaries between the other French and British colonies; for practically no Englishmen had crossed the Appalachian divide, up to 1713. There were still vast areas of unbroken wilderness left to the English east of the mountains; and it seems probable that most Englishmen, if they ever thought of it at all, looked upon the Allegheny Mountains, "far to the westward," as the natural and ultimate boundary of British expansion. The old "sea-to-sea" charters had been issued in ignorance; even when the provision was repeated in the charter of Georgia twenty years after Utrecht, it could have had no real significance in the minds of the authors of that charter.

Immediately after the peace both the French and the British

began to clarify their thinking with regard to the great interior of the continent. Governor Spotswood of Virginia called attention to the possibilities of westward expansion in the famous cavalcade of the "Knights of the Golden Horseshoe" to the Shenandoah in 1716, and in 1721 the Board of Trade strongly recommended to the Crown the fortification of the passes over the mountains as the best means of defending the colonies from "the insults of the French." But, said the Board,

. . . although these Mountains may serve at present for a very good frontier, we should not propose them for the boundary of your Majesty's Empire in America. On the contrary, it were to be wished, that the British Settlements might be extended beyond them, & some small forts erected on the great Lakes, in proper places, by permission of the Indian proprietors [the Iroquois]; & we would particularly recommend the building of a fort on the Lake Erie, as hath been proposed by Colonel Spotswood . . . whereby the french communications from Quebec to the River Mississippi, might be interrupted, a new trade opened with some of the Indian nations, and more of the natives engaged in your Majesty's interest. . . .

Such was the imperialistic policy of the Board of Trade; and this policy was in general the one followed by the British, toward both French and Spanish territories in the period between the Peace of Utrecht and the Seven Years War (1756). Examples of the policy are numerous: the most striking are the building of Fort Oswego on Lake Ontario, in lands claimed by France, in 1726; the establishment of Georgia in lands claimed by Spain, in 1733; and the attempted seizure of the strategic island of St. Lucia in the West Indies from the French in 1722.

The French, on their side, realized the tendencies of British expansion, and sought to anticipate it by a defensive line of forts. They had rebuilt Fort Niagara in 1725 and had established Fort Toulouse on the Alabama River facing South Carolina in 1714. To meet the expansion of population in the Hudson and Connecticut valleys they fortified Crown Point on Lake Champlain in 1731, while in the West Indies they sought to secure St. Lucia and the adjacent islands from British seizure by both fortifying them and quietly filling them with French settlers. Negotiations, meanwhile, were carried on between French and British governors from Canada to Barbados, each striving to establish the claims of his royal master to the greatest possible extent of territory, while more or less consciously preparing for the day when the issues must be settled by war. Spain, weakened by the stupidities and the dynastic preoccupations of her Bourbon monarchs, could do no more than protest the settlement of Georgia and gradually draw near to France for united action in the face of the British threat.

In the realm of commerce, the British commercial colonies of North America developed a clandestine trade with the French West Indies which rapidly came to be of prime economic importance both to themselves and to the French islands, since it provided them with quantities of sugar and molasses at lower prices than the English sugar islands could afford to charge, and supplied the French planters with foodstuffs, lumber, livestock, and manufactured goods more cheaply and more efficiently than the merchants of France could do it. Of course this commerce ran counter to France's mercantilist monopoly of her colonial markets, and the merchants of France repeatedly protested; but the diplomatic protests to England on the subject were hardly more than gestures of appeasement for the French merchants, since both governments realized the importance of this trade to both their empires.

British commerce with the Spanish colonies, however, was not such a simple matter. Under the terms of the Assiento Treaty (1715) English merchants were given a monopoly of the slave trade in the Spanish colonies, and were also given the privilege of sending one ship each year to the Fair at Porto Bello for the purposes of general trade. But the South Sea Company, to whom this monopoly was given, abused its privileges scandalously and apparently indulged in wholesale smuggling into the Spanish colonies under cover of their legitimate trade. But to make matters worse the Yankee traders found it profitable to violate Spain's mercantilist monopoly of colonial trade by small-scale smuggling ventures of their own, with the result that the trade of Spain with her colonies dwindled perceptibly in the second and third decades following Utrecht. It was to correct this situation that Spain instructed its coast-guard vessels to seize and search British and other vessels in the waters of the Gulf of Mexico and the Caribbean, and to confiscate them if they contained evidence of a contraband trade. The Spanish coast guards did not limit themselves to smugglers, however, and there were numerous seizures of innocent colonial and English ships that were little short of piracy. Britain thus found itself in the position of defending the freedom of the seas, a position that the imperialists in Parliament found useful in preparing an aggressive war against Spain.

In general, then, by reason of British territorial and commercial expansion, France and Spain were gradually drawn together in a common defense of the balance of colonial power established at

Utrecht. This process was retarded by their antagonistic interests on the continent of Europe, but it bore tangible fruit in the first Family Compact (1733), in which they agreed, in addition to European matters, to act jointly in defense of their colonial empires, and to cooperate to reduce the exaggerated commercial power of England.

Peaceful efforts had been made, meanwhile, to settle the colonial disputes between France and Spain on the one side and England on the other. The commission charged with settling the Anglo-French boundary of Hudson Bay had actually convened in Paris in 1719, and to its labors was added a dispute over the extent of Acadia. At about the same time, after England had protested the grant of the island of St. Lucia to the Marshal d'Estrées, the two countries agreed to evacuate St. Lucia until its ownership could be determined by a joint commission, and this agreement was renewed in 1730. Similarly, by the Treaty of Seville (1729), by which Spain agreed to settle her colonial disputes with England in return for permission to garrison the duchies of Parma and Modena, in Italy, with Spanish troops, England and Spain agreed to set up a joint commission to settle the troublesome questions of the freedom of the seas in America and of boundaries between English and Spanish colonies there. A final effort at peaceful settlement of the Anglo-Spanish disputes was made in the convention of the Pardo (1739), which repeated the provisions of the Treaty of Seville. But by that time the imperialists had gotten control of the British Parliament; the convention of the Pardo was rejected, and England went to war with Spain for the extension of her American empire.

This imperialistic war, called the War of Jenkins' Ear (in honor of Captain Robert Jenkins, who lost his ear in a fracas with Spanish guardacostas), began with an ambitious expedition against Cartagena, one of the richest prizes in Spanish America, in which there were numerous volunteers and soldiers of fortune from the British continental colonies as well as from the West Indies. But the expedition bogged down before Cartagena, and the attention of both belligerents was diverted to Europe by the outbreak of the War of the Austrian Succession.

France had remained neutral in the Anglo-Spanish conflict in the colonies, although favoring the Spanish cause. But now, in the European war, France and Spain were drawn more closely together, and by the Second Family Compact (1743) they again undertook a mutual guarantee of their respective territories in

America and Europe, and France specifically undertook to aid Spain in the destruction of Georgia and in the termination of the much-abused Assiento contract, which the king of Spain promised henceforth to award only to Spaniards. The entry of France into the war against England precipitated in America the so-called King George's War, which lasted until 1748. France immediately occupied strategic St. Lucia, and the English colonies, cooperating with the British fleet, sent a successful expedition against the fortress of Louisbourg, on Cape Breton Island, in 1745. But the war in Europe was a stalemate, and by the Peace of Aix-la-Chapelle all colonial conquests were to be restored. Cape Breton was returned to France to the great chagrin of the English colonists, but France continued to occupy St. Lucia on the ground that it had always been a French island, anyway. After the peace, new negotiations were set afoot to settle the old quarrels; but the eight years following Aix-la-Chapelle were hardly more than an interlude of uncertain peace in a new era of inter-imperial warfare.

AN INTERLUDE OF TROUBLED PEACE

The War of Jenkins' Ear and King George's War might well be called interludes of European war which interrupted the race of imperial expansion in America. For as soon as the war was over the protagonists again began to race into positions to block each other's colonial expansion while the diplomats in Europe continued their struggle for diplomatic advantages with which to support their respective players in the game of colonial expansion.

As soon as the peace was made, England sought to separate France and Spain by concessions to the latter with regard to the still unexpired Assiento. This she succeeded in doing by surrendering, by the Treaty of Madrid (1750), the remaining portion of the Assiento in return for a cash payment to the South Sea Company of £100,000 sterling—probably a profitable bargain for both sides. Georgia seems to have been forgotten. At the same time France and England made another effort to settle by joint commission their disputes over St. Lucia, Acadia and the island of Tobago. But while the commissioners were losing time over inconsequential details, both sides resumed the race for empire in the depths of the American wilderness.

The British made several expansive moves all at once. The Hudson's Bay Company undertook an extension of its trading area in the distant northwestern plains of North America, thought by the

French to be a part of Canada; the British government decided to build a military colony in Nova Scotia, at Halifax, to counter-balance the French fortress of Louisbourg; and they sought to occupy St. Lucia and the other "neutral islands" in the West Indies —only to find themselves forestalled by the French. Clearly, to the French mind, the English were already on the march, and the Marquis de la Galissonière, Governor of Canada, took steps to block British expansion in Acadia (Nova Scotia) by building new forts at the mouth of the St. John River and on the isthmus. At the same time new forts were begun inland, at Ft. Rouillé (Toronto) on the north side of Lake Ontario, and at Presqu'ile (Erie) on the south side of Lake Erie, while Crown Point and Ticonderoga on Lake Champlain were strengthened.

But the most famous and dramatic episode in this race for em-pire was caused by the third great element in British expansive-ness, the westward expansion of the old continental colonies. This movement found expression in the formation of great speculative land companies, the most famous of which was the Ohio Company of Virginia. Hearing of British penetration of the upper Ohio Valley from Pennsylvania and Virginia, the governor of Canada had sent Céloron de Blainville down "The Beautiful River," as they called it, to reassert the sovereignty of the king of France over that area, to impress the Indians, and to warn the British traders and settlers to get out and stay out. Blainville buried leaden plates at strategic points, proclaiming French sovereignty. He also ha-rangued the Indians, but he failed to impress them. And the British traders followed him through the Indian country to offset any good for France that he might have done. But the French took more effective action by the building of forts LeBoeuf and Venango on the upper Allegheny, and made plans to build another at the junction of the Allegheny and Monongahela rivers.

The French action in Acadia had nearly precipitated war at the isthmus in 1750, but Governor Edward Cornwallis had been restrained by his government in the hope that the joint commis-sion meeting in Paris might be successful in settling all the Amer-ican disputes. Similarly, friction in the West Indies over St. Lucia and the other "neutral islands" was prevented from causing war. Even the seizure of British traders in the Ohio Valley was smoothed over while Lieutenant-Governor Robert Dinwiddie of Virginia was sending young George Washington to Fort LeBoeuf to summon the French to retire from British soil. Failing in this, Dinwiddie sent William Trent to the forks of the Ohio to build a fort, but he was interrupted by the French expedition sent down the river for the same purpose, and forced to retire. George Washington, sent to support Trent, had a skirmish at Great Meadows early in July, 1754, and was forced himself to retire to Virginia.

Even now, however, England and France seem to have hoped to settle their colonial differences amicably, and while France was preparing a strong expedition to reinforce Canada and England was preparing the Braddock expedition to support Virginia's claim to the Ohio, the American disputes were practically taken out of the hands of the dawdling joint commission, and a genuine last-minute effort was made to preserve the peace. This direct negotiation turned upon Acadia and the Ohio Valley, and it reached its climax in a British offer to accept the Allegheny Mountains as the permanent boundary between the British colonies and the French in the interior if the French would grant England enough of their claim to a greater Nova Scotia to give them a broad band of land along the Bay of Fundy that would constitute a continuous land connection between Nova Scotia and New England. But the French, fearful of British control of the strategic St. John River, which was Canada's only open-water outlet to the sea in wintertime, refused the offer! When the negotiations then appeared to be certain of failure Braddock was ordered to depart, and the French fleet put out for Canada. The French expedition was intercepted off Newfoundland by the British fleet under Admiral Edward Boscawen and two vessels, the *Alcide* and the *Lys*, loaded with men, provisions, and money, were captured; but Braddock was disastrously defeated in the forests of western Pennsylvania.

Diplomacy had failed, and arms had been resorted to. The war that followed, known as the French and Indian War in America and as the Seven Years War in Europe, was the climax of a long rivalry between France and England in North America and the West Indies. But it also involved the interests of Spain, and, once again, Spain was drawn to the side of France in defense of the colonial balance of power in the Third Family Compact (1762). But to no avail. England had become too powerful and William Pitt played the game of diplomacy on the continent of Europe all too well. The American balance was successfully upset, to be only partially restored by the separation of the thirteen continental colonies from the British empire and their formation into the first free and independent American nation in 1783. But that is material for a later story.

THE ORGANIZATION OF COLONIAL DEFENSE

The approach of war led to military preparations in both France and England, and the Braddock expedition against Fort Duquesne in the summer of 1755 was only one of a number of attempts made by the British to take possession of lands which they believed to be theirs, and by the French to defend what they considered to be their land along the Bay of Fundy and in the valley of the Ohio. While the military preparations on both sides went on apace, the British colonial officials also made an effort to co-ordinate the defenses and the military operations to be carried on by the continental colonies. It was with this aim in view that representatives of seven of the colonies met at Albany in the summer of 1754 to consider ways and means, first, of unifying the colonies for military efforts, and, second, to win the support or at least the neutrality of the Indians in the expected war.

The Albany Conference turned its attention first to a consideration of Indian affairs. The Iroquois chiefs protested their friendship for the English but complained that their British friends had neglected them and had left them to fight the French alone. They said, moreover, that the French had been very attentive to their needs and had done everything possible to promote good feeling and a prosperous commerce between them. Now, the "Virginians," said the Iroquois chiefs, were moving into the Indian lands and were beginning to fight the French over the possession of these lands without consideration for the needs and desires of the Indians who were their rightful owners. The feelings of the Indians were soothed, but their fears were not satisfied. It was agreed, however, that there should be one general plan for treatment of the Indians, which would be supported at the general expense of all the colonies. The Indians had requested that William Johnson be named British agent to conduct affairs between themselves and their English neighbors, and this request was granted in 1755. At the same time, Edmund Atkin was placed in charge of Indian affairs in the southern department—that is to say, the lands lying south of the Ohio.

A committee had been appointed to consider the problem of inter-colonial union, and this committee drew up a proposal, drafted by Benjamin Franklin, for inter-colonial organization which has come to be known as the Albany Plan of union. This plan proposed that "humble application be made for an Act of the Parliament of Great Britain, by virtue of which, one General Government may be formed in America, including all the said Colonies, within, and under which Government each Colony may retain its present constitution, except in the particulars wherein a change may be directed by the said Act, as hereafter follows." The plan proposed that the colonial union should have a president-general to be appointed and supported by the Crown, and a grand council to be composed of representatives chosen by the assemblies of the various colonies. It was proposed that the president-general be given the power to conduct all Indian relations, "with the advice of the general council," and to make peace or declare war. The general council, on its part, would make laws regulating the Indian trade, make all purchases of lands from the Indians, and authorize and regulate all new settlements in the new lands to the west. The grand council would be empowered to make and lay taxes on the provinces and to appoint a general treasurer responsible to itself. Laws made by the general council would be submitted to the king for approval. Military commissions were to be issued by the president-general with the approval of the general council.

This remarkable proposal is one of the most significant documents in American history, for it is the first really important recognition of the need for a union of all the colonies on the continent. The sort of government it proposed would have been a sort of glorified royal colony with a one-chamber legislature and a royally appointed governor. It would have perpetuated the system of checks and balances between the royal prerogative as represented by the governor and the popular or local interest in government represented by the representative general council, and the separation of powers between the two. On the other hand, it gave tacit recognition to the increasing importance of the legislature in colonial political affairs and by providing for the appointment of a treasurer by the general council who would be responsible to it, the Albany Plan seems to reflect the tendency of colonial legislatures toward assumption of control of certain administrative offices. The plan was most important, perhaps, as a recognition of the fact that there were certain inter-colonial problems for the administration of which there was no constitutional provision in the British empire. Such problems were those presented by relations with the Indians who faced the westward march of British colonization all along the line, the problem of abuses in the conduct of Indian trade, which overlapped and outreached colonial boundaries, and the major problem presented by the need for a common defense against the common French enemy.

As might have been expected, the Albany Plan of union, unanimously adopted by the congress, was unanimously rejected by the colonies to which it was submitted. The colonies were not yet ready to surrender any part of their independence from each other in the name of union, although all realized the need for union. Furthermore, they were not willing to delegate to England the amount of control of colonial affairs that the adoption of the plan would have involved. Some of the colonies, indeed, already had become accustomed to royal control, but Connecticut and Rhode Island, particularly, were not for a moment willing to submit themselves to such a large measure of royal review and administration.

On the other hand, while the colonies rejected the plan because it involved a surrender of a certain part of their autonomy and seemed to give England an increasing amount of control over them, the British government ignored it. The Board of Trade, indeed, had recommended another plan, which would have established simply a military union which proposed that there be established a general-in-chief for the colonies who would be aided by Indian agents in the northern and in the southern colonies. Even this plan failed of execution, and the whole affair had little or no practical effect. It would be difficult to exaggerate its significance, however, as a recognition of the need for a more centralized plan of colonial administration for problems that overlapped colonial boundaries.

THE SEVEN YEARS WAR IN AMERICA

The war that broke out between England and France in 1754 began, so far as those two countries were concerned, as a war for empire. It had its origin in colonial rivalry and it was fought for the determination of a colonial problem. In this case at least, American and imperial interests led the two major European powers into a war which for them had only secondary European causes. Although the war was not formally declared until 1756, it should be considered as having begun with the battle of Fort Necessity in the summer of 1754. To avenge the defeat of Washington and to drive the French out of the Ohio Valley, General Braddock was sent to Virginia and over the passes toward Fort Duquesne in the summer of 1755. Braddock was a brave man and, judged by European standards, a good general; but he was not familiar with the methods of warfare in the American forest and he had little respect for the fighting qualities of the Americans. The expedition against Fort Duquesne was attacked in the forest beyond the headwaters of the Potomac on July 9 by the French and their Indian allies, who ambushed Braddock's forces and mowed down his soldiers from behind rocks and trees according to the approved frontier fashion. The general refused to modify his tactics, and as a result his forces were defeated and he himself mortally wounded. For the time being at least, the French remained in complete possession of Fort Duquesne and the valley of the Ohio.

During this same year, 1755, a second expedition was led against Fort Niagara by Governor Shirley of Massachusetts, but this expedition failed as ignominiously as had that of Braddock. In Acadia, however, the British were more successful, for they succeeded in seizing Fort Beauséjour, built by the French shortly after the Peace of Aix-la-Chapelle at the head of the Bay of Fundy. This fort had been established partly with a desire to retain the loyalty of the French Acadians to the French cause. These people had never really acquiesced in the British rule and ever since the Peace of Utrecht had constituted a military liability to the British colony of Nova Scotia. Because they seemed to constitute a menace to the safety of the colony, Governor Lawrence decided to deport them, and in the fall of 1755 some seven thousand Acadians were shipped away, many to the northern colonies, some to Georgia, others to South Carolina, and still others elsewhere in the more southerly colonies. Some escaped and went to Canada or Louisiana, where their descendants remain to this day.

Still another British expedition was sent against the French at Crown Point during this year, under the command of Sir William Johnson. The expedition was successfully foiled by the French, but the English constructed Fort Edward and Fort William Henry at the southern end of Lake George to block any attempt of the French to take the aggressive across the pass leading from Lake George to the Hudson River.

All these military operations took place before the actual declaration of war, which did not occur until the French attacked the island of Minorca in the Mediterranean. As a matter of fact, the two principal contestants were not ready to declare war until the spring of the year, for England, in search of allies on the European continent, had succeeded in making an alliance with Frederick II of Prussia. But Frederick had hitherto been the ally of France and Frederick's diplomatic *volte face* drove France into the arms of her erstwhile enemy Austria. The British alliance was consummated in January, 1756, and the French alliance with Austria was created in the Treaty of Versailles early in May. France succeeded in preventing a British declaration of war by encouraging Frederick to offer his mediation early in the spring, but as soon as the Austrian alliance was completed, all thought of diplomatic negotiation was dropped, and England declared war more or less according to the French plan.

The year 1756 was one of British losses. Frederick II was defeated in Germany by a coalition of French, Austrian, and Russian armies. The English squadron of Admiral Byng was outmaneuvered if not actually defeated in the Mediterranean, and the French succeeded in capturing Minorca as a result. An English attack on Louisbourg failed, and the Sieur de Montcalm, who took over command of the French forces in Canada, succeeded in capturing Fort Oswego on Lake Ontario and Fort William Henry at the southern end of Lake George.

The year 1757, however, marked the turning point in the war. The fortunes of war probably had something to do with this result, and the superior resources of England certainly did, but the change was also due in very large part to the force and personality of one man, William Pitt, who became Secretary of State in charge of the war in the fall of that year. Pitt was a man of energy, enthusiasm, extraordinary ability, and supreme self-confidence. He is said to have remarked to one of his friends, "I know that I can save England, and that nobody else can." His spirit, his energy, and his ability were infused into the British forces in America, in India, in Europe, and upon the high seas. He recalled inefficient and superannuated generals and appointed young, energetic men to take their places. He avoided sending forces to the continent of Europe but regularly paid Frederick II a large subsidy to support his ally on the continent while he directed English forces to the war on the sea and in the colonies. The chief point of Pitt's strategy, however, was America. General John Campbell, Earl of Loudoun, was recalled and General Abercrombie was sent out to relieve him. Abercrombie was assisted by two younger officers, Lord Jeffrey Amherst and James Wolfe, both of them men of great ability. Pitt directed the seizure of Louisbourg and appealed to the colonies for help in the expedition. To win colonial support he offered a greater amount of recognition for the colonial officers, compensation for expenses that might be incurred by the colonies, and the active aid of the British navy, with adequate supplies of arms and ammunition. In the summer of 1758 Wolfe, Amherst, and Boscawen undertook the siege of Louisbourg, and with the aid of about 500 colonial soldiers and with about 9,000 English soldiers and 40 warships they laid siege to the fortress early in June. After a series of heroic actions on both sides, the city fell to the English besiegers on the 28th of July, 1758. The fall of Louisbourg not only removed the menace of this strong point toward the British colonies, but gave the English forces a vantage point for destroying French shipping passing in and out of the Gulf of St. Lawrence.

During the same summer, Brigadier-General John Forbes took an expedition of English soldiers, colonials, and Indians against the French Fort Duquesne. Forbes and his adjutant, Colonel Bouquet, arrived before the fort in November, only to find it abandoned by the French. A third expedition against Fort Ticonderoga on Lake Champlain resulted in failure, but a fourth, against Fort Frontenac, succeeded in destroying that post and opening the way down the St. Lawrence to the British.

THE PASSING OF NEW FRANCE

The next year, 1759, is called "the wonderful year" in British history because it was in that year that the war was really won. Pitt's plan of campaign for that year involved four major actions. In Europe, he continued the subsidy to Frederick II and encouraged his Prussian ally in every way. In faraway India, the campaigns of the able Clive were continued. On the sea, the British blockade of the French coast was made so effective that French ships were prevented from reaching the French colonies in any considerable numbers, so that the colonies were left without adequate reinforcements and supplies and thus became relatively easy prey to the British armies. In America it was Pitt's plan to conquer Canada by a double expedition. Wolfe was to attack Quebec by sea and Amherst was to march against Montreal by way of Ticonderoga and Lake Champlain. The English operations in India were successful and culminated in the siege of Pondicherry, which lasted until January, 1761. The European campaign was successful and culminated in the great battle of Minden, where on the first of August a Hanoverian army under the command of Frederick of Brunswick met a great French army and almost totally destroyed it. On the sea, the British Navy succeeded in almost completely preventing French aid from reaching America. Both the Atlantic and the Mediterranean coasts of France were blockaded. One French fleet that came out of Toulon was met by Admiral Boscawen and chased into Lagos Bay in August. Another, which sailed out of Brest in an effort to get to America, was met by an English fleet under Edward Lord Hawke and was partially destroyed. Its remnants took refuge in Quiberon Bay. This occurred late in November. In America, meanwhile, General Amherst marched up the Hudson River and over the divide to Lake Champlain, where he found Ticonderoga and Crown Point abandoned by the French. He moved on down the lake and found the French established on the Ile aux Noix, where his progress was delayed by the fact that he was compelled to stop and build boats. Winter caught him before he could go farther, however, and he went into winter quarters near the outlet of the lake. Meanwhile, General Amherst had sent an expedition under Colonel John Prideaux and Colonel William Johnson against the fort of Niagara, which was still in the hands of the French, and this expedition was successful, thus partially cutting off French communication with the west.

In the meantime, General Wolfe had sailed into the St. Lawrence River and up that river to Quebec. All his efforts to draw Montcalm out of the citadel failed, however, and Montcalm, believing his position almost impregnable, merely waited for the winter, which he knew would force the English out of the river. Wolfe tried for months to find a landing which would lead him up the precipitous cliffs to the plains above the city. Finally, in desperation, early in September he decided to risk all to ascend one of the ravines leading up to the plains, and early on the morning of September 13, 1759, he landed his army, captured the outpost at the top, and succeeded in drawing up his forces in battle array before the French general got word that he was there. Montcalm, when he found the British drawn up before the city on the Plains of Abraham, at last went out to the attack, and the battle that followed is one of the most significant—perhaps the one most significant—in the history of North America. Time after time the French attacked, only to meet the withering volleys of musketry delivered by some of the best troops of Europe. As a matter of fact, from a military point of view this was a European rather than an American battle, for it was fought upon an open plain by two European-trained armies using European tactics and ordnance. The French finally took panic and fled within the walls, whereupon the British settled down to a regular siege. Both Montcalm and Wolfe were mortally wounded, and the Marquis de Vaudreuil, now in command of the French, escaped from the city and made his way to Montreal. Quebec surrendered to the British on the 18th of September, whereupon the British army went into winter quarters there, fully realizing that it was now hardly more than a matter of time before Montreal, the last French stronghold in Canada, must fall. In the next year, 1760, three British columns converged upon Montreal. General Amherst came down the river from Lake Ontario, General Haviland led the British army that had wintered on Lake Champlain down the Richelieu River, and General James Murray moved up the river from Quebec. With three armies thus concentrated on the city, Governor Vaudreuil surrendered Montreal to the British on September 8, 1760, almost exactly a year after the fall of Quebec. With the fall of Montreal, the British found themselves in complete and practically uncontested possession of all of French Canada.

Meanwhile, in the Caribbean, the English had captured the French islands of Guadeloupe and Dominique. France was exhausted by her efforts in Europe, and the colonies were incapable of defending themselves because of the almost complete British domination of the sea. France was prepared to make peace, but Pitt's obstinacy drove that country into a desperate bid for Spanish aid, which brought Spain into the war on the side of France and prolonged it for yet another year.

THE PEACE OF PARIS, 1763

The Duke of Choiseul, chief minister to the king of France, was faced by a delicate situation by the end of 1760. France was almost exhausted financially because of its great efforts in the conduct of the war. It had lost Canada and some of its islands in the West Indies, and was in a fair way to losing what remained of its possessions in India. The impossibility of getting aid to the colonies made it almost certain that France would not be able to recover any of its colonial losses. At the same time the war in Germany, while not altogether unfavorable to French arms, had proved to be a severe drain upon French military and financial resources. France might make peace, but it was bound by the Treaty of Versailles to its ally Austria, and Maria Theresa, the empress queen, would listen to no proposal for peace until her detested enemy Frederick II of Prussia should be completely and forever humbled. Choiseul did not dare to jeopardize the Austrian friendship for France by making a separate peace with England, and it was only with extreme difficulty that he won the Austrian approval for an effort early in the year 1761.

At the same time he hoped that, should his peace effort fail, he might be able to draw to his support the military and naval resources of Spain, and he sedulously cultivated the friendship of Charles III, who had succeeded to the Castilian throne in 1759. Charles had no love for England, and he was very much influenced by the French argument that the balance of power in America should be maintained at all costs. The Peace of Utrecht had established such a balance of power, according to the French argument, and were Spain to sit idly by and allow the British to destroy the French colonies, England would thereby become so powerful that it could not be long before the voracious British would be knocking at the gates of New Spain and South America. Aside from this, there was no very good reason why Spain should have entered this war except Charles' irritation over the continued procrastination of the British on the question of the illicit logwood settlements on the coasts of Yucatan and the adamant refusal of the British to allow Spanish ships to fish on the Grand Banks of Newfoundland.

Yet Choiseul had his way, and while with one hand he was negotiating with William Pitt for peace, with the other he was negotiating with Charles III for the signing of the so-called Family Compact which must inevitably lead to war. His negotiations with Pitt failed, largely through the stubbornness of William Pitt himself; and with the signing of the Third Family Compact in August, 1761, Spain became committed to war with England. The actual beginning of the Spanish phase of the war was delayed until the treasure fleet came home from America, but England declared war early in January, 1762, and in the fighting that followed British expeditions in quick succession took Cuba, the Philippines, and Florida.

Choiseul's new allies had proved to be a broken reed, and the renewal of the war had led not only to the seizure of valuable Spanish possessions but the conquest by the British of the French island of Martinique and the occupation of the "neutral islands." Choiseul, now thoroughly disgusted, made a final bid for peace; but until the fall of Havana, late in the summer of 1762, he found difficulty in bringing the belligerent and obstinate Charles to a realization that his efforts were futile. Peace negotiations were renewed by the British under the direction of Lord Bute, who had succeeded Pitt as the moving spirit in the British cabinet, at the point where the Pitt negotiation had broken off in the preceding year, and the negotiations were practically completed by the time news of the fall of Havana arrived in Europe to break down the last Spanish resistance to the idea of surrender.

The Treaty of Paris, signed on February 10, 1763, was perhaps the most significant treaty dealing with America that was ever signed in Europe. France gave up Canada to the British, retaining only the small islands of St. Pierre and Miquelon in the Gulf of St. Lawrence, and all the land east of the Mississippi River except the island and city of New Orleans. To recover Cuba, Spain gave up Florida to the British, and accepted the bitter necessity of admitting the British for the first time to a foothold on the shores of the Gulf of Mexico. England retained the islands of Tobago, St. Vincent, Dominica, and Grenada; Martinique, Guadeloupe and St. Lucia were returned to France. St. Lucia was a sort of *quid pro quo* for the eastern half of the Mississippi valley, surrendered by the French to England. The Philippine Islands were returned to Spain, and the French possessions in Africa and India were practically annihilated. In a separate treaty France, partly to compensate Spain for its losses in the war and partly to get rid of a burdensome colony which seemed to offer no prospect of profit, surrendered the western half of Louisiana, together with the island and city of New Orleans, to Spain.

By this settlement France was practically eliminated from America as an important colonial power. By the same token, England was left supreme in North America, Africa, and India. England was now the greatest colonial power in the world, rivalled only by a decadent Spain. British supremacy in the colonial world, indeed, was seriously contested only once again, in the War of the American Revolution, but it was never again effectually overthrown. For America the Treaty of Paris meant that eastern North America, at least, was to be Anglo-Saxon, not French, and the old question as to whether the British were to remain forever hemmed in behind the Allegheny Mountains by a French empire extending through the heart of the continent was answered once and for all in the negative. For the Treaty of Paris removed the French danger that had held the English back and opened the Allegheny passes to the traders, settlers, and land speculators who soon began to flow in an ever-increasing stream into the great interior valleys which had been one of the chief stakes of the war.

In England the treaty was severely criticized. William Pitt criticized it on the ground that England should have taken all the

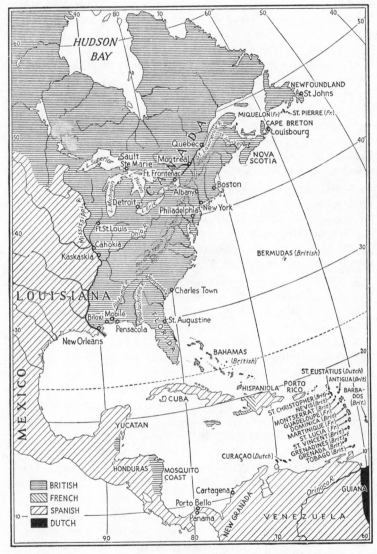

MAP 16. European Possessions in North America After the Peace of Paris (1763)

French colonies. Others believed that the restoration of St. Lucia, Guadeloupe, and Martinique to France was a mistake. Still others criticized the acquisition of Canada on the ground that the removal of the French menace would encourage the American tendency toward independence. On the whole, however, the treaty was well received and was welcomed by the masses as the end of a long and burdensome war.

For England the settlement of Paris meant the acquisition of a great new colonial empire in North America and the West Indies, and it established the British in a position of unchallenged supremacy upon the sea. For France, on the other hand, it meant not only the loss of her colonial empire but at least a temporary financial ruin and a disastrous loss of prestige in the councils of European diplomacy. So great a disaster was it that the country could face with equanimity the risks and the burdens involved in an attempt to recover the old French position of international leadership during the American Revolution. For the colonists in America the settlement of Paris opened vast new areas of western land to exploitation. It removed the French menace from their frontiers, and brought to them a realization of the strength of colonial military effort. For the empire as a whole, the settlement of Paris meant not only the addition of new territories but of new populations as well: the problems of defense of the new empire, of government of the newly acquired areas and peoples, and of inter-colonial and international relationships; and most of all the problem of imperial finance, forced upon imperial statesmen the necessity for a thoroughgoing reorganization of British colonial policy.

The reorganization of British colonial policy, however, coming as it did at the moment when the colonies felt themselves to be self-sufficient economically and politically, and when the French menace had been removed from their borders, was almost certain to precipitate colonial opposition, and even, perhaps, imperial civil war.

RECOMMENDED BOOKS FOR FURTHER READING

CONTEMPORARY NARRATIVES

Cadwallader Colden, *The History of the Five Indian Nations of Canada.*
Cadwallader Colden, *The Letters and Papers of Cadwallader Colden, 1711-1755,* IV, 120 ff., and 34-44.
William Johnson, *The Papers of Sir William Johnson,* edited by James Sullivan and Alexander C. Flick.

Louise P. Kellogg, *The French Régime in Wisconsin and the Northwest.*

Edna Kenton, *The Indians in North America* [Selections from the *Jesuit Relations*].

Edmund B. O'Callaghan, ed., *Documents Relative to the Colonial History of the State of New York*, VI, X.

Charles O. Paullin, ed., *European Treaties bearing on the History of the United States and its Dependencies*, Volume IV: 1716-1815.

Theodore C. Pease, ed., *Anglo-French Boundary Disputes in the West, 1749-1763.*

William Pitt, *Correspondence of William Pitt*, edited by Gertrude S. Kimball.

Peter Wraxall, *An Abridgement of the Indian Affairs Transacted in the Colony of New York from 1678 to . . . 1751*, edited by Charles H. McIlwain.

MODERN ACCOUNTS

Clarence W. Alvord, *The Illinois Country, 1673-1818.*

Hayes Baker-Crothers, *Virginia and the French and Indian War.*

John B. Brebner, *New England's Outpost, Acadia before the Conquest of Canada.*

The Cambridge History of the British Empire, I, Chapters 11-12, 16-19; VI, Chapter 4.

Julian S. Corbett, *England in the Seven Years' War.*

William L. Grant, "Canada versus Guadaloupe," *American Historical Review*, XVII, 735-743.

Hubert Hall, "Chatham's Colonial Policy," *American Historical Review*, V, 659-675.

David J. Hill, *A History of Diplomacy in the International Development of Europe*, Volume III.

George T. Hunt, *The Wars of the Iroquois.*

Harold A. Innis, *The Fur Trade in Canada.*

Louis K. Koontz, *Robert Dinwiddie.*

John C. Long, *Lord Jeffrey Amherst, a Soldier of the King.*

Ralph G. Lounsbury, *The British Fishery at Newfoundland, 1634-1763.*

Lawrence S. Mayo, *Jeffrey Amherst.*

Lewis B. Namier, *England in the Age of the American Revolution.*

Herbert L. Osgood, *The American Colonies in the Eighteenth Century*, III, Part II, Chapter 17: Part III, Chapter 3; IV, Part III (continued) Chapters 14-17.

Richard Pares, *Colonial Blockade and Neutral Rights, 1739-1763.*

Richard Pares, *War and Trade in the West Indies, 1739-1763.*

Stanley M. Pargellis, *Lord Loudoun in North America.*

Francis Parkman, *Montcalm and Wolfe.*

Max Savelle, "The American Balance of Power and European Diplomacy, 1713-1778," *The Era of the American Revolution*, edited by Richard B. Morris, pp. 140-169.

Max Savelle, *The Diplomatic History of the Canadian Boundary, 1749-1763.*

Nancy M. M. Surrey, *The Commerce of Louisiana during the French Régime, 1699-1763.*

Basil Williams, *The Life of William Pitt.*

Basil Williams, *Stanhope, a Study in Eighteenth-Century War and Diplomacy.*

Justin Winsor, *The Mississippi Basin.*

William C. H. Wood, *The Fight for Canada.*

William C. H. Wood, *The Great Fortress.*

George M. Wrong, *The Conquest of New France.*

George M. Wrong, *The Rise and Fall of New France*, Volume II.

PART V

The Growth of the Provinces in the Eighteenth Century

THE UNITY of the Anglo-American culture that exists today is the product of a slow process of assimilation of many diverse elements. These elements were sometimes racial, sometimes cultural, sometimes social. But the greatest diversity in the elements that went into the making of what is now the United States, Canada, or the British West Indies is to be observed in the peculiarities of the different provinces. For though the English colonies were, indeed, units in the larger entity of the empire, yet each province was distinct from all the rest in a manner and to a degree often overlooked by the twentieth-century student, who is likely to take American cultural unity for granted. Only in New England was there such a common outlook on life as to justify a discussion of this whole region as a unit. To a somewhat less degree, there was a unity of culture and of life in Pennsylvania, Delaware and West New Jersey, and in the West Indies; but in the latter case the mere physical separation of the islands made for certain differences in institutions and in culture. These separate English-speaking communities, scattered along the Atlantic seaboard of North America from Newfoundland to Barbados, were the human laboratories in which were gradually distilled the ideas, the ideals, and the institutions of the three major sectors of Anglo-American civilization. And although it is impossible to arrive at a correct understanding of the true nature of American development without considering the colonies in their larger setting in the British empire, it is equally impossible to understand American nationality without observing also the social, economic, political and cultural growth of each of the provinces separately. Sharply differentiated from each other in many ways, it was only toward the end of the colonial era that they began to discover the ties, economic, political, and cultural, that were to draw them together, first into "sections" and then—in two of the four sections—into a union which was to be perfected in nationhood. The very question why some of the colonies were developing toward eventual independent nationhood while others were being drawn ever closer to the mother country can only be explained by the individual and sectional differences, of experience and of outlook, among them. It seems appropriate, therefore, to give some attention to the individual growth of the colonies and to the differences, provincial and sectional, which set them off from each other.

31

New England in the Eighteenth Century

THE EVOLUTION OF POLITICAL INSTITUTIONS

WITH the ejection of Edmund Andros from New England upon the accession of William and Mary to the throne of old England, the Dominion of New England collapsed. Connecticut and Rhode Island quietly resumed their old charters, which had "gone into hiding" in 1686, and New Hampshire, the lands of which were sold by the Mason heirs to one Samuel Allen in 1691, remained to all intents and purposes a proprietary province until the Earl of Bellomont came over as royal governor of New York, Massachusetts and New Hampshire in 1697 and visited New Hampshire for the only time in 1700.

Massachusetts, however, was in 1690 a house divided. The old-line Puritans, led by Increase and Cotton Mather, father and son, were hoping that the original charter of 1629 might now be restored. Increase Mather, already in England to protest against the Andros government, exerted all his power to have the old charter restored by the new sovereigns. But there were many people in Massachusetts, non-Puritans or those who merely wished religion taken out of politics, who were determined never again to permit the return of the Puritan oligarchy to its old powers. Nor did the government of England have any intention of restoring to Massachuetts its old quasi-independence. On the contrary, it was now the settled policy of official England to draw the colonies more closely to itself and to strengthen and increase the effectiveness of the Crown's control over the colonies wherever possible.

Mather was compelled, therefore, to accept for Massachusetts a charter which, while retaining some of the features of the old government and enlarging Massachusetts itself, yet brought the colony directly under the Crown. The charter of 1691 thus provided for the annexation of the former colony of Plymouth and the Duke of York's (James II's) old domain of Maine to the province of Massachusetts. The enlarged colony was made a royal province, with a royally appointed governor. The council, however, instead of being named directly by the Crown, was nominated by the "Great and General Court," that is, the assembly. Members of the

443

lower house were to be elected by freemen owning property of a value of at least forty pounds sterling. The religious qualification for voting was thus omitted; at the same time it was provided in the new charter that there should be complete freedom of conscience for all Christians except Roman Catholics. Acts of the legislature might be vetoed by the governor, or disallowed (within three years) by the Crown. Such was the charter under which Massachusetts lived from 1691 until the Revolution. The hold of the Puritan oligarchy upon the government in Massachusetts was legally broken. Practically, they still exerted an enormous influence upon affairs; it was only very gradually that their places in the commonwealth were taken by more secular-minded leaders.

Sir William Phips, hero of the war against the French, was named the first royal governor of Massachusetts, and the political history of New England during the eighteenth century is largely the history of Massachusetts. For Connecticut and Rhode Island went their own ways, and New Hampshire was, for the first half-century, virtually a part of Massachusetts. Two important incidents, however, affected New England as a whole. One of these was the new effort to unite New England under one government, and the other was the move made by the Board of Trade in the direction of suspending or revising the New England charters in order to bring them still more directly and effectively under the control of the Crown.

The first of these experiments was inspired by the need of common action in war, which had been so clearly demonstrated in King William's War (War of the League of Augsburg). Moved by the desire to place New England under one military command, the king in 1697 appointed the Earl of Bellomont governor of New York, Massachusetts and New Hampshire, with military command, also, over Connecticut, Rhode Island, and the Jerseys. The experiment was a failure, however, and ended with Bellomont's death in 1701. The move to revoke the charters originated in the persistent complaints that the chartered colonies not under the direct control of the Crown had violated the navigation acts with impunity, had interfered with their administration, and had harbored pirates and illegal traders. A bill for the revocation of the charters failed, but the effort was renewed and narrowed to an effort to break the charters of Connecticut and Rhode Island, which were the worst offenders. The movement had lost its force by 1710, but continued intermittently until piracy and illegal trade declined after the Peace of Utrecht. For many years Connecticut and Rhode Island were nervous over the possibility that their charters, and therefore their independence, might be taken away. Happily for them it never happened.

The political history of Massachusetts during the eighteenth century presents a number of problems and conflicts that were common to practically all the English colonies in America. The first of these was the constitutional struggle between the colony on the one side and the "prerogative" on the other—a conflict that might be defined as one between two amorphous but developing constitutions—the constitution of the colony versus the constitution of the British empire. This conflict expressed itself in many ways; but the most important phase of the conflict was that having to do with the control and administration of the colony's finances. For as one of the unquestioned rights of Englishmen was that of giving money to the government only by their own consent, the assembly jealously refused to permit any disbursement of the colony's funds without its permission.

This quarrel got under way early in the history of the colony, but it flared up under Governor Joseph Dudley, who took office in 1702, particularly over the governor's salary. For the assembly was in the very convenient habit of voting the governor's salary annually and of varying the amount of it from year to year according as the governor had complied with its wishes. Dudley was instructed to secure the establishment of a permanent salary for the governor and other Crown officials; but the assembly refused to do so. Nor did it ever surrender on the issue. The contest continued until the administration of Jonathan Belcher, who in 1730 was finally instructed by the Crown to accept the annual grants of money, provided they were made at the beginning of the year instead of at the end—a proviso to which the assembly agreed. The surrender of Belcher was a significant victory for the assembly, for its practical effect, whatever the theory, was to keep the colonial governor in a position of at least partial subjection, and, therefore, responsible to the elected representatives of the people. As Belcher himself said, "They are daily endeavouring to incroach upon the little power reserved to the Crown in the Royal Charter."

Another issue between governor and assembly arose over the right of the governor to veto the General Court's nominations for the Council, a point on which the governor was eventually sustained by the home government. He was also sustained in his claim to the right to veto the choice of a speaker by the lower house. Other perennial issues in dispute were those which arose out of provision for the defense of the colony, the specification by the assembly of expenditures of public moneys by the Crown officials, and, most important of all, over the question of paper money. In general, the governors claimed, as did William Shirley, who became governor in 1740, that their instructions were binding upon the legislature, as a part of the provincial constitution. To which the colonials replied that the governor's instructions, far from being a part of the constitution of Massachusetts, were not binding upon them, but only upon the governor himself. The fundamental question involved in the political struggle in Massachusetts therefore, was, as elsewhere, the question of the relationship of the colonial constitution to the constitution of the Crown and the empire. How far might the Crown go in interfering in the internal affairs of the province? Did the laws made by Parliament apply in Massachusetts? And did the instructions to the governor, formulated by the Board of Trade and the Privy Council, have the force of law in the colony?

These questions were not clearly answered in Massachusetts during the colonial period. That colony, as the others, was struggling to achieve control of its own affairs—but that seemed to the British government essentially to mean independence; and as the Privy Council put it in connection with the struggle of Belcher with the assembly in 1733, "their design is to assume to themselves the executive power of the government of the said province, and has a direct tendency to throw off their dependence upon Great Britain." Actually, what the assembly most desired seems to have been autonomy, rather than independence; but neither side saw the issue quite clearly, and the conflict went on, to break out in its mature form in the Revolution of 1776.

SOCIAL AND ECONOMIC EXPANSION

While the political institutions of Massachusetts, along with those of the other New England colonies, were slowly and painfully growing toward maturity, this section was rapidly expanding its economic life as one of the wealthiest sections of the British empire in America. The basic industry was still farming, in the sense that the majority of the people still lived on farms and made their livings by raising a food supply for themselves and for the men engaged in the more profitable occupations of fishing, manufacturing, and commerce. Population was expanding steadily, and in 1750 small farms and villages dotted the landscape from the Kennebec River in Maine to Greenwich in Connecticut, at the boundary of New York. These "settlements" had struck inland, and had pushed far up the Connecticut and westward across the Housatonic River to involve Massachusetts in a long and bitter boundary controversy with the province of New York. This steady expansion "outward," if not precisely "westward," from the older settlements gave New England a new frontier along the upper waters of the rivers—the Kennebec, the Merrimac, the Connecticut and the Housatonic, and placed a premium upon cultivable land. The result was the appearance of a considerable amount of land speculation. In the first century of New England's history, lands had been granted only to new communities and in relatively small quantities. But in the eighteenth century the old communal system of land-administration was breaking down. Powerful individuals found it possible to buy large tracts of land or to get individual grants from the legislatures, and resell the land to the small settlers at a profit. The land of New Hampshire, of course, had always been entirely privately owned, and still was. Elsewhere in New England, where propriety of the land was vested in the colony as a whole townships had been granted to the town corporations. Certain grants, all of which were small, had been made to individuals, and in the eighteenth century there was nothing to prevent the wealthier members of the town corporations from buying out the poorer ones. These dispossessed heirs of former landowners found that they had a common grievance with the immigrant newcomers, with whom they tended to drift toward the frontiers, against the wealthy. The process was accelerated by the fact that Massachusetts and Connecticut practically abandoned the "town plan" of granting lands about 1725 and began to grant prospective town sites to individual promoters. By 1762 Massachusetts was allowing a single individual to purchase from the colony an entire township at one time, with the proviso that the purchaser settle a certain number of families upon his land within a specified period. Such a purchaser would then sell his land, either to bona fide settlers or to lesser speculators.

The result of these two parallel developments was a change in the structure of New England society amounting almost to a social revolution. For while it broke up the communal unity of the early New England villages, it also created a deep cleavage between the landowning, or creditor class, and the land-purchasing, or debtor class. Further, it set the people of the small farms and the frontier against the merchants and the speculators of the seaboard cities, which were the centers of wealth. The economic and social solidarity of Puritan New England had gone, and in its place had come a division which set class against class, section against section, debtor against creditor, and "west" against "east"—cleavages which were to bedevil American development from that day to this.

But farming was not an industry that was directly profitable in the export trade of New England, except for a few commodities such as the horses shipped to the West Indies. As a matter of fact, Massachusetts was now importing a part of its own food supply in the form of wheat, flour, pork and Indian corn, from the provinces farther south. Fishing was still the most important of the export industries. By 1750 four hundred vessels were said to be employed in the offshore cod fisheries off Nova Scotia and Newfoundland, and two hundred more were engaged in the "inshore" mackerel fisheries along the coast. Some 280,000 quintals of fish were taken every year, and most of this was exported. By this time, too, whaling, based upon Gloucester and New Bedford, had become an important branch of the fishing industry. Indeed, by 1771 it was estimated that in Massachuetts alone there were 304 ships regularly engaged in whaling. The products of this industry found a ready market in England; of the fish, from one-fourth to one-half was exported to the West Indies as "refuse" or "Jamaica" fish, and about one-fourth to one-third, or practically all the first-class product, was shipped abroad to the Roman Catholic countries of southern Europe and to the Azores and Madeira. The rest, which might be called good, but second class, was consumed at home. The fishing industry was the foundation for many New England fortunes, notably that of Peter Faneuil, of Boston; it is not without reason that a great gilded codfish, symbol of New England prosperity, is still mounted in the position of greatest honor over the desk of the Speaker of the House of Representatives in the State House in Boston.

Closely related to the fishing industry was the building of ships and the sawing of lumber. Not only did the New England merchants own and operate their own ships; ships could be built in New England more efficiently than elsewhere in the empire, and New England-built ships competed on favorable terms with those built in the yards of England itself. In Massachusetts alone about one hundred and fifty ships were launched annually. But the center of the lumbering and shipbuilding industries was now Portsmouth, in New Hampshire. Another business that was closely related to fishing was the manufacture of rum. This industry, centering in Newport, Rhode Island, employed thousands of men. By 1750 some 15,000 gallons were exported annually from Massachusetts alone—to say nothing of the enormous quantities consumed at home. Rum, indeed, was also called the foundation of New England prosperity—"the great support of all their trade and fishing; without which they can no longer subsist." Men could not—or would not—work without it, and it was the staple commodity of exchange for the slave trade from Africa to the southern colonies; a commerce which had its great American center, as distinguished from the activities of the Royal African Company of England, in Rhode Island. Here great quantities of molasses (14,000 barrels in 1764) were imported and made into rum, which was then shipped to the coast of Guinea and exchanged for Negroes; the blacks were then taken to the West Indies and the southern continental colonies to be sold as slaves.

Other important industries in New England were the manufacture of iron, woolens, and hats. Massachusetts was exporting certain iron products—nails, axes, and the like—to the southern colonies in 1722, and by 1733 there were six furnaces and nineteen forges operating in New England. Curiously enough, the New England ironmakers were actually importing bar iron from England for manufacture in New England—to the great distress of the iron manufacturers of old England, who, as already noted, did what they could to have that business stopped. Similarly, the home manufacture of woolens had now grown into a considerable industry in New England, despite the legislative efforts of the mother country to discourage it, as had, also, the manufacture of shoes and hats.

But the great source and basis of New England prosperity was still commerce. From its extractive and manufacturing industries New England drew many commodities for export; but a very important part of its exports was in reality made up of goods imported from England or elsewhere and re-exported to the colonies toward the south—or vice versa. Thus Boston, the great emporium of New England commerce, needed 160 warehouses to accommodate the goods that were constantly coming and going. In these warehouses might be found cloth, furniture, hardware and East India goods from England, tobacco from Virginia, rum, molasses, sugar, mahogany and dyewood from the West Indies and the Spanish Main, rice, timber, lumber, tar and turpentine from the Carolinas or from New England itself, and thousands of barrels of the lowly fish, brought from just offshore. It required upward of a thousand ships a year to bring these commodities into Boston and to take them away again.

But Boston was not alone. Portsmouth, Salem, Plymouth, Newport, Providence, New London, and New Haven were all centers of commerce, and flourishing, if small, foci of urban life. Everywhere in New England, in the eighteenth century, economic life was expanding. And in these places, the nerve centers of the expanding economic organism, there was taking place a steady accumulation of wealth.

However, the economic expansion of this region created another problem that was of both economic and political significance, the problem of an expanding currency. For, while wealth was accumulating in New England, as elsewhere in the colonies, this wealth was in the form of goods of one sort or another, and there was practically no accumulation of money. As a matter of fact, money acquired by the New England merchants from their favorable trade balances in the south or the West Indies tended to fly immediately to England to pay the region's adverse balance there; but this was taking place precisely at the moment when the expansion of the new era demanded a plentiful supply of some flexible medium of exchange. It was to meet this need that New England, along with practically all the other colonies, turned to the device of printing paper money.

Paper money was at once a boon and a curse to all the colonies, and New England was no exception. Massachusetts, faced with the need of money with which to pay the expenses of the expedition against Quebec in 1690, had issued promissory notes which were to be retired by future tax-receipts. This scheme worked well, and was repeated in Massachusetts and copied in other colonies. By 1715 the paper money outstanding in Massachusetts amounted to some £474,000. Naturally enough, as the issues increased, the value of the provincial paper declined, and in 1729 amounted to only about one-fourth that of sterling. But the situation in Massachusetts was still further complicated by the paper money issued in Rhode Island and Connecticut, which tended to gravitate toward Boston as the economic metropolis, and which was worth even less than Massachusetts money. So scandalous was the reputation of Rhode Island money, indeed, that at one time it stood against sterling at a ratio of about thirty-two to one.

The need for a circulating medium was great, nevertheless, and it was in an effort to meet this need that in Massachusetts it was proposed in 1701 to form a bank which would issue bank notes based upon land mortgages. The scheme came to nothing at the time, and was revived in 1714 and again in 1740. But the merchants of England were afraid of this depreciated currency, especially that proposed to be issued by private banks, and prevailed upon the Board of Trade to discourage it as much as possible. When the Massachusetts legislature issued a new emission of £106,000 of bills in 1733, the Crown instructed Governor Belcher to sign no more such acts for more than £30,000, and to see to it that all outstanding bills were canceled at the appointed time. Had this been done, it would have had a disastrous effect upon daily economic life in the colony, so dependent had business become upon this paper. The need, despite the depressed value of the paper, was actually for more paper rather than less.

Far from being able to suppress the money, therefore, Governor Belcher had to face the new scheme for a land bank to issue money which would be outside the governor's control. The bank, organized in September, 1740, proposed to lend money on mortgages at three per cent interest. It was supported by the farmers and debtor classes generally, but it was bitterly opposed by the large merchants, who were creditors, because they stood to lose heavily by a depreciated land bank currency. The merchants organized a silver bank of their own, refusing, at the same time, to accept the land bank bills. This only roused the farmers the more, and they marched to Boston at election time in 1741 and by influence and intimidation brought about the election of an assembly favorable to the land bank. The governor, favoring the merchants, who were now allied with the merchants of Britain, dissolved the assembly and appealed to the mother country for aid. Parliament responded by extending to the colonies the old so-called "Bubble Act" of 1720, originally passed to prevent speculative financial ventures in England. The Massachusetts land bank hardly came under the provisions of the old Bubble Act, which had prohibited the formation of joint-stock companies without permission of Parliament; the act, moreover, had not applied to the colonies. But at the urging of the merchants Parliament extended it to the colonies by statute in 1741, and by so doing effectively destroyed the bank and forced it to close its doors. Many of the subscribers to the bank were ruined; one of these was Samuel Adams, Sr., father of the radical leader of the Revolutionary era; and it is probably not too much to say that much of the younger Adams' bitterness against the Massachusetts conservatives and England had one of its sources in this episode.

But the destruction of the land bank did not solve the problem. In 1749 Parliament paid the colony of Massachusetts £175,000 sterling to reimburse the colony for its share in the Louisbourg expedition of 1745, and the General Court decided to use this money to retire the outstanding provincial bills of credit—at a ratio of 10 to 1. The immediate effect of the resumption of specie payments was a shock upon Massachusetts business; but the long-term effect was salutary, for it toned up, if it did not permanently stabilize, Massachusetts currency.

Rhode Island and Connecticut were not so fortunate—or unfortunate. In Rhode Island, particularly, where the small farmers controlled the legislature, paper money had its heyday. Not only did the province issue bills of credit, but land banks flourished as well: nine land banks were formed between 1710 and 1750, which issued a total of £465,000 in currency.

Money was "easy" in Rhode Island; in 1740 it was estimated that £340,000 in paper currency was in circulation; by 1750 the amount had risen to £525,000. The lot of the merchants, in this situation, was a bitter one. Although Rhode Island bills were not by statute legal tender, public opinion forced their acceptance. Governor Jenks, alarmed for the merchants, in 1731 vetoed a bill creating a new land bank, only to lose the veto power—if he ever had it. The merchants appealed to England for help, but the Board of Trade could do nothing because, since the paper was not legal tender, the merchants could not honestly say that they were compelled to accept it in payment of their bills.

Finally, in 1751, Parliament came to the aid of the merchants by passing the so-called Currency Act, which prohibited any New England colony from creating land banks and from declaring their bills of credit legal tender. This act, later extended to all the colonies, stopped the paper-money orgy in New England. But it was another interference in the internal affairs of the colonies, in the name of "hard money," which still further broadened the breach between debtor and creditor, frontier and city, and embittered the feeling of the debtors and the frontiersmen against the mother country.

RELIGION AND EDUCATION

Partly because of the economic, social and political movements just surveyed, and partly because of the influence of intellectual currents moving beyond its borders, New England in the eighteenth century was passing through a religious and intellectual transformation that was no less profound and significant than those in the social and political realms of life. For there had now set in a steady trend away from the religious, other-worldly outlook on life that had characterized the seventeenth century, toward one which was increasingly secular and this-worldly. This phenomenon was common to all the colonies, to be sure; and as such will be discussed later; but there were certain aspects of it which were peculiar to New England, and must be considered here.

The Mathers, Increase and Cotton, were the last great exponents of the Puritan Age. But even during their generation there was observable a worldliness and a lack of wholehearted devotion to the Puritan way. It seemed to them that the people were failing to live up to their covenant with God from the establishment of a Zion in the wilderness, and, therefore, as the poet Michael Wigglesworth put it, God had a "controversy" with New England. Cotton Mather complained that the people were sunk in a worldliness displeasing to God: they were wearing outlandish hats, and wigs; they were indulging in too much drinking, cock-fighting, and Sabbath-breaking; creditors were oppressing their debtors by high interest and profiteering; fortune tellers had appeared among them; and it was even said that there was a brothel in Boston! The Puritans had made a contract with God and he had made them prosperous; now, because of that very prosperity, the people were forgetting their covenant, and drifting away from God.

Such, in the minds of the Mathers, was the deplorable condition of New England when, deliberately or otherwise, they precipitated the witchcraft hysteria of 1691 and 1692. A belief in witchcraft was, of course, a very old and widespread superstition, and numerous people had been hanged in New England on the ground that they were witches before this. But the belief seemed to be waning; and at the suggestion of his colleagues Increase Mather published, in 1684, a little book relating to numerous cases of what seemed to him to be well-authenticated cases of witchery. In 1689 Cotton Mather published his *Memorable Providences,* in which he sought to sustain the superstition by stating that disbelief in witchcraft was a step in the direction of atheism. In the spring of 1691 two little girls of Salem proclaimed they had been bewitched, and accused various people of bewitching them. In the hysteria that followed, many persons were accused, and twenty persons were hanged and fifty-five more had "confessed" that they were witches. The hysteria subsided quickly, however, when some of the most important people in the colony—among them the wife of the governor—were accused. There then took place a revulsion of public opinion against the instigators of the affair, and the influence of the clergy was perceptibly weakened by the reaction.

The turn of the century saw other important developments in the religious and intellectual life of New England. A group of ministers sought to strengthen the churches by a "consociation" that would have amounted almost to Presbyterian government, but they were ably opposed by others who feared a centralization of church government. The protagonist of this group was Rev. John Wise, of Ipswich, who gave expression to a philosophy of democratic government that, in its thoroughgoing advocacy of that form, was a century before his time. Wise's ideas triumphed in the churches; but they were too advanced for the politically minded Americans of his day, who turned for their political philosophy to his somewhat more conservative English contemporary, John Locke. Only Samuel Adams, among the American leaders of the eighteenth century, seems probably to have been influenced by Wise's philosophy.

But this division of the churches over government was as nothing to the division that was developing over doctrine. For a number of the preachers of the churches, notably Charles Chauncy and Jonathan Mayhew, were coming to question the rigid, amoral nature of the Puritan concept of God. Charles Chauncy, as a reaction both to the emotionalism of the great religious revival known as the Great Awakening and to the cruel and arbitrary nature of the Calvinistic God portrayed by Jonathan Edwards, preached and wrote of a God who was benevolent and kind, rejoicing in the happiness of men. Such a concept inevitably led him away from the rigid Puritan doctrine of predestination to a belief in free will; for, said Chauncy, any talk of morality without freedom of will is against common sense. Nor is God the capricious, arbitrary deity of the Puritans; God rules the universe by physical laws which he has laid down, but which he does not himself violate—a suggestion of the Deism that was seeping into religion under the influence of Newtonian science. Mayhew, younger than Chauncy, went even further in the departure from the older Puritanism. For Mayhew, strict Puritan in his personal way of life, yet taught a "rational and practical" Christianity based on the Bible—a Christianity which taught a freedom of the will, the right of private judgment, and, perhaps most significant of all, a unitarian, as against the older trinitarian concept of God.

Opposed to these intellectual liberals were the revivalists, Jon-

athan Edwards, at Northampton, and the itinerant George Whitefield, who precipitated and led the great mid-century revival known
as the Great Awakening. These men, as will be noted later, appealed
to the emotions rather than the intellect, to "enthusiasm" rather
than reason. Despite the fact that Edwards was perhaps the greatest native intellect to appear in America in the colonial period,
and despite the fact that he thought of himself as a Puritan, his
appeal to "enthusiasm" was a departure from strict Puritanism
that would have scandalized the Puritan fathers—as it had, indeed,
in the case of Mrs. Hutchinson—and gave rise to other "enthusiastic" sects which departed from Puritanism even further than he
himself would have gone.

Thus did the religion of New England become a house divided.
But neither the "intellectuals" nor the "enthusiasts" clung to the
Puritanism of their fathers. Rather, they both showed tendencies
which were characteristic of their age. On the one side, the "intellectuals" showed clearly the influence of the scientific rationalism
which was the product of Newtonian science. On the other, the
"enthusiasts" displayed the emotionalism and the individualism
which were at once a counterpart of the pietistic reaction to intel-
lectualism in religion that was sweeping the common people of
Europe and a product of the condition of life on the American
frontier. Both, in any case, were a far cry from the earlier Puritanism.

This major division in religion, which resulted in a further
"atomization" of the Protestant sects, was symptomatic of the
times. For it was paralleled by an extension of the secularization
of the outlook on life of which Cotton Mather had complained.
Secular literature appeared and flourished in New England, as will
be noted later; secular interests everywhere tended gradually to
crowd out the once overwhelmingly dominant other-worldliness of
the Puritan fathers. The advance of science was largely responsible for this change; but it was also due in considerable measure to
the heavily secular intellectual influence of the frontier. Be that
as it may, the secularizing influences of the complex social, religious, and scientific developments of the century are to be seen
in the breakdown of the old public-school system and its replace-
ment by the rise of the so-called "academies"—private, aristocratic
preparatory schools—whose curricula, while still strongly religious,
were increasingly secular in nature. The trend is seen in the colleges, too. Yale, founded in 1701 as a reaction against the increasing "ungodliness" of Harvard, was slow in admitting the influence

of the scientific age which even Yale, however, could not escape. Harvard, on the other hand, gave increasing emphasis to science, mathematics, secular literature, and a contemporary foreign language, French, while giving relatively decreasing emphasis to questions of religion and theology.

It must not be gathered from all this that New England shed the Puritan mantle quickly and completely. On the contrary, even in the face of these diversifying tendencies religion remained a dominating influence in the lives of individual men. The Puritan tradition, in the form of a moral and intellectual discipline, retained its influence in the intellectual life of New England for another century and more, continually radiating from its New England matrix into the broadening culture of America. The eighteenth century, nevertheless, was a century of secularization, of diversification, and of humanization of the New England mind.

RECOMMENDED BOOKS FOR FURTHER READING

CONTEMPORARY NARRATIVES

The Boston News-letter.

Guy S. Callender, ed., *Selections from the Economic History of the United States, 1765-1860.*

Charles Chauncy, *The Benevolence of the Deity.*

Andrew M. Davis, ed., *Tracts Relating to the Currency of the Massachusetts Bay, 1682-1720.*

Clarence H. Faust and Thomas H. Johnson, eds., *Jonathan Edwards: Representative Selections.*

Sarah K. Knight, *The Private Journal of a Journey from Boston to New York in the Year 1704.*

Percy Miller and Thomas H. Johnson, eds., *The Puritans*, pp. 162-179, 256-280, 720-727, 750-764.

New England Courant.

William Shirley, *Correspondence of William Shirley*, edited by Charles H. Lincoln.

John Wise, *A Vindication of the Government of New England Churches.*

MODERN ACCOUNTS

James T. Adams, *Revolutionary New England, 1691-1776.*

Roy H. Akagi, *The Town Proprietors of the New England Colonies.*

Charles M. Andrews, *Connecticut and the British Government.*

Alice M. Baldwin, *The New England Clergy and the American Revolution.*

Alice M. Earle, *Customs and Fashions in Old New England.*

William H. Fry, *New Hampshire as a Royal Province.*

Lawrence H. Gipson, *The British Empire before the American Revolution*, III, Chapters 1-4.

Maria L. Greene, *The Development of Religious Liberty in Connecticut.*

Matt B. Jones, *Vermont in the Making, 1750-1777.*

Jacob C. Meyer, *Church and State in Massachusetts from 1740 to 1833.*

John C. Miller, "Religion, Finance, and Democracy in Massachusetts," *New England Quarterly*, VI, 29-58.

Herbert L. Osgood, *The American Colonies in the Eighteenth Century,* III, Part II, Chapters 12-16; Part III, Chapter 4.

Vernon L. Parrington, *The Colonial Mind, 1620-1800*, Book I, Part II.

Susan M. Reed, *Church and State in Massachusetts, 1691-1740.*

Lois K. M. Rosenberry, *The Expansion of New England.*

Henry R. Spencer, *Constitutional Conflict in Provincial Massachusetts.*

Williston Walker, *A History of the Congregational Churches in the United States.*

William B. Weeden, *Economic and Social History of New England, 1620-1789,* Volume II.

Ola E. Winslow, *Jonathan Edwards.*

Justin Winsor, ed., *The Memorial History of Boston,* III, Chapters 4, 8-9, 16.

George A. Wood, *William Shirley, Governor of Massachusetts, 1741-1756.*

Thomas G. Wright, *Literary Culture in Early New England, 1620-1730.*

32

New York and New Jersey

THE PROVINCE of New York had no representative institutions until Governor Henry Sloughter, sent over by William and Mary in 1691, called its first genuine representative assembly shortly after his arrival. New York, until the "Glorious Revolution" the personal property of James II, now became a royal province, and such it remained until the American Revolution. New Jersey was still divided into two sections, owned by two different, but overlapping, sets of proprietors; East New Jersey was economically dependent upon New York, and West New Jersey upon Philadelphia. But the proprietors had difficulty in maintaining political order, and voluntarily surrendered their political rights to the Crown in 1702. Their ownership of the land and their right to collect quitrents upon it were confirmed to them, however. When the Crown took over, and the united New Jersey became a royal province, one legislature was created for the entire colony. But Lord Cornbury, Governor of New York, was also made governor of New Jersey, and the two colonies continued to have a common governor until 1738.

ECONOMIC AND SOCIAL GROWTH

New York, as all the colonies, enjoyed in the eighteenth century a rapid expansion of population and economic activity. In the year 1720, for example, the province contained some 30,000 people; in 1756 it numbered roughly 85,000. Its commerce showed a similar expansion; for the value of New York exports rose from £52,000 in 1717 to £231,000 in 1769, and that of its imports from £21,000 to £188,000 in the same years. Drawing its exportable commodities from New Jersey, the Hudson Valley, Connecticut and Long Island, the province sent abroad large quantities of wheat, flour and bread, other cereals, livestock, lumber, whale oil, and furs. The fur trade, although still large, suffered a relative decline in importance in the economic life of the colony as the production and export of foodstuffs steadily increased. These foodstuffs were shipped largely to the West Indies, and were supplemented in that trade by lumber, horses, and other livestock. Some of the products of New York and New Jersey, however, went to Massachusetts and other parts of New England, and considerable quantities went to the southern colonies and the countries of southern Europe. In general, the commerce of New York, as, indeed, also of Pennsylvania, was comparable to that of New England, with the important difference that these middle colonies built up their favorable balance of payments by exporting goods produced in the region itself, whereas New England's prosperity grew largely, even chiefly, out of buying and selling goods produced elsewhere. It was, perhaps, for this reason that the middle colonies were less interested in ships and carrying services than were the merchants of New England. On the contrary, the merchants of New York and Philadelphia, while they did own a considerable amount of shipping of their own, depended heavily upon British and New England ships to carry their cargoes for them.

The expansion of New York is illustrated by the rapid extension of the area of settlement up the Hudson and Mohawk rivers. But immigration into this province was greatly discouraged by the aristocratic and monopolistic system of land distribution, which reached in New York an extreme not equaled, probably, anywhere else in the British colonies. For the process that had been started in good faith by the Dutch in the patroon system of grants (only one of which succeeded) was expanded by the early royal governors, particularly Benjamin Fletcher and Lord Cornbury, to the point where it was nothing short of scandalous. For these governors allotted great tracts of land, ranging in size from fifty or one hundred thousand acres to a million or more, to their political friends. These tracts lay mostly in the strip of the province lying east of the Hudson, in the area between the Hudson and the Delaware south of the Catskills, and on Long Island; many of them paid only "token" quitrents to the Crown, twenty or thirty shillings or a beaver skin, annually. By the mid-century this process had carried the great landholders into the Mohawk Valley and into the territory between the Hudson and the Connecticut that was later to become Vermont. In this latter area, however, Governor Benning Wentworth of New Hampshire established the town of Bennington in 1749 on the ground that the territory was part of New Hampshire. Governor Clinton of New York quickly resisted the New Hampshire claim on the basis of the original grant to the Duke of York, which made the Connecticut River the eastern boundary of the province, and on the ground that much of this very territory had been granted to, and occupied by, New Yorkers.

There thus began a bitter boundary dispute which was not settled until after the Revolution. A similar boundary dispute, with a similar cause and only a little less bitter, arose between New York and Massachusetts. The "westward movement" in Massachusetts and New Hampshire was beginning to infringe upon the vested interests of the New York aristocracy.

The great landowners thus held a monopoly of practically all the desirable land not occupied by Indians. Some of the lands were sold to settlers, but the proprietors generally asked prices that were prohibitively high, preferring to rent them to the settlers on a tenancy basis. This policy had the effect of discouraging many prospective settlers, who tended to move on into the areas where the more liberal land policies of Pennsylvania or Massachusetts prevailed. On each of the great "manors" there was usually a nucleus of land operated by the owner himself, with the aid of indentured servants and slaves. At such a point would be a mill, a brewery, a smokehouse, a warehouse, a wharf for ships (where the "manor" was on a navigable river), and other buildings and equipment useful to the entire community, from the use of which the owner exacted from his tenants the customary feudal fees.

Despite the discouragement to free settlement, however, immigration continued, and many of these newcomers "squatted" upon the lands of the great owners. Sometimes satisfactory arrangements were made between "squatter" and owner; at other times the "squatter" moved on toward a farther frontier. It was by this process that the newer lands of the Mohawk Valley were filled up, and that, by the era of the Revolution, the frontier between whites and Indians stood, roughly, at the watershed between the Mohawk and the Great Lakes. Here William Johnson, the greatest land speculator in the Mohawk region, and a picturesque frontier leader with an almost uncanny influence with the Indians, had erected his residence, Johnson Hall, which was a stopping place for the fur-traders on the route from Oswego to Albany, and the scene of many an Indian treaty.

The fur trade was still a business of enormous economic and political importance to the province. Albany, the second town of the province, was the emporium of this traffic, the most important in British North America. It was from this town that there went out, every spring, fur traders carrying the merchandise of the Dutch and English merchants of Albany to Oswego, built on Lake Ontario as a trading port in 1726. To this point came Indian traders, bearing canoe-loads of furs, from the western lakes and from Canada. There were one hundred eighty-six such canoes at Oswego in 1749, carrying over 1,600 people and 1,435 bundles of furs with a total value of some £22,000. It is estimated that the value of those furs today would be about $2,000,000. This commerce, carried on by dint of much bargaining and plying of the Indians with liquor, was as unsavory as it was profitable, and the merchants of Albany had a reputation for cheating and sharp practice. "The avarice and selfishness of the inhabitants are very well known throughout North America," wrote Peter Kalm in 1749. "If a Jew, who understands the art of getting forward perfectly well should settle amongst them, they would not fail to ruin him."

Be that as it may, the fur trade was doubly important to New York because it brought that province into direct rivalry with the French in Canada. The French had always claimed the lands of the Great Lakes-St. Lawrence Basin, but as the fur-bearing animals became more and more scarce in the face of the advancing white frontier, the Indians had to draw more and more upon the fur-producing areas of the farther west. Rivalry increased to bitterness and became an issue in international diplomacy about the turn of the century. Both sides employed every device known to human knavery to dominate the Iroquois Indians, who controlled this strategic water route, and the erection of Fort Niagara (1716, rebuilt 1726) by the French and of Fort Oswego by the English (1725-27) were incidents in the international rivalry for the control of the great fur-producing domains of the west. In this sense, and largely because of this trade, New York had become one of the most important strategic outposts of the British empire.

THE STRUGGLE FOR LEGISLATIVE AUTONOMY IN NEW YORK

The political history of New York shows a similarity to that of Massachusetts in its slow but steady growth to maturity. Here, as elsewhere in the colonies, the most persistent and significant theme is the conflict between the assembly, or popular branch of government, against the "prerogative," or the vaguely defined but vigorously maintained claim of the governor and other Crown officials to a rather large, even decisive, role in the internal affairs of the province. Here as elsewhere, too, the contest was most intense on the subject of finance. The last decade of the seventeenth century and the first decade of the eighteenth were largely taken up with factional struggles between the "Leislerians," followers of the ill-starred Jacob Leisler, and the "anti-Leislerians," who had dominated the government after Leisler's overthrow during the administration of Governor Sloughter. Both these factions were made up of wealthy, aristocratic politicians, and their rivalry was not one of class so much as a conflict of nearly equal aristocratic groups.

But the arrival of Lord Cornbury in 1702, followed by his avaricious attempts to exploit the governorship to his own personal profit, reduced factional rivalries to a position of less importance in the political life of the province than the struggle against the avarice of the governor. Thus, in an effort to check the spendthrift ways of the governor, the assembly in 1704 appointed a treasurer to keep account of special appropriations. At the same time, the assembly, following the precedent of the British House of Commons, denied the right of the council to amend money bills. This called forth the pronouncement by the governor of the position so often taken by the Crown representatives, that representative government in the colonies was the result of a mere act of grace on the part of the king, and not the expression of any inherent right the colonists might claim to have as Englishmen. Thus, he warned them, the Crown had bestowed upon them the favor of representative government; but what the Crown had given, it might also—if they became too "saucy"—take away.

The assembly had formerly provided the governor with a fixed sum for the support of government over a period of years; but Cornbury lived so extravagantly, and so scandalously used his position to promote the interests of himself and his friends, that the assembly, from about 1709, made certain taxes payable only to the treasurer elected by, and responsible to, itself, reduced the inflated salaries of officials who had been friends of Lord Cornbury, and voted many of its appropriation bills for only one year at a time. During the regime of Governor Robert Hunter (1710-20), the assembly steadily sought to extend its power, and regularly appropriated money for the support of government for only one year at a time; but Hunter was able to win a compromise in the form of a five-year grant in 1715.

This success of Hunter established a sort of balance in the government, which was not seriously disturbed until the regime of George Clarke, who became lieutenant-governor in 1736. For Clarke inherited a bitter conflict with the assembly, left to him by the unpopular Governor William Cosby. In the course of the controversy, the assembly reasserted its determination to maintain its control of the purse, and compelled the lieutenant-governor to agree not only to yearly grants of financial support but also to the principle that expenditures might be made only for specified purposes and by specified persons. Thus by 1739 the assembly had won recognition of its right to complete and itemized control of expenditures. The years from 1743 to 1753 were marked by strenuous efforts of Governor George Clinton to free himself of the restrictions placed upon him by the assembly, but his efforts were without success. Lieutenant-Governor James DeLancey, who was in sympathy with the assembly, succeeded in parrying the interference of the Board of Trade by slight compromises which, at DeLancey's death in 1760, left the assembly's control over provincial finances—and, therefore, most of the other affairs of the province—almost unimpaired.

Another continuing element of conflict in New York between the provincial assembly and the governor revolved about the question of control of the court system. Under Governor Francis Nicholson courts had been established by the governor and had been under his control. After the establishment of representative government, however, the assembly had advanced the claim that courts should be created by it. But the royal governors had been given the power of appointment in their instructions, and they had set up courts of chancery and other special courts without consulting the assembly. The assembly naturally and consistently opposed this as an arbitrary invasion of the legal rights of the legislature, and this brought the assembly into direct opposition to the Board of Trade, which advanced the claim that the establishment of courts was a right of the royal prerogative. The issue was never clearly settled, but the further question arose as to the judges' term of office. Did the governor have the right to dismiss the judges? If so, it would make possible a corrupt control of the courts for the purposes of arbitrary government. The assembly consistently claimed that judges should be appointed during "good behavior," whereas the governors claimed that judges were appointed only during "His Majesty's pleasure." It is to be noted that this claim of the British representatives was in direct contradiction of the British Act of Settlement of 1707, under which the judges in England itself were always appointed during "good behavior," which meant that they could be removed only by regular impeachment and conviction.

In 1751 the governor was instructed to appoint judges for the courts of the province only during the pleasure of the king. In 1760, however, the assembly tried to pass a law establishing the principle of tenure of the judgeships during good behavior. The law was blocked by the governor, whereupon the assembly refused to grant salaries for the judges for more than a year at a time. This was the situation when, upon the death of George II, it became necessary to make new appointments; and the judges of the province, siding with the assembly, practically went on strike by refusing to serve except on the basis of tenure to be assured during good behavior. The assembly was thus trying to get control of the judiciary, or at least to remove it from the control of the governor. The Board of Trade, on the contrary, was attempting to keep control of the courts in the hands of the governor and the Crown. In view of the fact that under the Act of Settlement the judges in England held office during good behavior, the Americans demanded to know why the royal prerogative should not be limited in America just as it was in England. The assembly was sincerely anxious to make impossible the corrupt control of the courts by the governor. The Board of Trade, on the other hand, was with equal sincerity trying to prevent the assembly from controlling the courts. Implicit in the Board of Trade's demands were the union of the judiciary with the executive to check the assembly. Equally implicit in the demands of the assembly was the separation of the judiciary from the executive functions; but such a separation in actual practice would probably have thrown a considerable measure of control to the assembly, and the fact that the council acted as the supreme court of appeals in the province would have meant, in effect, that the legislative and judicial branches of government would have been united.

For a time, as a result of the refusal of the judges to serve, the administration of justice in New York was practically paralyzed. The deadlock came to an end in 1762, when one of the judges finally agreed to serve during the pleasure of the Crown, and the Crown won an apparent victory. The struggle was not ended, however; and its significance lies in the clearness with which it illustrates the conflict between the popular branch of government and the prerogative. For the "popular interest" was working for a weakening of the executive and a concentration of governmental power in the hands of the assembly; against it stood the royal prerogative, determined to make both the governorship and the courts serve to check the "democratical" tendency in the popular branch of government toward provincial autonomy.

The assembly, as a matter of fact, about the middle of the century, did attempt to establish in New York what would have amounted to responsible government. The movement even went so far as to call the governor's chief assistant the "prime minister" and to attempt to have appointed as executive assistants to the governor only the individuals who could command a majority of the votes in the assembly, following the precedent then being set in the Parliament in England. This movement failed; and the practical stalemate that came into New York politics about 1750 remained more or less in effect in the province until the time of the Revolution. The tendency toward self-government, however, was clearly marked throughout the eighteenth century; and the governors repeatedly sounded alarms to the mother country and suggested that something be done to stop it. Governor Clinton, for example, appealed to the king "to make a good example for all America by regulating the government of New York"; for he was convinced that "the remedy must come from a more powerful authority than any in America." It seemed to him that the colonies were headed straight for independence. To be saved for the empire, he thought, they must be governed firmly and a definite limit must be placed on that tendency by a rigid system of checks, to be manipulated by the mother country, to control the "democratical" tendencies of the American legislatures. How prophetic his insight was, he hardly knew.

FREEDOM OF THE PRESS

It was in connection with the struggle over the judiciary that there took place in New York the famous Zenger trial. This incident had its origin in a series of articles published by John Peter Zenger in his newspaper, *The New York Weekly Journal*. When Governor William Cosby came to the colony in 1732, he found Rip Van Dam, president of the council, acting as executive head of the government. Cosby immediately claimed payment of his salary from the time of his appointment, but Van Dam maintained that, as *ad interim* governor, he was entitled to at least a part of the salary. Cosby refused to grant Van Dam's claim and created a special court of exchequer before which he proposed that Van Dam's case should be tried. Lewis Morris, the chief justice, denied the jurisdiction of such a court in questions of equity such as the one involved in this conflict, and he further denied the right of the Crown to set up special courts without the consent of the assembly—thus taking the assembly's side in the perennial conflict over control. Morris was forthwith dismissed, the court was convened, and Cosby's claim to the salary was upheld. Morris retaliated by writing a series of articles pointing out the illegality of the governor's position and attacking the governor for his apparent manipulation of the courts for his own benefit.

These articles were published in Zenger's *Journal*. Zenger himself had come to America from Germany in 1710 and his paper had become the organ of opposition as against the older newspaper of William Bradford, the *New York Gazette,* established in 1725, which favored the governor and his party. The Morris articles infuriated Governor Cosby, and Zenger was arrested and tried for libel. Morris and his friends came to Zenger's support and secured for his defense one of the most famous lawyers in the colonies, Andrew Hamilton of Philadelphia. The case was tried before a jury in a court of judges who were obviously opposed to Hamilton, Zenger, and Morris. They took the position that the only question to be decided by the jury was whether or not Zenger published the articles in question. If he had, then he was to be adjudged guilty of libel and punished therefor. But Hamilton very dramatically appealed to the jury on the ground that the articles were true; if true, he said, they constituted no libel, and, therefore, Zenger was not guilty. He pointed out the importance of their decision for the rights of free speech in America and for the future of fair and honest journalism. The jury, impressed by Hamilton's argument, and in direct departure from the instructions given them by the judges, found Zenger not guilty.

This is a significant event in American history, for according to English law, the judges were right in their position that they should decide whether the articles were libelous or not, and that the jury should decide simply whether the articles were published by the defendant. This was not the only case of the sort in the colonies, and not all of the others were decided in favor of the freedom of the press. Yet it set an important precedent, amounting almost to a legal principle, that in cases of libel the question of libelous matter was to be decided not by the judges but by the jury. More important still, the case established a precedent in support of the principle that, if statements published by a newspaper were true, they did not constitute libel. Thereafter, the newspapers could and did become the defenders of clean government and felt more and more free to publish articles explaining constitutional matters and supporting or condemning the proceedings of legislatures and Parliament. The Zenger trial thus became an important landmark in the evolution of the newspaper in America as a vehicle for public debate of political issues.

THE CITY OF NEW YORK

New York City, center of New York's provincial commerce, and now rapidly becoming the economic and military gateway to the continent, was also the capital and the center of New York provincial society. Third of the continental cities in the importance of its commerce (after Boston and Philadelphia), it was also a center of such industries as flour mills, sugar refineries, rum distilleries, and sawmills. Hundreds of ships, mostly "hired," were required each year to carry the commodities of commerce to and from the city. Its exports, as already noted, consisted of wheat, flour, bread, livestock, butter and cheese to the West Indies, in return for which the New York merchants took rum, sugar, and molasses. To the Azores, Madeira and Lisbon went a similar list of food products, plus lumber, in return for wines and fruits. To England went furs from the Indian trade, together with logwood, rum, cotton, sugar and tobacco collected in the southern colonies; these were exchanged for dry goods, blankets, hardware, furniture, and tea.

The population of the city, as always, was very cosmopolitan. The old Dutch nucleus remained and there had been added to it many newcomers. Some of these were from New England; there were also numerous French Huguenots, Scotch-Irish immigrants from Ulster, Germans from the Rhineland, Jews, and Negro slaves. These groups had a tendency to cliquishness, and in 1741 there was a great fear of a Negro uprising; by 1768 the Irish and German vote was already a political force to be conjured with. On the whole, there was a great deal of tolerance in religious matters and even in thought, for the Zenger trial had given a considerable filip to freedom of expression. The city could boast one college, Kings College, established in the year 1754. There were one theater and two newspapers, the *Gazette,* established in 1725 and the *Journal,* established in 1733. Social life was a good deal freer and more urbane than that of Boston. For the men there were numerous clubs and for the women there were concerts and "assemblies." Fashions, furniture, and customs were patterned after those of London. The city was notable for its hospitality, in connection with which food was plentifully dispensed and beer, cider, punch, and Madeira were said to flow freely. This being a commercial city, its standards were commercial and its outlook on life somewhat materialistic, as compared to the Puritan outlook of Boston. Fortunes were rapidly made from piracy and smuggling as well as from legitimate commerce, so that among the wealthy there were numerous *nouveaux-riches*. People from Boston looked down upon the social and intellectual life of New York as being "unintellectual, and material," whereas the people of the south looked upon the New Yorkers as "pushing, unrefined, and, in general, somewhat crude." To John Adams, "that cultured prig" from New England, it seemed that "with all the opulence and splendor of this city, there is little good breeding to be found. . . . At their entertainments there is no conversation that is agreeable; there is no modesty, no attention to one another. They talk very loud, very fast, and altogether."

RECOMMENDED BOOKS FOR FURTHER READING

CONTEMPORARY NARRATIVES

Henry J. Carman, ed., *American Husbandry*.

Cadwallader Colden, *The History of the Five Indian Nations of Canada*.

William Johnson, *The Papers of Sir William Johnson*, edited by James Sullivan and Alexander C. Flick.

Peter Kalm, *Travels into North America.*

New York Weekly Journal.

Edmund B. O'Callaghan, ed., *Documents Relative to the Colonial History of the State of New York*.

John P. Zenger, *A Brief Narrative of the Case and Trial of John Peter Zenger, Printer of the New York Weekly Journal*.

MODERN ACCOUNTS

Carl L. Becker, *The History of Political Parties in the Province of New York, 1760-1776*.

Edgar J. Fisher, *New Jersey as a Royal Province, 1738 to 1776*.

Alexander C. Flick, ed., *History of the State of New York*, II, III.

Dixon R. Fox, *Caleb Heathcote, Gentleman Colonist*.

Lawrence H. Gipson, *The British Empire before the American Revolution*, III, Chapters 5-6.

Francis W. Halsey, *The Old New York Frontier*, Part III.

Harold A. Innis, *The Fur Trade in Canada*.

Samuel McKee, *Labor in Colonial New York, 1664-1776*.

Herbert L. Osgood, *The American Colonies in the Eighteenth Century*, II, Part I, Chapter 19, Part II, Chapters 4-5; IV, Part III, Chapters 5, 10.

Arthur Pound, *Johnson of the Mohawks*.

Montgomery Schuyler, *The Patroons and Lords of Manors of the Hudson*.

Flora W. Seymour, *Lords of the Valley, Sir William Johnson and his Mohawk Brothers*.

Charles W. Spencer, *Phases of Royal Government in New York, 1691-1719*.

33

The Quaker Commonwealth: Pennsylvania, Delaware, and West New Jersey

CONSTITUTIONAL DEVELOPMENTS

THE POLITICAL history of Pennsylvania and Delaware in the eighteenth century begins with the "Charter of Privileges" of 1701, granted by William Penn to his two provinces (after some negotiation) just before his last departure for England. This new "frame of government" served as a sort of constitution for both Delaware and Pennsylvania until the Revolution. West New Jersey was politically united to East New Jersey under a royal government in 1702; but that region, peopled largely by Quakers and economically dependent upon Philadelphia, still regarded Quaker city as its social and cultural metropolis.

By the terms of the Charter of Privileges, the framework of government in Pennsylvania was left extremely vague. Its first article provided for religious toleration for all those who worshiped one God—a long step beyond the more limited toleration of most of the other colonies—and that all persons believing in Christ might hold office. It provided for an elected assembly with great power, and for the direct nomination of sheriffs and coroners by the voters. The "lower counties" of Delaware were authorized to separate from Pennsylvania if they so desired (which they promptly did); but the document made no mention of a legislative council for either of the provinces. Practically, therefore, from this point on both Pennsylvania and Delaware were governed by one-house legislatures; and by the terms of the charter these legislatures were given many of the powers for which other colonial legislatures were to struggle against the prerogative for a century—powers such as fixed annual meetings, the right of the assembly to choose its own speaker, the right to pass upon the qualifications of its members, adjournment, and "all other Powers and Privileges of an Assembly, according to the Rights of the Freeborn Subjects of *England,* and as is usual in any of the King's plantations in *America*." By this last remarkable phrase Penn appears to have granted the contention of the colonists (later to be eloquently denied by Governor William Keith) that their assembly was a parliament, built upon the rights of Englishmen to representation in their government.

In any case, the assembly was the central organ of government. The "prerogative," in Pennsylvania, was the prerogative of the proprietor; but even this was effectively nullified by the successful denial by the assembly, in 1704, of the proprietors' right to veto laws passed by it, after such laws had been approved by the governor. The right of the king to disallow Pennsylvania legislation, reserved in the original charter to William Penn, was, of course, still effective; but it was seldom exercised. The governors early showed a tendency to encourage the appointive council to assume legislative powers, which the council proceeded to exercise in the guise of "advice" to the governor; but the assembly resisted this tendency, too, on the ground that, under the Charter of Privileges, no such legislative power for the council was intended—a contention that was confirmed in practice by Governor William Keith (1717-28).

Partly because of the autonomous nature of the Pennsylvania government, partly because of the settled policy of the Crown already noted, and partly also because of Penn's financial difficulties, the Crown made an agreement with the proprietor in 1712 to purchase his rights for £12,000, and actually paid him £1,000 on account, but the deal fell through, largely because of Penn's protracted illness. Upon his death in 1718, the Board of Trade revived the idea, and in 1721 strongly recommended that Pennsylvania be made a royal province—as was done for South Carolina at about the same time. But the Whig government now in power declined to act upon this recommendation, and the movement collapsed.

Under the "young proprietors," John, Thomas, and Richard Penn, the political history of the province revolved around two major problems—the hold of the Quakers on government in the face of a growing non-Quaker population, and the relationship of the province to the proprietors. Out of the first problem grew the political factions of the province; out of the second grew a conflict between the province and the proprietors that foreshadowed the struggle for independence.

At the beginning of the century, when the Quakers constituted a majority of the population, political factions were built upon "proprietary" and "anti-proprietary" groups. But as the colony expanded, the interest-groups gradually shifted. With the great influx of newcomers, the Quakers found themselves in a numerical minority; but because many of the newcomers, particularly the Germans, were willing to accept the Quaker leadership, the Quaker "party" retained its control over Pennsylvania politics long after their numbers had ceased to justify it. As the Quakers became affluent, they tended to become more conservative—some of them even relaxed their principles to the point of owning slaves. They were less and less sympathetic to the problems of the frontier and, being opposed to war, they successfully blocked appropriations for provincial defense. At the same time, the "young proprietors" had become communicants of the Anglican Church, which separated them from the Quakers, and, by their avaricious attitude toward their "estate," they alienated the Indians and made them a danger to the frontiers of the province for the first time in its history. The newcomers on the frontiers, naturally enough, were embittered both toward the proprietors for their avarice and carelessness and toward the Quakers and their associates for their lack of understanding and their refusal to provide for frontier defense. The political alignments in the province thus tended to take the form of the "gentlemen's party" composed of wealthy Quaker merchants and their German followers, as against the "popular" or "country" party made up of small farmers and frontiersmen. The Quaker group was able to maintain its political hold upon the province until 1757, when their stubborn refusal to provide any defense for the frontiers against the Indians left that region to become the scene of a brutal and barbarous Indian war, and the British Crown, determined to break the impasse, threatened to make members of the assembly take the oaths usually required of officials and representatives throughout the empire. The threat was sufficient, and a number of the Quaker representatives resigned to make way for men more in sympathy with a policy of military defense. The conflict between the "gentlemen's party" and the "popular party," which was social and sectional as well as political, was thus brought to a resolution, for the time being, over the question of defense.

It was this same question of defense which precipitated the struggle against the proprietors. For although the Penns withheld much of the best land in the province for speculative purposes, they refused to contribute to the colony's defense until the assembly threatened to tax the proprietary lands for the purpose. The Penns then agreed, in 1755, to contribute £5,000 to the cause, but the fury of the province was roused when it was found that this sum was to be paid from the money that might be collected from quitrents already in arrears! Many of the provincial leaders determined to seek the overthrow of the proprietors and the assumption of control by the Crown. They cited the fact that the proprietors had speculated in provincial lands for their own selfish profit; they had alienated and antagonized the Indians while refusing to contribute to the colony's defense; they refused to permit the organization of a militia by the province unless they should be permitted to name the officers; now they finally refused to accept petitions for improvement from the provincial assembly—thus denying one of the oldest and most treasured rights of Englishmen. It was for reasons such as these that the assembly finally sent Benjamin Franklin to London in 1764 to present to the Privy Council the prayer of the province that the proprietary regime be brought to an end. But the plea came to England just at the moment when the British imperial system was being revised. In the face of the Sugar Act of 1764 and the Stamp Act that was to follow, Pennsylvania enthusiasm for direct royal control cooled; and the resentment against the "tyranny" of the proprietary was swallowed up in the bitter contest that now broke out against the "tyranny" of the king.

Pennsylvania had enjoyed what was by far the most autonomous provincial government in all British America, with the exception of Rhode Island and Connecticut. Andrew Hamilton exulted, in 1739, that

It is our great happiness that instead of triennial assemblies, a privilege which several other colonies have in vain endeavored to obtain, ours are annual and for that reason less liable to be practiced upon or corrupted. We sit upon our own adjournments when we please and as long as we think necessary and are not to be sent a-packing in the middle of a debate and disabled from representing our just grievances to our gracious sovereign. . . . We have no officers but what are necessary . . . and those generally elected by the people or appointed by their representatives. . . . Our foreign trade and shipping are free from all imposts except those small duties payable by the law to Great Britain. The taxes we pay for carrying on the public service are inconsiderable, for the sole power of raising and *disposing* money is lodged in the Assembly, who appoint their own treasurer and to them alone is he accountable. Such is our happy state as to civil rights.

But even that amount of autonomy was not enough. Governor Robert Hunter Morris wrote in 1755 that the Pennsylvania assembly had been "most remarkably indulged, both by the Crown and Proprietaries, and are suffered to enjoy Powers unknown to any Assembly upon the Continent, and even such as may render them a very dangerous Body hereafter; but not content with Privileges granted to them by Charter they claim many more and among others an absolute exemption from the Force of Royal and Proprietary Instructions."

There was something inherent in their situation that was propelling the men of this new community, as in the other American communities like it, toward an ever more complete autonomy. This phenomenon, illustrated both by the movement against the proprietor and the move for independence with which it merged, was a movement, hardly self-conscious but none-the-less real, toward a complete and independent control of their own affairs.

SOCIAL AND ECONOMIC EXPANSION

At the base of the political evolution, just reviewed, lay the phenomenal social growth and economic expansion of the Quaker provinces during the same period. For Pennsylvania was that one of all the British colonies which received the greatest influx of new settlers during the eighteenth century. By 1755 the population of the province had risen from some 20,000 in 1701 to about 200,000, and about half the population of the province was made up of Germans. Of the other half perhaps two-fifths were Quakers, two-fifths were Scotch-Irish Presbyterians from Ulster, and the remainder were a miscellany of Englishmen—Anglicans and Baptists—a few Jews, and some French Huguenots. In Delaware, where the population was about 25,000, the Quakers were probably a little less submerged by the influx of "foreigners."

The stream of Germans flowing into Pennsylvania was part of the larger flood pouring into all the colonies that has been discussed elsewhere. But by far the major volume of this flood came into this province, and from it flowed on into the back-country areas of the colonies farther south. It was estimated that, at the height of the movement, in the period from 1750 to 1754, at least 25,000 Germans arrived in Philadelphia alone. This wave of emigration from Europe brought to Pennsylvania crowds of indentured servants and "redemptioners" from the poor and the persecuted classes of Germany. Great numbers of these served terms on the lands of Englishmen or long-established Germans in the older parts of Pennsylvania and Delaware; as a matter of fact, the farmers drew upon this stream of immigrants for their chief labor supply. But land in the older parts of the province was high, and the redemptioner, when he finished his term of service, would go farther away, into the frontier region where land could be had more cheaply. Thus it fell out that, whereas the land along the Delaware was settled largely by Englishmen, the lands between this strip and the Susquehanna River were settled by Germans, who, by their industry and thrift, became prosperous and widely known as the "Pennsylvania Dutch."

Beyond the lands settled preponderantly by Germans, the Scotch-Irish became the settlers of the farthest frontier, along the branches of the upper Susquehanna. Many of these men, who made poor laborers because of their combativeness and their adventuresome spirit, merely squatted on land where and as they found it, and made trouble for anyone who might try to make them pay for it or to put them off—since, as they said, it was "against the law of God and of nature that so much land should remain idle while so many Christians wanted it to labor on." But they were Indian fighters *par excellence;* and they had scant patience with the pacifism of the Quaker majority in the assembly. It was they who were exposed to the marauding ferocity of the savages—for which they generally gave as good as they received—and it was chiefly they who finally forced an abandonment of the Quaker policy of pacifism in 1757. As the lands east of the higher ranges of the Alleghenies in Pennsylvania filled up, the Scotch-Irish mingled with the Germans in a steady, slow-moving stream of population southward along the natural barriers into Western Maryland and the Great Valley and the Piedmont of Virginia and the Carolinas.

Naturally enough, this extraordinary influx of people into Pennsylvania tended to raise the price of land, and land speculation became an important part of economic life. The Penns themselves, as already noted, held back much of their best land for speculative purposes; but the older English merchants and planters of Philadelphia and New Castle also saw the opportunity and seized upon it, buying up large quantities and selling it again at advanced prices. Thus, by the middle of the century, a man who purchased land from the proprietor would have to pay £15.10. per hundred acres, or, roughly, three shillings an acre, in addition to which all land in the province paid the proprietors a permanent quitrent of one penny per year per acre. Prices charged by speculators were, of course, much higher, but even the proprietors' terms seemed high to many prospective settlers, and this was partly responsible for the continued march toward the regions farther south.

Incidentally, the high price of land, the economic dependence of the frontiersmen upon the merchants of Philadelphia, and the political conservatism of the Quaker-controlled assembly, all combined to produce a sectional feeling between the frontiersmen and the farmers who composed the bulk of the "popular party," on the one hand, and the relatively wealthy and aristocratic merchants and land speculators who made up the "gentlemen's party" on the other. The newcomers might, indeed, early have gotten control of the provincial government had it not been for the fact that the Germans, most of whom spoke little or no English, and many of whom were not yet English citizens anyway, tended to follow the political leadership of the Quakers, with whom, religiously, most of the Germans had much in common.

Be that as it may, the rapidly expanding economy of Pennsylvania made it, in the eighteenth century, probably the most prosperous area in the British colonial empire. In addition to a rich soil and an equable climate, the province was fortunate in the fact that so many of its people were serious-minded, industrious workers. The Quakers had set the style in the beginning, but the industrious Germans continued the tradition, and Pennsylvania became the producer of a great variety of exportable products. Predominantly a farming area, the province produced in great abundance such foodstuffs as wheat and flour, rye, Indian corn, oats and other grains, and cattle, swine, horses, and other livestock. These foodstuffs were exported to the West Indies, to the southern colonies and to the countries of southern Europe. But the province also could already boast several considerable industries: pig and bar iron were shipped to some of the northern colonies and directly to England; Philadelphia was second only to New York as a market for the western fur trade, and the pelts were shipped to the mother country; from the forests of the province came lumber, barrels, and ships—of which considerable numbers were built along the Delaware. Thus the colony had a great surplus of exports of its own production, and had them in greater variety, probably, than any other colony.

The great wealth of the colony was thus based upon its own agriculture and its industry, the products of which were sold abroad. During the century, as population, agriculture and industry expanded together, the commerce of the province showed a parallel expansion. For example, the Board of Trade in 1721 estimated the annual imports of Pennsylvania from Great Britain to be some £20,000 and its exports to the mother country to be, roughly, £5,000. But in 1769 imports from England amounted to £203,000 and exports to the mother country totaled £28,000. But the trade with the mother country was only a part of the total commerce of the colony, for its best customers were the West Indies and the countries of southern Europe. From the West Indies were imported rum, sugar, and molasses; from southern Europe came fruits and wines: "port" and "Madeira" were the drinks of gentlemen; rum was the drink of working men. The import trade from both places, and particularly the latter, were highly profitable to the province, and from them was made up the province's favorable balance of payments. Thus in 1769, while the trade with England ran heavily against the colony, Pennsylvania's total exports were some £410,000 as against total imports of £400,000—and there were certain invisible items, such as freights and services on credits, which would make the favorable balance even greater than it appears.

Thus did Pennsylvania grow, and it rapidly accumulated wealth. But the unfavorable balance in England's favor drained the hard money out of the province at a time when it greatly needed a circulating medium with which to finance its expansion. Commodities, such as wheat, were used as money, but many men, among them Governor William Keith and Benjamin Franklin, favored the issuance of paper money. This was done, and the money was lent to borrowers on the security of their gold and silver, at interest; and it was so well managed as to enjoy an enviable record among the colonies for stability. This same canniness made it possible for Pennsylvania to boast that it was practically without direct taxes, since the expenses of government were paid from this interest on the provincial money and the income from certain excise taxes on the sale of liquor. That was indeed a happy land of which Governor Robert Hunter Morris could write in 1755, "We are burthened with no taxes and are not only out of Debt, but have a Revenue of Seven Thousand [pounds] a year and Fifteen Thousand in Bank, all at the Disposal of the House of Assembly."

THE CULTURE OF THE MELTING POT

In provincial Pennsylvania, as in the other colonies, the cultural development of the province in the eighteenth century shows a distinct trend toward a general secularization of life and thought. But the most characteristic features of the budding civilization of Pennsylvania and its cultural dependencies were its cosmopolitan make-up and its relatively broad tolerance. It was not ill-advisedly that Benjamin Franklin "fled" from Boston to Philadelphia as a boy! Franklin, indeed, is a symbol of the development of intellectual life in Pennsylvania as well as a figure transcending provincial boundary lines, for within a period of some six years he wrote *A Dissertation on Liberty and Necessity, Pleasure and Pain* (written in London in 1725), a materialistic discussion of religion— later revised in the more conservative *Articles of Belief and Acts of Religion,* and his *Modest Inquiry into the Nature and Necessity of a Paper Currency* (1729), which argued the necessity of a larger supply of money with which to finance the rapidly expanding provincial economy, organized "the Junto" (1727), a debating society interested in moral, political and philosophical questions, and began, in partnership with Hugh Meredith, the publication of *The Pennsylvania Gazette* (1729), which was the most distinguished newspaper in Pennsylvania for half a century or more. A little later he took a leading part in the organization of the American Philosophical Society (1743), in the establishment of a city hospital in Philadelphia (1751), and in the founding of the Philadelphia Academy (1753) which became the nucleus of the University of Pennsylvania. Meanwhile, he was studying and experimenting in various branches of science, bringing his studies to a brilliant climax in his experiments with electricity. Thus in his interest in science and its influence upon his thought, in his economic thinking, itself the outgrowth of the actual situation in his province, in his newspaper work, and in his active support of secular education, Franklin illustrates the influence of science and the general secularization of life that were working themselves out in Pennsylvania. In his publication of books in German, too, and his writings dealing with the problems of defense and Indian relations, he gives voice to the peculiar cultural developments inherent in Pennsylvania's polyglot population and its experience on the frontier.

But Franklin was far from being the only cultivated man in Pennsylvania. For one of his contemporaries, John Bartram, was the first notable American botanist; David Rittenhouse, another contemporary, achieved great distinction in the realm of mathematics and astronomy; Doctors John Morgan and Benjamin Rush founded the first medical school in the colonies; and William Smith, headmaster of the Philadelphia Academy, was a distinguished educator and writer. And there were many others.

If Pennsylvania was one of the most conglomerate colonies in point of population, it was also one of the most conglomerate in point of religion. For surely here was the greatest mixture of religions in the western hemisphere. The original settlers had been Quakers, with a few Anglicans and German Lutherans, who mixed with the remnants of the old Dutch Protestants and Swedish Lutherans along the lower Delaware. With the influx of newcomers after the Peace of Utrecht (1713), the Scotch-Irish brought their Presbyterianism, French Huguenots brought their Huguenot faith, and among the newcomers there began to appear both English and German Baptists and a number of Jews. The greatest variety was to be found among the Germans. For the German pietist movements had split the Germans into literally dozens of slightly differing sects; and members of many of these sects had fled to America to escape the religious persecution at home. It thus fell out that some of the most important of the new German communities in Pennsylvania were strongly religious in character. Such was the case, for example, at Bethlehem, founded by the Moravian Brethren. There were many such sects, in communities and out of them; and they contributed a strong cultural influence in the province. The most influential of all the Germans was Christopher Sauer, a printer and editor, who published a German-language newspaper, the *Pennsylvania Berichte,* along with many religious and secular books in German. Sauer was a real leader of his people, and exercised a remarkable influence upon their political opinions and cultural life.

Naturally enough, the existence side by side of such a variety of religions, encouraged to come to Pennsylvania in the first place by William Penn himself, made for an increasingly broad tolerance in the province, and the provision of the Charter of Liberties of 1701 that all who worshiped one God should be tolerated was probably even exceeded in practice; and Gottlieb Mittelberger could write, in 1750, that Pennsylvania "possesses great liberties above all other English colonies, inasmuch as all religious sects are tolerated there. . . . But there are many hundred unbaptized souls there that do not even wish to be baptized." Education, in the absence of any sect sufficiently dominant to establish a public system such as existed in New England, was left in the hands of the churches, with the result that each sect usually supported its own denominational school.

Philadelphia was the metropolis of Pennsylvania, Delaware, and western New Jersey, as New York was the metropolis of Connecticut, New York, and eastern New Jersey. By the time of the Revolution, it was the richest city on the coast and could boast a public library, a theater, and a university. It was a commercial city, shipping out the wheat and other foodstuffs produced round about, as well as furs and lumber. Its exports, like those of New York, went to the West Indies, to Madeira, to the Mediterranean, to the British Isles, and to the continent of Europe itself. In return for foodstuffs, lumber, and furs, the merchants of Philadelphia received sugar and molasses from the West Indies, fruits and wines from Madeira and the Mediterranean, and manufactured goods from northern Europe. Of particular interest is the expansion of the western trade with the Indians, for a large item in the imports of the Philadelphia merchants was "Indian goods," such as blankets, shirts, shoes, hatchets, knives, guns, and gunpowder, which were shipped westward over the mountains into the valley of the Ohio. The commerce across the mountains began about the end of King George's War and had grown to considerable proportions by 1754. It was this economic penetration of the Ohio Valley that precipitated the conflict between the British and the French in that region.

Social life in Philadelphia was relatively gay. There was no permanent theater until about 1756 but there were many clubs and taverns for social intercourse, and the denizens of the city enjoyed such sports as skating, dancing, sleighrides, and the like. By the end of the period the city could boast many churches, a hospital, regular street sanitation, street lights, and other municipal improvements.

In general, then, the cultural life of "the Quaker empire" was extremely mixed. For here mingled not only races, nationalities and languages, but religions and cultures as well. At the same time, the influence of the frontier experience upon culture was one making for individualism, a sort of philosophical pragmatism, and a broader tolerance than existed, probably, elsewhere in the western world. Pennsylvania was making many contributions to the emerging "American" culture; but in the characteristics just reviewed, the cultural life of the province was still peculiarly "Pennsylvanian."

RECOMMENDED BOOKS FOR FURTHER READING

Contemporary Narratives

Andrew Burnaby, *Travels through the Middle Settlements in North America . . . 1759 and 1760.*
Benjamin Franklin, *Autobiography.*
Alexander Graydon, *Memoirs of a Life, Chiefly Passed in Pennsylvania.*
Gottlieb Mittelberger, *Gottlieb Mittelberger's Journey to Pennsylvania in the Year 1750.*

Francis Daniel Pastorius, *Pastorius' Description of Pennsylvania, 1700* (Old South Leaflets, no. 95).

William Smith, *A Brief State of the Province of Pennsylvania.*

The Universal Instructor in all Arts and Sciences: and Pennsylvania Gazette.

John F. Watson, *Annals of Philadelphia and Pennsylvania in the Olden Time,* Volume I.

MODERN ACCOUNTS

Lucy F. Bittinger, *The Germans in Colonial Times.*

Beverley W. Bond, *The Quit-Rent System in the American Colonies.*

Edward Channing, *A History of the United States,* II, Chapter 9.

Frank R. Diffenderffer, *German Immigration into Pennsylvania through the Port of Philadelphia from 1700 to 1775,* Part II: *The Redemptioners.*

Sydney G. Fisher, *The Making of Pennsylvania.*

Paul L. Ford, *The Many-Sided Franklin.*

Karl F. Geiser, *Redemptioners and Indentured Servants in . . . Pennsylvania.*

Lawrence H. Gipson, *The British Empire before the American Revolution,* III, Chapters 6-8.

Lawrence H. Gipson, *Crime and its Punishment in Provincial Pennsylvania.*

Cheesman A. Herrick, *White Servitude in Pennsylvania.*

James O. Knauss, *Social Conditions among the Pennsylvania Germans in the Eighteenth Century.*

Herbert L. Osgood, *The American Colonies in the Eighteenth Century,* II, Part I, Chapter 24, Part II, Chapter 7; IV, Part III, Chapter 6.

Winfred T. Root, *The Relations of Pennsylvania with the British Government, 1696-1765,* Chapter 7.

Julius F. Sachse, *The German Sectarians of Pennsylvania, 1708-1800,* Volume I.

Max Savelle, *George Morgan, Colony Builder,* Chapters 1-4.

John T. Scharf and Thompson Westcott, *History of Philadelphia, 1609-1884,* Volume I.

Isaac Sharpless, *A Quaker Experiment in Government.*

William R. Shepherd, *History of Proprietary Government in Pennsylvania.*

Carl C. Van Doren, *Benjamin Franklin.*

34

Proprietary Maryland

IN THE troublous times in Maryland attendant upon the accession of William and Mary to the throne of England, a "revolution" had taken place in the province that had resulted in the seizure of power by the "Protestant"—or Anglican—faction, and the Roman Catholic Calverts had lost their governmental powers. Thus Maryland became a royal province in 1691. The proprietor still retained his title to the land, however, so that Maryland was in effect half-royal, half-proprietary; and this mixed status the colony retained until 1715. As the "revolution" had been chiefly an effort to wrest control of government from the Roman Catholic faction, then in a minority, the conversion of Charles Calvert, the young proprietor, to Protestantism in 1715 furnished a plausible excuse for restoring to him his political power. Thus the original charter to the first Lord Baltimore became again completely operative. In the light of the clearly defined policy of the imperial administration in this period, however, this event was obviously an aberration from the direction then being taken in the control of colonial affairs, which was tending definitely toward bringing all the colonies under royal control. It must be regarded as something of a step backward, too; for nowhere, probably, had proprietary government ever been as efficient or as beneficial, in the long run, as the royal form.

THE LEGISLATIVE TROUBLES OF A PROPRIETOR

Be that as it may, Maryland remained a proprietary province from 1715 until the American Revolution; and its political history presents an interesting chapter in the series of experiments in provincial government being conducted in the American colonies of that period. To begin with, the period of royal government had established a tradition of direct relationship with the Crown which nourished an anti-proprietary movement that flourished toward the end of the colonial era. For a long time the Anglican faction in Maryland, still in control of the government, looked with distrust upon the young proprietor's "conversion" to Protestantism, and this distrust was fanned into a flame by a long-drawn contest be-

481

tween Governor John Hart, who had also been governor under the Crown, and Charles Carroll, the proprietor's Roman Catholic agent, over the extent and limits of the agent's powers and prerogatives. The dispute finally ended in limiting the agent, in general, to affairs which concerned the property rights of the proprietor. But the prerogative of the proprietor himself was called into question when he persisted in vetoing a series of laws providing for the application of English statutes to Maryland. His disallowance of these legislative acts was probably wise; but it infuriated the legislators, who, under the leadership of Daniel Dulany, complained that the proprietor was denying the people of Maryland the rights of Englishmen to the protection of English law. The legislature even went so far, in 1729, as to pass a resolution questioning the proprietor's right to veto laws passed by the assembly at all, since, they said, "ample and full power of legislation is lodged in this province," and "it is we (the assembly) that are the people's representatives for whom all laws are made and human government established." The contest with the proprietor continued from this point on at an accelerated pace, and in 1739 the house of delegates attacked the proprietary system itself, under which, it asserted, "the people of this province [are] made a property to his lordship's officers," and new settlers were discouraged from coming to the province by the exorbitant fees charged by the proprietor's land office. As time went on the assembly steadily increased its powers; and, especially during the Seven Years' War, it used the need for assembly action in the maintenance of the colonial defenses to reduce the powers of the proprietary. In 1756 the assembly passed a revenue law which taxed the proprietor's lands, and in 1762 the house of delegates commissioned Benjamin Franklin to act as its agent in presenting its complaints against the proprietary system in general—a move, by the way, which paralleled the similar anti-proprietary movement in Pennsylvania. The complaint was without result, as far as Maryland was concerned.

The anti-proprietary movement in Maryland accomplished little in the direction of ending the proprietary regime. It is significant, however, as one aspect of the struggle of the house of delegates, that is, the lower house of the assembly, to extend its powers to the point of dominating the entire government. For here in Maryland, as elsewhere, the elected representatives of the people looked upon themselves as constituting a sort of local House of Commons, with all the powers and privileges that that involved. They quarreled with the governor and the council over their powers as well as with the proprietor. Thus the house of delegates insisted that it had the sole right to initiate money bills, and that it might eject from its membership individuals accepting appointments by the proprietor or his agents. On the other hand, it claimed the right to name certain officials, particularly the provincial treasurer and an agent of the colony in London, and make them responsible to itself.

In this struggle to increase its powers over government, the assembly did achieve a good deal. In the minds of most of the delegates, who constituted what was called the "country party," the council and the appointed officials were identified with the proprietary interest in the "court party." Against this group, in which the executive branch of government was identified with the upper house of the legislature as well as the "prerogative," the assembly succeeded in establishing its power over money bills, the governor's salary, and military appropriations, the right to name commissioners to assist the governor in the conduct of Indian relations, and in many other matters.

In general, it may be said that here, as elsewhere in the colonies, the representatives of the people were feeling their way toward a set of political institutions that would place the ultimate control of affairs in the hands of the voters or their representatives. Steadily and consistently claiming to have all the rights and privileges of a House of Commons in Maryland, the house of delegates sought, and expected, to have the evolution of government in the province follow the pattern of political evolution in England. Against this claim the proprietor's governor, Horatio Sharpe, followed the attorney-general Charles Pratt (later Lord Camden) given in 1760 to the effect that the

House of Commons stands upon its own laws, the *Lex Parlamenti;* whereas assemblies in the colonies are regulated by their respective charters, usages, and the common law of England, and will never be allowed to assume all those privileges which the House of Commons are entitled to . . . neither the Crown nor Parliament will ever suffer these assemblies to erect themselves into the power and authority of the British House of Commons.

But the house of delegates based its position upon the Lockeian doctrines of natural law and the rights of free-born Englishmen, and continued the contest with the prerogative as exercised by the proprietary, while public opinion tended more and more to demand the end of the proprietary regime and the return of the province to royal status—that is, until the disputes of the era of the Stamp Act raised the question whether royal status might not be just as oppressive as the proprietary regime. In its broadest aspects the parliamentary struggle in Maryland was a struggle for legislative autonomy against the arbitrary limitations placed upon the popular will of the province by a proprietary government resident three thousand miles away. Throughout the later proprietary period the executive, acting for the proprietor, was on the defensive, and sought to check the growing power of the lower house of the legislature. The house, on the other side, was constantly and increasingly aggressive in its long struggle toward provincial political autonomy.

AN ECONOMIC HOUSE DIVIDED

The older parts of Maryland, lying about the shores of Chesapeake Bay and the lower Potomac had always been devoted to the production of tobacco. In the eighteenth century, the tobacco plantations in eastern Maryland continued to export this Chesapeake staple—at the rate of some thirty-two thousand hogsheads annually, requiring two hundred ships manned by four thousand men, to carry it to England.

But concentration upon the production of tobacco made the colony subject to all the vicissitudes of a temperamental market, and one of the major themes in Maryland's history—as in Virginia's—is the succession of efforts to meet the situation. There were two main factors involved. One was the behavior of the market itself, which could not be influenced except by controlling the amount of tobacco offered for sale, and the other was the quality of the tobacco offered, which determined its relative value in a competitive market. On both these lines Maryland and Virginia attempted to manage the tobacco trade for the benefit of their planters.

The first efforts at control of production and quality were made by private individuals in London and in Maryland under the leadership of Henry Darnell, a Maryland planter. These efforts failed of success, and the Maryland legislature in 1727 passed a law which went much further in the direction of regulating the handling of tobacco intended for export than any previous law had done. But this law, which tried to establish a standard of quality in tobacco for export, was thought to be too favorable to the great planters, and it failed to achieve its intended effect. The next year a new law was passed which limited the number of tobacco plants a planter might set out according to the number of workers on any given plantation—a provision intended to favor the small planters. But this law was disallowed by the proprietor because it reduced by one-fourth the amount of tobacco to be paid the members of the Anglican clergy for their salaries. Another effort at crop-limitation was made in 1730. This law was approved; but as Virginia in the same year passed a more stringent law along the same line, thus making sure that exported Virginia tobacco should be superior to the Maryland product, the situation of the Maryland planters was not much improved. After another decade and a half of depression and uncertainty a new and stronger inspection law was passed in 1747, requiring that all tobacco for export be inspected at public warehouses, and that tobacco not meeting the standard be destroyed. In order to meet the need for a negotiable currency—already partially supplied by the provincial currency which had its beginning in 1733—the tobacco inspectors were empowered to issue notes for the value of the tobacco received, and these were circulated as money. This law remained the basis of Maryland's control of its tobacco production until the eve of the Revolution; but it was not entirely successful, and the tobacco planters continued to face the discouragements presented by warfare, competition and an uncertain market.

Meanwhile, the people and the legislature of Maryland had sought to improve their economic condition by a diversification of their products. As early as 1727 the legislature placed a bounty upon hemp, and a similar bounty was later placed upon linen. Similarly, encouragements were given to men engaged in the production of iron. This industry, in fact, did develop to a considerable degree; by the mid-century Maryland had eight furnaces and nine forges, and was exporting iron to the value of some £16,000. Maryland was second only to Pennsylvania in the production of iron. The province also exported considerable quantities of furs, lumber and grain.

But it was the increase in population, particularly in the "up-country" counties, that was most effective in diversifying Maryland's economic life. For the population of the province had risen from some thirty-five thousand at the beginning of the century to, roughly, one hundred and fifty thousand at the middle of the century, and a very considerable proportion of the newcomers went into the back-country and settled on relatively small farms, where they devoted themselves to the raising of livestock and grain. The town of Baltimore, founded at the head of tidewater on Chesapeake Bay about 1730, because of its proximity to the rapidly developing back-country, quickly became an important center of commerce in these back-country products, particularly grain.

Thus, in 1753, a list of exports from Maryland included tobacco, wheat, corn, iron, pork, beans, fish, and lumber. The province was rapidly achieving a degree of diversification, but it was still dependent upon England and the northern colonies for its manufactured goods as well as for the markets for its own products, and its position, therefore, was in general that of a debtor community. There was little or no protest against British regulation of Maryland's commerce; yet the diversification of Maryland's products, with a consequently increased interest in markets other than the old protected tobacco market in England, tended to range Maryland, in its economic interests and in its economic thinking, alongside of the northern commercial colonies. The staple, tobacco, had failed to provide a basis for a permanent prosperity; diversification was a contributing influence in the trend in the province toward economic self-sufficiency, even independence.

SOCIAL AND INTELLECTUAL CHANGE

The tobacco planters of the Maryland tidewater were divided into several levels. At the top of the planter society were the aristocrats, operating their plantations by a system of slave labor; the slave population increased from some five thousand at the beginning of the century to nearly fifty thousand in 1756. Frontier conditions had practically disappeared by about 1730; life in the red brick Georgian houses of the planters was of a refined, sophisticated sort, fashioned after an English model. Anglicanism was the predominant religion, although there were still a good many Roman Catholics, many of whom rose to great distinction in the history of the colony and of the subsequent nation. Among the greater landowners, estates might be from twenty thousand to forty thousand acres in size, often broken into sections located in several counties, although holdings of such size were not as common as might be supposed; estates of five thousand acres were much nearer the average. About one-fourth of the land was held in small parcels of about two hundred acres; but such small plantations could hardly be called profitable, and their owners were not of the same social status of the large landowners. On the contrary, they were looked upon as "the poor," standing only a little above the landless whites and the indentured servants in the social scale.

The sons of the wealthiest planters were educated in England,

and the great planters' houses were decorated with furnishings imported from London. Devoted to horsemanship, they produced a famous breed of race horses. Hospitable and cultivated, they dispensed a lavish hospitality marked by good food and imported wines. Annapolis, seat of the government, was also the center of society. By 1752 Annapolis could boast occasional theatrical performances, and in 1772 was built a permanent theater. The *Maryland Gazette,* published here, was one of the most distinguished colonial newspapers. Annapolis, indeed, according to the Reverend Jonathan Boucher, was "the genteelest town in North America."

In sharp contrast to the gay, sophisticated life of the planters and the "court" was that of the farmers on the frontier, which, in Maryland, lay along the Pennsylvania boundary and in the Piedmont lying east of the mountains. This country began to fill up rapidly in the fourth and fifth decades of the century, and its population was a mixture of Englishmen from the tidewater areas of Maryland and Germans who were moving in through Pennsylvania, bringing with them their language and their customs. In religion the English were liable to be Presbyterians or Quakers; but the Germans were Lutherans, Reformed, Moravians, or members of other pietist sects.

In its economic life, the "old west" of Maryland—centering in Frederick County and the town of Frederick—was devoted to farming on a relatively small scale. The soil was fertile, and the people were industrious; an anti-slavery tradition and transportation difficulties discouraged the cultivation of tobacco. This region, therefore, turned to wheat, corn and livestock, and shipped its surpluses to Baltimore and Philadelphia. Naturally enough, the society and social ideas of this section of Maryland were sharply different from those of the tidewater. Baltimore was the metropolis of this new society as Annapolis was the center of the older tidewater, and its society quickly became a society of sober businessmen, as contrasted with the gay, aristocratic society of the "court."

Maryland was thus a province with two distinct sectional societies. The frontier was bound to the older area in several ways, however. Many of the wealthy planters, such as Daniel Dulany, speculated in frontier lands; some even arranged for the transportation of immigrant families. The new areas were given representation in the house of delegates, but the Germans, because, largely, of language difficulties or to religious scruples over the taking of oaths, took little interest in politics, and this side of life fell largely into the hands of Scotch-Irish Presbyterians. The newcomers to Maryland were interested in settlement and social growth, not politics. Government remained largely in the hands of the Anglican upper class; and in the absence of any acute issue between the two sections, Maryland was singularly free from sectional conflict.

RECOMMENDED BOOKS FOR FURTHER READING

CONTEMPORARY NARRATIVES

Jonathan Boucher, *Reminiscences of an American Loyalist, 1738-1789*, edited by Jonathan Boucher.

William Eddis, *Letters from America, Historical and Descriptive.*

Philip Vickers Fithian, *Journal and Letters, 1767-1774*, edited by John R. Williams.

The Maryland Gazette.

Newton D. Mereness, ed., *Travels in the American Colonies.*

MODERN ACCOUNTS

Matthew P. Andrews, *The Founding of Maryland.*

Charles A. Barker, *The Background of the Revolution in Maryland.*

Kathryn L. Behrens, *Paper Money in Maryland, 1727-1789.*

Beverley W. Bond, *The Quit-Rent System in the American Colonies.*

Paul H. Giddens, "Trade and Industry in Colonial Maryland, 1753-1769," *Journal of Economic and Business History*, IV, 512-538.

Lawrence H. Gipson, *The British Empire before the American Revolution*, III, Chapter 2.

Clarence P. Gould, *The Land System of Maryland, 1720-1765.*

Clarence P. Gould, *Money and Transportation in Maryland, 1720-1765.*

Lewis C. Gray, *History of Agriculture in the Southern United States to 1860.*

Newton D. Mereness, *Maryland as a Proprietary Province.*

Margaret S. Morriss, *Colonial Trade of Maryland, 1689-1715.*

Herbert L. Osgood, *The American Colonies in the Eighteenth Century*, II, Part I, Chapter 22; III, Part II, Chapter 8.

John T. Scharf, *The Chronicles of Baltimore.*

St. George L. Sioussat, *Economics and Politics in Maryland, 1720-1750.*

Lewis W. Wilhelm, *Local Institutions of Maryland.*

Lawrence C. Wroth, *The History of Printing in Colonial Maryland, 1686-1776.*

35

The Expansion of Virginia

A CHANGING POPULATION

AT THE beginning of the eighteenth century Virginia was a
society of slaveowning planters. Even the planters just
beyond the fall line, who in Nathaniel Bacon's time had
revolted against the aristocratic oligarchy of Sir William Berkeley
and his favorites, had been absorbed into the pattern of the planter-
aristocracy. The colony was expanding, and, during the regime of
Lieutenant-Governor Alexander Spotswood (1710-22) settlement
moved steadily westward into the Piedmont. Spotswood himself
was intensely interested in this filling up of the west. About 1712 he
acquired a great estate on the Rapidan, in Spotsylvania county,
and about 1724 he established there a colony of Germans and
founded an iron works. In 1716 he led an expedition to the crest
of the Blue Ridge, where the explorers looked down upon the
beautiful and fertile valley of the Shenandoah. They took possession of the western lands in the name of King George II to the
accompaniment of copious libations, after which they popularized
the interest in the west by the formation of the "Knights of the
Golden Horseshoe."

But it was not until the second stream of immigration reached
Virginia, flowing southward along the great valley and the Piedmont from Pennsylvania and western Maryland, that Virginia began to grow so rapidly as to form, in the back-country, a new society, in many ways quite distinct from the older tobacco aristocracy
of the tidewater. This phenomenon got under way a little before
1730, and continued until a few years before the Revolution, or
until the tide of population movement turned westward over the
mountains from its former direction southward along the mountains and the Piedmont. The population of Virginia in 1721 was
some 95,000, of whom perhaps 72,000 were whites and 23,000
blacks. In 1756 Lieutenant-Governor Dinwiddie reported the population as nearly 300,000 souls, of whom about 175,000 were whites
and 125,000 were Negroes. By 1774 Governor Dunmore could report
(with, perhaps, a little exaggeration) that the population was now
half a million people, of whom three-fifths were white. Virginia's

population was multiplied, roughly, by five in approximately half a century; and the bulk of the increase settled in the Piedmont and "the valley."

These newcomers were largely Scotch-Irish and Germans from Pennsylvania, although another stream of immigrants made its way inland directly from the coast. Because these newcomers were Scotch-Irish Presbyterians or Germans of one dissenting sect or another, they resented the established power of the Anglican church. Many of them disapproved, moreover, of slavery. Most of them, indeed—partly because of religious principles, partly because frontier life had made them fiercely individualistic, even democratic —resented the aristocracy of the tidewater and its hold upon the political life of the province. They were, for the most part, industrious, thrifty farmers, who worked their farms and their herds with their own hands, and they looked with scorn upon the men of the tidewater who felt that work with one's hands was a sure sign that one was not a gentleman.

THE TOBACCO ARISTOCRACY OF THE TIDEWATER

In the tidewater area, on the other hand, lying roughly between the fall line and the sea, Virginia clung to its staple crop, tobacco, to its "capitalistic" plantation system of production based upon slavery, and to its aristocratic ways of life. The size of plantations in this area had steadily increased, until estates ranging up to eighty thousand acres were not uncommon, and in exceptional cases a single man might own as many as a thousand slaves. The methods of slave-production were wasteful, however, and continuous cultivation of the soil resulted in a soil exhaustion which compelled the planters constantly to bring new soil under cultivation. Because of these factors, combined with the effect upon Virginia of fluctuating conditions in the world market, the planters found it increasingly difficult to make both ends meet.

Throughout the eighteenth century there was a steady, if uneven, decline in the profits derived from tobacco culture. The planters did their business through agents in England, called "factors," who purchased whatever the planter needed and charged the cost, along with his commission, against the yearly harvest of tobacco that the planter would ship him in the fall. As often as not the shipment would not pay the factor entirely, with the result that debts were carried forward from year to year, and even from father to son. Many, if not most, of the planters of tidewater Virginia were thus permanently in debt to the British merchants who served them as factors, and there was little hope of relief, either, so long as tobacco remained the staple crop; for all the tobacco raised in Virginia had, as an "enumerated" commodity, to be shipped only to England.

Many expedients were tried in the effort to break these strengthening ties of financial bondage that grew out of the unfavorable balance of payments. Laws were passed limiting the amount of tobacco that might be grown or providing for the destruction of inferior tobacco, only to be disallowed by the Crown. Tobacco was used quite generally as currency, but the colony also printed paper money; and in 1749 the legislature passed a law making this paper money legal tender for the payment of debts to British merchants at a fixed ratio to sterling. But this law, too, was disallowed, and in 1754 the governor was instructed not to sign any more laws like it. At other times import duties were placed upon slaves in order to prevent the tobacco-raising area from increasing, and efforts were made to have the British government reduce the duties on tobacco imported into England. In every case the Virginia efforts failed by reason of the opposition of British interests concerned in the tobacco business or the slave trade, and the condition of the planters grew progressively worse.

In the absence of industrialism, there seemed to be only one other way for the use of their capital upon which the planters could depend. For with the rush of newcomers during the fourth, fifth and sixth decades of the century, land was at a premium, and the planters found it profitable to rent their lands, especially those in the Piedmont and the valley, to tenants. But the practice of renting soon grew into the practice of selling, or, rather, of buying large quantities of land and selling it in small quantities to the settlers. This fact, with its resultant era of land speculation, is of profound importance in the history of the province; for, had the planters not found this method of employing their capital in a profitable way, it seems clear that the tidewater planters must eventually have found themselves in complete bankruptcy.

Be that as it may, the slow deterioration of the financial condition of the province was not visible on the surface, and life on the plantations followed a pattern that was distinctive and, in its own way, delightful and attractive. The planter and his family lived in the big house around which, at a convenient distance, were grouped the cabins of the slaves. As the century wore on the great planters attached more and more land to their plantations and bought more and more slaves. The poor whites moved on to the frontier, with the result that in the tidewater region there gradually took place a greater stratification of society than had ever been the case before. Plantations now lined the rivers flowing into Chesapeake Bay, and the ships from England came into the bay and spent several weeks going from plantation to plantation picking up cargoes and delivering packages of manufactured goods, some of which came from England, some of which came from New England. At the beginning of the century there were no towns worthy of the name. There was, indeed, no need for them; for London was the great metropolis of the Chesapeake colonies, and to a less degree Boston, New York, or Philadelphia served as markets for the plantation industry. Time and time again the house of burgesses tried to legislate towns into existence by requiring that exports be cleared through central warehouses, but to no avail. The people did not feel the need of towns, and towns did not develop. It was not until the growth of population beyond the fall line precipitated a need for an entrepôt between the upland farmers and the sea that towns began to appear. Thus it came about that Richmond, founded in 1737, at the falls of the James, gradually became Virginia's first city worthy of the name.

So far as the tidewater planters were concerned, commerce was still carried on directly with London. The planter shipped his tobacco from his own wharf directly to a factor or merchant in London or Boston, who credited his account and shipped him the manufactured goods that he needed in return. When the planter sent his son to Oxford the merchant was the son's banker, and when the planter wished to buy something in another country, such as France or Italy, he drew a bill of exchange upon the London merchant who handled the entire transaction. As already noted, under this system it was so easy to buy practically anything that was desired without cash that the Virginia planters were generally in debt.

This did not prevent the Virginia gentleman from living in a very comfortable, even luxurious, style. On the contrary, it seemed to make for a gay, easy-going, aristocratic social life. The town of Williamsburg, the capital, was the center of Virginia society and it became fashionable for all the planters who could afford it to spend at least a part of the year there, especially when the legislature was in session. The town was built about 1699 and the capitol was removed there after the disastrous fire at Jamestown during that same year. By 1720 Jamestown had become a ruin and Williamsburg had taken its place as the political and social center of the province. It was there that William and Mary College, founded in 1693, was located, and as a result the town also became the educational center of the province. Williamsburg, indeed, was one of the loveliest little towns in America. It was small and, as colonial towns went, somewhat crowded; but with the governor's palace and the Bruton parish church nearby, with the building of the college, designed by Christopher Wren, and with its lovely shaded streets, Williamsburg presented an aspect of beauty that was hardly rivaled by any other colonial city, except, perhaps, Charleston. Raleigh tavern, near the capitol, was the center of official and unofficial gaiety and witnessed many balls and parties. About 1716 there was built a theater in which the first play seems to have been Shakespeare's *Merchant of Venice*. The established religion in the colony was still Anglicanism; but the Church of England was never as puritanical in its outlook on life as the more extreme Protestant sects.

In the country as well as in the town, Virginia society of the tidewater was classified according to wealth. The "gentlemen," plantation owners and their sons, educated at the Inns of Court in London or at Oxford or Cambridge or William and Mary, constituted a privileged class. Their plantation homes were relatively remote from each other and communications were relatively infrequent. News of the outside world was fairly infrequent, as were indeed all contacts with people from any considerable distance. The planters, therefore, kept their houses open to each other, and travelers were particularly welcome. Sometimes servants were stationed at the crossroads to invite travelers on the road to stop and partake of the hospitality of the planter's home. Southern hospitality, at least among the favored aristocratic classes, became a proverbial feature of the plantation system.

The plantation itself was in large measure self-sufficing. It produced practically all its own food supply, with plentiful beef, pork, poultry, and wild life, and imported the luxuries of dress and furniture, books, and wines for the table. Horseback riding became as essential a part of the education of Virginia youth as the driving of an automobile has come to be in the twentieth century. For the planters in the course of their work of supervising their plantations spent hours and even days in the saddle. Horse racing, indeed, was a sport for "gentlemen only," and those not gentlemen were on occasion punished for indulging in it. By 1730 there had been established a regular race track at Williamsburg with two racing seasons, in the autumn and spring of every year. Among the students at William and Mary cockfighting seems to have been a prevalent sport, and the college authorities felt it necessary to pass legislation against it. For the laborers, that is, for the "poor whites," there were occasional picnics or fairs and such sports as cudgeling, wrestling, and musical competitions.

In the aristocratic society of the southern gentlemen, women occupied a position of exaggerated importance. Women were looked up to by the gentlemen and there grew up a romantic exaltation of women and a consequent refinement and artificiality of manners in regard to them which has been perpetuated in the term "the southern gentleman." Girls married at fifteen, sixteen, and seventeen; at twenty-five a girl was an old maid and considered somewhat peculiar. As already noted, the official religion of the province was Anglican; but religion was not allowed to interfere with gaiety. "A man might be a Christian in any church, but a gentleman must belong to the Church of England."

LAND SPECULATION AND THE TRANSMONTANE WEST

The rapid influx of newcomers into Virginia in the eighteenth century brought with it, as an almost inevitable consequence, a great wave of speculation in western lands. Land speculation, to be sure, was a phenomenon that was common to all the colonies and had played an important part in the development of all of them. Some great proprietary tracts, such as the Granville holdings in North Carolina and the Fairfax claim to the Northern Neck and the Shenandoah valley in Virginia, dated from the preceding century. But land speculation was peculiarly significant in Virginia, both for the development of Virginia itself and for the future history of civilization on this continent. In that colony most of the lands east of the mountains had been allotted to owners— speculators or settlers—by the middle of the century; now, for the first time, the tide of population began to trickle down the western slopes, and the speculators, sensing the turn and in anticipation of the profits to be derived from it, sought to get control of the lands into which the moving population would flow.

One of the earliest speculative requests for lands beyond the watershed appeared in 1743, when James Patten petitioned the Virginia Council for 200,000 acres of land along the upper reaches of Woods River, or the Kanawha, which flows into the Ohio. As the upper branches of the Woods River lay within the great valley, east of the Allegheny ridge, and only a few miles distant from the upper waters of the Roanoke and the James, Patten and his associates were probably not conscious of the significance of their proposed settlement. Yet in this region, in the extreme southwestern corner of Virginia, where the divide is almost imperceptible and where the rivers flowing east and those flowing west lie within a few miles of each other, the earliest settlers were already beginning to arrive, and it was only a few years later that the village of Draper's Meadows, between the upper waters of the Roanoke and the New River, or southern branch of the Kanawha, came into being.

In 1745 John Robinson, president of the Virginia council, received a grant of 100,000 acres on the Greenbrier River, northern branch of the Kanawha. In the same year similar grants were made to Henry Downs; and John Blair, another member of the council, was given, for himself and his associates, 100,000 acres on the Youghiogheny River, which flows into the Monongahela. Many similar grants followed, all for speculative purposes. Many of the leading speculators were members of the legislature, or otherwise prominent leaders in Virginia political life. But the most famous of these grants was a group of them made by the council in a wholesale fashion on July 9, 1748. On that day alone nearly 2,000,000 acres of land were handed out to prominent Virginia planter-politicians in six great companies, the most famous of which were the Loyal Company, headed by Dr. Thomas Walker, and the Ohio Company, led by Thomas Lee, a member of the council.

The Ohio Company was given 200,000 acres of land along the Ohio, and Christopher Gist, a surveyor and Indian trader, was sent over the mountains in 1749 to select the best lands for settlement. As a beginning the company fixed upon a tract of land between the Youghiogheny and the Monongahela, and prepared to send in settlers. But the French had heard of this wave of British expansion into the Ohio valley, and in 1749 Céloron de Blainville was sent down the Allegheny and the Ohio to reassert the French claims to the valley and to warn the British in general and the Ohio Company in particular to stay off of what the French governors considered French soil.

The province of Virginia considered the lands west of Pennsylvania and Maryland as belonging to it under the charter of 1609. The French, on the other hand, claimed all the lands west of the Allegheny watershed by right of prior discovery; in the case of the Ohio valley their claim was based upon the reported discovery and exploration of the river by La Salle in 1670. In any case, each side looked upon the other as trespassers. It was logical, therefore, for the Ohio Company to appeal to Lieutenant-Governor Dinwiddie for protection, and for Dinwiddie to grant it. By 1753 the French had built a fort at Erie (Presqu'ile), on Lake Erie, and Fort le Boeuf on the Rivière aux Boeufs, a branch of the Allegheny, and were planning to extend their chain of forts down the Ohio to block the Virginia expansion. Dinwiddie then sent a young surveyor, George Washington, whose brother was a member of the Ohio Company, to warn the French that they were trespassing upon Virginia soil. The French refused to budge, and the next summer Washington was sent to establish a fort at the forks of the Ohio to forestall the French there, but he was himself forestalled, and the fight that took place at Great Meadows July 3 and 4, 1754, between his forces and those of the French who had anticipated him at Ft. Duquesne (Pittsburgh), was the beginning of a new Anglo-French colonial war.

So far as Virginia was concerned, the great wave of land speculation was symptomatic of a great sociological phenomenon—the population movement that, moving southward, had filled up the Virginia Piedmont and the great Allegheny valley. Just at the middle of the century this movement began to turn westward over the mountains into the valley of what the French called "The Beautiful River." For the time being, the transmontane movement was checked by the activities of the French in the valley and the outbreak of a war which was destined to upset and revise the international balance of colonial power on this continent.

THE CONSTITUTION OF THE OLD DOMINION

From the point of view of England, Virginia was almost an ideal colony. It produced a great staple, tobacco, which enriched the coffers of British tobacco merchants, but it also made Great Britain self-sufficient so far as that commodity was concerned, and, therefore, practically independent of foreign tobacco producers. Further, Virginia was a royal province under the direct supervision of the Crown; and, best of all, the royal governor was not dependent upon the provincial assembly for his salary, since this was provided out of a fund that had been earmarked for the purpose as far back as 1680.

The Virginia government was built upon the usual royal pattern; but, as in certain other colonies, the titular royal governors resided in England, leaving the actual administration of affairs to less noble but more energetic "lieutenant-governors." Thus Alexander Spotswood (1710-22) was lieutenant-governor for the Earl of Orkney, and Sir William Gooch (1727-49) was lieutenant-governor for the Earl of Albemarle—as was Robert Dinwiddie, who held office from 1751 to 1758. But the Virginia lieutenant-governors were sympathetic and energetic administrators, and it is probable that the "absentee-governor" practice actually operated to Virginia's benefit. The governor's council, here as elsewhere, was appointed by the Crown from among the wealthiest and most distinguished planters; the eighty-four members of the house of burgesses were elected by a franchise enjoyed by men who owned one hundred acres of unimproved, or twenty-five acres of improved land. In 1748, four new counties were created to provide political representation for some of the nearer parts of the Piedmont affected by the increase of population, and this raised the number of burgesses to ninety-two. The council, as elsewhere, served as a supreme court of appeals, but it also had original jurisdiction in some cases; on the other hand, as the upper house of the legislature, the council seems to have had no power to initiate legislation, but could only veto or suggest amendments to bills passed by the house of burgesses. Justices of the peace, who administered the affairs of the counties, executive as well as judicial (in small cases), as well as judges, sheriffs, and other officials, were appointed by the Crown and held their offices during the pleasure of the king. The smallest unit of local government was the parish, which took its name from its originally ecclesiastical character. The parish was presided over by a body of twelve men, known as the vestry, who were originally elected but who in practice constituted a self-perpetuating closed corporation made up of members of the best families. This was the group which elected the local rector of the legally established Anglican church, allocated land belonging to the parish, provided for the care of orphans, and assessed taxes for local purposes. On the whole the governor, by his power of appointment, his social influence, and, most of all, his financial independence of the assembly, enjoyed an exceptional position among royal governors; and the royal prerogative was probably more powerful in Virginia than in any other colony except Jamaica.

Yet Virginia was not without its struggle between the prerogative and the popular branch of government represented by the house of burgesses. On questions of defense, for example, the burgesses on occasion made it impossible for the governors to carry out the royal instructions by their refusal to appropriate money.

On one such occasion, in 1723, when the burgesses sought to discourage the increase of the slave population by the imposition of a tax upon Negroes imported into the province, the Virginia law was disallowed by the Crown because it affected unfavorably the business of the Royal African Company, which had a monopoly of the slave trade. Similarly, when, in 1730, the colony attempted to meet the disastrous effects of declining prices by a law requiring rigid inspection of all tobacco to be exported and the destruction of poor tobacco, the Board of Trade, influenced by the tobacco-merchants of England, opposed the law, and it was allowed to stand "on probation" only because of the earnest appeal of Lieutenant-Governor Gooch.

The interests of England, represented by the prerogative, and the interests of the colony, most often expressed by the burgesses, came into conflict on other occasions, although the conflict was softened by the tact of Virginia's long series of genuinely able lieutenant-governors. But the fundamental nature of the conflict of political interest between the colony and the prerogative was driven home only by the disillusionment that arose over the attempt to revise the Virginia code of laws, just at the end of Gooch's administration, in 1749. For in that year the assembly, in an effort to bring the body of Virginia law down to date and adapt it to new conditions, repealed a number of old and obsolete laws, retained others, and passed certain new laws to replace those which had been repealed. It was a notable event in Virginia legislative history, and it was a long step forward in the direction of modernization of the laws affecting land-holding, slaves, wills, the tobacco trade, the care of orphans, court procedure and jurisdiction, and many other questions of great importance to the province. But ten of the acts repealing or revising old laws were disallowed by the Crown because they did not contain the customary clause providing that they should not go into effect until approved by the king. The omission of the suspending clause from these acts violated the instructions to the governor requiring him to see that it was included. The Crown took the position that this was a dangerous precedent liable to "destroy that check which was established not only to preserve the just and proper influence and authority which the crown ought to have in the Government of its colonies . . . but also to secure to its subjects their just liberties and privileges." But the colonists had not thought of the lieutenant-governor's instructions as a part of their constitution in general, nor that part of them in particular as any such check upon their legislative freedom. A fundamental constitutional question had been posed by this disallowance, and from this moment onward the question of the place of the prerogative in the Virginia constitution became increasingly important in Virginia's constitutional development.

This break between the mother country and the colony occurred at about the same time as another which illustrated a deep cleavage, then beginning to appear in the colonial-imperial relationship. This incident, involving both Virginia's relationships as a debtor province and the generally detestable question of colonial paper money, arose out of a law passed that same year, 1749, called "An Act declaring the Law Concerning Executions and for the Relief of Insolvent Debtors." For many Virginia planters were now almost inextricably involved in debts to their British creditors, and sought some legislative relief from their difficulties. The act in question, therefore, provided that debts in British money might be paid in Virginia currency at the fixed ratio of five to four, whereas the real exchange rate varied, and was often much less favorable to Virginia currency, the ratio sometimes reaching as much as seven to four. The effect of this law upon the British factors was, therefore, electrical when they discovered it, some two years after its passage. Petitions and memorials swamped the Board of Trade, which had carelessly approved the law when it was passed, and the Privy Council, which interfered in 1754 to get the obnoxious law revised. This the assembly reluctantly did in 1755, probably only because of its pressing need for imperial protection against the French in the Ohio valley.

During the Seven Years War Virginia issued more and more paper money. Thus for the first time in its history, the colony got into serious difficulties over depreciation, and a sharp division between debtors and creditors appeared within the province itself. The colony compromised somewhat in 1764, and the retirement of part of the outstanding paper slightly eased the money problem just at the time when Parliament, at the insistence of British merchants, was extending the Currency Act of 1751 to all the colonies. At the same time, however, the conflict between prerogative and colony was taking other forms, one of which was over the attempt of Governor Francis Fauquier in 1759 to force the burgesses not to allow the two offices of treasurer and speaker to be held by the same man. But the most explosive, and therefore the most famous, issue was reached in the so-called "Parson's Cause," which first called Patrick Henry's fiery eloquence to the support of autonomous government in Virginia.

This famous case, usually taken as one of the opening explosions of the American Revolution, arose out of a series of Virginia laws providing for the payment of the parsons' salaries in tobacco—generally accepted as effective currency throughout the province. The law of 1748 had fixed the salaries at 17,280 pounds of tobacco. A law of 1755 provided for the payments in specie of debts owed in tobacco, at the rate of two pence per pound of tobacco. But the price of tobacco was more than two pence per pound, and the rectors, naturally enough, preferred to take their salaries in tobacco. They did not have their way, however. On the enactment of a similar law in 1758 the rectors, finding themselves allied by common interest with the London creditors against their Virginia parishioners, decided to fight for payment of their salaries in tobacco at the higher price. At the insistence of the London merchants and the parsons, the Crown disallowed the law, and the parsons brought suit for a recovery of the difference their parishes now owed them. It was in the county court of Hanover County that the young county lawyer named Patrick Henry challenged the right of the Crown to disallow a Virginia law that was once approved by the governor, on the ground that such a disallowance was a violation of the compact between king and people, a violation, that is, of the British constitution and the fundamental rights of British subjects.

The significance of this pronouncement is easy to see. But it was a climax, rather than the beginning, of a dispute between the colony and the mother country as to the real nature of the Virginia constitution—and, for that matter, of the constitutions of all the colonies—that had been going on since the first settlements along the seaboard. Henry's way of thinking had been consciously brewing in Virginia at least since the disallowance of the laws of 1749, but unconsciously for a much longer time. It was one of those dramatic sparks that mark the end of a long period of accumulation of political and economic feeling—and the beginning of a period of readjustment in political and economic relationships which sometimes necessarily take the form of revolution.

RECOMMENDED BOOKS FOR FURTHER READING

CONTEMPORARY NARRATIVES

Andrew Burnaby, *Travels Through the Middle Settlements in North America . . . 1759 and 1760.*

William Byrd, "A Progress to the Mines," *A Journey to the Land of Eden, and Other Papers,* edited by Mark Van Doren.

William Byrd, *The Secret Journal of William Byrd of Westover, 1709-1712,* edited by Louis B. Wright and Marion Tinling.

Harry J. Carman, ed., *American Husbandry.*

Robert Carter, *The Letters of Robert Carter, 1720-1727,* edited by Louis B. Wright.

Robert Dinwiddie, *Official Records of Robert Dinwiddie, Lieutenant-Governor of the Colony of Virginia, 1751-1758,* edited by Robert A. Brock.

Christopher Gist, *Christopher Gist's Journals . . . ,* edited by William M. Darlington.

Henry Hartwell [and others], *The Present State of Virginia, and the College.*

Thomas Jefferson, *Notes on the State of Virginia.*

William S. Perry, ed., *Historical Collections Relating to the American Colonial Church,* Volume I.

Alexander Spotswood, *The Official Letters of Alexander Spotswood, Governor of Virginia, 1710-1722,* edited by Robert A. Brock.

The Virginia Gazette.

George Washington, *The Diaries of George Washington, 1748-1799,* edited by John C. Fitzpatrick, Volume I.

MODERN ACCOUNTS

Charles H. Ambler, *Sectionalism in Virginia from 1776 to 1861.*

Kenneth P. Baily, *The Ohio Company of Virginia and the Westward Movement, 1748-1792.*

James C. Ballagh, *A History of Slavery in Virginia.*

Richard C. Beatty, *William Byrd of Westover.*

Beverley W. Bond, *The Quit-Rent System in the American Colonies.*

Philip A. Bruce, *The Virginia Plutarch,* Volume II.

Julian A. C. Chandler, *The History of Suffrage in Virginia.*

Julian A. C. Chandler, *Representation in Virginia.*

Avery O. Craven, *Soil Exhaustion as a Factor in the Agricultural History of Virginia, and Maryland, 1606-1860.*

Leonidas Dodson, *Alexander Spotswood, Governor of Colonial Virginia, 1710-1722.*

Hamilton J. Eckenrode, *Separation of Church and State in Virginia.*

Percy S. Flippin, *The Financial Administration of the Colony of Virginia.*

Percy S. Flippin, *The Royal Government in Virginia, 1624-1775.*

Lawrence H. Gipson, *The British Empire before the American Revolution,* II, Chapters 1, 3.

Meyer Jacobstein, *The Tobacco Industry in the United States.*

Henry R. McIlwaine, *The Struggle of Protestant Dissenters for Religious Toleration in Virginia.*

Herbert L. Osgood, *The American Colonies in the Eighteenth Century,* I, Part I, Chapters 21, 23; IV, Part III, Chapters 7, 12.

Ulrich B. Phillips, *American Negro Slavery.*

William Z. Ripley, *The Financial History of Virginia, 1609-1776.*

Halsted L. Ritter, *Washington as a Business Man.*

John W. Wayland, *The German Element in the Shenandoah Valley of Virginia,* Chapters 1-10.

Thomas J. Wertenbaker, *Norfolk.*

Louis B. Wright, *The First Gentlemen of Virginia.*

36

North Carolina Grows Up

"LUBBERLAND"

THE EARLIEST settlements along Albemarle and Pamlico Sounds had originally been made by emigrants from other colonies. These settlements had been sharply differentiated, by their development, both from the tobacco-plantation society of Virginia to the north and from the rice-plantation society of South Carolina to the southward. They had never paid profits to the Carolina proprietors. On the contrary, they had been a constant source of irritation and worry, and there had existed, right from the first, a conflict of interest between the proprietors on the one side and the colonists on the other. The proprietors had made a number of half-hearted attempts to impose upon these settlements the Fundamental Constitutions of 1669, but in this they had been uniformly unsuccessful.

In 1711, toward the end of the War of the Spanish Succession (Queen Anne's War), the Tuscarora Indians, resident in the western parts of North Carolina, fell upon the frontiers with exceptional fury. The savages, driven to desperation by the steady encroachment of the whites upon their lands and by the kidnaping of Indians to be sold into slavery in the West Indies, had formed a conspiracy with other tribes to drive out the white men. The war lasted two years and was brought to an end only with the aid of troops sent into the northern colony by South Carolina. The Indians were finally broken by the capture of their fort at Nahucke, on the Neuse River, after which the remnants of the tribe migrated northward to New York, where they joined their Iroquois kinsmen of the Five Nations.

This bloody war opened new lands for settlement, but it further embittered the relations between the proprietors and the colonists, who deeply resented the failure of the proprietors to protect them. The conflict was still further embittered by the insistence of the proprietors upon payment of the quitrents in money, whereas the colonists, who had practically no money, could only pay the quitrents with the produce of their farms. Produce, as a matter of fact, in the absence of any other easily acquired currency, was widely

503

used in exchange, and economic life was based quite largely upon
barter. Nineteen commodities—beef, butter, wheat, Indian corn,
tobacco, etc.—were listed in a law of 1715 as legal tender in the payment of both public and private indebtedness; and this system of
exchange persisted until well past the middle of the century. Paper
money had, to be sure, made its appearance about 1712. As more
and more issues were printed, its value declined, and the breach
between the colonists and the proprietors was still further widened
by their refusal to accept this depreciated currency in payment of
quitrents.

The poverty of the colony was due in large measure to its lack
of commerce with the outside world. The shallow waters of Pamlico and Albemarle Sounds precluded direct, ocean-borne commerce
with the mother country, but permitted a coast-wise traffic which
was carried on chiefly by small sloops from New England. There
was little enough commerce of any sort, however, and North Carolina remained a frontier community, without luxury, depending
upon its own crude industry for most of the manufactured goods
it used. The inhabitants raised some cattle, some Indian corn, and
some tobacco. Its tobacco market was partially cut off by Virginia,
however, which, for the protection of its own planters, prohibited
the importation of tobacco from other colonies, even for re-export.
As the century wore on, naval stores became one of the most important products, and cattle also, especially as the high lands of the
Piedmont were opened to settlement, became increasingly so.

Socially the scattered settlements around the shores of Pamlico
and Albemarle Sounds were still pretty backward. Colonel William
Byrd, II, one of the Virginia members of the joint commission
which marked out the boundary between North Carolina and Virginia in 1728, described the slovenliness and backwardness of the
country, which he called "Lubberland," as follows:

One thing may be said for the Inhabitants of that Province [he said],
that they are not troubled with any Religious Fumes, and have the least
Superstition of any People living. They do not know Sunday from any
other day, any more than Robinson Crusoe did, which would give them
a great advantage were they given to be industrious. But they keep so many
Sabbaths every week, that their disregard of the Seventh Day has no manner of cruelty in it, either to Servants or Cattle. . . . To speak the Truth,
tis a thorough Aversion to Labor that makes People file off to N Carolina,
where Plenty and a Warm Sun confirm them in their Disposition to Laziness for their whole Lives.

The colony had an assembly, composed of twenty-six representatives; but when the assembly sought, in 1715, to regulate the

granting and settlement of land, the proprietors disallowed many
of the laws, requiring, on the contrary, that sales of land should
take place only in their office in England. New settlers were now
coming in, but the proprietors charged such a high price for the
land that immigration was discouraged. On the other hand, the
governors connived at the violation of the regulations by their
friends and members of the council, with the result that much of
the land fell into the hands of speculators. These developments, in
turn, brought about a cleavage between the lower house, representing as it did the poorer landholders, on the one side, and the
council, composed of friends of the governor and the proprietors,
on the other.

Such was the situation in North Carolina when the events took
place in South Carolina which led to that colony's becoming a
royal province. Proposals began to be made that North Carolina
be made a royal province, but the movement was retarded by the
good work of Governor George Burrington, who did much for the
welfare of the colony, especially by opening to settlement the lands
in the Cape Fear region.

The Crown had now been negotiating with the proprietors for
some years for the purchase of the rights under their charters of
1663 and 1665, and the deal was finally consummated in 1629.
Seven of the proprietors sold their claims (in both North and
South Carolina) to the Crown for £17,500; the eighth, Lord Carteret, accepted as his one-eighth share a strip of land seventy miles
wide along the northern boundary of the colony with Virginia—
an estate which was to cause the colony much grief later on. With
the purchase of the colony by the Crown, North Carolina became a
royal province, and like South Carolina, which had actually made
the change to royal government nearly a decade earlier, became
legally a possession of the Crown.

SOCIAL AND ECONOMIC EXPANSION

A turning point in the history of North Carolina came at about
the time when it became a royal province. The population of the
province was estimated at some thirteen thousand; but a rapid influx of newcomers more than doubled the population between 1733
and 1754, and carried the population figures upward, until, on the
eve of the Revolution, North Carolina numbered three hundred
thousand souls.

There were several reasons for this increase. In the first place,

North Carolina participated in the general wave of immigration into all the seaboard colonies already discussed. A steady stream of newcomers entered the colony by the Chowan, the Roanoke, the Tar, the Neuse and the Cape Fear rivers. Among these were Palatines, Scotch Highlanders, French Protestants and Scotch-Irish Presbyterians. Another stream, made up of Germans and Scotch-Irish moving southward from Pennsylvania along the great valley and the Piedmont spread out eastward to meet those coming inland from the seaboard. Many of the newcomers in the coastlands went in for the cultivation of tobacco; but tobacco was never an important staple in this colony.

The newcomers sometimes bought their land, but more often they merely squatted on land that appealed to them, counting upon making a satisfactory arrangement with the proprietor when he discovered them. Land prices soared, however, and there was great confusion in land titles—a confusion made yet more confused by the enormous holdings of private individuals and private companies. The largest of these was the Carteret "share," now owned by the Earl of Granville. The Granville claim was estimated to contain half of the province. But there were others, such as the grant of one million two hundred thousand acres given in 1737 to Henry McCulloh, and the grant of two hundred thousand acres to Arthur Dobbs a few years later. Land speculation was at its height, and many even of the old settlers along the seaboard who had acquired large holdings became wealthy because of the rush for lands.

Yet North Carolina could not be said to be genuinely prosperous. The poor soil of the "pine barrens" along the coast, coupled with the difficulty in getting to a deep-water port, held back the development of the country. Tobacco continued to increase in importance, along with the naval-stores industry of the "pine barrens" and the cattle-raising industry of the interior, and plantations similar to those in Virginia began to appear along the principal rivers. But the North Carolinians were notoriously indebted to British creditors, who were further alarmed by the increase of paper money and the attempts of the legislature to make this depreciated currency a legal tender at a fixed value. Using their influence with the Board of Trade, the merchants had the governor of the colony instructed to make every effort to have the legislature pass a law making these bills acceptable only at their real value. But he accomplished nothing, and it was largely on account of the North Carolina situation that Parliament, in 1764, passed the currency act of that year which prohibited the colonies from passing legal-tender acts in the future.

It was in the production of naval stores that North Carolina most nearly achieved economic stability. Under the encouragement of the bounties offered by the Naval Stores Act, the production of these pine products steadily increased, until in 1753 the colony exported 60,000 barrels of tar, 12,000 barrels of pitch, and 10,000 barrels of turpentine, in addition to 750,000 barrel staves. Slowly but surely North Carolina was moving, in this industry at least, toward prosperity.

POLITICAL STRIFE AND SECTIONALISM

North Carolina's political history was peculiar in several ways. The royal government set up after the purchase of the province from the proprietors followed, to be sure, the general plan of the royal governments elsewhere. Here, too, there took place the series of bickerings and contests between the assembly and the prerogative that have been observed elsewhere. In the very first assembly under the royal regime, the lower house came into immediate conflict with the first governor, the same George Burrington who had been governor for the proprietors in 1724 and 1725, over the right of the governor to appoint the clerk of the house. Thereafter, there was an almost continual contest over such questions as a permanent revenue for the Crown, the election of a colonial treasurer, the regulation of fees charged by government officials, paper money, land administration, and others. In general, there was inherent in this continued and varied conflict the vague feeling on the part of the colonists, represented by the lower house, that the governor was the agent of a "foreign" power that must not be allowed to become too despotic in the internal affairs of North Carolina.

The bitterest controversy in North Carolina's legislative history arose over the question of lands. The Crown, naturally enough, was interested in actually collecting the quitrents; to further this aim Governor Burrington busied himself in clarifying the titles to land formerly granted, and this meant, in many cases, re-surveying the old grants. But the landowners resented the attempt to collect the quitrents efficiently, and, especially, the attempt to collect them in money rather than in produce. In the period covered by the administration of Governor Gabriel Johnston (1734-52) the population of the province was rapidly increasing, the vacant lands were being filled up, and those who had land to sell were becoming wealthy. Such was the scramble for lands that preceding administrations had issued many blank patents for land without troubling to have it surveyed. These blank patents had been issued to the friends of the government, and Johnston found half a million acres of the best land in the hands of these speculators. Johnston refused to confirm many of these grants, and sought to secure legislation aimed at systematizing both the granting of lands and the collection of quitrents. Most of all, he sought to protect the actual settlers on the land who were being victimized by the speculators.

As the assembly was composed largely of men holding patents, blank and otherwise, for large areas of land, Governor Johnston had to face a long and bitter battle on this issue. He managed to get a compromise bill through the assembly in 1739, but the Board of Trade, not really understanding the North Carolina situation and advised by North Carolina speculators and merchants who were opposed to Johnston, opposed the bill and it was disallowed by the Crown. Johnston had to begin again. The incident was one of the many unfortunate instances in which a colonial governor was handicapped by the poorly informed or badly advised agencies of the Crown residing three thousand miles away from the scene of his duties.

Meanwhile, the population was steadily increasing. The region along the Cape Fear River developed rapidly, and the town of Wilmington, founded about 1733, provided the colony, at last, with a deep-water port, at which there developed a considerable export and import business. Most of the newcomers went inland to the Piedmont, however, and after the unsuccessful effort of the Stuart pretender to recover the throne of England with the aid of loyal Scots in 1745, many Scotchmen came to North Carolina and settled in the beautiful rolling back-country. It was these newcomers, Swiss, Scotchmen, Irishmen and Germans, who suffered most from land speculation; and out of this problem grew an unfortunate sectionalism between the older tidewater region and the newer regions—which might be called "the west" but for the fact that they also included the region about Cape Fear, which was a southern rather than a western area.

Under a law of 1715, the counties along Albemarle and Pamlico Sounds each had five representatives in the assembly; the other, newer precincts had only two each. Now, despite the increase of population in the new areas, the older counties held to their five representatives each, which gave them control of at least half the

lower house, even when the population of the new counties surpassed their own. The result was that the lower house of the legislature was effectively controlled by a minority of the population.
Naturally, the new counties became increasingly insistent upon an
equalization of representation, and Governor Johnston attempted
many times to have passed a law redistributing representation—
only as often to have it blocked by the representatives of the tidewater counties. He also attempted to have the government of the
province permanently established at New Bern. In this, too, the
tidewater counties were able, for the time being, at least, to defeat
him. The struggle came to its climax in 1746 when, at an assembly
arbitrarily held at New Bern, at which the old colonies refused to
be present, the governor had passed a law reducing the number of
representatives from the older counties to two instead of five. For
eight years the older counties refused to attend the New Bern
assembly.

Johnston died in 1752, and was succeeded by Arthur Dobbs an
Irish businessman already mentioned as heavily interested in North
Carolina lands. Dobbs' sympathies were on the side of the landholders, naturally enough, and when the "Representation of the
People Act" of 1746 was disallowed in 1754, the older counties
resumed their hold on the legislature; which, by the way, they
retained until the sheer force of the number of new western counties at last overcame their numerical superiority.

Dobbs, however, never really got along well with the colony.
He was an arch-royalist, a strong "prerogative man" and ardent
British patriot, and he found himself in constant conflict with the
assembly. That body passed a court bill providing for tenure
during good behavior, which was disallowed by the Crown; but
the assembly circumvented the Crown's intention to appoint judges
"during the king's pleasure" by re-enacting its own law every two
years. Similarly, on the rights of the assembly to name an agent of
the colony in London, to name treasurers responsible to itself, to
fix fees and otherwise to control the purse, and on his own desire
to provide for the support of the Church of England—the established church since 1729—the old governor rehearsed the experience of other governors of royal and proprietary provinces. Here
in North Carolina, as elsewhere, the people of the colony were
gradually assuming control over their own provincial affairs, and
hammering out on the anvil of their experience a provincial constitution which admitted less and less interference in the name

of the prerogative, and which moved more and more directly, if unconsciously, in the direction of complete provincial autonomy.

But North Carolina also illustrated, perhaps more dramatically than any other colony, the sectionalism between tidewater and frontier that has been noted in general terms elsewhere. For the conflict between "north" and "south" over the reapportionment of seats was but symptomatic of a conflict involving also the question of land prices, the exorbitant fees charged by provincial officials responsible to the tidewater-dominated assembly, the suppression of paper money, and the low prices of farm produce resulting from the post-war depression after 1763. This conflict, which was social as well as sectional—the poorer farmers versus the wealthy land speculators and their officials—came to a climax about 1765 in a movement sponsored by a farmers' organization known as the "Regulators." The Regulators were quieted by a show of force by Governor William Tryon in 1768; but when the Regulators won a majority of the provincial assembly in 1769 and Tryon dissolved the assembly in an effort to evade the inevitable reforms, the Regulators resorted to violence. It was only after a pitched battle between the Regulators and Tryon's "forces of law and order" on the banks of the Alamance River on May 16, 1771, that the movement was suppressed. This battle has sometimes been called the first bloodshed of the American Revolution; but the Regulators had no intention of overthrowing the government. In fact, many of the Regulators became loyalists in the Revolution; against the men of the tidewater, in the hope that the mother country would protect them from their American exploiters. Their cause was a social and sectional conflict with the vested interests of the seaboard, not with England. It began long before the era of the Revolution; it was, in truth, one of the bitter chapters in the history of the rise of the American west.

RECOMMENDED BOOKS FOR FURTHER READING

Contemporary Narratives

William K. Boyd, ed., *Some Eighteenth Century Tracts Concerning North Carolina*.

William Byrd, *William Byrd's Histories of the Dividing Line betwixt Virginia and North Carolina*, edited by William K. Boyd.

Hugh T. Leffler, ed., *North Carolina History, Told by Contemporaries*.

Janet Schaw, *Journal of a Lady of Quality*, edited by Evangeline W. and Charles M. Andrews.

Modern Accounts

Alex M. Arnett, *The Story of North Carolina.*

Samuel A. C. Ashe, *History of North Carolina,* Volume I.

John S. Bassett, "The Regulators of North Carolina (1765-1771)" in *American Historical Association Annual Report, 1894,* pp. 141-212.

John S. Bassett, *Slavery and Servitude in the Colony of North Carolina.*

Robert D. W. Connor, *History of North Carolina (1585-1783).*

Charles S. Cook, *The Governor, Council, and Assembly in Royal North Carolina.*

Lawrence H. Gipson, *The British Empire before the American Revolution,* II, Chapter 4.

Shirley C. Hughson, *Carolina Pirates and Colonial Commerce, 1670-1740.*

Herbert L. Osgood, *The American Colonies in the Eighteenth Century,* II, Part II, Chapter 3; IV, Part III, Chapter 9.

Charles L. Raper, *North Carolina, a Royal Province, 1729-1775.*

Charles L. Raper, *North Carolina; a Study in English Colonial Government.*

37

The Development of South Carolina

SOUTH CAROLINA BECOMES A ROYAL PROVINCE

IN CONTRAST to its less gifted twin to the north, South Carolina was a prosperous, even wealthy province from its earliest history. Almost from the beginning the Indian traders of Charleston had tapped the rich Piedmont Indian trade in deerskins, and after the introduction of rice culture the plantation system of society had taken root more strongly here than anywhere else on the continent. South Carolina's relations with the proprietors, however, had paralleled those of North Carolina, with the same unending conflict between the colony on the one side and the proprietors on the other. Well, indeed, might the colonists complain; for the proprietors' neglect of the colony was notorious. This colony stood as the English outpost against the Spanish in Florida and the French in Louisiana, to say nothing of the often hostile Indians around its borders, yet the proprietors did little or nothing for the colony's protection. Furthermore, the colonists were offended by the policy of the proprietors in insisting upon the support of the Anglican Church in this community of which only a minority of the people were Anglicans. The proprietors had disallowed laws of the assembly, and, although unable to defend the colony themselves, attempted to prevent the colony from issuing paper money or raising taxes to defray the expense the colony incurred in its own defense.

In 1715, just after the end of the War of the Spanish Succession (Queen Anne's War), the Yamassee Indians formed a conspiracy against the white settlements which were encroaching upon the Indian lands southward and westward. The Indians fell upon the frontiers and carried their ravages to within a few miles of Charleston. The colony, unable adequately to defend itself, appealed to North Carolina and Virginia for help. North Carolina sent a body of men to repay the aid given it by South Carolina in its own Tuscarora War, and Virginia sent aid in the form of ammunition and supplies. It was a year before the Indians were brought under control, and even after that the frontiers were for a long time disturbed by isolated incidents growing out of the hatred of the

512

Indians for the whites. The Yamassees were eventually driven into Spanish Florida; it was thought, in fact, that the Spaniards in Florida had incited the Indians to the war in the first place.

Naturally, during this war, the colony appealed to the proprietors for aid. But the proprietors protested that they could not give adequate help, whereupon the assembly appealed to the Crown to be made a royal colony, in order to receive the royal protection. Because of the colony's strategic position, as well as because of its mercantilist value as a producer of rice and naval stores, the Board of Trade urged that the request of the colony be granted. At the same time the Board entered into negotiations with the proprietors with a view to an outright purchase of the colony by the Crown, but the proprietors declined to sell. The colony continued its efforts, meanwhile, and was encouraged in them by the Board. But the bitterness of the colonists reached its height when several acts passed by the assembly were disallowed by the proprietors, among which were a new election law calculated to weaken the proprietary control, another law opening the former Yamassee lands to settlement, and even an old law of 1707 which legalized the practice of the lower house of the assembly of choosing a treasurer and other officials paid from public funds who were, therefore, considered responsible to the commons house and not to the proprietors.

Such was the situation between the colony and the proprietors when in 1719 war again broke out between England and Spain, and news arrived in South Carolina that the Spaniards were preparing at Havana an expedition against the colony. The governor called out the militia; but the militia took advantage of its gathering to circulate for signatures a resolution declaring the rule of the proprietors at an end and South Carolina a royal province. The governor, Sir Nathaniel Johnson, was asked to accept the governorship under the Crown, but, because of his loyalty to the proprietors, he declined. When the assembly met in December it declared itself a convention and proclaimed James Moore governor until the king's pleasure could be known. It also named a council, fashioned after the councils of other royal provinces. Then this "convention" changed itself back into an assembly—by the mere process of voting—and named a new chief justice to replace the odious and notorious Nicholas Trott. Colonel John Barnwell was sent to England to explain to the authorities there what had been done in this peaceful revolution.

The "revolution" caused surprisingly little concern in official quarters in London. On the contrary, the Board of Trade, which had long encouraged the colonists in their resistance to the proprietors, heartily approved of the change, and the Crown accepted the new status of the colony by naming Sir Francis Nicholson as its royal governor, with a royal council, and James Moore was elected speaker of the new assembly. The government of South Carolina was now a royal government; but the soil was still owned by the proprietors under the charter of 1665. It was not until 1729 that a final agreement with the proprietors was reached providing for the transfer to the Crown of their title to the soil.

ECONOMIC EXPANSION AND SOCIAL CONFLICT

The economic and social development of South Carolina followed a pattern peculiar to itself—a pattern that was due in large measure to the peculiarities of its soil, climate, and geographic location. Its position as the southernmost of the continental colonies, coupled with its contiguity to the country of the deerhunting Indians of the southern end of the Appalachian highland and the Piedmont, made Charleston the entrepôt for a very profitable export trade in deerskins that began early in the colony's history. The introduction of rice culture in 1693 found a very congenial environment for that important cereal in the swampy meadows along the coast, and rice became the great export staple of the colony. The beginning of successful cultivation of indigo gave South Carolina a third valuable staple for export, and the remarkable increase in cattle-raising and related industries that accompanied the development of the Piedmont—the "west"—beginning about the middle of the century, gave the colony a very important fourth item of export. Population grew enormously, but much of the increase was made up of Negro slaves, who were put to work on the plantations of rice and indigo. A very large proportion of the increase of whites was made up of those who went into the Piedmont, either from the coast or out of the stream moving down from the north along the mountains, to engage in farming and the raising of livestock. Thus the population of South Carolina was estimated at 9,000 whites and 12,000 Negroes in 1721; in 1750 it was some 25,000 whites and 39,000 Negroes; on the eve of the Revolution (1775) the population had grown to some 70,000 whites and about 100,000 Negroes.

Economically, the colony might be said to have labored in four or five zones, according to the industry, which was in each case largely determined by the soil. In the fresh-water swamps along the sluggish rivers near the sea, rice culture flourished. But the labor of clearing the land and cultivating the rice in the heat and humidity of those swamps could only be performed by Negroes; and slavery increased apace. Relatively small plantations were the general rule, each plantation being worked by about thirty slaves under an overseer; but an enterprising planter might, and quite often did, accumulate several plantations. England imported 1,400 tons of rice from South Carolina between 1712 and 1717, and a large proportion of this was re-exported to continental Europe. Shortly thereafter, in 1730, rice was removed from the list of "enumerated articles" to the extent of allowing the South Carolinians to export this commodity directly to the countries south of Cape Finisterre—which made it possible for South Carolina rice, then called the best in the world, to compete on a successful basis with Italian and East Indian rice in the markets of Portugal and Spain. By 1748 the export of rice from the colony amounted to 55,000 barrels, with a value of £618,750, South Carolina currency, or some £90,000 sterling. Eight years previously, in 1740, it had required 160 ships of 100 tons each to move the harvest of this commodity alone out of Charleston harbor!

In the higher, somewhat better lands back of the swamps, indigo had come to be cultivated, with handsome profits to its producers by 1750. This dye-plant, introduced into South Carolina from Antigua in 1741 by Miss Elizabeth Lucas (later Mrs. Charles Pinckney, and called "Eliza" Pinckney), had reached a stage of profitable production by 1745, and quickly took an important place in the colony's economy; for the demand for indigo dye in the markets of Europe was such that one pound of indigo was said to be worth one hundred pounds of rice. The fact that England was partly dependent upon French producers led, in 1748, to a law by Parliament placing a bounty of 6d per pound upon all indigo produced in the British colonies and shipped directly to Great Britain. The result was a rapid increase in production in South Carolina, and in 1754 that colony exported ten thousand pounds of the dye. This industry, too, was such that the labor involved could most economically be performed by Negroes, which contributed to the growing disparity between the numbers of the two races.

In the pine belt back from the coast there was a considerable industry devoted to lumbering and the extraction of naval stores, and this industry contributed quantities of these commodities to Charleston's export trade. Still farther back, along the upper reaches of the Savannah, the Edisto and the Santee rivers, the new-comers from Europe and the north had built their farms by the middle of the century, and there began to appear a sectional difference between the lowlands and the Piedmont similar to that in Virginia and North Carolina. These farmers raised grain, cattle, and hogs, which they sold to the planters of the tidewater area or exported to the West Indies. All these commodities, however, played a much less important role in the exports of the colony than rice and indigo.

This was not true, however, in the case of the deerskin trade. That picturesque business with the remote Indian tribes of the Creek and Cherokee nations was carried on by itinerant traders who carried their goods—blankets, shirts, guns and ammunition, knives, pots, and the like—right into the Indian country, taking in return the deerskins and others that the Indians had to offer in exchange. Sometimes the traders would take their goods to the Indian country on long trains of pack horses; but after the founding of Augusta, at the head of navigation on the Savannah River, in 1735, much of the "Indian goods" was shipped by boat from Charleston through the "Inland Passage" and up the Savannah to the falls. Augusta became the chief entrepôt for this Indian trade, and Georgia was able to derive a certain profit, even from the trade of the Carolinians, by its licensing system—much to the disgust and annoyance of South Carolina. The trade was said in 1735 to give permanent employment to some three hundred traders and enormous profits to the merchants of Charleston who furnished the "Indian goods" to the traders—goods that were furnished sometimes on a share basis and sometimes on credit against the anticipated profits from the deerskins with which the trader was expected to return from the Indian country.

The importance of this trade may be seen from the fact that in 1770 Charleston exported 799,837 pounds of deerskins, with a value of £57,738 sterling. But the deerskin trade was not only important merely because of the profits derived from it. For whereas, according to the *South Carolina Gazette,* in 1736 the trade accounted for one-fifth of the exports from the province to Great Britain, it also served as a very effective means of keeping the Indians at peace since they, by adopting the white man's weapons, dress, tools, and other aspects of his civilization, had become so dependent upon this trade with the whites that the Indians would starve if the trade should be cut off.

ARISTOCRACY AND SECTIONALISM IN SOCIETY

The cultivation of rice and indigo in the lowlands of South Carolina, involving the exploitation of slave labor, was the economic base upon which was built the South Carolina aristocracy. There was a wide social gulf between the plantation owners and their slaves; and as the Negroes came more and more to outnumber the whites, the cleavage between the two races became, if anything, wider. Fear of slave-insurrections became a constant psychological phenomenon in South Carolina society, and this fear lay behind the unwillingness of many Carolina slaveowners to educate their slaves or even to teach them the Christian religion, since a common education and a common religion might be liable to draw the Negroes together in a common cause against the whites. The fears of the whites were realized more than once; the worst slave-insurrection took place in 1739 and was suppressed with great cruelty. It resulted in a revision of the slave-code which, while it restricted the freedom of action of Negro slaves, also prevented the sort of extreme cruelty to the Negroes that would be liable to provoke them to insurrection. At the same time, the colony sought to check the increase of the numbers of the Negroes by placing high duties upon them when imported and by offering inducements in the form of free land, tools, provisions, and even cattle, to white Protestants willing to come into the colony to settle. All to little avail, however, since the Negroes continued to increase their own numbers by the simple process of natural reproduction.

Slavery was thus at once the mechanism of their prosperity and the "bête noire" of the tidewater Carolinians. Yet the life of the Carolina slaveowners, centering as it did in the city of Charleston, was pleasant, and this aristocratic society was, perhaps, the most sophisticated, if not the most cultivated, in North America. For Charleston, the metropolis of the Carolina aristocracy, was a wealthy, prosperous center of commerce from which nearly two hundred ships cleared in the year 1748, of which sixty-eight sailed for Europe, eighty-seven for the West Indies, and thirty-eight for the northern colonies, carrying, in all, exports to the value of £1,129,559, South Carolina currency. Charleston was famous for the shops of its merchants and the balconied brick town houses of its planter aristocrats. And it could boast an active annual "season" of balls, concerts, and plays almost half a century before the social ice began to thaw along the frigid shores of Puritan New

England. So many carriages, "chariots," and "chaises" crowded the thoroughfares in 1750 as to require traffic regulations to enable the good people to get to church!

Meanwhile, the back-country was rapidly filling up with new-comers. In accordance with its desire to offset the rapidly increasing slave population, the colony sent agents to Germany and to Switzerland to induce Protestants to come to Carolina; the immigrants themselves were offered a bonus of six pounds, with tax exemptions for ten years, and some even had their first years' planting financed as additional inducements to come into the colony. The encouragements offered were so far successful as to bring a great stream of newcomers pouring into the colony through Charleston; so successful, indeed, was the colony's immigration policy that it became embarrassing. In 1752 so many immigrants came to Charleston that it was almost impossible to handle them all, and the assembly hastily placed a limit upon the number of those who might be allowed to settle in the province in any one year.

As a result of this rapid "westward movement," land prices rose, and there ensued an era of land-speculation similar to those taking place in other colonies. William Livingston and his associates secured in 1742 a grant of 200,000 acres of land from the Privy Council, with the understanding that they would settle a thousand Protestants upon their land within ten years. Another company, under the leadership of James Peyne, received a grant of 500,000 acres for the settlement of poor European Jews. A third group, sponsored by John Hamilton, sought a grant of 200,000 acres for the development of the naval stores industry. As the land fell into the hands of speculators, the newcomers found it increasingly difficult to secure land on favorable terms, and sought to remedy the situation by land reform in the legislature. Progress toward democratization of the land, however, was pitifully slow.

Culturally, too, all was not well with the settlers in the back-country. Here society was still in the frontier stage of settlement: there were few slaves, and white men worked with their own hands at the clearing of land and the raising of houses. There was neither time nor money for luxury, nor were there schools for the children; and there were only a very few ministers even for the maintenance of religious worship. Separated as they were from the courts and the seat of government, the people of the frontier had only begun, in the 1730's and 1740's, that long, uphill battle for participation in the social and political life of the province. This struggle, indeed, coupled as it was with the struggle for a democratization of the land, is one of the major themes in South Carolina political history.

The government of South Carolina in the middle of the eighteenth century was completely in the control of the planter-merchant aristocracy of Charleston. The leaders of the aristocracy, such men as Charles Pinckney, Andrew Rutledge, Benjamin Smith, and Thomas Lloyd, were generally members either of the governor's council or of the commons house of assembly. The house was composed of representatives elected by voters who held the franchise upon the basis of what was probably the highest property qualifications in all the colonies. For under the franchise law of 1745 the vote was limited to citizens who owned either a cultivated plantation or three hundred acres of undeveloped land. This law had placed the franchise in the hands of the highly propertied classes; formerly the voter was required to own only fifty acres. The representatives themselves were required to own five hundred acres of land and twenty slaves. Further, the aristocratic parishes of the tidewater were allowed five representatives each; the newer parishes were allowed only four, three, two, or one representative each.

Thus the commons house of assembly, controlled by the Charleston aristocrats, merchants and planters, was by far the most powerful element in the South Carolina government. Its control of government was so complete that it had little trouble maintaining its grip upon the treasury as well as its right to name and instruct the treasurer, Indian commissioner, the colony's agent in London, and other officials. It was able in most instances to have its will against the governor, although the most successful of the royal governors, James Glen (1743-56) was both successful and popular because he worked with, rather than against, the governing oligarchy. Glen's sympathy with the problems of the colony, indeed, as in the question of paper money, often drew down upon him the criticism, even the rebuke, of the mother country.

The government of the colony by a benevolent, aristocratic oligarchy was not without its advantages, and South Carolina was certainly one of the most prosperous of the units in the British empire. As one contemporary boasted, there was probably no other community in the world where such a large proportion of the population enjoyed annual incomes of from £5,000 to £10,000. And

yet, with the rapid settlement of the back-country, with the resultant economic and social differences between the two sections,
the hold of the oligarchy upon government was bound to be challenged.

For the small farmers of the Piedmont, the Scotch-Irish and German men of the cowpens—the first American "cowboys"—were
fiercely individualistic, strongly democratic, and not liable for long
to submit without protest to an oligarchic rule in which they had
little voice. No provision had been made by the colony for local
government among the newcomers, and the result was that, for
a long time, the frontier communities had neither courts, nor officials, nor representation in the assembly. The "west" simply did
not enter into the calculations of the oligarchy. But as settlement
increased, and the absence of authority encouraged disorder, a
demand arose for local government and for representation in the
assembly. Now, in the decade of the 1750's, with the increasing
imminence of war with France, the problem of the west was made
more acute than ever by the necessity of defense against the French
in Louisiana. Measures were taken by the assembly for the erection
of forts and the organization of militia; but the oligarchy was unwilling to surrender even a small part of its monopoly of government.

As early as 1752 the settlers along the Pedee River had petitioned
the assembly for the establishment of justices of the peace, but
without avail. In 1767 several petitions were received from this
same region and that along the Congaree. These petitions cited
the difficulties involved in going long distances to Charleston to
find courts, complained about the exorbitant fees charged by officials, and raised objection to the necessity of trying their cases
before juries picked solely from residents of Charleston. They asked
again for the establishment of local courts and juries; but again
without avail. Although at this time more than half the white population lived in the western parts of the colony; yet the men of
the tidewater still labored under the impression that this was a
sparsely settled area. Moreover, they distrusted these newcomers,
many of whom were foreign-born, and feared to give them a share
in government. Even had they been native-born "Americans," however, the oligarchy would hardly have been more inclined to surrender their own hold upon the government. Many reasons occurred to them—social, economic, and political—why the westerners
should not be given greater political power. These conservatives
were no democrats; and they were encouraged in their conserva-

tism by the Crown and the royal governor, for much the same reasons. A petition sent to the assembly in 1768, asking for a division of the west into parishes with representation in the assembly, was, indeed, submitted to a committee for study and recommendation, and this committee recommended that the reform be made; but nothing was done.

The situation was by this time getting desperate. Encouraged by the absence of authority, disorder steadily increased. The law-abiding citizens, despairing of having a local government and judiciary set up by the assembly, took matters into their own hands and, much like the vigilantes of California a century later, began to enforce order, driving out of the country idle and disorderly persons whom they considered undesirable. They called themselves the "Regulators," as their neighbors in North Carolina were doing. But because, as he said, they were illegally trying and punishing people without authority, the governor sent a series of military expeditions against them. Some blood was shed, especially at Saluda Creek in March, 1769. But it was not until the provincial congress which set up a state government during the Revolution that the west was given representation; even then, the west was given only forty seats out of a total of one hundred eighty-four!

The Regulator movement of South Carolina, then, as that in North Carolina, was social and sectional in nature; it was a phenomenon precipitated by the filling up of the "old west" rather than an outgrowth of the colonial conflict with the mother country with which it happened to coincide.

RECOMMENDED BOOKS FOR FURTHER READING

CONTEMPORARY NARRATIVES

Bartholomew R. Carrol, ed., "A Brief Description of the Province of Carolina" in *Historical Collections of South Carolina*, II, 193-272.

Alexander S. Salley, ed., *Journals of the Commons House of Assembly of South Carolina.*

The South Carolina Gazette; and Journal.

Pelatiah Webster, *Journal of a Voyage to Charlestown in South Carolina . . . in 1765,* edited by Thomas P. Harrison.

MODERN ACCOUNTS

Verner W. Crane, *The Southern Frontier, 1670-1732.*

Shirley C. Hughson, *The Carolina Pirates and Colonial Commerce.*

Edward McCrady, *The History of South Carolina under the Proprietary Government, 1670-1719.*

Robert L. Meriwether, *The Expansion of South Carolina, 1729-1765.*

Ulrich B. Phillips, *American Negro Slavery.*

Harriott H. R. Ravenel, *Charleston, The Place and the People.*

Harriott H. R. Ravenel, *Eliza Pinckney.*

Alexander S. Salley, *The Introduction of Rice Culture into South Carolina.*

William A. Schaper, "Sectionalism and Representation in South Carolina" in *American Historical Association Annual Report, 1900,* Volume I.

William R. Smith, *South Carolina as a Royal Province, 1719-1776.*

David D. Wallace, *Constitutional History of South Carolina from 1725 to 1775.*

David D. Wallace, *The Life of Henry Laurens.*

Edson L. Whitney, *Government of the Colony of South Carolina.*

38

Georgia: A Refuge and a Fortress

T HE COLONY of Georgia presents a history which is in many ways unique among those of all the British colonies in America. It was founded in a region that had already been occupied by Spain, and this fact, coupled with its proximity to Florida, made Georgia both a military outpost and a subject of long and acrimonious diplomatic controversy between the two mother countries. Unlike any other American colony, too, Georgia was founded largely for philanthropic purposes, and its sponsors neither hoped for nor received any financial return for their efforts. The management of the colony was in the hands of a board of trustees; it was thus neither a corporate, nor a royal, nor a proprietary province: it was a trusteeship. Finally, the humanitarian impulses of the trustees led them to prohibit slavery and the importation of hard liquors in the province, in an age when both were recognized and accepted social institutions in the new world as well as in the old. In all these ways Georgia was different from the other colonies; as a result, during the twenty years of the trusteeship, the history of Georgia follows a pattern that was peculiarly its own.

THE ANGLO-SPANISH CONTEST OVER "GUALE"

The coastal region northward from St. Augustine had been occupied by the Spaniards shortly after the founding of that city in 1565 by Pedro Mendez de Aviles. Seven large missions and numerous smaller ones were built along the coast, the most northerly of which were San Felipe Mission on Parris Island, now in South Carolina, and at Chatuache, about twenty miles still farther north. The Spaniards had also penetrated the back-country, and had built a number of missions in the neighborhood of the Apalachicola River centering about San Luis, the present Tallahassee. After the English came to Charleston, the Spaniards built a mission far to the northward, at Sabacola, on the Chattahoochee.

At the time of the coming of the English into the neighborhood, particularly to Charleston, the Spanish mission stations along the coast were garrisoned by Spain, and St. Augustine itself was heavily fortified. The English, on their side, sought to displace the Spaniards, and stirred up the Indians in the region against them. The result was a bitter Indian War, led by Englishmen, which forced the abandonment of the most northerly missions in 1680. Three years later the more southerly missions were plundered by the notorious pirate Agramont, who was followed by other pirates and more Indian attacks sponsored by the English. The Spaniards struck back at the English-Scotch colony of Port Royal in 1686, but the line of missions was still farther retired, to the region immediately surrounding Amelia Island, which lies just north of the St. John's River. Meanwhile, a similar contest had developed in the interior, where the Apalachicola Indians took the side of the English. The war of the Spanish Succession brought active warfare to this frontier, instead of the skirmishing that had preceded, and the Spaniards retired to their settlements in the Apalache region. Later efforts were made by the Spaniards to recover the lost ground, both on the coast and in the interior; but they did not achieve any permanent success.

In 1663 the coast as far south as the thirty-first degree of north latitude had been given by King Charles II of England to the proprietors of Carolina, and this was later extended to the twenty-ninth degree. But the proprietors had never undertaken to settle the area south of Charleston and Port Royal; only a few hardy individuals, traders and squatters, had penetrated the region, and it had remained, for all practical purposes, a wilderness. The disastrous Yamassee War in 1715, however, was attributed by many to the evil machinations of the Spaniards in Florida, and suggestions were brought forward in England for the settlement, or at least the fortification, of the intervening lands as a measure of protection for Carolina against both the Spanish and the French neighbors of the colony.

Such a suggestion was made by Sir Robert Montgomery in 1717, when he applied for a grant of the land between the Savannah and the Altamaha rivers, where he proposed to set up a military colony to be called the Margravate of Azilia. Nothing came of this, however, for the Carolina proprietors refused to surrender to him their claims to this land. The Board of Trade was nevertheless convinced of the need of fortifying the Altamaha region, and in 1720 strongly recommended that it be done. As a result of this recommendation and the advice of Francis Nicholson, the new royal governor of South Carolina, a fort, called Fort King George was built at the mouth of the Altamaha in 1721. The Spanish government promptly protested to London against the building of this fort, on the ground that this was territory recognized as Spanish under the Treaty of Madrid of 1670 and guaranteed to Spain by the Anglo-Spanish Treaty of Utrecht of 1713, both of which claims were legally correct. Spain's protest was ineffective in the face of British expansiveness; but it did raise the question of the boundary between Carolina and Florida, which had never been determined. The British insisted that Spain owned nothing north of St. Augustine, whereas Spain could show that in 1670, when the principle of actual possession was written into the Treaty of Madrid, England had not occupied a single square yard of land south of Charleston. Spain now proposed that the colonial governors be empowered to arrange a boundary, to which England agreed. Spain appointed two commissioners, and in 1725 they made their way from St. Augustine to Charleston, only to find that England had neither named commissioners nor even ordered the governor to deal with the Spaniards.

The situation was eased somewhat by the accidental burning of Fort King George in 1726, after which it was abandoned and its garrison was withdrawn to Port Royal. The question of ownership was still unanswered, however, and remained so, even after the founding of Georgia in 1733. This colony was thus always considered by Spain as a usurpation of Spanish territory. The issue was not finally resolved until the cession of Florida, with "Guale," to England in the Treaty of Paris of 1763.

THE GENESIS OF GEORGIA

The colony of Georgia was the product of two sets of motives, one imperialistic and the other philanthropic. The British government as well as private individuals had long been considering ways and means of building in the "debatable land" a bulwark against the potential enemies of the empire on that frontier, and the Board of Trade was definitely planning a settlement on the Altamaha in 1730. It was at about this time that a group of philanthropists, led by James Oglethorpe and John Viscount Perceval, proposed to fill the imperial need by founding in that region a colony of debtors out of England's prisons.

Oglethorpe and Perceval were members of a charitable organization, known as "The Associates of the Late Doctor Bray," that had been founded to carry on the charitable work of Doctor Thomas Bray, such as founding and maintaining of libraries and providing educational opportunities for Negroes. Bray and his two younger colleagues were all exponents of a growing humanitarianism in England and Europe generally. At the same time, Oglethorpe and Perceval were members of Parliament, and all three were interested, among other things, in the conditions existing in the prisons of England. Oglethorpe secured the appointment of a committee of Parliament for the investigation of prison conditions. The state of affairs in the prisons was found to be thoroughly deplorable, many people were in prison because of their inability to pay relatively insignificant debts, and the treatment they received, to say nothing of the living conditions in which they were kept, was shockingly bad. The reports of the Oglethorpe committee, in 1729 and 1730, resulted in a reform of the condition of the prisons themselves and the freeing of several thousand people.

The difficulties of these people in finding employment suggested to Oglethorpe the possibility of giving them a new start in a colony. He won the support of Perceval in the formation of a group to constitute a trusteeship for the purpose, a group which was merely an enlargement of "The Associates of the Late Doctor Bray" (Bray himself died in 1730), and proceeded to apply to the Crown for a charter. The request was granted, and resulted in the founding of the colony of Georgia.

The charter granted to Perceval, Oglethorpe, and their associates on June 20, 1732, was a curious document among colonial charters. Proclaiming first the new colony's double military and philanthropic purpose, the charter created the body known as the "Trustees for establishing the colony of Georgia in America," of which Viscount Perceval was named president. This board of trustees was granted, for the purposes of the colony, the land lying between the Savannah and the Altamaha rivers and two lines extending directly westward from their sources to the Pacific Ocean. Within this area the trustees were authorized to grant land in the colony, appoint governors, make the laws, and set up courts, much as the proprietor of a proprietary province, with the important exception that the trustees were prohibited both from receiving any pay for their services and from owning estates in the colony. The size of grants of land was limited to not more than five hundred acres, in the hope that this colony, as a military outpost, would become a society of small farmers. Liberty of conscience was granted to all except Roman Catholics. The charter was to run for twenty-one years, at the end of which period the Crown reserved the right to revise the government of the colony as it might consider proper.

Having gotten their charter giving them the authority to proceed, the trustees now set about preparing to make their colony a reality. Their first task was to publicize their enterprise in such a way as to attract gifts and other popular support; pamphlets were printed, ministers preached sermons upon the religious and humanitarian aspects of the proposed colony, and the imperialists

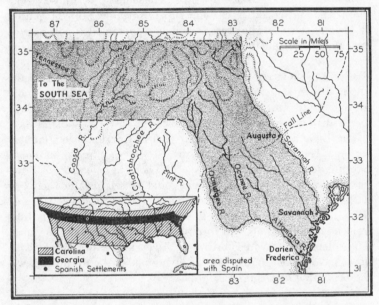

MAP 17. The Boundaries of Georgia Under the Charter of 1732

NOTE: Because of the vagueness of geographic knowledge at the time and the vagueness of the language of the charter itself, the boundaries shown on this map must be considered only approximately accurate.

debated its military and imperial worth. Gifts poured in upon the trustees in the form of money, books, and equipment. The merchants gave seeds, vines and trees; the militarists gave guns, swords, bayonets and powder flasks. Popular interest in this, "the greatest social and philanthropic experiment of the age" was at fever heat. Parliament itself, under the leadership of Sir Robert Walpole, made a grant of £10,000 to the enterprise, and this grant was followed by many others, which were justified, in general, by the value of the colony as a military outpost. It was the first time the government of England ever contributed to the support of an American colony.

When the trustees began to select the men who were to go to

the colony, they found that there were many more applicants than could be accommodated and that, therefore, they could maintain a high standard of personnel—as well they might, since the colonists must also be ready to bear arms. Toward the end of 1732 enough people had been selected to make a beginning, and the ship *Anne,* with about one hundred emigrants, set sail about the middle of November, 1732. On board the ship went Oglethorpe himself, now one of the trustees, charged with supervising the work of getting the colony started. The trustees had not appointed a governor of the colony; nor did they ever do so, preferring to govern it themselves, directly, in order to avoid interference by the Crown. It was for the same reason that they passed only three laws for the colony during the entire period of the trusteeship, finding it more convenient to govern the colony by "regulations" than by laws that had to be approved by the Crown.

The *Anne* and her passengers arrived at Charleston on January 13, 1733. Here they were received by the governor and other South Carolina leaders and given Godspeed. Then they went on to Beaufort, where they stayed until a site could be selected for their first settlement. Oglethorpe sought a site on the Savannah River, and there, on a bluff on the south side of the river some eighteen miles from its mouth, he decided to build his first settlement, Savannah. The colonists came on February 13, 1733, and, establishing themselves in four big tents, began the laying out of the town. This was the beginning of Georgia.

THE GEORGIAN UTOPIA

While the building of Savannah was going on, Oglethorpe turned his attention to the establishment of good relations with the Indians. At the time of his arrival he had found a group of Yamacraw Indians, one of the Creek tribes, encamped beside the Savannah on the site of his proposed town. The chief of this group was one Tomo-chi-chi, and, fortunately for Oglethorpe, among them was Mary Musgrove, the Indian wife of a South Carolina trader. Oglethorpe engaged Mary as an interpreter, and she was able to arrange an agreement between him and Tomo-chi-chi which was agreeable to both, and which, indeed, was the beginning of a lifelong friendship between the Indian and the Englishman. Through Mary's influence and the aid of Tomo-chi-chi, Oglethorpe was able to have a meeting of Creek chieftains at Savannah in May, 1733, at which he came to an agreement with them concerning land and trade. The Indians sold him the land between the Savannah and the Altamaha as far as the upper limits of tide-water, and he, on his side, agreed to regulate carefully the trade of the white settlers with the Indians, going so far as to set the prices, then and there, of the most important English products in the Indian trade.

It was well that Oglethorpe came thus early to an agreement with the Indians, especially with regard to the land. For new settlers came in rapidly, and some of them pushed inland, where they might have been seriously endangered by an unfriendly attitude among the Indians. The town of Savannah grew rapidly, too; but it was not the intention of the trustees to limit the population of their colony either to poor debtors or even to Englishmen. Thus they invited the persecuted Lutherans of the bishopric of Salzburg, in Austria, to go to Georgia; a considerable group of them did, setting up the town of Ebenezer at Red Bluff, on the Savannah River, as the center of an industrious German-speaking community of farmers. Other groups of Germans also came to Georgia, among them a group of Moravians sent there by Count Zinzendorf. But the Moravians were pacifists in the midst of a military community, and with the approach of war with Spain they decided to remove to the less warlike province of Pennsylvania. From Scotland, and with the definite intention of bringing more fighting men into the colony, the trustees brought over one hundred highlanders and their families and settled them on the Altamaha, at New Inverness, in the district they called Darien, where they constituted one of the first lines of defense of the colony facing the Spaniards to the southward. On St. Simon's Island, opposite the mouth of the Altamaha, Oglethorpe selected—also for military reasons—a site for another town, which he called Frederica. Still farther south he established outposts on islands along the coast; the most southerly of which, and most irritating to the Spaniards, being Fort St. George, on an island opposite the mouth of the St. John's River, and hardly one hundred miles from St. Augustine itself.

It was the benevolent purpose of the trustees to make their colony a community of small farms supporting a sturdy English yeomanry who would also be fighting men in time of war. Thus the men to whom lands were granted were expected to be ready to give military service when called upon, much as on a feudal military fief. Nor could the owner dispose of his land without the consent of the trustees. The land was granted under the legal form called "tail-male"; that is to say, it could be inherited only by male heirs. If a man died without sons, his land reverted to the trustees; for if a daughter inherited the land, she might marry an enemy of England or someone unfriendly to the ideals of the colony, and the land would thus fall into unfriendly hands. Colonists whose expenses were paid by the trustees received fifty acres of land; those who came to the colony at their own expense and brought from four to ten men servants might receive as much as five hundred acres. This was the upper limit, however. All land thus granted was to pay a quitrent of ten shillings sterling per one hundred acres after a free period of ten years. To encourage the production of commodities desired by the English merchants, and particularly the culture of silk, the colonists were required to plant a certain number of mulberry trees (1,000) for every one hundred acres of land in each grant. If the colonist failed to bring his land under cultivation and fence it within eighteen years, it was to revert to the trustees. Indentured servants, at the end of their term of servitude, were given from twenty-five to fifty acres.

But the colonists had to work their lands with their own hands. The trustees could hardly promote the greatest humanitarian enterprise of their age and run so far counter to their own humanitarianism as to permit Negro slavery within their colony. Nor could Negroes do the work demanded by the wine and silk industries the trustees were so anxious to promote; were Negroes allowed in the colony, both the humanitarian ideal and the commercial purpose of the trustees would be defeated. They therefore prohibited slavery in the colony, thus setting it apart from all the others. But here, in a terrain very similar to that of South Carolina, the Georgia colonists had to do all their own hard labor in an enervating climate while just across the Savannah River their South Carolina neighbors were waxing wealthy and comfortable merely by the use of Negro labor. They might, indeed, cross the river into South Carolina; for there they might both accumulate landholdings of any size and have them worked by Negroes, provided only that they could raise the necessary capital. Many of the settlers did, indeed, exactly that.

Another law of the trustees which irked the colonists was the one prohibiting the importation of rum, brandy or other hard liquors. This would have been irksome enough, in that age of hard liquors, if the only desire of the colonists for the stuff was to drink it. But the fact was that Georgia was in a favorable position to sell lumber from its great forests to the West Indies, and this golden opportunity was lost, largely because the colony could not receive West Indian rum in exchange.

Thus for three reasons the Georgia colonists were discontented: they desired to be allowed to amass larger holdings of land and to be free of the prescribed military restrictions; they desired to be allowed to import slaves and employ them on the plantations; and they desired to be allowed to import rum and other hard liquors, either for consumption or for re-export. Finally, in addition to all these, there existed among these Englishmen accustomed to self-government a growing dissatisfaction with the arbitrary and unrepresentative nature of the colony's administration.

The government of the colony was, indeed, an anomaly. The trustees, back in England, made all grants of land and formulated the regulations of life and commerce, and appointed all the officials of the colony. While the trustees never actually appointed a governor, Oglethorpe, the trustees' "agent," was to all intents and purposes a governor with a large measure of military and civil power. Oglethorpe, however, was an extremely busy man, voyaging back and forth to England, fighting the Spaniards, and promoting the colony, with the result that he was unable to give much time to the internal conditions of his settlement. Nor could the trustees promptly and effectively administer the detailed problems of local government. It thus fell out that, from sheer necessity if for no other reason, local government came to be left in the hands of the local officials. Each important town had its own bailiffs, constables, and justices of the peace, but there was no connection between the towns. Oglethorpe himself, as agent for the trustees, was the only cohesive element. As time went on, however, the local bailiffs, acting in Oglethorpe's absence, assumed an increasing amount of responsibility for the conduct of affairs. The most important of these officials was the "storekeeper" for the trustees at Savannah, who naturally had business with practically every colonist who came over. Little by little this man, Thomas Causton, became Oglethorpe's chief lieutenant in the entire colony. The colonists complained about his arbitrary "rule," however, and the trustees, partly because of the colonists' complaints and partly because Oglethorpe was preoccupied with military affairs, decided in 1741 to divide the colony into two counties, one about Savannah as a center and the other about Frederica, each with its local magistrates. Each county was to be provided with a "president" and four "assistants," all of whom were to be appointed by the trustees. The scheme was actually set up only in the Savannah area, however, and in 1743 the "president" of Savannah became "president" for the whole colony. The three bailiffs at Savannah became his assistants. Thus Georgia became, in effect, a province governed by an appointed governor and council; this was as near as it came to representative government until 1751, just a year before Georgia became a royal province. One advantage the Georgians had, however, because of the popular interest in the colony and the military interest of Parliament, popular subscriptions and parliamentary appropriations made taxation unnecessary throughout the period of the trusteeship. In one respect, at least, Georgia was indeed a Utopia!

GEORGIA AND SPANISH FLORIDA

The colony of Georgia, as already noted, was settled upon land claimed by Spain. Spain had protested the English infiltration into "Guale" southward from Carolina since the Peace of Utrecht, and now protested violently against this apparent British seizure of Spanish territory in what seemed to be a clear violation of the Anglo-Spanish treaties of Utrecht (1713), Madrid (1721), and Seville (1729). Oglethorpe was apparently determined to make the St. John's River the boundary between Georgia and Spanish Florida; Fort St. George, near the mouth of that river, was to be the southern bastion of the Utopia.

With the intention of conciliating the Spaniards in Florida, Oglethorpe in 1736 sent Charles Dempsey to St. Augustine to express his friendship to the Spanish governor, Don Francisco Moral Sánchez. The governor, frightened by the British encroachments, and impressed by Oglethorpe's show of force, sent an emissary, Don Antonio Arredondo, to Oglethorpe at Frederica, and there it was agreed that Fort St. George should be dismantled. The question of a boundary between Florida and Georgia was to be referred to the Spanish and English courts in Europe, and, pending a settlement of the boundary, it was agreed that the English and Spanish colonists in Georgia and Florida would keep the peace. This agreement by Arredondo and Oglethorpe was ratified by Governor Sánchez and the boundary question was duly referred to his sovereign. Oglethorpe, too, reported the agreement to his home government, and received the commendation of the Georgia trustees. Madrid, however, refused to ratify the agreement, on the ground that Governor Sánchez had had no authority to make it.

Sánchez himself was recalled to Spain, and was rumored to have been hanged for having given tacit recognition to the British occupancy of the area south of Charleston.

Spain strengthened the garrison at St. Augustine, while protesting, through diplomatic channels, against the British occupancy of Georgia. Mingled as it was with other diplomatic differences between England and Spain, the Georgia question became one of the major causes of the War of Jenkins' Ear. There were several of these differences, which the Walpole ministry sought to settle by peaceable means in the ill-fated Convention of the Pardo of January, 1739. This convention provided that the question of a boundary between Georgia and Florida should be left to the joint commission to be set up under the convention for the adjudication of the other disputes between the two countries. But the British imperialists, eager to expand the empire at the expense of Spain, were now in control of the British Parliament, and the Convention of the Pardo was rejected. The imperialists were determined upon war; and war—the War of Jenkins' Ear—began in 1739.

The outbreak of war brought the military functions of Georgia into play, and Oglethorpe soon had a chance to demonstrate his generalship. He immediately took the offensive against Florida, and in the spring of 1740 led an expedition against St. Augustine. He succeeded in taking two Spanish forts on the St. John's River, but failed ignominiously before St. Augustine itself, and was compelled to return ingloriously to Frederica. In the summer of 1742 the Spaniards took the offensive and attacked Frederica, only to fail as ingloriously as Oglethorpe had failed at St. Augustine. Thereafter the fighting between Florida and Georgia resolved itself into nothing more serious than border raids. The interest of the European powers had been diverted by the outbreak of the War of the Austrian Succession; and what had started as a war of British imperial expansion was soon submerged by the struggle upon the larger stage. Georgia continued to play a role in the European conflict, however, for in the second Franco-Spanish Bourbon "Family Compact," signed at Fontainebleau in 1743, one of the stated objectives of the alliance of France and Spain in the war was agreed to be the restoration of Georgia to Spain. Practically, possession of Georgia proved to be "nine points of the law," and the Spanish were never able to dislodge the English from their Georgia plantations. After the campaign of 1742, indeed, the Spaniards never made another serious effort to do so.

THE RATIONALIZATION OF THE UTOPIA

The colonists of Georgia had never been satisfied with the economic and social regulations under which they were expected to live. From the first the humanitarianism and the defense-mindedness of the trustees had run counter to the natural economic and social tendencies of the colony, on three main issues: land, rum, and Negro slavery. As already explained, the trustees had limited the size of an individual's holdings in land to five hundred acres, and had provided, for military reasons, that inheritance of land might take place only in the male line. But this land policy placed a serious handicap upon the economic development of the colony. For these small Georgia holdings, worked by the colonists themselves and such indentured servants as they could afford, had to compete with the large holdings just across the Savannah River, in South Carolina, worked by slave labor. The climate made it difficult for white men to compete with slave labor in any case, while the larger units of land could produce more, at a lower proportionate cost than the Georgia farms. With the outbreak of war with Spain, the movement of discontented settlers away from the colony became serious, and the trustees gradually modified their land policy. In 1740 the settlers were permitted to rent lands, thus making it possible to bring larger amounts under the control of single individuals, and the maximum amount that could be inherited was raised from five hundred to two thousand. Daughters as well as sons were now permitted to inherit land. The law of tail-male was completely discarded in 1742, and the quitrents on all land were substantially reduced. This gradual modification of the land policy opened the way for large estates, and with it the establishment of a landed aristocracy, in a colony that had originally been dedicated to the alleviation of the distress of the poor!

But there were other restrictions that must be removed before the economic life of the colony could flow freely. The trustees, in their desire to protect their colony from the dangers which had beset the colonists in the old world, had enacted a law, in January, 1734, prohibiting the importation of and use of rum and other strong liquors in their colony. Beer might still be used, of course, and it was hoped that the colony might itself become a great producer of wine. But wines and beer did not satisfy these hard-drinking Englishmen, and there was a good deal of nullification of the law. As there was no real public sentiment against the use of strong drink, the law was practically impossible to enforce. Moreover,

Georgia was heavily wooded, and might achieve prosperity by the sale of lumber to the West Indies, in return for which the Georgians would have to import the great West Indian staples, sugar and rum. As they could not consume or re-export sufficient amounts of sugar, the difference between commercial prosperity and poverty seemed to be involved in this "hot, hellish liquor." Many were the complaints that came to the ears of the trustees, and because of these, coupled with the outright nullification, the trustees in 1742 instructed William Stephens, "president" at Savannah "to wink at the Importations of rum and to discourage seizures."

A petition from the colonists to the Board of Trade against the policies of the trustees with regard to land, rum, and slaves was brought to England by Thomas Stephens (son of William) late in 1742, and this led to a parliamentary investigation of the trustees' affairs. It was probably as a result of this investigation that the land policy was modified, and that the trustees finally agreed to repeal the law prohibiting the importation of rum, at least so far as to permit its import from other British colonies. This was not a complete surrender of their principles, however, for the trustees straightway enacted measures strictly regulating the conduct of public drinking houses, in order at least to control "the odious and loathesome Sin of Drunkenness."

But the greatest sacrifice of their ideals that the trustees had to face for the prosperity of their colony was that involved in the institution of Negro slavery. They had hoped to found a colony of poor men, who would earn their living by their own labor, and they had looked with disgust upon a social system, already developed in the plantation colonies, which permitted the exploitation of the labor of black men by whites, and which resulted in the appearance of an aristocratic society containing all the social ills of which their colonists were the unhappy victims. One of their earliest laws for the colony, therefore, had been the one prohibiting slavery in the colony. The settlers were discouraged to find that they could not do the back-breaking labor of clearing and cultivating the land as well as Negroes, and that they could not compete with Carolina plantations that employed slaves. Actually, too, numerous slaveowners moved into Georgia and settled in remote areas where it was difficult to control them, and these nullifiers of the law succeeded where the law-abiding citizens were failing. As early as 1738 a number of the colonists petitioned the trustees to remove the restriction on slavery, but nothing was done until Thomas Stephens won the ear of Parliament in 1742.

The colony itself was divided—torn between humanitarianism and economic prosperity—and ardent anti-slavery crusaders appeared to oppose the change. But Negroes continued to come into the colony in increasing numbers, while public opinion clamored for a removal of the restriction. Despite the stubborn persistence of the trustees in the name of humanitarianism, thrift, and military danger, they were forced to give in; in August, 1750, they surrendered this last of their great ideals, and repealed the anti-slavery law—not, however, without retaining numerous restrictions upon the practice.

One more important change was made by the trustees in the administration of their colony. As the period provided by their charter drew towards its end, a number of the original sponsors of the colony lost interest in it. Oglethorpe himself took less interest than formerly, and the political administration of the colony fell more and more into the hands of the "president" at Savannah. The settlers, on their side, many of whom were not in sympathy with the humanitarian objectives of the trustees, were discontented with a system of government which denied them any voice in the management of their political affairs. Partly to relieve themselves of the burden, therefore, partly to avoid criticism that might be leveled at them at home, and partly to satisfy the desires of the settlers, the trustees decided, in 1751, to call an assembly of representatives of the people to discuss the laws. This assembly, which was composed of delegates from all the towns or settlements of ten families or more, had no power to pass laws but only to discuss proposed laws and make suggestions for others. The result was quite satisfactory to the trustees, and another assembly was held in 1752. Georgia never achieved a truly representative legislature, however, under the trusteeship.

GEORGIA BECOMES A ROYAL PROVINCE

The period of the trusteeship was, indeed, drawing to a close. The trustees might ask for a renewal of their charter, to be sure, but there were numerous reasons why they might not do so. The colonists were not satisfied with the administration of the trustees, despite all the compromises they had made, and most of the humanitarian efforts of the founders had failed of their objectives among the very people they had most hoped to serve. The colony had demonstrated its military usefulness, to be sure; but practically the colony was almost a complete failure. Five thousand people, perhaps, had come to the colony before 1751; 2,500 of these, of whom one thousand were foreign Protestants, had come at the expense of the trustees. But at the time of the surrender of the charter there were in the colony only about three thousand souls, of whom one thousand were Negroes, and only about 153,000 acres of land—about fifteen square miles—had been brought under actual cultivation. Furthermore, South Carolina, from which Georgia had been carved out in the first place, was now desirous of acquiring control of the Georgia area once more, and the trustees were afraid they could not resist this movement. The trustees themselves were losing interest, and many of the private donors of funds for the support of the experiment had long since ceased to make any contributions. The result was that the financial administration of the colony was becoming increasingly difficult.

In 1751 the trustees asked Parliament for a grant of money—as they had regularly and successfully done in the past, but the request was refused. They then turned to the king, who also refused to aid with the decision that he would give no financial aid to the colony until the trustees should give up their charter. As the charter was to expire in 1753 in any case, the trustees decided to surrender it immediately, which was done in June, 1752. In order to protect Georgia from annexation by South Carolina, however, the surrender was made with the proviso that the colony was to retain its separate provincial status, which was accepted by the Crown.

In taking on the administration of Georgia, the Crown provided that it should be a royal province, with institutions similar to the other royal governments. Thus the colony was to have a royally appointed governor, a royally appointed council of fourteen, and an elected representative lower house of nineteen men, called the commons house of assembly. All males owning fifty acres of land or paying taxes on other property worth fifty acres were given the vote. Similarly, a judicial system was established, including justices of the peace, county courts and a general or superior court; the Governor's Council, as in other royal provinces, served as a supreme court of appeals, as well as the upper house of the legislature and as an executive council for the governor.

The first governor, Captain John Reynolds, was a naval officer who sought to rule Georgia as a captain ruled his ship—with consequent unpopularity to himself. He did not arrive until 1755, when he called the first really representative assembly Georgia ever had. Because of his unpopularity, as also because of his ineffective handling of the problems presented by the necessities of defense of the frontiers in the French and Indian War, Reynolds was soon recalled, to be succeeded by Henry Ellis, who was more successful.

The war did not touch Georgia directly, but the Spanish danger became a reality when Spain entered the conflict on the side of France in 1762, and Georgia had once more to face the possibility of invasion from Florida. Happily, however, the war soon ended, and by the Treaty of Paris, 1763, Florida was ceded to England by Spain, and the land east of the Mississippi by France; which ended the old Spanish and French threats—at least for the remainder of the colonial period. By the royal proclamation of October 3, 1763, the boundary between Georgia and Florida was definitely fixed at the St. Mary's River, and Georgia ceased to be a "frontier" settlement.

RECOMMENDED BOOKS FOR FURTHER READING

CONTEMPORARY NARRATIVES

Antonio de Arredondo, *Arredondo's Historical Proof of Spain's Title to Georgia*, edited by Herbert E. Bolton.

Elizabeth Donnan, ed., *Documents Illustrative of the History of the Slave Trade to America.*

Albert B. Hart, ed., *American History Told by Contemporaries*, II, Chapter 6.

MODERN ACCOUNTS

Herbert E. Bolton and Mary Ross, *The Debatable Land.*

Edward Channing, *A History of the United States*, II, Chapter 12.

Ellis M. Coulter, *A Short History of Georgia*, Chapters 1-10.

Elizabeth Donnan, "The Slave Trade into South Carolina before the Revolution" in *American Historical Review*, XXXIII, 804-828.

Amos A. Ettinger, *James Edward Oglethorpe, Imperial Idealist.*

Ralph B. Flanders, *Plantation Slavery in Georgia*, Chapters 1-5.

Lawrence H. Gipson, *The British Empire before the American Revolution*, II, Chapter 6.

John T. Lanning, *The Diplomatic History of Georgia.*

John T. Lanning, *The Spanish Missions of Georgia.*

James R. McCain, *Georgia as a Proprietary Province.*

Herbert L. Osgood, *The American Colonies in the Eighteenth Century*, III, Part II, Chapter 9; IV, Part III, Chapter 13.

Robert Wright, *A Memoir of General James Oglethorpe.*

39

The Heyday of the British West Indies

THE BRITISH colonies in the West Indies were the most important section of the British empire in the eighteenth century. In the first place, the amount of sugar produced by the islands made them extremely valuable to the entire empire. But the sugar trade was doubly important because of its international character, and the production of sugar within the empire gave England a commodity for export which was of supreme importance in English foreign trade. The West Indies were important also because of their strategic position relative to the other parts of America. They were a great problem of defense in time of war, and they formed a base of operations for the slave traders and the South Sea Company in its conduct of trade under the Assiento in time of peace. The islands furnished a market for the products of the colonies on the North American mainland and for the Negroes who were brought by the Yankee traders from the coasts of Africa. Incidentally, in the purchase of goods produced by the northern colonies the West Indies paid for their purchases, in part at least, in cash; and this hard money they got from their own trade with the neighboring colonies of France, Spain and Holland. The balance of direct trade between the West Indies and the mother country, as a matter of fact, was unfavorable to the mother country; but because such a large part of the imports from the West Indies was re-exported from England, and because the islands served as a pivot for so much of the trade of the other parts of the empire, they assumed in the minds of the British statesmen a position of unmatched importance as justifying the mercantilist theory of the self-sufficient empire. It is no accident, therefore, that the West Indies were generally considered, from the English point of view, the most profitable and most important of all the colonies.

THE CONSTITUTIONAL STRUGGLE IN THE ISLAND COLONIES

Politically the West Indies colonies were still divided into three units: Barbados, the Leeward Islands, and Jamaica. All were royal provinces, each with a governor appointed by the king, an appointive council, and an elected assembly. Of the four Leeward Islands, however, each had its own legislature and lieutenant governor, with one governor for the entire group. In the political history of the islands generally there is to be observed the same struggle between the popular branch of government and the royal or proprietary prerogative that has already been noted in the history of the continental colonies; for here, as elsewhere, there was a consistent effort to lodge control of government in the hands of the representatives of the people, with a consequent distrust of a strong executive representing the conservative influence of the imperial administration far from the colonies themselves, in London.

In Jamaica, almost alone among the British colonies, the struggle was won by the prerogative. The governors were instructed to procure a permanent revenue for the Crown which would make the executive independent of the legislature. This the assembly refused to grant, since it would thus deprive itself of a check upon the behavior of the governor. Governor Hamilton, who arrived in 1711, was reduced to receiving funds for only three months at a time. When one assembly failed to provide funds for the support of troops defending the island and Governor Hamilton advanced the money, the next assembly refused to reimburse the amounts advanced, on the ground that the money was spent without legal authorization, and, therefore, the assembly could not pay it without "infringing the liberties of subjects of this island, and betraying the trust reposed in them." The struggle continued, however; and the breach between the assembly and the executive was widened by John Ayscue, president of the council, in 1726, when he complained that the assembly, in disregarding the governor's instructions, was violating the king's "commands." The assembly replied that the king's instructions were but "recommendations" to a "free legislature," and refused to pass any laws until reparation should be made. The arrival of Robert Hunter as governor in 1727, after having passed through a similar struggle in New York, brought the conflict to a head. Hunter succeeded in defeating the assembly on the issue by refusing to sign any law passed by the assembly until provision had been made for a permanent revenue to the Crown. The island was practically without law for a period, until the assembly, fearful of the effect upon the large slave population, finally gave in and granted a permanent income to the Crown of £8,000 per annum. The executive was to this extent made independent of the legislature; but the assembly had its way in lesser matters of parliamentary procedure such as the election of the speaker, self-adjournment, and others.

In Barbados and the Leeward Islands also, as in Virginia and Jamaica, the Crown had now a permanent revenue, derived from the old four and one-half percent export duty on "dead" articles, which had been established as early as 1663. By the middle of the eighteenth century this fund had become quite large; and from it were paid the salaries of the governor of Barbados and the Leeward Islands and of the lieutenant governors of St. Christopher, Antigua, Nevis, and Montserrat. Since it was used for other purposes as well, it became a standing grievance between the colonists and the Crown. In all the islands, nevertheless, the struggle for legislative autonomy went on, with varying degrees of success. The fact that the West Indies did not achieve the measure of independence enjoyed by the northern colonies was due, not to any lack of desire for it or of vigor in the struggle, but, rather, to the exposed position of the islands, which made them utterly dependent upon the mother country for defense and the fear of insurrection by their own great slave populations, which could only be kept in subjection by the sanction of British arms.

PROSPERITY AND THE BEGINNING OF ECONOMIC DECLINE

All the island colonies had gone in heavily for the production of sugar, and this commodity remained the staple item of export for all of them. Barbados, one of the most profitable of all the British possessions, had in 1748 a population of some 25,000 whites —Scottish, Irish, Dutch, French, Portuguese, Jews, and Englishmen— and probably 70,000 Negroes. It was importing some 2,500 Negro slaves annually. In this year over 220 ships entered the harbor of Bridgetown, the principal port, to carry away some 15,000 hogsheads (= 1,500 lbs.) of sugar and 12,000 puncheons (= 84 gallons) of rum. This island exported little or no molasses, but manufactured it into rum at the distilleries in Bridgetown.

The Leeward Islands presented a similar picture. The seat of the governor of this group of small island colonies was on the island of Antigua, at the town of St. Johns, where the harbor was one of the few good ones possessed by the group. This island had a good soil, but it had no springs or streams, and was entirely dependent upon the rains for its water supply. The size of its sugar crop, therefore, varied from year to year. Yet its exports at the mid-century averaged about 15,000 casks of sugar, 10,000 casks of rum, 3,000 to 4,000 bags of cotton, and some 6,000 bags of ginger.

Its population was made up of some 3,500 whites and 28,000 blacks, a ratio of one to eight.

St. Christopher, or St. Kitts, was next to Antigua in size, and was the oldest of the British settlements in the West Indies. It had been occupied jointly with the French until 1713, but was taken over entirely by the British under the terms of the Treaty of Utrecht. Its soil was extremely fertile, and it was famous for its rugged, mountainous beauty. It was handicapped, however, by the lack of good harbor facilities. This small island exported annually some 11,000 casks of sugar, 85,000 gallons of rum, and 33,000 gallons of molasses. St. Christopher also exported considerable quantities of a fine grade of cotton. Its population was made up of about 10,000 whites and 20,000 Negroes.

Nevis and Montserrat, the other two islands in the group, were smaller and less important; their general economic situation was much the same, however. Nevis had a population of 900 whites and 7,000 blacks; Montserrat, 3,500 whites and 5,500 blacks. These small islands, like the rest, were devoted to the raising and export of sugar and its by-products. The exports of Nevis, however, were rapidly declining in 1750, while Montserrat was barely holding its own. The decline in the prosperity of the West Indies seems to have struck the smaller islands first.

Jamaica was now by far the most important of the island colonies, partly by reason of its relatively diversified economic life, and partly because of its exposed position as an outpost of the British empire in the direction of Spanish America. Its population included perhaps 10,000 whites and 120,000 Negroes, or a ratio of one to twelve. Its exports at the mid-century amounted to some £1,500,000 annually, and included, besides the usual sugar, rum and molasses, considerable amounts of cotton, ginger, cocoa, pimento and spices. Coffee, introduced into the colony early in the century, soon became an important item of export, and another important commodity was fustic, a wood that was much used by European dye-makers in the making of dyes. This wood, along with considerable quantities of mahogany, which was just making its appearance in the product of the fine furniture-makers of the period, was cut in large quantities on the coasts of Spanish Central America, and imported to Jamaica, whence it was re-exported to England, to Philadelphia, Boston, and other colonial towns, and to the continent of Europe.

Jamaica's relative proximity to the Spanish colonies had made it a convenient depot for the slave-trade carried on by the British

South Sea Company under the Assiento. This agreement, or contract, awarded by Spain to the British company under the terms of the Anglo-Spanish Treaty of Utrecht, had given the company a monopoly of the business of supplying the Spanish colonies with slaves, and the company had found Jamaica the most convenient point for refreshing and sorting their cargoes before landing them on Spanish soil. Here, also, they received orders from their agents in the Spanish colonies, and from here the slaves were distributed to Cartagena, Porto Bello, Vera Cruz, Cuba, and other nearby Spanish places. The Spanish purchasers paid for the Negroes with specie, and much of this welcome hard money found its way to the continental colonies to pay for the food (fish, wheat, etc.) and the horses and pipe-staves imported by the island from the north. The slave trade under the Assiento practically stopped with the outbreak of the War of Jenkins' Ear in 1739, and the treaty itself came to an end in 1750. Some clandestine trade with Cartagena and Porto Bello continued; but the end of the Assiento was a severe blow to the prosperity of the island.

None of the island colonies raised its own food supply. For this they turned to the continental colonies, whence they imported fish for the slaves, wheat, lumber and staves, and horses, and to Ireland, whence they imported barreled beef and pork, butter, and other provisions. From England, of course, came practically all their manufactured goods such as furniture, machinery for the sugar mills, harness, carriages, clothes and hardware. All of them, dependent as they were upon an abundant supply of slaves, imported large numbers of Negroes every year. Barbados averaged about 3,000 annually, Antigua about 1,500, St. Christopher 1,500, Nevis 400, Montserrat 350, and Jamaica, exclusive of those re-exported, about 4,000. With the exception of Jamaica, the slave trade was carried on by independent traders of the islands themselves, or by New Englanders, or by English slavers.

The islands were thus heavy importers of foodstuffs and slaves. Yet so profitable was the production of sugar that the value of the islands' exports far exceeded that of the imports, and the islands were greatly prosperous, so long as the market for their staple product maintained its steady demand. Yet these communities, like the expanding colonies on the North American mainland, were in need of capital for their expanding industry. Much of the capital that went into the development of the sugar industry of the West Indies—much more, indeed, than in any other section of the empire —came from England, and much of the profits of the industry

went into the amortization and interest charges of these investments. Most of the investment thus made was in the form of credit,
and the planters of the islands, especially the smaller ones, like
the planters of Virginia, were generally heavily in debt to their
British creditors.

Another severe drain upon the profit-making capacity of the
islands was the custom of the great planters of residing in England rather than in the islands, leaving their plantations to be
operated by overseers. It was this group, associated with the English factors of the planters remaining in the islands, that constituted the famous "West India lobby." The system was a vicious
one for the islands, however, for aside from its inefficiency the
planters in London drew as much from their distant plantations
as the traffic would bear, and profits that otherwise might have contributed to the increased prosperity of the islands were drawn out
to be spent in England.

The result of this combination of circumstances was a shortage
of money similar to that in the continental colonies. To meet the
need in Barbados an attempt was made in 1706 to establish a land
bank, but it was suppressed by action of the Crown. One of the
most satisfactory ways of getting a money supply was by a clandestine trade with the Spanish colonies, in which slaves and British
manufactures were sold for gold and silver. Unfortunately, this
trade was not sufficiently large to be very effective in solving the
problem. Colonial legislatures attempted to make sugar the medium
of exchange by fixing the price at which certificates of deposit
might circulate; but this scheme always failed because of the inevitable fluctuation of the price of sugar in the open market.
Sugar was, nevertheless, consistently used as a medium of exchange.
Aside from the Barbados Land Bank of 1706, which lasted only
one year, the West Indies seem not to have attempted, as did the
continental colonies, to issue paper currencies, although the proposal was often made. The scarcity of money was certainly a great
handicap upon the economic life of the islands, and was doubtless
one important factor in their decline.

In any case, by the middle of the eighteenth century the fabulous prosperity of the islands had already begun to recede. The
reasons were manifold. To begin with, the islands, now having
been cultivated for sugar for a century, began to show signs of
soil-exhaustion, and it required an increasing number of slaves—
at a consequently greater cost—to cultivate a given area of land.
But the French islands near by, which had begun the business

somewhat later and probably did it somewhat more efficiently, were offering serious competition to the sugar of the British islands in the world market. In this they were encouraged by the traders of the northern continental colonies, and an effort was made to equalize the cost of French sugar imported into the British empire by the Molasses Act of 1733. This act did not affect the situation in the world market, however, where French and Dutch sugar continued to undersell the British product. The situation was aggravated by the fact that sugar was on the list of enumerated articles which had to be landed in England before being sent to the continental market, and efforts were made to equalize the delivery costs of British sugar in the world market, first by drawbacks of import duties on sugar re-exported out of England, and then, in 1739, by the entire removal of sugar from the enumerated list.

But all to no avail. The increased cost of production due to soil exhaustion, foreign competition, the end of the Assiento and other conditions brought about a gradual decline, so far as world trade was concerned, which became more rapid in the second half of the eighteenth century and amounted almost to collapse with the abolition of slavery in the British empire early in the nineteenth. It should be noted, however, that, though the islands never again recovered their position in the world market, the steady increase in sugar consumption in England, where the product of the British islands had a monopoly, gradually rectified the loss, and in the second half of the century the islands were actually exporting more sugar than ever before, practically all of it going to England. This fact had a profound effect upon their relationship to the rest of the empire; for because of it their very economic survival now depended upon the English market. Thus, in the era of the American Revolution, when the colonies on the continent threw off the leading strings of English economic control, the West Indies were in such a state of economic dependence upon the mother country that to have joined the continental colonies in the move for independence would have been nothing short of suicidal.

THE SOCIETY OF THE WEST INDIES PLANTERS

The society of the British West Indies was an aristocratic society, dominated by the wealthy planters. Because of the fact that the islands depended upon local cities as points of shipment and deposit, there existed in these island colonies a more considerable mercantile group of people than existed, say, in Virginia. For this and other reasons society here was more mixed, and the "spread" of social classes was, if anything, broader. Thus at the top of West Indies society stood the wealthy planters. Many of the more affluent plantation owners, however, particularly in St. Kitts, had moved back to England where they constituted a well-organized and powerful lobby to promote the interests of their islands and themselves in Parliament and out of it. For these men, England was their home; their plantations in the islands were but investments to pay them profit. Their sons were educated in England; by the middle of the eighteenth century many of the proprietors of large sugar plantations had never seen their properties in the islands, since they had inherited them from their fathers. For the absentee planters there was nothing like the local loyalty of the Virginian for his province or the Pennsylvanian for his; their patriotism was all for England.

But the most deplorable social effect of absenteeism upon the islands was that it drained off the most cultivated and able colonials, leaving the leadership of society, to say nothing of economic and political life, in the hands of second-rate men. Those who remained resented the desertion of the islands and tried to force the absentees to return. But to no avail. Conditions in the colonies, indeed, discouraged white immigration of any sort. In any case the climate was not congenial to white men; but the increasing proportion of blacks to white, and the relative lack of economic opportunity, discouraged white men from going to the islands when it was so much easier to go to the colonies on the continent, where conditions were much better. The island colonies made every conceivable effort to encourage white immigration. Jamaica offered headrights of fifty acres of land for adults and twenty acres for children. All the islands passed laws requiring planters to import proportionate numbers of whites for all the slaves they bought, or to pay fines. It was found to be easier to pay the fines, and this constituted a steady source of income for the island treasuries.

As it was, at the top of the society of the islands stood the resident planters. But as each of the islands had at least one important town where the business of exporting and importing had to be done, there developed in those towns something of a "bourgeois" class of lawyers, officials, agents, and merchants, who led a life of considerable gaiety and sophistication, in which they mingled with the resident planters. Below these more well-to-do groups, across a wide social gulf, stood the poor whites—free and often idle workers, indentured servants, and Jews. The free Negroes consti-

tuted a class of their own; at the bottom of the social scale stood
the Negro slaves. One of the vicious results of absenteeism was
the increasingly harsh treatment of the slaves by the overseers.
The fear of slave insurrections, which were, indeed, more numerous than they needed to be, led to harsh laws against the Negroes
and deliberate discouragement of any attempt to educate them or
to convert them to Christianity, on the ground that they should
not be given even these innocuous bonds of common interest.
Negro slavery was at its utterly deplorable worst in the West Indies
in the eighteenth century.

Religion in the West Indies was likewise at a low ebb. There
had been little or no religious motive in the minds of the first
settlers, and the frontier conditions of settlement had diluted such
religion as there was. Anglicanism was the most generally accepted
form, but the practice of religion was at an even lower ebb than
in Virginia. On the other hand, gambling was very prevalent in
all the island colonies, as were other vices, such as miscegenation
between whites and blacks which resulted in the appearance of
a race of mulattoes. Attempts were made to limit this practice,
but without much success. In the absence of whites, indeed, some
of the islands permitted certain mulatto descendants of white men
to become voters.

Education, like religion, was also at a low ebb. There were few
schools of any sort: those who could afford it sent their children
to England to be educated; others engaged tutors. There was one
school of higher grade at Bridgetown, in Barbados. Codrington
College was founded by the Society for the Propagation of the
Gospel on a bequest made by Governor Christopher Codrington
in 1710. Between 1740 and 1750 this school had about forty pupils
each year.

Of the towns, Bridgetown, in Barbados enjoyed the most active
social life. In contrast to other West Indian towns, Bridgetown
presented a neat, "English" appearance with its twelve hundred
houses, many of them built of brick and stone and having glass
windows. It contained a handsome Anglican church and Codrington College, and the governor's residence was famed for the
elegance of its "court" society. Bridgetown was noted for its hospitality and its gay social life, with such amusements as card parties,
balls and concerts. There seems to have been a theater there at an
early date; there was also a theater at Spanish Town, in Jamaica.
Of Bridgetown one traveler said "There is in general a greater ap-

pearance of order and decency than in any other colony of the West Indies."

On the whole, the West Indies presented, in the eighteenth century, the most depressing social scene to be found in all the British colonies in America. The lack of social vigor, absenteeism, the general loyalty to England rather than to the local islands—all contributed to the decline of the islands. These conditions also explain, in considerable measure, why the islands did not feel the same independence and resentment against England in the revolutionary era that led to the successful revolt of the continental colonies.

RECOMMENDED BOOKS FOR FURTHER READING

CONTEMPORARY NARRATIVES

Charles Leslie, *A New and Exact Account of Jamaica.*

William Perrin, *The Present State of the British and French Sugar Colonies . . . Considered.*

Janet Schaw, *Journal of a Lady of Quality,* edited by Evangeline W. Andrews and Charles M. Andrews, Chapters 1-2.

Hans Sloane, *A Voyage to the Islands Madera, Barbados, Nieves, S. Christophers and Jamaica . . .*

MODERN ACCOUNTS

Herbert C. F. Bell, "The West India Trade before the American Revolution" in *American Historical Review,* XXII, 272-287.

Vera L. Brown, "The South Sea Company and Contraband Trade" in *American Historical Review,* XXXI, 662-678.

The Cambridge History of the British Empire, I, Chapters 11, 15.

Lawrence H. Gipson, *The British Empire before the American Revolution,* II, Chapters 7-9.

Richard Pares, *Colonial Blockade and Neutral Rights, 1739-1763.*

Richard Pares, *War and Trade in the West Indies, 1739-1763.*

Lillian M. Penson, *The Colonial Agents of the British West Indies,* Chapters 1-9.

Lillian M. Penson, "The London West India Interest in the Eighteenth Century" in *English Historical Review,* XXXVI, 373-392.

Frank W. Pitman, *The Development of the British West Indies, 1700-1763.*

Lowell J. Ragatz, *Absentee Landlordism in the British Caribbean, 1750-1833.*

Lowell J. Ragatz, *The Fall of the Planter Class in the British Caribbean, 1763-1833,* Chapters 1-3.

Agnes M. Whitson, *The Constitutional Development of Jamaica, 1660 to 1729.*

James A. Williamson, *A Short History of British Expansion,* Part IV, Chapters 2-3, 5.

40

The Mind of Provincial America

BY THE middle of the eighteenth century the population of the British colonies in America had grown to about two million souls, of whom perhaps 400,000 lived in the West Indies and some 1,500,000 had their homes in the continental colonies stretching from Georgia to Newfoundland. On the continent, probably 500,000 people lived in New England, 400,000 in the middle colonies, and 700,000 (of whom 300,000 were Negroes) in the colonies south of Pennsylvania. Of those who lived in the West Indies, probably not more than one-third were white. These widely spread settlements, each one different from the mother country and strongly sectional in economic life, in social forms, and in culture, were still bound together by the old ties of language and tradition, fundamental political and economic ideas, and a common English cultural heritage. Yet in many ways the civilization of these young communities was new, an amalgam of old-world cultures with indigenous cultural factors that sprang from the American soil, and as the century wore on they found themselves being drawn together by certain new ties—ties that sprang from propinquity, from economic and cultural intercourse, from the frontier struggle against common enemies, and from the common cause that all of them were waging against the prerogative of the Crown in their pursuit of political autonomy. The West Indies colonies were not so subject to these new influences as were the continental colonies. For this reason, as well as for reasons growing out of their insularity and their exposed position as outposts of the empire, this section of the colonies did not participate in the growing cultural unity that characterized the communities on the continent of North America. On the continent, however, the new ties of cultural exchange and common endeavor were drawing the colonies, despite their disunity, their rivalries, and their jealousies, into an ever-increasing understanding of each other and a growing feeling of kinship and loyalty which emerged, in the ensuing years, in a genuine American patriotism.

THE SOCIAL MIND OF THE AMERICANS

As has so often been the case in human history, the social status of an individual living in the British empire in America in the middle of the eighteenth century was in large measure determined by the way in which he made his living. Or, to put it another way, his social status depended upon the degree of his economic independence from other individuals, and this depended upon his economic affluence; this, in turn, depended upon the amount of property he owned, if any, or the amount of his wages, or his status as servant or slave. The fact that saved America from becoming a rigidly stratified society in the eighteenth century seems to have been the possibility that a man could, by initiative, industry, and thrift, pass from one rank in society to another. Indeed, very few people in British America believed in anything like social democracy. On the contrary, the Americans had inherited the British form of a mild caste system, and most of them had a thorough fear of democracy. Democracy was exactly as abhorrent to the good people of the eighteenth century as communism is to the good people of the twentieth.

The eighteenth-century Americans certainly did not believe in the equality of men in the modern sense of the phrase. There was no true aristocracy in the old-world sense, it is true; but those who rose to affluence and assumed the right to put "mister" before their names and "gentleman" after them, became, in a very real sense, a colonial aristocracy, widely separated from the indentured servants and artisans at the bottom of the scale by a social gulf that it became increasingly difficult to cross. The great landowners of New York, Virginia, Maryland, South Carolina and the West Indies stood at the top of American society. These men looked upon themselves as the elite of America, and upon manual labor of any sort as below their dignity. Furthermore, the laws of primogeniture and entail that existed in many of the colonies tended to fix this aristocracy of landed families upon colonial societies, since under the law or custom of primogeniture an estate descended from the father to the eldest of his sons instead of being divided among them, and by the law of entail a man might by will or deed prevent his estate from being broken up. As the eighteenth century wore on the size of the large estates in these colonies increased rapidly, and with them the number of the aristocracy.

The merchants of the growing commercial cities constituted a sort of bourgeois aristocracy of their own, especially in Boston, New York, and Philadelphia. While their wealth was derived from commerce, there was a strong tendency among them to acquire landed estates in the country, and thus to identify themselves with the landed aristocracy.

Yet the backbone of American society was made up of the small farmers who, at the middle of the century, were by far the most numerous single group in the colonial population. There were few of this class in the West Indies—a profound difference, to be sure, with important implications for intellectual and political life— but the homesteads of the continental farmers stretched in a broad, almost unbroken band across New England and the middle colonies from the seacoast to the frontier, and southwestward into the southern colonies along the Allegheny highland and the Piedmont. By the mid-century this social group was becoming conscious of the difference between itself and the aristocracy, landed or commercial, of the tidewater. These were the "agrarians" of a later day, who were already making their liberal views known on the question of paper money, or on the redistribution of seats in colonial assemblies in favor of the west; these were the men who made up the "popular" faction as against the "gentlemen's" faction of the tidewater and the cities.

There were relatively few professional men of any sort. There were some professional medical men, and some professional lawyers, who had been looked upon with scorn in the seventeenth century and were now, with the increase of wealth and property, rapidly on the increase. In the towns the skilled artisan or small shopkeeper and his mate still enjoyed the title of "goodman" and "goodwife." Below them in the social scale stood the indentured servants, and below them, the slaves.

An age-old recognition of social differences had been inherited by the Americans from their English ancestors, and this attitude had persisted. Yet in America it tended to break down. For there was little place for social distinctions on the frontier; there every man was expected to make his own way and there ability was respected more than social rank. And in a still new society, where land was plentiful and where the rapidly expanding economy made opportunities for many, it was relatively easy for a man to move from a lower class to a higher. Indentured servants were generally given "headright" land upon the termination of their contracts; once having made a beginning, it was not difficult to procure more

land and, by thrift, energy, and persistence, to win a competence,
or even wealth. Thousands of men actually did it.

The flexibility of American society and the steady expansion
made for two typically American ideas: one was the conviction
that if a man worked hard and used his intelligence, he could be
successful—he could be a "self-made man"; the other was a deep-
rooted optimism, and a belief in the inevitability of "progress."
Further, the constant struggle with the soil, the forest, and the
climate made for a pragmatic outlook on life that valued the practical thing more highly than the theoretical, adaptability more
highly than book-learning. Out of the frontier experience the
Americans had already established the tradition of American ingenuity. One of them wrote, just before the Revolution, "I am
convinced that America abounds in Natural Genius as [there is]
hardly a town but has its Genius."

The social mind of the Americans, then, was a composite of ideas
derived from the double background of their experience. From
their European "old-countries" they had inherited a respect for
social stratification and the institutions that went along with it.
But out of their experience as frontier people had come a "leveling" influence and a flexibility of social life which inevitably un-
dermined the aristocracy. Their expanding economy made for a
belief in progress and equality of economic opportunity made
for a confidence in the ability of the individual, as well as an
inarticulate faith in the validity of "enlightened self-interest"
which was the native American counterpart of the doctrines just
then being put into classic expression by Adam Smith in England.
It was out of the leveling influences of nearly two centuries of
frontier life that came the first true impulses toward American
democracy.

Probably the most provocative thinker upon social themes to
appear in the colonies in the eighteenth century was John Woolman, a quietist Quaker tailor, who was born at Rancocos, in West
Jersey, October 19, 1720. Woolman made a series of journeys up
and down the colonies between 1741 and 1765, and wrote, besides
a remarkable *Journal,* a series of notable pamphlets on social problems, such as *Some Considerations on the Keeping of Negroes* and
A Word of Remembrance and Caution to the Rich. He attacked
the institution of slavery on humanitarian and religious grounds,
and on the belief, as he put it, "that liberty was the natural right
of all men equally." He preached a more humane treatment of the
Indians, and was much interested in the amelioration of the con-

ditions of the poor. In his discussion of the relationship between the rich and the poor he dwelt upon the idea of the stewardship of the rich and the fatal tendency of wealth to promote laziness and vice; but he adduced economic arguments, as well, which showed a faint tendency toward social utopianism. For, he said,

If such who had great Estates lived in that Humility and plainness which belonged to a Christian life, and laid much Easier Rents and Interests on their lands and moneys, and so led the way to a right Use of things, so great a number of people might be employed in things Usefull that Labour both for men and other Creatures would need to be no more than an agreeable Employ . . . as [God] is the perfection of Power of Wisdom and of Goodness so I believe He both provided that so much labour shall be necessary for mens support in this world as would, being rightly divided, be a suitable Employment of their time, and that we cannot go into superfluities, nor grasp after wealth in a way contrary to his wisdom without having connection with some degree of Oppression, and with that Spirit which leads to Self exaltation and strife, and which frequently brings Calamities on countries by parties contending about their claims.

Woolman was a literary figure as well as a social thinker, and left a profound and lasting impress upon the American mind, particularly in the growing movement against slavery.

POLITICAL THOUGHT AMONG THE AMERICANS

While the social leaven of the American frontier experience was making for an approach to social democracy, the more formal and institutionalized political experience of the Americans was making for an American political philosophy. For out of the complex of developing provincial life, economic, social, and political, there was emerging, about the middle of the eighteenth century, a body of political ideas that were peculiarly American. Into this body of ideas there had gone, to be sure, much that was borrowed from Europe, and this was particularly true of the ideas of the English thinker, John Locke. But the greatest formative force operating upon the emerging American political theory was experience—the experience of Englishmen with a rich heritage of political traditions attempting to apply their traditional ideas and institutions to a situation in which at least two of the fundamental conditions were unique. In the first place, these men had had to build an entirely new governmental system where none had existed before. At the beginning they were without the aristocratic framework of English society upon which to build their institutions. A society had to be created before political institutions could appear: there was not even a voting electorate; and one of the first and most fundamental problems the early settlers had to solve was the problem of creating an electorate. In the second place, there were no precedents for the formation of colonial constitutions. Did the English constitution apply, partially or fully, to the new communities, or were the colonial charter and the laws made by the colonial legislature the sum total of the colonial constitution? In other words, did the colony have two constitutions, a double constitution, or simply one constitution peculiar to itself? The first problem, the creation of a new governmental form where none had existed before, had been accomplished, in a rough way, by the end of the seventeenth century. The second problem, as to the relationship of the colonial constitution to the constitution of England, was the one about which revolved much of the political debate of the eighteenth century, and to solve which, indeed, the American revolution eventually had to be fought. In solving the first problem the Americans had hit upon a territorial property-basis scheme for an electorate which made the popular base of government in America much broader than that in England. Out of the effort to solve the second came the thought which was to produce the two constitutions of the United States, the Articles of Confederation and the Constitution of 1789, to say nothing of the plethora of state constitutions formulated in the Revolutionary era. It was the experience of the colonists in their struggles over these two problems out of which American political ideas were born. If the political philosophies of Locke, Pufendorf, and Montesquieu were popular among the Americans of the mid-century, it was because those theories merely confirmed and expressed more eloquently than they could themselves the conclusions to which the Americans were coming as a result of their own experience in their own political strife.

Thus, in the development of the colonial constitution in the eighteenth century, two major sorts of struggle are to be observed. The internal struggle was concerned with such problems as the issuance of paper money, the redistribution of seats in the representative branch of the legislature to accommodate the growth and spread of population, and the relationship of the lower house to the provincial council. Throughout this internal aspect of the colonial experience there runs a theme of faction based on economic interest: hard-money merchant against agrarian farmer; politically intrenched tidewater against the new political west; popular, less wealthy lower house against appointive, wealthy, and conservative council. By and large, also, it may be said that the factions representing the wealthier interests were conservative, devoted to the maintenance of the *status quo,* and that the factions representing the less wealthy, debtor class of people were more liberal, generally devoted to change in the direction of more popular government. This in itself was not democracy, nor was there anything like political democracy in the twentieth-century sense; but every step toward the broadening of the popular base of government was certainly a step in that direction. Judged upon that ground, the colonial governments were the most democratic in the world at the time.

The other aspect of the constitutional struggle had to do with such questions as the right of the colonial assembly to control money affairs, to elect its own speaker, to act as a high court of appeals, to appoint certain officials responsible to itself, or to appoint, or confirm the appointment of judges. Throughout this aspect of constitutional development runs the theme of colonial autonomy, expressed by the colonial legislature, but especially the lower house, against the insistence of the Crown that the prerogative, personified in the governor and expressed in the governor's instructions or the rulings of the Board of Trade, was an equally important element in the colonial constitution with the recognized right of Englishmen to be taxed only by their own consent or the documentary institutions laid down in the colonial charters. The English position was, in general, that the colony was no more than a municipal corporation like those within the framework of the English constitution in England. According to this point of view the only constitution in force in the colonies was the English constitution. One defender of the prerogative in New York, probably Archibald Kennedy, went so far as to claim that the colonies were in fact only fiefs of the Crown, and that they were permitted to have assemblies, not by any right, but merely by the grace of the king. From the colonial point of view, the colonial constitution was their own and inviolable, co-powerful with, if not superior to the English constitution, within the borders of the colony.

Out of these two aspects of the colonial political experience, the local and the imperial, came American political theory, and it was easy for them to find in such English apologists for parliamentarianism as John Locke a rationalization of their own experience. For the English revolution of 1688-89 had been a revolution growing out of a struggle between an arbitrary king and the representatives of the people in Parliament, to which, in the mind of the colonial liberals at least, their own struggle against the royal prerogative was perfectly analogous. Locke, basing his system upon the doctrine of natural rights so typical of the thinking of his time both in Europe and America, attributed the origin of government to a voluntary association of men hitherto living in a state of natural liberty and equality. For the purpose of protection of their natural rights of life, liberty and property, men had delegated their own right to punish violators of these natural rights to government. They surrendered this power, however, only to the government established by themselves. They were under no obligation to any other; and if the government failed to protect them, the people had a right to discharge it from its position, by force, if necessary. For the proper operation of government, Locke defined three branches, the legislative, the executive, and the judiciary; and for their effective functioning he believed that they should be separate from each other. According to Locke, "the great end of men's entering into society is the enjoyment of their properties in peace and safety." Thus the chief function of government is the protection of property; to the politically minded eighteenth-century American this idea coincided exactly with the fact that, in America, government itself rested solidly upon a property-determined franchise.

The colonists had begun very early in their history to believe in, and actually to practice, the compact theory of government, and they looked upon their charters as written constitutions. They had had occasion to exercise their right of resistance at the time of the English revolution, and they had, without exception, built their governments upon the ownership of property. It was neither an arbitrary nor an accidental fact, therefore, that Locke's philosophy of government became the favorite political philosophy of the Americans.

The earliest and the greatest of American political philosophers in the pre-revolutionary era was John Wise, pastor of the church at Ipswich, in Massachusetts. Wise was prompted to express his ideas by the move of the Mathers in favor of establishing a presbyterian form of government among the New England churches. He wrote two pamphlets, *A Vindication of the Government of the New-England Churches* and *The Churches Quarrel Espoused,* in which he defended the democratic form of government then in vogue in the Congregational churches. His motive was thus to defend democracy in church government; but in demonstrating democracy's virtues for church government he very successfully demonstrated its superiority as a governmental form for secular society as well, and thus made himself the earliest American philosopher of democracy, a century before the United States had achieved even universal manhood suffrage. Taking his lead from Pufendorf, the German political philosopher, Wise, like Locke, based his system upon the doctrine of natural law, natural liberty and natural equality. "The End of all good Government," he said, "is to Cultivate Humanity, and Promote the happiness of all, and the good of every Man in his Rights, his Life, Liberty, Estate, Honour, &c. without injury or abuse done to any." Since democracy is the form of government most calculated to do just this while preserving the natural equality of men, he concludes that democracy is the best form.

Another political thinker of merit was Jeremiah Dummer, agent for Massachusetts in England, who wrote *A Defence of the New England Charters* as a plea for the preservation of these liberal colonial constitutions against a proposal to withdraw them by act of parliament. Jonathan Mayhew, in a sermon preached in 1750 in commemoration of the execution of Charles I, on the text "the powers that be are ordained of God; whosoever therefore rebels against the powers that be rebels against God"—in which he found that, though the powers that be are ordained of God, they are charged with governing for the good of the people; when they fail to fulfill this obligation the people are no longer bound to obey, but may, in fact, depose their rulers and get new ones.

Mayhew marks the sort of political thinking that was going on in America at the mid-eighteenth century. Strongly tinctured with the ideas of Locke, American political thought held to the ideas of the social compact and natural law, the equality of all property owners, constitutions embodying a law superior to the government, and the right of revolt. In practice, they had arrived at an advanced stage of political maturity. In their political theory they had arrived at a mature set of ideas that vindicated their experience and set them apart from England, and gave them the self-assurance to resist, with increasing determination, the efforts of the mother country to interfere with their normal and apparently inevitable growth toward complete political autonomy. Their political philosophy was becoming increasingly the philosophy of free men.

SECULARIZATION OF OUTLOOK AND THE PROGRESS OF RELIGIOUS TOLERANCE

The seventeenth century in America had been a period when religion was by far the dominant intellectual interest. By the mid-eighteenth century several major events had taken place in the western world to modify, if not greatly to reduce, the influence of religion in human thought. Religion was still a matter of dominant interest, to be sure, to the masses of the people. But the intellectual triumphs and implications of Newtonian science, the secular emphasis of life on the frontier, the increasing multiplicity of religious sects, and a general preoccupation with matters other than religious—economic, political, and literary—were making rapidly for an increasing secularization of the outlook on life, on the one hand, and an ever increasing amount of religious toleration on the other.

Into the world of religion, in the early eighteenth century, came two influences. The discoveries of Sir Isaac Newton, Gottfried Wilhelm Leibniz, René Descartes and a host of other physicists and mathematicians had demonstrated that the universe was ruled by physical laws, and implied that much of the older belief in divine interference in human affairs in the form of miracles, signs and portents was erroneous. God was thought to be bound by the same laws that governed the universe, with which he, once having created it and set it in motion, did not interfere. The methods of science, likewise, gave rise to the beginnings of biblical criticism, the study of comparative religion, and new philosophies of "natural" religion, the most characteristic of which was Deism. This great intellectual ferment in religion in Europe had its counterpart in America, and found expression in the writings of Benjamin Franklin, Thomas Paine, and Thomas Jefferson.

But the "natural religion" of the scientists was for the intellectuals, not for the common people. In Europe and America the great masses of the people could neither understand the intellectual complexities of scientific criticism nor derive much emotional satisfaction from the cold and static dogmas of the older Protestant faiths or the apathy of a decadent Roman Catholicism. The result was that there appeared in Europe and America such emotional preachers as John and Charles Wesley, George Whitefield, and, above all, Jonathan Edwards, who preached a gospel of emotional individualism against the intellectual generalities of the scientists. Their preaching brought on that vast, emotional religious revival known in American history as the Great Awakening.

It was at Northampton, Massachusetts, that, in the year 1732, this religious phenomenon had its American beginning. Here Jonathan Edwards, preaching the wrath of an angry God against sinners, aroused his hearers to such a pitch of emotional fervor that, on occasion, "there was such a breathing of distress and weeping, that the preacher was obliged to speak to the people, and desire silence that he might be heard." Such an appeal to the emotions would never have had the approval of the rationalist leaders of the Puritan migration to Massachusetts Bay. Yet its appeal to the emotions was precisely the secret of the Great Awakening's success. For its emphasis was upon feeling, not thought; upon the individual and God's interest in him individually. These were things the common people could understand.

The religious revival spread all over New England, and then, early in the next decade, to the middle colonies and the south. George Whitefield, still a member of the Anglican Church, arrived in America in 1739 and toured the colonies preaching with great power to immense audiences. He, like the other evangelists, emphasized the necessity of regeneration from sin and God's interest in the individual sinner. Benjamin Franklin, that tough-minded skeptic, went to hear Whitefield in Philadelphia, largely, as he said, out of curiosity, and determined not to be moved by his preaching. But under the spell of the orator Franklin decided, first, to put into the collection all the copper he had in his pocket, then all the silver, and then all the coin he had. Other powerful preachers of individual regeneration were Theodore Frelinghuysen, a pastor of the Dutch Reformed Church, and William Tennent and his son Gilbert, Presbyterian revivalists who founded the "log college" for the training of preachers that eventually developed into the college at Princeton.

But the Great Awakening hardly touched the educated classes of the people, who were largely under the influence of the rationalistic influences associated with Deism. Even among those most affected by it the excitement soon wore off and a reaction set in. Jonathan Edwards himself was criticized for the excitement he had caused, and was eventually driven from his pulpit. The significance of the movement thus seems to have been largely negative; for it divided the older sects into "new lights" and "old lights," factions which corresponded roughly to the poor and wealthy classes of society. Some of the "new lights" formed new sects, others joined the more pietistic of the older groups, such as the Baptists. Its greatest significance, however, lay in its great emphasis upon the worth of the individual and a consequent "leveling" tendency that was closely akin to an impulse to social democracy. As an intercolonial movement, also, it was one of numerous influences that were drawing the sections of the colonies together into a cultural unity, a tendency that was underlined by the foundation of four new colleges, Princeton (1746), Brown (1764), Rutgers (1766), and Dartmouth (1770)—all of them for the purpose of training preachers.

One other significant result of the Great Awakening was the added impulse it gave to the long growth of religious toleration. Notice has already been taken of the beginnings of toleration in the colonies—the work of Roger Williams, the Maryland Toleration Act, and the provisions for religious toleration in the proprietary colonies of Carolina, Pennsylvania and New York. Starting as a "defense mechanism" for the protection of persecuted religious minorities, it became, toward the end of the first century, a selling-point for the attraction of prospective colonists. As the eighteenth century advanced, and as the number of religious sects continued to multiply, toleration became a matter largely of indifference. The chief interests in life were becoming more and more secular, and it mattered less and less what other men believed. Gradually freedom of individual worship came to be looked upon as a matter of right, and with Thomas Paine and many others religious freedom took its place along with other natural rights of man. For Paine, freedom to believe as one wished was like freedom to breathe: "Toleration," he says, "is not the opposite of intolerance, but is the counterfeit of it. Both are despotisms: the one assumes to itself the right of withholding liberty of conscience, the other of granting it." Toleration was becoming a positive principle.

Broadly speaking, America was overwhelmingly Protestant in religious belief. By the middle of the century, there were in the colonies three major groups of Protestant religions; and these religions were roughly identifiable with the three major social groupings among the people. In the plantation colonies of the south and the West Indies, and in New York, Anglicanism was the officially established form of worship. In no one of these colonies were Anglicans now in a majority, but Anglicanism was the religion followed by the majority of the aristocratic, landowning class. Anglicanism was conservative, rational and formal, with an elaborate ritual, and tended to emphasize the ritual more than individual experience. It was supported by the conservative, aristocratic and official classes; but, by the same sign, it found little response among the poorer groups in society.

Anglicanism was associated in the popular mind with the British Crown; and with the growth of the breach with the mother country the Anglican Church was to a considerable degree condemned as an agency of British tyranny. It was true, of course, that the hierarchical government of the Anglican Church centered the government of the American churches in the Bishop of London. The bishop exercised his authority in America through the agency of commissaries; but this proved unsatisfactory. It was difficult to enforce church discipline, questions requiring the decision of the bishop were delayed, sometimes for years, and the difficulty of going to London for ordination all proved the system to be unworkable. The result was a move to establish a resident bishop in America; but this move was opposed by many Americans as an unwarranted extension of British control, and nothing came of it until after the Revolution.

A second group, composed of the Congregationalists, Presbyterians, Lutherans and members of the Dutch Reformed Church, was strongest in New England and urban New York and Philadelphia. These were the religions of the merchants of the cities and the farmers of New England. By the middle of the century they were generally conservative in their outlook, but they were split by the opposing democratic, or liberal, and conservative tendencies represented by the "new lights" and the "old lights." As the merchants accumulated wealth, they tended to become conservative in politics and religion. To this group should also be added the Quakers of Pennsylvania who became progressively more conservative in their politics and more formal in their worship. Thus these middle-class groups were divided by the social and political divisions that were appearing among the people.

The third group of religions, which were essentially democratic and made their great appeal to the poorer and less sophisticated classes of the people, was made up of the Baptists of Rhode Island, New Jersey, and Pennsylvania, the German pietists of Pennsylvania and the frontier, and the original English Quakers. All these groups emphasized the worth of the individual man, piety, and social equality, and generally opposed hierarchical forms of church government, tax-supported churches, military service, and slavery. Because of the radicalism of their religious and social ideas these groups had been persecuted in the seventeenth century; in the eighteenth they were still feared by the conservative elements in society as dangerous to the *status quo* and as the advance guard of a "numerous democracy"—as indeed they were. With the growth of toleration, however, these sects found religious peace.

Thus religious beliefs and institutions, among the Americans of the eighteenth century, tended to follow the lines of economic interest and social class. In general, religion in America was characterized by the multiplicity of its forms, its relative decline in the face of an increasing secularization of life, and by a growing and an increasingly genuine tolerance.

THE SPREAD OF EDUCATION

The earliest schools in America, like so many of the other institutions in the seventeenth century, were strongly religious in character. Thus the town schools in New England, supported by public funds, were designed chiefly to teach prospective Puritans to read and understand the Bible. The early schools in the middle colonies, since there was no state-supported system of education, were supported and managed as sectarian enterprises, each sect having its own schools. In the south, such schools as existed were under the supervision of the Anglican rectors, or were taught in the families of the planters by private tutors. In New England education was looked upon as a matter of vital interest to the state itself; in the middle colonies it was a religious concern of the sects; in the south it was a matter of interest only to the individual parent. Yet in all cases education was closely allied to, and dominated by, religion.

As the eighteenth century wore on, and as life in general became more secular in its interests, education itself became more secular in its aims and outlook. Thus the New England academies, which replaced the earlier Latin schools in the eighteenth century and spread to all the colonies, while they still retained Greek and Latin as the core of the curriculum, added other subjects not so confined in their usefulness to prospective ministers. English composition, mathematics, foreign languages and natural science, all of them subjects of a secular nature and usefulness, became standard parts of the curriculum. Particularly striking as an example of this tendency was the Philadelphia Academy, which later became the University of Pennsylvania, established in 1754 under the inspiration and patronage of Benjamin Franklin. In 1749 Franklin had formulated a plan for an institution which would be non-sectarian and whose curriculum would emphasize the useful sub jects such as English, foreign languages, astronomy, geography, mathematics, history, politics, and logic. In its non-sectarian character and in the emphasis upon the useful studies in its curriculum the Philadelphia Academy typified at once the increasing secularization and the growing utilitarianism of American educational thought.

These same trends are to be observed elsewhere. Even Harvard, oldest of American universities, established chairs of natural science, literature, foreign languages, mathematics and other secular subjects in the course of the eighteenth century. Yale did likewise, although more slowly. King's College, established in New York in 1754, while somewhat Anglican in flavor, was committed to a curriculum which included such utilitarian subjects as foreign languages, mathematics, surveying, navigation, geography, history, husbandry, commerce and government, and natural history, which included the sciences of astronomy, geology, and biology. A medical college was founded in Philadelphia in 1765 under the leadership of the eminent Doctor Benjamin Rush, and King's College added a medical department in 1767. Brown University, founded in 1764, also showed the non-sectarian trend, for, although it was founded as a Baptist institution, it admitted both students and teachers from all Protestant sects, and gave a broad course of study which carefully avoided any sectarian bias.

In education, as in life, the Americans of the eighteenth century were rapidly shaking off their medieval preoccupation with the other worldly interests of theology and religion and taking on the more brightly hued and variegated cloak of secular, this-worldly humanism.

THE STUDY OF THE UNIVERSE

The most brilliant chapter of American intellectual life in the eighteenth century is, perhaps, that dealing with the progress of experimental science. For in this realm of knowledge are to be found the names of Franklin, famous for his studies of electricity, John Winthrop IV, of Harvard, most famous of American astronomers in the eighteenth century, David Rittenhouse, astronomer and mathematician, John Bartram, botanist of Philadelphia, John Mitchell and Lewis Evans, geographers, and Cadwallader Colden, John Morgan and Benjamin Rush in clinical medicine. These men were in step with the scientific progress of the Enlightenment in Europe, and all of them received recognition for their accomplishments among their European colleagues. Many, indeed, were fellows of the British Royal Society.

The studies of electricity by Franklin, with his kite and leyden jars, are known to every American schoolboy. John Winthrop IV, professor of mathematics and natural philosophy at Harvard from 1738 to 1779, is not so well known. Winthrop established a physics laboratory at Harvard, and introduced the study of calculus there in 1751. He also studied earthquakes and comets, and shocked the old-line Puritans by his demonstrations that these phenomena had natural causes—a demonstration that carried with it the implication that these phenomena were not at all the manifestations of the anger of God. David Rittenhouse of Philadelphia, self-taught mathematician and astronomer, made notable contributions to the study of the planets and the behavior of comets. John Bartram, also of Philadelphia, made a notable collection of plants at his home and traveled from one end of the colonies to the other collecting, identifying and classifying plant life. Known to Peter Kalm and Karl von Linné (Linnaeus), the great Swedish naturalist, Bartram corresponded and exchanged plants with botanists in Europe, thus contributing greatly to European knowledge of American flora. Lewis Evans of Philadelphia and Dr. John Mitchell of Virginia made maps of America that were widely used in both Europe and America as bases for further geographical study and exploration. Mitchell is also to be classed with Colden, Morgan, and Rush for his contributions to the study of medicine. These men, living in the age before the promulgation of the germ theory of disease, were still far from the scientific medicine of a later day. Yet by their emphasis upon clinical study, by their empirical approaches to scientific practice in sanitation and segregation, and by their constant theorizing about the causes of the diseases they observed, they made certain progress toward a more perfect medical science. Rush, the most brilliant of them all, is particularly notable for his contribution to the study of insanity; he was among the first men to treat insanity as a disease rather than as a crime.

THE AMERICAN TRADITION IN LITERATURE

In literature, as, indeed, in all the aspects of the budding American culture, two streams of development may be observed. One is the indigenous, or native element, springing from the experience of the Americans themselves in this, their now native land. The other is a borrowed element, copied from Europe, and particularly England, by a society just becoming conscious of the cultural refinements of the older civilization, and which, feeling itself out on the periphery of the cultural world, was seeking to improve itself by the importation of culture from abroad.

In literature, the most poignant experiences of the Americans are to be found in the writing of the frontier. Mary Rowlandson's tragic, gripping story of her captivity among the Indians during King Philip's War remained one of the most widely read books among the Americans throughout the eighteenth century, and there were many others like it. Cadwallader Colden's *History of the Five Nations of Indians* went through edition after edition. The most truly native literary form, however, was probably the Indian treaty itself, wherein the simply quaint, allegorical and sometimes beautiful language of the Indians passed through the minds of American or half-breed translators to form a literary fusion of the cultures of Indian and Anglo-Saxon.

The eighteenth century is also the first century of the American newspaper. Beginning with the *Boston News-Letter,* which began publication in 1704, the newspapers became, in the course of the century, increasingly important as organs of information and opinion. At the beginning the newspaper was made up of months-old news items from abroad, a few literary "fillers," and advertisements. Local news was generally ignored; everybody knew what was happening in the community anyway—why print it? James and Benjamin Franklin introduced a new idea into American journalism in 1719 in their *New England Courant* by patterning it after the sprightly *Spectator.* So new and so sprightly was the *Courant,* indeed, that it was frowned upon by the conservatives of Boston, and it eventually stopped publication after Benjamin Franklin departed from the chilly atmosphere of Boston to find a more congenial intellectual climate in Philadelphia. There, in 1729, he bought and developed the *Pennsylvania Gazette.* Elsewhere in the colonies newspapers were appearing, in the form of Bradford's *New York Gazette* and Zenger's *Weekly Journal,* the *Maryland Gazette,* the *Virginia Gazette,* and the *South Carolina Gazette and Country Gentlemen.* In the West Indies similar journalistic progress was exemplified in the *Jamaica Weekly Courant,* the *Barbados Gazette,* and others.

By the middle of the eighteenth century the newspapers were devoting an increasing amount of space to politics and even local news. It became customary for men of opinions to publish their ideas in the form of letters to the publishers, signed with the names of Roman or Greek patriots or by Latinized American names, such as Cato, Publius, Pericles, Massachusettensis, and so on. This was the era when the newspapers began to come into their own as organs of opinion. Naturally enough, they began to take sides and to represent one faction against another. In the course of the debates, such subjects as the relationship of the colonies to the mother country, the struggle of the assembly against the prerogative, the advantages of free trade for the colonies, and similar topics came in for discussion. The style of the discussions was academic and stiffly literary, to be sure; but it was such publications that gradually built up an informed public opinion. Such an organ was, indeed, doubly necessary now that population had spread over such large areas of the seaboard, and it was no longer possible to disseminate news and opinion by word of mouth.

The greatest agency in the success of the newspaper as an organ of information and opinion, and, indeed, one of the most important agencies in the promotion of the new sense of cultural unity was the post office. For aside from the cultural exchanges that took place in the form of letters, it was the post office which delivered the newspapers to their readers. Massachusetts had established a provincial postal service as early as 1677, and Pennsylvania had established its own in 1683. But the postal service was necessarily an intercolonial enterprise, and King William III made a beginning at an intercolonial post office in 1691, when he gave a monopoly of the post-carrying business in Massachusetts, Pennsylvania, and New York to Thomas Neale. Neale surrendered his monopoly in 1707, and Parliament created an American post office in 1710. In 1753 Benjamin Franklin became postmaster-general, and his administration was notable for his speeding up of the mails and the improvement of post roads. He was responsible for a reduction of the postal rates, and for the fixing of a standard postage rate for newspapers. The post riders now went to nearly every important town and village; and with them went news. By 1770 a man could travel over a fairly good road all the way from Portsmouth, in New Hampshire, to Charleston or even Savannah. Along this road moved ideas; the mere existence of this highway gave the colonies a tie binding them together as they had never been before.

Another form of literature that was peculiarly American, and one that was probably read by more Americans in the eighteenth century than any other, was the almanac. This homely literary creature arose to meet the need of common men for some sort of calendar. Published annually, the almanac contained astronomical data such as the dates and phases of the moon, a schedule of the tides, and a list of dates and days of the year, with weather forecasts for every day. It contained instructions when to sow and when to reap, how to care for livestock, homeopathic remedies for illness, and a host of other miscellaneous items of information useful to the farmer and the sailor. These little handbooks poured from the presses annually in every important provincial town and were in nearly every American home. As the eighteenth century wore on, the almanacs began to take on a distinctly literary and scientific flavor, with articles on slavery, on medicine, on temperance, or on history, with short stories and essays on a vast variety of subjects. *Poor Richard's Almanac,* published by Benjamin Franklin at Philadelphia, was only the best known of a host of these annual "poor men's magazines." Interspersed with wise or thrifty sayings, advice to the lovelorn, and a rough, racy humor, *Poor Richard* was both utilitarian and entertaining. By and large, the almanac furnishes what is probably the best index to the tastes and the thoughts—the "mind"—of the eighteenth-century American.

In the more formal literary efforts of the Americans there appears a different strain. The literary products thus far mentioned, the narrative of Indian captivities, the Indian treaty, the newspaper, the almanac, the literary product sprang directly from the experience of the people, and furnish the best possible record of their own reactions to that experience. But one intellectual aspect of life in America was the growing feeling of cultural inferiority and a consequent urge to imitate the refinements of the mother country. The southern and West Indian plantations had long looked to England for cultural leadership, sending their children to England for education and buying books directly from London. But as the colonists became more and more wealthy and more and more conscious of the refinements of life, they felt increasingly that they were far out on the periphery of civilization, and as poets and writers appeared among them, these looked to English writers as their models. Thus Benjamin Franklin, who was doubtless the greatest writer of prose the colonial period produced, consciously fashioned his style after that of the *Spectator.* Similarly, the poets patterned their writings after those of Englishmen, and after none so much as Dryden, Pope, and, later, Goldsmith.

Thus the Reverend Mather Byles deliberately imitated Pope's couplets for his own poems, but brought to them a native wit of his own. A friend and contemporary of Byles, a literary-minded distiller, was Joseph Green. Green, too, was of a humorous turn, and his poems are noteworthy if only as symptomatic of the trend away from the somber Puritan outlook on life of an earlier day. Later in the century William Livingston of New York wrote, in imitation of Pomfret, his *Philosophic Solitude, or the Choice of a Rural Life.* Goldsmith's works had hardly reached this country before he had a host of imitators, as did James Thomson. It was not until near the end of the century that American poetry, even while imitating English models, begins to have a flavor that is genuinely American. The best of the imitators was Timothy Dwight, tutor at Yale and later its president, whose *Greenfield Hill* written in the era of the Revolution and filled with patriotism, is probably his best. John Trumbull, associated with Dwight as one of the "Hartford Wits," achieved distinction by a long, patriotic satire called *McFingal.*

The best poet to appear in America in the eighteenth century was Philip Freneau, born in New York in 1752. He began his writing on the very eve of the American Revolution, and, while still showing much of the imitativeness of earlier American writers, demonstrated, on the one side, a genuine feeling for nature and a fine romantic imagination, and, on the other, a biting satire that found good use during the Revolution. His best poems are his lyrics, and he rises to his greatest expression in *The House of Night, Pictures of Columbus,* and *The Indian Burying Ground.* Freneau wrote of the American scene and of American subjects—nature, the Indian, the sea, the West Indies. His poetry, for the first time, genuinely and beautifully expressed the living experience and the true feeling of America. In him, at last, at the very end of the colonial period, the American colonies had produced a poet.

THE AMERICAN TRADITION IN ART

In the realms of painting and architecture the same two streams of the American "mind" may be observed as have just been noted in literature. The native strain in painting began with the New England primitives of the seventeenth century and the Dutch painters of New York. Thus the earliest American paintings, while they apparently show the influence of both Elizabethan England and Rembrandt's Low Countries, yet have a simplicity and a crude directness that their old-world forbears do not show. This difference was probably due in part to the very ineptitude of the American amateur, in part to a different idea as to what he wished to do.

In any case, the paintings of the seventeenth century are without exception portraits; and the portraits of children are portraits of little adults, which is the way in which the Puritans thought of them! The early American paintings are extremely "factual"—factual as only amateurs could paint them; at the same time, they have been called "ideographs" because they present the facts as the author thought they ought to be.

It was this set of characteristics that marked the earliest native American paintings. During the eighteenth century these characteristics continued, but with a more refined sense of composition and a perfected technique, to produce such artists as Robert Feake and John Singleton Copley. In the work of these artists the earlier combination of factualness and ideography flowers in their superb character studies, which are done with a freshness, a directness, and an absence of the stylized painting of contemporary England which set them off as American, representing a native American art.

In art, however, as in literature, the Americans who could afford to indulge their interest, conscious of their own provincialism, thought more of imported paintings and painters than they did of their own. Thus John Smibert, a Scotchman trained in England and Italy, came to America with Bishop Berkeley in 1729 as a professor of art in Berkeley's proposed college in Bermuda; when the college did not materialize he stayed on in New England, where he was hailed as the greatest artist in America. Smibert brought with him the English tradition, and from his time on the English style parallels the style of the native Americans. As American artists fell under the influence of the British school, some of them, like Benjamin West and Gilbert Stuart, went to England to work and study. But their work was English, not American, giving expression to an English, not an American mode of life and thought.

Similarly, in architecture, the earliest styles in colonial America stem from Elizabethan or Jacobean England and seventeenth-century Holland and Germany. After a century of adaptation to the environment and the social conditions of America these styles had become something that might well be called American. With the growing cultural consciousness of the eighteenth century, however, wealthy Americans began to build their houses on plans showing the influence of Sir Christopher Wren and the later transition toward the classical called the Georgian style of architecture. This imported style, often—and rather incorrectly—called "colonial," flourished in the middle and second half of the eighteenth century, and culminated in the great classical revival at the end of the century. The Georgian style of architecture differed somewhat in the different sections of the colonies—more severe in the north, more genial in the south—but it practically eliminated other fashions for those who could afford it, and the older styles in architecture persisted only in older houses and churches.

In both painting and architecture, two parallel streams are thus to be observed, one springing directly out of the experience of the people in a new land, the other resulting from an awakened interest in cultural things which led them to import styles and artists other than their own. It is only relatively recently in their history that Americans have overcome their self-conscious provincialism and have gone back to that which grew up with them, as it were, out of the American soil.

AMERICAN PHILOSOPHY AND PHILOSOPHERS

At the apex of the intellectual pyramid of civilization stands philosophy, mother of the sciences. Formal philosophy has always been a province reserved to the intellectual elite, for only relatively few men have had both the education and the intellectual ability to pursue its study successfully. In the British colonies in America every prospective minister studied philosophy in college, and, as leaders of their religious flocks, brought a modicum of its intellectual discipline to the people of the towns and villages where they preached. In a sense, every college-bred man was a philosopher, and the leadership of the people was distinctly in the hands of such men. It is not surprising, therefore, that philosophic thinking played a very important role in the intellectual life of the Americans of the eighteenth century, or that America should have produced such important philosophic minds as those of Jonathan Edwards, Samuel Johnson, John Witherspoon, Cadwallader Colden, Benjamin Rush, Benjamin Franklin and Thomas Jefferson.

Flowing into the American mind were the streams of thought of Europe: the sensationalism of Locke, the idealism of Berkeley, the Scottish realism of Reid, and the materialism of the French school, particularly La Mettrie. As in literature and art, however, there was also an indigenous tendency in American thought which grew out of the frontier experience of the colonists, a sort of utilitarianism which was eventually to take the form in American pragmatism. American philosophy of the eighteenth century, therefore, represented many different schools of thought about the universe and man's relationship to it. Everyone, however, was influenced more or less by the peculiar intellectual and social environment presented by the American scene.

Jonathan Edwards and Samuel Johnson were idealists. Edwards, "the ablest metaphysician of the period between Leibniz and Kant," apparently arrived at his idealism independently, perhaps after studying Locke; Johnson, the first president of King's College, was a disciple of Bishop Berkeley. As the intellectual descendants of Puritanism these idealists, basing their beliefs upon Locke's demonstration that all knowledge is derived through the senses, concluded that all knowledge is subjective, or internal within the thinker. Thus, ideas are the only reality, and these ideas come from the mind of God, which is the perfect source of all ideas and all knowledge. Accordingly God, as the source of ideas, is immanent in human beings, and they approach him to the degree in which they partake of his knowledge. Both Edwards and Johnson were important figures in the intellectual life of their century, and their philosophy was one of the sources of the later American transcendentalism.

A second stream of thought flowing into America from Europe was that of the materialists. Curiously enough, the materialists, starting, as did the idealists, with the sensationalism of Locke, believed, in direct contrast to the idealists, that the knowledge of the material world derived by the senses is true; that the material world presented to the mind by the senses, in other words, not only is real, but is the only reality. Cadwallader Colden and Benjamin Rush, both physicians, were of this school of thought, and it found a number of important exponents in the south. This philosophy, based as it is upon direct observation of the phenomena of nature, was peculiarly congenial to the American mind, and there is some reason to believe that its influence upon the subsequent development of American philosophy might have been much greater had it not been crowded out, as it were, by the success of the system of thought called Scottish realism, which radiated, always through ministers and schoolmasters, from Princeton University in the second half of the eighteenth century.

As a reaction against the extreme immaterialism of the English idealists, Thomas Reid, a Scottish thinker, had fallen back upon "common sense." According to his way of thinking, natural phenomena, as presented by the senses, are real. But the human mind knows three different kinds of reality: first, matter; second, the thinking human self—a reality just as definite as matter, but perceived by the mind without the aid of the senses; and third, the reality of good and evil, perceived by the human conscience. This philosophy, brought to America by John Witherspoon, president of Princeton, was probably the most influential in America in the late eighteenth century. It has been called, indeed, "the American philosophy," and its popularity may perhaps be attributed to its appeal to a people who, by and large, were accustomed to a constant, everyday contact with "reality" in the work they did with their hands, while also feeling the ever-present influence of conscience prompted by their high-powered religions.

A fourth stream of thought flowing into America from Europe was Deism, which had its beginning in a rationalistic reaction against the miraculous, or irrational nature of accepted Christianity. It was a conscious effort to bring religion into a more reasonable harmony with the reign of law in the natural world. Thus it was rather more of a religion than a philosophy, explaining the universe in terms of a God who was its maker and lawgiver, and a universe itself which operated invariably according to the natural laws God had laid down for it. Its greatest appeal was to men imbued with the scientific spirit of the eighteenth century, such as Benjamin Franklin and Thomas Jefferson. With these men religious practice reduced itself pretty much to a system of ethics; but this, too, had a strong appeal in a society which was becoming progressively more secular in its interests and in its outlook on life.

Franklin, indeed, exemplifies a sort of outlook on life which was perhaps more typical of American thinking than any of the others. Without being formally philosophical, this was an attitude toward life which emphasized the practical, the utilitarian. Americans in general tended not to be as deeply interested in philosophy as in solving the practical problems of life by thought, adaptability, and inventiveness. This strain of thinking, which was hardly more than attitude, may probably be attributed to the century and a half of frontier experience—a century and a half of experience in which survival itself often depended upon adaptability and ingenuity. The history of the Americans during the first two centuries, indeed, is a record of adaptability writ large; it is no wonder that, in the American mind, one of the tests of virtue, in ideas and institutions as well as in tools, should be, even in the eighteenth century, "does it work?"

In philosophy, then, as in the other departments of the young American culture, the Americans borrowed much from Europe. But what they borrowed they molded to their American needs. At the same time, in their own experience in the building of a civilization where none had been before, they had made the beginning upon a way of thought and an outlook on life that was peculiarly their own.

TOWARD THE FORMATION OF A NATION

Out of the diverse elements of life in the colonies on the North American continent there were being formed, about the middle of the eighteenth century, many ties that were drawing the colonies together. Economic ties had long existed between the northern colonies and the south, as, indeed, they also existed between these same colonies and the West Indies. But as the continental colonies expanded to the point where they became contiguous and roads were built connecting one colony with another, there took place an assimilation between them that was forever impossible to the West Indies because of their insularity. The great north-and-south highway along the continental seaboard has already been mentioned; over this highway, in certain sections, regular stage-coach service was provided for the small but increasing number of intercolonial travelers, and inns sprang up at convenient points for their overnight accommodation, where they exchanged ideas which inevitably drew them out of their provincialisms. Along the roads, too, went the post-riders, carrying intercolonial mail, and perhaps most important of all, newspapers. More and more travelers, European and American, were touring the colonies and publishing their observations for readers both here and in their homes. By these exchanges of news, essays, and personal relationships, the people in every colony discovered that they had much in common with their neighbors in all the others.

They found, for example, that nearly all of them were engaged in the same or similar contests between the popular factions among them and those representing an authority three thousand miles away in England. All, or nearly all, had the same grievances against the British laws of navigation and trade. On the other hand, they were now conscious, perhaps more than ever before, of their common enmity for the French—an enmity that was heightened by the fact that New France stood across the path of westward expansion. Many men realized the need for common policies in the face of the French and Indian threat to the colonial frontiers. The Albany Congress, with its plan for colonial union, failed; but it was a clear evidence, nevertheless, of a growing feeling of unity among the leaders of American business and politics.

Other, more subtle influences were also at work. A number of writers were at work upon histories of the colonies or of groups within the colonies which overlapped colonial boundaries. Such, for example, was William Douglass' *Summary, Historical and Political, of the British Settlements in North America,* published in Boston, 1748-53, which had a wide sale throughout the colonies. The widespread popularity of this book is evidence of the desire of the colonists to know more about themselves as a whole—evidence, that is, of an awakened self-consciousness among them as a budding nation. Education, too, was becoming increasingly intercolonial in its influence. The Presbyterians of the southern frontier sent their sons to Princeton in New Jersey to be educated, instead of England; the Baptists sent their sons to Brown, in Providence. The influence of all the colleges, indeed, was becoming increasing intercolonial. Not only did their graduates traverse colonial boundaries; there were many more of them, and they were going in increasing numbers into law and politics rather than the ministry. Even language itself— "American English"—was becoming self-conscious, Americans were noticing their linguistic difference from their English cousins, and newspapers engaged in discussions of the origins of the term "Yankee." Nor was this nationalistic urge unobserved by the Americans themselves. For there was appearing and finding expression with increasing assurance and eloquence that consciousness of growth and future grandeur that later came to be called the idea of "manifest destiny." Nathaniel Ames, in his almanac of 1758, could write:

> The Curious have observ'd, that the Progress of Humane Literature (like the Sun) is from the East to the West; thus has it travell'd thro' Asia and Europe, and now is arrived at the Eastern Shore 'of America. . . . Arts and Sciences will change the Face of Nature in their Tour from Hence over the Appalachian Mountains to the Western Ocean; . . . O! Ye unborn Inhabitants of America, when your Eyes behold the Sun after he has rolled the Seasons round for two or three centuries more, you will know that in Anno Domini 1758, we dream'd of your Times.

Many were the college commencement orators and colonial leaders who were beginning to glory in the future greatness of America. Christopher Gadsden, in the Stamp Act Congress of 1765, was to give this sentiment classic expression when he cried, "There ought to be no New England man, no New Yorker, known on the Continent; but all of us Americans"—and, ten years later, at the very end of the era of colonial dependence, Patrick Henry could say, "I am not a Virginian, but an American."

RECOMMENDED BOOKS FOR FURTHER READING

Contemporary Narratives

Andrew Burnaby, *Travels through the Middle Settlements in North America . . . 1759 and 1760.*

William Byrd, *History of the Dividing Line betwixt Virginia and South Carolina,* edited by William K. Boyd.

Bliss Carman, ed., *The Oxford Book of American Verse.*

Charles Chauncy, *The Benevolence of the Deity.*

Cadwallader Colden, *History of the Five Indian Nations of Canada.*

Michel G. St. J. de Crèvecœur, *Letters of an American Farmer.*

Ellwood P. Cubberley, ed., *Readings in Public Education in the United States,* Chapters 1-3.

Jonathan Edwards, *Selected Sermons . . .* edited by Harry N. Gardiner.

Benjamin Franklin, *Autobiography.*

Benjamin Franklin, *The General Magazine.*

Benjamin Franklin, *Poor Richard's Almanac.*

Thomas Jefferson, *Notes on the State of Virginia.*

Samuel Johnson, *Samuel Johnson, President of King's College, His Career and Writings,* edited by Herbert W. and Carol C. S. Schneider.

Carl C. Van Doren, ed., *Benjamin Franklin and Jonathan Edwards, Selections from Their Writings.*

Harry R. Warfel [and others], eds., *The American Mind,* Volume I.

Modern Accounts

James T. Adams, *Provincial Society, 1690-1763.*

Charles M. Andrews, *The Colonial Background of the American Revolution.*

Charles M. Andrews, *Colonial Folkways.*

Carl Bridenbaugh, *Cities in the Wilderness.*

Arthur W. Calhoun, *A Social History of the American Family from Colonial Times to the Present.*

The Cambridge History of American Literature, Volume I.

Wilbur L. Cash, *The Mind of the South.*

Verner W. Crane, *Benjamin Franklin, Englishman and American.*

Arthur L. Cross, *The Anglican Episcopate and the American Colonies.*

William E. Dodd, "The Emergence of the First Social Order in the United States" in *American Historical Review,* XL, 217-231.

Foster R. Dulles, *America Learns to Play.*

Alice M. Earle, *Child Life in Colonial Days.*

Alice M. Earle, *Colonial Dames and Goodwives.*

Alice M. Earle, *Stage-Coach and Tavern Days.*

Ernest Earvest, *John and William Bartram.*

Harold D. Eberlein, *The Architecture of Colonial America.*

Wesley M. Gewehr, *The Great Awakening in Virginia, 1740-1790.*

Nathan G. Goodman, *Benjamin Rush, Physician and Citizen, 1746-1813.*

Oskar F. L. Hagen, *The Birth of the American Tradition in Art.*

Richard T. H. Halsey and Elizabeth Tower, *The Homes of Our Ancestors*.

Samuel Isham, *The History of American Painting*.

Marcus W. Jernegan, *Laboring and Dependent Classes in Colonial America, 1607-1783*.

Sidney F. Kimball, *Domestic Architecture of the American Colonies and of the Early Republic*.

Michael Kraus, *Intercolonial Aspects of American Culture on the Eve of the Revolution*.

John A. Kreut, *Annals of American Sport*.

Arthur C. McGiffert, *Jonathan Edwards*.

Frank J. Mather [and others], *The American Spirit in Art*.

Charles H. Maxson, *The Great Awakening in the Middle Colonies*.

Henry L. Mencken, *The American Language*.

Mary H. Mitchell, *The Great Awakening and Other Revivals in the Religious Life of Connecticut*.

Herbert M. Morais, *Deism in Eighteenth Century America*.

Samuel E. Morison, *Three Centuries of Harvard, 1636-1936*.

George C. D. Odell, *Annals of the New York Stage*, Volume I, Book I.

Vernon L. Parrington, *The Colonial Mind, 1620-1800*.

George H. Payne, *The History of Journalism in the United States*.

Isaac W. Riley, *American Philosophy, the Early Schools*.

Edwin E. Slosson, *The American Spirit in Education*.

Preserved Smith, *A History of Modern Culture*, Volume II.

Luke Tyerman, *The Life of the Rev. George Whitefield*.

Moses C. Tyler, *A History of American Literature*.

Carl C. Van Doren, *Benjamin Franklin*.

Luther A. Weigle, *American Idealism*.

Thomas J. Wertenbaker, *The Founding of American Civilization; The Middle Colonies*.

Stanley T. Williams, *The American Spirit in Letters*.

Ola E. Winslow, *Jonathan Edwards, 1703-1758*.

Lawrence C. Wroth, *An American Bookshelf, 1755*.

PART VI

The Break-up of an Empire and the Birth of a Nation

T HE AMERICAN empire of which Great Britain found itself possessed in the year 1763 included all the eastern half of the continent of North America and a large number of the islands in the Caribbean area. It included a conglomeration of communities and peoples of great diversity—the fur-trading stations of Hudson Bay; the fishing stations of Newfoundland; the military colony of Nova Scotia; the feudal, French community of Quebec; thirteen autonomous communities of the continental seaboard; the Indian-inhabited eastern half of the Mississippi Valley; Spanish Florida; and a group of islands in the West Indies that included the old English islands, some new French islands, and most of those islands that had formerly been called "neutral." This congeries of geographic and ethnographic oddities was anything but a unity— much less so, indeed, than had been the English empire of the era before the Seven Years' War. But it demanded a co-ordinated administration and defense, and British imperial statesmen hoped it might assist the mother country out of the slough of financial despond into which she had fallen as a result of the great imperial war. The years following the Peace of Paris, therefore, were marked chiefly by the effort of the British imperial administration to rationalize its policy in the light of the new acquisitions and in the direction of a more efficient commercial and fiscal control. All the colonies acquiesced in the reorganization and "tightening" of the imperial administration except the two sections, north and south, composed of the thirteen autonomous communities along the Atlantic seaboard of the continent. These thirteen colonies, however, having achieved a high degree of maturity in their economic, social, and political life, and finding their future development and expansion to depend upon a freedom, in all these aspects of their life, that was not envisaged by the new imperial policies, suddenly found themselves standing squarely in opposition to the will and purpose of the mother country. The empire was split wide open, by forces of which Americans and Britons alike were only barely conscious, if at all. The political and economic thinking of the men involved being what it was in that era, it was impossible to close the rift in the empire, and the section of it made up by the thirteen continental colonies seceded and became a separate, sovereign nation. It was this segment of the old British empire that formed the nucleus of the new United States of America. It is the story of the rift in the empire and the struggle of these thirteen still disparate provinces to join themselves together in an organic nation that is the theme of this, the concluding section of this volume.

41

The Reorganization of the British Empire in America, 1763-70

THE PROBLEM OF THE ENLARGED EMPIRE

THE Peace of Paris of 1763 left the British colonial empire enormously enlarged and diversified. The domain of the British East India Company in the Far East may be left out of consideration as the private preserve of a company of English merchants trading with peoples possessed of a high degree of native civilization, and the British territories in Africa may be passed over as mere areas of exploitation of primitive peoples. But the British empire in America was a conglomerate affair composed of the cosmopolitan English islands and settlements, French Canada, Spanish Florida, certain French islands in the West Indies, and the great interior valley, peopled chiefly by the semi-savage Indians. It was this expanded and enlarged set of possessions that gave most concern to the administrators of the empire; for it was imperative that this odd assortment of colonies be brought under the central colonial administration; and that it be exploited, in accord with the ruling principles of mercantilism, to the greatest possible profit of Englishmen.

The problem of reorganization was fourfold. To begin with, the expense of the war had been enormous, and the national debt of England had risen to the unheard of figure of £140,000,000. The charges on this debt had to be met by taxation, the burden of which, for a population of perhaps 8,000,000, had now reached staggering proportions. The war had been fought in large measure for the defense of the colonies, yet they had contributed relatively little to their own defense. It was not now expected that they could raise money to pay England a part of the vast sums already expended; but in view of the apparent advisability of maintaining a defensive military force in the colonies, it was thought only reasonable that they should pay at least a part of the cost of its maintenance for the future.

Thus, the most pressing question with regard to the empire was the question of defense, and the solution of the problem depended upon the raising, in the colonies, of a part of the necessary money. But the establishment of a standing army in America was not entirely for the purpose of defense. For colonial administrators had long been complaining about the independent tendencies of the Americans, and many acute observers had predicted the day when they might attempt to throw off the yoke of the mother country. There were, indeed, evidences of a hardening colonial spirit manifested during the Seven Years' War. Many colonists looked upon the proposal to establish a standing army as a plan to keep the colonies in a state of due submission; it is probable that they were not entirely without reason for this suspicion.

A third problem confronting the imperial administrators was presented by the necessity of establishing governments in the newly acquired territories. All of the colonies ceded to England by France were French in language and culture, devotees of the Roman Catholic religion, and, far from being capable of governing themselves, knew only the French law and the absolute, paternalistic French form of government. The colony of Florida was Spanish in culture and religion, and the Mississippi and the Great Lake basins were inhabited by Indians, many of the tribes of which had been bitter enemies of the British for over a century. What was to be done with these new, non-English-speaking communities? Evidently it would be difficult, if not impossible, to impose the British form of government upon them; yet it was extremely inadvisable, even impossible, to administer them under their original governmental forms.

But the most vital problem of all, in the minds of the British ministry, was to restore the prosperity of English merchants, lost through seven years of war and a collapse of the overexpanded war market. The system of colonial commerce and navigation regulated by the great act of navigation and the various acts of trade had failed of effectiveness, and British agents in the colonies still complained that they were effectively nullified by the smuggling of colonial merchants and the connivance of colonial officers and juries.

THE PROCLAMATION OF 1763

When the government of George Grenville came into office, therefore, after the ratification of the Treaty of Paris, some of its first actions were directed to a consideration of the problems of the empire. And, since the prosperity of England was thought in large measure to depend upon imperial trade, the reorganization of the empire was inseparably coupled with the tightening of the entire navigation system, calculated as it was to assure the profits of empire to the English merchants. Thus the series of laws and proclamations enacted by the Grenville government between 1763 and 1765 had the double objective of reorganizing the empire and of restoring trade.

In May, 1763, the British ministry directed a series of questions to the Board of Trade, asking (1) what sort of governments should be set up in the new colonies; (2) how much of an army would be necessary for the safety of the colonies, old and new; (3) how could the colonies be brought to pay a reasonable part of the expense of maintaining the new forces; and finally (4):

By what regulations, the most extensive commercial advantages may be derived from those cessions, and how those advantages may be rendered most permanent and secure to His Majesty's trading subjects.

Here was the case of British colonial policy: the new additions to the empire, as the older parts of it, were to be made to pay a profit.

The Board of Trade made its report during the summer. The result of the recommendations of the Board was the Proclamation of October 7, 1763, which enunciated a permanent policy for the new French and Spanish additions, and a temporary policy with regard to the Indian lands of the interior of North America. Under the proclamation, the "extensive and valuable acquisition in America, secured to our crown by the late definitive treaty of peace" were divided into two major parts. The "civilized" colonies taken over by Great Britain were organized into separate governments after the English pattern. Canada (bounded on the south by the line of 45° north latitude), East Florida (the boundary of Georgia was moved south, from the Altamaha to the St. Mary's), West Florida (south of the line of 31° and west of the Appalachicola River), and the group of islands of which Grenada was the most important, were to have governments patterned after the older "royal" provinces, with representative assemblies and royally appointed governors and councils. The provision of a British representative government and the guarantee of religious liberty were included with a view to attracting new colonists. It was soon found, however, that the French- and Spanish-speaking inhabitants of the new colonies were not prepared to exercise their "rights of Englishmen," nor to understand the intricacies of English justice. It became necessary, therefore, to make other provisions for them.

That part of the new acquisitions lying west of the Allegheny

Mountains and inhabited chiefly by Indians was restored, until further notice, to the Indians themselves. This last territory was a rich fur-bearing country, and the fur-merchants of England and the colonies were opposed to opening it to settlement. But the most pressing reason for this arrangement was the desire to appease the Indians by the preservation to them of their hunting grounds. The promulgation of the proclamation was hastened, indeed, by the outbreak, late in the spring of 1763, of the most disastrous Indian war experienced by the British colonies. As this war and its significance are part of the larger history of the west, however, its relationships to the Proclamation of 1763 will more properly be discussed in another place.

THE REVENUE ACT OF 1764 (THE "SUGAR ACT")

Grenville and his advisers had already made up their minds, in May, 1763, to maintain an army in the colonies, and to raise a part of the expense by colonial revenues. Thus the American Revenue Act of March, 1764 (often called the Sugar Act), stated that "it is just and necessary, that a revenue be raised, in your Majesty's . . . dominions in America, for defraying the expences of defending, protecting, and securing the same." At the same time, a second major objective of the act was to discourage smuggling "to and from the said colonies and plantations, and improving and securing the trade between the same and Great Britain."

Thus the first purpose of this famous act was to raise a revenue, and for this purpose certain duties were laid on foreign goods imported into the colonies by way of England itself. Portuguese and Spanish wines were to pay ten shillings a ton; silks and other oriental fabrics were to pay two shillings per pound of weight, and European fabrics were to pay three shillings per piece. High duties were laid upon foreign goods imported into the colonies directly without stopping in England; thus foreign-made white sugar was to pay twenty-seven shillings per hundredweight; foreign indigo was to pay sixpence per pound; foreign coffee was to pay £2-19-9 per hundredweight; Madeira wine was to pay seven pounds per tun. Coffee imported into the colonies by way of England, on the other hand, was to pay only seven shillings per hundredweight. It was hoped thus to discourage the direct trade, benefit the coffee merchants of London, and at the same time raise a revenue.

Of particular concern to the framers of the act was the prevalence of smuggling in the colonies, and they were determined to stop it. Smuggling had been a common practice in America for many years, especially since the Molasses Act of 1733. It had recently been on the increase, and, during the war just ended, it had continued to such a degree as to have the character of trading with the enemy. The British government had taken active steps to suppress this unpatriotic trade, by the use of warships and by the issuance of general search-warrants known as "writs of assistance." James Otis, a brilliant young lawyer of Boston, was retained by the "smuggling interest" to attack the legality of these writs, but without success. Despite this setback, however, the business of smuggling went on.

This smuggling was of two kinds. One form consisted of the importation of European manufactured goods and non-European products, directly, in competition with British manufacturers and merchants, and in direct violation of the "Staple Act" of 1663. The other chief form of smuggling was the importation of molasses and sugar from the foreign West Indies colonies without paying the duties required by the act of 1733. The economic livelihood of the northern colonies actually depended in large measure upon this foreign trade, for the supply of sugar and molasses provided by the British sugar islands was inadequate for the continental demand. Such was the extent of this sugar-smuggling, that probably seven-tenths of the sugar consumed in the continental colonies came from the foreign islands without paying any duty.

Evidently, could the established legal duties on colonial imports be collected, they would provide a handsome income for the Crown. But when news reached the colonies that the Molasses Act of 1733 was to be renewed and revised, there was an outburst of protest from the colonial merchants, especially those of New England. As early as the fall of 1763, the merchants of Boston, New York, Providence, Philadelphia, and other ports formed organizations to bring pressure to bear upon Parliament and the British government not to renew the hated legislation. The merchants of Rhode Island, for example, pointed out that of the 184 ships that had cleared from Newport in 1763, 150 went to the West Indies and returned with 14,000 hogsheads of molasses, of which only about 2,500 hogsheads came from the British islands. They showed, in fact, that the British sugar colonies could not furnish more than two-thirds of the molasses used by Rhode Island alone. The molasses was made into rum, most of which was shipped to Africa and traded for Negroes, ivory, or gold dust. The Negroes were taken to the West Indies to be sold, and bills of exchange on London, with which to buy British manufactured goods, were taken in payment. The collection of a duty upon foreign molasses, said the merchants, would utterly ruin their business.

The protests were made in vain. The West Indies planters desired a prohibitive duty of foreign molasses as encouragement to British sugar. But the Grenville ministry was interested chiefly in revenue, and instead of maintaining the high former duty of 6d per gallon, the Sugar Act (the Revenue Act) reduced the duty to 3d per gallon. After the Sugar Act was passed, the merchants and the legislatures of the northern colonies protested through their agents in London, and invited the southern colonies to join them in protests, not only against the Sugar Act, but against the Stamp Act, the next proposed item in the Grenville program, as well. Their efforts were successful, and the southern colonies cooperated by sending in vigorous protests to London.

The Sugar Act, while it did not go as far in the direction of protecting the West Indies planters and sugar merchants as they might have wished, did discriminate against the northern colonies in their favor. It was only natural that the rift between the Caribbean colonies and the continental colonies should have been widened as a result. But by the same token, the cooperation of the continental colonies with each other in their common protest to the mother country drew them together as never before, and prepared the way for more active and effective cooperation against the Stamp Act of the following year.

But by far the most significant and far-reaching provisions of the Revenue Act of 1764, were those looking to the enforcement of the laws, old and new, for the regulation of colonial commerce and navigation. No one questioned the right of the Crown to regulate imperial commerce, and to collect duties on it; but for years the existing laws had not been vigorously enforced. This laxity was due in some cases to the inefficiency of the laws themselves, in others to the inactivity of the customs officials, and in other cases to outright corruption, even among the most responsible officers, not even excepting colonial governors. In any case, the money collected by the customs officers in America did not pay the expenses of their own establishment. In a year when they collected £2,000, the costs of the service were £7,000.

The Grenville government was determined that this anomalous situation must end. It was for this reason that the Sugar Act contained certain provisions for its enforcement that affected the application of the entire navigation system. High bonds were required of ship captains that enumerated articles would be landed in a British colony or in England, and that dutiable foreign molasses would be brought in properly and the duties paid; ships taken within six miles of shore which could not show certificates of such deposits were to be arrested and confiscated; and the list of enumerated articles was extended to include practically all the major products of the American colonies.

This act of 1764 placed American commerce in a straitjacket. It increased the list of enumerated articles, it discriminated against the free colonial molasses trade with the foreign West Indies, it strengthened the hold of British manufacturers upon the colonial market, and it heavily penalized the direct trade in wines and European products formerly brought to the colonies directly. Not only did it seek deliberately to promote the welfare of British merchants and manufacturers at the expense of the Americans, but it actually reached over into the colonies to hamper trades that affected British interests only indirectly, if at all. It sought to raise for the Crown a revenue for the protection and the subjection of the colonies; it discriminated against the continental colonies in favor of the British West Indies; and it tried to force colonial commerce under the control of the merchants of England by tightening up the acts of trade and navigation; and all at the expense of the continental colonies. It is no wonder they were alarmed for the future of American commerce and expansion!

THE CURRENCY ACT OF 1764

The willingness of the southern continental colonies to cooperate with the northern colonies in their protest against the Sugar Act was increased by the passage of another measure of Parliament in the summer of 1764. This was the so-called Currency Act of that year, which applied the principle of the Currency Act of 1751 to all the colonies. The fact that the balance of trade of the colonies with the mother country was an unfavorable balance, coupled with the chronic indebtedness of the southern planters to their English factors, had made specie scarce in all the colonies, and encouraged them to seek relief in the issuance of paper money. During the Seven Years' War this practice had been increased by the needs of the war. In Virginia, for example, paper money had been made legal tender at the rate of five to four for sterling, so that £125 in Virginia currency would pay a sterling debt of £100. But the Virginia currency was rapidly decreasing in value, and the British merchants complained to their government that debtors in Virginia were now in a position to pay off their debts at much less than their real value. It was then that the government came to their rescue and extended the provisions of the Currency Act of 1751 to all the colonies, forbidding them to make their paper money legal tender and subjecting any colonial governor who might sign a legal tender law to a fine of £1,000. The act further required that all such legal tender paper issued during the war just ended be retired on the date specified by the law that had created it.

The problem of how the Americans might pay their indebtedness to England thus became one of major importance. The northern merchants were forced to reduce their orders for British goods. Some of them, indeed, entered into agreements to import smaller quantities of British goods. Less "mourning cloth" was to be worn at funerals; the tradesmen of Boston agreed to wear Massachusetts leather for their aprons; and—crowning blow of all—the students of Yale College unanimously voted to abstain from the drinking of imported liquors! A natural concomitant of this incipient boycott of British imports was the encouragement it gave to home manufactures. For manufactured goods such as woolen cloth must be had; if the colonial merchants were to overcome their economic indebtedness to England, they must manufacture the goods at home —a sort of mercantilism for America! Thus the "Society for the Promotion of the Arts, Agriculture and Economy" formed in New York in December, 1764, was only one of numerous such societies formed in the course of the widespread attempt of American economic life to find some way of escape from the British-built economic walls that hemmed it in.

THE STAMP ACT OF 1765

It had been estimated that the cost of the new British establishment in America, civil and military, would be about £350,000 annually. And it was thought only fitting and proper that the colonies should pay at least £100,000 per year, which was actually less than one-third of this sum, all of which would be spent exclusively for their benefit. But it was thought improbable that the Sugar Act, even if vigorously enforced, could raise such a large amount as £100,000 a year. The practice of requisitioning contributions from the colonies had woefully failed during the war just ended, and the government decided to raise the balance of the colonial share of the needed money in the colonies by means of a stamp tax. Grenville announced the government's intention at the time of the debate over the Sugar Act, but because he anticipated colonial opposition, he delayed bringing in his stamp bill for a year, in order to allow time for the colonies to express themselves on the subject. He even went so far as to call in the colonial agents resident in London, and told them of his plan. When he asked them whether they could suggest any better way of raising the money, they had nothing to offer as a substitute. Opposition was strongly articulate, however, and petitions were sent to Parliament against the act, both from the colonies and from the merchants of London, the latter of whom realized that this proposal was bound to react against their trade in the colonies. But the government was at the moment more interested in raising an American revenue than in the merchants, and the petitions were refused under the provisions of an old parliamentary rule which forbade petitions on money bills. Grenville proceeded to have the legislation passed, and the Stamp Act became a law on March 22, 1765. This act provided that, with certain specified exceptions, legal documents executed in the American colonies should bear a stamp varying from two pence to six pounds in value according to the nature of the instrument. Similarly, dice, playing cards, pamphlets, newspapers, advertisements, calendars, and almanacs were to be stamped. All money received from these several duties was to be earmarked for use only for the defense of the colonies. One of the most irritating provisions was that making cases involving violations of the act cognizable by the courts of vice-admiralty, at the option of the informer—for the vice-admiralty courts were not jury courts.

This act reaped the whirlwind. Parliament had often taxed imperial commerce, and its right to do so was unquestioned. But no British Parliament had ever ventured to legislate in such a way as to tax practically every business transaction and almost every individual within the bounds of every colony in America. For a body of Englishmen sitting in London thus to dispose of the fortunes of Englishmen resident three thousand miles away in America, with no means of making their wishes known on the floor of the legislature, seemed monstrous in the extreme. And this feeling, coupled with the accumulated grievances growing out of the Proclamation of 1763, the Sugar Act and the Currency Act, inflamed American opinion to the point of violence, and called forth the first genuinely representative convention of the colonies acting in unison, the so-called Stamp Act Congress of 1765, the deliberations of which must be noted in some detail.

THE QUARTERING ACT

News of the passage of the Stamp Act had not reached America when the Grenville government took the legal steps necessary for the establishment of a permanent armed force in the colonies. The annual mutiny act authorized the sending of troops to America, and, because the number was expected to be greater than the regular military posts could accommodate, and in order to force the colonies to assume a further share in the cost of their support, the quartering act was passed, about a month after the Stamp Act, to provide quarters for them at colonial expense.

This act required the colonies to billet the soldiers in colonial barracks, or, failing that, in inns and alehouses, or, finally, failing sufficient room in them, in empty houses, barns, or other buildings belonging to private citizens. The government and council of each province were made responsible for cooperating with the military; quarters, food, and vehicles furnished would be paid for at the regular established rates.

New York was the most strategic military point in America, and the largest number of troops were stationed there; General Gage, commander-in-chief of the British army in America, established his headquarters there. The operation of the act thus placed a disproportionate burden upon the province of New York, and the legislature was quick to refuse to carry it out, at least in certain of its provisions, whereupon the governor was instructed to sign no laws until the legislature made the required provisions for the troops. The resultant stalemate lasted for months, until New York, faced with a complete legislative paralysis, finally gave in, but the crisis presented a fundamental constitutional conflict for all the colonies that was far from settled by New York's acquiescence.

COLONIAL RESISTANCE: THE STAMP ACT CONGRESS

The series of acts for the administration, defense and exploitation of the empire promulgated by the Grenville government cut off the western lands of the continental colonies, restricted colonial currency, shackled colonial commerce, taxed the colonists within the boundaries of their own provinces, and now quartered troops upon the colonists themselves. The king and the British government were pleased with their cleverness, for it seemed that the principle of maintaining troops permanently in the colonies at colonial expense was now established. Furthermore, the navigation system had been tightened and the control of American trade placed more effectively than ever in the hands of the British merchants and manufacturers. The mercantilist doctrine that colonies exist only for the benefit of the mother country had been written into these laws. It is true that the British merchants opposed the stamp act because they knew their trade with the colonies would suffer by it. But their mercantilist thinking was unchanged; their quarrel with the ministry was essentially a rivalry between merchants and government for the profits of colonial trade. Nor did the merchants protest the Sugar Act. It mattered little that this system, if enforced, would strangle the American colonies as northern Ireland had been strangled before them. The British statesmen, with a few exceptions, did not realize the true effect of what they were doing. Indeed, they hardly thought of the American side of the question, and would probably not have believed it, if told. It took the united protests of the British merchants and of the American people, expressed in the Stamp Act Congress, to drive the point home. And even then their conviction was temporary and superficial—"a conviction of the head, not of the heart."

The colonial resistance to the stamp act was immediate, practically universal, and extremely effective. For the stamp act, in contrast with the other acts in the Grenville program directly affected interests of practically every element in the population, and it gave the colonies a common issue around which to rally as none of the others had done. Popular resentment flared up everywhere; upon arrival of the news of passage of the act, bells were tolled, flags were lowered to half-mast, and newspapers appeared with broad black borders—"in mourning," as they explained, "for the death of liberty." Rioting took place in many sections of the colonies, the stamp-collectors were hanged in effigy many times over, and all of them were forced or prevailed upon to resign. The house of Governor Hutchinson of Massachusetts was broken into and sacked. Mob leaders formed strong-arm associations called the "Sons of Liberty" for the coercion of British officials and sympathizers; merchants formed non-importation agreements to order no goods from England until the "black act" should be repealed; and companies were formed for the development of home industries. Young ladies of two Rhode Island cities agreed among themselves that they would refuse any and all swains who approved of the stamp act!

Provincial legislatures added official protest to popular clamor by passing resolutions condemning the stamp act. Of these, the "Virginia Resolves," passed on the motion of Patrick Henry, May 29, 1765, were the first, and were typical of all the others. Reviewing the history of colonization, the resolves proclaimed that the English settlers in the new world brought with them their rights of Englishmen, the most obvious and inalienable of which was to be taxed only by their own representatives. Thus the Virginians, it was claimed, could be taxed only by their own representative assembly, and any usurpation of that right by the British Parliament was a violation of American and British liberty. The Pennsylvania resolves even went so far as to say that the government of the province, founded on natural right and English liberty, "is and ought to be perfectly free."

This was going pretty far. But the most significant development of all was the invitation sent out by the Massachusetts General Court, inviting the other provinces to send delegates to a congress for consideration of "the difficulties to which they are . . . reduced by the operation of the acts of Parliament for levying duties and taxes on the colonies" and of measures to be taken for the amelioration of their condition. Evidently it was the intention of its Massachusetts sponsors that the congress should consider both the sugar act and the stamp act; but the congress of delegates that met in New York on October 7, 1765, has come to be known popularly as the Stamp Act Congress.

This congress was a fairly conservative body. Nine provinces were represented, and among the missing was Virginia, which had not had time to designate delegates. The congress, which was on the whole fairly moderate in opinion, prepared an address to the king, a declaration of rights and grievances, and petitions to the House of Lords and the House of Commons. Protesting their loyalty to the king and "due subordination to that august body the Parliament of Great Britain," they took their stand on the principle that the Englishmen in America were entitled to exactly the same rights as Englishmen born in England. One of those inalienable rights was that they might not be taxed but by consent, either by themselves or by their representatives. But it was manifestly impossible, said the resolution, for the colonies to be represented in Parliament; therefore the only bodies qualified to tax the colonists were their own elected provincial legislatures. Another right of every British subject, it continued, was trial by jury; but the stamp act provided that violations might be tried in vice-admiralty courts, without juries. Finally, the resolutions pointed out that the duties of the sugar act were "extremely burdensome and grievous; and from the scarcity of specie, the payment of them absolutely impracticable."

Thus the work of the Stamp Act Congress was essentially a protest against the limitations placed by the Grenville legislation upon American commerce. The effect of that legislation was disastrous, also, as the resolution pointed out, upon British trade as well; for it tended to make the colonies "unable to purchase the manufactures of Great Britain." Therefore, the congress asked for "the repeal of the Act for granting and applying certain stamp duties, of all clauses of any other Acts of Parliament, whereby the jurisdiction of the Admiralty is extended as aforesaid, and of the other late Acts for the restriction of American commerce," presumably the Sugar Act.

This was the first time the American colonies had shown such unanimity on any subject. Even so, it is doubtful whether the colonial protest would have had any effect had it not had the support of the British merchants. The non-importation agreements, coupled with the general disorder following the passage of the Stamp Act, had resulted in the enormous falling-off of over one million pounds in the exports of goods to America during twelve months— a decrease of over one-third. As England was already suffering from the post-war depression, the decline in American trade greatly increased unemployment and decreased shipping, with the result that petitions from all parts of England poured in upon Parliament to repeal the hated stamp act.

The Marquess of Rockingham had succeeded Grenville as head of the government in the summer of 1765, and, moved by the outcry against the legislation as well as by the advice of such men as William Pitt and Benjamin Franklin, the new government had the stamp act repealed. The principle of parliamentary tax action was maintained, however, in the declaratory act, which stoutly affirmed that Parliament had the right to legislate for the colonies "in all cases whatsoever."

The repeal of the stamp act thus brought no solution to the real problem involved. But the colonists were overjoyed, and the king's birthday in June, 1766, was celebrated with more genuine feeling by the Americans than on any other occasion, probably, before or since.

The Rockingham ministry also made some slight revision in the sugar act. Among other things, the three-penny duty on foreign molasses was changed to a one-penny duty on all molasses imported into the colonies, regardless of whether it was of foreign or British origin, thus making it a duty purely for revenue. But the fundamental problem remained: did the English Parliament, elected by about fifteen thousand voters in England, have the right to legislate for the colonies, even to the extent of "internal taxation," the suppression of industrial expansion, and the strangulation of American commerce? England had never ceased to believe that it did have that right; the colonials continued to insist that it did not. Things being as they were, and given the new attempts by England, soon to follow, to control American economic and political life, the question could only be answered by war.

THE CONFLICT RESUMED: THE TOWNSHEND PROGRAM

The government that followed the Rockingham ministry in 1766 was headed by the Duke of Grafton, with the great William Pitt, now Earl of Chatham, as Lord Privy Seal and the real leader of the ministry. The liberal Earl of Shelburne, as Secretary of State for the Southern Department, was in charge of the colonies, and Charles Townshend was Chancellor of the Exchequer. But Pitt was ill, and, unfortunately for America, Townshend was able to convince his other colleagues that he could raise enough money in America to pay for the military establishment there, merely by levying duties upon certain American imports—and by making sure that they were collected. The "Townshend Acts," therefore, were similar to the series of acts passed by the Grenville government between 1763 and 1765 in that they were calculated to raise a revenue for support of the military establishment in America and to tighten up the enforcement of all the laws relative to the colonies. But the Townshend program went even further, for it was hoped that enough money would be raised also to support the civil list of Crown appointees in the colonies, thus making the governors and judges and other imperial officials independent of the colonial assemblies on questions of money and salaries. This, in turn, might bring to an end the century-old debate with the assemblies in a victory for the prerogative and block the growing tendency of the colonial assemblies toward "independency."

Thus the Townshend Revenue Act of June 29, 1767, laid duties upon glass, painters' lead and colors, tea, and paper shipped from

England to the colonies. It also ominously and specifically authorized the use of writs of assistance in the colonies for the enforcement of the act. The old "plantation duties" were still in effect,
as were those from the Sugar Act of 1764 (as modified in 1766),
so that the colonies were paying duties, in 1768, on the enumerated
articles shipped from one colony to another, Madeira, Spanish and
Portuguese wines, foreign sugar and indigo, all molasses, coffee,
and pimento, glass, lead, painters' colors, paper and tea.

For the collection of these duties, the Grafton ministry passed
an act in June, 1767, establishing in America a board of customs
commissioners. Under this act, a board of customs commissioners
similar to the one in England was established in America, with
headquarters at Boston. This board had complete control of the
administration of the American customs, and it was responsible
directly to the Lords of the Treasury, bearing no responsibility
to the customs commissioners of England. It went immediately
to work, and was soon showing a profit, as against the consistent
losses incurred in the customs service prior to this time. Thus before 1767, the American customs had brought in about £2,000
per year, at a cost, for collection, of some £9,000—a real loss of
£7,000 per year. But after the reorganization of 1767-68, the American customs produced some £30,000 annually, at an administrative cost of some £13,000—a real gain of £17,000 annually. Never
had the customs system in America been so effectively and profitably
administered. In the long run, however, this was money out of
the pockets of the Americans; it is no wonder they objected!

The third step in the Townshend program was the reorganization of the system of vice-admiralty courts in America. The sugar
act and the stamp act had extended the jurisdiction of the vice-
admiralty courts to cases under those acts, and a court of vice-
admiralty had been set up at Halifax. The Lords of the Treasury,
in charge of American customs, recommended that the court be
removed, but it was not until the act of 1767 that this was done.
Under this legislation, four vice-admiralty courts were erected in
America; at Halifax, Boston, Philadelphia, and Charleston. These
courts had both original and appellate jurisdiction, and were courts
of last appeal. But since cases in admiralty courts might be tried
without juries, many cases which, under the old system, would have
been tried before civil juries partial to colonial defendants would
now be more impartially considered. This, again, would be expensive to American violators of the navigation acts; but the American objection to the new arrangement was based chiefly upon

the complaint that it was a partial suspension of the "right of Englishmen" to a jury trial.

One other step in the reorganization of the imperial administration should be noted here, and that was the creation of the office of Secretary of State for the Colonies. Hitherto, colonial affairs had been handled chiefly by the Secretary of State for the Southern Department, acting on the advice of the Board of Trade. The adoption of the Townshend program had caused the resignation of Shelburne, and the new office was created in October, 1767. In January, 1768, it was given to Wills Hill, Earl of Hillsborough, who was committed to the program of coercion of the colonies.

The Townshend program of reorganization was only too successful. For not only had the enforcement of the laws of navigation and trade been made effective; all the duties now imposed upon the colonies were "external" duties, and it appeared that all the logic of the colonial opposition to the reorganization had been met. Best of all, from the mother country's point of view, the colonial system of administration was now being enforced; smuggling was brought almost to a stop, and the duties were actually being collected. But that was precisely its greatest fault, in the eyes of the colonies. Under the old order of things the colonies had enjoyed a large measure of free trade; now their commerce was to be vigorously restrained and to be made to pay duties into the British exchequer, to be used in maintaining a system of government which was the negation of their own impulse to self-government.

In the face of the colonial opposition that now broke out afresh, the imperial officials found themselves utterly helpless. With or without writs of assistance, they met increasing resistance in collecting the duties. In Boston the popular temper was such that the customs commissioners asked for a ship to protect them and the British man-of-war *Romney* was sent to Boston harbor. Rioting broke out upon the seizure of the sloop *Liberty,* belonging to John Hancock, and troops were sent to Boston to protect the officials and their families. Meanwhile, the colonial protest over the Townshend duties had spread over the entire length of the continental colonies. On February 11, 1768, the house of representatives of Massachusetts addressed a circular letter to the other provinces, inviting them to cooperate in a common resistance to the British system. Hillsborough then added fuel to the already brightly blazing discontent by instructing colonial governors ·to dissolve any assemblies that showed a disposition to cooperate with Massachusetts. The Massachusetts assembly was dissolved when it refused to rescind its action, and the other colonies quickly came to its aid.

To make matters worse, the New York assembly continued to resist the quartering act, which was renewed in 1767, with the result that Parliament ordered the governor of New York to sign no legislation until the support for the troops under the act was granted. Its normal functions thus nullified, the assembly was compelled to give in; but the coercion exercised by the government left a residuum of bitterness that New York was not soon to forget. The New Yorkers, therefore, the more readily joined in the agitation against the Townshend duties.

Colonial opposition was now thoroughly aroused, and many of the American leaders expressed their opinions, pro and con, in a sort of pamphlet warfare. Greatest of the protagonists at this juncture was John Dickinson of Pennsylvania, whose *Letters of a Pennsylvania Farmer* were widely read all over the colonies. In these letters, Dickinson retreated from the "no taxation" and the "external taxation" arguments, to the argument that Parliament has the right only to "regulate" imperial commerce; duties for regulation were permissible, but duties for revenue, being a form of taxation, he could not accept. Thus Dickinson, who doubtless represented the feelings of the majority of Americans, acknowledged the need of some central, co-ordinating agency in the empire; but he claimed that the powers of this agency could not and did not include taxation.

The colonial legislatures took up the cause, and the first to take action was that of Virginia, which, on the motion of George Washington, passed the so-called "Virginia Resolves of 1769," which were copied, in one form or another, by most of the other colonies. In these resolves, actually written by George Mason, the Virginians reasserted the principle that taxation in Virginia rested in the hands of the house of burgesses and the king, and they begged the king to prevent the suggestion of Lord Mansfield, that Americans resisting Britain be transported to England for trial, from being carried into effect.

But as in the case of the stamp act, the most effective form of pressure exerted upon the government of Great Britain was the non-importation agreements of the colonial merchants. In Virginia, an "association" was formed by a number of the rich planters who agreed to import no more English goods upon which were laid import duties for revenue. In the mercantile centers similar associations were formed, and the mobs again supported their merchant and planter leaders with violence. The non-importation agreements were unequally effective in the various colonies—less effective in Georgia and Carolina, for example, than in New England. But on the whole, these agreements, coupled with the new stimulus they gave to colonial manufactures, had a terrifying effect upon the British merchants who shared in the American trade. Lord North, therefore, who had now come to the head of the government, brought about the repeal of most of the Townshend duties early in 1770. The old duties on tobacco, wine, sugar, molasses and tea, however, were retained.

Again colonial resistance had been successful. Again a part, at least, of the offending duties had been repealed. But the principle of parliamentary legislation remained, as did the problem of supporting a military establishment in the colonies. Colonial economic life was still in large measure in British leading strings. In the light of the inevitable expansion of the American economy, those leading strings had, eventually, in one way or another, to be broken.

RECOMMENDED BOOKS FOR FURTHER READING

CONTEMPORARY NARRATIVES

Samuel E. Morison, ed., *Sources and Documents Illustrating the American Revolution, 1764-1788*, pp. 1-54.

Thomas Pownall, *The Administration of the Colonies*.

Richard T. Grenville-Temple, *The Grenville Papers*, edited by William J. Smith.

MODERN ACCOUNTS

Charles M. Andrews, *The Boston Merchants and the Non-Importation Movement*.

Charles M. Andrews, *The Colonial Period of American History*, IV, Chapter 11.

Arthur H. Basye, "The Secretary of the State for the Colonies, 1768-1782," *American Historical Review*, XXVIII, 13-23.

Carl L. Becker, *The Eve of the Revolution*.

George L. Beer, *British Colonial Policy, 1754-1765*.

Alfred L. R. Burt, *The Old Province of Quebec*.

Edward Channing, *A History of the United States*, III, Chapters 1-4.

Hugh E. Egerton, *The Causes and Character of the American Revolution*.

Lawrence H. Gipson, *The British Empire before the American Revolution*, Volume I.

Lawrence H. Gipson, *Jared Ingersoll*.

William L. Grant, *Colonial Policy of Chatham*.

Ralph V. Harlow, *Samuel Adams*.

Emily Hickman, "Colonial Writs of Assistance," *New England Quarterly*, V, 83-104.

George E. Honard, *The Preliminaries of the Revolution, 1763-1775*.

Kate Hotblack, *Chatham's Colonial Policy.*

Eugene I. McCormac, *Colonial Opposition to Imperial Authority during the French and Indian War.*

John C. Miller, *Sam Adams.*

Arthur M. Schlesinger, *The Colonial Merchants and the American Revolution, 1763-1776.*

Margaret M. M. Spector, *The American Department of the British Government, 1768-1782.*

Charles J. Stillé, *The Life and Times of John Dickinson, 1732-1808.*

Moses C. Tyler, *Patrick Henry.*

Claude H. Van Tyne, *The Causes of the War of Independence.*

42

The New West

THE EXPANSIVE movement of population across the Allegheny divide was a major sociological phenomenon that had had its beginning during the decade of King George's War. In the previous period, from about 1700 to about 1750, the first phase of the American westward movement had filled up most of the space remaining between the fall line and the crest of the mountains. This process was relatively complete by the end of King George's War, and the wave of westward moving population began to trickle down the western slope into the fertile valleys of the Allegheny, the Ohio, the Great Kanawha, and the Tennessee about the middle of the century. This movement was greatest in the area south of New York. Far to the east, in Maine, the English settlements were still confined to a relatively narrow strip along the seaboard, held there by the proximity of the French in Canada and Acadia and the antagonism of the pro-French Micmacs and Abenaki Indians. In the valley of the Connecticut, settlement had been moving northward as far as Keene, New Hampshire, and Putney, on the west side of the river, but had not yet approached the northern divide between the Connecticut valley and the valley of the St. Lawrence. It was not very attractive land to begin with, and just over the divide to the west, in the valley of St. Sacrement (Lake George) and Lake Champlain, the French were well established around the fortress at Crown Point. On the English side of the divide, again, along the Hudson and the Mohawk, settlement had proceeded to the heads of the valleys. But here, too, held in check by the proximity of the French and the opposition of the powerful tribes of the Iroquois confederacy, settlement, if the British port at Oswego be excepted, seemed hesitant to cross the divide.

Further to the south, however, it was a different story. As the settlers, following the trails of the fur-traders before them, made their way up the valleys of the Susquehanna, the Potomac, the James, and the Roanoke, they found the ascent easy, and the soil good. At the top of the divide they found low passes which opened to easy access the western slopes watered by the Allegheny, the

Youghiogheny and Monongahela, the Great Kanawha and its branches, the Greenbrier, and the New, or the Tennessee with its upper branches, the Holston and the Clinch rivers. As a matter of fact, the divide between the Shenandoah and the James, on the one side, and the New River on the other, lies in the Great Valley, and is almost imperceptible. Westward expansion in this direction was hardly more than a continuation of the movement that had already occupied the great north-and-south valleys of the Appalachian range. Descent of the western slope was here merely a matter of following the line of least resistance.

Pennsylvania and Virginia traders had penetrated the lands of the "western waters" probably before 1740. During King George's War they had gone into the Ohio valley with increasing frequency, and had set up trading posts in some of the Indian villages. The most noted of these were at Pickawillany, the village of the chieftain LaDemoiselle, on the Great Miami River north of the Ohio, and at Logstown, on the upper Ohio. Other traders, from Virginia and the Carolinas, were going to the country of the Cherokees, around the upper reaches of the Tennessee, even earlier. Already, the attractiveness of the western lands was known, and the land speculators began to anticipate the increase in values that was bound to occur with the expected settlement. As early as 1743, one James Patten petitioned the Crown for a grant of two hundred thousand acres of land on the Great Kanawha. In 1745 John Robinson and others were given one hundred thousand acres along the Greenbrier, a branch of the Great Kanawha lying just beyond the Allegheny range. Numerous other grants followed, and by 1747 the wave of speculation was in full swing. Altogether, there were more than a score of land companies from Pennsylvania to Georgia seeking lands in the Mississippi valley about 1750.

The most famous of all these companies was the Ohio Company of Virginia. This company, composed of wealthy speculators in Virginia and England, was organized in 1748, and was granted 200,000 acres of land on the upper Ohio on condition that it build a fort and settle one hundred families upon it within seven years. The Ohio Company was thus chiefly interested in the profits to be derived from the sale of lands; it counted also, however, upon a profitable fur trade with the Indians. In 1750 the company sent Christopher Gist to inspect its land, and built a trading post at the mouth of Will's Creek on the upper Potomac, as a base of operations, whence it planned to build a road to the Monongahela River. But the activities of the Ohio Company brought it into conflict both with the French in Canada, as already noted, and with the traders and settlers from Pennsylvania, of whom the best known was George Croghan. Croghan had land grants near the forks of the Ohio, and a trading house on the Muskingum River. But the rival claims of Virginia and Pennsylvania to the lands along the upper Ohio were submerged in the developing conflict with the French, and did not come to a head until after the war. When the fighting started, and it became necessary to raise an armed force, Lieutenant-Governor Dinwiddie of Virginia issued a proclamation, on February 9, 1754, in which he offered 200,000 acres of land west of the mountains to men who would volunteer for the service against the French. This proclamation became the basis of the claims of the Virginia soldiers in which George Washington became interested. For the time being, however, the actual occupation of this land was delayed by the war.

Thus by 1754, when the first hostilities with the French took place, the British had actually begun to settle on the western slope of the Allegheny divide. The settlements were still relatively few, to be sure; but English-speaking farmers had built their homes along the upper Allegheny, the Monongahela, at Draper's Meadows on the New or Kanawha River, and at Stalnaker's post on the Holston, in what is now Tennessee. The land speculators had seen this movement coming, and had sought to anticipate it and exploit it by getting control of the most valuable lands in the west. It was the importunities of the land speculators, their quarrels among themselves, and the reaction among Englishmen at home that forced the British government not only to claim the new west as against the claims of France, but also to formulate a policy with regard to how the west should be treated among Englishmen themselves.

The Albany Congress of 1754 had sought to deal with the problem of western expansion, and the power of establishing new colonies in the west as buffer-states against the French would have been given the central government under the Albany plan of union. A little later, Benjamin Franklin, author of the plan and himself a speculator in the lands of the west, proposed that two new colonies be set up back of the mountains, between the Ohio River and Lake Erie. Thomas Pownall, governor of Massachusetts, proposed a similar scheme.

What would have happened to these schemes had the war not intervened, it is of course impossible to say. However, the Earl of Halifax, president of the Board of Trade and an aggressive imperialist, was already convinced of the desirability of settling the trans-Allegheny west, merely to forestall the French. Most of the British ministers agreed with him, and it was chiefly for this reason that they had favored the project of the Ohio Company. Similarly, in order to hasten the process of settlement, the ministry, on August 27, 1754, instructed Virginia to grant lands west of the mountains in lots of one thousand acres, which were to be freed of quitrents for ten years as an inducement. That same summer, at about the time of the Albany Congress, the Board of Trade recommended to the ministry that a unified imperial policy be adopted with regard to the Indians, and that the military forces in America be placed under one command. Both these recommendations were carried out. Two imperial agents for Indian affairs were appointed, William Johnson in the north and Edmund Atkin (followed by John Stuart) in the south; and General Braddock was sent to the colonies as commander-in-chief of all British forces in America.

The chief objective of British policy up to this point, however, was strategic; that is to say, the British policy makers were more interested in occupying the Mississippi valley and holding it against the French than they were in the American westward movement as such. In America, colony was already pitted against colony in the race for the speculative profits of the west; English speculators were just beginning to be interested. When the time should come when the great British speculators would discover the possibilities of the American west—as come it did, soon after the war then starting—the competition between colonial speculators and British speculators would have a profound effect upon the formation of British policy toward the west, and would pit the colonies against the mother country.

THE WEST IN THE PROCLAMATION OF 1763

Prior to 1748 the British government had left matters pertaining to the Indians, the fur trade, and the lands in the west in the hands of the provincial governments. A great deal of confusion and corruption had been the result, and the provinces had gradually come to assume that these were matters that should be left to them. But when the general nature of the westward movement and the dangers inherent in intercolonial conflict over the development of the west became apparent about 1750, and when the great potential profits from speculation in western land also began to be seen, it seemed high time for the formulation of a general imperial policy. Just prior to the Seven Years' War, therefore, the Crown had adopted a policy of encouraging settlement in the west, as already noted. But this policy, such as it was, had never been clearly formed, and it seemed to have as its chief purpose the forestalling of the French in the occupation of the Mississippi valley. With the elimination of the French as a result of the war, however, and with abundant evidence that a great wave of settlers was poised, as it were, ready to roll down the western slope as soon as peace should be declared, and with the sure knowledge that such an event would cause trouble with the Indians, the British ministry was compelled to consider the problem of the American west in a much more thoroughgoing fashion than it had ever done before.

British opinion on this question was of two minds. One school of thought opposed the settlement of the American west, and proposed that the westward movement be stopped at the Allegheny divide. They had two major reasons: belonging to the "raw materials" school of British mercantilists, and representing such vested interests as the Hudson's Bay Company, they believed that the fur trade, which centered in this great western area, should be left untouched, and that these lands should be left to the Indians in order that this "essential raw material" might continue to flow to Great Britain. Moreover, they said, communication and trade with new inland communities would be difficult because of the mountain barrier; the settlers there would be led to devote themselves to manufacturing. Not only would this separate them from the market for British manufactures and make them competitors of British manufacturers; once independent of the need for British supplies and support, the west would separate from the empire and become independent in fact.

The ministry, however, was composed of imperialists, or expansionists, who believed that the west should be opened, if gradually, to settlement. Representative of wealthy investors and merchants—as distinguished from manufacturers—eager to expand their American markets, this school of thought held that, far from becoming manufacturers, the emigrants to the Mississippi valley would turn their interest to farming, whereas, if compelled to remain in the old colonies where land was getting scarce, they would there turn to industry as a way of making a living. Thus the "markets" wing of the mercantilists and imperialists favored the opening of the American west for reasons quite similar to those of their opponents for keeping it closed.

Be that as it may, the letter of May 5, 1763, from the ministry to the Earl of Shelburne, president of the Board of Trade, asking for recommendations as to the new territories just acquired from France referred to the Mississippi valley as well as to Quebec, Florida, and the West Indies, and the Board set to work to formulate its recommendations for that section along with the others. The problem of the west really involved three major issues. The first of these was the difficult question of the regulation of Indian affairs: should a strong imperial agency be created for this purpose, or should this business be left in the hands of the colonial governments? It was generally agreed, even by those who wished the west entirely closed, that some sort of a boundary line must be established between the white settlements and the lands to be reserved for the Indians; but where should this line be drawn? The second issue arose out of the question how far and how fast white settlement should be permitted to go. The settlers were already moving in; should new colonies be established to accommodate them and control them, or should this be left to the old colonies? Should an attempt be made to make the movement westward a gradual one, or should it be allowed to proceed in a rush, as it threatened to do? The third issue was the question of how the great Mississippi empire was to be administered. Should it be left under the administration of the old colonies, the general-in-chief of the British army in America, or—since the settlements along the Mississippi itself were French and since much of the area's trade was with Quebec—should it be placed under the administration of the governor of Quebec?

The Proclamation of October 7, 1763, embodied the results of the effort to find answers to these problems. But the policy inherent in the proclamation also included certain features that were precipitated by the outbreak, in May, of the most disastrous Indian war in all American history, the war known as the Conspiracy of Pontiac.

In this bitter frontier war the Indians gave expression to all the bitterness and hatred that had been nourished in them by two centuries of British abuses, but particularly those of a more recent sort. Chief among these abuses was the unscrupulous profiteering of the British and American traders at the expense of the Indians. For the traders used every known device to cheat the Indians, and the savages had gradually come to realize it. The most devilish practice was the custom of furnishing the Indians with rum, in such quantities that the traders were enabled to take from the intoxicated natives the most valuable furs without giving anything of comparable value in return. Another cause of discontent among the Indians was the sudden decision of the British ministry at the end of the war to curtail, in the name of economy, the old custom of making gifts to the Indians to keep their friendship. But by far the most deep-seated cause for discontent was the way in which the whites were encroaching upon the Indian hunting grounds. The settlers had begun to pour into the Fort Pitt region even as soon as the French had been driven out by the Forbes expedition in 1758, and the Indians looked upon this influx with dismay. Their bitterness was increased by the individual land speculators, who used the same tricks as the trader to cheat the Indians out of their birthright. It was a matter of life and death for the Indians, for upon the preservation of their hunting grounds their very existence depended. The feeling of the Indians was still further inflamed by the French traders still among them, who encouraged them to believe that a French army was coming to help them.

Pontiac, an Ottawa chieftain, had formed a great confederacy of tribes from the Lakes to the Gulf of Mexico to take up the hatchet against the British, and in May and June, 1763, these tribes fell upon the now British posts in the territory north of the Ohio and captured them, one after the other. Such important posts as those at Michilimackinack, Miami, Sandusky, and St. Joseph fell before the Indian assault; only Detroit and Fort Pitt were able successfully to hold out. British captives were tortured and killed; along the frontier the Indians attacked farms, massacred people, burned houses and crops, and killed or drove off livestock. Fortunately the southern Indians had been pacified at a conference held at Augusta, and those tribes did not join in carrying out Pontiac's original plan for a simultaneous attack all along the frontier from the Lakes to the Gulf. Colonel Henry Bouquet was sent into the west with an expedition composed of British regulars and frontiersmen, and succeeded, on August 6, in a pitched battle at Bushy Run, between Fort Pitt and the Allegheny Mountains, in putting the Indians to flight. The war went on, however, and it was only after a series of actions in the trans-Ohio region that Bouquet was able to bring the Indians to sign a peace in September, 1764.

The outbreak of the war, and the pusillanimous unwillingness of the colonial legislatures to assist in their own defense, strengthened the British government in two convictions: one, that a policy must speedily be devised for the administration of the American west, and the other, that the only way in which the colonies could be effectively defended was by a force of British regulars, the support of which, in all justice, ought to be borne, even if only in part, by the colonies themselves. The Earl of Shelburne resigned the presidency of the Board of Trade in September, 1763, and was succeeded by Viscount Hillsborough. The policy enunciated in the Proclamation of October 7, 1763, was, nevertheless, substantially the policy proposed by Shelburne.

Under the terms of the proclamation, an effort was made to effect a real, if temporary, solution of the three basic problems with regard to the west. For the appeasement of the Indians, a line was drawn along the Alleghenies through the sources of the rivers that flow into the Atlantic, which line, for the time being, was to be a boundary between the white settlements and the Indian hunting grounds of the west. The trade with the Indians was to continue, but the traders were required to acquire licenses from the governors of the colonies where they resided and to post bond for the loyal observance of any regulations regarding the conduct of the Indian trade. With regard to the problem of western lands, the proclamation provided that, in general, and for the time being, the lands beyond the boundary were to be reserved to the Indians as their hunting grounds. New colonies were to be set up in East Florida, West Florida, and Quebec; but the southern boundary of Quebec was fixed at the forty-fifth degree of latitude, and the northern boundary of Florida was fixed at the thirty-first degree. Thus all the immense area between these lines, the mountains, and the Mississippi was a sort of great Indian reserve. Within this reserve the colonial governors were forbidden to issue patents to land; and settlers on land within it that was not already ceded to the Crown were ordered forthwith to remove. Finally, no new purchases of land from the Indians anywhere were to be made by anyone but authorized agents of the Crown, who were to make such purchases at public meetings of the Indians themselves. On the question of administration the proclamation was silent. Somehow, in the haste to get the proclamation issued and the Indians pacified, the great west was left without any provision for civil government. This omission worked a particular hardship upon the French communities already founded along the Mississippi and the Wabash; and the fault was not corrected until the Quebec Act of 1774.

THE FORT STANWIX LINE, 1768

Although the Proclamation of 1763 closed the trans-Allegheny lands to settlement, and sought thus to check the westward movement, this arrangement was not expected to be permanent. On the contrary, Shelburne, its real author, was convinced of the desirability of opening the west, and it was expected that a permanent boundary line between the whites and the Indian reserve would be drawn farther west, and the intervening territory filled with settlers. But the settlers could not—or would not—wait. Just as soon as peace was made with the Indians the old settlers rebuilt their abandoned farms and new settlers began moving in, despite the proclamation line, especially into the region around Fort Pitt.

The proclamation did, however, have the effect of forcing the land speculators to turn to the British Crown, rather than to their colonial governments, for approval. The speculators, indeed, had begun to formulate their schemes as soon as the Treaty of Paris was signed, and were merely marking time during the Indian war, and they were soon to awaken to its full force the speculative mania of the capitalists of England. In Virginia, the soldiers who had been promised land by Lieutenant-Governor Dinwiddie as a bonus for their enlistment organized themselves under the leadership of George Washington, who was himself one of the claimants, and petitioned the Crown for a confirmation of their titles in the spring of 1763. The Ohio Company revived its scheme and sent a representative to England to seek a confirmation of its grant. A group of Indian traders, who had lost goods at the hands of the Indians at the beginning of the war, called the "Sufferers of 1754" petitioned the Crown for land in the west as compensation for their losses, and to their plea was now added the claims of others, the "Sufferers of 1763," who had been surprised by the outbreak of Pontiac's war in the latter year. During the summer of 1763 a number of wealthy landowners of Maryland and Virginia formed a group called the Mississippi Company, which sought to obtain a vast stretch of land upon the Mississippi, Wabash, Ohio, and Tennessee rivers. In New York another company planned to settle a colony, to be known as New Wales, on the upper Ohio.

This wave of speculative fever was, as yet, confined to America. The western interest in America was intense; and, as the various projects overlapped, the colonies became rivals in the race for the west, each colony supporting its own particular group of speculators against the others. The British government of the Marquis of Rockingham, however, discouraged the interest in the west. It never made any pronouncement on the subject, but Lord Barrington, one of its members, drew up a plan for the permanent closing of the Mississippi valley to settlement—a plan which would permanently have made of that area one vast Indian reserve, valuable to England only for its fur trade.

By the time of the accession to power of the Grafton ministry, in 1766, the American west had again become a pressing problem. The government of the Marquis of Rockingham had attempted to force the squatters west of the proclamation line back eastward, but had found it to be impossible because of their numbers. The Indians, too, were still discontented; despite the stringent regulations of the Indian trade put into effect by the two Indian agents, Stuart and Johnson, abuses in the Indian trade continued. Moreover, the question of adequate defense was still unsolved, for the resistance to the Stamp Act which had led to its repeal in 1766 demonstrated conclusively that some other means of raising money for the support of the army must be found. This combination of circumstances led, as already noted, to the revision of the plan of imperial reorganization, including the west.

The Earl of Shelburne, now Secretary of State for the Southern Department in charge of American affairs, proposed to make a revision of England's western policy a part of the general revision. Shelburne was still considering the possibility of forming new colonies in the west, and the old schemes for colonization, which had been discouraged by the Rockingham government, lost no time in presenting themselves to him, along with several new ones.

Among the new schemes was that of General Phineas Lyman, of Connecticut, who was the agent for a group of "military adventurers." Lyman proposed that no less than five or six new colonies be erected in the Mississippi valley, beginning with a large colony at the mouth of the Ohio, where Lyman promised to locate ten thousand settlers within four years. Major Thomas Mant proposed to colonize the area about Detroit. The most promising of these schemes, however, was that of the Illinois Company, organized by Benjamin Franklin and George Croghan. This company proposed to set up a colony in the Illinois country, between the Wabash and the Mississippi, a fertile region already containing several French villages, and badly in need of some sort of civil government. Franklin was a personal friend of Shelburne, and, although the plan of the Illinois Company never materialized, Franklin's ideas had considerable influence upon the formation of Shelburne's western policy.

Like Franklin, Shelburne believed that the American westward movement was the inevitable result of the natural increase of the American population. At the same time he was one of those who believed that British policy, by thus providing an outlet for the surplus population of the old colonies, would divert the Americans from their tendency to turn to manufactures which would compete with the industries of England. He therefore favored the erection of two new colonies in the west. One of these he would establish about Detroit as a center, and the other he would locate in the Illinois country. As for the expense of defending the country, he believed that the revenue from the sale of lands, and the quitrents, would be adequate for this purpose.

Shelburne's ideas were approved by the cabinet, but news of increasing discontent among the Indians and warnings of the imminent danger of a new Indian outbreak brought a revival of the old plan for a permanent Indian boundary line, and the suspension of the projects for new colonies in the Illinois country and at Detroit. Shelburne instructed Sir William Johnson to arrange a permanent boundary line with the Indians, and this was done at the Treaty of Fort Stanwix, in the fall of 1768. In the southern colonies the beginnings of a permanent line back of Georgia and South Carolina had already been drawn by the Indian agent John Stuart in his meeting with the Indian chieftains at Augusta in 1763, and this line had been extended northward in 1764 and 1765 until it reached to the northern boundary of North Carolina. Now, in October, 1768, Stuart met with the Cherokee chieftains at the frontier town of Hard Labour, and arranged a boundary line to the west of Virginia. The line already run to the southward was ratified, and the new extension of it was defined as running from Chiswell's Mine on the Great Kanawha in a straight line northward to the confluence of the Great Kanawha with the Ohio. As this new line cut off much land already acquired or claimed by Virginia speculators, it aroused the bitter opposition of that colony; the speculators, indeed, actually nullified it by their continued penetration of the area west of the new line, as will be noted later.

Thus, by the end of 1768, a permanent line had been arranged with the Indians from the Great Lakes to the boundary of Florida. In the meantime, however, the new office of Secretary of State for the Colonies had been created, and American affairs were taken out of Shelburne's hands and turned over to the Marquis of Hillsborough, the first Secretary of State for the Colonies to occupy the new office. Under Hillsborough's administration, Shelburne's plan to create two or three new colonies in the interior was dropped. The Fort Stanwix and Stuart lines, therefore, marked a return in part to the policy of restraining the westward movement and of setting up a large Indian reserve. This plan, naturally enough, had the support of the Scottish fur merchants doing business through Quebec, who were rapidly coming to control the fur trade of the Great Lakes and adjacent territories.

The Congress at Fort Stanwix, held in October, 1768, resulted in two acts of considerable interest for the history of the west. The first was the establishment of the boundary line, which was to run from the east end of Lake Ontario to the Allegheny River, and thence along the Allegheny and Ohio rivers to the mouth of the Tennessee. The land east of the line was purchased from the Indians for some £10,000. Beyond the line, the British promised the Indians, the whites would not be allowed to go. The land just purchased was acquired by the imperial government, and it seems to have been assumed that the imperial government would administer it. Such a policy would inevitably conflict with the interest of such colonies as Virginia, which desired these lands for themselves. Such a conflict did, indeed, result.

The other act which grew out of the Congress of Fort Stanwix was the specific cession, by the Indians, of a large tract of land between the Allegheny Mountains and the Ohio River to the group of "suffering traders" who had lost goods at the hands of the Delaware and Shawnee Indians in 1763. This vast tract of land, just south of the Pennsylvania boundary, lay in land claimed by Virginia, and therefore excited that colony's antagonism. At the same time, however, the Iroquois chieftains ceded their title to the lands along the back of Virginia, which had been cut off by the Treaty of Hard Labour. This cession by the Iroquois was actually of land claimed by the Cherokees, and Virginia's claim, now reinforced by the Iroquois deed, brought that colony squarely into conflict with John Stuart, the agent for Indian affairs in the southern colonial district.

COLONIAL VERSUS IMPERIAL POLICY IN THE WEST: VANDALIA

The establishment of the Fort Stanwix line marked the end of the first stage of British interest in the new west. In the course of those few years, however, the general intent of British policy had become fairly clear, and that policy was soon seen to be running counter to the interests of certain colonies, particularly Virginia. In the years that followed, British policy swung back still farther toward the complete abandonment of the west, and in 1771 Hillsborough ordered Gage to abandon Fort de Chartres in the Illinois country and Fort Pitt on the Ohio. This meant the evacuation of the lands west of the Ohio. The regulation of the fur trade was left in the hands of the individual colonies. As for the lands east of the Ohio, these too were for the time being left to the mercies of the rival colonies claiming them.

Virginia, in fact, claimed all the lands between the mountains and the Ohio, and as far west as the mouth of the Tennessee. The Virginia speculators were now becoming impatient at the vacillating and interfering policies of the imperial government, and began to take matters into their own hands. Their first step was to have the Hard Labour boundary line moved farther westward to include the Holston and Louisa or Big Sandy, the present western boundary of West Virginia, at the treaty of Lochaber in 1770. The Virginians had already taken charge in the area ceded at Fort Stanwix. But they again found themselves frustrated by a new plan to establish a colony, to be called Vandalia, in the newly ceded area—a plan which, if carried through, would cut off Virginia claims to the west forever.

The Vandalia project had its origin in the "Indiana" grant to the "suffering traders" at the Treaty of Fort Stanwix. Those traders, doubtful of the validity of their title, sent Samuel Wharton to London as their agent to win the official confirmation of the Crown. In London, however, Wharton found that the interest of English speculators in the American west had now become thoroughly aroused, and he became absorbed in a scheme for the development of the Ohio valley that dwarfed the Indiana project by comparison. With the aid of Benjamin Franklin, Sir William Johnson, and interested politicians in England, Wharton was able to win the support of many of the wealthiest and most influential men in England. The result was the formation of the Walpole Company, so-called after Thomas Walpole, a nephew of Sir Robert Walpole and a well-known banker. This company, composed chiefly of English speculators, petitioned the Secretary of State for the Colonies to be allowed to buy from the Crown 2,500,000 acres of land between the Alleghenies and the Ohio. At the suggestion of Lord Hillsborough, however, the project was expanded to include enough land to establish an entirely new colony. The company was now reorganized as the Grand Ohio Company, which proceeded to ask the Crown to sell it the territory now occupied by the state of West Virginia, with a part of the present Kentucky, in return for which they proposed to pay the Crown some £10,460, plus a quit-rent of two shillings per hundred acres after twenty years. The colony, as proposed, would have been a proprietary province to be known as Vandalia, in honor of the Queen, who was said to have descended from an ancient Vandal line, in which the civil government would have been supported by the proprietors, but from which quitrents would be paid to the Crown.

The Vandalia project was approved by the Lords of the Treasury in 1770, and its apparent approval by both Hillsborough, as Secretary of State for the Colonies, and the Lords of the Treasury made it apparent that the Crown looked upon the lands in the Mississippi valley ceded by France in 1763, including especially those acquired from the Indians at Fort Stanwix in 1768, as imperial domain. The assumption seems to have been that the claims of Virginia and other colonies to transmontane lands had been extinguished by the Proclamation of 1763. But Virginia still regarded this land as belonging to the province under the charter of 1609 and by subsequent purchase from the Indians. Virginia speculators were already at work in this area, and settlers from both Pennsylvania and Virginia were pouring over the mountains in a steady stream. It was not to be assumed that Virginia would surrender her claims, in favor of the empire-sponsored Vandalia project, without a struggle.

Chief among the groups of speculators in Virginia were the old Ohio Company, the Loyal Company, and George Washington's group of military claimants to lands under Governor Dinwiddie's Proclamation of 1754. Wharton's Grand Ohio Company prevailed upon the Virginia Ohio Company and Washington's military claimants to merge their interest with the Vandalia project, but ignored the Loyal Company. It seemed as though the Virginia opposition had been overcome. But Hillsborough now evinced opposition to the scheme, due partly, perhaps, to his growing conviction that the westward movement must not be allowed to pass beyond the mountains, and partly to the influence of those Virginians who still opposed the Vandalia scheme. Wharton's company was powerful enough to bring about the resignation of Hillsborough, and when Lord Dartmouth, who favored the project, became Secretary of State for the Colonies, the new colony of Vandalia seemed assured. The Privy Council approved the project on August 14, 1772, and instructed the Board of Trade to draw up a constitution for the new colony. The northern and southern Indians were notified of the plan by Johnson and Stuart late in the fall. It seemed as though the first fruits of the American westward movement were about to appear.

Under the proposed constitution for the new colony, its government would have followed the general pattern of the older royal colonies. The governor and council were to be appointed by the Crown, and the assembly was to be composed of representatives elected by the property owners in the colony, who must also be Protestants. Laws passed by the legislature were to be subject to the disallowance of the Crown. The colony was to have three sets of courts (courts of the justices of the peace, a court of assizes, and a superior court), and the judges were to be appointed by the king. The Anglican Church was to be established, as in Virginia, but toleration of all other Protestants was provided for, and dissenters were to be excused from paying tithes for the support of the Anglican clergy. Here was a new sort of proprietary colony— one in which the profits from the sale of land would go to the proprietary, but whose government would be responsible to the king.

The Privy Council ordered the necessary papers drawn in July, 1773. But there was a delay, due, probably, to the opposition of Virginia. In January, 1774, news came to England of the "tea parties" that had taken place in the colonies in December, and the new colony was lost sight of in the wave of resentment that swept through England. The Vandalia project was lost in the clouds of approaching war. It was later to be revived in the Continental Congress of the new United States, only to be lost again before the determined opposition of Virginia.

THE FINAL IMPERIAL POLICY TOWARD THE WEST

Meanwhile, the movement of population into the west continued to flow. Emigrants from the northern colonies found their way as far as West Florida, along the eastern shore of the lower Mississippi. Phineas Lyman revived his plans for a western settlement near the junction of the Ohio and Mississippi rivers, to be called "Georgiana," and actually succeeded in getting some grants of land north of Natchez from the governor of West Florida, to which he took a number of settlers. Meanwhile, too, squatters continued to pour into the lands along the upper Ohio, the Monongahela, the Great Kanawha, and the Holston, without waiting for the British ministry to make up its mind.

Groups of settlements had been founded in the neighborhood of the Watauga River, a branch of the Tennessee, and formed what was known as the Watauga Association, which, when the settlements were found to be outside the boundaries of Virginia, set up its own government. These settlements were later incorporated into North Carolina. Another speculative enterprise was Richard Henderson's Transylvania Company, which proposed to settle the area between the Tennessee and Cumberland rivers. It was this group which, on the eve of the Revolution, employed Daniel Boone to run a trail for them to the lands they proposed to settle. These settlements, too, formed their own government, but were later absorbed into Virginia's County of Kentucky.

In Virginia, the speculators who had been left out of the Vandalia enterprise continued to maintain the claim that the lands on the upper Ohio belonged to Virginia and not to the empire. With the arrival of Lord Dunmore as governor of the colony in 1771, these Virginians found a champion. He was opposed to the Vandalia project; he favored the settlement of the west under colonial auspices, and he was quite ready to make money out of western lands himself. The Proclamation of 1763 had prohibited colonial governors from making grants of lands beyond the proclamation line, and this prohibition had been reinforced by various instructions, particularly a circular sent to the governors in May, 1773, which stopped all land grants whatever in anticipation of a new plan under which the imperial government was expected to take over the sale of lands itself. But Dunmore took advantage of the recognition, in the Proclamation of 1763, of the claims of soldiers who had been promised land bonuses for enlistment in the war, and proceeded to grant lands to former provincial officers. The rush of settlers continued, and in 1773 Harrodsburg and Louisville were founded far down the Ohio. The speculators advertised their lands, and George Washington even sent an agent to Ireland to find settlers for him.

Naturally, the Vandalia Company protested against this activity, which threatened the occupation of the best lands in the contemplated new colony, and succeeded in having an order sent to Dunmore to stop his activity. But to no avail. Dunmore seized the town of Pittsburgh in 1773, on the grounds that the region fell within the bounds of the Virginia charter of 1609. The Pennsylvania officials threw Dr. John Connolly, Dunmore's agent, in jail, and a state of tension existed between the two colonies that amounted almost to civil war. But this dispute was lost sight of in 1774 when the Shawnee Indians, living in the area now being overrun by the whites, took up the hatchet in a vain effort to stop the inevitable flow of the hated "long-knives" into their hunting grounds. The Indians were crushed by the militiamen raised against them, and sued for peace in the fall of 1774. The war ended, but no actual terms of peace were made. Nor were there to be; for soon all thought of the west was to be lost in the conflagration that had already broken out along the seaboard.

In England, however, the west had not been entirely forgotten. The Earl of Shelburne had often recommended that the imperial government take the sale of land out of the hands of the speculators and reap the rich profits from land sales for itself, and this idea had received an increasing amount of attention. Even while the Vandalia colony seemed to be approaching reality the idea was tentatively adopted by the Privy Council, and orders were sent, in April, 1773, to all the governors of royal provinces to stop granting lands altogether until a new policy could be devised. It was found that the powers of the governors to grant lands varied greatly, and that literally millions of acres had been granted away without any appreciable return to the Crown. Then, as a result of its deliberations, the Privy Council sent out orders to the colonial governors which embodied a new policy.

Henceforward, according to these new orders, all new grants of land were to be surveyed before granting—contrary to the previous custom. Surveys were to be made in lots of from one hundred to one thousand acres, and were to be sold at auction for the profit of the Crown. The net effect of this policy, had it been carried into effect, would have been to stop, or discourage, speculation in vast areas of land, and to encourage the small purchaser and landowner. Unfortunately, however, it never had a fair trial, since it was promulgated in the fatal year of the coercive acts against Massachusetts and Dunmore's Indian war on the frontier.

It did, however, excite the antagonism of the ·land speculators, and was immediately and violently branded as another example of British tyranny. It was formulated in a genuine effort to remedy the too-long tolerated abuses in the administration of western lands. But, taken in connection with the efforts of the Crown to control American commerce, it certainly did appear to have the effect of strangling the potential outlet of American capital through investment in the west. In the American view the lands of the west belonged to the colonies by charter; the assumption, since 1763, of imperial administration of those lands on the ground that they belonged to the empire rather than to the colonies, appeared to be both a violation of the charters and an unwarranted interference in a realm where the colonies believed themselves legally autonomous under their colonial constitutions.

THE QUEBEC ACT, 1774

While the vacillating British government was slowly and fumblingly finding its way toward an intelligent policy regarding the territory between the "ministerial line" and the mountains, the region farther west, and particularly the region lying north and west of the Ohio, was practically forgotten. In general, British policy envisaged a great Indian reservation to the west of the "ministerial line" where the fur trade would be preserved and the Indians kept at peace. But this policy of neglect worked a special hardship on the fertile region lying between the Wabash and Mississippi rivers known as the Illinois country, where the French had built the villages of Kaskaskia, Cahokia, and Vincennes and the military post at Fort Chartres. The fort and village at Detroit and the trading posts at Michilimackinack and Green Bay were in much the same case; but as they were garrison posts under the control of the commander-in-chief of the military forces, and trading posts under the general supervision of the Indian agent, they were not so badly off.

The French farmers and traders in the Illinois settlements had resided there, now, nearly a century. They had been fairly prosperous, and they had generally been considered as belonging to the colony of Louisiana, although they also had important connections with Canada, and stood on the main route of communication between the two French colonies. Now, cut off from Louisiana by the terms of the Treaty of Paris (1763), and from Quebec by the royal proclamation of the same year, these communities were without civil government of any kind except such local makeshifts as they could arrange for themselves. For the Proclamation of 1763 had made no provision for the civil government of the vast territory cut off from the other colonies by the proclamation line.

When peace was finally made with Pontiac, in 1765, the merchants of the eastern seaboard hastened to bring these western posts into their economic orbit. The posts on the Great Lakes maintained their trade connections with Quebec, as formerly, where a group of enterprising Scottish merchants rapidly took over the western trade formerly controlled by Frenchmen. But the merchants of Philadelphia seized upon the Illinois country as their own special province. Thus it came about that when peace was made with Pontiac the Philadelphia firm of Baynton, Wharton and Morgan had already sent large quantities of merchandise over the mountains to Pittsburgh, and began shipping them down the Ohio River in flatboats in the spring of 1766. Thereafter, year after year for several years, this company and David Franks and Company, a rival group in Philadelphia, made of the Ohio a highway for their traffic to the Illinois. There they hoped to make large profits from the trade with the French and with the Indians and from the business of supplying the troops in the Illinois country. But the rivalry of interloping French and Spanish traders from across the Mississippi and of the Scottish fur merchants of Montreal diminished their profits from the fur trade, and the gradual withdrawal of troops diminished their commissary business, with the result that Baynton, Wharton and Morgan withdrew from the Illinois country entirely, and Franks and Company fared little better.

The penetration of the Illinois country, however, called attention to its attractiveness and to its need for civil government. Colonel John Wilkins did attempt, with the aid of George Morgan, one of the Philadelphia merchants, to set up a court of justice in 1768. The court was split by factions, however, and Daniel Bloüin, one of the native French residents, journeyed to New York to ask General Gage to permit the establishment of a colonial government in the Illinois country patterned after that of Connecticut.

Nothing came of this effort, but the merchants, having failed to make money from their trade, turned to the possibilities of land speculation. The result was the formation of the Illinois Land Company, organized by David Franks and Company, and the Wabash Land Company, organized by William Murray with the patronage of Governor Dunmore of Virginia, for the exploitation of the lands of this area in what later came to be known as the Northwest Territory. But it was not the intention of the British Crown to encourage a larger settlement in the Illinois country. The "ministerial line" of 1768 was regarded as final, and the ministry, far from encouraging the growth of this area, so far to the west of the line, sought to discourage it, even, if necessary, to the point of removing to Quebec the French families already there.

Meanwhile, the province of Quebec was itself a problem of no small importance before the British ministry. The Proclamation of

1763 had provided that Quebec, like East Florida, West Florida, and the West Indian colony of Grenada, should have a government patterned after those of the old royal provinces, that is to say, with a governor and a council appointed by the king, and an assembly elected by the property holders among the people. Further, the

MAP 18. Colonial Projects in the New West, 1748-1775

people of the new provinces were to have the benefit of English law and English courts.

Governor James Murray had not been long in Canada, however, before he discovered that, in these provisions, a blunder had been made. The French *habitants* of the province did not understand English law nor the English court system. Nor did they have any understanding of the institutions of representative government. They spoke the French language, and were Roman Catholics, whereas the newcomers were English-speaking Protestants. Any effort, therefore, to impose the English system, either of law or of government, upon them, was sure to arouse their resentment, and Murray astutely delayed the application of these provisions of the proclamation while appealing to the home government to make an exception for Quebec with special provisions for governing the Canadians in a way more like that to which they were accustomed.

Murray's task was made especially difficult by a small group of English-speaking merchants and others who had swarmed into Canada after the conquest, who demanded their "rights of Englishmen" in the form of English law, jury trials and representative government. Murray finally resigned in disgust, and was succeeded by Sir Guy Carleton (later Baron Dorchester), in 1768.

Governor Carleton lent a sympathetic ear to the French citizens of Canada. He realized that a too abrupt break with the past of the province would be a blunder, and that some concessions must be made in the matters of language and law. In the matter of the government, Carleton was convinced that the French were not prepared for representative institutions, the establishment of which could only result in a government of this all-French population by a small, if noisy, minority of Englishmen. Furthermore, as time wore on, and as the breach between the old colonies and the mother country widened after 1770, Carleton realized that, were the discontent of the Canadians not wisely dealt with, Canada would be likely to join the rebellious colonies to the south. On the other hand, were the Canadians to be pacified, and should the troubles with the old colonies eventuate in civil war, Canada would provide a loyal base of operations against the rebels.

In 1770, therefore, Carleton returned to England to urge upon the ministry the desirability of a liberal policy toward Canada. His urging was not heeded, however, until the tea disturbances of late 1773 and the retaliatory actions of 1774 had convinced the British government that the Canadian problem must be solved. Meanwhile, also, the unanswered question of the ultimate disposition of the settlements in the Illinois country had become increasingly troublesome by reason of the demands of the inhabitants for a civil government and the activities of land speculators in this land, which the ministry definitely did not wish to settle. Early in 1774, Parliament turned its attention to these two problems, and found the solution to both of them in the famous Quebec Act of June, 1774.

The Quebec act provided that, so far as law and government were concerned, the province should remain much as it had been before the conquest. French civil law was to remain in force, but English law should apply in criminal cases, thus providing the jury system for such cases. The plan for a representative assembly was abandoned, and, instead, the act provided that government should be merely by the governor and his appointed council. The Roman Catholic religion was specifically recognized, "subject to the King's Supremacy," together with its right to collect tithes from its communicants. Finally, the bounds of the province were extended to include all the lands between the Ohio and Mississippi rivers and the southern edge of the Hudson Bay basin.

For the people of Quebec, this was an eminently wise and states-manlike law. It was a recognition of the fact that the culture and the institutions of a people cannot be changed completely over-night. As such, it pacified the French-Canadians, and may have saved their loyalty for England during the Revolution. Histor-ically and geographically, too, there was much to justify the annexa-tion of the northwest territory to Quebec, and it had the long-desired effect of providing a civil government for that region. But by this time the passions of the Americans were roused against the mother country, and the Quebec Act was assailed as another glar-ing example of British tyranny. The suspension of jury trial in civil cases and the abandonment of representative government were fixed upon as violation of those sacred shibboleths of the British consti-tution and the rights of Englishmen, and an augury of the fate that awaited the Americans. The recognition of the Roman Catholic establishment was bitterly denounced by the Protestant colonists, especially as a precedent for the establishment of some state church, perhaps the Anglican, over them as an agency of the royal tyranny.

But the bitterest outcry was with regard to the new boundaries. For by this act the claims of Virginia to the northwest territory were seemingly cut off forever. The plans of the land speculators in the area received a severe setback, and this, coupled with the apparent intention of the Crown to set up the Vandalia colony by royal de-cree and the new "small-holdings" policy with regard to lands elsewhere in the colonies, seemed to shut off completely the trans-Allegheny west from exploitation by the old colonies. It raised again the troublesome question whether the lands west of the moun-tains belonged to the Crown or to the colonies under their "sea-to-sea" charters. There was only one side most of the Americans could take; and the Quebec act, therefore, greatly widened the already growing breach between the colonies and England.

THE WEST AND THE IMPERIAL CONFLICT

The problem confronting the British government with regard to
the American west after the Treaty of Paris was thus fundamentally
a sociological one. The expanding population of the old colonies
had begun to sweep into the Mississippi valley to occupy the inviting lands to be found there; and it is probable that nothing could
have stemmed that tide. This movement of population, however,
brought to a new crisis the old conflict between the two races of
white men and Indians, the issue of which was inevitable but un-
reached for another century. Supporting the movement stood the
wealthy and influential men in the colonies, many of whom were
personally interested in the development of the west, who were prepared to insist not only that the stream of population flow on, but
that the old colonies have the direction and the financial benefits
from it.

The British ministry, shackled by factional politics, stumbled
falteringly along the inevitable path toward a policy for the American west, now favoring the expansionist school of mercantilist politicians, now favoring the conservative, raw-materials school. In general, the policy followed by the ministry in the eleven years following the Peace of Paris was a policy of gradual expansion. But the
details of that policy, as they appeared in the Vandalia project and
in the final land policy of 1774, brought the ministry into sharp
and fundamental conflict with the very men who were opposed to
the recent policies of the mother country on other grounds.

Fundamental to the conflict over the west was the question of
imperial ownership as against colonial ownership; and the British
assumption of imperial ownership after a long period when the
administration of vacant lands had been left largely in the hands
of the colonial governments opened an economic and jurisdictional
conflict which was just as bitter and just as profound as the conflicts over commerce and colonial autonomy that were shaking the
eastern seaboard. In order to see how these major elements in the
struggle worked together to produce the American Revolution it is
now necessary to turn back and trace the story of the widening rift
in the empire from 1770 to 1774.

RECOMMENDED BOOKS FOR FURTHER READING

CONTEMPORARY NARRATIVES

Clarence W. Alvord, ed., *The New Régime, 1765-1767.*
Jonathan Carver, *Travels through the Interior Parts of North America in the Years 1766, 1767, and 1768.*
John Dickinson, *Letters of a Pennsylvania Farmer.*
Illinois State Historical Library, *Collections,* IX-X, XVI.
William Johnson, *The Papers of Sir William Johnson,* edited by James Sullivan and Alexander C. Flick, I-IV.
Louise P. Kellogg, ed., *Frontier Advance on the Upper Ohio, 1778-1779.*
Louise P. Kellogg, ed., *Frontier Retreat on the Upper Ohio, 1779-1781.*
Theodore C. Pease, ed., *Anglo-French Boundary Disputes in the West, 1749-1763.*
Reuben G. Thwaites and Louise P. Kellogg, eds., *Documentary History of Dunmore's War.*
Reuben G. Thwaites, ed., *Early Western Travels,* I-II.

MODERN ACCOUNTS

Thomas P. Abernethy, *From Frontier tô Plantation in Tennessee.*
Thomas P. Abernethy, *Western Lands and the American Revolution.*
Herbert B. Adams, *Maryland's Influence upon Land Cessions to the United States.*
George H. Alden, *New Governments West of the Alleghenies before 1780.*
Clarence W. Alvord, *The Illinois Country, 1673-1818.*
Clarence W. Alvord, *The Mississippi Valley in British Politics.*
Clarence E. Carter, *Great Britain and the Illinois Country, 1763-1774.*
Charles Gayarré, *History of Louisiana,* Volume III.
Lawrence H. Gipson, *The British Empire before the American Revolution,* Volume IV.
Charles A. Hanna, *The Wilderness Trail.*
Louis Koontz, *Robert Dinwiddie.*
George E. Lewis, *The Indiana Company, 1763-1798.*
Francis Parkman, *Conspiracy of Pontiac and the Indian War after the Conquest of Canada.*
Frederic L. Paxson, *History of the American Frontier, 1763-1893,* Chapters 1-3.
Arthur Pound, *Johnson of the Mohawks.*
Theodore Roosevelt, *The Winning of the West,* Volume I.
Max Savelle, *George Morgan, Colony Builder.*
Frederick J. Turner, *The Significance of the Frontier in American History,* Chapters 4-6.
Albert T. Volwiler, *George Croghan and the Westward Movement, 1741-1782.*
Justin Winsor, *The Mississippi Basin.*

43

The Rift in the Empire, 1770-76

THE ROOTS OF FRICTION

THE REPEAL of the Townshend duties by Lord North's government in 1770 left certain fundamental questions still unanswered. Did Parliament have the right to legislate for the colonies—and, if so, did that right extend to taxation, "internal" or "external"? Did the Crown have the right to coerce colonial legislatures? Did the British government have the right to quarter troops in America contrary to the wishes of the colonial legislatures, and ask the Americans to pay for the troops' support? Most important of all, must the Americans humbly submit to economic discrimination by the mother country—economic discrimination that threatened to stifle American commerce and reduce the colonies to the status of "another Ireland" and that threatened effectively to block the capitalistic development of the west by Americans in favor of land speculators resident in England? From the point of view of responsible, thoughtful businessmen in America, to submit to the revised British colonial system would bring America perilously near to economic suicide by strangulation.

It should be noted that the more important features of the revised colonial system remained: in the vice-admiralty courts, the board of customs, the actual "external" taxation in the remaining import duties, and the centralized administration of colonial affairs in the office of the Secretary of State for the Colonies; in the Defense of America and the quartering acts; and in the changing, pro-British policy toward the American west. Yet the repeal of the major portion of the Townshend duties quieted American disturbances for the time being, and there was a distinct lull in American resistance. The merchants, even before the repeal, had begun to be dissatisfied with the non-importation agreements. The paralysis of business was just as discouraging to them as to the English. The import trade fell off, though not entirely because of the non-importation agreements, and the export trade went into a slump from which it recovered only slowly. Goods were scarce, prices had a tendency to rise, and the merchants found themselves severely criticized for their "lack of patriotism."

Far more important and disturbing, however, was the breach that was appearing between the merchants, who had originally instigated colonial resistance, and the popular elements upon whom they had depended for popular support. The "Sons of Liberty" had taken the merchants at their word when they based their resistance upon high constitutional argument and the "rights of Englishmen." Now, as prices began to rise, the popular elements began bitterly to criticize their merchant leaders. Thus, when news of the partial repeal of the duties arrived in America in the spring of 1770, the merchants were not only divided among themselves as to what to do next, but they also found themselves facing the antagonism of the non-mercantile population. Some of the colonial ports agreed to keep the non-importation agreements in force; others were willing to relax them. The merchants of New York and Philadelphia were divided; but a good many colonial merchants merely nullified the agreements by renewing their trade with England. The non-mercantile consumers, however, now having been aroused by the argument that the Townshend duties constituted taxation, would not be satisfied as long as even a single one of the old duties remained in force. Despite the popular opposition, the New York merchants abandoned non-importation early in July, 1770, and the other commercial ports gradually followed suit. A rift had appeared between the merchants and the non-mercantile public; and this rift had given birth to two diverging points of view, those of the "moderates" and the "radicals"—of which more must be said later.

The breakdown of non-importation marked the beginning of three years of relative prosperity. American imports from Great Britain doubled and trebled. Even the tea duty was acquiesed in. Good times meant good feelings; and had nothing happened to drive the "moderates" again into the hands of the "radicals," Great Britain might not have lost an empire. The merchants and men of property had come to fear and distrust "the mob" more than they did the British navigation system; and they were willing to submit to the restrictions being placed upon them rather than promote, or even face, the social forces that had so frighteningly displayed their power. As Cadwallader Colden wrote, "All Men of property are so sensible of their danger, from Riots and tumults, that they will not rashly be induced to enter into combinations, which may promote disorder for the future, but will endeavour to promote due subordination to legal authority."

The "radicals," however, were not disposed to let the fires of discord die. They had seen what force and organization could do;

and they made the most of the lull to improve their organization while keeping alive, by every device of publicity and organization, the emotions of distrust and fear that had flared up after the Grenville acts and the Townshend acts. Nor were they entirely without excuse. The British warships along the coast had precipitated occasional riots by the impressment of seamen, and distrust of the soldiers in Boston was increased by friction between them and the working people. On March 5, 1770, a clash between the soldiery and the citizenry that started with the snow-balling of a sentry at the customs house resulted in the soldiers firing upon the citizens and killing four of them and wounding several others. The soldiers were withdrawn to Castle William, in the harbor, but the "Boston Massacre" became a rallying cry for the radicals, at the head of whom stood Samuel Adams. Adams, with his close friend and fellow revolutionary, Joseph Warren, now proceeded to organize committees of radicals in the town meetings of Massachusetts, and these committees cooperated in keeping alive the issues. The response to their efforts was feeble, however, until the *"Gaspee* incident" furnished a new spark for the smoldering emotions of distrust and fear.

The *Gaspee* was a schooner employed by the customs collectors as a revenue cutter in Narragansett Bay, where smuggling was rife. On June 9, 1772, the *Gaspee* ran aground near Providence. During the night a large body of civilians boarded the schooner, set the crew ashore, and burned the hateful symbol of British oppression. The incident enraged the British officials in America and the British government at home, but the inquiry into the affair failed to produce any culprits. On the other hand, it did result in the formation of an intercolonial system of committees of correspondence like those organized in Massachusetts by Samuel Adams. Led by Virginia, where Patrick Henry, Thomas Jefferson, and Richard Henry Lee, in the Virginia assembly, furnished the leadership, radicals in some of the colonies formed such committees for discovering and exchanging information and ideas relative to the troubles with the mother country. This was the nucleus of the new intercolonial organization which was to be in large measure responsible for the formation of the common intercolonial front presented to the mother country in 1776.

THE TEA PARTY AND AFTER

The British blunder which really gave the radicals an issue and brought the intercolonial organization to life was the famous Tea

Act of 1773. The British East India Company, for a century and a half the greatest of British commercial enterprises, had fallen on evil days. Mismanagement, troubles in India, Dutch competition and graft had nearly bankrupted the company. Its stock was selling far below par, and it was heavily in debt. It had 17,000,000 pounds of tea on its hands, and the American market, greatly reduced by non-importation, seemed to be permanently lost to it. For a flourishing illicit tea business had sprung up in the colonies, so flourishing that perhaps nine-tenths of the tea imported into America after 1770 was foreign (mostly Dutch), and was brought into the colonies without paying even the three-penny duty of the old Townshend act. The British Parliament, therefore, in order to assist the failing company as well as to stamp out the illegal tea business in America, passed the tea act, which provided that the British East India Company might ship its tea to America without previously paying the duty on tea imported into England, and that it might sell its tea directly to American merchants instead of by auction in London as heretofore. One result of this bill was that the company was now required to pay only the three-penny Townshend duty on tea imported into America, which actually made the price of its tea lower to American consumers than to Englishmen and made possible successful competition with illicitly imported foreign tea. Another result was that now the British East India Company, through its favored agents in the colonies—merchants who had opposed non-importation—might become the direct competitor of American merchants. In general, this was an extreme case of short-sighted discrimination against the Americans and American economic life in favor of merchants in England. Submission would have been a real, if not very great, economic loss to American business; but the precedent would have been set for more important and deep-reaching discriminations later on.

The effect in America was immediate and violent. The merchants, who had come to fear the mob, were once more driven to call the "popular elements" to their support. Thus the "little people"—laborers, farmers, and small shopkeepers—united their efforts to those of the merchants, and the radical leaders made the most of their opportunity to arouse public opinion all over the colonies against British "oppression." When the company's tea arrived at Charleston it was locked up in warehouses, and it was not allowed to be sold. At Philadelphia and New York the popular outcry was such that some of the tea ships were sent back to England without unloading the tea. When the tea ships came to Boston, popular meetings demanded of Lieutenant-Governor Hutchinson that he send them home. But he refused to allow them to clear until they had unloaded; whereupon, on the night of December 16, 1773, a group of men dressed as Indians boarded the ships, took the tea, valued at about £15,000, from the holds and threw it overboard into the waters of the harbor.

This incident completely and permanently ended the calm of the preceding three years. In England it was looked upon as an outrage, and Lord North immediately asked Parliament for legislation authorizing him to suppress the disorders in the colonies and to insure a proper "dependence of the colonies upon the crown and Parliament of Great Britain." Parliament responded handsomely, in April, 1774, by enacting the series of laws known to Americans as the "intolerable acts." The first of these was an act closing the port of Boston to all business, in or out, until the British East India Company should be reimbursed for the loss of the tea that had been thrown overboard. A second act provided that British officials or agents charged with offenses committed in the line of duty while suppressing disorder or enforcing the law might be tried in other colonies or in England, in order that they might have fair trials. A third act provided for the quartering of soldiers in the localities where they might be needed; and if the barracks were not in convenient places, the soldiers might be quartered in taverns and vacant buildings on the spot. These three acts were of a more or less temporary and disciplinary nature.

The fourth group of laws in this series was of a more permanent sort. The governors of the colonies of Massachusetts, long at odds with the legislature and the people, had often recommended that the Massachusetts charter of 1691 be revoked and that the government of the colony be reorganized along the lines of the royal provinces of New York or Virginia. Now the question came up again, and, at the suggestion of Lord George Germain, later Secretary of State for the Colonies, the old charter was amended by a group of laws which completely revised the Massachusetts government. Under these laws the councilors of the colony, formerly nominated by the assembly under the provisions of the charter, were to be appointed directly by the Crown, as in Virginia. The town meetings were severely restricted: they might meet only by permission of the governor; and jurors, formerly chosen by the town meetings, were henceforth to be named by the sheriffs, thus assuring juries more favorable to the Crown than heretofore. At the same time, General Thomas Gage was made temporary governor of Massachusetts to replace Thomas Hutchinson, who left for England on June 1, 1774, the day the Boston Port Act went into effect.

This series of enactments by Parliament, coupled, in the minds of the Americans, with the Quebec Act—which, as we know, had no connection with the dispute with Massachusetts—precipitated a wave of resentment in the colonies surpassing anything that had gone before. At a meeting of representatives of the towns of Suffolk County, Massachusetts, a set of resolutions was adopted which denounced the coercive acts as contrary to the right of the Americans—rights which were theirs by "the laws of nature, the British constitution, and the charter of the province." This appeal to constitutions based on natural law was typical of the American Revolution. It was also a distinct step in the direction of independence. The fourth resolution proclaimed that "no obedience is due from this province to either or any part of the acts above-mentioned, but that they may be rejected as the attempts of a wicked administration to enslave America." These resolutions were later endorsed by the First Continental Congress. Meanwhile, the Suffolk meeting recommended that the new government of Massachusetts be disregarded; that sheriffs and other officials continue to perform their duties as before the act; and that the citizens arm themselves and be prepared to defend their right by force, if necessary. The Virginia assembly, on the motion of Thomas Jefferson, set aside a day of fasting and prayer. When the assembly was dissolved because of this act, Jefferson and eighty-four of his associates joined in an expression of sympathy for Boston and suggested that a general meeting of all the colonies be called to consider the formation of a common front against British oppression. In Virginia and elsewhere food and supplies were collected for the relief of the Bostonians, and a great wave of sympathy for the oppressed colony swept over all the others.

Public opinion in America was now aroused as never before. Pamphlets poured from the presses, and newspapers were filled with letters from "Spartacus," "Cincinnatus," "Massachusettensis," and many another Greek or Roman patriot. Patriotism, indeed, was of two conflicting kinds. One brand placed loyalty to America and the American cause first; the other placed loyalty to the king and the empire above all other loyalties. Even the "American patriots" still claimed to be loyal to the Crown; but they, more or less like Thomas Jefferson, now appealed to the Crown against the usurpation of authority by the Parliament of Great Britain over other equal parts of the empire and its encroachments "upon those rights which God and the laws have given equally and independently to all." Jefferson rejected the entire colonial policy of Great Britain since 1763, especially proclaiming the doctrines of free trade and legislative autonomy for the colonists as natural rights. "No longer persevere," he cried to the king, "in sacrificing the rights of one part of the empire to the inordinate desires of another; but deal out to all equal and impartial right."

On the other hand, those Americans who reprobated the violence and the insubordination of the colonies found in the coercive acts an entirely proper set of disciplinary measures against a colony that had let "independency" and mob violence go entirely too far. They, like Jonathan Boucher, a loyalist Anglican clergyman of Annapolis, believed in the divine right of the king of England to rule over his people in America, and also that, in the last analysis, all the people could in right do was to accept the king's authority and have faith in his benevolence. It seemed to these writers that it was now squarely up to the king, after such rebellious acts as the "Boston tea party," to assert his authority once and for all. If he did not do so, the colonies were, and would remain, totally independent of the empire—a condition which the loyalists could envisage only with the deepest horror.

THE FIRST CONTINENTAL CONGRESS

It was under these conditions that the first Continental Congress met on September 5, 1774. From the colonial point of view, the very existence of all the colonies seemed to be wrapped up in the struggle of Massachusetts. For if Great Britain succeeded in crushing Massachusetts, the same fate would probably await them all. The "rump" meeting of the Virginia burgesses had suggested the advisability of a meeting of representatives of all the colonies. Now the suggestion was taken up, and representatives of twelve of the thirteen colonies came together to discuss their common grievances and formulate a common policy. Fifty-five delegates attended; some of them had been elected by their colonial assemblies, others had been chosen at extra-legal meetings. More than half of the delegates hoped, and believed, that the disputes with the mother country could still be settled without violence. These men, such as John Dickinson and Joseph Galloway of Pennsylvania, John Rutledge of South Carolina and John Jay of New York, representing the body of "moderate" opinion in the colonies, were fearful of the "popular" and "democratic" tendencies in America, and looked upon the power and authority of the empire as the only sure guarantee of law and order. For them, oppression by the mother country was bad, but might be alleviated by petition and protest; "democracy" would be infinitely and intolerably worse. But these men also sought to preserve the constitutional gains that had been made by the colonies in the direction of legislative autonomy. Their problem was thus to formulate a conception of the British empire that would preserve both the sheet-anchor bond of imperial authority and the degree of freedom inherent in the colonial constitutions. It was with this idea in mind that Joseph Galloway brought in a plan for colonial union that closely resembled the Albany plan of 1754. Under this plan he proposed that a federation of the colonies be formed under a president general to be appointed by the Crown and a grand council to be elected by the colonial legislatures. The president general would be given authority to regulate intercolonial affairs, as an American section of the British Parliament, thus providing an answer to the problem of parliamentary representation. Either the American or the British section of Parliament would be allowed to initiate legislation pertaining to intercolonial affairs, but the approval of both sections would be necessary before any such legislation could take effect.

This moderate and promising plan failed of adoption by only one vote. But that slender margin determined the temper of the Congress as sufficiently "radical" to take a firm, even revolutionary stand against the mother country. The radical leaders were Samuel Adams and John Adams of Massachusetts, Richard Henry Lee and Patrick Henry of Virginia, Roger Sherman of Connecticut, Charles Thomson of Pennsylvania, and Christopher Gadsden of South Carolina. These men, in contrast with the moderates, were most fearful, not of democratic tendencies, but of the oppressive tendencies of the mother country. Basing their position upon the general idea of natural law and its derivative natural rights of men, they maintained that the rights of Englishmen, for which they insisted they were struggling, were natural, inalienable rights under natural law. These rights were thus inalienable by Parliament. On the contrary, the radicals rejected completely all parliamentary authority over the colonies, implying that they were independent states, each with its own legislature, and were bound together only by their common loyalty to the Crown as the symbol of British unity.

As the Congress proceeded with its work, the hold of the radicals upon it strengthened. On September 18 the "Suffolk Resolves" were endorsed by the Congress, and on October 14 it adopted a "Declaration of Rights" setting forth the American position. After reviewing the various acts of the British Parliament since 1763 which seemed calculated to restrict American liberties, the declaration listed the following as rights of the inhabitants of the British Colonies in North America: (1) "life, liberty and property," and the right to have these taken away or modified only by their own consent; (2) "all the rights, immunities of free and natural-born subjects within the realm of England"; (3) the right to tax themselves and legislate for themselves through their representatives, though nevertheless the right of Parliament to legislate for the empire as a whole, but only for "regulation" and not for "revenue," was recognized; (4) the right of trial by jury, in the neighborhood where the offense was committed; (5) the right to "all the immunities and privileges granted and confirmed to them by royal charters, or secured by their several codes of provincial laws"; (6) the rights of orderly assembly and petition to the king; (7) the right of the colonial legislature only to decide whether a standing army should be maintained within its borders; (8) the right of the colonists to elect both houses of their legislatures. On the resolutions accompanying the statement of these rights, the Congress declared the coercive acts and many of the acts of Parliament in the Grenville and Townshend series, as also the Quebec Act, "infringements and violations" of the above-mentioned rights, and stated that all these acts must be repealed before harmony could be restored between the colonies and the mother country.

The most significant action of the Congress, perhaps, was the adoption, on October 20, of an intercolonial agreement known as "The Association." By this agreement a stringent non-importation was revived; no British goods were to be consumed, and no goods were to be exported to Britain. Furthermore, for the purpose of bringing additional pressure to bear on the mother country, the non-import and non-export aspects of the Association were extended to the British West Indies as well as to England and Ireland. Every encouragement was to be given to home manufactures, especially the manufacture of wool. All extravagance and dissipation was to be discouraged, even to the point of discarding mourning dress and the habit of giving gifts at funerals! In order that the agreement might be fully and faithfully carried out, committees were to be chosen in every county, city and town by the voters, and these committees watched and publicized the conduct of all persons who were suspected of disloyalty to the American cause.

Before the Congress adjourned, on October 26, it adopted ad

dresses to the people of Great Britain and of the province of Quebec, and a petition to King George III. The address to the people of Great Britain protested against the establishment of Roman Catholicism in Quebec and sought to convince the British people of the reasonableness of the American position; the address to the people of Quebec sought to incite them to rebel against British "tyranny." The Quebec Act had very effectively quieted the complaints of the people of that province, however, and there was but little response. As its last act the Congress called for a second meeting to take place in May, 1775.

The acts of the first Continental Congress indicate the extent of the victory of the "radicals" over the "moderates." With no legal basis for its existence, the Congress had assumed the right to speak for all the colonies. It had "nationalized" the issue between the colonies and the mother country, and it had created in the local communities the machinery which made it possible for a vigorous minority to block economic life, interfere in the lives of citizens with whom it was not in sympathy, and completely to shut off freedom of speech. The moderates, representing chiefly the class of merchants, were confounded at what they had done. For they had called into being a movement which now threatened rebellion and independence, and they were faced with a choice of going along with the movement or of turning back to the mother country and submitting to all the economic and political disabilities that that would mean. It is not surprising that many of them, like Joseph Galloway, chose the latter, and became "tories." Others, like John Dickinson, who went along with the revolutionary movement, did so with the determination to keep it in as conservative bounds as possible.

THE ROAD TO REVOLUTION

The members of the first Continental Congress protested their loyalty to the Crown, and spoke of themselves, in the preamble to the Association, as "We, His Majesty's most loyal subjects." But the publication of the various acts of the Congress precipitated a storm of protest and opposition, both in England and in America. If anything, the Congress widened the breach between the colonies and the mother country rather than healed it.

In England, the reaction was severe. The elections for the new Parliament that met on November 1, 1774, had shown that the sentiment of the country was clearly behind the coercive policy of the Lord North government. It was felt that conciliation had been tried, in the repeal of the stamp act and the Townshend duties, but that conciliation had only encouraged the Americans to increase their demands. In the eyes of Englishmen, the Americans either were subjects of the Crown, or they were not. Since Parliament was the supreme legislature for all British subjects, the American colonies were subject to Parliament's laws, just as were the unrepresented areas of England of which there were many—by the principle of "virtual representation." The resistance of Massachusetts and the other American provinces clearly challenged the principle of parliamentary authority, which was essentially a challenge to the authority of the Crown itself. Thus to accept the American position was tantamount to admitting that the colonies were essentially independent, which no Britisher was willing to do. As conciliation had failed, therefore, the logic of the situation seemed to demand not less, but more, coercion.

It was for reasons such as these that Lord North now proposed new coercive measures against the "rebellious" Americans. The military forces already in the colonies were to be reinforced. A counter-blow against New England and non-importation was struck in the New England Restraining Act of March 30, 1775, which provided that no New England province would be allowed to trade with any country in the world except Great Britain or the British West Indies, nor would such a province be permitted to use the fisheries. Then, when it was seen that the other provinces were in sympathy with New England, the provisions of this act were extended to all the others except New York, Delaware, North Carolina and Georgia. Thus all the colonies, with these exceptions, were practically blockaded, so far as foreign trade was concerned. Yet there were those in England who urged a more moderate course. The Earl of Chatham, the great William Pitt, proposed that an effort be made to win American recognition of Parliament's right to taxation, after which annual American congresses might be held for the purpose of making free grants to the Crown; if this were done, Parliament might then promise never to exercise its right to tax the colonies.

Lord North himself, realizing the determination of the Americans and pushed by the merchants who were losing money by American non-importation, had decided in the meantime upon one last effort at appeasement of the colonies. This was made on February 20, when he proposed that as soon as any colony should make a satisfactory offer for the support of its own defense and its Crown officials, it would be exempt from any imperial taxation other than for the simple regulation of trade. But this offer was spurned by the colonies; indeed, by the time when it arrived in America it was already much too late for reconciliation.

For events in America were now taking place with great rapidity. The "Committees of Safety" created with the Association were effectively enforcing its provisions. England's exports to the twelve "associated colonies" shrank in one year by nearly ninety-seven per cent. Persons suspected of British sympathies were sedulously watched; they were abused and insulted, and were even subjected to personal violence. Many tories were tarred and feathered, burned in effigy, or driven from their homes. The "committees of correspondence," organized after the tea act and the coercive acts, working with the local committees to enforce the Association, took almost complete charge of the situation in practically all the provinces. By the end of 1774, the committees in ten of the colonies had succeeded in organizing provincial congresses. Most of these congresses were extra-legal, and were formed in defiance of the governors; but they generally contained many of the same men who had sat in the provincial legislatures. These provincial congresses stood strongly together in their support of Massachusetts, and it was these bodies that designated provincial representatives to the second Continental Congress.

The local committees had also begun to gather stores of arms and ammunition in case of need. This was particularly true in Massachusetts, where General Gage had orders to seize such stores and to arrest Samuel Adams and John Hancock, the leaders of the provincial congress, and send them to England for trial. It was his attempt to seize the military stores at Concord and to arrest Adams and Hancock, on April 19, 1775, that led to the bloodshed on the village green of Lexington and all along the road back from Concord to Boston.

The road to Lexington and Concord was the road to revolution; for at Lexington and Concord the War of American Independence had begun.

THE SECOND CONTINENTAL CONGRESS

Three weeks after Lexington and Concord, on May 10, 1775, the second Continental Congress met in Philadelphia. Lord Dartmouth, Secretary of State for the Colonies, had instructed the colonial governors to prevent the naming of delegates to the new Continental Congress, with the result that they were selected by radical conventions instead of by the provincial assemblies. The membership of the Congress was consequently much more radical than that of its predecessor, and it had even less legal basis for its existence. All thirteen of the older continental colonies were represented, and among the new members were Benjamin Franklin and Thomas Jefferson, the latter of whom took George Washington's seat for Virginia when Washington left to take charge of the American army.

One of the first acts of the second Continental Congress was a declaration of war on Great Britain. Still protesting its loyalty to the king, the Congress created a continental army that included the "minute men" around Boston, and named George Washington its commander-in-chief. Then the Congress issued, on July 6, 1775, almost exactly a year before the Declaration of Independence, an eloquent "Declaration of Causes of Taking up Arms." This declaration reviewed again the steps by which the breach had grown between the colonies and England, culminating in the "unprovoked assault" of Gage upon the people of Massachusetts at Lexington.

His troops have butchered our countrymen [it read], have wantonly burnt Charlestown, besides a considerable number of houses in other places; our ships and vessels are seized; the necessary supplies of provisions are intercepted, and he is exerting his utmost power to spread destruction and devastation around him. . . . We are reduced to the alternative of choosing an unconditional submission to the tyranny of irritated ministers or resistance by force. The latter is our choice. . . . Our cause is just. Our union is perfect. . . . In our own native land, in defense of the freedom that is our birthright, and which we ever enjoyed till the late violations of it; for the protection of our property, acquired solely by the honest industry of our forefathers and ourselves, against violence actually offered, we have taken up arms. We shall lay them down when hostilities shall cease on the part of the aggressors, and all danger of their being renewed shall be removed, and not before.

As a final gesture toward conciliation, the Congress, led by the moderate John Dickinson, in July adopted a last humble appeal to the king—the so-called "Olive Branch petition"—which declared again the fundamental loyalty of the Americans to the Crown and appealed to the king to intervene to protect their rights from the tyranny of Parliament. This petition was brought to the king in August, but George III could not see how men who had fired upon English soldiers could still be loyal, and refused to receive it. Nearly a year before, in November, 1774, he had written Lord North that the colonies were then in a state of rebellion and that "blows must decide whether they are to be subject to this country or independent." Lexington and Concord, and the spread of violence over all the colonies, had not changed his mind.

Meanwhile, the Congress had sent emissaries to the West Indies and to Canada to win support for the "American" cause. In the West Indies there was much sympathy; for, while the island colonies were dependent upon the British navy for protection, they also came under the provisions of the acts of trade, and had gone through the same struggle with the prerogative for political autonomy. They were dependent upon the continental colonies for their food supply, and they had participated in the profits of the smuggling business in North America. The assemblies of Jamaica and Barbados therefore passed resolutions supporting Boston. The Bahamas were openly sympathetic, lending the Americans arms from the forts in the islands; Bermuda actually sent delegates to the Continental Congress. Yet the insular position of these colonies, their weakness, their exposure to foreign attack, and their essentially stronger attachment to the mother country made it a foregone conclusion that they could never successfully resist, even if they wished to do so. The crisis in the relationship between the continental colonies and the mother country had also brought a crisis in the relationship between the continent and the islands. The island colonies, faced with the choice, could not but choose to remain loyal. As between them and their continental brethren, the American Revolution brought a parting of the ways, forever.

As for Canada, the situation was different, but the result was the same. In the spring of 1776, the Continental Congress sent Benjamin Franklin and Charles Carroll, a Roman Catholic from Maryland, and Carroll's cousin John Carroll, later Archbishop of Baltimore, to Canada, already occupied in large part by American armies, to try to persuade the Canadians to join forces against the "tyranny" of England. They went to Montreal, where Franklin put to work the printing press he had brought with him, printing propaganda. But they found the Canadians acutely hostile. Canada had been, on the whole, well pleased by the Quebec Act, and the invasion of Canada by two American armies under Benedict Arnold and Richard Montgomery had done nothing to soften the bitter distrust, even hatred, of the older English colonies that was their heritage from two centuries of border wars. When the American forces were finally driven out of Canada in the summer of 1776, Franklin, the commissioners, and the printing press went with them. Canada was lost to the Americans.

Meanwhile, elsewhere in the colonies, during 1775, the Americans had been moving, step by step, toward the complete extinction of British control. The news of Lexington and Concord had aroused and inflamed American emotions everywhere. Washington, at his home at Mount Vernon, declared, on hearing the news, that it now was either war or slavery. On the frontier, feeling ran high. At Charlotte, in Mecklenburg County, North Carolina, a group of the men of the Piedmont met on May 31, 1775, and adopted resolutions declaring all royal commissions null and void, and "the constitution of each particular colony wholly suspended." This was hardly more than an expression of opinion, but it was an opinion that drew very near to independence.

As the breach rapidly widened, the normal functions of government were widely suspended, and extra-legal provincial congresses took charge. In some cases, the shift of control was accompanied by violence. In Virginia, for example, when Patrick Henry, in defiance of Governor Dunmore, secured the election of delegates to the second Continental Congress, Dunmore began to transfer ammunition from Williamsburg to a British warship, but he was compelled to return it. Then, with the news of Lexington, Dunmore tried to raise a force of loyalists to suppress the incipient rebellion. Failing in that, he went aboard a British warship and departed—not, however, without burning Norfolk, which had fired on the king's ships, on his way. The Virginia convention then assumed charge in that province, declared Dunmore had deserted his post, and proclaimed Virginia's title to the disputed lands in the west. Similarly, in practically all the colonies, the king's authority collapsed and the revolutionary bodies took over.

Such was the situation as the year 1775 wore toward its end. Fighting had taken place in several areas, but as yet the Americans still insisted they were fighting only in defense of their rights as Englishmen, without any thought of independence. On October 26, George III made the usual speech from the throne to a new Parliament, in the course of which he announced his intention of dealing vigorously with the colonies and his plan to engage foreign mercenaries to do the fighting—a plan which placed the Americans in the position, not of Englishmen, but of a foreign enemy. Then appeared, in January, 1776, Thomas Paine's *Common Sense*.

Thomas Paine was an Englishman who had arrived in America only in 1774. Endowed with the peculiar faculty of interpreting the popular mind to itself in popular terms, Paine quickly saw the trend events were taking, and presented, in his pamphlet, the popular, radical solution to the problem—a solution toward which events by this time seemed to be moving inexorably. To begin with, Paine was a republican—a revolutionary characteristic, in the mind of the eighteenth century. He ridiculed the institution of hereditary monarchy in general as "the most prosperous invention the Devil ever set on foot for the promotion of idolatry." But the British monarchy in particular, supported, as he said, by the ruling class as an instrument for the exploitation of the poor both in England and in the colonies, came in for his most eloquent scorn. "The royal brute," George III, was endeavoring to keep the colonies in perpetual slavery; men had fled to America to escape the persecution of the monster at home; now the time had come to separate from such a perverted parent once and for all. The true interest of America lay in the direction of free trade, independence and unhampered expansion in the limitless hinterland of the continent. Small islands need protection, to be sure, "but there is something absurd in supposing a Continent to be perpetually governed by an island." No; nothing short of independence, it seemed to him, could preserve the peace, prosperity and happiness of the Americans. Let them throw off their false reverence for the British Crown, set up their own republican government, and, while preserving friendly economic relations with all countries, turn their backs upon all of Europe and its wrangling oppressors of mankind, and devote themselves to the happy business of developing this continent as free men.

Paine's pamphlet struck a responsive chord in the minds of the hesitating Americans, and gave them the impetus that carried them to independence.

THE DECLARATION OF INDEPENDENCE

During the spring of 1776, the drift toward independence became increasingly clear. The division between "loyalist" and "patriot" became ever more marked and more bitter, and the loyalists began to form armed bands to counter-balance the armed bands of the patriots. This was no longer merely rebellion against Great Britain; it was civil war as well. The North Carolina provincial congress instructed its delegates in the Continental Congress to vote for the independence of all the colonies, and Virginia, shortly afterward, on May 15, instructed its delegates to introduce the necessary motion into the Congress. This was done by Richard Henry Lee early in June.

Meanwhile, during that spring, other significant steps had been taken, both by the Congress and by the provinces. Congress had ordered the disarming of all loyalists and the issuance of letters of marque to privateers against England in March, and, in April, it had recommended the opening of all American ports to foreign ships. Various colonies, uncertain as to how to proceed after the collapse of British authority, had requested advice, and the Continental Congress had responded by a resolution to the effect that it be "recommended" to the colonial assemblies and conventions, "where no government sufficient to the exigencies of their affairs have been hitherto established, to adopt such a government as shall, in the opinion of the representatives of the people, best conduce to the happiness and safety of their constituents in particular, and America in general." As these new governments were to be established without the usual "oaths and affirmations necessary for the support of any government under the Crown of Great Britain," this was tantamount to the organization of independent states.

Thus was the situation prepared for a declaration of independence. On June 7, 1776, Richard Henry Lee introduced three resolutions into the Continental Congress. The first of these stated that "these United Colonies are, and of right ought to be, free and independent States, that they are absolved from all allegiance to the British Crown, and that all political connection between them and the State of Great Britain is, and ought to be, totally dissolved." The second resolution proposed that these independent states form foreign alliances for the maintenance of their independence; the third proposed the formation of a confederation of the united colonies in some sort of a constitution to be approved by them individually. The conservatives in the Congress, led by John Dickinson, succeeded in delaying consideration of the resolution on independence nearly a month, but the radicals had all three resolutions turned over to a committee for study in preparation for the discussion. On this committee were Thomas Jefferson, Benjamin Franklin, and John Adams. The task of making the draft of a declaration of independence was confided to Jefferson, and his draft was then edited by the others.

The debate on Lee's first resolution took place on July 1. The conservatives opposed the move. Dickinson, although at last resigned to independence, sought to delay the step on the ground that the proper moment had not yet come. The radicals were determined, however, and by a certain amount of political maneuvering succeeded in winning the approval of all the thirteen colonies except New York. Thus Lee's resolution was approved by twelve delegations on July 2. Then the draft of the Declaration of Independence was taken up, and, with certain slight amendments, adopted on July 4, 1776.

The Declaration of Independence, which formally announced the separation of thirteen of the British colonies from the old empire, is an eloquent statement of the political theory of the radical wing of American thought of the moment. Though couched in the language of John Locke, it is a crystallization of the political experience of the colonists through two centuries of political evolution. It begins with the basic doctrine of the operation of natural law in human affairs: "We hold these truths to be self-evident, that all men are created equal, that they are endowed by their Creator with certain unalienable rights, that among these are life, liberty, and the pursuit of happiness." Governments, according to this philosophy, are instituted among men to secure these natural rights, "deriving their just powers from the consent of the governed." Thus government is the instrument of the popular will, or social compact, and "whenever any form of government becomes destructive of these ends [the securing of the natural rights of men], it is the right of the people to alter or to abolish it, and to institute new government, laying its foundation on such principles and organizing its powers in such form, as to them shall seem most likely to effect their safety and happiness."

The colonies had suffered, said the Declaration, under a British government that had long evinced "a design to reduce them under absolute despotism," and they were now under the necessity of throwing off that old, destructive government and setting up a new one "to provide new guards for their future security." The major part of the document, like a lawyer's brief, is given to a list of the violations of the compact between the American people and the Crown committed by the latter that compelled the American people to dissolve it. This list merely reviews, in a devastating summary, the long list of events by which the colonists had been alienated from their ruler. Finally, the American idea as to the proper relation between the colonies and Parliament comes out in the penultimate paragraph: "Nor have we been wanting in attention to our British brethren. We have warned them from time to time of attempts by their Legislature to extend an unwarrantable jurisdiction over us. . . . They too have been deaf to the voice of justice and of consanguinity. We must, therefore, acquiesce in the necessity, which denounces our separation, and hold them, as we hold the rest of mankind, enemies in war, in peace friends." Thus it was the

American position that the Americans and the British were two separate peoples, that is, two distinct parts of one nation, each with its own legislative arrangements, united only by the Crown. Now, with the Declaration of Independence, they became two distinct nations, each one foreign to the other. There is a note of genuine regret, representing, probably, the feeling of the vast majority of Americans, in the phrase in Jefferson's original draft, omitted by amendment during the debate, to the effect that "we must endeavor to forget our former love for them . . . we might have been a free and a great people together."

It was not without genuine regret, therefore, that the Americans separated themselves from their mother country. The step was taken solemnly, almost sadly. But when it was done they were no longer British colonies: they were now "the United States of America."

THEORIES OF EMPIRE

The events that had taken place between 1763 and 1775 in the contest between the mother country and the continental colonies precipitated a break between England and those colonies which had now culminated in complete separation. This estrangement was the result of not one, but several issues. Chief of these was the strengthening of the system of British laws calculated to control, even to strangle, the economic life of the colonies in the interests of the mother country. The second issue was the question of taxation by Parliament, which in its larger aspects involved the more fundamental question of colonial self-government. The third was the conflict that arose out of the attempts of England to station and support troops in the colonies in time of peace. A fourth was the interference of the British government in the governmental affairs of the provinces of New York and Massachusetts, and the restriction of civil liberties which seemed to be threatened by the precedent set in the Quebec Act of 1774. A fifth issue grew out of the apparent intention of the British government to cut off the claims of the old colonies to the lands in the west and to establish new colonies there. The central theme, perhaps, was taxation; at least more was said about it than about anything else. But there were many others, and it was the combination of issues rather than any single one that precipitated organized resistance to the mother country in the form of committees of correspondence and the militia for armed conflict, should it be necessary. This organized resistance of the colonies had culminated in the first Continental Congress and the creation of new popular governments which gave no recognition to the Crown, and, finally, in the Declaration of Independence.

In a more profound sense, however, the essential question involved was not that of taxation, nor that of quartering of troops, nor that of the administration of western lands. The fundamental question at issue was the one involved in the colonial claim that all these matters should be managed by the colonies themselves. The most significant thing about the break is the fact that it raised for the first time, on both sides of the Atlantic, the fundamental question as to what the relationship of the colonies to the mother country should be. Up to the time of the Seven Years' War Great Britain had generally assumed that the colonies were and should remain subservient to it. This assumption had been challenged by individual colonies in 1650 and in 1689, but without permanent result. Now, in 1775, it was challenged by all the older continental colonies, who had gradually come to assume, on their side, that they had all the rights of self-government within their colonial boundaries. How far did the rights of the mother country extend in the direction of coercion, and what real right did England have to make laws for the people who lived in America? No one knew the answers to these questions. From the American point of view Englishmen obviously could not rule Americans. But from the English point of view, either the people living in America were Englishmen and therefore subject to English law or they were not Englishmen at all, and, therefore, independent and outside the pale of the British empire. As the fundamental issue in the conflict became clearer, various theories were advanced to explain or justify one system or the other. The most conservative view, represented by Lord Grenville and Lord Chief Justice Mansfield, was that Parliament was the sovereign authority for the whole British empire. The Americans had protested at the time of the stamp act that the British Parliament had no right to tax them because they were not represented in that body; but there were parts of England itself that were not directly represented in the British Parliament. They were, however, "virtually represented"; that is, in the sense that the Parliament represented the whole of the British people wherever they might be, rather than specific parts thereof. Now, either the Americans were Englishmen or they were not Englishmen. If they were, as they themselves claimed over and over again, then according to this view they were subject to the laws made by the British Parliament. Thus, according to this way of thinking, there existed a dual authority in each of the colonies, the authority of the colonial legislature and the authority of the British Parliament. Those two existed, theoretically, side by side, but the ultimate sovereignty resided in the British Parliament rather than in the colony.

A more liberal English view, represented by William Pitt and Lord Camden, was that while the British Parliament was indeed the supreme authority for the empire as a whole, yet the colonial legislature could not be superseded in such matters as internal taxation within the colony. This group looked upon the principle of virtual representation as "so absurd as not to deserve an answer," as Camden put it. Taxation could only be imposed upon the colonists by representatives elected by themselves, therefore the British Parliament had no right to impose taxes that would affect the situation within any colonial boundaries. On the other hand, it was recognized that there were certain matters, such as intercolonial trade and defense, which overlapped colonial boundaries and which could be regulated only by the central authority residing in the Parliament of Great Britain. Thus the Pitt-Camden position was that Parliament had the authority to regulate imperial commerce, and even tax it for the purposes of regulation; but for the purposes of taxation Parliament had no authority within any colony. With regard to other things, however, and particularly matters which might affect the fate of the empire as a whole, Parliament would have the authority to legislate even on matters within any given colony.

A third body of opinion with regard to the structure of the empire, represented by Franklin in the earlier phases of his thought on the subject, and implicit in the resolutions of the Stamp Act Congress, was built upon the idea that the colonies might have direct representation in the British Parliament, and that that body, instead of being composed of representatives of Great Britain alone, might become a legislative council composed of representatives of all parts of the empire. But this proposition was by many considered impractical because of the great distances involved, and, indeed, undesirable.

A fourth way of thinking was that presented by Joseph Galloway in the first Continental Congress. Galloway believed that there might be established two parliaments in the empire, one in Great Britain and one in America. Under such an arrangement, the consent of both parliaments, or branches of a single parliament, would be necessary for the passage of imperial legislation.

The empire would in effect be divided into two equal units, united only by attachment to the British Crown. The American parliament under this scheme of things would be composed of representatives of the American colonies, and any legislation affecting America passed by the British Parliament would have to be approved by it. But this idea was rejected by the first Continental Congress, as already noted.

Still another theory as to the structure of the empire was advanced by Benjamin Franklin a little later in the conflict. According to this way of thinking, the British Parliament was considered the lawmaking body for Great Britain and for the regulation of imperial affairs, but the colonial legislature in each province was considered a parliament for that province, which was not subject to legislation by any other. The British Empire was thus thought to be composed of many separate and independent provinces united only by their tie to the British Crown. The one exception to the rule was the British Parliament, which was recognized as being the necessary legislative body for general imperial affairs. Although vaguely expressed, and clearly realized by only a few, this position probably most nearly represented the traditional American view of the structure of the empire.

In actual practice, the structure and function of the Continental Congress was not unlike the plan suggested by Galloway. The Continental Congress recognized the authority of the provincial parliaments within the provinces and considered itself authorized to act only on matters which concerned the colonies as a whole. Moreover, it thought of itself as having no subservient relationship to the British Parliament, but it looked directly to the British king as sovereign. Except for the fact that it recognized the sovereignty of the British Parliament outside the three-mile limit, it considered the continental colonies practically independent of England, and it assumed that with regard to matters pertaining to its member provinces its authority was superior to that of the British Parliament. Curiously enough, this theory of empire bears a striking resemblance to the theory expressed in the Durham Report of 1839 in respect to Canada and eventually carried out in practice in the organization of the relationships between the self-governing dominions in the modern British Empire.

There was one other way of thinking about the relationship of the American colonies to England. This was the extreme American view represented by Samuel Adams and Thomas Paine. According to these men, America was by nature free and independent of England. Can an island govern a continent? cried Tom Paine. America, he urged, must throw off the leading strings that bound her to the mother country and boldly assert her independence. This, at last, was the position finally accepted by the Americans in the Declaration of Independence.

It would be a mistake to believe that these theories caused the American Revolution. They were but rationalizations of a break that had taken place before the theories were formulated. The fact was that the American continental colonies had already reached a maturity, economic, political, and cultural, that demanded, not subservience, but autonomy; not more and more imperial restraint, but, rather, more and more freedom for independent self-direction. The theories were but intellectual attempts to justify an event of which the contestants themselves were hardly conscious. The continental colonies constituted in effect a new nation. The theories of empire that resulted from the contest with England were rationalizations of that fact. The war that was fought between the colonies and the mother country was fought not so much for independence, as for the recognition of a maturity and a *de facto* nationhood that already existed.

RECOMMENDED BOOKS FOR FURTHER READING

CONTEMPORARY NARRATIVES

Jonathan Boucher, *Reminiscences of an American Loyalist, 1738-1789, Being the Autobiography of the Revd. Jonathan Boucher,* edited by Jonathan Boucher.
William B. Donne, ed., *The Correspondence of King George the Third with Lord North from 1768 to 1783.*
Benjamin Franklin, *The Writings of Benjamin Franklin,* edited by Albert H. Smyth, V, VII.
Thomas Hutchinson, *Diary and Letters,* edited by Peter O. Hutchinson.
The Interest of the Merchants and Manufacturers of Great Britain in the Present Contest with the Colonies Stated and Considered.
Thomas Jefferson, *A Summary View of the Rights of British America.*
Thomas Paine, *Selections from the Works of Thomas Paine,* edited by Arthur W. Peach.
Margaret W. Willard, ed., *Letters on the American Revolution, 1774-1776.*

MODERN ACCOUNTS

Charles M. Andrews, *The Colonial Background of the American Revolution.*
James T. Adams, *Revolutionary New England, 1691-1776,* Chapters 15-17.
Randolph G. Adams, *The Political Ideas of the American Revolution.*

Alice M. Baldwin, *The New England Clergy and the American Revolution.*

Carl L. Becker, *The Declaration of Independence.*

Carl L. Becker, *The Eve of the Revolution.*

Carl L. Becker, *The History of Political Parties in the Province of New York, 1760-1776.*

Carl L. Becker [and others], *The Spirit of '76.*

Mary A. Best, *Thomas Paine, Prophet and Martyr of Democracy.*

The Cambridge History of the British Empire, Volume I, Chapter 22; Part 2; Chapter 24.

Clarence E. Carter, *Great Britain and the Illinois Country, 1763-1774.*

Edward Channing, *A History of the United States,* III, Chapters 3-12.

Gilbert Chinard, *Honest John Adams.*

Gilbert Chinard, *Thomas Jefferson, The Apostle of Americanism.*

Edward D. Collins, "Committees of Correspondence of the American Revolution," in *American Historical Association Annual Report,* 1901, Volume I, 243-271.

Philip Davidson, *Propaganda & the American Revolution, 1763-1783.*

Bernard Faÿ, *Benjamin Franklin, the Apostle of Modern Times.*

Paul L. Ford, "The Association of the First Congress," *Political Science Quarterly,* VI, 613-624.

Herbert Friedenwald, *The Declaration of Independence.*

Ralph V. Harlow, *Samuel Adams.*

Fossey J. C. Hearnshaw, ed., *The Social & Political Ideas of Some Representative Thinkers of the Revolutionary Era.*

William W. Henry, *Patrick Henry.*

James K. Hosmer, *The Life of Thomas Hutchinson.*

George E. Howard, *The Preliminaries of the Revolution, 1763-1775.*

William E. Lecky, *The American Revolution, 1763-1783.*

Charles H. Lincoln, *The Revolutionary Movement in Pennsylvania, 1760-1776.*

Charles H. McIlwain, *The American Revolution: A Constitutional Interpretation.*

Charles E. Merriam, *A History of American Political Theories.*

Lewis B. Namier, *The Structure of Politics at the Accession of George III.*

Arthur M. Schlesinger, *The Colonial Merchants and the American Revolution, 1763-1776.*

Robert L. Schuyler, *Parliament and the British Empire.*

Charles J. Stillé, *The Life and Times of John Dickinson.*

Moses C. Tyler, *Literary History of the Revolution, 1763-1783,* Volume I.

Carl C. Van Doren, *Benjamin Franklin.*

Claude H. Van Tyne, *The Causes of the War of Independence.*

George M. Wrong, *Canada and the American Revolution.*

44

The War for American Independence

T**HE ARRIVAL** of General Gage in Boston early in 1774 to succeed Thomas Hutchinson as governor of Massachusetts was an ominous event in the history of all the continental colonies. For Gage was a military man, sent to Boston as to a military post; and his appointment made it clear that Britain was determined to enforce the "intolerable acts" and British authority over the colonies by force, if necessary.

Gage had instructions to arrest Samuel Adams and John Hancock, ringleaders of the Boston "rebels," and send them to England for trial. But colonial resistance was not easily to be crushed. The local committees of safety were gathering arms and ammunition, and "minute men" began to drill on the village greens of New England in preparation for the conflict that now seemed imminent. As the countryside bristled more and more with the warlike attitude and preparations of the Americans, Gage found himself practically besieged in Boston. Finally, on April 18, 1775, he sent a force of some one thousand men to arrest Adams and Hancock, who were at Lexington, and to seize the arms and ammunition stored at Concord. Paul Revere, a silversmith of Boston, rode out into the country to arouse the people, and the British force was met at Lexington next morning by a party of about fifty "minute men," who opened fire on the "invaders."

In the skirmish that took place some of the Americans were shot down, and the rest dispersed. The British pushed on to Concord and destroyed a small amount of war supplies. Then, on their return march to Boston, the soldiers were harassed by a continuing fire from the Americans practically every step of the way. Strong reinforcements were hurried out to their aid, and joined them at Lexington; but the effectiveness of the American fire was such that, out of a total of twenty-five hundred soldiers who set out from Boston that day, 273 men were killed, wounded, or taken prisoner. The Americans suffered 93 casualties in all.

This, the "battle of Lexington and Concord," was the first skirmish in the war that eventually became a war for the complete independence of thirteen of Britain's American colonies. It was still more than a year before independence was declared, and the colonists still thought of themselves as fighting for the rights of British citizens. But the effect of this clash upon the other colonies was electrical, and it drew the thirteen continental provinces together as nothing, hitherto, had done. For the first time Britain had deliberately used force; and the Americans, aroused to a white heat of anger and exasperation, had met force with force. Hitherto, the conflict with the mother country had been largely an affair of the intellectuals and the merchants; the common man had little interest in it, and had been only slowly aroused by the various organizations and committees for propaganda and "safety." Now, however, common men had been deliberately shot down by British soldiers; and that was something the common people could clearly understand. From this point on, therefore, the issue, in the popular mind, was clear: Britain was determined to deprive the Americans of their self-government and their liberties. The tendency toward British tyranny must be stopped now, at all costs; otherwise the Americans would be reduced to economic and political servitude to England. Nor was this an idle imagining; it was a real fear, probably, in the minds of many, if not most, of the men who swarmed around Boston as Gage shut himself in and prepared to withstand siege.

THE FIRST YEAR OF WAR, 1775-76

After the battle of Lexington and Concord, military action spread to many points up and down the coast. At Boston, General Gage found himself and his army cooped up in the town by a motley American "army" of some 16,000 men. Gage received reinforcements under General Sir William Howe, who eventually succeeded him in command. The Americans occupied Breed's Hill, on the Charlestown peninsula overlooking Boston, and, since this would make it possible for them to fire into the city, it became necessary for the British to drive them out. This General Howe attempted to do, and, scorning the obvious plan of cutting them off by occupying the neck of land joining the peninsula to the mainland, he chose to storm the hill. The entrenched Americans withheld their fire until the British were within almost point-blank range, then wreaked such havoc in the British ranks that probably one third of the British soldiers were killed. It was only on the third charge that the Americans, whose ammunition was running low, were compelled to withdraw.

The hard-won benefits from this, the so-called battle of Bunker Hill, were almost immediately lost, however, when George Washington, newly appointed general-in-chief of the Continental army, arrived and took command of the American besiegers. For Washington occupied Dorchester Heights, on the south side of Boston, and his position there made Boston untenable. Because of this, as well as because of the fact that Boston was of little strategic value anyway, General Howe abandoned the city on March 17, 1775, and moved his army to Halifax, from whence he began his campaign against New York later in that year.

Meanwhile, hostilities had begun elsewhere. In May, 1775, while the Americans were besieging Boston, Ethan Allen of the Green Mountains (the region later to become Vermont), aided by Benedict Arnold of Connecticut, succeeded in seizing the totally unprepared forts of Ticonderoga and Crown Point. Arnold then went on to take Fort St. John, at the outlet of the lake.

Arnold then proceeded to Boston and proposed that an expedition be sent against Quebec. This expedition was undertaken largely on the assumption that the French Canadians were discontented under the British, and would rise to aid the Americans in driving the British out. The Continental Congress had sought to take advantage of this supposed situation by sending a commission to stir up the Canadians to rebellion. The commission had met with little success, however, as already noted; the Canadians were equally lukewarm toward both sides. The American commission was still at work when the military expedition got under way.

The Canadian expedition was in two parts. One, under the command of General Richard Montgomery, was to follow the old Lake Champlain route, take Montreal, and then go on to Quebec. The other, commanded by Arnold, was to hurry through the Maine wilderness and descend the Chaudière to surprise Quebec. Montgomery's expedition succeeded in entering Montreal on November 12, 1775, and Arnold, after an epic march through extreme hardship and difficulty in the Maine woods, finally joined him before Quebec. The town had been warned, however, and the combined American forces were unable to take it. In a desperate attempt to storm the place, on the last day of 1775, Montgomery was killed and Arnold was wounded. In the spring and summer of 1776 Governor Guy Carleton succeeded in driving the

Americans out of Canada. With them went Franklin and his propaganda printing press.

Meanwhile, in the summer of 1775 and early in 1776, fighting had taken place in the southern colonies. News of the fighting around Boston brought to a head the warlike preparations in all the colonies from Connecticut and Rhode Island to Charleston in South Carolina. Opposed to the "rebels" in North Carolina were numerous Scottish loyalists who had been granted land directly by the Crown and had participated in the "Regulator" movement against the land speculators of the North Carolina tidewater region. These loyalists organized themselves into a force under the leadership of Donald MacDonald to cooperate with the British army operating out of Wilmington to keep the southern provinces from joining the rebellion. The American frontiersmen, however, met them at Moore's Creek Bridge on February 27, 1776, and in the battle that ensued this loyalist force was completely destroyed. General Sir Henry Clinton and Admiral Sir Peter Parker, who had sought to cooperate with MacDonald, then turned south and attacked Charleston on June 28. William Moultrie, in command at the fortress on Sullivan Island, in Charleston harbor, repulsed a land attack under Clinton, and the British turned back out to sea. The success of the Americans in holding Charleston was of great importance to the American cause, for it effectively preserved the south.

In October, 1775, a British fleet burned the town of Falmouth in Maine, and in Virginia Governor Dunmore, who went on board a British man of war in Chesapeake Bay to escape the Americans under Patrick Henry, succeeded in burning the town of Norfolk on January 1, 1776. The burning of these towns had little significance, however, except for their effect in further inflaming anti-British feeling.

Thus, for a year prior to the Declaration of Independence, active civil warfare had been going on between Great Britain and thirteen of the colonies on the continent. But by the summer of 1776 it had become clearly apparent that this "rebellion" was not to be quelled overnight. The Declaration of Independence made the issue abundantly clear, and both sides settled down to a systematic war.

THE OPPOSING FORCES

At first glance it would appear that the Americans were doomed to lose. It would have been so even had all the American colonies of Great Britain stood in a solid front of opposition to the mother country's imperial policy. But not all the colonies resisted, nor were those that did so genuinely united. As it was, only thirteen of the colonies on the continent of North America were irrevocably involved, and even they hesitated to carry their resistance so far as an appeal to force.

The population of these thirteen colonies was now about 2,500,000 souls; that of the mother country was probably in the neighborhood of 10,000,000. The comparative resources of the two protagonists showed a similar discrepancy. In the thirteen revolting colonies there were probably 200,000 "fighting men," but only some 90,000 of them were in service in 1776. Great Britain probably had some 2,000,000 fighting men, but her army was surprisingly small. Parliament had provided for an army of 55,000 men in 1775, but its actual numbers were closer to 30,000, and Britain found it necessary to "purchase" a supplementary force of some 20,000 men from certain impecunious German princes, chief of whom was the landgrave of Hesse-Cassel. In addition to these forces, the British eventually had the service of perhaps 25,000 American loyalists, and a majority of the Indian tribes in the interior of the continent. But the British armies in America probably never totaled over 75,000 or 100,000 men. The British and German armies were composed of professional soldiers, engaged for long terms of enlistment. The Americans, on the other hand, were chiefly raw militia, serving on short terms and generally disposed to suspend warlike operations whenever some pressing matter, such as a harvest, demanded their attention at home. As the war wore on the Americans were more and more disinclined to enlist, even for short terms, and the states were forced to offer large bounties for enlistment and even resort to such extreme measures as compulsory military service. After the arrival of French armies to aid the Americans, the difficulty in getting the Americans to fight was even greater than before.

It was in naval power that the greatest discrepancy in strength appeared. Great Britain was now the undisputed mistress of the seas, whereas the Americans, accustomed to depend upon the British navy for protection at sea, had practically nothing in the way of a navy. This British superiority becomes especially significant in view of the fact that the Americans possessed neither arms nor munitions factories, and had to import their military supplies from friendly nations abroad. British control of the sea was bound to make such importations difficult.

Financially, too, Great Britain had an enormous advantage; for British financial resources were hundreds of times as great as those of the Americans. It is true, of course, that the national debt of Britain had mounted, during the Seven Years' War, to the hitherto unheard of sum of £140,000,000. Britain would not welcome the additional burden of taxation that would result from a new war—a war undertaken, in part, at least, to force the Americans to bear a part of this same burden of taxation for imperial defense.

One great advantage the Americans had in the fact that the British invading armies had to be transported three thousand miles by sea, and in the difficult nature of the American terrain over which they must operate after they arrived. The fact, also, that the Americans were the defenders, fighting in their homeland on "interior lines" gave them an advantage that was both psychological and strategic.

All in all, however, the British had an enormous superiority of strength over the Americans; by all calculations, it appeared that the Americans could not win.

THE CAMPAIGNS OF 1776-77

The British campaign for the summer of 1776 had as its chief objective the seizure of New York, which was the strategic center of the colonies. Thus Howe, after receiving reinforcements in Nova Scotia, sailed south and landed his army on Staten Island, where he was joined by the forces of Henry Clinton and Admiral Peter Parker, who had returned north after their failure at Wilmington and Charleston. From Staten Island Howe's army rowed over to Brooklyn Heights in August. Washington, meanwhile, anticipating this move by the British, had brought the American army from Boston to New York. Since Brooklyn Heights overlooked the city, Washington had fortified that spot to prevent the British from coming closer. Howe here attacked the Americans, outflanked them, and captured a large portion of the American army under General John Sullivan. As he could no longer hold the city, Washington withdrew northward along the Hudson. After victories at Fort Lee, on the west side of the Hudson, and at Fort Washington, at the north end of Manhattan Island, Howe attacked Washington at White Plains, and succeeded in occupying the town. This placed him in a position either to strike at New England or to drive across New Jersey toward Philadelphia, so

Washington divided his army into two parts, placing one, under Charles Lee, to the north of White Plains, while he took the other into New Jersey to protect the road toward Philadelphia. Lee succeeded in getting himself and his army captured by the British, and Washington led his weakened and dwindling army across the Delaware into Pennsylvania in December.

The American cause now seemed to be in a desperate situation. The Continental Congress abandoned Philadelphia and moved to Baltimore, while the British systematically occupied the eastern parts of New Jersey. But Washington watched the movements of the British and Hessian army from the Pennsylvania side of the Delaware, and then, on Christmas night, he made a surprise attack upon the Hessians occupying Trenton. The stroke was a complete success, for it netted about one thousand Hessians, and resulted in a most opportune bolstering of American morale. A few days later Washington struck the British again at Princeton, and the British withdrew into the region immediately surrounding New York.

Thus stood the scales of war in the winter of 1776-77. When spring came, in 1777, the campaigns opened that were to tip them definitely in favor of the American side. The British had seized Newport in the fall of 1776, and Howe contemplated three expeditions against the Americans—one from Newport against Boston and two from New York, one up the Hudson and one against Philadelphia. The large force of British and Hessians that had gone to Canada was still there, and General "Gentleman Johnny" Burgoyne proposed to march southward over the Lake Champlain route to join these forces with those under Howe at New York. This movement, if successful, would have cut off New England from the rest of the rebellious colonies. But Howe, partly because he was determined to invade Pennsylvania and partly because of the failure to receive needed reinforcements, abandoned his plans for a campaign against Boston and even for an expedition up the Hudson, in order to concentrate upon an attack upon Pennsylvania by sea. Thus Howe went on to Delaware Bay, confident that Burgoyne would succeed in cutting through from the north without his help. He was sent orders to cooperate with Burgoyne, but he received them, fatefully, when it was too late to change his plans.

Howe's operations in Pennsylvania were entirely successful. He landed his army at the upper end of Chesapeake Bay, and marched against Philadelphia. Washington, who had been waiting to see what Howe's game was, met him at Brandywine Creek. Here again, as at Brooklyn, the Americans, whose exposed flank was again under General Sullivan, were outflanked. Washington had to retreat, and the British occupied Philadelphia. Washington struck at them at Germantown on October 4, but without success.

Of far greater significance were the operations in the north. For Burgoyne, who had seized Ticonderoga just before Howe left New York, had advanced southward while Lieutenant-Colonel Barry St. Leger was entering New York State by way of Oswego, with the intention of joining Burgoyne at Albany. St. Leger arrived before Ft. Stanwix (henceforth called Fort Schuyler), at the portage of the Mohawk, only to be beaten back at a place called Oriskany. Burgoyne, moving southward from Ticonderoga, found the going increasingly slow and hazardous, by reason of the roughness of the terrain and the difficulty in getting supplies. This difficulty inspired him to send a foraging expedition eastward. But the New Hampshire legislature quickly raised a force of frontiersmen under the command of John Stark. Stark met Lieutenant-Colonel Baum's foraging Germans at Bennington, and completely destroyed them, together with a large part of a second detachment sent out to their aid. Meanwhile, the "embattled farmers" of New England and New York were gathering around Burgoyne in such numbers that his army was outnumbered four to one, and completely surrounded. When he began to move south in mid-September, 1777, he found the Americans under General Horatio Gates in a strong position at Bemis Heights, above Freeman's Farm, near Saratoga. In the battle that followed, the British, practically surrounded, were pretty badly beaten, and on October 17, 1777, Burgoyne surrendered with his army of over five thousand men—and between three and five hundred women and children!

Burgoyne's surrender was the major British disaster of the war. It not only prevented the junction of the British from Canada with those in New York to split the Americans and thus provided a brilliant success for the Americans to balance that of Howe at Philadelphia, but it gave France an occasion to throw its weight on the side of the Americans—an aid without which the Americans probably could never have carried the war through to a successful conclusion.

FRANCE SENDS AID

France had already been helping the Americans, with money, arms and ammunition, and supplies. But this had been secret aid, responsibility for which might be repudiated, in case of need. For France had hesitated to recognize the independence of the United States before she felt sure they could win their fight against the mother country. For recognition of the independence of a part of the British empire was bound to be considered an act of hostility against Great Britain and to result in war. The surrender of Burgoyne was the first significant victory of the Americans over a British army, and it was so complete a victory as to demonstrate the ability of the Americans to win when they met the British on something like equal terms. So far as France was concerned, it was just the sort of demonstration that country had been waiting for, and when the French ministry learned that England was about to send a peace mission to the Americans, France decided the moment to redress the American balance of power, so badly upset in the Seven Years' War, had arrived.

The Franco-American alliance of February, 1778, therefore, brought the full force of France to the side of the Americans. Greatly did they need it, indeed; for despite the rejoicing over the victory at Saratoga, which was a victory won by the militia, the forces under Washington were in a desperate plight. This was the ghastly winter of 1777-78—the winter of Valley Forge. Washington had gone into winter quarters there, but he saw his men in need of shoes and clothing, badly fed, short of arms and ammunition. It was nearly impossible to procure such supplies, for the credit of the Continental Congress had fallen to a low ebb; the value of the paper money had fallen to a point at which the expression "not worth a Continental" had a real and terrible meaning. At the same time, while Washington's army was on the verge of starvation, the British in Philadelphia were well fed. The farmers could not resist the appeal of the hard money the British paid for their produce. Washington was almost in despair over the future.

Active French aid, therefore, came just when the Americans needed it most. Two months after the signature of the alliance, on April 5, 1778, the Count d'Estaing sailed for America with a fleet of twelve ships and a considerable body of soldiers. He entered Delaware Bay on July 8. For the British, the American war was now of secondary importance to that with France, into which Spain entered the following year. For the time being, therefore, General Sir Henry Clinton, who had succeeded Howe at Philadelphia, was ordered to evacuate that city and return to New York, which was the strategic center of the Atlantic seaboard. This he did on June 18, leading his soldiers across New Jersey while most of their baggage and belongings went by sea to New York under the command of Admiral Lord Howe (brother of the retired General Sir William Howe).

When Estaing arrived in the Delaware Bay in July, therefore, he found the British fleet gone, and he followed it to New York by sea while Washington was harrying Clinton's flanks by land. Finding the entrance to New York harbor too difficult, Estaing then went on to Newport, which was still in the hands of the British, apparently with the idea of cooperating with the Americans in an attempt to recover that place. The attempt was made in August, with an American army cooperating with the French fleet. But by this time Admiral Howe had received reinforcements for his fleet, and sailed out of New York to drive Estaing from Newport. Both fleets were battered by a storm, however, and Estaing went to Boston for repairs, leaving the American army to retire from its positions on Rhode Island without having accomplished anything. Estaing, having refitted, sailed for the West Indies to pass the winter.

Meanwhile, the British had decided to make an effort to conquer the south, using Georgia as a base. Urged on by the former royal governors of Georgia and South Carolina, and hoping to be reinforced by hordes of loyalists, they seized the town of Savannah on December 29, 1778. They then overran Georgia and South Carolina and laid siege to Charleston. Washington sent General Benjamin Lincoln south with a small force to dislodge the British. The French admiral Estaing came to Savannah to aid Lincoln, but the joint effort to recover that city failed. Late in the fall of 1779 Clinton started for the South from New York, landed an army of seven thousand men on the coast north of Charleston, and succeeded in capturing the city, with Lincoln's army in it, in May, 1780. Another American army was sent south, this one under General Gates. It was met at Camden, in North Carolina, by a force of British regulars under Lord Cornwallis, and, composed chiefly of raw militia, it turned and fled. The British were still not in complete possession of the field, however, as from this time on the Americans resorted to a sort of guerrilla warfare, led by Thomas Sumter, Francis ("the Swamp Fox") Marion, and Andrew Pickens, that kept the British forever on the alert and made it extremely difficult for them even to hold the country they had conquered.

While these events were taking place, a campaign of a heartening nature had been taking place far out in the west. The frontiersmen of Kentucky, anxious for a blow at the British and their Indian allies, organized an expedition under the command of George Rogers Clark to seize the British posts in the Illinois country. This expedition crossed the Ohio in the spring of 1778, and by a combination of trickery and daring, succeeded in seizing the villages of Kaskaskia and Vincennes. Colonel Henry Hamilton, the British commandant at Detroit, then recovered Vincennes, but Clark, in the midst of the winter of 1778-79 and in the face of the utmost difficulties, captured the place once more, together with Colonel Hamilton. The Illinois country was then organized as a county of Virginia, which it remained until the reorganization of the Northwest Territories after the war.

France finally sent a land army to America under the command of the Count de Rochambeau, who sailed into Newport—which had been abandoned by the British in 1779—on July 10, 1780. There the French remained almost a year; but in the spring of 1781 Rochambeau received word that the French West Indies fleet, now under Admiral de Grasse, was coming north for the summer campaign. Washington suggested that the American and French armies cooperate with the French fleet to take New York from the British, but Rochambeau preferred to operate against the British in the south. He therefore asked de Grasse to make Chesapeake Bay his objective.

Thus it came about that in 1781 French and American allies took, for the first time, the offensive. General Cornwallis, who had defeated the Americans at Camden, had been given a free hand, and had gone forward with his plan of systematically conquering the south. He had been harried by the American guerrillas, and one of his lieutenants, Major Patrick Ferguson, had lost his entire regiment at the battle of King's Mountain in October, 1780. But Cornwallis persisted in his plan. Opposed to him were General Nathanael Greene, generally considered the best military officer of the Revolution, and General Daniel Morgan. Greene and Morgan had only small forces, but they used them well, and Morgan succeeded in destroying, at Cowpens, in western North Carolina, on January 17, 1781, a strong tory detachment under

Lieutenant-Colonel Tarleton, which Cornwallis had sent against him. But Greene and Morgan were separated, and Cornwallis sought to strike at Greene. Morgan and Greene succeeded in joining forces, however, and turned on Cornwallis at Guilford courthouse. The battle was severe, but indecisive, and Greene retreated after inflicting severe loss upon his enemy. Cornwallis, on his side, though he called it a victory, made the best of his way to the sea at Wilmington to get supplies and rest his men. Greene turned southward again, and succeeded in clearing the British out of western South Carolina and North Carolina; but he had to return to the conflict against the refreshed Cornwallis, who had started from Wilmington toward Virginia. General Clinton had already sent a force of loyalists under Major-General Benedict Arnold, now in British uniform, into Virginia, and Cornwallis hoped to join forces with this expedition.

Washington and Rochambeau sent the young Marquis de Lafayette south to stop Arnold. He was unable to prevent the junction of Arnold's force with that of Cornwallis, but Cornwallis, on the other hand, was unable to win a decisive action over the Marquis. The British general, hampered by contradictory orders from Clinton, his commander-in-chief at New York, fortified Yorktown, on the York River, as a base from which to operate while keeping in touch with the British fleet.

It was at this moment, in the summer of 1781, that word came to Washington that Admiral de Grasse would reach the Chesapeake with the French fleet and an army of three thousand men about the first of September, and Washington decided to take the offensive. Marching to the Chesapeake with an army of two thousand Americans and five thousand Frenchmen, he joined his force to that of Lafayette, and proceeded to Yorktown. Fortunately for the Americans, the French fleet, under de Grasse, had reached the Chesapeake on time, just three or four days before a British fleet under Admiral Graves, that had come down from New York to forestall de Grasse and cooperate with Cornwallis. In the naval action that followed, on September, 1781, though the action itself was indecisive, the British fleet was sufficiently discomfited to cause Graves to turn back to New York for repairs, whence he did not return to the Virginia capes until October 21.

This was the decisive moment of the war. For during the six weeks when the French fleet held the mouth of the Chesapeake, the allied army laid siege to Yorktown with sixteen thousand men, while Cornwallis, with his seven thousand, could do nothing but hold on and wait for aid from the British fleet—the aid that never came. Cornwallis did, indeed, make a half-hearted effort to escape with his army across the York River, but this effort failed, and on October 19, 1781, two days before the second arrival of Graves with his fleet off the Virginia capes, he surrendered.

His surrender marked the virtual end of hostilities in America. British armies still occupied Charleston, Savannah, New York and sundry small places along the coast. But the British people were sick of the war. Britain, moreover, by this time found itself at war with France, Spain, and Holland. The final outcome of the American segment of the war thus depended in large measure upon the course of events elsewhere.

A WORLD WAR

The war that broke out between France and England in 1778 quickly became a world war. For a year, to be sure, France stood alone, of the European nations, against Britain. Yet the entrance of France alone into the war gave the war a worldwide aspect. The continuance of the British invasion of America depended upon the maintenance of the British dominance of the sea. But the French were able to challenge the British so successfully as to threaten the British lines of communication; later, the French navy's achievement of a merely local and temporary mastery of the waters about the mouth of Chesapeake Bay had a vital and conclusive effect upon the fighting in America. During the summer of 1778, while Estaing was in American waters with one French fleet, the French admiral the Count of Orvilliers met the British channel fleet under Admiral Keppel off Ushant (July 27, 1778). The action was indecisive, but the failure of the British to stop the French fleet there resulted in an increase of the French fleet in America.

In the West Indies the French had promptly seized Dominica, ceded to the British in the Treaty of Paris of 1763, and the British retaliated, late in 1778, by taking St. Lucia from the French. In June, 1779, Estaing seized St. Vincent from the British, and then went on to take Grenada on July 6.

In June of that year Spain joined its forces to those of France, although it refused to ally itself with the United States. Spain hesitated to recognize American independence; for Spain had a great American empire of its own, and open recognition of the independence or of the right of the British colonies to rebel against the mother country would be an extremely risky example for her own. Nevertheless, Spain continued to send secret aid to the Americans and the addition of the Spanish navy to that of France gave the allies a force of about one hundred and twenty first-class fighting ships, sufficient to challenge very seriously the British mastery of the sea. Not only that, the joining of French and Spanish forces again raised the possibility of invasion of England itself. Fifty thousand French troops were gathered on the French coast along the English Channel, and in the summer of 1779 a great Franco-Spanish armada sailed into the Channel to cover the transport of troops to English soil. But the French and Spanish fleets were poorly co-ordinated, and when an easterly gale blew them out of the Channel again, the plan for an invasion was abandoned. Once again the weather had saved England from invasion.

The Spaniards then turned their attention to Gibraltar, the fortress at the gateway to the Mediterranean which the British had acquired from Spain by the Treaty of Utrecht. A blockade was established both by land and by sea; the fort was in a serious condition when its supplies ran low; and it was relieved by Admiral George Rodney only in January, 1780. After relieving Gibraltar and Minorca from the Spanish threat, Rodney sailed to the West Indies to face the possibility of a Spanish invasion of Jamaica. But the Spaniards failed to attack. Then, in the last month of 1780, news arrived that Holland had joined the war against England, and Rodney turned his attention to the Dutch island of St. Eustatius.

Holland had long complained of British arrogance on the sea. The British navy had small regard for the rights of neutrals, and the Dutch complaints dated back to the Seven Years' War. Now, the maritime nations of northern Europe, exasperated by Britain's disregard of their rights, formed, in the year 1780, an "armed neutrality" to enforce their rights. Holland, while a neutral, had used its West Indian island of St. Eustatius as a base for an extremely profitable trade with the Americans—a trade composed chiefly of arms, ammunition, and supplies. Even British merchants engaged in this trade, buying American produce and selling to the Americans supplies that were of use to them in the war. The news that England was at war with Holland, therefore, was good news to Rodney, for he quickly fell upon the island and, on February 3, 1781, captured it, taking with it booty of an enormous value.

His preoccupation with St. Eustatius, however, was fatal. For it permitted de Grasse to arrive at Martinique with a large French fleet, and the French admiral then sailed north to the capes of the Chesapeake to cooperate with Washington and Rochambeau, as already related. After Yorktown he returned to the West Indies, where he joined forces with Admiral the Marquis of Bouillé, who had already recaptured St. Eustatius from the British. He then attacked the British island of St. Christopher, which surrendered on February 23, 1782. Once more the French and Spanish planned to attack Jamaica, but while de Grasse was on his way to join the Spaniards, Rodney, with a strongly reinforced fleet, caught him off Dominica, near a group of small islands called the Saints, and captured him with a part of his fleet. The rest of the French fleet succeeded in joining the Spaniards, but the projected invasion of Jamaica, delayed by Rodney's victory, was eventually canceled by the news of peace.

It should be noted that fighting in this war had spread to South Africa and to India, where the British were generally successful. The African and Indian engagements had little actual influence on the outcome of the war, however. In the North Sea, a Dutch squadron had met a British squadron with indecisive results; and in the Mediterranean the French and Spanish allies had succeeded in wresting Minorca from the British in February, 1782. Gibraltar, however, the siege of which had been renewed, still held out. A final desperate effort was made to take it on September 8, 1782, and continued for five days of bitter fighting. The attack failed, and "the rock" was once more relieved by a British fleet on October 19.

The Battle of the Saints in the West Indies and the relief of Gibraltar saved Britain from the complete loss of the war. But vital British supplies from the Baltic had been shut off, and Britain could not much longer continue to face the antagonism of the armed neutrality of northern Europe and active warfare with Holland, France and Spain in the south. It was, indeed, the entry of these nations into the war that won independence for the Americans. For it is difficult to see how Washington, who, as he said, was "at the end of our tether" in 1781, could have beaten Cornwallis without the aid of French troops and the French fleet, or even how he could have carried on the war as long as he did, without the aid of France and Spain. As it was, the naval and military campaigns round the world diverted British attention from the American phase of the war. Indeed, winning that part of the war had become actually less important to England than beating the French and the Spaniards. The fatal failure of Britain was the failure of the British navy to maintain, at the crucial moments, the vaunted British mastery of the sea.

In any case, the British public was sick of the war and humiliated by its outcome. Criticism of Lord North's government, which had been in power throughout, resulted in its overthrow in March, 1782, and a new ministry was formed with the Marquis of Rockingham at its head. Into this ministry went Edmund Burke, the Earl of Shelburne, and Charles James Fox, all of them known for their friendship or moderation toward the Americans in the difficult years preceding the war. As yet, no one would propose to the king that the independence of the former colonies be recognized, but Shelburne opened a correspondence with his old friend Benjamin Franklin, then in Paris, and later sent Richard Oswald, another of Franklin's friends, to Paris to talk with him about possible terms of peace. Thus began the negotiations for peace between Britain and her former colonies. On Rockingham's death, in the summer of 1782, Shelburne became prime minister; with his accession the peace—and independence for the new United States of America—was practically assured.

RECOMMENDED BOOKS FOR FURTHER READING

CONTEMPORARY NARRATIVES

John Adams, "Autobiography" in *The Works of John Adams,* edited by Charles F. Adams, II, III.

Edmund Burke, *On Conciliation with America* (Old South Leaflets, No. 200).

Edmund C. Burnett, ed., *Letters of Members of the Continental Congress,* I, II.

Nicholas Cresswell, *The Journal of Nicholas Cresswell, 1774-1777.*

William B. Donne, ed., *Correspondence of King George the Third with Lord North,* Volume II.

Thomas Gage, *The Correspondence of General Thomas Gage,* edited by Clarence E. Carter.

Joseph Galloway, *A Candid Examination of the Mutual Claims of Great-Britain, and the Colonies.*

Albert B. Hart, ed., *American History Told by Contemporaries,* II, Chapters 28-29, 31-32, 34-35.

Samuel E. Morison, ed., *Sources and Documents Illustrating the American Revolution, 1764-1788,* pp. 34-54, 62-87, 104-162.

Thomas Paine, *Common Sense.*

William Pitt, *Speeches on the American Revolution* (Old South Leaflets, No. 199).

Ambrose Serle, *The American Journal of Ambrose Serle, Secretary to Lord Howe, 1776-78,* edited by Edward H. Tatum, Jr.

Carl C. Van Doren, ed., *Secret History of the American Revolution*.
George Washington, *The Writings of George Washington*, II, III, edited by John C. Fitzpatrick.

MODERN ACCOUNTS

Wilbur C. Abbott, *New York in the American Revolution*.
Gardner W. Allen, *A Naval History of the American Revolution*.
Albert J. Beveridge, *The Life of John Marshall*, Volume I.
Edward Channing, *A History of the United States*, Volume III.
Hamilton J. Eckenrode, *The Revolution in Virginia*.
Bernard Faÿ, *The Revolutionary Spirit in France and America*.
Sydney G. Fisher, *The Struggle for American Independence*.
John Fiske, *The American Revolution*.
Paul L. Ford, *The True George Washington*.
John W. Fortescue, *A History of the British Army*, Volume III.
Francis V. Greene, *The Revolutionary War and the Military Policy of the United States*.
George W. Greene, *The Life of Nathanael Greene*.
Louis C. Hatch, *The Administration of the American Revolutionary Army*.
Rupert Hughes, *George Washington*.
William E. H. Lecky, *The American Revolution*.
Alfred T. Mahan, *The Influence of Sea Power upon History, 1660-1783*, pp. 330-376.
Alfred T. Mahan, *The Major Operations of the Navies in the War of American Independence*.
Hoffman Nickerson, *The Turning Point of the Revolution*.
Charles O. Paullin, *The Navy of the American Revolution*.
James B. Perkins, *France in the American Revolution*.
Phillips Russell, *John Paul Jones: Man of Action*.
Charles C. Sellers, *Benedict Arnold, The Proud Warrior*.
Nathaniel W. Stephenson and Waldo H. Dunn, *George Washington*.
George O. Trevelyan, *The American Revolution*.
Claude H. Van Tyne, *The War of American Independence*.
William C. H. Wood, *The Father of British Canada*.
George M. Wrong, *Canada and the American Revolution*.

45

The Internal Revolution

THE War for American Independence has been called the American Revolution. As a successful rebellion that broke the leading-strings of England, such, indeed, it was. But the real revolution of the United States was an internal one—a revolution which involved a fundamental modification of the old ways of life in order to bring them into line with American experience. It was a weakening of inherited ancient English social and economic attitudes and prejudices, and an emergence of ideas and institutions which had long been struggling toward the surface in American society—ideas which were more genuinely American—more expressive of the American mind and more satisfactory in the American way of life—than the old borrowed institutions and ideas that had been brought to America from Europe and adapted to the American environment. The internal revolution, considered in this light, might well be called a flowering—a first flowering, perhaps—of the political, social, and intellectual aspects of a genuinely American civilization that had been slowly but surely evolving since the first colonist set foot on American soil. It was a revolution, to be sure; but in the sense that it threw off old, imposed forms and followed the lines of its own genius.

THE POLITICAL REVOLUTION: THE ARTICLES
OF CONFEDERATION

In its political aspects the internal American revolution meant a substitution, for that section of the old empire, of a government of the united thirteen revolted colonies for the old British imperial government that had served as a central administration of their intercolonial and international problems throughout the colonial era. It meant, similarly, a substitution of independent, self-sufficient state governments for the dependent, regulated provincial governments of the era of colonial dependence. The Americans were faced with the task of creating new institutions in both these fields. They had only their experience, supplemented by their reading of the eighteenth-century political philosophers, to instruct them; it was out of these two bodies of materials that they built their state.

The union of the states had its origin in the Continental Congress, and its expression in the Articles of Confederation. The Congress itself had been hardly more than a response to an immediate need: it had no real basis in law or precedent—except, perhaps, the Stamp Act Congress of 1765 or the Albany Congress of 1754—and it had no constitution of its own. It was nothing more than its name implied: a congress of representatives of the states, meeting together to discuss their common problems and to concert their common actions. But it had absolutely no power to impose its decisions upon the states; any state might cooperate or not as it chose. As a matter of fact, the states jealously guarded what they considered their sovereign independence, and were quick to resent anything that smacked of coercion.

The sheer necessities of the struggle, nevertheless, forced a certain system of procedure upon this "government by sufferance." When the first Continental Congress met at Philadelphia in the autumn of 1774, it thought and acted as a temporary body, with no thought of renouncing the ancestral allegiance to the British Crown. The Congress was composed of some of the ablest men in the colonies, called together rather informally to discuss ways and means of resolving their differences with the mother country. But they differed widely among themselves as to how those difficulties were to be resolved. Men of all shades of opinion were there, from "tories" to extreme "radicals"; men of widely differing faiths, Quaker, Puritan, Anglican, and Roman Catholic; men from all sections, from commercial New England, from cosmopolitan New York and Pennsylvania, and from the aristocratic agricultural south. The Congress was fairly representative of "continental" society; the differences between its members were to a fair degree the differences among the people.

Because the work of the first Continental Congress was chiefly devoted to the task of formulating the American case and enlisting support in bringing pressure to bear upon the ministry among those colonies not so bitterly aroused, the parties in the Congress were able to agree upon such a statement of the American cause, even to the point of recognizing the authority of Parliament to legislate for the empire in the regulation of commerce. The Congress acted pretty much as a whole, feeling that a permanent mechanism of organization was unnecessary. Faced with the prospect of a continuance of the crisis, however, it called for a new Congress to meet the following May—should the grievances of the colonies, in the meantime, not be redressed.

But when the second Continental Congress met in May, 1775, armed conflict had taken place in Lexington and Concord, and men knew that the struggle now beginning would be long and trying. The Congress itself was of a much more "radical" shade of opinion than its predecessor. Moreover, the thirteen colonies were now in full rebellion, and the Continental Congress found itself faced with the immediate necessity of setting up fairly permanent mechanisms for the conduct of the war, for the organization and administration of a treasury, for the accumulation of materials of war, and for the securing of aid from abroad. Without any precedent to go by, other than the prior experience of its members in the colonial legislatures, this amorphous body organized itself into a series of committees for the administration of its various and rapidly multiplying functions. For an entire year the Congress was little more than a congeries of committees.

As yet the idea of a severing of the political connection with the mother country had not posed the necessity of establishing a more formal plan of government. But with the steady increase of the sentiment for independence a corresponding realization of the need for a formal union of the states to replace the old central authority of the imperial government began to take place, and this realization led, in June, 1776, to the appointment of a committee to formulate a plan for the new government. The plan was presented to the Congress by John Dickinson on July 12, 1776, only eight days after the final adoption of the Declaration of Independence. Dickinson, a conservative, proposed a government with a strong, centralized authority. But this plan was too conservative, in its authority too much like the imperial government from which the former colonies had just declared their independence, to suit the agrarian "states-rights" group in the Congress. The Dickinson plan was therefore modified, in the course of the debate, in the direction of a more loose-jointed arrangement, which finally emerged as the Articles of Confederation, the first Constitution of the United States of America.

The division of the second Continental Congress into parties over the form of a proposed central government was thus basically social and economic. Political divisions followed, roughly, the lines of class or professional interests. The agrarians held a majority of the votes in the Congress, and the result was that the Articles of Confederation, as finally adopted by the Congress and submitted to the states in 1778, expressed the "states-rights," or "particularist" theory of government.

The Articles of Confederation left to each state "its sovereignty, freedom and independence, and every Power, Jurisdiction and right," which was not expressly delegated to the central government. The central government was given the authority to conduct relations with other nations as the agent for all the states, and the Congress was to be the last court of appeals in cases between states. Both the central government and the states were to have the power to coin money. The national armed forces were to be raised by a system of state quotas, and the central government could not make war, sign treaties, or borrow money without the approving vote of nine states. Under this constitution the national government was given no machinery for enforcing its decisions upon the states; its effectiveness was bound to depend, in the last analysis, upon the good will and the loyalty of the state legislatures. Weak as it was, however, it was under this constitution that the Revolutionary war was fought and won.

The Articles of Confederation, though submitted to the states for approval in 1778, were not finally ratified by all of them until March 1, 1781. The reason for the delay is to be found in the cleavage between the states which had claims to land in the west and those which had no such claims. In Pennsylvania, New Jersey, and Maryland, particularly, several powerful land companies had applied directly to the Crown, in the period just preceding the war, for large areas of lands in the west for the purpose of settlement and population. Two of these groups, indeed, the Indiana Company and the Vandalia Company, had already received a certain amount of encouragement prior to the adoption of a "small-holdings" policy by the Crown, whose unquestioned right it was to dispose of the land acquired from France in 1763, regardless of the "sea-to-sea" clauses in some of the old colonial charters, upon which the claims of the "landed" states were based. The members of these land companies held to the theory that, with independence, the Crown's title to the western lands had devolved upon the United States as a whole. The speculators of the "landed" states, not unnaturally, claimed that the title to the lands in the west rested, as it had always rested, with the states, according to the terms of their original charters, regardless of what had happened to their charters in the meantime.

This was essentially only a cleavage between two rival groups of land speculators. But Virginia supported its sons and refused to surrender its claims under its charter. Maryland, on the other hand, stood staunchly by Samuel Chase and the Illinois-Wabash Company, formed in 1779 to exploit the lands north of the Ohio claimed by Virginia, and refused to ratify the Articles of Confederation unless Virginia surrendered its claims. After much obstinate debate on both sides, Virginia finally surrendered to the Continental Congress, on January 2, 1781, its claims to the north and west of the Ohio. This induced Maryland to ratify the Articles, but it effectively destroyed the hopes of the Indiana and the Vandalia companies, since Virginia retained its title to lands south and east of the Ohio, where the lands claimed by these companies lay.

At long last, then, in 1781, five years after the Declaration of Independence, the first Constitution of the United States went into effect. It would be a mistake to suppose the country to have been without a government all that time, however, for the government legally established was to all intents and purposes identical with the government which had existed, *de facto,* at least since the meeting of the second Continental Congress in May, 1775. In the long struggle over the Articles the social and economic forces that were to determine the shape of political opinion and institutions had become visible, and the general lines of American political divisions had been laid down. The passage and the ratification of the Articles of Confederation marked the ascendancy of the "agrarians" in the new state; but the demonstrated strength of the conservative opposition was such as to indicate that the agrarian ascendency could not be expected to last forever.

However that may be, the break from the British control was now complete, and a central government of the United States of America had been set up in its place. That, alone, was a considerable revolution.

STATE CONSTITUTIONS

When thirteen of the British colonies in North America sent delegates to the Continental Congress, first to protest against and then to resist the policies of the mother country, they took the steps which, for themselves, led to the demolition of the old imperial institution and the erection of a new "union" to take its place. The destruction of the imperial tie and its function in the colonial governments was not followed, however, by the creation of a similar tie with the new central government of the Confederation. On the contrary, the Confederation's capacity to interfere in the politics of the individual states as Britain had formerly done was clearly and unequivocally limited. Yet the "prerogative" and its mechanisms had been a real and important part of the colonial constitution, and it performed a function that was by independence left unprovided for. For the individual states, therefore, independence meant more than mere separation from the mother country: it also presented them with the compelling necessity of creating new state constitutions to replace the old provincial constitutions under the Crown.

In all the new states political opinion was divided into two groups. The loyalists were early practically eliminated from political life; but the balance of the population was sharply divided over questions growing out of the new situation. The "radicals" were those who, like Samuel Adams and John Adams, Patrick Henry, Thomas Jefferson and Benjamin Franklin, favored a vigorous stand against the mother country in defense of American rights, and had not flinched even before the thought of ultimate independence. The "conservatives," led by such men as Alexander Hamilton, John Jay, George Washington, Robert Morris, and John Dickinson, had clung to the hope that the colonies might still preserve the old loyalty to the mother country, if only she could be brought to a recognition and a generous adjustment of colonial grievances. In general, also, it was the radicals who favored more popular forms of government in the states, while the conservatives advocated governments which would place political control in the hands of a propertied, aristocratic upper class. The local provincial political divisions were thus largely social in nature, based upon a greater or a lesser faith in popular control.

Thus the radicals, in their plans for new state constitutions, drawing upon the lessons of the colonial experience, favored governments in which the dominant element would be an elected legislature, with low property qualifications, or none at all, limiting the right to vote. They distrusted any established church and the legal aspects of aristocracy and they were especially opposed to the old methods of apportionment of representation which had placed the control of colonial legislatures in the hands of the wealthy seaboard communities as over against the settlements in the west. The conservatives, on the other hand, were afraid of popular control. Though they eventually came to support the move for independence, they did not think of independence as involving such thoroughgoing social reform as seemed to be inherent in the radical program. The conservatives, therefore, stood for a preservation of the old order of things: the continuation of the Anglican establishment in religion, wherever it had been established before, the retention, unchanged, of the old political system which left control of affairs in the hands of "the rich, the well-born, and the able," and the preservation of the aristocratic social order based upon wealth— especially those aspects of the system that depended upon large estates in land.

In most of the states the radicals were in control of the situation, if not of the legislatures, and it was the radical elements who set up new governments to replace the old. As the old royal governments began to lose control, in the latter half of 1775, the revolutionary leaders in the states turned to the Continental Congress for advice. The response of the Congress was a general recommendation that temporary governments be set up in the states, pending a settlement of the quarrel with the mother country. As the move for independence gained momentum, the temporary arrangements tended to become permanent; and in May, 1776, two months before the Declaration of Independence, Congress advised the states to form permanent governments. Connecticut and Rhode Island, the most autonomous and the most "popular" of the former colonies, found the transition easy: all that was necessary was a slight revision of their colonial charters, deleting all reference to the Crown and all phrases binding these colonies to England, in order to produce new state constitutions. Virginia very quickly adopted a permanent constitution, and New Jersey adopted an arrangement that depended upon the outcome of the dispute. New Hampshire, Massachusetts, and South Carolina quickly formed governments of a semi-temporary nature. The other states followed, and by 1780 all the states had fashioned their state constitutions.

These documents were hastily, and often crudely, put together. Some were formed by the temporary congresses or conventions that had been elected by the local committees and that had assumed control of the government, sometimes even in defiance of the state legislatures; others, such as those of Delaware and Massachusetts, were drafted by conventions especially created for the purpose. In all of them were reflected, in one way or another, the colonial experience, together with the political ideas of certain of the eighteenth-century political philosophers, chiefly John Locke and the great French political philosopher, the Baron de Montesquieu.

The most radical or "democratic" of this crop of new constitutions were those of Pennsylvania, North Carolina, Delaware, and

Georgia. Pennsylvania, for example, drawing upon its colonial precedent, adopted a constitution providing for a unicameral legislature, the members of which might be any taxpayer, without further property qualification; all taxpayers, moreover, could vote. The executive branch of the state was to be a council of twelve, one of whom would be elected "president" by joint vote of assembly and council. The council appointed judges and other non-elective officials, but it had no veto power over the legislature. The control of the legislature was taken out of the hands of the wealthy eastern counties by a redistribution of representation which now placed the weight of influence in the west. Another remarkably democratic feature of this constitution was the provision of a system of free, public schools to be supported by public funds. On the whole, this constitution, which stemmed back to the Charter of Privileges of 1701 and the ideas of William Penn, made Pennsylvania almost a pure democracy. For this very reason, however, it was greeted by a storm of criticism and opposition by the conservatives, who, in their distrust of democracy and their fear of the future under such a radical plan, made every possible effort to prevent its going into operation. They were successful, after fourteen years, in having it revised during the conservative reaction which swept over the country in the late seventeen-eighties and led to the drafting of the federal Constitution of 1789.

At the other extreme from the Pennsylvania constitution was that of South Carolina. In the second constitution, adopted in 1778 (the first constitution was in effect only from 1776 to 1778), a two-house legislature was provided, which was composed of a senate and a house of representatives. The Anglican Church, which had been "established" under the first constitution, was disestablished, and the senate was made elective by popular vote. But it remained essentially a conservative document, for the plantation counties of the coastlands were given one hundred forty-four representatives as against fifty-eight for the upland counties. Members of the senate were required to possess property worth not less than £2,000 if they lived in the parish they represented, or £7,000 if they did not; the governor was required to possess property worth not less than £10,000. A member of the house of representatives had to possess fifty acres of land or a town lot—or property worth £3,500 if he did not live in the parish he represented. Every voter had to have at least fifty acres of land or a lot in town. The effect of all this was to place the control of government in the hands of the wealthy aristocrats of Charleston and the eastern counties. The influence of the western frontier counties was distinctly curbed. One reaction resulting from the colonial experience, however, is to be observed in the provision for the election of the governor by the legislature and the restriction of his power to that of making certain appointments; he was not even allowed the veto power. The possibility of an executive check upon the legislature was thus removed; the legislature was the predominant element in the government, but the legislature was "owned" by the aristocrats.

The other state constitutions fell somewhere between these two extremes. Virginia, New York, and Massachusetts adopted constitutions which were only less conservative than that of South Carolina. North Carolina was much more democratic; its constitution was remarkable for the provision permitting universal free white male suffrage in the election of members of the lower house of the legislature. Even here, however, democracy failed to overcome completely the prevailing idea that government must somehow be anchored in property, for the voter was required to own fifty acres of land in order to be allowed to vote for senators, and senators themselves were required to own at least three hundred acres.

In general, then, the state constitutions show the influence of certain clearly defined trends which appear in the colonial period of institutional growth. The legislatures were made the predominant element in the government while the executives were made correspondingly weak. Little check was placed on the legislature, although some provisions were made to prevent hasty action, such, for example, as the clauses in the Pennsylvania constitution requiring the publication of laws before final passage, and the providing of "censors" to review the work of the legislature. The fact is that the legislatures everywhere assumed that they alone were to judge of the constitutionality of their own measures. This attitude, again, was the outgrowth of the tendency already observed in the evolution of parliamentary institutions in the colonies prior to the Revolution, as well as a reaction against the system of checks and balances imposed upon the colonies by the British system of administration. For inherent in that struggle was the principle of parliamentary autonomy and responsibility—an ideal at last achieved in the constitution of the colonies now become states.

Complete parliamentary self-government, however, must not be mistaken for democracy. The state constitutions, under the influence of the radicals, were, indeed, far more democratic, in a relative sense, than the colonial constitutions had been. But without exception they placed the control of government in the hands of property owners, and in most cases created a hierarchy of political responsibility and privilege that followed the pattern of the graduations of wealth. The years from 1776 to 1789 were a period of "radical" or "democratic" control; but both the radicalism and the democracy of the period were relative only to the position of the conservatives. It was another generation before even universal manhood suffrage was established, to say nothing of the newer mechanisms of democracy invented in the twentieth century.

LEGAL AND SOCIAL ASPECTS OF THE INTERNAL REVOLUTION

That the mind of the Americans was moving toward a broader conception of civic and social relationships, however, there can be no doubt. The eighteenth-century "Enlightenment," with its doctrine of natural rights based upon natural law, had made a profound impression in America. But there was also a leaven of equalitarianism that arose from the American scene itself, and especially from the economic and social conditions in the expanding frontier.

The equalitarian trend is to be observed in various ways. To begin with, the most ardent supporters of the Revolution, and those whose day-by-day efforts made it a reality, were the common people—small farmers and frontiersmen, supported in some measure by the poor artisans in the towns, so that, in its social aspects, the Revolution was their revolution. These were the men who benefited from the extensions of the suffrage, such as they were, that were written into the new state constitutions; and "the elevation of whole classes of people to the status of voters elevates them also in their social status." The old acceptance of a stratified society as a matter of course was broken, and this reform was symbolic of a trend toward social "leveling" that has persisted in American life ever since.

One of the most significant aspects of the equalitarian trend in American life during the Revolution is to be found in the legislation, passed by the states, having to do with the ownership of land—legislation which struck at one of the economic foundations of the aristocratic stratification of society. In the words of J. Franklin Jameson, "Political democracy came to the United States as a result of economic democracy . . . this nation came to be marked by political institutions of a democratic type because it had, still earlier, come to be characterized in its economic life by democratic arrangements and practices." But the democratization of economic life in the Revolutionary era meant the democratization of the land, since agriculture was the basic element in economic exchange. This process began with the mere act of throwing off the allegiance to Great Britain; for by that act alone the still ungranted lands of the thirteen provinces ceased to be the property of the Crown, as in the royal provinces, or of great proprietors, as in the case of Maryland and Pennsylvania, and became the property of the people of the states. This alone was an extremely significant change; for it marked the end of a medieval concept of land-holding and the beginning of a distinctly modern one. In addition to the Crown lands, many great estates belonging to tories were confiscated and appropriated to state use. How were these lands to be administered? Should the states continue the system of collecting quitrents? Should the old semi-feudal systems of land-holding, calculated to create and preserve a landed aristocracy, be continued in force?

The states thus found themselves in possession of large areas of "public lands." One of the first internal problems to be faced was that of administering these public lands, and the social trend of the times is to be seen in the methods devised. The states needed money with which to pay the expenses of the war; the sale of public lands offered a sure and substantial income; either the land could be sold outright for money, or it could be used in the place of money to pay the land-hungry soldiers for their wartime service. The latter plan was followed in several states, with the result that the number of small landowners was substantially increased. In other cases the states sold large blocks of land to speculators for cash, and the speculators then resold the land in small parcels at large profits. In either case, however, the net result was an extension of the number of small landowners, an effective democratization of land-holding, and a rapid increase in the numbers of people moving past the Alleghenies to build a new frontier society in the trans-Allegheny west.

Perhaps the most typical of the old land-holding institutions were the twin laws of entail and of primogeniture. These laws, which seem to have had their origins in the medieval need for a social order based upon powerful landed families, had as their object the preservation of the stability of large estates in land. Thus the law of entail made it possible to prevent the division of large estates, and the law of primogeniture provided for the inheritance of an entire estate, in cases where the owner died intestate, by the oldest son instead of allowing it to be divided equally among the children. The net effect of these two laws was a tendency to preserve the great estates, once formed, for centuries in the hands of the same direct line of family descent. Some of the colonies had already abolished one or both these laws, even before the Revolution. But during the Revolutionary era almost all the states abolished both entails and primogeniture. While the freeing of the land from these old restrictions was not immediately and fully effective, the ultimate result was to prevent the crystallization of an aristocracy of great landed families. For the constant break-up and re-forming of estates brought about a fluidity of ownership which tended both to prevent the formation of great units of land and constantly and increasingly to broaden the numbers and the classes of people owning land. Obviously, this process had a distinctly "leveling" effect upon society.

The social significance of the broadening boundaries of land-ownership was complemented by its political significance. For the reformers in the state legislatures were not content to do away with the aristocratic restrictions upon land transfers; as already suggested, they also broadened the base of political control by a reduction in the amount of land required for participation in political activity. Thus, prior to the Revolution, every colony had a property qualification for voting, and this generally meant land. The most common requirement was that the voter own land that produced an income of at least forty shillings a year or a house in town worth £5. Another requirement was that he own a stated amount of land, say, fifty acres, without reference to its value. But during the Revolution most of the states reduced the property qualification for voting to the point where almost any taxpayer could vote. In some of the states property qualifications for office-holding, generally higher than those for voting, were proportionately reduced. Property qualifications for political responsibility were retained, however, and in some of the states those qualifications were very high.

Thus, in the liberalization of the laws regulating the purchase, holding, and transmission of land, and in the reduced property requirements for participation in political life, there may be seen a distinct tendency toward an increase in the number of small land-owners, a democratization of the social system based upon land, and a corresponding democratization of politics.

Another indication of the "leveling" process going on in American society is to be seen in the changing attitude toward slavery. Thoughtful men could not fail to see the inconsistency between the sentiment for liberty and freedom, proclaimed in the Declaration of Independence that "all men are created equal," and the presence of half a million Negroes as slaves in the thirteen states. Even before the Revolution, the influence of eighteenth-century humanitarianism was challenging the practice of slavery. Many Americans had seen the inhumanity of the institution and had denounced it; such an apostle of freedom was the Quaker saint, John Woolman of New Jersey. Slaveholders themselves saw the inhumanity of it; Patrick Henry, one of the most eloquent and powerful of the Virginia leaders of the Revolution, wrote:

Would any one believe that I am the master of slaves of my own purchase! I am drawn along by the general inconvenience of living without them. I will not, I can not justify it. . . . I believe a time will come when an opportunity will be offered to abolish this lamentable evil. Everything we can do is to improve it, if it happens in our day, if not, let us transmit to our descendants, together with our slaves, a pity for their unhappy lot, and an abhorrence of slavery. . . . It is a debt we owe to the purity of our religion, to show that it is at variance with that law which warrants slavery.

But the anti-slavery sentiment went well beyond private opinion. As early as 1774 the first Continental Congress took cognizance of the evil by including the slave trade among the wrongs to be remedied by the non-importation agreements, and it is difficult to avoid the conclusion that, in part at least, the motive behind this action was a desire to limit the evils of the slave trade itself. Already, in July, 1774, the legislature of Rhode Island, moved by the conviction that personal liberty should be the natural quality of everyone regardless of color, had enacted a law providing that any slave brought within the bounds of the province should automatically become free. Similar laws were passed by other states; some prohibited the importation of slaves altogether, others sought to discourage the trade by placing prohibitive duties on imported slaves. Some states even went so far as to abolish slavery; Pennsylvania enacted, in 1780, a law providing for the gradual abolition of slavery, and Massachusetts accomplished the same end by a judicial decision of the superior court, which ruled that the phrase in the state constitution that "all men are born free and equal" made slavery unconstitutional in that state. Virginia, one of the states where slavery was strongest, encouraged the manumission of slaves, with the result that ten thousand slaves were freed in less than ten years. The struggle for liberty was thus not merely a struggle for freedom from British control. For many men, even in the slaveholding states in the south, the declaration that "all men are created equal" meant exactly what it said.

The "leveling" tendencies already noted may also be seen in certain intellectual and religious changes that were taking place at the same time. Among other things, a new humanitarianism had already begun to manifest itself before the era of the American Revolution. Now, some states reduced the number of criminal offenses punishable by death, and others modified their laws with regard to imprisonment for debt. This humanitarianism, along with the increasing interest in natural science and philosophy, is to be traced, in some measure at least, to the influence of the intellectual phenomenon in the eighteenth century known as the Enlightenment.

Other changes, however, may be traced to the influence of the war itself. Such, for example, was the wave of patriotism that swept over the new states during and after the Revolution, and is clearly reflected in the literature of the period—in the writings of Philip Freneau, Joel Barlow, Francis Hopkinson, Jonathan Trumbull, and others. Another observable intellectual change was a broadening of the American horizon to include the appreciation of other nations such as France, Holland and Spain, which had aided us in the war. This was particularly true of France. From the deathless enmity of the colonial days for all things French, an enmity that sprang both from provincialism and from the long series of Anglo-French wars, the Americans swung to an admiration of French culture and French customs that became something of a fad. People who could, studied French, read French books, wore French clothes, and adopted French manners. Chairs of French were established at William and Mary in 1779 and at Harvard in 1780.

Still another intellectual aspect of the "leveling" tendencies of the American Revolution is to be seen in the liberalization of education. The most notable example of this, perhaps, were the efforts made in Pennsylvania and Virginia to establish systems of free, public schools. Hitherto education in Virginia, as in most of the states, had been a privilege of the rich; but the Virginia plan, formulated by Thomas Jefferson, would have provided a minimum of education for all the children in the state, regardless of their social or economic status. Jefferson, himself an aristocrat, distrusted the aristocracy based on wealth; and his educational plan was calculated to produce an aristocracy of intellect that, by a process of selection, would be composed of the most intelligent individuals in society, drawn from all classes. In its provision for elementary education for all children, however, Jefferson's educational plan was essentially democratic. What he desired was an intellectual aristocracy drawn from, and based upon, a social democracy. His plan failed of adoption in Virginia by a narrow margin; but it is typical of the sort of thinking about education that was going on in the new states.

Much more obvious, in the realm of intellectual and religious progress, was the effect of the Revolution upon religion. At the beginning of the Revolution, nine of the thirteen rebellious colonies had "established" churches—that is to say, churches that were officially recognized and supported by the state. In the New England colonies, except Rhode Island, Congregationalism had been "established" from the beginning. A majority of the people were Congregationalists and the churches were supported by public funds. In six of the colonies the Anglican Church was the established form, but in none did it number a majority of the inhabitants among its adherents. In the southern colonies, particularly, there was great resentment among the Baptists, Presbyterians, Quakers, and others over the laws that required them to pay taxes to support an Anglican clergy or those that forbade them from maintaining their own denominational schools for their children. Only in Pennsylvania and Rhode Island did complete religious freedom prevail on the eve of the American Revolution.

In New England, where the established Congregational Church was the church of the vast majority of the people, the Revolution had little or no effect upon the establishments; the Congregational Church was not separated from the state in Connecticut until 1818, and in Massachusetts until 1833. In the states where the Anglican Church was established, however, it was identified both with British control and with the local aristocracy. The move of resentment which swept it from power during the Revolution was thus both anti-British and anti-aristocratic in nature. The Americans had long been suspicious of the power of the Anglican Church, and this feeling had been manifest in the long-continued opposition to the establishment of an American bishopric. Thus it came about that with the establishment of new state governments religious toleration became in most states one of the fundamental rights of the citizen, and churches of all denominations, or their adherents, were brought to a position of equality before the law. The clause concerning religious toleration in the constitution of Virginia, where the Anglican Church had hitherto been established, also written by Thomas Jefferson, is typical. It provides that:

No man shall be compelled to frequent or support any religious worship, place, or ministry whatsoever; nor shall be enforced, restrained, molested, or burdened in his body or goods, nor shall otherwise suffer on account of his religious opinions or belief; but that all men shall be free to profess, and by argument to maintain, their opinions in matters of religion.

The Anglican Church was disestablished elsewhere, and its disestablishment had a two- or a three-fold significance. Associated, as it had been in the popular mind, with the forces of aristocracy, "toryism," and reaction, the stripping of its power indicated the popular trend toward democracy and independence. The establishment of legal religious equality, therefore, was a long step toward complete religious toleration, despite the fact that religious qualifications for office-holding were retained in most of the states. Toleration of practically all shades of private belief had become, after the long, slow growth of toleration through the colonial period, a reality; and it may perhaps fairly be said that the United States was one of the first countries in the world to arrive at this advanced stage of enlightenment. As Jameson puts it:

If religious freedom and equality is America's chief contribution to the world's civilization, as has been conspicuously declared—and surely much could be said for this view—great honor belongs to the men of the Revolutionary period, for then it was, more than at any other time, that this principle, so distinctive of America and so invaluable to her prosperity and development, was put into actual practice.

THE LOYALISTS

It should be clear from what has been said that the American Revolution was social as well as political in nature, and that many profound internal changes took place along with the separation from England. The general direction of this social revolution was toward more democracy than had existed in the colonies in the era just prior to the Revolution—by the extension of economic opportunity, by the social leveling that resulted from this, and by a corresponding broadening of the social base of political control. Another social phenomenon of the Revolution, a tragic incident, to be sure, but one calculated to increase the relative strength of the radical, "democratic" elements in American society by the removal of a large body of its aristocratic, conservative members, was the emigration of the loyalists.

The loyalists were those Americans who held their loyalty to their king more sacred and binding than any other loyalty. They were the men and women who, in the face of the "rabble-rousing democracy" and the radical demand for independence, maintained their British patriotism. They had been raised under the British Crown, and had learned to love it. For them the Crown was the symbol of order, of security, and of the rights of Englishmen; most of all, it was the symbol of the British nation, of which they considered themselves wholeheartedly a part. Most of them were conservatives, whether because of their positions in politics or society, because of large properties that they feared to lose, or because merely of temperament and a love for the old regime. But there were also many who were convinced that the mother country was mistaken in its colonial policy and that the Americans should be given greater autonomy in the administration of their affairs. Such a one was Joseph Galloway. These liberal tories were even willing to demand reforms in the name of their rights as Englishmen. But they could not bring themselves to break the bonds of love for the mother country and sacrifice their ideals and their futures to a new state and a new society being formed by men whose ideals of society and of government were repugnant to their own.

At the time of the Declaration of Independence the loyalists still constituted probably one-third of the population of the thirteen colonies. Practically all the members of the "courts" of the royal governors were loyal to the king, as were the placemen appointed by them. Similarly, the Anglican clergy and the military officers were for the most part loyal. Many others who clung to the old ties were large landowners or businessmen, and many were members of the professions and intellectual occupations. In general, it may be said that the tories were thoughtful, well-educated, moderate, and conservative men, who included in their numbers many of the most intelligent and enlightened members of American society.

The loyalists were able to defend themselves eloquently in press and pulpit, for the loyalist position was ably presented by such writers as "Massachusettensis" in Massachusetts, Samuel Seabury in New York, and Jonathan Boucher in Maryland. But the popular clamor of the radicals called down upon the tories an increasing amount of persecution. Gradually, the loyalists found it more and more difficult to get the public ear, as their printing establishments were throttled or shut up and the writers of pro-British literature were exposed to personal violence.

As the conflict deepened into violence in Massachusetts, in the spring of 1775, many of the loyalists of the province moved into Boston in order to be under the protection of General Gage. Feeling became more and more bitter; the conflict was becoming a civil war with one part of the population arrayed in bitter hatred against the other. As the rebellion spread to the other colonies the social breach became wider and deeper. Families were divided; and the local "committees of safety" began hysterically to ferret out the tories to "save" the communities from their influence. Many were thrown into jail; many were tarred and feathered; many were driven from their homes, to which they were never to return.

As time wore on, the feeling against the loyalists mounted ever higher and higher. Loyalist property was often destroyed by radical mobs. With the Declaration of Independence, loyalty to the Crown of Great Britain became treason, punishable by the confiscation of the loyalists' property, or by exile, or even death. Several states enacted laws disfranchising loyalists, or otherwise depriving them of the rights of citizens. Other states banished them. All the states enacted laws confiscating loyalist property. These confiscations were not entirely without justification, for many loyalists actually joined the military service of Britain and fought against their former fellow-citizens. It has been estimated that in the single colony of New York no less than 23,000 men joined the British flag. Other devices were used by the tories to handicap the independence party, devices such as tampering with the mails, sniping, proselyting, and spying upon the American armies.

In any case, the persecution of the loyalists led many of them to leave the country. As early as the fall of 1776, when General Gage had been forced to evacuate Boston, about a thousand loyalists had left with him to seek refuge elsewhere under the British flag. Some went directly to England, some went to the British West Indies, and others went to Florida and Nova Scotia. With the occupation of New York by the British that city became the haven for the loyalists, and when, the war lost, the British gave up that place also, thousands of loyalists decided to go with them. Elsewhere, especially in the interior parts of New York and New England, loyalists were emigrating all during the war. Of these rural loyalists many went to Canada, there to take up land in the region which later became the province of Ontario, where they were recognized and indemnified by their grateful king.

All in all, probably 60,000 Americans emigrated from the United States because of their loyalty to the king of England. In their eyes, the Americans were traitors to their king and nation; in the eyes of the Americans, the tories were themselves traitors to their country, to their friends and relatives, and to the cause of American liberty. So deep was the division of loyalties which found loyalty to one's king pitted against loyalty to one's country; so strong was the bitterness and the passion of civil war!

RECOMMENDED BOOKS FOR FURTHER READING

CONTEMPORARY NARRATIVES

Jonathan Boucher, *Reminiscences of an American Loyalist, 1738-1789, being the Autobiography of the Revd. Jonathan Boucher,* edited by Jonathan Boucher.

Albert B. Hart, ed., *American History Told by Contemporaries,* II, Chapters 26-27, 30, 33.

Old South Leaflet, No. 2, *Articles of Confederation.*

Old South Leaflet, No. 173, *Samuel Adams on the Rights of the Colonists, 1772.*

MODERN ACCOUNTS

Thomas P. Abernethy, *Western Lands and the American Revolution.*

James T. Adams, *New England in the Republic, 1776-1850.*

Charles A. and Mary R. Beard, *The Rise of American Civilization,* I, Chapters 6-7.

Gilbert Chinard, *Thomas Jefferson, Apostle of Americanism.*

Robert A. East, *Business Enterprise in the American Revolutionary Era.*

Edward Channing, *A History of the United States,* Volume III.

John Fiske, *The American Revolution.*

Alexander C. Flick, *Loyalism in New York during the American Revolution.*

Lawrence H. Gipson, *Jared Ingersoll.*

Isaac S. Harrell, *Loyalism in Virginia.*

Francis W. Hirst, *Life and Letters of Thomas Jefferson.*

Homer C. Hockett, *The Constitutional History of the United States, 1776-1826,* Chapters 7-9.

Edward F. Humphrey, *Nationalism and Religion in America, 1774-1789.*

John F. Jameson, *The American Revolution Considered as a Social Movement.*

Merrill Jensen, *The Articles of Confederation.*

William E. H. Lecky, *The American Revolution, 1763-1783.*

Charles E. Merriam, *A History of American Political Theories,* Chapters 1-3.

Allan Nevins, *The American States During and After the Revolution, 1775-1789.*

Vernon L. Parrington, *The Colonial Mind, 1620-1800,* Part III.

Enoch W. Sikes, *The Transition of North Carolina from Colony to Commonwealth.*

William G. Sumner, *The Financier and the Finances of the American Revolution.*

William G. Sumner, *Robert Morris.*

Moses C. Tyler, *Literary History of the American Revolution, 1763-1783.*

Claude H. Van Tyne, *The Loyalists in the American Revolution.*

Claude H. Van Tyne, *The War of Independence.*

William S. Wallace, *The United Empire Loyalists.*

George M. Wrong, *Canada and the American Revolution,* Chapters 18-22.

46

The Diplomacy of Independence

AMERICA AND THE EUROPEAN BALANCE OF POWER

IT WAS one thing for thirteen of the twenty-six British colonies in America to revolt against the mother country and declare themselves an independent nation. To make good their independence and to be accepted into the family of nations was quite another matter. Indeed, it probably would have been quite impossible had not the international situation in Europe been propitious for just such a series of events.

The nations of Europe, in their relations with each other, had long been under the sway of the idea of an international balance of power. This doctrine, as expressed in terms of the contemporary mercantilist philosophy of national well-being, held that the wealth and power of a state derived chiefly from its favorable balance of trade, and that, therefore, no state should be allowed to become too great commercially, since it would thereby be so enriched as to enable it to lord it over the others. But, since colonies were the most profitable and dependable market for exportable products, the weight of a nation in the scales of international power was determined chiefly by the size and the commerce of its colonial empire. The Seven Years' War had been fought largely to maintain the colonial balance of power in the face of the expanding wealth and power of Great Britain in America, and Britain's victory was pointed to as clearly confirming this mercantilist doctrine of the American balance. France and Spain had been defeated, with a consequent loss of colonies, commerce, power, and prestige, in 1763. Now they were resting, waiting for a time when the American balance of power might be redressed.

The mounting dispute between Great Britain and thirteen of the continental colonies was therefore watched with great avidity by France and Spain, but particularly by the former. For this quarrel might be the beginning of a rift which would lead to a complete separation serving French interests enormously, since the richest source of British wealth and power, the heart of the British colonial empire, would be cut off, and British commercial and military

682

power would be correspondingly reduced. To that degree, at least, the balance of power would be redressed to the advantage of France.

FRANCE IS INTERESTED

It was for reasons such as these that, as early as 1764, the Duke of Choiseul sent secret French agents to the colonies to observe their relations with the mother country and to give such encouragement as might be discreetly possible to any tendency to independence. This policy was continued until Choiseul went out of office in 1770. During the next four years French foreign policy sank to the nadir of ignominious passivity and humiliation in the eyes of Europe. The year 1774, however, saw the accession of a new king, Louis XVI, to the French throne, and the advent of a new and vigorous French patriot to the foreign ministry in the person of the Count de Vergennes. Vergennes was a disciple of Choiseul, and immediately revived the policy of sending agents to America.

The Americans, on their side, were delighted, and rightly looked upon French interest as a source of assistance that might be a deciding factor in their struggle. The French agent, Bonvouloir, who came to America in September, 1775, had instructions to assure the Americans that France had no desire to regain Canada, thereby to restore the old French menace on the American frontier; that it looked with benevolence upon the efforts of the Americans to free themselves of British exploitation; and that it would welcome American ships in French ports should the Americans choose to go there regardless of the British navigation laws.

This encouragement was both secret and unofficial. But the Continental Congress, in November, 1775, appointed a secret committee of correspondence to establish and cultivate relations with foreign governments. This committee charged Arthur Lee, colonial agent for Massachusetts then in London, with the task of establishing contact with representatives of other powers. Lee's experience as a "minister" [agent] from Massachusetts to England served him fairly well in his duties as agent for the Continental Congress in its diplomatic relations with foreign powers. Lee succeeded in meeting Caron de Beaumarchais, popular French playwright and secret political agent, in London. Beaumarchais saw in the American revolt the opportunity for which France had been waiting, and began vigorously to urge the Count de Vergennes, and even the king himself, to extend secret aid to the American rebels. His urgings were without result, however, until the spring of 1776.

Meanwhile, Bonvouloir, the French agent in America, was extending encouragement to the Continental Congress while reporting to his superior that the thirteen discontented colonies were about to break off their relationship with the mother country. Thus both Bonvouloir and Beaumarchais probably hastened the growing conviction of Vergennes and the king that the moment to strike at England in the name of the American balance of power had almost arrived.

The Americans, for their part, encouraged by both Beaumarchais and Bonvouloir, finally decided to send an agent directly to France. The Continental Congress selected Silas Deane of Connecticut for the purpose, and sent him abroad with instructions to negotiate for the purchase (on credit) of miltary supplies and Indian goods with which to win the support of the Indians in the expected frontier conflict with Canada, and to sound out the French government with regard to a formal miltary alliance. Deane, a somewhat naive Connecticut Yankee at King Louis XVI's court, was not very successful. Between Deane and Beaumarchais, however, the king was finally persuaded to give secret aid to the colonies in the form of money and military supplies.

Thus, many months before the Declaration of Independence, the Continental Congress had set up what was effectively a committee of foreign affairs; it had sent agents abroad to negotiate with foreign powers and had received considerable military aid from one of them; and it had thrown open American commerce to the world in defiance of British imperial law. In doing these things, the thirteen revolted colonies had assumed the prerogatives of a sovereign state. This assumption of both sovereignty and independence was publicly and legally announced by the Declaration of Independence.

THE FRENCH ALLIANCE

Upon the assumption of full and independent national sovereignty, the new states were faced with the necessity of formulating a permanent foreign policy. This they did in the summer of 1776, and the major outlines of this policy are to be seen in the instructions given the three diplomats, Arthur Lee, Silas Deane, and Benjamin Franklin, who were officially named to present the American case for recognition and assistance to France.

Naturally, the immediate problem was to win recognition of the independence and nationhood of the United States, and, following that, to arrange, if possible, for military assistance. The United

States had no desire for permanent foreign alliances. Far from it, the American colonies had been founded in large measure by men who were attempting to escape from the insecurity of life in Europe, and this idea of escape and isolation from European dangers persisted as one of the most deeply rooted features of the American attitude toward the outside world. As Thomas Paine said when he appealed to the Americans to declare their independence, the connection of the colonies with England "tends directly to involve this continent in European wars and quarrels, and sets us at variance with nations . . . against whom we have neither anger nor complaint. As Europe is our market for trade, we should form no partial connection in any part. It is the true interest of America to steer clear of European contentions, which she never can do while . . . she is made the make-weight in the scale of British politics." This desire to avoid unnecessary entanglements in European wars was hardly more than a feeling, in the late eighteenth century, but it was a real feeling and Paine was appealing to it knowing that the argument would be effective. On the other hand, the normal economic development of the colonies, and particularly those of the north, had brought them very early to a realization of the need for a constantly expanding market for their trade, and the ideal of a free commerce was deeply rooted in the thinking of Americans with regard to their relations with foreign countries. Thus it came about that the two basic ideas influencing the Continental Congress when it approached foreign nations for aid seemed to be military isolation and freedom of commercial intercourse. But the necessities of war convinced the members of the Congress that it might have to make an actual alliance with a foreign power in order to win that power's active military assistance in the struggle against Great Britain. The three objectives of American diplomacy then were the winning of recognition of American independence, the acquisition of supplies and military assistance in the conduct of the war, and the establishment of commercial relations with the nations with whom commerce, under British control, had been largely prohibited.

The committee that drew up the "Plan of Treaties" and the instructions for the new agents to France had no precedents by which to guide their policy except the British precedents, which they all knew. In the meetings of the committee, which was composed of Benjamin Franklin, John Adams, John Dickinson, Benjamin Harrison, and Robert Morris, Franklin took a collection of British treaties and apparently selected the Anglo-French commercial Treaty of Utrecht (1713—never ratified), marked the desirable articles in that treaty, and then handed them to John Adams, who copied them. The text arrived at by this method followed closely— in some places word for word—this abortive Anglo-French commercial treaty of sixty-odd years earlier, and embodied the principle of freedom of commerce together with the wartime principle that free ships make free goods. The text was approved by Congress on August 27, 1776, and was subsequently used by American diplomatic representatives abroad.

Lee and Deane were already in Europe, and Franklin joined them in December. The American agents were permitted to reside in Paris, where they were unofficially welcomed. They received no official attention, however, since an official reception would be tantamount to a recognition of American independence. The American agents did keep in touch with the French government, and succeeded in getting for their people continued loans in the form of money and supplies. It was not until the fall of 1777 that the cautious reserve of France broke down, for France was not prepared to risk an outright war with England in aid of the Americans unless there were some promise that the American rebellion would be a success. But the promise came when news arrived in Europe that on October 1, 1777, General Burgoyne had been forced to surrender himself and his army to the Americans at Saratoga. France was spurred into a more definite policy toward the Americans, moreover, by the news that England was preparing to make peace overtures to the Americans on terms that would grant them practically everything they had demanded before the Declaration of Independence. A reunion of the colonies with the mother country would frustrate the French desire to strike at Britain through America. Vergennes, therefore, convinced the king that France must strike now or never, in the name of complete American independence, and appealed to Spain to help in the cause against England lest England, reunited and reconciled with its rebellious colonies, turn against the Spanish colonial empire, to upset the American and European balance of power as it had done in 1739. Spain was cautious, however, and did not come to the aid of France until 1779.

The understanding between France and the United States was signed on February 6, 1778. Two treaties were signed, one commercial and the other military. The commercial treaty followed closely the "Plan of Treaties" that had been copied from the Anglo-French commercial Treaty of Utrecht. It provided for commercial intercourse between the two countries, and embodied the principle, of great interest to the United States as a commerce-carrying maritime nation, that "free ships make free goods." The other treaty provided that, should war break out between France and England as a result of this French recognition of American independence, France and the United States would fight together and neither would make a separate peace with the enemy without the other's consent. Territory that might be conquered from England in the West Indies was to go to France after the war; British territory conquered on the continent of North America was to go to the United States; and each one guaranteed the other's possessions in America "forever."

News of the alliance with France reached America about the same time as news of the British effort at conciliation. The Americans were tempted to accept the British terms, but not for long. They were now committed to the achieving of complete independence or nothing. As expected, the recognition of the United States precipitated war between France and Great Britain, and French soldiers found themselves fighting beside the Americans on American soil.

A WORLD WAR

The war soon spread to include Spain and Holland. Spain was afraid a British victory over the colonies might lead to a new attack upon the Spanish possessions and hoped that a successful war might bring about the restoration of Gibraltar, taken from Spain in 1713. But Spain was afraid that an American victory might set up a republic that would be more of a threat to the Spanish possessions in America than ever Britain was. Furthermore, a successful rebellion in the British colonies might be a very bad example for the Spanish colonies—which, indeed, had reason enough to complain, and which, also, eventually followed the American example, just as the Spanish monarch feared.

Spain finally made up its mind, about a year after the Franco-American alliance, to declare war on Great Britain. Not, however, as the ally of the Americans. Spain was willing to send them aid, which she did; but she would not recognize them. John Jay, whom Congress sent to Spain to do there what Franklin and his colleagues had done in France, was allowed to cool his heels for two years without ever being received at the Spanish court. He finally gave up in disgust, and joined Franklin and the other American agents at Paris. The mere fact that Spain was at war with England, however, was a help to the American cause. Another indirect aid, however slight, came from concerted effort made by the European neutrals, jealous of the high-handed British treatment of their sea-borne commerce, and urged on by France, to place a limit upon British disregard for neutral rights. This was the so-called "Armed Neutrality of 1780." Under the leadership of Catherine IV of Russia, the Baltic nations and Holland united in a formal declaration of certain principles governing the rights of neutrals on the high seas, such as the principle that "free ships make free goods" and the rule that blockades, to be respected, must be enforced.

The "Armed Neutrality" was significant for its advance position with regard to maritime law and for the fact that it completely isolated Great Britain from the continent. Under the circumstances, Great Britain seized upon a pretext to declare war on Holland. For from England's point of view, it was better to have Holland as an enemy than as a neutral since Holland was carrying on a lucrative trade in supplies and contraband of war with the revolted colonies by way of the Dutch colony of St. Eustatius. The British declaration of war against the Dutch turned out to be a boomerang, because the British admiral Rodney, who captured St. Eustatius, had his attention diverted by this task just long enough from the French West Indian fleet to allow Admiral de Grasse to run up the coast and cooperate with the American army in those few, crucial days when Cornwallis found himself caught on the York peninsula with his escape to the sea cut off by the presence of the French vessels off the mouth of Chesapeake Bay.

Great Britain now found itself isolated, with no friends and three dangerous enemies in Europe, and with rapidly dwindling prospects of success in America. The British people were discontented and restless over the lack of military success, and the public was beginning to demand peace. It was under this combination of circumstances that negotiations for peace were finally begun in April, 1782.

THE TREATY OF VERSAILLES: PEACE WITH INDEPENDENCE

When the news of the defeat of Cornwallis reached England, Lord North resigned. He was succeeded by the Marquis of Rockingham, in whose cabinet the Earl of Shelburne, friend of the colonies of an earlier day, held the portfolio of Secretary of State for the Southern Department, in charge of colonial affairs (the office of Secretary of State for the Colonies was abolished). Soon after his accession to office he sent Richard Oswald to Paris, and Henry Laurens, an American diplomat who had been captured at sea en route to Europe, to Holland, to sound out Benjamin Franklin at Paris and John Adams, then representing the United States at the Hague, on possible terms of peace. When Oswald reached Paris he saw both Franklin and Vergennes, and learned from them that they were prepared to negotiate for peace. Thomas Grenville was appointed to assist Oswald, but just as the negotiations were getting under way, the Rockingham ministry fell from power, and Shelburne himself became prime minister, after which the negotiations went forward rapidly.

The turn the negotiations now took was due largely to the prejudices of John Jay, who, after his long and unpleasant stay in Spain, had developed a definite distrust of that country and its government. Congress had already named its peace commissioners, in 1781: Franklin, Jay, Henry Laurens, Thomas Jefferson, and John Adams. By the instructions of June 15, 1781, they were instructed to act with the other belligerents in the negotiations for peace, and to secure as much as they could for the United States, depending for aid upon the pressure that would be exerted on their behalf by France and Spain. But Spain had failed to take Gibraltar from England, and Vergennes looked with sympathy upon Spain's claim to the eastern half of the Mississippi valley—to be taken at the expense of the United States as "compensation" for the failure to regain Gibraltar. John Jay was suspicious of the Franco-Spanish aims, which were not divulged to the Americans, and his suspicions seemed confirmed when he found out that Gérard de Rayneval, Vergennes' secretary, had made a secret trip to London. Shelburne, on his side of the triangle, was anxious to separate the Americans from their allies in the hope of getting better terms, and encouraged the Americans to negotiate independently of the French, contrary to the instructions they had received from the Continental Congress. The negotiations thus eagerly begun on both sides ended on November 30, 1782, in the signature of the preliminary treaty of peace, between the United States and England. This treaty was embodied in the general peace signed September 3, 1783.

By this treaty, Great Britain recognized, first of all, the independence of the United States of America. The western boundary of the new country was agreed upon as the Mississippi River. Its southern boundary was the northern boundary of Florida, now re-ceded to Spain by the defeated England. To the northward the Americans had first asked the cession of all of Canada, then the southern boundary of Quebec as established by the Proclamation of 1763 (the line of 45° north latitude from Lake Nipissing to the

Connecticut River and thence along the divide between the St. Lawrence River and the Atlantic Ocean to the St. Croix River and the sea). They had finally accepted a line which ran up the St.

MAP 19. The United States of America, 1783

Lawrence from 45° north latitude through the Great Lakes to the Lake of the Woods, and thence to the Mississippi. The new nation retained certain rights, such as a share in the Newfoundland fisheries, that it had enjoyed during the period when the present states were colonies. Great Britain insisted that the loyalists be provided for, with the result that the treaty included the promise that the

United States Congress would "earnestly recommend" to the states that confiscated loyalist property be restored. The article containing the promise was a dead letter before it was signed, however, for Congress had no way of compelling the states to restore confiscated property, nor was it probable that the states would even listen to the suggestion, the state of feeling against the loyalists being what it was. England finally compensated the loyalists herself, through the agency of a loyalist claims commission.

This treaty has been called "The American birth certificate," and so it was. But though they were independent, at long last, of their mother country, the American states had given up her protection; and in their eagerness to win freedom from her commercial and economic restrictions, they had had, perforce, to give up a large part of the wide imperial market for their goods, which for them had been both free and protected. More important still, though the Americans were citizens of independent states, they were not yet a thoroughly united nation; for still another internal revolution had to take place before a genuine union, without which independence meant relatively little, could be achieved.

RECOMMENDED BOOKS FOR FURTHER READING

Contemporary Narratives

John Adams, "Diary" in *The Works of John Adams,* edited by Charles F. Adams, III, 298-383.
Benjamin Franklin, *The Writings of Benjamin Franklin,* edited by Albert H. Smyth, VII, VIII.
Albert B. Hart, ed., *American History Told by Contemporaries,* II, Chapter 35.
James B. Scott, ed., *The Armed Neutralities of 1780 and 1800.*

Modern Accounts

Thomas P. Abernethy, *Western Lands and the American Revolution,* Chapter 21.
Thomas A. Bailey, *A Diplomatic History of the American People,* Chapters 2-3.
Samuel F. Bemis, *The Diplomacy of the American Revolution.*
Samuel F. Bemis, *A Diplomatic History of the United States,* Chapters 2-4.
The Cambridge History of the British Empire, Volume I, Chapter 25.
French E. Chadwick, *The Relations of the United States with Spain, Diplomacy.*
Edward Channing, *A History of the United States,* III, Chapters 10, 12.
Gilbert Chinard, *Honest John Adams.*

George L. Clark, *Silas Deane, a Connecticut Leader in the American Revolution.*

Edward S. Corwin, *French Policy and the American Alliance of 1778.*

Bernard Faÿ, *Benjamin Franklin, the Apostle of Modern Times,* pp. 404-477.

Bernard Faÿ, *The Revolutionary Spirit in France and America.*

Frank Monaghan, *John Jay, Defender of Liberty.*

James B. Perkins, *France in the American Revolution.*

Paul C. Phillips, *The West in the Diplomacy of the American Revolution.*

Carl C. Van Doren, *Benjamin Franklin.*

Claude H. Van Tyne, *The American Revolution, 1776-1783,* Chapters 7-13, 16.

Claude H. Van Tyne, "French Aid before the Alliance of 1778" in *American Historical Review,* XXXI, 20-40.

47

Independence Has Its Problems

THE War for American Independence was brought to a definitive conclusion by the Peace of Paris. A feeling of relief and rejoicing swept over the country and it seemed to many citizens that under a government free from the domination of England there could be no limits to the prosperity and happiness which was in store for America. Indeed, one observer, nearly overcome by the prospect, was moved to call upon his countrymen to gaze upon the fair opportunity presented "for converting this immense northern continent into a sea of knowledge and freedom, of agriculture and commerce, of useful arts and manufactures, of Christian piety and virtue; . . . thus making it . . . an asylum for the injured and oppressed in all parts of the globe; the delight of God and good men; the joy and pride of the whole earth; soaring on the wings of literature, wealth, population, religion, virtue, and everything that is excellent and happy to a greater height of perfection and glory than the world has ever yet seen."

Brilliant and expansive as the prophet's vision was, the prospects were slight that the dream would achieve immediate crystallization, for independence had its problems and they were not slow in manifesting themselves. The country was politically unstable, for by severing the bonds tying the colonies to Great Britain thirteen states emerged, each jealous of its rights and privileges as sovereign powers and each dominated by ambitious and often shortsighted men. True, the necessities of war and peace demanded cooperation among the states, but the resulting confederation bound the whole together in a tenuous union of free and independent sovereignties. Economic life in the former colonies was likewise unsettled by the war and by the new independent status outside of the British Empire. Moreover, the new west, expanding rapidly as it was, presented numerous knotty problems crying for careful statesmanship. The position of the new American regime in the realm of international affairs was not clear, so that a revival of commerce, an essential to the economic well-being of America, was long delayed. Finally, the social conflict between the two powerful elements in American society which had flared up during the war continued with increasing intensity during the first years of peace.

THE WAR AND PROBLEMS OF POLITICAL ORGANIZATION

The outbreak of hostilities between England and thirteen of its colonies in 1775 had led to a shift from colonial to state organizations in which both colonial and English practice and theory found expression. The new state constitutions establishing fundamental frameworks of government for the new entities had not been adopted without political conflict between conservative and popular factions within each society. These constitutions continued in force throughout the period under consideration with few changes.

The organization of a central government proved to be a greater political problem confronting the Americans than that of state government. Indeed, the question of central control was an old one that had plagued not only the patriots but their predecessors in England and in the colonies. The outbreak of the war was itself testimony to the failure of efforts thus far attempted to achieve a workable organ of central control acceptable to both England and the colonies, and, with war a reality, a renewed impetus was given to the search for a plan of union. The first two Continental Congresses were little more than committees of advice, with no basis in law and with little faith placed in them as permanent governing bodies; clearly something needed to be done to place the affairs of the emergent nation in the hands of some legally constituted and recognized institution. It is instructive to note that the conservatives among the revolutionists wished to provide for a strong union before issuing a declaration of independence from Great Britain, fearing, as they had reason to, that the war would open the flood gates of radical agrarianism. The social conflicts of the seventeenth and eighteenth centuries between representatives of the agricultural west and the coastal aristocracy were reminders of the ever-present dangers of militant radicalism and men of substance wished to proceed cautiously in throwing away the restraints provided by the old British connection. "Farewell aristocracy," cried Gouverneur Morris. "If the disputes with Great Britain continue, we shall be under the worst possible dominions . . . [that] of a riotous mob."

The story of the writing and of the adoption of the Articles of Confederation has already been recounted. The advocates of strong government found themselves temporarily thwarted under the Articles, and majorities in the state legislatures continued to rule unhampered by the exercise of external controls. The conservatives, however, routed in the early engagements, were not defeated for

long. They made continued efforts during the eighties to nation-
alize the Articles of Confederation, but since the constitution required a unanimous vote to effect major changes, nothing significant was accomplished toward the goal of strong government until
the "revolution of 1787-89." In the meantime, conservatives saw
what to them represented basic weaknesses in the Articles of Confederation. Congress had no taxing power, internal or external; all
groups in society had had enough of that as part of the old empire.
Each state in the Confederation was left free to levy its own taxes
through its own legislature. The Congress could only make requests
for money from the states—"government by supplication," as the
opponents of the Articles described this process. Without taxing
power and without control over the issuance of money, in keeping
with radical theories of outside control developed in pre-revolutionary days, the Confederation was powerless to redeem its bonds
or to provide for a stable currency—both essentials of good government in the eyes of the business and commercial elements of society.
Twice Congress endeavored to effect changes in the Articles in
order to secure an independent source of revenue for the union
by taxing imports, but each time one or more states objected and
the proposals were abandoned.

Another weakness of the Articles, which soon became apparent,
lay in the fact that the central government was without authorization to regulate commerce among the various states. The Confederation's prestige among foreign states, moreover, was not great
enough to secure favorable commercial treaties abroad. Such conditions engendered endless confusion and bad feeling among the
various states, and, in addition, a genuine disgust developed on the
part of the commercial classes for the Confederation.

Finally, the union lacked an executive and a judiciary which
might carry into effect the little legislation which the Congress was
allowed to pass.

It is difficult fully to appreciate the value of the Articles of Confederation since its opponents have been so effective in propa-
gandizing against the tenuous union therein provided. "Too often
the propaganda of one generation becomes the classic of the next"
is a statement that could well be applied to *The Federalist,* which
was written in 1787 and 1788 in support of the new constitution
of the United States. Scholars in recent years have been revaluing
the Articles of Confederation and have been giving this first American constitution its just due. Certainly the Confederation was in

keeping with the more radical theories of empire, which had developed among leading Americans in the pre-war period. Agrarian groups, representing the bulk of the population, seemed satisfied with the instrument of government. Thomas Jefferson described the Confederation as a model government. "With all the imperfections of our present government [he said], it is without comparison the best existing or that ever did exist. A comparison with the governments of Europe is like a comparison of heaven and hell." As an experiment in confederation the Articles are not to be despised. They were weak enough, to be sure, but it is by no means certain that, given better times and a longer term of life, they might not have developed into a satisfactory form of government for the Americans.

ECONOMIC LIFE

The Confederation period was one of economic readjustment attendant upon the break-up of the old empire. The eight years of warfare had resulted in a feverish and unhealthy prosperity which lasted in most states until about 1785. In that year the fictitious wartime prices of farm produce collapsed with disastrous consequences to the farmer elements in society. The new manufacturing enterprises fostered by the conflict suffered, following the peace, from British competition and the dumping of English goods upon glutted American markets. The Confederation seemed powerless to check these hurtful trade practices by erecting tariff barriers. The currency of the country, moreover, had fallen into hopeless confusion; and Congress was unable readily to establish a sound financial structure for the business of the states.

Congress, despairing of other devices for raising revenue during the war, had printed more than $240,000,000 of paper money, while the states had issued a similar amount to bolster up their own finances. Nor was the situation improved following the war, since the normal sources of supply of gold and silver had all but disappeared. No gold or silver was mined in the new states and bullion was very difficult to get from the West Indies, owing to trade restrictions set up by the foreign governments. Then, too, privateering no longer brought specie to the states and the gold left by the British army purchasing agents was rapidly drained off to meet unfavorable trade balances. As a result of these conditions the cry for printing press money persisted unabated and many states continued to resort to the policy of issuing paper in order to provide for the money needs of their peoples.

Perhaps the worst feature of economic activity during the period resulted from a failure of the states to revive the once profitable commerce and fisheries so well developed during colonial times and so badly damaged by the war. The first necessity for a restoration of the prosperity of the eastern cities was the re-establishment of normal commercial relations with Great Britain; but there were grave difficulties in the way of such a restoration. First, under the navigation acts England refused to allow foreign merchants, and this category now included Americans, to participate in the trade of the empire. The Americans, fighting for freedom from commercial restraints, apparently had overlooked the benefits enjoyed as members of the empire. In 1783, by certain English Orders in Council, American vessels were excluded from Canadian and West Indian waters. Nor were the French, Spanish, and Dutch any more anxious to give up their mercantilistic practices in order to benefit the new nation and its merchants. As a result, the triangular trades built up during a century and a half were badly disrupted and the traditional sources of bills of exchange were closed to Americans.

A second difficulty blocking a rapid restoration of trade was the impotence of the Confederation in securing favorable commercial treaties and in controlling commerce among the states. Each state acted as it saw fit, with disastrous results to some of them. Each had its own tariff laws and each its own currency. Some states, by virtue of superior locations, were in favorable positions to take advantage of neighbors less favorably situated. For example, New Jersey, having no convenient port of its own, was actually subject to taxation by New York and Pennsylvania, through whose ports its commerce was carried on. Placed between Philadelphia and New York, it was like a cask tapped at both ends, as James Madison once observed.

Economic activity in the union revived a little following the post-war depression, but slack times had left its trail of discontent among all classes of society. The business elements looked to stronger government to assist in stabilizing commercial, financial, and industrial activities, while the agrarians and their sympathizers put their trust in moratoria and continued issues of paper money to ease the strains of economic change.

THE NEW WEST

A national domain had been secured in 1780 by the refusal of Maryland to adopt the Articles of Confederation until the states having western lands should promise to cede them to the proposed central government. This was a significant decision on the part of Maryland. When the Treaty of Paris gave the western lands to the new nation, a prize of immense value was placed in the hands of the Confederation, and the question raised by Maryland, although doubtless inspired in part by jealousy, was entirely pertinent. What was to be done with this land and how was the area to be governed were insistent questions. One of the most significant social movements of the decade and a half beginning in 1776 was the new westward movement of population. Before the outbreak of hostilities there were between six and eight thousand people living west of the Allegheny mountains; by 1790, when the first census was taken, over 110,000 people made their homes west of the mountains, or five per cent of the total population of the union.

During the Confederation period, as indeed during the revolutionary and pre-war years, there had been a continuous search to discover effective means of controlling the west and of providing for its swelling population. A variety of possible solutions was suggested. Among them was the idea of organizing western counties under the control of older eastern states—for example, Illinois county in Virginia. Another experiment was the creation of new colonies in the west—such were the ill-fated colonies of Transylvania and Franklin. But these and other expedients failed to meet the essential problems, and by the end of the war no policies existed for dealing with the survey, the sale, and the governing of the newly acquired public domain. As the states made cessions of land to the Confederation, Congress was hard put to it to redeem its pledges made at the time of Maryland's exactions. For the Congress was committed to a policy of disposing of the lands for the common good, and of providing the means whereby new states could be fashioned and admitted to the Confederation.

Congress eventually rose to the challenge and provided for the west in a statesmanlike fashion. The Land Ordinance of 1785, providing for the survey and sale of western lands, was the first significant piece of legislation passed by the new nation dealing with the public domain. The entire area was to be laid out in townships six miles square, subdivided into sections of 640 acres, of which a certain portion were set aside for the support of public education. In thus providing for the survey of land preceding its occupation by settlers much of the confusion and litigation over land titles attendant upon the westward movement during colonial days was avoided. In order to raise revenue for the distraught government the ordinance enabled Congress to sell half of the townships intact and the remainder in sections one mile square at the minimum price of $1.00 an acre. Experience later proved that 640 acres was too much for most men to buy, since the migration west in the America of these years was accomplished by individuals who could ill-afford to purchase such large quantities of land. It was not until 1832, however, that the minimum purchase was reduced to forty acres.

With the problem of survey and sale of lands out of the way, the Congress next turned its attention to government in this area. As long as government was lacking, population moved slowly, since there was inadequate security of title to land and little protection from Indians. Congress responded to this problem in the Ordinance of 1787, which was, indeed, the first adequate answer to the frontier problem. Drawing upon a policy-defining ordinance passed in 1784 for precedent the Ordinance of 1787 provided for territorial government and for admission of the western settlements into the Confederation on terms of equality with the older states. The new government under the Constitution of 1789, which supplanted the Confederation, adopted the principles laid down between 1784 and 1787 and the work of the Continental (Confederation) Congress in regard to the west furnished the political and legal basis for the expansion of the American people westward to the Pacific. The solution to the problem of the west was a monument to the Confederation as well as a wise handling of America's colonial question, for it served to strengthen the bonds of unity which were in danger of loosening during these years.

In addition to the pressing necessity of dealing with the survey and sale of land and of providing a government for the west, the Confederation faced serious competition for control of that region from foreign neighbors—British from the north, and Spanish on the south and the west. The situation was made doubly serious by eastern unconcern for the fate of westerners and for western problems, particularly as they touched economic affairs. As a result of these factors—foreign competition and eastern indifference—there was a possibility that the Confederation might lose its newly acquired public domain in spite of the Ordinances of 1785 and 1787. Indeed, toward the end of the Confederation period schemes were on foot for western independence, for Spanish control of the southwest, and for an extension of British influence. Thus, to a few Americans interested in western problems there was an incentive to work for a strong national government to enforce a vigorous policy in that region.

DIPLOMATIC UNCERTAINTY

The relationships established by the new regime in America with the older European states were characterized by distrust and unfriendliness. Republics were in bad repute among the ruling classes in Europe, for they might set bad examples to the discontented and oppressed of the old world—as indeed was the case in France. America, moreover, continued to be looked upon as a field for colonial expansion and more than one state hoped to see the new nation kept weak in order to improve the opportunities of fishing in troubled waters. Finally, the success of the Americans in winning independence had done nothing to alter the mercantilist practices or theories of the great European commercial states.

Considerable friction with the erstwhile mother country continued to plague the Americans. First, the Orders in Council of 1783 resulted in a loss of trading privileges for American merchants within the British empire. England was unwilling, for obvious reasons, to negotiate a commercial treaty with its former colonies—free trade was still more than a half century in the future. As a matter of fact, there was no compelling reason why England should make a treaty, since her merchants already enjoyed the American trade and the Confederation lacked means of retaliation. Second, trouble developed over the terms of the treaty of 1783. The Confederation, for its part, complained, not unjustly, that Britain had refused to evacuate a number of fur trading posts held in the American northwest and that the Indians were being given moral and material encouragement from these very posts to oppose the American agricultural advance into the west. For its part, Britain complained, not less justly, that the Americans were not carrying out the pledges given in respect to colonial debts and the treatment of loyalists and their property. Third, Vermont, having proclaimed its independence from England, New York, and New Hampshire alike, was dickering with Britain for re-incorporation within the empire. Congress was placed in a difficult position, for it was fearful of alienating New York; but despite the Confederation's inability to act with decisiveness, Americans were extremely irked at British meddling. Finally, ill-feeling was further aroused when John Adams, sent to England in 1785 to negotiate concerning the differences existing between the two nations, was ostentatiously ignored. The British government refused even to send a minister to the Confederation, alleging that it could not afford to send thirteen ambassadors, and to send less than that number would be futile.

The friction developing on the American southwestern frontier with Spain was scarcely less important to the new nation than the difficulties with England. Spain was growing more concerned with the trans-Allegheny migration of Americans toward the Spanish Floridas, whose boundaries were in dispute. Moreover, Spanish control of the mouth of the Mississippi gave Spain a stranglehold on the one feasible outlet for western trade, which hold was made effective in 1784 when Spain announced the closing of the Mississippi to American shipping. The "men of the western waters" were universal in their demands for a satisfactory solution to this problem of the navigation of the Mississippi and the correlative question of deposit and transference of goods to ocean-going vessels at New Orleans.

An effort was made to deal with all of the issues outstanding between the two powers in the unsatisfactory negotiations between John Jay and the Spanish minister, Diego Gardoqui, in 1786. Jay endeavored to secure three concessions (1) a line drawn at 31° north latitude as the Florida boundary, (2) a treaty of commerce, and (3) the right of the Americans to the free navigation of the Mississippi River. The negotiations resulted only in securing a treaty of commerce, but in return the United States was expected to abate its claim to free navigation of the Mississippi for a term of thirty years. This last provision was highly unsatisfactory to the west and to southern states with western interests. Moreover, this part of the treaty revealed a disposition on the part of the commercial north and east to sacrifice western interests to the demands of the east; a disposition which might easily have driven the west or portions of it out of the Confederation. Needless to say, no treaty embodying such provisions was ever drawn up and ratified.

With France there was less trouble, during these post-war years. Efforts were made to improve Franco-American commercial opportunities, since by the terms of the alliance of 1778 only limited trading privileges had been granted and after 1783 American ships were denied access to the French West Indian ports. Friction developed also over the failure of the Confederation effectively to deal with the debts still due France, and over French efforts at securing extra-territoriality rights in America for French citizens.

To summarize: the Confederation proved unable to command respect among foreign powers or too weak to wring concessions from unfriendly European governments—"We are the lowest and most obscure of the diplomatic tribe," complained Thomas Jefferson, American Minister to France. Whether or not time would have worked to place the new nation in a better position is unknown, but the Confederation's uncertain international status proved a distinct disadvantage to the struggling nation and added many recruits to the ranks of those seeking a modification of the Articles of Confederation.

SOCIAL CONFLICT AND THE MOVE TOWARD STRONG GOVERNMENT

In the midst of these domestic and foreign difficulties the social conflict, temporarily abated during the short period of post-war prosperity, tended to sharpen in intensity and to jeopardize the welfare of the new states and the Confederation. The slight efforts that were made to stabilize economic life only resulted in increased burdens of taxation and debt, bringing additional hardship upon the agrarian classes of society. As a rule the latter looked to further issues of paper money to keep prices up and taxes spread out over the population. During the elections in 1786 the paper money men won control of the legislatures of eight states—Vermont, Rhode Island, New York, New Jersey, Pennsylvania, North and South Carolina, and Georgia. Generally, the legislatures of these states passed "stay" laws or debtor's moratoria and increased the output of paper currency. In New Hampshire, where an outlet for agrarian discontent was blocked by a failure to carry the legislature, several hundred men armed with muskets, swords, and staves confronted the lawmakers and demanded a release from taxes and an issue of paper money. Although the effort was without immediate effect the tenor of the times was revealed. In Massachusetts, following the refusal of the General Court to pass legislation to relieve debtors or to provide an equitable and systematic program of taxation, open rebellion occurred, led by Daniel Shays, a one-time Revolutionary war officer. There ensued in the Bay State a period marked by open attack upon lawyers and courts trying debtor cases. In one Massachusetts county having a population of about fifty thousand, over 4,000 suits were brought; in many towns the courts, jammed with debtor cases, were forcibly closed. When the debtors tried to intimidate the legislature in an effort to secure a repudiation of debts, the business community of the state began to act. Early in 1787 the Commonwealth, refusing aid from the Confederation, placed General Benjamin Lincoln in command of the troops supplied by men of wealth and principle. General Lincoln himself collected approximately $20,000 from Boston businessmen with the warning that it was, "Some of your property now, or all of it later."

Perhaps the most significant result of the uprisings in New Hampshire, Massachusetts, and in such states as Rhode Island, which was controlled by the agrarians, was the effect upon those men in the Confederation who depended upon law and order, maintained by strong government, for a continuance of their economic well-being. George Washington, for example, when he heard of Shays's rebellion in Massachusetts, was led to exclaim, "There are combustibles in every state which a spark might set fire to . . . I feel . . . infinitely more, than I can express to you, for the disorders which have arisen in these states. Good God! Who besides a Tory, could have foreseen, or a Briton predicted them."

"What is to give us security against the violence of lawless men?" asked General Henry Knox of George Washington in October, 1786. "Our government must be braced, changed, or altered to secure our lives and property. We imagined that the mildness of our government and the wishes of the people were so correspondent that we were not as other nations, requiring brutal force to support the laws. But we find we are men—actual men, possessing all the turbulent passions belonging to that animal, and that we must have a government proper and adequate for him. . . . The men of property and the men of station and principle . . . (in Massachusetts) are determined to establish and protect them in their lawful pursuits. . . . Something is wanting and something must be done."

Following Shays's rebellion there developed among the moneyed classes a rapid crystallization of sentiment against the Confederation as an instrument of government. Astute politicians like Alexander Hamilton of New York saw the lack of discipline and organization among the farmer element. He and others argued forcibly that the troubles of the day arose from agrarian policies such as stay laws and paper money issues which were the outcomes of too much democracy. The root of the trouble, it was argued, was the "pernicious slackness" of the Articles of Confederation to which the agrarians were wedded. Was it not the patriotic duty of the sound and principled men of society to erect strong legal barriers to protect the rights of property from being swept away? Thus it was that a small but strong minority of the population came to identify its interests with the establishment of a strong coercive power to replace the weak government under the Articles. During the years between 1785-87 persistent efforts were made by such men as Hamilton to organize a body of men having some show of authority to sponsor a reorganization of the governing power in America. That body was found, after several failures, in the convention which met at Philadelphia during the summer of 1787 for the express purpose of revising the Articles of Confederation. Clearly the Articles of Confederation had failed, in the eyes of the conservative portions of American society, to accomplish its elemental tasks; a new instrument was essential to the well-being of these groups. Success attended their efforts in the "revolution of 1787-1789."

RECOMMENDED BOOKS FOR FURTHER READING

CONTEMPORARY NARRATIVES

François J. de Chastelleux, *Travels in North America in the Years 1780-81-82.*

Joseph Hadfield, *An Englishman in America, 1785,* edited by Douglas S. Robertson.

Albert B. Hart, ed., *American History Told by Contemporaries,* II, Chapters 33-35; III, Chapters 2-8.

Thomas Jefferson, *Notes on the State of Virginia.*

Samuel E. Morison, ed., *Sources and Documents Illustrating the American Revolution, 1764-1788,* pp. 203-233.

MODERN ACCOUNTS

George H. Alden, *New Governments West of the Alleghanies before 1780.*

Thomas A. Bailey, *A Diplomatic History of the American People,* Chapter 4.

Samuel F. Bemis, *Jay's Treaty.*

Alfred L. Burt, *The United States, Great Britain and British North America,* Chapters 1-7.

Edward Channing, *A History of the United States,* III, Chapters 14-15, 17-18.

Gilbert Chinard, *Thomas Jefferson, the Apostle of Americanism.*

John Fiske, *The Critical Period of American History, 1783-1789.*

Alexander C. Flick, ed., *History of the State of New York,* IV, V.

William W. Henry, *Patrick Henry.*

Francis W. Hirst, *Life and Letters of Thomas Jefferson.*

Merrill Jensen, *The Articles of Confederation.*

Andrew C. McLaughlin, *The Confederation and the Constitution, 1783-1789.*

John B. McMaster, *A History of the People of the United States, from the Revolution to the Civil War,* Volume I.

Samuel E. Morison, *The Maritime History of Massachusetts, 1783-1860,* Chapters 1-4.

Allan Nevins, *The American States During and After the Revolution, 1775-1789.*

Ellis P. Oberholtzer, *Robert Morris, Patriot and Financier.*

Frederick S. Oliver, *Alexander Hamilton.*

Frederick L. Paxson, *History of the American Frontier, 1763-1893,* Chapters 3-8.

Kate M. Rowland, *The Life of George Mason, 1725-1792.*

Max Savelle, *George Morgan, Colony Builder.*

Nathaniel W. Stephenson and Waldo H. Dunn, *George Washington.*

William G. Sumner, *The Financier and Finances of the American Revolution,* II, Chapters 16-23.

Payson J. Treat, *The National Land System, 1785-1820,* Chapters 1-3.

Frederick J. Turner, *Western State-Making in the Revolutionary Era.*

Claude H. Van Tyne, *The Loyalists in the American Revolution.*

Joseph P. Warren, "Confederation and the Shays Rebellion," *American Historical Review,* XI, 42-67.

Arthur P. Whitaker, *The Spanish-American Frontier, 1783-1795.*

48

The Welding of a Nation

THE DEMAND FOR CONSTITUTIONAL REFORM

THE ECONOMIC depression, social demoralization, and political uncertainty that seemed to characterize the situation in the thirteen states during the years following the War of Independence created among the conservatives a nervousness and a lack of confidence in the future that precipitated a determined movement to revise the Articles of Confederation. The feeling of nervousness was not shared by the agrarian-democratic elements in society; they felt that, with only slight changes, the old Articles of Confederation would do well enough. They feared, indeed, the establishment of a strong central government that might be expected to oppress both the states and the citizens as the British government had done before the war. They feared, also, the creation of an aristocratic government and an aristocratic society that might undo all the gains of the "leveling" and the local autonomy that had been achieved during the war.

It would be a mistake, therefore, to think of the movement for a stronger constitution as expressing the unanimous desire of the entire people. On the contrary, the movement was set going and pushed forward by the propertied, conservative leaders, from the very first, in the sincere belief that a strong national government with authority was the only institution that could save the country from complete disintegration. Nor were these sponsors of revision at one among themselves; there were deep and bitter differences as to the form the proposed union should take, just how its powers should be organized, and so on. But in the early stages of the movement it was fairly easy for them to unite upon the need of revision, in the face of the common danger, which they called a "universal democracy."

The final accomplishments of the revision and the inauguration of a new constitution marked the beginning of a new conservative era, as the revolutionary years had been a "radical" or "progressive" era, in the dialectic of American history. The pendulum swung to the left during the war, to win independence; it swung to the right, after the war, and the American constitution was the

706

result. It is this alternation of "progressive" and "conservative" eras, this swinging of the historical pendulum from left to right and back again, that is one of the most striking features of American political history, from the War of Independence to the present day.

The movement for revision got under way even before the Articles of Confederation had been ratified. As early as September 3, 1780, Alexander Hamilton of New York, an influential conservative, wrote to James Duane suggesting the necessity of a "solid coercive union" and the desirability, if Congress did not assume more power, of calling at once a general convention for the formulation of a stronger union of the states. "There is something . . . diminutive and contemptible," he wrote, "in the prospect of a number of petty states, with the appearance only of union, jarring, jealous, and perverse, without any determined direction, fluctuating and unhappy at home, weak and insignificant by their dissensions in the eyes of other nations." Hamilton was already building up support for revision, and in 1782 he succeeded in getting the legislature of his own state, New York, to recommend to the Continental Congress the calling of a convention for revising the Articles of Confederation. The Congress, however, failed to act upon this recommendation.

Another leader in the movement for revision was James Madison, a member of the Continental Congress from Virginia. Madison was particularly anxious to endow the Continental Congress with the power to coerce the states members of the Confederation, even by the use of force, if necessary. Madison was a member of a committee of the Continental Congress which recommended that the Articles of Confederation be amended by the addition of an article clearly recognizing the power of Congress to compel states to fulfill their engagements to the Confederation. Another committee recommended still further changes, particularly in the direction of giving Congress the power to collect the revenue due it from the states. But the states complied with the demands of Congress only reluctantly, if at all.

In April, 1784, Congress requested authority from the states to pass a "navigation act" to be fashioned after the British navigation acts of the colonial period. This act, which was proposed as a retaliation for the restrictions placed by Great Britain upon American trade with the old British empire, would have prohibited the importation or exportation of commodities in the ships of any nation not having a treaty of commerce with the United States. But this request from Congress was not granted. Some of the states were willing that Congress should have the power asked; others would have granted it with such reservations as to make it meaningless; by others, particularly among the southern states, which were jealous of the already great commercial power of the north, the request was flatly refused. The states, on the other hand, tried to regulate and protect their commerce individually and independently of each other, with the result that the need for some sort of central, co-ordinating power was intensified.

The merchants of Boston, greatly interested in interstate, as well as international trade, prevailed upon the Massachusetts state legislature to pass resolutions, in July, 1785, which proposed that a general convention be called for a thoroughgoing revision of the Articles of Confederation. But the Massachusetts delegates to the Continental Congress, not in sympathy with the movement, actually refused to present the resolutions to that body, on the ground such a convention might encourage "the friends of an aristocracy to send members who would promote a change of Government."

But the era of radical reform and decentralization of government was drawing to a close. There was a real need for a central government with power to co-ordinate the efforts of the states for the solution of national problems. It was realized, of course, that in order to create such a government the states must surrender at least a part of their sovereignty. The great problem was how to preserve the gains of the radical era represented by independence and the large amount of social and legislative reform that had been achieved, and at the same time to set up a central, national authority with power to promote the national interest, but without the power to exercise over the states the same sort of "tyranny" against which they had fought to be free.

The train of events which finally culminated in the adoption of a new constitution had its beginning in 1786. This movement really grew out of the local need, as between Virginia and Maryland, for a body of regulations controlling the use of the Potomac River. The charter to Lord Baltimore had provided that the southern shore of the Potomac should be the southern boundary of Maryland, which meant that planters in Virginia using the Potomac must pass under Maryland jurisdiction and submit to Maryland's regulations of their traffic. It was for the formulation of a set of regulations mutually acceptable to Maryland and Virginia, therefore, that, as early as 1777, a joint commission representing the two states had been appointed and had begun its work. The difficulty had remained unsolved, however, and in 1784 and 1785 new commissioners were appointed to attack the problem again. Five of the commissioners met at Mount Vernon, George Washington's home on the Virginia shore of the Potomac, early in 1785, and drafted a set of recommendations which were accepted by both states. It was realized, however, that Pennsylvania and Delaware were both interested in the problem of the Delaware and Chesapeake waterways, and, at the suggestion of Maryland and Virginia, a further conference was called at Annapolis to meet in September, 1786, to consider the advisability and practicability of setting up a code of commercial regulations governing all the states.

The convention met, but only five states were represented. It had been hoped, by Madison and others, that the Annapolis convention might not only devise a set of commercial regulations for the union, but might also be the entering wedge for a thoroughgoing revision of the Articles of Confederation in their entirety. But the smallness of the attendance and the manifest distrust of the convention demonstrated how great was the agrarian distrust of the movement and its sponsors. The convention moved with great circumspection, therefore, though it adopted a resolution drawn up by Alexander Hamilton calling upon the Continental Congress to call a general convention of the states for a revision of the Articles of Confederation in such a way as to render them "adequate to the exigencies of the union." In order to avoid the appearance of radicalism, and to win the confidence of the agrarian opposition, the resolution also specified that any revision made by the proposed convention would have to be submitted to the states for ratification.

The Continental Congress granted the request for a new convention, and issued its call to the states in February, 1787. All the states except Rhode Island accepted the invitation to send delegates, but most of them did so with great caution and specific reservations guaranteeing that the product of their deliberations should be sent back to the states for ratification. Thus it came about that in the summer of 1787 there met at Philadelphia a convention of delegates from the states whose purpose was to revise the Articles of Confederation. Representative as it was almost wholly of the commercial and well-to-do and conservative elements in American society, probably no one realized how thoroughgoing was to be the revision it was to produce, nor how big with significance for the future of the United States would be the document that was to be the product of their deliberations.

THE CONVENTION OF 1787

The fifty-five men who met at Philadelphia in the Convention of 1787 probably represented a higher level of ability than any similar political meeting in this country before or since. Seven of these men had been governors of states; eight had signed the Declaration of Independence; twenty-eight had been members of the Continental Congress. George Washington, successful leader of the military forces during the war, was chairman of the convention, and among the delegates were such men as Benjamin Franklin, Alexander Hamilton, James Madison, Robert Morris, John Dickinson, Pierce Butler and many others of great distinction in the service of the country during the revolutionary era. They were almost without exception from the mercantile, professional, or land-speculating groups of well-to-do men throughout the colonies. Most of them held securities of the Confederation government that would be worthless were that government to fail; most of them were investors either in commercial enterprises that would benefit from an effective system of regulations or in western lands, the administration of which was now a function of the national union. Not one of the so-called "radicals" of the early revolutionary movement was present. Thomas Jefferson was in Paris as United States minister to France; Patrick Henry, who was designated as delegate, refused to attend because of the conservative nature of the revisionist movement; Thomas Paine was in Europe; Samuel Adams was not a delegate.

It would be a mistake, however, to conclude from the composition of the Convention of 1787 that its members were concerned only with bolstering up their personal interests by the establishment of a strong government in the face of the "universal democracy." Businessmen they were, to be sure, and each stood to gain by the establishment of a strong national government. But they, conservative in social position and in economic interest, were genuinely and deeply convinced that the welfare not only of themselves but of the people at large and of the nation they had all helped to establish was bound up with their deliberations. Their personal interests were identified with the interests of the whole people; and they dedicated themselves wholeheartedly and sincerely to the task of taking such steps as seemed to them best calculated to promote the common welfare. They were conservative in their philosophy of government, and the document that resulted from their labors was a conservative document; but it is probably safe to say that, at that moment in American history, the discipline of the conservative reaction was exactly what the new nation most greatly needed.

The convention began its deliberations in May, 1787, and continued its work in secret through a hot and trying summer. The first and most fundamental question was whether the convention should merely revise the Articles of Confederation or throw over that first constitution in favor of an entirely new one, based upon a radically different and more conservative philosophy of government. There was deep disagreement upon this point. Under the Articles of Confederation all the states were equal, the small states were as powerful as the great, and the small states therefore feared any change that might threaten to reduce them to positions of secondary importance. The majority, however, favored a thoroughgoing change of government, and this opinion prevailed.

This point having been tacitly agreed upon, the convention proceeded to the working out of its plan for the new government. Here the differences of opinion among the delegates as to the most desirable form of government began to make themselves felt, and the work of the convention came to revolve about these major differences and the corresponding compromises that were made to resolve them. At the beginning·Edmund Randolph, representing Virginia, presented a plan for the government that would have created a legislature of two houses, the members of which would have been apportioned among the states on the basis of white population, and an executive branch of government which would have been elected by the legislative.

But this plan was immediately attacked by the small states, led by William Paterson of New Jersey. Paterson's objection to the Randolph plan focused upon the apparent preponderance of power it would give to the states with large populations and the corresponding disadvantages under which the small states would be placed. Paterson therefore submitted a contrary plan, according to which the legislature of the new government would be composed of one house only, in which the states would be represented equally, regardless of the numbers of their populations.

Neither one of these plans was adopted. Instead, a "great compromise" was reached according to which the legislature should be a two-house body, of which the upper house, or Senate, was to be made up of the states, equally represented, and the lower house was to be composed of representatives elected by popular vote

and apportioned to the states on the basis of population, including three-fifths of the Negroes. By this arrangement the large states
had an advantage in the lower house, but all the states would have
equal weight in the Senate; and as it was agreed that all laws must
be passed by both houses, either one was in a position to check
the other.

The struggles over this great basic question were bitter and prolonged, and the convention was more than once on the verge of
dissolution. Another problem that nearly wrecked it grew out of
the sectional nature of the economic life of the country. The
northern states were devoted chiefly to commerce and industry,
and the south was almost purely agricultural, depending for its
livelihood upon the sale of its agricultural surplus in a free world
market, from which it imported the manufactured goods in the
ships, American or other, which carried those goods most cheaply.
It was the fear of the southern states that the north, dominating
the proposed legislature both by the weight of population in the
lower house and by sheer numbers of states in the Senate, might,
by taxation and commercial regulation, reduce the south to a
position of economic subjection and political inferiority in the
new union. Thus the north, which had so furiously resented the
effect of the British navigation system upon its commerce and had
demanded a freedom of trade instead, now found itself in the position of demanding a government which would set up just such a
navigation system and customs duties for its own protection at
the expense of the south, whose interest now, more than ever, demanded freedom of trade.

The convention was at this point deeply divided along lines of
sectional interest—a division which was to run through much of
the subsequent history of the United States. Thus, on questions of
taxation, or of commercial regulation, or of the numbering of
the population for the purposes of representation, the debates,
some of them bitter in the extreme, followed sectional lines. The
south, with its small white population, asked that direct taxes be
apportioned according to the numbers of the white population.
But three-fifths of the Negroes were to be counted for the purpose
of representation; why not for taxation also? On this point the
south was compelled to compromise, and it was agreed that the
slaves should be counted for both representation and taxation.

On the question of commercial regulation, the power of regulating interests and foreign trade was given to the national government, but the slave states, led by South Carolina, insisted that

the government should have no power to prohibit the slave trade, at least within the next twenty years. Similarly, since the national government must carry on all relations with foreign nations, especially those dealing with commerce, the southern states succeeded in placing a check upon the treaty-making power by insisting that all treaties be ratified by not less than a two-thirds vote of the Senate, where the states were equal and where the southern states felt reasonably sure they would always be able to muster more than one-third of the votes for the defeat of any international commercial agreement that was distasteful to them.

The Constitution that was at last submitted to the states was thus the result, not of immediate and complete agreement among the statesmen composing the convention, but of long and bitter argument, which ensued at last in compromises, "second best" provisions that could be accepted by all. These compromises were made imperative by the very nature of American life—by the differences in size between the states, and by the differences in the economic and social structure of the states of the two great sections, north and south. The most remarkable thing about it, perhaps, is that they were able to harmonize their differences at all. This is perhaps to be explained by the deep conviction in the minds of the members of the convention, from the north and the south alike, that some workable national constitution must ensue from their labors if the union were to be saved at all.

A NEW CONSTITUTION

The Constitution that emerged from the deliberations of the great convention of the summer of 1787 was a curious product of political theory, revolutionary experimentation and the experiences of the colonies prior to independence. The Articles of Confederation and the state constitutions made during the Revolution were the logical outgrowth or continuation of the trend of political development during the colonial period. For the Articles of Confederation, embodying the American sentiment against the strong centralization of the British empire, provided a maximum of the provincial autonomy toward which the colonies had been struggling for upward of a century, and a minimum of coercive power—amounting practically to zero—in the hands of the central government. Inspired by the teachings of Locke and their local struggles with the mother country over questions of taxation, the framers of the Articles had consistently adhered to the principle of taxation only by the actual representatives of the taxpayers, with the result that the Confederation government had been given no power to tax, and the power of taxation had been reserved strictly to the states. The Articles had thus attempted to correct the faults of the old imperial constitution and to guarantee to the states the autonomy that the imperial constitution had denied them.

Similarly, the state constitutions had marked the culmination of the evolution of the colonial constitutions. Thus the general trend in the state constitutions had been toward a strong legislature at the expense of the executive, and a strong lower house at the expense of the upper house. The legislatures had assumed various forms of control over the power of appointment, and some of them even appointed officials and judges and held the officials responsible to themselves. It is probably safe to say, in general, that the state constitutions represented a reaction against the cramping system of checks and balances imposed upon the colonies by the British Crown in the form of a royal executive who was theoretically independent of the legislature and superior to it, and in a judiciary appointed by the Crown and responsible to it.

Now, in the Constitution of 1787, there was a distinct reaction back toward the separation and a balancing of the powers of government—a strong, independent executive, an independent judiciary, with implied powers of judicial review of legislation, and a legislature with powers that were strictly limited, both with regard to its relations with the executive and to the judiciary, and with regard to the relations of the two houses with each other. True, the framers of the Constitution retained the principle of state autonomy in the "residual powers"; but within the limits of the powers that were specifically delegated to it, the national government was made supreme and unchallengeable.

Thus the three great articles of the Constitution provided, first, that the legislative functions of government were to be performed by a bicameral Congress composed of a Senate and a House of Representatives. All legislation must pass both these houses, but certain special powers were given to each. Such, for example, was the provision that the House of Representatives alone might initiate bills for raising revenue; similarly, the Senate alone was given the power to collaborate with the President in the appointment of ambassadors, judges of the Supreme Court, and other high officials, and in the making of treaties with foreign powers. In general, the Congress was empowered to levy taxes (for national pur-

poses) and customs duties, to regulate commerce with foreign states
and between the states, to set up courts inferior to the Supreme
Court, to raise an army and navy and declare war, to create and
regulate the value of a national monetary system, and to administer the public domain. The new Congress was thus a genuinely
national legislature, and the states were specifically prohibited from
interfering in the matters assigned to it.

The thoroughly national nature of the new government was also
seen in the provisions made for the executive. For this branch of
government, while neither as strong as the administration of the
old empire operating from London had been in colonial days nor
as weak and spineless as the corresponding branch, such as it had
been, of the Confederation, yet had a very considerable power.
The head of the government was the President, elected by an indirect method (later abandoned), who was to hold his office for four
years. This executive was to be the commander-in-chief of the
army and navy, and was to have the authority, "by and with the
advice and consent of the Senate," to carry on the relations of the
United States with other nations. Similarly, with the advice and
consent of the Senate, he was to have the power to appoint ambassadors and other diplomatic agents, judges of the Supreme Court,
and other officials of the national government. While not clearly
stated, the President was also assumed to have the power to name
heads of such executive departments as he might wish to create
to assist him in his duties as chief administrator of the laws that
Congress might pass. All these powers made the President of the
United States one of the most powerful national executives among
the constitutionally governed states of the world. All laws must
be signed by him before they would become effective, and he had
the power of checking an unwise Congress by vetoing legislation.
Congress, on its own side, might override the obstinacy of the
President by a two-thirds vote of a vetoed bill, or, should worst
come to the worst, it might oust him from his office by the method,
extremely difficult in itself, of impeachment by the House of Representatives and trial before the Senate.

Thus, in the creation of the legislative and the executive
branches of government, the new Constitution provided for an
almost complete separation of their functions. This separation was
not of such a nature as to make them entirely independent; quite
the contrary—for mechanisms were provided, as already noted, to
prevent either the executive or the legislature from assuming too
much power. Again, it might be noted that this feature of the Con-

stitution was a sort of compromise between the strong executive of the former royal colonies and the weak executives set up as the opposite extreme by the constitutions of the Confederation period. It was a compromise that grew out of the experience of the Americans, and the conviction in the minds of its framers that neither of these two kinds of political institutions had been entirely satisfactory.

Similarly, the national court system was made independent of both the legislature and the executive, and was endowed with the power to check both of them. The Constitution created a Supreme Court, with original jurisdiction in some cases, such as those concerning ambassadors, cases between states, and those to which the United States might be a party, and appellate jurisdiction in others involving the matters entrusted to the national government. Congress was given the power to create lower federal courts, which it eventually did. In all the courts, judges were to hold their office "during good behavior"—a reaction against the old royal custom of appointing judges "during his Majesty's pleasure," which had meant they might be removed if the king disliked their interpretation of the law.

The judiciary was thus made entirely independent of the legislature and the executive except that appointments of judges were to be made by the President and confirmed by the Senate. Once appointed, the judges could not be removed. The power of the federal judiciary was greatly enhanced by the power of judicial review of congressional legislation, which, although not explicitly stated in the Constitution, yet seems, from their correspondence and other evidence, clearly to have been in the minds of the framers, and which has generally been assumed to have been one of the powers of the courts, especially since the time of Chief Justice John Marshall.

In general then, this Constitution set up a strong national government to replace the old, loosely federal government of the Confederation. For it was recognized as "the supreme law of the land; . . . anything in the Constitution or laws of any State to the contrary notwithstanding." Under it, its framers encouraged the fusing together of a nation of one people, instead of the former confederation of thirteen sovereign states. This alone constituted a major revolution in the political philosophy dominating the country. Nor was it immediately accepted; for a very large proportion of the people clung to the old "federal" conception of the government that expressed itself in the "states-rights" doctrines of the ensuing decades. The triumph of the "national" doctrine was not complete, indeed, until a great civil war had been fought to test it.

RATIFICATION OF THE CONSTITUTION

Such was the Constitution as it was framed by the convention at Philadelphia in the summer of 1787. But the mere framing of it, great achievement as· that was, was only a step in the political revolution its framers sought to bring about. For it still had to be ratified by the people of the new nation.

The method of ratification prescribed was typical of the convention. The framers of the Constitution realized that the state legislatures were in large part still controlled by the "agrarian" or "radical" elements among the voting population; and that these elements would offer an almost insurmountable opposition to the ratification of an instrument which so completely reversed their own "loose" philosophy of government. The new Constitution was sent to the old Continental Congress, therefore, with the provision that it was to be submitted to the states for ratification by conventions to be called specifically for that purpose; as soon as nine states should have ratified it, it was to be considered as standing in full force among them. The Continental Congress took the first step of providing for its own end by submitting the Constitution to the states, and the state legislatures issued the call for conventions to consider the new proposal.

The calling of the state conventions was the signal for a political campaign that divided the voters into two camps, for and against the Constitution. For the members of the conventions had to be elected, and a candidate was to be judged chiefly on the basis of the simple question whether he was for or against. The chief aim of one party, of course, was to convince the voters that the new Constitution was desirable, and that they should therefore elect the delegates pledged to ratify it; the task of the other party was precisely the opposite. The campaign thus became one in which the arguments for and against the Constitution were presented to the voters in every conceivable way. The campaign was a bitter one, from one end of the union to the other; numberless speeches were made, and vast quantities of printed matter were thrown off the presses in the effort to convince the voters.

The most dignified and profound of the publications issued in the course of the struggle was a series of essays written by John Jay, James Madison, and Alexander Hamilton, which, taken together, have come to be known as *The Federalist*. These essays, published serially in New York, were in effect a profound study of the ends and functions of government. According to the philosophy expressed in them, the first object of government is the protection of the diversity in the faculties of men, from which rise differences of opinion as well as differences in wealth. For "from the protection of different and unequal faculties of acquiring property, the possession of different degrees and kinds of property immediately results; and from the influence of these on the sentiments and views of the respective proprietors, ensues a division of the society into different interests and parties."

Thus government, to the authors of *The Federalist*, had as its chief objective the protection of individual and group liberties. Yet as the best index to the diverse interests and abilities of the people in the manner and extent in which the diverse groups acquire property, government becomes a sort of umpire among propertied groups and between propertied groups on the one side and propertyless groups on the other.

This identification of government with property is typical of the best political theory of the eighteenth century. Locke, expressing the theory of natural rights in political terms, gave man's natural rights as "life, liberty, and property." The American Constitution does pretty much the same thing, and it is no criticism of it to say it was an instrument of the propertied, conservative classes. This it was, to be sure; but it was a genuine attempt by able and sincere leaders to establish the most effective political institution possible, a government that expressed the best political thought of its century. As such it has endured for a century and a half; it is only in the twentieth century that the eighteenth-century conception of government as the guardian of property as the measure of individual liberty has been seriously and effectively challenged.

The appeal made to the voters in the convention elections of 1788 was thus an appeal to property owners. There were as yet very few propertyless voters in any of the states. As already noted, in every state there was some sort of a property-qualification for voting. The vast preponderance of property was of course in land; but fairly large fortunes existed in the form of commercial assets, securities issued by the old Confederation (which, now far below par, would be greatly increased in value by the establishment of a strong national government), and other forms. The great cleavage in the electorate, therefore, was not between the property owners and the propertyless, but rather, between the agrarian property owners and the non-agrarian propertied classes.

The election campaign was bitter, and in several states political manipulation was employed by both the proponents and the opponents of the Constitution to bring about its ratification or its rejection. In New Hampshire, where the majority of the delegates appeared to be opposed, the convention was adjourned temporarily to give time for the proponents to bring pressure to bear upon the doubtful ones. In Pennsylvania, on the other hand, the opponents to the Constitution in the state legislature tried to win delay in setting the date for the election of delegates to the convention by walking out of the assembly and destroying the quorum; but a mob of "federalists" sought them out at their homes and dragged them to the assembly, where their presence made up the quorum and made possible the further conduct of business. The proponents of the Constitution then forced a vote setting the date of the convention at a date so early as not to allow time for a thorough public debate of the Constitution or its merits.

One by one, however, the states ratified the Constitution. Connecticut, New Jersey, Delaware, and Georgia ratified promptly, and the quick action of the Pennsylvania assembly soon brought that state into line. There was a bitter debate in Virginia, which finally ratified. But in New Hampshire, New York, and Massachusetts the majority of the members of the conventions were opposed to the Constitution. The majority was won over in New Hampshire, as already noted; in New York and Massachusetts enough delegates were won over to bring about ratification. South Carolina and Maryland ratified with little opposition, due in part, at least, to the high property qualifications for voting in those states. North Carolina and Rhode Island, on the other hand, held out to the last, and the Constitution went into effect without them.

By the beginning of 1789 the battle had been won. But it must not be thought that the institution of the new government was at the expressed wish of the whole "American people." Far from it. Only men, and as a general rule, only those with property, could vote in any state. Of the adult males in the United States in 1788 it has been estimated that only about 25 per cent voted in the elections of delegates to state ratifying conventions. And as probably two-fifths of those delegates opposed the Constitution, it appears that the Constitution, as adopted, represents the expressed wishes of probably less than 15 per cent of the male population, or less than 10 per cent of the total white population—to say nothing of the Negroes.

Be that as it may, the wisdom of the makers of the Constitution has been demonstrated in the passage of time. It had been ratified by the requisite number of states by the summer of 1788, and the Continental Congress of the old Confederation, as its last official act, called for elections of the members of the new Congress and the President of the new union. George Washington was unanimously elected President of the United States by the presidential electors, and his inauguration, in New York, April 30, 1789, marks the beginning of a new era in the history of the United States.

RECOMMENDED BOOKS FOR FURTHER READING

CONTEMPORARY NARRATIVES

The Constitution of the United States (Old South Leaflets, No. 1).

Jonathan Elliot, ed., *The Debates in the Several State Conventions on the Adoption of the Federal Constitution.*

Max Farrand, ed., *The Records of the Federal Convention of 1787.*

Alexander Hamilton, John Jay, and James Madison, *The Federalist*, edited by Edward M. Earle.

James Madison, *Notes on the Proceedings of Federal Convention.*

Samuel E. Morison, ed., *Sources and Documents Illustrating the American Revolution, 1764-1788,* pp. 233-362.

MODERN ACCOUNTS

Charles A. Beard, *An Economic Interpretation of the Constitution of the United States.*

Charles A. Beard, *The Supreme Court and the Constitution,* Chapters 1-2.

Albert J. Beveridge, *The Life of John Marshall,* Volume I.

Edward Channing, *A History of the United States,* III, Chapters 16-18.

Max Farrand, *The Fathers of the Constitution.*

Max Farrand, *The Framing of the Constitution of the United States.*

Allan M. Hamilton, *The Intimate Life of Alexander Hamilton.*

Homer C. Hockett, *The Constitutional History of the United States, 1776-1826,* Chapters 10-11.

Gaillard Hunt, *The Life of James Madison.*

Andrew C. McLaughlin, *The Confederation and the Constitution, 1783-1789,* Chapters 11-18.

Andrew C. McLaughlin, *Foundations of American Constitutionalism.*

C. E. Merriam, *A History of American Political Theories,* Chapter 3.

Kate M. Rowland, *The Life of George Mason, 1725-1792.*

Arthur M. Schlesinger, *New Viewpoints in American History,* Chapter 8.

Robert L. Schuyler, *The Constitution of the United States.*

Ernest W. Spaulding, *New York in the Critical Period, 1783-1789.*

49

Postscript. Elements in the Making of a Nation

T HE COLONIAL period of Anglo-American history was one of the major incidents in the expansion of European civilization round the basin of the Atlantic Ocean. Upon the shores of North America, which in the year 1600 presented the aspect of an unbroken wilderness, in 200 years Europeans and their sons built a new civilization. The first settlers were themselves Europeans and their culture was a European culture; but the men of 1789 were not Europeans. They were Americans, and the civilization of the United States, Canada, and the West Indies was distinct both from all those that had preceded it and from its contemporaries in the old world and the new. Each of these divisions of the old British empire was a new land and the people who lived upon the land were a new people. Their economic practices were in large measure new and different from those of their European kinsmen. Their social and political institutions were different from those of the old world and their outlook on life was a new and fresher attitude.

The United States of America, one of the three great segments of the former British empire on this continent, had become sharply differentiated from the other two, and, because impelled to do so by the genius of its own peculiar economic and political development, it had broken away from the old empire to become an independent state. And now, the process of fusion and organization complete, it stood proudly alone, united, and in every sense a nation. What had been the elements that had gone into the making of that nation?

First of all must be considered the land itself. The unfriendly soil and the rigorous climate of New England, coupled with the presence of magnificent forests upon the land and countless myriads of fish in the nearby ocean, had directed the firstcomers in New England into the ways of shipping and the sea. The fertile soil and salubrious climate of the middle colonies, taken together with the advantages offered by natural water highways up into the land, had contributed largely to the making of a civilization in that region which was at once agricultural and commercial. Farther to the south, the soil and climate of Virginia, the Carolinas, and Georgia had been found appropriate for the cultivation of tobacco, rice, and indigo. The settlers in these regions, following the line of least resistance, had adopted those means of making a livelihood which had been found easiest and most profitable. But the dedication of economic activity to the cultivation of these staple products had made necessary a supply of cheap labor which could stand the rigorous southern sun, thus leading to the adoption of the institution of slavery. This institution had brought in its train the practices and prejudices of an aristocratic agrarian society, and on the whole had discouraged the development of large urban centers of population. In the windswept islands of the Caribbean, after various experiments had failed, the European newcomers had hit upon the cultivation of sugar; and sugar, as tobacco and rice in the southern colonies on the continent, had become the commodity the production of which had come almost to dictate what the social and cultural institutions of the West Indian society were to be. In every section of the English-American empire, soil conditions, climate, natural resources, mountains, and natural waterways had profoundly influenced the sort of things the Europeans did and the sort of social and political institutions they established for their own guidance.

But it would be a mistake to believe that the natural environment was the sole determinant in the formation of a civilization on the shores of North America. After all, the new culture that was founded there was established by men who were members of the most highly developed civilization that the world had yet seen. They brought with them their institutions, their religions, their philosophies, and their attitudes toward life. True it is that they came from many different parts of Europe: from England, France, Germany, Holland, Denmark, Sweden, Spain, and Portugal, and each one of these national groups brought with it a cultural heritage that was peculiarly its own. The civilization that they founded in America was basically English; but even had the natural environment had no effect, the new civilization would have been greatly changed by the admixture of so many additional and divergent streams from the differing national cultures of old Europe. Thus it must be said that while the base of American civilization was English, the English heritage was changed and remolded by the necessity of adaptation to a new and compelling environment and was given a cosmopolitan character by the mixture of other cultures with the English. The old institutions and ideas were changed to meet new conditions, and when an old institution could not be found for adaptation, new ones were invented; so that at the end, when an American nation came to stand alone, its culture was a new thing under the sun.

Thus the two major determinants in the formulation of an American culture were the natural environment and the nature and the heritages of the people who came to America to live. Once they had arrived here and established their institutions, however, those very institutions exercised a strong, even decisive influence upon the course of their history. The New England town meeting was not precisely like any institution that had ever existed before, nor were the tobacco plantations of Virginia, or the sugar farms of Barbados; but once the New England town meeting was established it asserted a predominant influence in the lives of the people who lived under it. Once the plantation slavery system was established in Virginia, the entire history of that province came to be affected, even in large measure determined, by that institution.

The third determinant directing the course of history in the American colonies was thus the very set of institutions and ideas that was established there by the newcomers, and which might properly be called American. In general, the influence of such a set of institutions and ideas was exercised in a conservative manner—in a way, that is, to retard rather than to promote change. Perhaps the most important single consideration with regard to the colonial period of American history lies in the fact that it was a new civilization, and that the student of that period is privileged to see how institutions and ideas are made.

Once American institutions became established and relatively fixed in the state constitutions of the revolutionary period and the federal Constitution of 1789, the rate of change in American ideas and institutions perceptibly slowed down; and it was not until a new disruptive force, the industrial revolution, brought with it new institutions and ideas and a new demand for a readaptation of the old, that the rate of social change was again to equal the rapidity of the social change that took place in the colonial period.

The significance for Europe of the colonial period of the British empire in America thus resides in the fact that it is an incident in the expansion of western civilization. It presents the spectacle of a great migration of Europeans into a new area of the world where, under the influence of geographic conditions and the necessity for adaptation, they discarded their cultural heritage or re-molded it into a new form.

For Americans—that is to say, for the people of Canada, the United States, and the British West Indies—this chapter of human history is significant as showing the origins of their present-day society and its institutions. It may not be amiss to say that the citizen of the twentieth century can hardly understand the institutions and the customs of the nation of which he is a part without having studied with considerable care the reasons for their existence, which are to be found only in their origins.

Appendix I

DECLARATION OF INDEPENDENCE

In Congress, July 4, 1776,

THE UNANIMOUS DECLARATION OF THE THIRTEEN UNITED STATES OF
AMERICA,

WHEN in the Course of human events, it becomes necessary for
one people to dissolve the political bands which have connected
them with another, and to assume among the Powers of the earth,
the separate and equal station to which the Laws of Nature and
of Nature's God entitle them, a decent respect to the opinions of
mankind requires that they should declare the causes which impel
them to the separation.

We hold these truths to be self-evident, that all men are created
equal, that they are endowed by their Creator with certain unalienable Rights, that among these are Life, Liberty and the pursuit of
Happiness. That to secure these rights, Governments are instituted
among Men, deriving their just powers from the consent of the
governed, That whenever any Form of Government becomes destructive of these ends, it is the Right of the People to alter or to
abolish it, and to institute new Government, laying its foundation
on such principles and organizing its powers in such form, as to
them shall seem most likely to effect their Safety and Happiness.
Prudence, indeed, will dictate that Governments long established
should not be changed for light and transient causes; and accordingly all experience hath shown, that mankind are more disposed
to suffer, while evils are sufferable, than to right themselves by
abolishing the forms to which they are accustomed. But when a
long train of abuses and usurpations, pursuing invariably the same
Object evinces a design to reduce them under absolute Despotism,
it is their right, it is their duty, to throw off such Government, and
to provide new Guards for their future security.—Such has been the
patient sufferance of these Colonies; and such is now the necessity
which constrains them to alter their former Systems of Government.
The history of the present King of Great Britain is a history of repeated injuries and usurpations, all having in direct object the

establishment of an absolute Tyranny over these States. To prove this, let Facts be submitted to a candid world.

He has refused his Assent to Laws, the most wholesome and necessary for the public good.

He has forbidden his Governors to pass Laws of immediate and pressing importance, unless suspended in their operation till his Assent should be obtained; and when so suspended, he has utterly neglected to attend to them.

He has refused to pass other Laws for the accommodation of large districts of people, unless those people would relinquish the right of Representation in the Legislature, a right inestimable to them and formidable to tyrants only.

He has called together legislative bodies at places unusual, uncomfortable, and distant from the depository of their Public Records, for the sole purpose of fatiguing them into compliance with his measures.

He has dissolved Representative Houses repeatedly, for opposing with manly firmness his invasions on the rights of the people.

He has refused for a long time, after such dissolutions, to cause others to be elected; whereby the Legislative Powers, incapable of Annihilation, have returned to the People at large for their exercise; the State remaining in the mean time exposed to all the dangers of invasion from without, and convulsions within.

He has endeavoured to prevent the population of these States; for that purpose obstructing the Laws of Naturalization of Foreigners; refusing to pass others to encourage their migration hither, and raising the conditions of new Appropriations of Lands.

He has obstructed the Administration of Justice, by refusing his Assent to Laws for establishing Judiciary Powers.

He has made Judges dependent on his Will alone, for the tenure of their offices, and the amount and payment of their salaries.

He has erected a multitude of New Offices, and sent hither swarms of Officers to harass our People, and eat out their substance.

He has kept among us, in times of peace, Standing Armies without the Consent of our legislature.

He has affected to render the Military independent of and superior to the Civil Power.

He has combined with others to subject us to a jurisdiction foreign to our constitution, and unacknowledged by our laws; giving his Assent to their acts of pretended legislation:

For quartering large bodies of armed troops among us:

For protecting them, by a mock Trial, from Punishment for any Murders which they should commit on the Inhabitants of these States:

For cutting off our Trade with all parts of the world:

For imposing taxes on us without our Consent:

For depriving us in many cases, of the benefits of Trial by Jury:

For transporting us beyond Seas to be tried for pretended offences:

For abolishing the free System of English Laws in a neighbouring Province, establishing therein an Arbitrary government, and enlarging its Boundaries so as to render it at once an example and fit instrument for introducing the same absolute rule into these Colonies.

For taking away our Charters, abolishing our most valuable Laws, and altering fundamentally the Forms of our Governments:

For suspending our own Legislature, and declaring themselves invested with Power to legislate for us in all cases whatsoever.

He has abdicated Government here, by declaring us out of his Protection and waging War against us.

He has plundered our seas, ravaged our Coasts, burnt our towns, and destroyed the lives of our people.

He is at this time transporting large armies of foreign mercenaries to compleat the works of death, desolation and tyranny, already begun with circumstances of Cruelty & perfidy scarcely paralleled in the most barbarous ages, and totally unworthy the Head of a civilized nation.

He has constrained our fellow Citizens taken Captive on the high Seas to bear Arms against their Country, to become the executioners of their friends and Brethren, or to fall themselves by their Hands.

He has excited domestic insurrections amongst us, and has endeavoured to bring on the inhabitants of our frontiers, the merciless Indian Savages, whose known rule of warfare, is an undistinguished destruction of all ages, sexes and conditions.

In every stage of these Oppressions We have Petitioned for Redress in the most humble terms: Our repeated Petitions have been answered only by repeated injury. A Prince, whose character is thus marked by every act which may define a Tyrant, is unfit to be the ruler of a free People.

Nor have We been wanting in attention to our British brethren. We have warned them from time to time of attempts by their legislature to extend an unwarrantable jurisdiction over us. We have reminded them of the circumstances of our emigration and settlement here. We have appealed to their native justice and magnanimity, and we have conjured them by the ties of our common kindred to disavow these usurpations, which would inevitably interrupt our connections and correspondence. They too have been deaf to the voice of justice and of consanguinity. We must, therefore, acquiesce in the necessity, which denounces our Separation, and hold them, as we hold the rest of mankind, Enemies in War, in Peace Friends.

We, therefore, the Representatives of the united States of America, in General Congress, Assembled, appealing to the Supreme Judge of the world for the rectitude of our intentions, do, in the Name, and by Authority of the good People of these Colonies, solemnly publish and declare, That these United Colonies are, and of Right ought to be Free and Independent States; that they are Absolved from all Allegiance to the British Crown, and that all political connection between them and the State of Great Britain, is and ought to be totally dissolved; and that as Free and Independent States, they have full Power to levy War, conclude Peace, contract Alliances, establish Commerce, and to do all other Acts and Things which Independent States may of right do. And for the support of this Declaration, with a firm reliance on the Protection of Divine Providence, we mutually pledge to each other our Lives, our Fortunes and our sacred Honor.

JOHN HANCOCK.[1]

[1] The remaining signatures are omitted.

Appendix II

THE CONSTITUTION OF THE UNITED STATES
OF AMERICA [1]

WE THE PEOPLE of the United States, in Order to form a more per
fect Union, establish Justice, insure domestic Tranquility, provide for the common defence, promote the general Welfare, and
secure the Blessings of Liberty to ourselves and our Posterity, do
ordain and establish this CONSTITUTION for the United States of
America.

ARTICLE I.

SECTION 1. All legislative Powers herein granted shall be vested
in a Congress of the United States, which shall consist of a Senate
and House of Representatives.

SECTION 2. The House of Representatives shall be composed of
Members chosen every second Year by the People of the several
States, and the Electors in each State shall have the Qualifications
requisite for Electors of the most numerous Branch of the State
Legislature.

No Person shall be a Representative who shall not have attained
to the Age of twenty-five Years, and been seven Years a Citizen of
the United States, and who shall not, when elected, be an Inhabitant of that State in which he shall be chosen.

[Representatives and direct Taxes shall be apportioned among
the several States which may be included within this Union, according to their respective Numbers, which shall be determined by add-
ing to the whole Number of free Persons, including those bound to
Service for a Term of Years, and excluding Indians not taxed,
three fifths of all other Persons.] The actual Enumeration shall be
made within three Years after the first Meeting of the Congress of
the United States, and within every subsequent Term of ten Years,
in such Manner as they shall by Law direct. The Number of Repre-

[1] This version of the Constitution is that published by the Office of Education,
United States Department of the Interior, in 1935. It follows the original document closely in matters of spelling and capitalization, whereas our practice
throughout this book has been to follow more modern rules in both capitalization and spelling.

sentatives shall not exceed one for every thirty Thousand, but each State shall have at Least one Representative; and until such enumeration shall be made, the State of New Hampshire shall be entitled to chuse three, Massachusetts eight, Rhode-Island and Providence Plantations one, Connecticut five, New-York six, New Jersey four, Pennsylvania eight, Delaware one, Maryland six, Virginia ten, North Carolina five, South Carolina five, and Georgia three.

When vacancies happen in the Representation from any State, the Executive Authority thereof shall issue Writs of Election to fill such Vacancies.

The House of Representatives shall chuse their Speaker and other Officers; and shall have the sole Power of Impeachment.

SECTION 3.   The Senate of the United States shall be composed of two Senators from each State, chosen by the Legislature thereof, for six Years; and each Senator shall have one Vote.

Immediately after they shall be assembled in Consequence of the first Election, they shall be divided as equally as may be into three Classes. The Seats of the Senators of the first Class shall be vacated at the Expiration of the second Year, of the second Class at the Expiration of the fourth Year, and of the third Class at the Expiration of the sixth Year, so that one-third may be chosen every second Year; and if Vacancies happen by Resignation, or otherwise, during the Recess of the Legislature of any State, the Executive thereof may make temporary Appointments until the next Meeting of the Legislature, which shall then fill such Vacancies.

No Person shall be a Senator who shall not have attained to the Age of thirty Years, and been nine Years a Citizen of the United States, and who shall not, when elected, be an Inhabitant of that State for which he shall be chosen.

The Vice President of the United States shall be President of the Senate, but shall have no Vote, unless they be equally divided.

The Senate shall chuse their other Officers, and also a President pro tempore, in the absence of the Vice President, or when he shall exercise the Office of President of the United States.

The Senate shall have the sole Power to try all Impeachments. When sitting for that Purpose, they shall be on Oath or Affirmation. When the President of the United States is tried, the Chief Justice shall preside: And no Person shall be convicted without the Concurrence of two thirds of the Members present.

Judgment in Cases of Impeachment shall not extend further than to removal from Office, and disqualification to hold and enjoy any Office of honor, Trust or Profit under the United States: but the Party convicted shall nevertheless be liable and subject to Indictment, Trial, Judgment and Punishment, according to Law.

SECTION 4. The Times, Places and Manner of holding Elections for Senators and Representatives, shall be prescribed in each State by the Legislature thereof; but the Congress may at any time by Law make or alter such Regulations, except as to the Places of Chusing Senators.

The Congress shall assemble at least once in every Year, and such Meeting shall be on the first Monday in December, unless they shall by Law appoint a different Day.

SECTION 5. Each House shall be the Judge of the Elections, Returns and Qualifications of its own Members, and a Majority of each shall constitute a Quorum to do Business; but a smaller Number may adjourn from day to day, and may be authorized to compel the Attendance of absent Members, in such Manner, and under such Penalties as each House may provide.

Each House may determine the Rules of its Proceedings, punish its Members for disorderly Behavior, and, with the Concurrence of two thirds, expel a Member.

Each House shall keep a Journal of its Proceedings, and from time to time publish the same, excepting such Parts as may in their Judgment require Secrecy; and the Yeas and Nays of the Members of either House on any question shall, at the Desire one fifth of those Present, be entered on the Journal.

Neither House, during the Session of Congress, shall, without the Consent of the other, adjourn for more than three days, nor to any other Place than that in which the two Houses shall be sitting.

SECTION 6. The Senators and Representatives shall receive a Compensation for their Services, to be ascertained by Law, and paid out of the Treasury of the United States. They shall in all Cases, except Treason, Felony and Breach of the Peace, be privileged from Arrest during their Attendance at the Session of their respective Houses, and in going to and returning from the same; and for any Speech or Debate in either House, they shall not be questioned in any other Place.

No Senator or Representative shall, during the Time for which he was elected, be appointed to any civil Office under the Authority of the United States, which shall have been created, or the Emoluments whereof shall have been encreased during such time; and no Person holding any Office under the United States, shall be a Member of either House during his Continuance in Office.

SECTION 7. All Bills for raising Revenue shall originate in the House of Representatives; but the Senate may propose or concur with Amendments as on other Bills.

Every Bill which shall have passed the House of Representatives and the Senate, shall, before it become a Law, be presented to the President of the United States; if he approve he shall sign it, but if not he shall return it, with his Objections to that House in which it shall have originated, who shall enter the Objections at large on their Journal, and proceed to reconsider it. If after such Reconsideration two thirds of that House shall agree to pass the Bill, it shall be sent, together with the Objections, to the other House, by which it shall likewise be reconsidered, and if approved by two thirds of that House, it shall become a Law. But in all such Cases the Votes of both Houses shall be determined by Yeas and Nays, and the Names of the Persons voting for and against the Bill shall be entered on the Journal of each House respectively. If any Bill shall not be returned by the President within ten Days (Sundays excepted) after it shall have been presented to him, the Same shall be a Law, in like Manner as if he had signed it, unless the Congress by their Adjournment prevent its Return, in which Case it shall not be a Law.

Every Order, Resolution, or Vote to which the Concurrence of the Senate and House of Representatives may be necessary (except on a question of Adjournment) shall be presented to the President of the United States; and before the Same shall take Effect, shall be approved by him, or being disapproved by him, shall be repassed by two thirds of the Senate and House of Representatives, according to the Rules and Limitations prescribed in the Case of a Bill.

SECTION 8. The Congress shall have Power To lay and collect Taxes, Duties, Imposts and Excises, to pay the Debts and provide for the common Defence and general Welfare of the United States; but all Duties, Imposts and Excises shall be uniform throughout the United States;

To borrow money on the credit of the United States;

To regulate Commerce with foreign Nations, and among the several States, and with the Indian Tribes;

To establish an uniform Rule of Naturalization, and uniform Laws on the subject of Bankruptcies throughout the United States;

To coin Money, regulate the Value thereof, and of foreign Coin, and fix the Standard of Weights and Measures;

To provide for the Punishment of counterfeiting the Securities and current Coin of the United States;

To establish Post Offices and post Roads;

To promote the Progress of Science and useful Arts, by securing for limited Times to Authors and Inventors the exclusive Right to their respective Writings and Discoveries;

To constitute Tribunals inferior to the Supreme Court;

To define and punish Piracies and Felonies committed on the high Seas, and Offenses against the Law of Nations;

To declare War, grant Letters of Marque and Reprisal, and make Rules concerning Captures on Land and Water;

To raise and support Armies, but no Appropriation of Money to that Use shall be for a longer Term than two Years;

To provide and maintain a Navy;

To make Rules for the Government and Regulation of the land and naval Forces;

To provide for calling forth the Militia to execute the Laws of the Union, suppress Insurrections and repel Invasions;

To provide for organizing, arming, and disciplining the Militia, and for governing such Part of them as may be employed in the Service of the United States, reserving to the States respectively, the Appointment of the Officers, and the Authority of training the Militia according to the discipline prescribed by Congress;

To exercise exclusive Legislation in all Cases whatsoever, over such District (not exceeding ten Miles square) as may, by Cession of particular States, and the acceptance of Congress, become the Seat of the Government of the United States, and to exercise like Authority over all Places purchased by the Consent of the Legislature of the State in which the Same shall be, for the Erection of Forts, Magazines, Arsenals, dock-Yards, and other needful Buildings;—And

To make all Laws which shall be necessary and proper for carrying into Execution the foregoing Powers, and all other Powers vested by this Constitution in the Government of the United States, or in any Department or Officer thereof.

SECTION 9. The Migration or Importation of such Persons as any of the States now existing shall think proper to admit, shall not be prohibited by the Congress prior to the Year one thousand eight hundred and eight, but a tax or duty may be imposed on such Importation, not exceeding ten dollars for each Person.

The privilege of the Writ of Habeas Corpus shall not be suspended, unless when in Cases of Rebellion or Invasion the public Safety may require it.

No Bill of Attainder or ex post facto Law shall be passed.

No capitation, or other direct, Tax shall be laid unless in Proportion to the Census or Enumeration herein before directed to be taken.

No Tax or Duty shall be laid on Articles exported from any State.

No preference shall be given by any Regulation of Commerce or Revenue to the Ports of one State over those of another: nor shall Vessels bound to, or from, one State, be obliged to enter, clear, or pay Duties in another.

No money shall be drawn from the Treasury, but in Consequence of Appropriations made by Law; and a regular Statement and Account of the Receipts and Expenditures of all public Money shall be published from time to time.

No Title of Nobility shall be granted by the United States: And no Person holding any Office of Profit or Trust under them, shall, without the Consent of the Congress, accept of any present, Emolument, Office, or Title, of any kind whatever, from any King, Prince, or foreign State.

SECTION 10. No State shall enter into any Treaty, Alliance, or Confederation; grant Letters of Marque and Reprisal; coin Money; emit Bills of Credit; make any Thing but gold and silver Coin a Tender in Payment of Debts; pass any Bill of Attainder, ex post facto Law, or Law impairing the Obligation of Contracts, or grant any Title of Nobility.

No State shall, without the Consent of the Congress, lay any Imposts or Duties on Imports or Exports, except what may be absolutely necessary for executing its inspection Laws: and the net Produce of all Duties and Imposts, laid by any State on Imports or Exports, shall be for the Use of the Treasury of the United States; and all such Laws shall be subject to the Revision and Control of the Congress.

No State shall, without the Consent of Congress, lay any duty of Tonnage, keep Troops, or Ships of War in time of Peace, enter into any Agreement or Compact with another State, or with a foreign Power, or engage in War, unless actually invaded, or in such imminent Danger as will not admit of delay.

ARTICLE II.

SECTION 1. The executive Power shall be vested in a President of the United States of America. He shall hold his Office during the Term of four Years, and, together with the Vice-President, chosen for the same Term, be elected, as follows

Each State shall appoint, in such Manner as the Legislature thereof may direct, a Number of Electors, equal to the whole Number of Senators and Representatives to which the State may be entitled in the Congress: but no Senator or Representative, or Person holding an Office of Trust or Profit under the United States, shall be appointed an Elector.

[The Electors shall meet in their respective States, and vote by Ballot for two persons, of whom one at least shall not be an Inhabitant of the same State with themselves. And they shall make a List of all the Persons voted for, and of the Number of Votes for each; which List they shall sign and certify, and transmit sealed to the Seat of the Government of the United States, directed to the President of the Senate. The President of the Senate shall, in the Presence of the Senate and House of Representatives, open all the Certificates, and the Votes shall then be counted. The Person having the greatest Number of Votes shall be the President, if such Number be a Majority of the whole Number of Electors appointed; and if there be more than one who have such Majority, and have an equal Number of Votes, then the House of Representatives shall immediately chuse by Ballot one of them for President; and if no Person have a Majority, then from the five highest on the List the said House shall in like Manner chuse the President. But in chusing the President, the Votes shall be taken by States, the Representation from each State having one Vote; A quorum for this Purpose shall consist of a Member or Members from two-thirds of the States, and a Majority of all the States shall be necessary to a Choice. In every Case, after the Choice of the President, the Person having the greatest Number of Votes of the Electors shall be the Vice President. But if there should remain two or more who have equal Votes, the Senate shall chuse from them by Ballot the Vice-President.]

The Congress may determine the Time of chusing the Electors, and the Day on which they shall give their Votes; which Day shall be the same throughout the United States.

No person except a natural born Citizen, or a Citizen of the United States, at the time of the Adoption of this Constitution, shall be eligible to the Office of President; neither shall any Person be eligible to that Office who shall not have attained to the Age of thirty-five Years, and been fourteen Years a Resident within the United States.

In Case of the Removal of the President from Office, or of his Death, Resignation, or Inability to discharge the Powers and Duties of the said Office, the same shall devolve on the Vice President, and the Congress may by Law provide for the Case of Removal, Death, Resignation or Inability, both of the President and Vice President, declaring what Officer shall then act as President, and such Officer shall act accordingly, until the Disability be removed, or a President shall be elected.

The President shall, at stated Times, receive for his Services, a Compensation, which shall neither be encreased nor diminished during the Period for which he shall have been elected, and he shall not receive within that Period any other Emolument from the United States, or any of them.

Before he enter on the Execution of his Office, he shall take the following Oath or Affirmation:—"I do solemny swear (or affirm) that I will faithfully execute the Office of President of the United States, and will to the best of my Ability, preserve, protect and defend the Constitution of the United States."

SECTION 2. The President shall be Commander in Chief of the Army and Navy of the United States, and of the militia of the several States, when called into the actual Service of the United States; he may require the Opinion in writing, of the principal Officer in each of the executive Departments, upon any subject relating to the Duties of their respective Offices, and he shall have

Power to Grant Reprieves and Pardons for Offenses against the United States, except in Cases of Impeachment.

He shall have Power, by and with the Advice and Consent of the Senate, to make Treaties, provided two-thirds of the Senators present concur; and he shall nominate, and by and with the Advice and Consent of the Senate, shall appoint Ambassadors, other public Ministers and Consuls, Judges of the Supreme Court, and all other Officers of the United States, whose Appointments are not herein otherwise provided for, and which shall be established by Law: but the Congress may by Law vest the Appointment of such inferior Officers, as they think proper, in the President alone, in the Courts of Law, or in the Heads of Departments.

The President shall have Power to fill up all Vacancies that may happen during the Recess of the Senate, by granting Commissions which shall expire at the End of their next Session.

SECTION 3. He shall from time to time give to the Congress Information of the State of the Union, and recommend to their Consideration such Measures as he shall judge necessary and expedient; he may, on extraordinary Occasions, convene both Houses, or either of them, and in Case of Disagreement between them, with Respect to the Time of Adjournment, he may adjourn them to such Time as he shall think proper; he shall receive Ambassadors and other public Ministers; he shall take Care that the Laws be faithfully executed, and shall Commission all the Officers of the United States.

SECTION 4. The President, Vice President and all civil Officers of the United States, shall be removed from Office on Impeachment for, and Conviction of, Treason, Bribery, or other high Crimes and Misdemeanors.

ARTICLE III.

SECTION 1. The judicial Power of the United States, shall be vested in one supreme Court, and in such inferior Courts as the Congress may from time to time ordain and establish. The Judges, both of the supreme and inferior Courts, shall hold their Offices during good Behaviour, and shall, at stated Times, receive for their Services a Compensation which shall not be diminished during their Continuance in Office.

SECTION 2. The judicial Power shall extend to all Cases, in Law and Equity, arising under this Constitution, the Laws of the United States, and Treaties made, or which shall be made, under their Authority;—to all Cases affecting Ambassadors, other public Ministers and Consuls;—to all Cases of admiralty and maritime Jurisdiction;—to Controversies to which the United States shall be a Party;—to Controversies between two or more States;—between a

State and Citizens of another State;—between Citizens of different States;—between Citizens of the same State claiming Lands under Grants of different States, and between a State, or the Citizens thereof, and foreign States, Citizens or Subjects.

In all Cases affecting Ambassadors, other public Ministers and Consuls, and those in which a State shall be Party, the supreme Court shall have original Jurisdiction. In all the other Cases before mentioned, the supreme Court shall have appellate Jurisdiction, both as to Law and Fact, with such Exceptions, and under such Regulations as the Congress shall make.

The trial of all Crimes, except in Cases of Impeachment, shall be by Jury; and such Trial shall be held in the State where the said Crimes shall have been committed; but when not committed within any State, the Trial shall be at such Place or Places as the Congress may by Law have directed.

SECTION 3. Treason against the United States, shall consist only in levying War against them, or in adhering to their Enemies, giving them Aid and Comfort. No Person shall be convicted of Treason unless on the Testimony of two Witnesses to the same overt Act, or on Confession in open Court. .

The Congress shall have power to declare the Punishment of Treason, but no Attainder of Treason shall work Corruption of Blood, or Forfeiture except during the Life of the Person attainted.

ARTICLE IV.

SECTION 1. Full Faith and Credit shall be given in each State to the public Acts, Records, and judicial Proceedings of every other State. And the Congress may by general Laws prescribe the Manner in which such Acts, Records and Proceedings shall be proved, and the Effect thereof.

SECTION 2. The Citizens of each State shall be entitled to all Privileges and Immunities of Citizens in the several States.

A Person charged in any State with Treason, Felony, or other Crime, who shall flee from Justice, and be found in another State, shall on demand of the executive Authority of the State from which he fled, be delivered up, to be removed to the State having Jurisdiction of the Crime.

No Person held to Service or Labour in one State, under the Laws thereof, escaping into another, shall, in Consequence of any Law or Regulation therein, be discharged from such Service or Labour, but shall be delivered up on Claim of the Party to whom such Service or Labour may be due.

SECTION 3. New States may be admitted by the Congress into this Union; but no new State shall be formed or erected within the Jurisdiction of any other State; nor any State be formed by the Junction of two or more States, or parts of States, without the Consent of the Legislatures of the States concerned as well as of the Congress.

The Congress shall have Power to dispose of and make all needful Rules and Regulations respecting the Territory or other Property belonging to the United States; and nothing in this Constitution shall be so construed as to Prejudice any Claims of the United States, or of any particular State.

SECTION 4. The United States shall guarantee to every State in this Union a Republican Form of Government, and shall protect each of them against Invasion; and on Application of the Legislature, or of the Executive (when the Legislature cannot be convened) against domestic Violence.

ARTICLE V.

The Congress, whenever two-thirds of both Houses shall deem it necessary, shall propose Amendments to this Constitution, or, on the Application of the Legislatures of two-thirds of the several States, shall call a Convention for proposing Amendments, which, in either Case, shall be valid to all Intents and Purposes, as part of this Constitution, when ratified by the Legislatures of three-fourths of the several States, or by Conventions in three-fourths thereof, as the one or the other Mode of Ratification may be proposed by the Congress: Provided that no Amendment which may be made prior to the Year One thousand eight hundred and eight shall in any Manner affect the first and fourth Clauses in the Ninth Section of the first Article; and that no State, without its Consent, shall be deprived of its equal Suffrage in the Senate.

ARTICLE VI.

All Debts contracted and Engagements entered into, before the Adoption of this Constitution, shall be as valid against the United States under this Constitution, as under the Confederation.

This Constitution, and the Laws of the United States which shall be made in Pursuance thereof; and all Treaties made, or which shall be made, under the Authority of the United States, shall be the supreme Law of the Land; and the Judges in every State shall be bound thereby, any Thing in the Constitution or Laws of any State to the Contrary notwithstanding.

The Senators and Representatives before mentioned, and the Members of the several State Legislatures, and all executive and judicial Officers, both of the United States and of the several States, shall be bound by Oath or Affirmation, to support this Constitution; but no religious Test shall ever be required as a Qualification to any Office or public Trust under the United States.

ARTICLE VII.

The Ratification of the Conventions of nine States shall be sufficient for the Establishment of this Constitution between the States so ratifying the Same.

DONE in Convention by the Unanimous Consent of the States present the Seventeenth Day of September in the Year of our Lord one thousand seven hundred and Eighty seven and of the Independence of the United States of America the Twelfth. In Witness whereof We have hereunto subscribed our Names.

G° WASHINGTON
Presidt and deputy from Virginia
[Other signatures omitted.]

ARTICLES IN ADDITION TO, AND AMENDMENT OF, THE CONSTITUTION OF THE UNITED STATES OF AMERICA, PROPOSED BY CONGRESS, AND RATIFIED BY THE LEGISLATURES OF THE SEVERAL STATES, PURSUANT TO THE FIFTH ARTICLE OF THE ORIGINAL CONSTITUTION.

[ARTICLE I.]

Congress shall make no law respecting an establishment of religion, or prohibiting the free exercise thereof; or abridging the freedom of speech, or of the press; or the right of the people peaceably to assemble, and to petition the Government for a redress of grievances.

[ARTICLE II.]

A well regulated Militia, being necessary to the security of a free State, the right of the people to keep and bear Arms, shall not be infringed.

[ARTICLE III.]

No Soldier shall, in time of peace be quartered in any house, without the consent of the Owner, nor in time of war, but in a manner to be prescribed by law.

[ARTICLE IV.]

The right of the people to be secure in their persons, houses, papers and effects, against unreasonable searches and seizures, shall not be violated, and no Warrants shall issue, but upon probable cause, supported by Oath or affirmation, and particularly describing the place to be searched, and the persons or things to be seized.

[ARTICLE V.]

No person shall be held to answer for a capital, or otherwise infamous crime, unless on a presentment or indictment of a Grand Jury, except in cases arising in the land or naval forces, or in the Militia, when in actual service in time of War or public danger; nor shall any person be subject for the same offence to be twice put in jeopardy of life or limb; nor shall be compelled in any criminal case to be a witness against himself, nor be deprived of life, liberty, or property, without due process of law; nor shall private property be taken for public use, without just compensation.

[ARTICLE VI.]

In all criminal prosecutions, the accused shall enjoy the right to a speedy and public trial, by an impartial jury of the State and district wherein the crime shall have been committed, which district shall have been previously ascertained by law, and to be informed of the nature and cause of the accusation; to be confronted with the witnesses against him; to have compulsory process for obtaining witnesses in his favor, and to have the Assistance of Counsel for his defence.

[ARTICLE VII.]

In suits at common law, where the value in controversy shall exceed twenty dollars, the right of trial by jury shall be preserved, and no fact tried by a jury, shall be otherwise reexamined in any Court of the United States, than according to the rules of the common law.

[ARTICLE VIII.]

Excessive bail shall not be required, nor excessive fines imposed, nor cruel and unusual punishments inflicted.

[ARTICLE IX.]

The enumeration in the Constitution, of certain rights, shall not be construed to deny or disparage others retained by the people.

[ARTICLE X.]

The powers not delegated to the United States by the Constitution, nor prohibited by it to the States, are reserved to the States respectively, or to the people.

[Amendments I-X, in force 1791.]

ARTICLE XI.

The Judicial power of the United States shall not be construed to extend to any suit in law or equity, commenced or prosecuted against one of the United States by Citizens of another State, or by Citizens or Subjects of any Foreign State. [1798.]

ARTICLE XII.

The Electors shall meet in their respective states and vote by ballot for President and Vice-President, one of whom, at least, shall not be an inhabitant of the same state with themselves; they shall name in their ballots the person voted for as President, and in distinct ballots the person voted for as Vice-President, and they shall make distinct lists of all persons voted for as President, and of all persons voted for as Vice-President, and of the number of votes for each, which lists they shall sign and certify, and transmit sealed to the seat of the government of the United States, directed to the President of the Senate;—The President of the Senate shall, in presence of the Senate and House of Representatives, open all the certificates and the votes shall then be counted;—The person having the greatest number of votes for President, shall be the President, if such number be a majority of the whole number of Electors appointed; and if no person have such majority, then from the persons having the highest numbers not exceeding three on the list of those voted for as President, the House of Representatives shall choose immediately, by ballot, the President. But in choosing the President, the votes shall be taken by states, the representation from each state having one vote; a quorum for this purpose shall consist of a member or members from two-thirds of the states, and a majority of all the states shall be necessary to a choice. And if the House of Representatives shall not choose a President whenever the right of choice shall devolve upon them, before the fourth day of March next following, then the Vice-President shall act as President, as in the case of the death or other constitutional disability of the President.—The person having the greatest number of votes as Vice-President, shall be the Vice-President, if such number be a majority of the whole number of Electors appointed, and if no person have a majority, then from the two highest numbers on the list, the Senate shall choose the Vice-President; a quorum for the purpose shall consist of two-thirds of the whole number of Senators, and a majority of the whole number shall be necessary to a choice. But no person constitutionally ineligible to the office of President shall be eligible to that of Vice-President of the United States. [1804.]

ARTICLE XIII.

SECTION 1. Neither slavery nor involuntary servitude, except as a punishment for crime whereof the party shall have been duly convicted, shall exist within the United States, or any place subject to their jurisdiction.

SECTION 2. Congress shall have power to enforce this article by appropriate legislation. [1865.]

ARTICLE XIV.

SECTION 1. All persons born or naturalized in the United States, and subject to the jurisdiction thereof, are citizens of the United States and of the State wherein they reside. No State shall make or enforce any law which shall abridge the privileges or immunities of citizens of the United States; nor shall any State deprive any person of life, liberty, or property, without due process of law; nor deny to any person within its jurisdiction the equal protection of the laws.

SECTION 2. Representatives shall be apportioned among the several States according to their respective numbers, counting the whole number of persons in each State, excluding Indians not taxed. But when the right to vote at any election for the choice of electors for President and Vice-President of the United States, Representatives in Congress, the Executive and Judicial officers of a State, or the members of the Legislature thereof, is denied to any of the male inhabitants of such State, being twenty-one years of age, and citizens of the United States, or in any way abridged, except for participation in rebellion, or other crime, the basis of representation therein shall be reduced in the proportion which the number of such male citizens shall bear to the whole number of male citizens twenty-one years of age in such State.

SECTION 3. No person shall be a Senator or Representative in Congress, or elector of President and Vice-President, or hold any office, civil or military, under the United States, or under any State, who, having previously taken an oath, as a member of Congress, or as an officer of the United States, or as a member of any State legislature, or as an executive or judicial officer of any State, to support the Constitution of the United States, shall have engaged in insurrection or rebellion against the same, or given aid or comfort to the enemies thereof. But Congress may by a vote of two-thirds of each House, remove such disability.

SECTION 4. The validity of the public debt of the United States, authorized by law, including debts incurred for payment of pensions and bounties for services in suppressing insurrection or rebellion, shall not be questioned. But neither the United States nor any State shall assume or pay any debt or obligation incurred in aid of insurrection or rebellion against the United States, or any claim for the loss or emancipation of any slave; but all such debts, obligations and claims shall be held illegal and void.

SECTION 5. The Congress shall have power to enforce, by appropriate legislation, the provisions of this article. [1868.]

ARTICLE XV.

SECTION 1. The right of citizens of the United States to vote shall not be denied or abridged by the United States or by any State on account of race, color, or previous condition of servitude—

SECTION 2. The Congress shall have power to enforce this article by appropriate legislation. [1870.]

ARTICLE XVI.

The Congress shall have power to lay and collect taxes on incomes, from whatever source derived, without apportionment among the several States, and without regard to any census or enumeration. [1913.]

ARTICLE XVII.

The Senate of the United States shall be composed of two Senators from each State, elected by the people thereof, for six years; and each Senator shall have one vote. The electors in each State shall have the qualifications requisite for electors of the most numerous branch of the State legislatures.

When vacancies happen in the representation of any State in the Senate, the executive authority of such State shall issue writs of election to fill such vacancies: *Provided,* That the legislature of any State may empower the executive thereof to make temporary appointments until the people fill the vacancies by election as the legislature may direct.

This amendment shall not be so construed as to affect the election or term of any Senator chosen before it becomes valid as part of the Constitution. [1913.]

ARTICLE XVIII.

[SECTION 1. After one year from the ratification of this article the manufacture, sale, or transportation of intoxicating liquors within, the importation thereof into, or the exportation thereof from the United States and all territory subject to the jurisdiction thereof for beverage purposes is hereby prohibited.

SECTION 2. The Congress and the several States shall have concurrent power to enforce this article by appropriate legislation.

SECTION 3. This article shall be inoperative unless it shall have been ratified as an amendment to the Constitution by the legislatures of the several States, as provided in the Constitution, within seven years from the date of the submission hereof to the States by the Congress.] [1919.]

ARTICLE XIX.

The right of citizens of the United States to vote shall not be denied or abridged by the United States or by any State on account of sex.

Congress shall have power to enforce this article by appropriate legislation. [1920.]

ARTICLE XX.

SECTION 1. The terms of the President and Vice President shall end at noon on the 20th day of January, and the terms of Senators and Representatives at noon on the 3d day of January, of the years in which such terms would have ended if this article had not been ratified; and the terms of their successors shall then begin.

SECTION 2. The Congress shall assemble at least once in every year, and such meeting shall begin at noon on the 3d day of January, unless they shall by law appoint a different day.

SECTION 3. If, at the time fixed for the beginning of the term of the President, the President elect shall have died, the Vice President elect shall become President. If a President shall not have been chosen before the time fixed for the beginning of his term, or if the President elect shall have failed to qualify, then the Vice President elect shall act as President until a President shall have qualified; and the Congress may by law provide for the case wherein neither a President elect nor a Vice President elect shall have qualified, declaring who shall then act as President, or the manner in which one who is to act shall be selected, and such person shall act accordingly until a President or Vice President shall have qualified.

SECTION 4. The Congress may by law provide for the case of the death of any of the persons from whom the House of Representatives may choose a President whenever the right of choice shall have devolved upon them, and for the case of the death of any of the persons from whom the Senate may choose a Vice President whenever the right of choice shall have devolved upon them.

SECTION 5. Sections 1 and 2 shall take effect on the 15th day of October following the ratification of this article.

SECTION 6. This article shall be inoperative unless it shall have been ratified as an amendment to the Constitution by the legislatures of three-fourths of the several States within seven years from the date of its submission. [1933.]

ARTICLE XXI.

SECTION 1. The eighteenth article of amendment to the Constitution of the United States is hereby repealed.

SECTION 2. The transportation or importation into any State, Territory, or possession of the United States for delivery or use therein of intoxicating liquors, in violation of the laws thereof, is hereby prohibited.

SECTION 3. This article shall be inoperative unless it shall have been ratified as an amendment to the Constitution by conventions in the several States, as provided in the Constitution, within seven years from the date of the submission hereof to the States by the Congress. [1933.]

Index

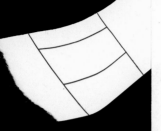